THE COMPANION GUIDE TO
Ireland

THE COMPANION GUIDES

GENERAL EDITOR: VINCENT CRONIN

*It is the aim of these guides to provide a Companion,
in the person of the author, who knows intimately
the places and people of whom he writes, and is able to
communicate this knowledge and affection to his readers.
It is hoped that the text and pictures will aid them
in their preparations and in their travels, and will
help them remember on their return.*

LONDON · OUTER LONDON · EAST ANGLIA
NORTHUMBRIA · THE WEST HIGHLANDS OF SCOTLAND
PARIS · THE SOUTH OF FRANCE
THE ILE DE FRANCE · NORMANDY · THE LOIRE
FLORENCE · VENICE · ROME · NEW YORK
MAINLAND GREECE · THE GREEK ISLANDS
JUGOSLAVIA · TURKEY
MADRID AND CENTRAL SPAIN

In preparation

OXFORD AND CAMBRIDGE
UNION OF SOVIET SOCIALIST REPUBLICS

THE COMPANION GUIDE TO

IRELAND

BRENDAN LEHANE

A SPECTRUM BOOK

PRENTICE-HALL INC.
Englewood Cliffs, N. J. 07632

COLLINS
8 Grafton Street, London W1

1985

William Collins Sons & Co. Ltd
London · Glasgow · Sydney · Auckland
Toronto · Johannesburg

Prentice-Hall, Inc.
New Jersey · London · Sydney · Toronto
New Delhi · Tokyo · Singapore
New Zealand · Rio de Janeiro

British Library Cataloguing in Publication Data

Lehane, Brendan
  The companion guide to Ireland. – (Rev.ed.)
  1. Ireland – Description and travel – 1981
  –Guide-books
  I. Title
  914.15′04824 DA980

Library of Congress Cataloging in Publication Data

Lehane, Brendan
  The Companion guide to Ireland.

  "A Spectrum Book"
  Includes index.
  1. Ireland – Description and travel – Guide-
  books. I. Title.

ISBN 0-13-154436-5

First published in Great Britain 1973
This revised edition published 1985
© Brendan Lehane 1973, 1985

ISBN 0-13-154436-5
ISBN 0 00 217518 5
ISBN 0 00 217336 0 (Collins trade paperback)

U.S. edition © 1985 by Prentice-Hall, Inc., Englewood Cliffs,
New Jersey 07632; William Collins Sons & Co., Ltd., and Brendan Lehane

A SPECTRUM BOOK

10 9 8 7 6 5 4 3 2 1

Prentice-Hall International (UK) Limited, *London*
Prentice-Hall of Australia Pty. Limited, *Sydney*
Prentice-Hall Canada Inc., *Toronto*
Prentice-Hall Hispanoamericana, S.A., *Mexico*
Prentice-Hall of India Private Limited, *New Delhi*
Prentice-Hall of Japan, Inc., *Tokyo*
Prentice-Hall of Southeast Asia Pte. Ltd., *Singapore*
Whitehall Books Limited, *Wellington, New Zealand*
Editora Prentice-Hall do Brasil Ltda., *Rio de Janeiro*

Maps by Charles Green, Reginald Piggott and H.A. Shelley
Made and Printed in Great Britain by
William Collins Sons & Co. Ltd., Glasgow

To Maureen and Peter

CONTENTS

ILLUSTRATIONS

unless otherwise stated, all the photographs
between pages 28 and 381
are reproduced courtesy of Bord Failte,
and those between pages 412 and 445
courtesy of
the Northern Ireland Tourist Board

MAPS

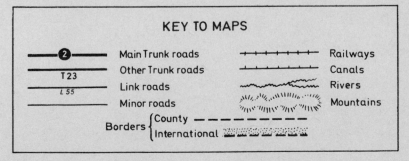

KEY TO MAPS

2 Main Trunk roads	Railways
T 23 Other Trunk roads	Canals
L 55 Link roads	Rivers
Minor roads	Mountains
Borders { County	
International	

Acknowledgments

Research on Irish art and architecture has progressed fast in the last few years, and I am extremely grateful to those pioneer authors and scholars who have been generous with their help. Dr Maurice Craig, whose *Dublin 1660-1860* is an essential and delightful source for any work on the capital city and much else in Ireland, read the book both in typescript and proof and did not, I am glad to say, confine his comments to his own special subjects. The Knight of Glyn, the Hon. Desmond Guinness, the Hon. Mrs Guinness, and Mr Terence de Vere White read the book in proof or typescript; Miss Anne Crookshank read the Dublin and the late Earl of Antrim the Ulster section. Almost all corrections and additions they suggested were made.

A book of this nature must draw on thousands of sources, both written and oral; I have moreover received help and hospitality over the last few years in all parts of Ireland. It would be impossible to acknowledge more than a fraction of my debts, but I cannot omit mention of works I used repeatedly: the *Shell Guide to Ireland* by Lord Killanin and M. V. Duignan, Murray's *Handbook to Ireland* (8th edition, 1912), *Ireland Observed* by Maurice Craig and the Knight of Glyn, *The Way that I Went* by R. Lloyd Praeger, *Irish Houses and Castles* by the Hon. Desmond Guinness and William Ryan, *Dublin Under the Georges* and *Country and Town in Ireland under the Georges* by Constantia Maxwell, and innumerable articles by Mark Girouard, Mark Bence-Jones, John Cornforth and others in *Country Life*. I have made full use of the books mentioned in the Bibliography, and of many more. For some months I received much help from the County Library at Lismore, County Waterford.

Finally I must thank the Irish Tourist Board for material help during the early phases of preparing this book and for supplying me with a lot of information; and particularly Mr Leacey of their Mullingar office for much time and valuable advice.

Introduction

EVERYONE coming to Ireland by sea or air lands near the coast, and this book follows the coast in a clockwise direction, making long circular tours inland from various points. Nothing is as magnificent as the mountains of Kerry or Galway, but Ireland's interior, showing its treasures with greater reluctance, can leave more lasting memories. Both coast and hinterland can be seen by means of buses, trains, motor cruisers or sailing boats, but none of these goes everywhere a car goes. In the directions given, use of a car is assumed.

Though I have tried to show how to get to most sites, some – across fields and tracks, or at the end of a maze of lanes – call for the use of a map. The best are listed in the appendix of book suggestions. Maps apart, asking the way can lead to enlightenment, entertainment or despair, but the increasing number of signposts is obviating the need.

There is a list of houses open to the public at the end of the book. Many houses besides these are described or mentioned in the text, some of which open rarely or irregularly. Others may open in the future, and still others, never officially open, seldom turn away a genuinely interested caller. These tend to be away from the main towns and tourist areas. I would not be thanked for giving the names of those whose owners, I know, show callers round, but they are not uncommon.

This natural Irish hospitality is unlikely to be altered radically by the tragedy being played out in the North. It is the worst of a series of outbursts that have occurred since Ireland was divided by an arbitrary border in 1921. It could, in spite of the horrors it has caused, lead to an enduring improvement if it softens a clash of interests that has existed for centuries. Without some knowledge of this clash both modern and historic Ireland can be infinitely puzzling to visitors, and a sketch of Irish history, absurdly brief, may still be helpful, if only in introducing more paradoxes and contradictions to a situation which can too easily be simplified. I have put this as an appendix at p. 445, together with notes on the language, the climate, food and drink, the Tourist Board, and a glossary of words or phrases that otherwise may prove obscure.

Because they occur so often, I have abbreviated the term Roman Catholic to RC, and Church of Ireland to C of I.

CHAPTER ONE

Dublin

DUBLIN on the map is a little like the front half of a lobster seen from above. Its claws curve into the sea to form Dublin Bay, which ends, on the north side, at the peninsula of Howth and on the south at Dun Laoghaire. The protuberances of Dublin Harbour, in the middle of the bay's shoreline, make the head. If a lobster had a spinal cord it would, in this case, be the Liffey, entering the town on its west side, cutting it in two, and debouching into the harbour itself. Near the river mouth are the sea-ends of two more rivers: the Tolka to the north and the Dodder to the south, each of which swings west, so that between them they enclose the major part of the city's suburbs. Two canals, the Royal on the north side and the Grand on the south, also start near the Liffey's mouth, and bend west to belt the town more closely. At a glance, Dublin has a symmetrical geography.

Its contents are not so orderly. The south has the larger part of Dublin's historic and architectural distinction and of its antiquity, art, and money. Most of the great maintained showpieces lie on an east–west axis through College Green, 300 yards south of O'Connell Bridge. The best shopping is to its south; and the rich suburbs spread south and south-east again. 'West End' in Dublin, unlike most western cities, equates with humble areas. However, the southern monopoly is not complete. Two of Ireland's finest buildings overlook the river on the north, and there is plenty of interest in the streets and suburbs behind, from the General Post Office, a kind of shrine of Irish patriotism, to the magnificent Botanic Gardens at Glasnevin.

Time has been harder on the north. Until recently poverty abounded, blotching and rotting dignified Georgian houses that had become slummy tenements. Streets are drearier, shops more gaudy, and the 1916 Rising left uglier scars on

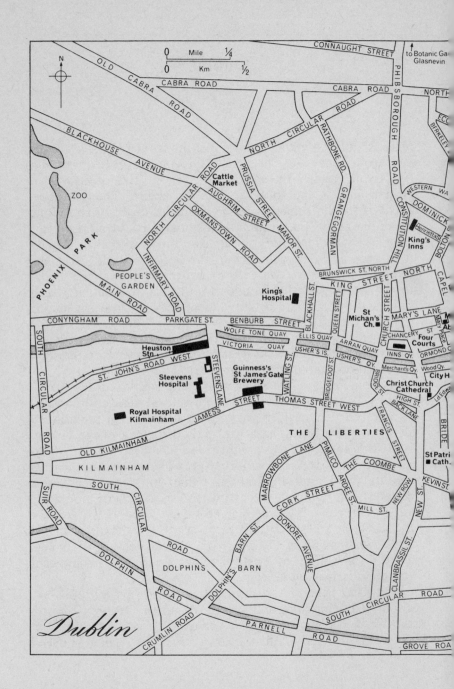

Dublin

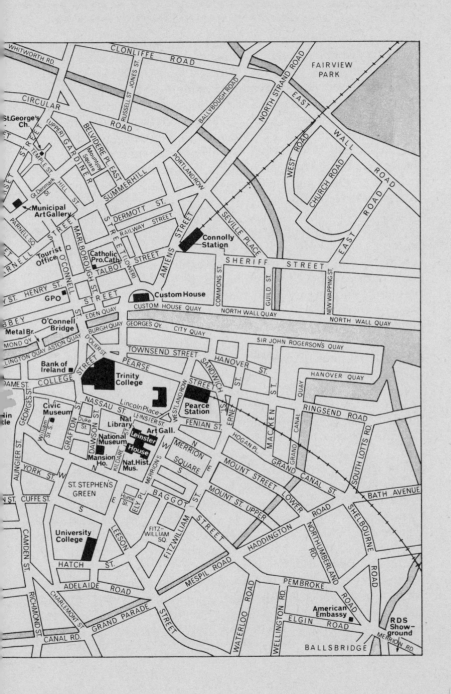

the main thoroughfares. Neglect and fighting felled and
pocked much of the eighteenth-century inheritance of north
Dublin, and that is the more disastrous since Dublin, like
Bath or Edinburgh, is essentially an eighteenth-century town.

It was old, of course, before the eighteenth century. Baile-
Ath-Cliath, its Gaelic name (pronounced Bawlaclee), means
'village of the hurdle ford' and that, like its more usual name
(which means 'black pool', from the peat-stained waters of
the Liffey) dates from prehistory. Vikings founded the town
and some surviving buildings went up in their ninth- and
tenth-century occupation. Anglo-Normans expanded and
strengthened it, and made it the centre of the Pale. It shared
its country's seesaw fate in subsequent centuries, and many
buildings and relics survive from the sixteenth and seventeenth
centuries. But a walk round the central area confirms the
eighteenth-century's predominance, in architecture and town
planning; and hundreds of street-names, even after twentieth-
century changes, still commemorate the ruling figures of the
eighteenth-century ascendancy.

College Green, with its statue of Henry Grattan and the
modern Thomas Davis memorial by Edward Delaney, is
flanked by two of the greatest eighteenth-century buildings,
the Bank of Ireland on the west and Trinity College, standing
in its own 25 acres, on the east. (There is a great coming and
going of statues in Ireland, due to nationalist feelings;
William III was helped off College Green by a land-mine in
1929.)

The **Bank of Ireland** was not built as such, but was started
in 1729 by Sir Edward Lovett Pearce, Irish Surveyor-General,
to house the Irish Parliament. Various seventeenth-century
parliaments had been held in its predecessor on the site,
Chichester House, named after James I's Lord-Deputy, Sir
Arthur Chichester. The new parliaments continued the
tradition of putty-like subservience to Westminster ('Tell us
what the pile contains?/Many a head that holds no brains'
Swift wrote) but strengthened as the century wore on, and
the Ascendancy's wealth and independence increased. At its
apogee, in the 1780s, it counted orators like Grattan, Flood
and Curran among its members and in 1783 achieved some

degree of self-government. But real power still lay with the English and their loyal claque. Before two decades were out, Wolfe Tone's 1798 rebellion, and the fear of French-style revolution or Napoleonic invasion, turned Pitt and the English firmly against independence. By means mostly foul (many Irish titles date from the period), the Parliament passed the Act of Union in 1800, and so voted its own extinction. Thomas de Quincey, on a visit, described the Lords' last sitting in his autobiographical sketches. Dublin was torn by riots. Grattan's heroic last speech brought him to a duel with the Lord Chancellor, whose hand his bullet smashed. But the Irish Parliament was dead for well over a century, and the building was sold to the Bank of Ireland for £40,000.

The handsome symmetry of the façade belies its own odd history. Pearce designed the main south-facing portico and central colonnade in their present forecourt. (Even in his day the Commons had the large central chamber, while the Lords were kept to the east wing.) Fifty years later, when more space was needed, the sensitive James Gandon designed a discreetly plain convex wall to screen new rooms southeast of the main block. His concern not to detract from Pearce's work still left him free on the east side, where he built a splendid Corinthian portico for the Lords. But when some time later similar development was needed on the west, Gandon was ignored and a committee produced a flamboyant Ionic colonnade that swamped Pearce's structure and left the whole lop-sided. However, after the Bank took over, Francis Johnston toned down the disastrous effect of the western colonnade by moving its wall forward *between* the columns, turning them into pilasters. Then he established the balance on the east by applying new columns to Gandon's wall, which he topped with a matching balustrade. The result of several efforts spread over a century is what to-day looks very like one man's work.

The British Government stipulated, when the building was sold in 1800, that the interior should be remodelled to preclude any future use as public debating rooms. Only the panelled House of Lords remains much as it was, like a large drawing-room with a fireplace, suitable for the thirty or so peers who deliberated there. It contains a magnificent 1233-piece chandelier of 1788, two vast Huguenot tapestries of the Siege of Derry and the Battle of the Boyne, woven in Dublin by 'Jan van Beaver, ye tapestry weaver', fine wood carving, and the 1765 House of Commons mace of silver gilt retrieved at a Belfast auction in 1937. Liveried guides are usually on hand to show visitors round, but most of the rooms are given over to banking activities; a pity, when independence offered a splendid chance of restoring the place to its original use, and plans had already been drawn for doing so, and for spreading the parliamentary demesne north to the quays. As it turned out those in power chose Leinster House, which has never wholly answered the needs.

The stern grey façade of **Trinity College** stands to the east of College Green. Beside its entrance are statues of Burke and Goldsmith, two alumni from a list that includes Congreve, Farquhar (supposedly expelled for a prank), Bishop Berkeley, Swift, Grattan, Emmet, Thomas Davis, Wilde, Synge, Edward Carson and many others. To look at, it could be in Cambridge, with elegant academic buildings round courtyards noisy with students. Being, as it is, in the middle of the capital, it has played at times a more active part in the nation's affairs, and political debate has often been more partial than at its English equivalents.

The college was founded in 1591 on the site of a dissolved monastery – then, like St Patrick's Cathedral, well outside the walls of the city, which was concentrated round the Castle. Other colleges, planned to rise beside it, were never built. It remained alone, a complete university, though the Government has recently considered plans to fuse it with University College in a newly constituted University of Dublin. Its founders – among them Archbishop Ussher, Primate of Ireland (who first dated the creation of Adam to the precise year 4004 BC) – hoped it would be a civilising influence in Popish Ireland, and it remained exclusively Protestant, with a short break in James II's reign, till 1793. Even then, senior offices and fellowships were withheld from Catholics till 1873. Women students, however, were admitted in degrees in 1903, earlier than in some British universities.

Until recently, English students who failed to get to Oxford or Cambridge often tried for Trinity, as a more socially approved option than English redbrick. To the Irish, for some good reasons, it has always had a smack of Ascendancy; though social, as opposed to religious, equality has been firm policy during most of its existence.

The oldest existing buildings date from the turn of the seventeenth century, a time when Whiggish tutors were resented – and one at least was murdered – by students of Jacobite sympathy, and the habit began of defacing King William's statue in College Green, to end only with the 1929 explosion. A tradition lasted long that 'Trinity Fellows made up in bad manners for what they lacked in learning'. As the eighteenth century was set into its rich, Augustan and optimistic mould, both buildings and reputation of the college rose. The main construction work took place in mid-century, substantially financed by the Irish Parliament, after which the first courtyard – Parliament Square – is named.

The 300-ft Palladian façade – one of Dublin's great elevations – dates from 1752–9, a time when the city, with a population approaching 150,000, was, bar London, the largest in the British Isles. This west front was the work of the London architects, Henry Keene and John Sanderson. It houses, on the upper floor, a hall known as the Regent House. The porch leads by the Porters' Lodge towards the clean, grey, slightly forbidding granite buildings surrounding the two main squares. On the left of Parliament Square is the **dining-hall**, built in the 1740s by Richard Castle, second only to Francis Johnston in the number of buildings he designed for Dublin. Much restored (it started falling down ten years after erection), it contains portraits of famous Trinity men. Projecting from the end of this wing is the darkly panelled **chapel**, added between 1779 and 1790, to the rough designs of Sir William Chambers (at the time heavily occupied with London's Somerset House). The elegant hundred-foot **campanile** to the front was built in 1853 on a spot supposed to mark the centre of the medieval priory church. (In spite of repeated attempts, no undergraduate has yet reached the top to plant a trophy.) Opposite and corresponding to the chapel on the right of the court is the **Examination Hall,** or theatre. Like the chapel, it was designed by the prolific and fastidious Chambers. It has, like the chapel, good ceiling stucco by Michael Stapleton, whose Adam style came into fashion after the more flamboyant work of Robert West. The theatre – with its 60-light gilt chandelier brought via St Andrew's Church from the Old Parliament House at the time of the Union – makes a lavish setting for the concerts often held there.

The 1906 bronze figure to the right of the Campanile and not far from a reclining figure by Henry Moore is of W. E. H. Lecky (1838–1903), a scholar of Trinity and author of the masterly *History of Ireland in the Eighteenth Century*. As MP for Trinity from 1895 he opposed Home Rule, but still comes over as progressive when compared with his contemporary, J. A. Froude. Beyond it, at the far end of the grassed Library Square, are the terraced **Rubrics,** apartments dating from the turn of the seventeenth century and the oldest extant college buildings. Goldsmith had his chambers here. Trinity's greatest treasure is the austere, 270-ft long **Library,** to the right of the court. Originally redbrick, it was begun in 1712 to the plans of Thomas Burgh (the first known Irish-trained architect). It opened in 1732, having cost £20,000. Until 1892, when sadly it was closed in, the ground floor was an open arcade, insulating the books from the damp ground below and supporting possibly the largest single-chamber library in the world. Its glory is the interior, lit by a hundred windows. The pinewood barrel-vault by Benjamin Woodward is an early Victorian replacement of, and arguably an improvement on, the original flat plaster ceiling which divided the chamber into two floors. Throughout the interior, whose lofty perspective is emphasised by book-lined recesses and a series of marble busts, there is an economy of decoration (except on the richly carved Corinthian capitals) and an atmosphere of clerical restraint. It contains nearly a million manuscripts and printed books and the number grows steadily, as Trinity is one of the four libraries in these islands entitled, by the Library Act of 1801, to a free copy of every book published in Britain and Ireland.

At the top of the staircase (by Richard Castle) leading up to the library there was until recently an inscribed tablet, and nearby a painting of the battle order at the 1602 Battle of Kinsale. These commemorated the £700 subscribed by the English victors – 'out of the arrears of their pay' – to found the library, in the hopes that what was never to be lastingly achieved by the sword might make steadier progress by the printed word. South of the building is the modern extension, planned by Paul Koralek (who won the commission in an open international competition and who also designed the Arts and Social Science building to the south) and opened in 1967 – an annexe of shuttered concrete that has a claim to be the best modern building in Ireland. Its inside arrangements are as advanced as any library's in the world. Outstanding manuscripts are kept on display in a building beside the new library. They include two of the greatest, but stylistically opposed, early Celtic manuscripts: the mid-seventh-century Book of Durrow, with its beautiful Irish majuscule text and inspired primitive illuminations; and the Book of Kells, compiled a century later, possibly at St Columba's monastery on Iona, showing at its most elaborate the whimsical extravagance of Celtic art. West of this is the neatly square **Provost's House,** facing out to Grafton Street, and built by John Smyth in 1759 following, externally, Lord Burlington's design for General Wade's house in London (of which Lord Chesterfield said its owner would do best to sell, and buy the house opposite, to be able to see without having to live in it). Closed to the public, it remains as it was originally, with one of its rooms, a finely ceilinged saloon, running the length of the building.

Along the north flank of Library Court is the unlovely Graduates' Memorial Building of 1892. If we pass to the right of the Rubrics we come to New Square, with Benjamin Woodward's **Museum Building** of 1853-7 on the right, now the School of Engineering – a building whose outside carvings and spacious domed staircase delighted Ruskin. On the left, in the square's north-west corner, is Castle's little Doric **Printing House,** a gift to the university from Bishop Stearne of Clogher in 1734. (Bishop Berkeley the philosopher gave a fount of Greek type in the same year.) It still contains, as it did throughout the eighteenth century, the University Press, which until this century used a picture of the delicate temple-like building as its title-page device.

Beyond the square lie the relieving grass and trees of **College Park,** which we can cross and emerge in Lincoln Place, close to the city's best preserved Georgian enclave. Lincoln's Inn was formerly Fanning's, and as such figures in Gogarty's *As I Was Walking Down Sackville Street.* A right and left turn outside the college's back gate bring us to the north-west corner of **Merrion Square.** Like central Dublin on both sides of the Liffey, this sector owes much to a 1757 Act of the Irish Parliament which set up the 'Commissioners for Making Wide and Convenient Streets', well ahead of other European cities. Their timely work up to 1840, when the Dublin Corporation took over, often evokes nostalgia in an age of ugly and quick-return development, but it sometimes involved fairly brutal appropriation of crowded buildings along narrow streets. Still, it has left the pleasing spaciousness, sometimes depressingly windy, of the modern town centre.

Another feature of the residential area that surrounds the square – and an impressive comment on eighteenth-century rationalism – is its shortage of churches. St Stephen's, at the end of Mount Street Upper, brought a magnificent vista to the square's south side, but only in 1824. Growing from empty marshland to be the city's chief residential district in the space of a century (1721–1825) it did, all that time, without any church building at all. The square itself was laid out in 1762 and completed by the end of the century. Most of the tall brick houses, whose small differences in height, style, doorways and wrought-ironwork were caused by the rivalries of aristocrats and merchants, have interesting histories, and most now house official institutions. Sir William and Lady Wilde (irascible surgeon and antiquary, and histrionic poetess) lived at No. 1, for a time with young Oscar; No. 39 was the British Embassy Chancery until it was burned early in 1972; Sir Jonah Barrington (1760-1834), judge, wit and diarist – who was deprived of office for appropriating money paid into his court, but is still known for his colourful, suspect *Personal Sketches* and *Historic Anecdotes and Secret Memoirs* – lived at No. 42. Daniel O'Connell owned No. 58 in his latter, respectable years. W. B. Yeats, who was born at Sandymount and spent years of his boyhood and adult life in London, lived for a while at No. 52; when, in 1922, he became a senator of the Irish Free State, he bought No. 82, staying till 1929 when he took a flat at 42 Fitzwilliam Square. The Duke of Wellington was born at No. 24 Upper Merrion Street, which runs from the south-west corner of the square, on 29th April 1769, his father the Earl of Mornington being Professor of Music at Trinity (but the Duke was brought up at Dangan). After the earl's time No. 24 was bought by the first Lord Cloncurry and rented, at the time of the Union, by Lord Castlereagh. The effect the Union had on prices as well as morale is shown by Cloncurry's paying £8,000 for the house and selling it ten years later – but *after* Union – for £2,500. It now houses the Land Commission. Good Georgian houses continue in the streets to the south, and one of the finest concentrations is in **Fitzwilliam Square**, built in the 1820s, and now, with doctors thick on the ground, Dublin's Harley Street. It connects with Merrion Square by Fitzwilliam Street, one side of which, despite spirited protest, was maimed in 1965 to make way for a new Electricity Supply Board building.

Facing Merrion Square on the west is Leinster Lawn, at the back of **Leinster House**, seat of the Irish Parliament or *Oireachtas*, which we can visit shortly. Two wings (built much later than Leinster House) flank the lawn, the right-hand of which houses Ireland's **National Gallery**. The statue on the lawn depicts William Dargan, the great Irish Railway King, who used the profits of the 1853 Dublin Exhibition, which he organised on the same site, to found the collection. The statue of Shaw near the entrance is by the Polish Paul Troubetzkoy, and it was the playwright's own favourite. Shaw left the gallery a third of his estate in his will. The filming of *Pygmalion* as *My Fair Lady* brought in a windfall. Even before this the gallery housed one of Europe's more important collections, especially in respect of continental works.

Inside, some impressive alterations and additions to the

rooms have been made recently, involving a rearrangement of the pictures. Of the 6,000 paintings in the collection, less than 2,000 are on view, but they make one of the finest smaller collections in Europe, due partly to the obdurate generosity of Sir Hugh Lane. Lane's nose for art-bargains and Old Masters of the future, as well as his generosity with an amassed fortune, were put repeatedly at Ireland's disposal, and all too often rejected. In 1903 the governing authority failed to appoint him – obvious and best candidate – Curator of the National Museum; and when later, as senator of the new university, he proposed a £350 salary for the new Professor of Art, the sum was reduced to £100. His sin in official eyes was admiring the Impressionists. When Lane proposed an art gallery spanning the Liffey (where the Metal Bridge now stands) to be built by Lutyens, he was thwarted at every turn. Yet Lane was offering the finance too, with American support. The architect should be Irish, said officials; (Lutyens in fact had an Irish mother). Dublin's spurning of Lane's love for it at last drove him to give London, then Johannesburg, what he wanted Dublin to possess. He even changed his will in London's favour. Before he died he recanted and added a codicil; but this was not witnessed, and London's National Gallery – legally right but morally equivocal – refused to part with the Lane Collection till a recent arbitration divided the pictures between London and Dublin on a five-yearly exchange basis. The Irish half is kept at the Municipal Gallery of Modern Art in Parnell Square.

Besides Lane's work for the gallery, there have been important bequests from Evie Hone in 1955, and Sir Chester Beatty in 1960. In the Irish section downstairs there is a good selection of the work of Nathaniel Hone (1831–1917), descendant of a prolifically artistic eighteenth-century family, and himself much influenced by twenty years spent at Barbizon. Several hundred of his oils and many more water-colours are stored out of sight, ensuring that, regardless of his merit, he is never well known. His skies and seascapes have great power and drama, and his detail is impeccable – the butcher who came to buy cattle at his home at Portmarnock was told to pick out wanted animals from the latest canvas, which might have been on the lines of his *Cattle at Malahide* here.

Outstanding the century before was James Barry (1741–1806), son of a Catholic bricklayer in Cork, who was taken up by Edmund Burke, and thereafter lived in Rome and England, where he failed to make the impact he hoped and allowed his choler to hamper his career, though he was Professor of Painting at the Royal Academy for seventeen years from 1782 and decorated the Society of Arts with many huge murals, still in place. His *Adam and Eve* here shows a typical attempt at sublime grandeur without the skill of his inspiration, Raphael. James Arthur O'Connor's (1792-1841) *The Poachers* is here too, showing Ireland in her turn move into the evocative landscapes of continental styles. Much of his best work is at Westport House, Co. Mayo. There is a well-known portrait of *W. B. Yeats* by his father, J. B. Yeats, as well as the *Artist's Wife* and *John O'Leary*. The twentieth-century room also includes twelve paintings by the poet's brother, Jack B. Yeats, as well as works by Sir William Orpen, Walter Osborne (an underrated painter, showing Impressionist influence, with a deep feeling for scenes of urban bustle and squalor), together with works by Picasso, Juan Gris, Segonzac and others.

The Italian collection includes Fra Angelico's little *Attempted Martyrdom of Saints Cosmas and Damian*; an unknown painter's *Battle of Anghiari* and *The Taking of Pisa* (both panels on a wedding-chest); Titian's *Portrait of Baldassare Castiglione*; Tintoretto's *Venice, Queen of the Adriatic*; Perugino's *Pietà*; and works by Giovanni Bellini, Correggio, Palma Vecchio, Veronese, Canaletto, and many others. There are French paintings from all periods, including Gerard David's *Our Lord bidding farewell to his Mother*, Claude's *Juno confiding Io to the care of Argus;* Poussin's *Entombment* and others; and ballet sketches by Degas. The famous *Saint Francis in Ecstasy* by El Greco is in the Spanish section, along with three brilliant Goyas, Murillo's *St Mary Magdalen*, and others. The Flemish, Dutch and German schools are richly represented by such masterpieces as Geerhardt David's *Christ Saying Farewell to his Mother;* Rubens' *St Dominic;* Brueghel's *Peasant Wedding;* and two Rembrandts. The large English section has nine Gains-

boroughs, four Hogarths, seven Reynolds's, and works by
Stubbs, Wilson, Turner, Raeburn, Lawrence, Crome, Romney
and Constable. The display of thirty-one Turner water-colours
is limited to the month of January by the terms of a 1900
bequest, but they may be seen in all their coddled freshness on
request. There is also an important collection of icons, recently
acquired.

The **Natural History Section** of the National Museum is
south of Leinster Lawn. It is, as such places tend to be, a little
musty, and many of its exhibits need renewing. But, without
pretensions to be anything but national, it contains a complete
and at the same time digestible representation of Irish
ecology. Some things are remarkable for their absence; as
well as the Romans, the Reformation, and, for a long while,
the Industrial Revolution, Ireland has done without moles,
weasels, polecats, voles, the Greater Shrew, two of the four
British mice, eight of the fifteen British bats, snakes, night-
ingales, reed warblers (one case of breeding is recorded),
tawny owls, and a few more. Most flora and fauna that it
has nourished are on display here, including (skeletally) the
Giant Irish Deer, with its eleven-foot antler span, an animal
that was not uncommon between twelve and four thousand
years ago, after the Ice Age's retreat. The antlers alone
weighed about a hundredweight, and were shed and regrown
every year. Exclusively Irish animals displayed include the
Irish hare and Irish stoat, a smaller, darker version of the
British one, and confusingly often called weasel, though no
such animal exists here. There are particularly good displays
of mammals, birds, insects and spiders – and enough specimens
of exotic sea creatures – shark, fire fish, sun fish, angel ray,
whip ray, blue skate – to deter all but the brave from the
growing tourist sport of sea-fishing.

Leinster House itself faces west to Kildare Street, and its
courtyard is flanked by two more repositories, the National
Library and the National Museum. It was built in 1745, to
Richard Castle's plans, for the Earl of Kildare, though the
north side of the river was then more fashionable. Castle built
it in the manner of a country house – two formal fronts,
with a central corridor dividing the house longways, in the

harsh, cold stone quarried at Ardbraccan. When the earl, whose country seat was Carton (rebuilt by Castle), was made Duke of Leinster in 1766, the house's name was changed. As Leinster House it was sold in 1815 to the Royal Dublin Society, whose headquarters it remained for a century, during which the great complex of museums and institutes that remain rose around it. The first independent government in 1922, rejecting the far more appropriate Bank of Ireland building in the centre, decided to make it the seat of government, and the Royal Dublin Society was evicted to Ballsbridge. Now the Dail Eireann (or Chamber of Deputies—148 of them) occupies the Society's old D-shaped lecture hall, and the Seanad (or Senate, of sixty) meets in the attractive north-wing saloon, with excellent stucco work on walls and ceiling. Visitors are shown round as much as current business of government allows. The similarity of design between this house and the White House in Washington may stem from the fact that the latter's architect, James Hoban, was born in Carlow in 1762 and trained in Dublin.

To the right of Leinster House on leaving it is the **National Library**, with a rich collection of manuscripts and over half a million books (the reading room can be seen by visitors). Attached to it is the **National College of Art**. On the left is the **National Museum.** Both these flanking buildings were designed in Renaissance style by Sir Thomas Deane and opened in 1890. Far the most splendid of the museum's displays is in the Great Hall on the ground floor – a priceless collection of Irish antiquities from Stone Age times, through the Bronze and Early Christian periods to the Middle Ages. In the entrance hall, or Rotunda, are casts made by the best Irish sculptor, John Henry Foley, of some notable High Crosses. Of Bronze Age items, the most striking are the gold ornaments – torques, lunulae and fibulae that date from as far back as 2000 BC – when immigrant craftsmen, working with gold mined in Co. Wicklow and elsewhere, produced work that was in demand as far as the Mediterranean. The Feakle Treasure of a gorget and other ornaments is dated to about 650 BC.

The Early Christian period, after St Patrick and other

missionaries converted the country in the fifth century, brought Ireland to an unlikely eminence in several branches of the arts and scholarship. Trinity Library possesses some of the best illuminated manuscripts. In the museum the greatest relics include the Ardagh Chalice, a superbly restrained eighth-century silver and copper two-handled cup, decorated with bands, bosses, enamelled beads and gold filigree, in styles which are echoed in most other Celtic crafts; the penannular Tara Brooch, of about the same time, of cast silver-gilt studded with glass and amber; and decorated with bird and animal designs in intricate filigree; the Moylough Belt-shrine of silvered bronze with enamel appliqué; and the Lough Erne reliquaries. The tradition is continued in later treasures, including the highly decorated brass Shrine of St Patrick's Bell, from the twelfth century; several crosier- and book-shrines, especially those of Lismore, Clonmacnois, and Cormac McCarthy of Cashel (all early twelfth century); the Cross of Cong from the same period, which originally contained one of the suspiciously numerous pieces of the True Cross; and the later Fiacal Padraig in which, at Killaspugbrone near Sligo, was preserved a tooth of St Patrick, for the edification of future generations. As a whole, the display rivals and perhaps surpasses all related collections in Europe; for Ireland, free of the Romans (Roman items on display were probably pilfered from Britain by third- and fourth-century Irish invaders) preserved and developed its Celtic origins as no other country could. However, it is not the only notable section of the museum, which houses also a fine assortment of musical instruments, good silver, glass, guns, so-called Irish Chippendale furniture, exhibits of country crafts; and memorials of all risings and wars up to 1922.

Kildare Street, outside, runs from Trinity to St Stephen's Green. At the north – Trinity – end, on the right, is the distinguished building which until 1977 housed the **Kildare Street Club,** in which the principles of the Protestant Ascendancy are said to survive unmoved by events of the last hundred years. Founded in 1782 in No. 6, near the Shelbourne, it moved for more room in 1860 (during the move the old premises caught fire and three maids were killed) to this Venetian style palace by Deane and Woodward, with its adornment of whimsical

The Custom House, seen from across the Liffey.
Below The Bank of Ireland, Dublin, once home of the Irish Parliament.

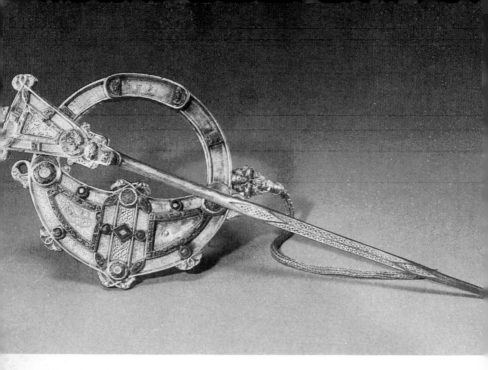

In Dublin's National Museum: The Tara Brooch, a paragon of Celtic intricacy. *Below* The Ardagh Chalice, an eighth-century marriage of restraint and ornament.

beasts. The new building is now leased, but the club goes on, amalgamated with the **University Club** in St Stephen's Green. No. 39 Kildare Street was home of Lady Morgan (1776–1859), who came to early fame as Sydney Owenson for her rattling wild-Irish novels, then married a learned doctor and became Dublin's leading hostess, a beacon in the drear post-Union days. Her drawing-room has been called 'the foyer of liberation'. Every visitor had to call on her. 'Fifty philosophers passed through my little salon last night', she wrote once. But developers have replaced philosophers and in 1972 the house and several others were demolished. In **Nassau Street** (left at the top of Kildare Street) is the modern Kilkenny Shop, an emporium of the best of Irish craftsmenship.

Molesworth Street is directly opposite Leinster House. It is smart, rich, and distinctive in some details, mainly the gable-ended houses whose style followed William III from Holland. The site, owned by Robert, 1st Viscount Molesworth of Swords, was the centre of a development scheme of 1725 and onwards, and the houses are Dublin's oldest this side of the river. In a city well endowed with fine Georgian doorways, No. 20 has one of the finest. This was until recently an old-world quarter, with plenty of solicitors, tailors, odd societies, and slightly *bijou* antique shops, but developers have begun their inroads by demolishing houses on the north side and replacing them with bland brick blocks. At the far end of Molesworth Street we meet **Dawson Street,** a busy bus route which, first laid out in about 1709, boasts mainly late Georgian houses, many rebuilt or converted into shops. Facing us is the **Royal Hibernian,** one of the best and best-known Dublin hotels. A few doors down on the left is **St Anne's Parish Church,** begun in 1720 to the plans of Isaac Wills, credited also with the design of St Werburgh's Church, and still as fashionable as it was in its early years, at the centre of this exclusive parish. Its curved apse and gallery carried on slender pillars keep the elegance which Victorian stained glass and the rebuilding of the west front (by Sir Thomas Deane) did their best to cancel out. Mrs Hemans, author of 'The Boy Stood on the Burning Deck' and various religious poems, is buried there: and there are curved shelves on either side of the chancel to hold a weekly twenty-five pence worth of bread for the poor of the parish, bequeathed, at the time of the church's founding, by Theophilus Lord Newtown.

Farther down on the left is the home of the **Royal Irish Academy**, originally built for Lord Northland of Dungannon in 1770 and converted in 1852 to its present use. (Wolfe Tone, close friend of Northland's son, spent a lot of time here.) The academy itself was granted a charter in 1785 to foster the study of 'Science, Polite Literature, and Antiquities', and is still the country's leading academic society. The original building, backed by additions begun in the 1850s, is handsome red brick with stone cornice, string-courses and window-cases. Its library can be visited and contains a priceless collection of ancient manuscripts which include the early ninth-century *Stowe Missal*, the *Book of Ballymote*, the *Speckled Book* (Leabhar Breac) – both of around 1400 – and the early seventeenth-century *Annals of the Four Masters*.

A little farther down on the left is the **Mansion House**, the Lord Mayor's official house since 1715. It was built ten years earlier as a private residence in red brick, then bought by the city; later Victorian stucco and cast-iron work prettified, and so spoiled it. Yeats hated its exterior and wrote at length of his hate. But the interior is closer to the original; and a hall, the Round Room, added hastily in 1821 for George IV's visit, is still, with a ninety-foot diameter, the largest public meeting hall in the city. It was here that the first Dail Eireann met at the end of 1918, setting up its own administration and bringing British Government to a standstill.

St Stephen's Green opens out at the end of Dawson Street, a fine stretch of green bordered, particularly on the east and south sides, by some good Georgian houses. Its origins as a park go back to Charles I's reign when, with the city population of 9,000 bursting at the walled seams, it was included in a 'green belt', 'wholie kept for the use of citizens and others, to walk & take the open aire.' Development of its precincts had to wait for the Restoration, which, resolving for a while the squabbles of centuries, encouraged the extension of Dublin's boundaries with less fear of marauding and attack from the mountains. Already, by the late seventeenth century, the green was fashionable, through the selling of sizeable plots of land around the 27-acre central area, and the prohibition of houses of less than two stories, or built of mud and wattle. During the eighteenth century, several (surviving) mansions of noblemen were built; but the land, thinly treed and without railings, was let out for grazing and put to uncongenial uses, hangings, whippings, riots and the like. The iron balustrade came in 1815, to commemorate Waterloo. In 1880 Lord Ardilaun, a Guinness philanthropist (a happily common combination) had the place converted to its present state, with ornamented lake and gardens, and gave it to the city. It saw havoc in 1916 when a contingent of the Citizen Army, like their comrades in the Post Office, disturbed the peace of a sunny Easter Bank Holiday, barricading themselves in and defending their position with guns. Countess Markievicz, commanding a contingent, gave her first order to kill and was rewarded with the blood of an English soldier. Her bust, by Seamus Murphy, stands in the park. Others include Henry Moore's bronze memorial to W. B. Yeats; Foley's Lord Ardilaun; the poet Mangan by Oliver Sheppard; the patriot Thomas Kettle by Francis Doyle; a German gift of a fountain portraying 'The Three Fates'; and a stately megalithic memorial, also by Murphy, to the Fenian leader, Jeremiah O'Donovan Rossa. Van Nost's 1758 equestrian bronze of George II shared the same fate as other memorials to English luminaries, being blown up before the last war. Less predictable was the damaging, in 1969, of Edward Delaney's Wolfe Tone statue opposite the Shelbourne. It is now restored.

Each building has a history, but we must confine ourselves to a select few. Walking clockwise round the green we pass, on the north side (called Beaux' Walk in the eighteenth century) No. 8, built in 1754, now the United Services Club; No. 9, built in 1756, now the Stephen's Green Club, and containing outstanding plaster-work; No. 16, earlier this century the palace of Dublin's Anglican Archbishop; and finally the **Shelbourne Hotel**, one of Dublin's best, certainly its most famous. The ingenious bureaucrat Sir William Petty had his home, Kerry House, here in the 1660s (his heirs were the Lansdowne family, one of whose titles was Shelburne).

Thackeray, Shelley (who released balloons from his bedroom windows), George Moore and other notables stayed here and Elizabeth Bowen has written its history. The present building dates from 1865, but Martin Burke opened his hotel in 1824. Beyond the hotel, at the beginning of Merrion Row, is a Huguenot cemetery of 1693, resting-place of many French refugees from Louis XIV's persecution; who brought their invaluable crafts to Dublin at a time, after Ormonde's planning of the modern city, when they were most needed.

The east side of the green has some dignified Georgian houses, several of them (Nos. 44, 52 and 53) with interior plaster-work by Dublin's master-stuccoist, Michael Stapleton. Hume Street, off this side of the green, leads the few yards to **Ely** (pronounced Eeligh) **Place,** a fairly unspoiled Georgian cul-de-sac of rich associations. No. 4 was the home of the intractable lawyer, John Philpot Curran (1750–1817), who violently disapproved of his daughter's involvement with the rebel Robert Emmet. George Moore lived in the house a century later, and owned the garden opposite. (When he moved in, all the front doors were painted white, by the landlord's orders. Moore, insisting that being an art critic demanded it, painted his green, and a feud began with his neighbours, two sisters. They dumped in his letter-box a torn-up copy of *Esther Waters* labelled 'too filthy to keep'. To retaliate, Moore rattled their railings at night to make the dogs bark. They hired an organ-grinder to play below his window, and he prosecuted the organ-grinder. He threw stones at their cat, which threatened his favourite blackbird in the garden; then bought a trap. They called the RSPCA; but in the end the trap caught the bird.)

W. B. Yeats told the story in his *Autobiographies*. He himself frequented No. 8 – Ely House, facing Hume Street – at the turn of the century, then the headquarters of Dublin's Theosophical Society. There, in company with George Russell (AE), Maud Gonne and others, he pursued that mysticism which had its effect on the Anglo-Irish culture of the Celtic Twilight. Michael Stapleton built this house (and Nos. 6 and 15) in 1770 for Henry Loftus, Earl of Ely. It shows strong Adam influence in its mahogany doors, plasterwork, carved chimney pieces, and magnificently flamboyant wrought-iron staircase with the labours of Hercules in gilt bronze inserted at intervals. The place comes to vivid life in the pages of Gogarty's Dublin classic (see below), but the days when he sat discussing George Moore's sex-life with the then owner Sir Thornley Stoker, brother of Bramley, Dracula's creator, amid appropriate period riches, and they were interrupted by the unexplained entry of an elderly naked lady crying 'I like a little intelligent conversation', are far away. The house is now the headquarters of the Knights of Columbanus, a kind of Catholic masonry. No. 6 was the home of John Fitzgibbon (1749–1802), Earl of Clare; who as Lord Chancellor was mainly responsible for the passing of the Act of Union which brought all hopes of a healthy independent Ireland to an end. Popular reaction to his policies was felt at No. 6 when a crowd of 6,000 men and women, with *ad hoc* armaments, chased the chancellor home, stoned the house and him, and tried to break in; but they were panicked into flight by the chancellor's sister mixing disguised in the crowd and spreading the canard that the army was on its way. No. 25 Ely Place was the home of Oliver St John Gogarty (1878–1957). It has been pulled down recently to make way for the Royal Hibernian Academy's art gallery: not a very clever thing for such a learned society to do. Gogarty, surgeon, poet and author (of, among others, *As I Was Going Down Sackville Street*, first of an autobiographical series) was a close friend of Joyce and figured as Malachi Mulligan in *Ulysses*.

Back at St Stephen's Green and continuing down the east side, we pass, some way along and among other Georgian buildings, the former St Vincent's Hospital, which in 1834 was adapted from Nos. 54, 55 and 56. Earlsfort Terrace leads away from the Green at the corner, and down it on the right is the dull granite face of **University College,** Dublin. This, the largest constituent of the National University of Ireland, with 9,000 students, has now largely moved to a new 400-acre estate at Belfield in Donnybrook. Part of the Earlsfort Terrace buildings were erected for the Great Exhibition of 1865, and enlarged in 1880 for the new Royal University (a makeshift, non-teaching institution whose function was simply to hold exams and grant degrees to those whom scruples or geography prevented from entering Trinity). In 1909 the National University was founded, comprising the colleges at Cork, Galway and Dublin. Douglas Hyde (1866–1949), first President of the Irish Republic, and his co-founder of the Gaelic League, the historian Eoin MacNeill (1867–1945), the poet Thomas MacDonagh and statesman Kevin O'Higgins, were at the university.

Second left off Leeson Street, which also leads from the Green's south-east corner, is Upper Pembroke Street, in which, between Nos. 25 and 26, a tunnel leads to the **Tower of Glass**, a studio founded by Sarah Purser in 1903 for the improvement of ecclesiastical art. Edward Martyn of Tulira overcame his misogyny to co-operate on the project. To it in part much of the best stained glass in Irish churches is owed, the work of pupils like Michael Healy, Evie Hone, Wilhelmina Geddes and Beatrice Elvery (later Lady Glenavy), and Kitty O'Brien. Sarah Purser died in 1943, but the studio continues. Its more recent output includes windows for the new cathedral of Galway.

We return to St Stephen's Green, on whose south side **Iveagh House**, now the Department of External Affairs, incorporates No. 80 (built by Castle in 1730) and No. 81. They were joined in the 1870s to make one house for the Guinness family. Castle also built No. 85, **Clanwilliam House** (with an elaborate rococo ceiling by the Francini brothers, perhaps their best work, in the upstairs saloon), and it is possible that with this house he introduced the Venetian window – of three lights, the central one arched – into Ireland. Both this and No. 86 – whose handsome grandeur clashes, probably on purpose, with its earlier neighbour – are combined as **Newman House**. They belong to University College and can be seen inside. From a first-floor window of No. 86, its owner, the MP, gambler and rake Buck Whaley, is said to have jumped into a standing coach for a bet. These two houses were formed, in 1853, into the Catholic University, over which Cardinal Newman was first rector. His neo-Byzantine church adjoins them. Among the university's teachers was Gerard Manley Hopkins, who died in Dublin in 1889; and James Joyce was a pupil in modern languages – his first writing appeared in the student magazine. After graduating he left Ireland to spend most of his life in Paris, Trieste and Zürich. (On one return visit, in 1912, he failed to find a publisher for *Dubliners*.) Patrick Pearse and Eamon De Valera were also students here.

Harcourt Street leads off the south-west corner of the Green. Mass conversion into hotels and offices disguises the excellent Georgian architecture of its terraces. Edward Carson was born at No. 4. No. 17 was the central part of Clonmell House, built for the parvenu rogue and Chief Justice, Jack Scott, 1st Earl of Clonmell. Yeats went as a boy to the C. of I. High School at No. 40, one of the best preserved houses. Shaw was born at No. 33 Synge Street, a quarter of a mile west of, and parallel to, Harcourt Street. Back in the Green, the best façade on the west side is that of the **Royal College of Surgeons**, designed in 1806 by Edward Parke (who also planned the dignified Commercial Buildings in Dame Street), but much altered later. It served as Headquarters of the St Stephen's Green contingent of the Citizen Army in 1916, and was pocked by bullets. A statue of Robert Emmet by Jerome Connor stands opposite Nos. 124-25, where he was born.

Having walked the four sides of the Green we pass an arch, commemorating those fallen in the Boer War, and then into **Grafton Street**, named after an unmemorable viceroy of the 1720s. It is a busy street, and good shopping centre, preserving in its windings the character of the country-lane it used to be before the construction of O'Connell Bridge made it a main north–south highway. The smell of coffee from Bewleys Coffee House (with its high-backed seats a link with an older Dublin), good bookshop, tobacconists, tailors, handicrafts and other shops, and the famous department stores of Brown Thomas and Switzer contribute to the street's cachet, something like Bond Street's, on an Irish scale. Some lanes and alleys off the street are worth following. Johnston's Court on the left leads past the oddly sequestered Carmelite Church of St Teresa. Beyond and parallel to Clarendon Street, at the end of the court, is William Street, in which, to the right, is the massive, granite, and in the present context, over-large façade of **Powerscourt House**. It was built in the early 1770s by Robert Mack for the third Viscount Powerscourt, an Opposition leader, who also owned the family house by Castle in Co. Wicklow. Its interior preserves good plaster work by Michael Stapleton, very much in the Adam style.

A little to the south, we come on the **Civic Museum**, built after 1765 for the Society of Artists, and used in 1920–2 as the Supreme Court of the outlawed Republican government. It houses a collection of Dublin drawings, models and relics of various kinds.

Back in Grafton Street, No. 79 is on the site of Samuel Whyte's Academy, where Sheridan the playwright, the future Duke of Wellington, Robert Emmet and Tom Moore were at school. Over the road is **Duke Street,** with the renovated Bailey restaurant, where once Parnell, and later Arthur Griffith, Gogarty and their friends used to meet regularly in the first-floor Smoking Room, between five and seven in the evening. Opposite is Davy Byrne's pub. Joyce frequented both, but both were unrecognisably different in his day. A religion grows up in Dublin round pubs with Joyce or Brendan Behan associations, but especially in Joyce's case the atmospheres congenial to him are seldom found now in the pubs he made famous.

*

At the top of Grafton Street we return to College Green (passing, on the right, a better view of Trinity's Provost's House than that from the college grounds). Now we turn left towards Dame Street, and the city's oldest quarters and buildings. **Dame Street** itself, whose name derives from a dam on the Poddle River, beside the castle, became important in the seventeenth century as the link between the old city and newly founded Trinity College, as well as the harbour beyond. Where before College Green had comprised a pasture where any citizen could graze his cattle, Dame Street now became the backbone of the city and stayed so till the nineteenth century, when the north–south axis from O'Connell (then Carlisle) Bridge took over. At one time the centre of the city's goldsmiths, it now mixes business and commerce

fairly evenly. Beyond the Bank of Ireland, on our right, is
the site of Daly's Club House, built in 1791 to house a society
of aristocrats and politicians. It was noted for intrigue, high
spirits and gambling; detected cheats being thrown from
upper windows. But it lost ground to the Kildare Street Club,
and closed in 1873. Fragments of the original survive in the
present structure.

Anglesea Street is just beyond on the right. Its name recalls
the Earls of Anglesey's estates in this area, granted in the
seventeenth century and subject, in the eighteenth, of one of
the longest Irish legal disputes, when one member of the
family was denied his titles by another through unending
claims of illegitimacy, bigamy, assault and murder. Characters
and episodes probably gave Scott models for the battle for
possession of Ellangowan in *Guy Mannering*. The incumbent
claimant was finally recognised by an Irish court but not by
the English House of Lords, and his titles had to be separated.
Edward Parke's 1799 **Commercial Buildings** stood just beyond,
a dignified granite structure recently reconstructed, in which
wholesale commercial business was conducted within easy reach
of the quays where, in those days, ships were moored. The
vestibule and inner courtyard have been destroyed. Of the
various narrow streets that lead down, in a period maze, towards
the river on the right, Fownes Street is named after a philanthropic friend of Swift who persuaded the dean to leave
his money to found a lunatic asylum; and **Crow Street** is
associated with a theatre that rivalled the Smock Alley
theatre to the west, at a time when Ireland's prosperity
attracted, not only native talent, but also the best actors and
writers of England as well, including Farquhar, Garrick, the
Kembles, Mrs Siddons, and Tate Wilkinson. Thomas
Sheridan, R.B.'s father, was the making of Smock Alley,
managing it in the mid-century, a time when shouts and
missiles from the gallery and invasion of the stage and
dressing rooms by bucks who thought actresses fair game at
any time made modern audience participation look somewhat
stilted. The Duke of Leinster himself, in a leap from box to
stage, was rumoured to have impaled, and virtually cas⁺rated,
himself on spiked iron bars erected for the players' defence.

Now the hill rises to the castle and the high ground to which most of medieval Dublin was confined. On the left, just before the Castle Gate, is the imposing domed **City Hall**, with its heavy Corinthian portico, the building of which first brought the architect Thomas Cooley to Dublin from London in 1769. He won the £100 prize for his design. It was built, in what a century before had been the Earl of Cork's garden, as the Royal Exchange, to replace the Old Tholsel; but marketing activities followed the city's movement eastwards, and it was left to serve various functions: prison for rebels of the 1798 Rising, military depot and Corn Exchange. In 1852 it was given its present role. The rotunda with twelve support columns is worth a glance from inside, but apart from some statues – the best by Edward Smyth of Charles Lucas – ancient charters and regalia the building is rather cold and unwelcoming. So, too, was Dublin, when Thomas Wentworth came as Viceroy in 1632 and found that his new home, the **Castle,** lay derelict and cruelly damp. From his study window he used to look at an old horse grazing as it could in the muddy ooze which was spread so wide there was barely space for 'taking the air'. He rebuilt it with his usual brusque efficiency but five years after a maid left a basket of hot ashes under a wooden staircase and it all burned to a shell. Wentworth wrote to the king that he had lost 'the worst castle in the worst situation in Christendom'.

Destruction, with or without intent, had been regular since its first building around 1220. It was the bastion of Englishry from the thirteenth century to 1922, when, after a period during which its prison function was revived, the English moved out. The rebels of 1916 were so awed by its prestige that they did not even try to take it, though at the time of the Rising it was not defended. In the past its reputation was as grim as that of the Tower of London, with severed heads of criminals riding its gates. To-day, hardly any of the medieval building survives. It is, in essence, eighteenth century, and it was in the eighteenth century, when feminine Anglo-Irish hearts all over Ireland beat fast in the hopes of an invitation to a ball or presentation to the viceroy, that 'the Castle' was synonymous with the Ascendancy. In its new version it was

divided into an upper court, with the viceroy's private and
state apartments off, and a lower court, giving on to the
Record Tower (now the State Paper Office – the only one
of the original Norman corner-towers to survive), and the
Chapel Royal, built by Johnston about 1814 (C of I till 1943;
now the Catholic Church of the Most Holy Trinity). The
Upper Yard, apart from the grandly porticoed Bedford Tower,
containing the Heraldic Museum and Genealogical Office
(whose staff, for a fee, help to trace Irish ancestors), and its
flanking triumphal arches on the north side, is almost sombrely
redbrick and domestic. (It was often pointed out that the
figure of Justice on the Cork Hill gate faced the viceroy and
kept her back to the people.) From a safe in the Bedford
Tower, in 1907, just before Edward VII arrived on a state
visit, the Irish Crown Jewels were stolen. The theft was followed
for years by a trail of rumour, reports of homosexuality in
high places, arrests and at least two murders, but the mystery
was never solved nor were the jewels ever found.

Recent years have seen extensive restoration of the Castle,
and some rebuilding of the east and south sides of the upper
courtyard. An incongruous office block has arisen on the east
of the lower courtyard. But the state apartments (open to the
public) are as sumptuous and imposing as they were in their
imperial heyday. St Patrick's Hall, at the top of the stairs, has
been called the most magnificent room in Ireland. Once used
for banquets, state balls, and the investiture of the knights of
St Patrick, it is now the setting for the seven-yearly inauguration
of presidents and other high-flown happenings. The three huge
ceiling paintings by Vincent Waldré date from 1778: their
forgotten theme the benefits England showered on Ireland.
Waldré's patron was the viceroy, the Marquess of Buckingham,
noted by Horace Walpole for his 'many disgusting qualities, as
pride, obstinacy, and want of truth, with natural propensity to
avarice'. It was here that Buckingham invested himself, in 1783,
first grand master of the Knights of St Patrick, a now defunct
order whose members' banners still decorate the walls. The
Supper Room, with elegant gothic plasterwork, is situated inside
Bermingham Tower, originally of 1411 but rebuilt in 1775. The
list of martyrs and rebels confined here is long and distinguished.

The State Dining Room was added for George V's visit in 1911. A long gallery leads to the gilded Throne Room, decorated in Buckingham's time; the medallions above the doors may be by Angelica Kauffman. Other rooms contain two fine eighteenth century plaster ceilings, brought here from Sarah Purser's demolished Mespil House.

Outside the castle Lord Edward Street leads up to Christ Church Cathedral, at the start of an area of the city which, because of the demolition of slums, and the failure to put anything much in their place, has a no-man's-land quality. Before the cathedral, **Fishamble Street** curves down to the river, and it was in the Charitable Musical Society's Hall here, long since demolished, that Handel's *Messiah* was given its first performance, on 13th April, 1742. This was a period of great musical activity in Dublin. Geminiani lived in Dame Street, and played and taught there for years. Thomas Arne and his son Michael (later an alchemist who tried to concoct gold in a house at Clontarf) gave many concerts – Arne senior's opera *Rosamund* was performed in 1743. Handel's stay was the high point of these years. Put out by rivalry in London with Bononcini, and the public's inability to choose the greater composer, Handel accepted an invitation from the Duke of Devonshire, then viceroy, to visit and compose a new work for Dublin. In six weeks he wrote *The Messiah*. Its performance was triumphant, and often repeated. It was only later that George II initiated the custom of standing for the *Hallelujah Chorus*, but on this occasion Dr Delany rose at the end of *He was despised* and cried to the soloist, Mrs Cibber: 'Woman, for this, be all thy sins forgiven.' Handel stayed a year and England had to wait nearly two for its first hearing of the new work. Before leaving he was taken to the by now demented Swift, who, on registering who his visitor was, cried out: 'Oh! a German, and a Genius! A Prodigy! Admit him.'

Christ Church Cathedral is the oldest building in Dublin. It is also mother church of the C of I diocese of Dublin and Glendalough, and one of the two C of I cathedrals, both originally RC, of a mainly RC city which lacks an RC one; there have been proposals to hand over Christ Church to the

Catholics, but they always come to grief. Founded by the Dublin Danes, about 1040, it was begun again on something approaching its present scale in 1172, Strongbow and St Laurence O'Toole being sponsors; and the basic building was complete fifty years later. Part of the crypt built by the Danes may have been preserved. A lot has changed since the main building period, and the central tower, though it looks perfectly in keeping with the rest, was built about 1600 after one original steeple was burned and another flattened in a storm. Its history reflects that of the town. Lambert Simnel, ten years old and supposed son of the Earl of Warwick – and so claimant to the throne – was crowned here in 1487 as Edward VI, with a golden tiara taken from a statue of the Virgin Mary (a year later, captured in England along with his ambitious backers, he was sent by a wryly merciful Henry VII to work out his days as kitchen-boy). The cathedral adopted Anglicanism in 1551. For a short period under James II it restored the Mass, though an Anglican thanksgiving was offered in 1691 after William III's victory at the Boyne. It was used for services and concerts in the eighteenth century, but the urgent need of repairs, as well as the growth of slums, closed its doors in 1829. Massive restoration costing Henry Roe, a Dublin distiller, a quarter of a million pounds, took place between 1871 and 1878. The architect was George Edmund Street, a prolific and distinguished Gothic Revivalist, and pupil of Sir George Gilbert Scott. Street's work – including the present east wing, west front, flying buttresses, baptistery, and the Synod Hall across St Michael's Hill, as well as the covered bridge that connects with it – has left more of its stamp on the building than that of any other period. Indeed little of the main structure – the transepts and sagging north nave wall are the exceptions – remains from before.

The interior does preserve some remarkable antiquities. In the south nave arcade is a supposed, and much worn, effigy of Strongbow, marking his burial place, with another said to be either of Eve, his wife and Dermot MacMurrough's daughter, or of Strongbow's son, whom according to legend he cut in two for being a coward. Just round the corner in the south transept is the magnificent, flamboyant and grimly lit tomb of Robert, 19th Earl of Kildare (1674–1742) and premier earl of Ireland, by Sir Henry Cheere, a popular Westminster sculptor. The statue is perhaps unique in showing the subject prostrate. Eighteenth-century dead are normally shown standing or reclining. In the chapel of St Loo or St Laud in the south-east corner of the cathedral, a bronze, heart-shaped case hangs from a chain, containing St Laurence O'Toole's embalmed heart. (St Laurence mediated between Danes and Normans at the 1170 conquest of Dublin, and died in France.) Most impressive of all is the vaulted crypt, one of the largest in these islands and extending the whole length of the church. Part of the 800-year-old walls are made of lime or mortar mixed with ox-blood and supported by wooden wedges, now supposedly petrified in the damp bog air. In medieval times the crypt was leased to stall-holders who held markets here. As late as the seventeenth century it housed taverns. In haphazard order, remains down here include statues of the last two Stuart kings, the candlesticks and tabernacle used for mass in James II's reign, and a melodramatic memorial to Nathaniel Sneyd by Thomas Kirk (1781–1845).

High Street, over the road, was medieval Dublin's main thoroughfare, and one of the two churches beside it dedicated to St Audoen was built in the twelfth century on the site of a Danish church. (Twice honoured St Audoen, or Ouen, was a seventh-century Bishop of Rouen, relics of whom were enshrined at Canterbury; the men of Bristol, granted Dublin by Henry II, introduced him to Ireland.) This, the C of I **Church of St Audoen**, preserves a west door from 1190 and three bells from 1423, the oldest in the country; as well as several early tombs and fragments. But most of its looks are owed to mediocre nineteenth-century restoration. North of the church is St Audoen's Arch, whose lower half, put up in 1240, is all that survives of Dublin's city gates. Above these wall fragments rises Patrick Byrne's **Catholic Church of St Audoen** of 1841–7, whose appearance is much enhanced by its position. On the other side of High Street, in Back Lane, is **Tailors Hall** (in the seventeenth century the Earls of Kildare had a house and the Jesuits, until evicted, a college, in this same street). The hall now gleams from restoration inspired in 1965 by the Irish Georgian Society. It had been closed as unsafe in 1960 and looked ripe for demolition, when an appeal was successfully launched. Built in Queen Anne's reign, it was used by various guilds for formal occasions, possessing as it did Dublin's largest public room. In 1792 the Catholic Convention – or 'Back Lane Parliament' – met here, with Wolfe Tone as secretary, and pressed demands which next year brought Catholics the vote. In the nineteenth century it was used as school, warehouse, temperance meeting-room, workmen's reading-room, coffee-room. It is now the headquarters of An Taisce, Ireland's equivalent of the English National Trust.

Thomas Street West leads away from Christ Church Place to the west, passing on the left the area of the **Liberties**, a poor and slummy area, so called because it was outside the Lord Mayor's jurisdiction. A colony of Huguenot weavers settled here in the seventeenth century, but it stayed poor. Swift, hero of Dublin's underlings, said he should be paid two pounds a year for wear and tear to his hats, caused by acknowledging greetings from residents of the Liberties. At the turn of this century part of the Liberty of St Sepulchre was demolished and replaced with the present blocks of flats by the first Earl of Iveagh, under a Guinness trust.

Guinness's St James's Gate Brewery is a mile on. The stout it produces is part of the Irish – not to mention British – way of life, but the firm is important in other ways – as a model of industrial relations and as a notable exporter (to some 120 countries). The brewery, covering sixty acres, and once the biggest in Europe, extends around the site of the business Arthur Guinness started to rent at £45 a year in 1759, and includes attractive architecture of the end of the eighteenth century, and the tallest windmill-tower in these islands. From Arthur's initiative the family – now incorporating the separate titles Iveagh and Moyne – has arrived at a kind of international status. Its members have, however, continued to help Dublin in many ways – with grants of land, sports, homes, conservation – both as company and private benefactors.

Beside the brewery, on the south side of James's St, is the 1769 **Church of St Catherine,** built to John Smyth's designs with a good Roman Doric façade – and until 1967 another candidate for demolition. Saved with the help of the Irish Georgian Society, it is now used as a community centre. The already hanged body of Robert Emmet was beheaded outside it in 1803. But this is taking us beyond the city centre and we return, by the way we came, to Christ Church, turn right just beyond it down Werburgh St, and pass on the left **St Werburgh's Church,** a sister foundation to the church of the same name in Bristol, its origins going back to Norman times. Its interior is the most elegant of eighteenth-century restorations, designed after a fire in 1754, by John Smyth. After Robert Emmet's rising of 1803, however, castle authorities took a dislike to this vantage point overlooking their fortress, persuaded seven venal architects to declare it unsafe, and pulled down the tall baroque tower and upper part of the façade. Under the chancel is the family vault of the FitzGeralds, which in 1798 was opened at dead of night to accommodate the body of Lord Edward Fitz-Gerald. Son of the first Duke of Leinster, and himself a good soldier and one-time MP for Athy, he was drawn to Paris by the revolution, and there shed his family tra-dition and joined the revolutionary United Irishmen. After 1796 he moved between Ireland and France, arranging for a French invasion of his country to time with the 1798 Rising, on the eve of which he was given away and arrested in nearby Thomas Street. He and some of his captors were wounded and he died, within a month, at Newgate. Major Henry Sirr, who led his captors, lies buried in the churchyard. The sump-tuous carved pulpit came from the castle's Chapel Royal; and the viceroy, particularly when Dr Delany was rector, often used the church – his vast pew still remaining in the gallery with a splendid view of the east window and interior.

Werburgh Street is also the site of Dublin's first theatre, founded by the tireless Thomas Wentworth, Earl of Strafford (whose genius and planning have been unfairly blackened by scheming contemporaries, and history thereafter). In 1636 he brought over the playwright James Shirley, whose play *The Royal Master* was first performed here. During one of

Wentworth's trips to London, pious Archbishop Ussher
closed the theatre down, claiming such licence would bring
on the plague. Wentworth reopened it on his return and it
did well for four years. No trace of it remains, nor of the
house (though there is a wall-tablet on the site) where Swift
was born in 1667: No. 7 Hoey's Court, between Werburgh
Street and Little Ship Street on the left.

Swift was Dean of St Patrick's Cathedral from 1713 to
1745. While, before this, he held the living of Laracor in
Meath, he hoped for a bishopric, but Queen Anne, non-
plussed by his satires, barred the promotion. Other women
were more vulnerable. 'Stella' – his name for Esther Johnson
– was a friend from early years who followed him to Laracor,
then Dublin, and was with him – possibly married him in
secret – until his death. She kept cool during his stormy
affaire with 'Vanessa', Esther Vanhomrigh, which ended with
the latter's death at Celbridge; and when he himself died in
1745, crazed by pain as he had been for years, he was buried
beside Stella in St Patrick's. Both romances live on, one in
his *Journal to Stella*, the other in his poem 'Cadenus and
Vanessa'; so do *Gulliver's Travels*, mostly written here and the
only work that earned him money; and satires like *The Tale
of a Tub*, the *Battle of the Books*, and the short *Modest
Proposal*, in which he dryly urges the fattening, slaughter and
sale of starving Irish children to the rich, as joints for eating.
But in Ireland his reputation rests on his championship of the
Irish against English rule. He was revered for his tireless
struggle in the slums and throughout the country, and it was
this fight that he most wanted remembered, as his own
famous epitaph shows: '*Ubi saeva indignatio* . . .', 'He is laid
where bitter rage can no more tear his heart. Go, traveller,
imitate if you can one who was, to the best of his powers,
a defender of liberty.' 'The greatest epitaph in history,' it
was called by Yeats, whose own has since been called the
same.

The odd situation of St Patrick's, on foundations often
waterlogged by the Poddle river flowing beneath it, led to a
macabre postscript. A flooding in 1835 dislodged flagstones and
brought various coffins to view. Swift's and Stella's were opened,

and the skulls kept for examination. Sir William Wilde, Oscar's father, traced symptoms of what is known as Menière's syndrome, a disorder of the inner ear causing the pain, giddiness, deafness and vomiting that marked Swift's last years. Stella, however, was 'a perfect model of symmetry and beauty'; and he singles out the teeth 'which for their whiteness and regularity were, in life, the theme of general admiration, are, perhaps, the most perfect ever witnessed in a skull.'

Inundations like that of 1835 happen no more, though there have been more recent leaks from aisles; but they were common – and sometimes rose to six or seven feet in depth – up to 1870, and caused frequent deaths in the lower floors of nearby weavers' slums. But the belief that St Patrick had baptised converts on the site overcame objections of this kind when Archbishops Comyn and Henry de Londres erected what became Ireland's largest church (300 ft long) from 1191 onwards. Another reason for its position was that it escaped the overlordship of Christ Church, with whose dean and chapter de Londres had quarrelled. The rivalry of the two cathedrals, and repeated attempts to turn St Patrick's into a university, continued to the sixteenth century, after which it fell gradually into disrepair. Cromwell's troops stabled horses here, and James II used it as a barracks. Patching took place from time to time – forty tons of new timber for the roof in 1671; a new Lady Chapel replacing what had virtually been a Huguenot parish church in the 1840s. There were also additions, like George Semple's incongruous granite spire of 1750. Then between 1863 – by which time the roof had fallen again and all but individual chapels were disused – and 1869, Sir Thomas Drew, paid by Sir Benjamin Lee Guinness, carried out almost total rebuilding; and added some touches of his own like the north and south porches, the west window and door, and the buttresses to the nave. But basically the cathedral remains truer to the original Early English and Gothic than Christ Church, keeping also some of the fortifications which had been needed when, being outside the walls, it was often attacked from Wicklow. Drew carried out further repairs in 1900, partly because the Caen stone he used before was not hard-wearing. Again a Guinness, in the person of

Lord Iveagh, son of Sir Benjamin, financed the work. The two cathedrals' rivalry had been resolved at the disestablishment of the C of I in 1869 when St Patrick's was made a national cathedral, standing in similar relation to Christ Church as Westminster Abbey to St Paul's.

Like Christ Church its exterior is not outstanding as compared to others in these islands. The surrounds – with cramped terraces and Nicholas Street market gone, and tenements raised up – are still poor, though a pleasure park has emerged from the debris. But its interior is of great interest and its length and profuse memorials are impressive. The most obviously striking feature is the Jacobean memorial in black marble and alabaster, still with its original paint, to the wife of the first Earl of Cork (there is a better Cork monument at Youghal), on the left of the entrance. It is the biggest in these islands. The earl, the most successful adventurer of his time and a great believer in his own importance, first had this erected beside the altar, at a cost then of £1,000. Viceroy Wentworth ordered it moved. The congregation, he said, could not worship without 'crouching to an Earl of Cork and his lady . . . or to those sea-nymphs his daughters, with coronets upon their heads, their hair dishevelled, down upon their shoulders,' Cork protested but Wentworth won at least this round in their prolonged tussle. On the monument itself, the men portrayed on the top two levels are Lady Cork's distinguished ancestors. She and the Great Earl are below, and eleven of their children below them. The infant is guessed to be Robert Boyle, physicist-to-be.

Swift's and Stella's graves are at the foot of the second column along this side, and against the south nave wall is a fine bust (of 1775, by Patrick Cunningham) and his ringing epitaph. An ancient cross in the north-west corner, removed from near the tower, was supposed to mark St Patrick's Well, where the saint once baptised. Opposite the second column in this north aisle is Lady Morgan's monument to Carolan, one of the last of the Irish bards, and farther along a memorial to Samuel Lover, the nineteenth-century novelist. In the north transept, once walled off from the main building and used as the parish church of St Nicholas Without (without, that is, the city walls), are memorials of the Royal Irish Regiment. Founded in Charles II's reign and disbanded in 1922, it had in the period defended the British Empire in most corners of the globe and been target, at Lexington, of the first shots fired in the American War of Independence. Much-married Dame St Leger's memorial in the right-hand corner carries an amusing Elizabethan marital tale. In the other corner is the pulpit used by Swift. In the north choir aisle on the right is Swift's caustic epitaph to Marshal Schomberg, killed at the Boyne, whose family were too mean to record his burial here themselves – 'The fame of his valour was more effective with strangers than his closeness by blood was with his kinsmen.' The choir itself was the chapel of the Order of St Patrick, founded in 1783 by George III to consist of the sovereign and twenty-two knights. Above the stalls are the banners of the knights, an order, which, numbering twenty-two knights in the years of the Union, quickly contracted after independence was granted in 1921 and finally ended on the death of the late Duke of Gloucester in 1974. The Lady Chapel at the east end served for 150 years as a Huguenot church; services being a translation from the C of I form. On the walls of the south choir aisle are four brasses, seldom found in Ireland. A tablet in the south transept commemorates the Rev. Charles Wolfe, known for little but his poem *The Burial of Sir John Moore after Corunna*. But this is only to pick out a few. All the walls are clustered with memorials and epitaphs, a cameo of Anglo-Irish distinction, piety and bombast.

A monument in the south transept commemorates Archbishop Narcissus Marsh, and when we leave the cathedral and turn left we can walk through the close to **Marsh's Library**, Ireland's oldest public library, built at his order between 1702 and 1707. It is still a public library, available for anyone's use, and from it micro-films of books, from what amounted in the early eighteenth century to the complete gentleman's library, are sent all over the world. The steep-roofed exterior has been often restored; the interior is much as it was – L-shaped, with whitewashed walls and dark ranks of oak shelves, and stalls. In the ground-floor windows is the only Queen Anne glass left in Dublin. Several books are chained to the shelves, a custom which, though obsolete, has never been succeeded by a better. Some of the many treasures are kept on display: notably Swift's personal copy – which he read four times – of Clarendon's *History of the Great Rebellion*. Among the marginal notes in Swift's hand are remarks like (on the Scotch) 'Mad treacherous damnable infernal for ever' and (on Montrose): 'a perfect Hero, wholly un-Scotified.'

NORTH DUBLIN

The River Liffey cuts Dublin in two. It rises with a westward flow near Sally Gap in the Wicklow Hills, curves round in almost full circle, comes into Dublin by Chapelizod (where it metamorphoses into Joyce's Anna Livia Plurabelle), flows east past the Phoenix Park and then under some dozen bridges within the city to form the harbour and reach the sea at Dublin Bay. Crossing any bridge from south to north we find a different feel in the air. Nowhere is the contrast more marked than over O'Connell Bridge – or the Metal Bridge one move up, sometimes called Ha'penny Bridge because of the toll charged earlier this century – leading from the centres of learning, journalism and finance to the once fine, still broad, but meretricious O'Connell Street.

There are two points of view. One was put by George Moore, quoting Somerville and Ross: 'Few towns are duller out of season than Dublin, but the dullness of its north side neither waxes nor wanes.' Brendan Behan stated the other: the *people* he liked lived mainly on a line between the Custom House and Glasnevin cemetery – 'between birth and death, come to think of it.' There is a lot of room between the extremes, and more good to be said of the north now that, through various agencies, the best of its old parts are being brought to the light again.

O'Connell Street was laid out in the late 1740s as Gardiner's Mall, by Luke Gardiner, first Viscount Mountjoy (d. 1755), founder of a family which in less than a century did more than any other to beautify Dublin. He widened the street (which he called Sackville Street) to 150 feet, let building sites, and

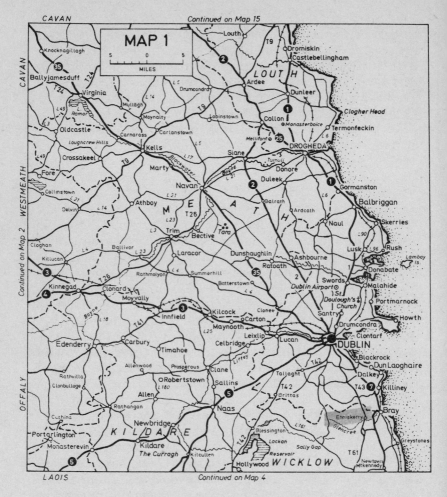

Continued on Map 15

Continued on Map 2

Continued on Map 4

planted the 48-foot-wide Mall with trees, planning it as a long residential square. It was one of the earliest components of fashionable north Dublin. After his time the street was extended to the river and gradually became the main north–south thoroughfare it is now. Only two original houses survive. Maurice Craig calls its prevalent style 'neon-classical'.

We can divert along the right-hand quay to the Custom House, a few hundred yards along, passing the skyscraper **Liberty Hall**, the trades union headquarters whose less obtrusive predecessor played a large part in the independence movement. The **Custom House** itself is in fact better appreciated as a unity from across the river (a nasty railway viaduct of 1889 cuts out views from the road bridge). It is often said to be, with the Four Courts, the finest building of Dublin. Both were designed by James Gandon, and Maurice Craig finds the Custom House expresses the 'feminine and predominantly horizontal' aspect of Gandon's mind; while the Four Courts upstream is 'masculine in feeling, built on a cubical if not vertical theme.' Gandon, born in England, and pupil of Sir William Chambers, was brought to Ireland in 1781 through friendship with Lord Charlemont, who combined statesmanship with lavish patronage of the arts. Soon John Beresford, Chief Commissioner for the Irish Revenue and later Pitt's right-hand man in gerrymandering the Act of Union, commissioned him to plan the new Custom House, to match London's Somerset House. Gandon rejected the 'meretricious elegance' of the popular Adam style, and looked more to France for models. His style was Palladian with baroque and neo-classical additions. So the great building rose – in spite of a partly submerged site, vicious hostile demonstrations (Beresford was much hated, and Gandon found 'a good cane sword' a useful escort), and initially a lack of skilled labour – in granite and Portland Stone, in isolated splendour. Finished in 1791, it was described as the greatest building in these islands since the time of Wren; and a friend wrote to Creevey in 1805: 'It is in every respect a noble edifice, in which there is no fault to be found except that old Beresford is sumptuously lodged in it.' Gandon proceeded to work on the Four Courts, the eastern portico of Parliament House, the King's Inns, and Carlisle Bridge (reconstructed in 1880 and renamed O'Connell Bridge, which we crossed just now).

But the building is not what it was. In 1921 followers of De Valera marked the Sinn Fein election victory by setting the place – the storehouse of British archives – on fire. It blazed for five days, and hardly more than the shell survived. So now Ardbraccan stone has replaced Portland, the interior is quite replanned, and the exterior differs in some small but important respects. But many of the sculptures are outstanding – Smyth's statue of 'Commerce' topping the 125-foot dome, the heads round its base, the arms of the Kingdom of Ireland on the end pavilions, and the keystones by the Doric portico on the south side representing the Atlantic and thirteen principal rivers of Ireland. The general impression is one of grandeur. Government business goes on inside and it is not open to the public.

We return to O'Connell Street by Lower Abbey Street, and pass on the left the new **Abbey Theatre**, opened in 1966 on the site of the disused Mechanics Institute, which Miss Horniman gave to the Irish National Theatre Society in 1904. It was here, in the original Abbey (which had in its time been both mortuary and pawnbroker's), with Yeats, Lady Gregory, Douglas Hyde, Lennox Robinson and the Fay brothers working together with actors like Sarah Allgood and her sister Maire O'Neill, that the theatre got its international reputation. Synge's *Playboy of the Western World* went on in 1907 and sparked off commotions through the use of the word 'shift' [*sic*]. (In 1912 the same play, on tour in America, led to arrest of the performers in Philadelphia.) Miss Horniman herself withdrew her backing in 1910 when, through an error, the theatre kept open on the day of Edward VII's death, 7th May. Later, some of Shaw's and most of O'Casey's plays produced violent audience reactions – uproar and salvoes of vegetables on the stage. Then, in 1951, after a performance of *The Plough and the Stars*, which ends with Dublin ablaze after rebellion, the back-stage of the theatre was burned down. The company took a long lease of the Queen's Theatre over the river until 1966, when the new theatre, designed by one of Ireland's best-known architects, Michael Scott, was opened.

No. 32 Abbey Street was the first headquarters of Maud Gonne's Daughters of Erin, a forceful group of female nationalists who, so their enemies said, taught children to answer the catechism question 'what is the origin of evil' with 'England'. We return to O'Connell Street, with its central line of statues (O'Connell himself, by Foley, is near the bridge), its garish cafés and amusement arcades, its two cinemas, shops and stores; and without its **Nelson's Pillar**.

The 134-foot column with Kirk's statue on top was blown to
bits in 1966 (a less drastic solution to the presence of this
tall affront had been suggested in a letter to the *Irish Times* –
change the eye and the arm, and call it Emmet).

It had already survived, what some nearby buildings did
not, a bombardment from a British ship in the harbour at
the time of the 1916 Easter Rising. The **General Post Office**
opposite Abbey Street, to the right, was the rebels' headquarters, and here thirty-seven-year-old Patrick Pearse, half-
English poet, barrister, journalist, teacher, and chosen
president of the Provisional Republican Government, and
forty-seven-year-old Scottish-born James Connolly, founder
of Irish socialism, and union leader, tried, during the week it
lasted, to control that idealist insurrection. They took over
the Post Office (a late, massive work of 1815–18 by Francis
Johnston) by simply walking in and ordering out the startled
staff and customers. Pearse proclaimed a republic to bemused
spectators. For a day or two Dublin disbelieved. Then the
troops came, and the guns. In four days, 450 Irish and 100
British were dead. Artillery had made a ruin of the inside of
the Post Office and much else around it (other parts of Dublin
suffered too), and the leaders surrendered. General Maxwell,
commanding the British, under martial law executed Pearse,
Connolly (wounded, and fatally ill, he had to sit for the ritual)
and thirteen others, at Kilmainham Prison. De Valera, condemned, was reprieved due, it was thought, to his being an
American citizen. Despite the agony, O'Casey called 1916 'the
year one in Irish history and Irish life'. Then in 1922 the Civil
War brought more destruction. Subsequently, the street's
damage was repaired, but faultily; and it never regained the
elegance it had boasted as Sackville Street. Nowadays election,
commemorative and other rallies are often held in front of the
GPO's still imposing façade.

Henry Street and North Earl Street join O'Connell Street
just beyond the GPO. The site of O'Connell Street, when
Luke Gardiner bought it in 1714, was called Drogheda
Street. Two nearby lanes are Moore and Off (formerly Of).
Together they commemorate the first owner, Henry Moore –
Earl of Drogheda. Another curiosity here is a line of London

plane trees, in the centre beyond the crossroads. For six months every winter a colony of pied wagtails roost here amid the lights, noise and fumes. They settle at dusk and leave at first light. There have at times been several thousands of them. This, in a species that would normally choose sequestered river banks and country villages, has been going on since 1929. 'In all my birding,' wrote Canon Raven, 'I have come across nothing so bizarre.' (I on the other hand have: a similar community winters in a plane tree near London's Hammersmith tube station).

Turning right up Cathedral Street and left at Marlborough Street, we can visit Dublin's Catholic **Pro-Cathedral**, begun in 1816, a monumental Doric building by John Sweetman. It is very grand outside but in a cramped situation (C of I interests kept it out of O'Connell Street, for which it was intended). The interior, with its dome and typical apse at the *west* end, contains some impressive details like the white marble altar, with a small marble canopy on eight pillars by Peter Turnerelli (1774–1839), an Italian born in Dublin. Count John McCormack was once a member of the church's Palestrina Choir, which was endowed by Edward Martyn, who spent fortunes in an attempt to raise the aesthetic standards of RC worship in Ireland. It was in this Pro-Cathedral that J. H. Newman made his first profession of the Catholic faith in public, in 1851. 'Ten thousand difficulties do not make one doubt' he had written shortly before. The building is in the middle of a district known in English days as Monto (from Montgomery, now Foley, Street); then a notorious red-light area, Joyce's 'Nighttown'. Prostitution was done away with in 1925. Before that, up to sixteen hundred ladies pursued their calling in half a dozen streets, whose names have all been changed.

Tyrone House, opposite, now houses the Government's Education Department, but was built in 1740 by Richard Castle for Sir Marcus Beresford, father of John. One of the first of the aristocracy's town houses, it is heavy, simple and solid, in Irish granite. It was decorated inside with excellent rococo stuccowork, on ceilings which still survive, by the Francini brothers. When John Beresford (patron of Gandon at the Custom House) took it over he used parts of the house and outbuildings as torture-chambers to discover plotters and rebels of the 1798 rebellion – work that was probably congenial to him. In 1835 it was bought by the Government, and later a replica was built to balance it, with the domed Central Model Schools (where Shaw was a pupil) in between. Tyrone House's portico and central Venetian window have suffered from later remodelling.

Back in O'Connell Street we turn right, pass on the left the CIE Passenger Bureau, in which can be seen (from the street) Evie Hone's stained-glass window designed for the Irish Pavilion at the 1939 New York World Fair; and on the right the Tourist Office and Gresham Hotel, owned by Charles Forte. At the end of the street stands the **Parnell Monument** and statue, with a long quotation engraved in gold. (With statues of O'Connell, Nelson and Parnell, wrote Yeats, a single Dublin street commemorated three of history's best-known adulterers.) Parnell, formerly Rutland, Square – the city's second oldest after St Stephen's Green – begins beyond the statue. Opposite is the **Rotunda** complex – hospital to the left, and Assembly Rooms, which were built to finance the hospital, on the right. The Round Room, designed by Castle's pupil George Ensor and altered by Gandon in 1786, nowadays houses the Ambassador Cinema, and its interior is changed for the worse. The New Assembly Rooms were built by Richard Johnston (Francis's elder brother) in 1784–6. They now contain the Gate Theatre, founded by Micheál MacLiammóir and Hilton Edwards, who were later subsidised by the fifth Earl of Lord Longford, and presenting often plays of fairly highbrow appeal. In 1783 the Rotunda witnessed the great Volunteer Convention, an Anglo-Irish attempt to throw off some of Westminster's control. To it, in expectation of his emergence as some kind of sovereign of Ireland, the flamboyant Frederick Augustus Hervey, Earl of Bristol and Bishop of Derry, drove in state in a coach and six, led by a squadron of dragoons in gold and scarlet attended by liveried lackeys, only to find Lord Charlemont elected above him. The original – and present – purpose of the Assembly Rooms was to provide funds for the **Maternity Hospital** adjacent, to the left, founded by Bartholomew Mosse, an obscure relation of the great Earl of Cork. Appalled by the squalor in which many Dublin mothers had preforce to produce their babies – the obverse side of the eighteenth-century boom – Mosse in the 1750s commissioned Castle to build a proper hospital, the first of its kind in the two islands. (Even in the hospital, for the first thirty years, the rate of mortality among babies was one in six.) Gem of the hospital is its chapel, a square-shaped riot of baroque, alive with aerial putti, by the French-Italian stuccoist Barthélemy Crémillion; its bane is the modern red-brick addition on the west side.

There are some imposing houses on the east of **Parnell Square**, erected in the mid-eighteenth century, a time when the optimism of the Anglo-Irish brought artistic talents from England, France and Italy to build and decorate rich men's homes. Oliver St John Gogarty, Joyce's 'Buck Mulligan' was born at No. 5. No. 9 was built in the 1750s for the philanthropic Dr Mosse; and No. 11 for the Earl of Ormonde. In the middle of the square is the sunken cross-shaped Garden of Remembrance, designed – rather heavily – by Daithí P. Hanly in 1966, fiftieth anniversary of the Easter Rising. Beyond that, set back from the north pavement of the square, is **Charlemont House**, now the Municipal Gallery of Modern Art. James Caulfeild, first Earl of Charlemont, had it built. He was a cautious Liberal, who having helped to win some self-government for Ireland in 1782 felt progress had gone far enough and opposed those colleagues – like the florid Earl Bishop of Derry – who wanted more. Charlemont was an eighteenth-century paragon, refined, rational, attractive, kind to everyone.

Macaulay said he 'gave the tone to the society and the age.' He had spent years in Rome, Paris and London (where he was friendly with Burke and Johnson), and settled in his native Ireland more from a sense of duty than desire. But, settled, he took up the causes he felt were right, was a great patron of the arts – architecture, painting, theatre, books – and when in old age he left Dublin for Bath, the streets from Charlemont House to the river were completely thronged. Long before, Charlemont House had earned the title 'the Holland House of Dublin'. It was designed in the 1760s by

Sir William Chambers, who also planned the Earl's Casino at Marino. Unpretentious, three stories built of brick faced with granite, it attracted through its owner all the notables of the country and many from outside: 'To see and converse with him,' said Burke, 'would alone induce me to pay a visit to Dublin.'

The porch is an incongruous addition of 1930. Inside, the staircase, some ceilings and isolated details are the only important internal features to survive. But the building still serves an artistic purpose, housing the collection of which Sir Hugh Lane's split legacy forms the nucleus. The collection is representative of Irish, British and continental artists born less than 110 years ago, though the Lane collection remains regardless of age. Outstanding are Lane's Impressionists (there are seven Constables, including the *Elder Tree*, by way of antecedents). There is Renoir's *Les Parapluies;* a fine group of Corot, including *Landscape* and *The Palace of the Popes at Avignon;* Manet's *Eva Gonzales* and *A Concert in the Tuileries;* Daumier's *Don Quixote;* Degas' *La Plage;* and several lesser works. Modern art is represented by, among others, Utrillo, Picasso, Bonnard, Piper, John Nash, Jack Yeats – and Rouault's *Christ and Soldier*, which, when first presented by the Friends of the Gallery in 1942 as a gift, was rejected, the Lady Mayoress finding herself 'offended, as a Catholic and a Christian'. A president-to-be of the Royal Hibernian Academy called it 'naïve, childish and unintelligent'. A Henry Moore in the small sculpture collection fared no better: 'that figure has got leprosy,' said a lady trustee. Fortunately for the gallery, there were second chances. The Rouault was borrowed by that eminently Catholic institution, St Patrick's College, Maynooth, until the gallery came round.

The Portrait Room brings to life great figures from the recent Irish past, the people whose names recur in the political and artistic rebirth of Ireland; and there is a poem by Yeats, 'The Municipal Gallery Revisited' – copies are on sale at the bookstall – which helps to evoke the period and its luminaries. Here is *George Russell* ('Æ'), a patriarch of the Gaelic Revival, by Casimir Markievicz (husband of the Rebel Countess); John S. Sargent's delicate *Hugh Lane;* and another by Mancini; Mancini's *Lady Gregory*; *Katherine Tynan and Douglas Hyde* by John B. Yeats (father of the poet and of artist Jack, who called his father the best portraitist since Goya); William Orpen's *Nathaniel Hone*, and his *Sir John Mahaffy* (the gallery has some of the best work Orpen ever did); one of *Orpen* himself by his pupil, James Sleator; and several politicians – *De Valera, Kevin O'Higgins, Redmond, Cosgrave, Arthur Griffith* – by Sir John Lavery (who once taught Churchill how to paint).

The path we follow now is off the axis of concentrated interest, but the walker will still get an impression of decayed glory, of the feckless side of modern Ireland, that the car-driver or selective sightseer misses. We turn left outside Charlemont House and at the end of the square continue straight along Great Denmark Street. On the left is the broad, five-bay **Belvedere House**, which has been the Jesuit Belvedere College since 1841. It was built in 1786 by Michael Stapleton, the great Dublin stuccoist, for the second Earl of Belvedere, son of the genial martinet who incarcerated his wife for thirty years because of her adultery with his brother. It has a fine façade, spoiled by twentieth-century alterations, particularly to the windows, and a splendid view downhill to the dome of the Custom House. Inside, the Venus Room, Apollo Room and Diana Room (the school's library, with original book-cases) still keep their magnificent Stapleton plasterwork. This being a Catholic boys' college, one indeed that James Joyce attended from 1893–8 and put into *Portrait of the Artist as a Young Man* – the authorities removed Venus herself from the Venus room. But much that is good remains.

Up Temple Street, the next turning to the left, is **Great St George's Church** (C of I) by Francis Johnston, with a 200-foot spire imitative of **St Martin-in-the-Fields in London. It is** perhaps Johnston's finest work. The broad flat ceiling, without any central support, shows his engineering as well as artistic skill. Below, at the foot of Hill Street, is the old square tower of the church St George's was built to replace. It was here, on 10th April, 1806, that the Duke of Wellington married Catherine Pakenham, sister of the second Earl of Longford. It has been called his bravest exploit, comparable to Waterloo,

so marred by smallpox was the bride he had returned from the
Peninsular Wars to join. The blemishes are questionable, but
the marriage was still a bad one.

Great Denmark Street leads into Gardiner Place and that
in turn to decayed **Mountjoy Square**, a model of Georgian
near-uniformity partly saved from demolition and redevelopment by recent efforts of the Irish Georgian Society. The name
commemorates Luke Gardiner, third Viscount Mountjoy,
grandson of the first viscount who laid out O'Connell Street.
The third viscount pushed the development of Dublin
farther east and north, and laid out Mountjoy Square and
the long avenue of Gardiner Street in the last decade of the
eighteenth century. On the east side Nos. 25 and 26, built by
Charles Thorp, are outstanding. The height of the first-floor
windows gives them an imposing elegance. Perhaps the best
houses in the square are Nos. 39 – now a Youth Hostel – and
40, by Michael Stapleton. No. 47, with a good hall-ceiling,
has recently been opened to the public – the first house in
Dublin to be opened – and No. 50 is to be headquarters of
the Irish Georgian Society, with Mrs Desmond Guinness's
splendid architectural library. No. 1 Mountjoy Place, off the
south-east corner of the square, was built and decorated by
Stapleton for himself, and he died here in 1801. The fight
against the slummy grubbiness of this quarter of Dublin has
a long way to go. Sean O'Casey and Brendan Behan were born
nearby, and lived impressionable years and set their plays in
the quarter.

We can follow the faded grandeur out of the north-west
corner of the square, along Gardiner Street Upper, then left
down **Dorset Street**, named after Lionel Sackville, first Duke
of Dorset, who was Lord-Lieutenant when the street was a
straggling country lane. Eccles Street is third on the right.
At No. 7 (now demolished) lived Bloom and his Molly, in
the longest twenty-four hours in literature – Joyce's *Ulysses*.
Francis Johnston, and later the Home Ruler Isaac Butt,
lived at No. 64, the latter causing distress to his neighbours with
early-hours gatherings. Off left is Nelson Street, in a house of
which Brendan Behan set *The Hostage*. No. 12 Dorset Street
was Richard Brinsley Sheridan's birthplace, in 1751; and

O'Casey was born, in 1884, in the house now occupied by the Hibernian Bank. Mary Place, another right turn off Dorset Street, farther along, leads to **St Mary's Chapel of Ease**, always called the Black Church from the colour of the calp limestone in which it was built in 1830. John Semple designed it with great ingenuity. The principles of his building are severity, a shearing away of classical ornamentation before Gothic introduced its own. It looks in a sense – what it certainly is not – unfinished Gothic. The ingenuity comes in the basic structure, a revival of simple corbelling techniques used in Ireland a thousand years before, and making the church's interior into one enormous parabolic vault, each course of stones overlapping the one beneath. Its solidity was said to be connected with Archbishop Magee's conviction that Protestant congregations were in danger of being massacred and that every church must needs be a fortress too. The church, deconsecrated in 1962, belongs now to the Dublin Corporation which uses it as an exhibition hall. Like others, it owes its survival to the Irish Georgian Society.

We return to Dorset Street and cross Dominick Street. No. 20 is the oldest house in Dominick Street, built for himself by the decorator Robert West, and now an orphanage. It has one of Dublin's best staircases. St Saviour's Dominican Priory beside it was an early building by J. J. McCarthy, known as Ireland's Pugin in spite of the fact that Pugin himself worked in several parts of Ireland. At this junction, Dorset Street becomes Bolton Street, and the next right turn is **Henrietta Street**, the saddest, because the oldest and once the finest of Georgian streets, built between 1725 and 1794, and now a forlorn and perhaps irreparable slum. In its time it was most exclusive, named after the wife of the ducal viceroy who in turn gave his name to Grafton Street. Seven peers lived here in the 1790s; and four successive Primates of Ireland had their houses here from 1725 to 1794. Luke Gardiner himself and later his son, Earl of Blessington, lived at No. 10, once Mountjoy House, which like No. 9 was built by Pearce in 1730. Both preserve some good interior work, especially No. 9's staircase and other details. These two and No. 8 together form a convent of the Sisters of Charity of

St Patrick's Cathedral, Dublin, treasury of Anglo-Irish piety and bombast.

Merrion Square, Dublin, and one of its famous fanlights.

St Vincent de Paul, an order devoted to helping the poor.
Nathaniel Clements (1705–77), whose skill as an architect
(he built Beauparc, Phoenix Park Lodge, Lodge Park,
Kildare and others) is being acknowledged for the first time
since his own day, built and lived at No. 7. His extravagance
there made his wife, according to Mrs Delany, 'finer than the
finest lady in England'.

In 1827 the archiepiscopal houses at the end of the street
were demolished to make way for the King's Inns Library.
But the real damage was done by a certain Alderman Meade
early this century, who bought up most of the houses, stripped
their interiors and staircases, and turned them into tenements.

The **King's Inns Building** itself was built to a late design
(1795) of James Gandon; and H. A. Baker helped to conceive
the great western façade. Francis Johnston added the cupola
in 1816, and the two three-bay wings on each side were mid-
nineteenth-century extensions. The wings on the Henrietta
Street side house, on the north, the dining-hall, recently
restored, where training lawyers have to eat a stipulated
number of meals; and on the south the Registry of Deeds.
The dining-hall is pure Gandon, with stucco figures by
Edward Smyth. This is the headquarters of the legal profession's ruling body, which moved here from the site of the
Four Courts.

We go back to Bolton Street and bear right where it joins
King Street. This ends, half a mile on, opposite the Blue Coat
School or **King's Hospital**, a building rarely noticed because
of its inconspicuous placing. Originally founded by Charles II,
in 1672, as hospital and school, it became exclusively a
school for the sons of 'decayed citizens' of C of I persuasion.
The present building was planned to order by Thomas Ivory
in the 1770s but, like Gandon at the King's Inns, he was up
against official interference and miserliness. He left the work
before the erection of a dome (the present inadequate one
was put up in 1894), nor could he build the quadrangle he
wanted to the rear. But the 300-foot façade, with its deep
rustication, Ionic columns and elegant balustrades is very
fine, and among the good points inside is a chapel, now lit
by an Evie Hone window. The school has lately moved out,

and the building has been refurbished at a cost of some half a
million pounds by its new owners, the Incorporated Law Society.

We can pass on to the quays, turn left at Ellis Quay,
continue through Arran Quay (Edmund Burke was born at
No. 12, no longer there; St Paul's Church of 1835–40 by
Patrick Byrne was one of the first RC churches to be built in
a conspicuous place) and, before visiting the Four Courts,
turn left to see **St Michan's** (pronounced Mikan's) in Church
Street. It is one of the oldest of Dublin's churches, first dedicated
in 1095 to a Danish saint (after the battle of Clontarf in 1014
Dublin's resident Danes remained, and took to Christianity). It
was then parish church for the Danish settlement of Ostmans-
town or Oxmantown. But most of the fabric dates from 1685–6
the time of the first post-medieval expansion of the town
beyond the castle precincts. It was largely restored in 1821,
and again in the 1920s after Civil War damage. The interior
is pleasingly plain, with some beautiful wood carving –
particularly that of seventeen musical instruments, made
from one piece of wood, below the organ – which is remini-
scent of Grinling Gibbons, but not – despite claims to the
contrary – by him. The organ dates back to 1724 and was
supposedly used by Handel in the 1740s. The fine carved
penitents' stool, used for some kind of public trial and
confession, is the only one of its kind in Ireland.

The church is mainly famous for its dark and sinister
vaults, reached by steps from the outside, and containing
extraordinarily well preserved bodies, probably of the seventeenth century. The misnamed 'Crusader' and a woman and
boy, blood vessels visible through their toughened leathery
skin, are on display and can be touched (in spite of the fact
that this is still a Christian church, and that whoever the
bodies once were probably looked forward to the sleep of the
just). Why they remain in such a state is not certain. Bog air
is a marvellous preserver, and the oak forest that once covered
the area might have something to do with it; more likely the
moisture-absorbing yellow limestone of the walls. One story
goes that a nearby whisky distillery once exploded and
provided the embalming spirit. The brothers John and Henry
Sheares, executed for rebellion in 1798, are buried here, and

the vilified Earl of Leitrim, murdered in Donegal. What was thought to be the executed patriot Robert Emmet's grave was found, on opening, to be empty.

Facing the river, the 436-foot façade of the **Four Courts** building – another of James Gandon's masterpieces – shows its scarred history to anyone familiar with Gandon's genius. It was begun in 1786, to take over from the previous site in Christ Church Place, and to incorporate the Public Offices already begun by Thomas Cooley on the west side. In the next sixteen years Gandon erected his great central block with its portico of six Corinthian columns, the vast and distinctive lantern-dome, the radiating extensions containing the original Courts of Exchequer, Common Pleas, King's Bench and Chancery, and the two quadrangles and their wings. It was all done against the heaviest odds – economic cutbacks, political attack, sneers against Gandon's Englishness, even a landslide at Portland, which delayed the stone being sent. But Dublin rallied as it neared completion. Gandon's favourite sculptor Edward Smyth did most of the many statues that still beautifully break the skyline, as well as a prodigious number inside. Throughout the nineteenth century the building served its legal purposes while inferior buildings were added to the rear. Then in 1916 it was occupied by rebels, but not for long and without great damage. Disaster came in 1922, when, after the Treaty, Republicans seized the building. Michael Collins ordered a bombardment from the other side of the river, and what had been an acrid debate became the Civil War. Shelling forced the besieged to surrender, but the building was wrecked by the land mines left behind by the defenders. The contents of the Public Records Office were irreplaceable; and in the rebuilding of the central block and wings, economies and even 'improvements' were incorporated, and the present building differs from its predecessor in many details, none of them for the better.

The return to O'Connell Bridge takes us along the quays (or Abbey Street in a car, the quays this side being for westbound traffic). The walk is worth taking, for an intangible quality of Dublin – river, bridges, elegant buildings crumbling or defaced by the signs of commerce, blue and white buses (recently changed from green), auction rooms with the variable bric-à-brac of domestic Ireland, chance vistas of spires and domes and towers. But we can make a final detour, left up Capel Street, the centre of the first expansion of Dublin outside the original walls. Mary's Abbey is the second turning left.

The abbey was supposedly founded in the tenth century, but comes into the light in the middle of the twelfth, when it was taken over by the Cistercians, an order grown hardy and expansive after its reformation by St Bernard of Clairvaux. At one time its territory stretched to the river, and its influence much farther. It was here that Silken Thomas proclaimed himself a rebel, throwing the Sword of State before the assembled council. Shortly after, Henry VIII dissolved the abbey, and by the seventeenth century it was derelict. (Apart from a cluster of buildings round St Michan's, there was by then almost nothing north of the river.) In the 1780s its site – most of its stones had already been used for bridge-building – was the home of Ireland's first national bank, and all that survives these vicissitudes are the Chapter House and part of an adjoining passage, topped now by a warehouse which fronts on Meetinghouse Lane. The rib-mouldings of the vault are its isolated treasure.

Farther along Capel Street we can turn left for the Daisy Market, a colourful slice of old Dublin, or first right for St Mary's, Dublin's oldest complete church, dating from 1697. Thomas Burgh, architect of Trinity Library, built it when the area was beginning to fill up. The exterior, apart from the east window, is heavy and dull; but inside shows a lighter touch, with good oak panelling and a fine west end. The organ, a rare survival of the work of Renatus Harris, one of the best early eighteenth-century organ builders, is virtually intact, but in need of restoration for which an appeal has been launched. A tablet commemorates the Ormonde family, and both Wolfe Tone (to whose memory the church-yard is dedicated) and the Earl of Charlemont were baptised here. In 1747 John Wesley preached his first Irish sermon from the pulpit. The poor flocked to hear him, and he returned to the city often, till shortly before he died. 'Alas, poor Ireland', he wrote near the end of his *Journal*: 'who shall teach thy very Senators wisdom?'

WEST DUBLIN AND BEYOND

A mile and a half west of O'Connell Bridge the **Phoenix Park** begins, and continues to run close to the Liffey for about three miles. With an area of nearly 1,800 acres – over five times the size of Hyde Park – this is one of Europe's biggest urban parks. Soon after the Conquest it was granted to Kilmainham Priory's Knights of St John, but the king took it back at the Reformation. From 1661 Charles II's Lord-Lieutenant, the newly created Duke of Ormonde, chose to live in Phoenix Lodge rather than the dank discomforts of Dublin Castle, and though he later built the viceregal lodge at Chapelizod he carried out the most extensive of his public works in the park, spending £31,000 on a perimeter wall, the planting of beech-mast and mustard, and a full-time ranger to care for his falcons, hounds, beagles, deer and partridges. He also stopped the king granting the park to the Duchess of Cleveland and earned a lifelong enemy at court.

But Lord Chesterfield, viceroy in the 1740s found the park 'a crude, uncultivated field'. He gave play to his Augustan passion for patterns of trees and well-framed vistas in laying it out at his own expense roughly as it has come down to the present. A philanthropic viceroy, he opened the park to the public, and it soon became a favourite area for robberies and duels, the papers often complaining of the perils of passage. It was also the setting for military reviews and pageants of great splendour. Chesterfield caused to be built the Phoenix Column, which owes its name, as does the park itself, to a semantic error. *Fionn Uisg*, though pronounced much like 'phoenix' is in fact Gaelic for 'clear water' that wells up not far from the pillar. The English took the sound at face value.

From the main gate at the south-east corner a straight road leads through to Castleknock Gate on the north-west. Over to the left is the 205-foot **Wellington Testimonial**, erected after Waterloo with bronze panels on the pedestal commemorating his battles in bas-relief. First on the right is the **People's Garden**, spattering its steep lakeside with bright spring and summer colours. Then comes the Zoo, thirty acres of it (five less than London's), and one of the prettiest and best stocked in the world. A *cottage orné* stands at the entrance. It was built by Decimus Burton in 1831, the founding year of the gardens, when the Zoological Society's collection consisted of one wild boar. Nowadays there are most things you can think of, but special pride is felt about the lions. Not only have nearly 600 cubs been born and bred here since 1857; they have improved on nature by arriving in bigger, healthier litters of up to five cubs and have at times been exported to Africa. But lions and others are well covered in the zoo's own guide.

Beyond, and still to the right, is **Aras an Uachtaráin**, the president's official residence. The house was built as his official lodge in 1751 by Nathaniel Clements, who enjoyed the sinecure of Park Ranger as well as the lucrative post of Deputy Paymaster-General. It was expanded to serve as viceroy's home by Francis Johnston in 1815, and given its formal garden by Decimus Burton in 1840-1. Johnston plastered over Clements's original red brick, wings were added for Queen Victoria's visit in 1849, and the interior has more recently been improved by ceilings and mantelpieces salvaged from Sarah Purser's dismantled Mespil House, and Riverstown House, Co. Cork. A tree by the road here marks the spot where in the evening of 6th May, 1882, Lord Frederick Cavendish, newly appointed chief-secretary who had only arrived in Dublin that morning, and his assistant, Thomas H. Burke, were stabbed to death with an amputation knife. Four 'Invincibles' – an extreme wing of the Fenians – were later hanged for the crime. For one of them, Joe Brady, the 'drop' was miscalculated, and Marwood, the executioner, had, on behalf of British Justice, to haul on his legs. The killers had been informed on by one of their number, James Carey, who was given a pardon and a one-way ticket to Cape Town. With the tidiness of Jacobean tragedy, Carey was shot dead on the boat, and his own murderer hanged in London.

What was then the under-secretary's residence, now the

Apostolic Nunciature, is on the right of the main drive, beyond Chesterfield's Phoenix (which was moved off the drive early this century to make way for motor-racing). The **US Ambassador's Residence,** formerly that of the chief secretary, is hidden from view on the left. Beyond and south of the ambassador's house lie the **'Fifteen Acres'** which in fact comprise over a hundred, with paths and copses and a number of playing fields, and turf dust gallops, where race-horses exercise early in the morning. St Mary's Chest Hospital, built in 1766 as a military school, stands on the south side overlooking a steep drop to a picturesque and park-flanked stretch of the river. The hospital's chapel, built in 1771, is by Cooley, and the main building was enlarged by Francis Johnston in 1808–13. Across the river is Chapelizod, whose name obscurely derives from Isoud, or Iseult, or Isolde, sister of the King of Ireland whom Tristan slew, setting in train a sequence of bliss and misery for himself and a recurring theme for writers and composers. Chapelizod, a popular recreation ground in the last century, comes into Joyce's *Finnegan's Wake.* It was here that the Liffey was sublimated in the motherly character of Anna Livia Plurabelle.

We have crossed the river. Palmerstown, a mile west of Chapelizod on the Lucan road, gave the Irish branch of the Temple family, and so a nineteenth-century Prime Minister, their title. But we turn back to Dublin along St Laurence Road and then Sarsfield Road, which leads straight to Kilmainham, passing the 1914–18 **War Memorial Park** on the left, a pleasant enough scene laid out by Lutyens, and surprisingly unknown to many Dubliners. Just before crossing the South Circular Road we pass, on the right, the gaunt pile of **Kilmainham Gaol,** whose list of past inmates – Parnell, William Smith O'Brien, Robert Emmet, Patrick Pearse – reads like a *Who's Who* of Irish patriotism. In old ballads, hanging is often euphemised as 'the Kilmainham minuet'. The disused building has been restored as a memorial, and on Sunday afternoons you can see the cells where various luminaries were locked, as well as the yard where the 1916 Rising leaders were shot.

Over the other side of the South Circular Road is **Kilmain-ham Royal Hospital,** also being restored, as an extension of the National Museum. For many years it has been declared unsafe and used as a dump for the museum's surplus, mainly of old carriages. The hospital, 'for the reception and entertainment of antient maimed, and infirm officers and soldiers' was built during 1680–4, a little before the Royal Hospital at Chelsea, but after the Invalides at Paris. It supported 400 inmates who had sixpence in the pound docked from their pay. The work was designed by the Irish surveyor, Sir William Robinson, who also designed Marsh's Library. The massive, plain hospital – it owes its ugly plaster mantle to nineteenth- century restoration – 306 feet by 288 feet – forms a quadrangle round a court with the main front facing the Liffey to the north. Between massive Corinthian pilasters, and below the arms of Ormonde, the main entrance leads into the magnificent pine-panelled Great Hall, to the right of which in British times lay the apartments of the Army's Commander-in-Chief. The gem is to the left, on the east side: the chapel, with its charming ceiling of fruit and flower designs, sadly a papier mâché copy of the original seventeenth-century plaster which, mounted on oak twigs, crumbled last century. The stained-glass window is supposed to contain fragments from the original Templar-cum-Hospitaller Priory dissolved by Henry VIII. This was on an adjacent site, as is Bully's Acre, burial ground for Murrough and Turlough, Brian Boru's son and grandson, both killed at Clontarf in 1014. The cemetery closed its gates to the dead after 500 had been buried there within ten cholera-ridden days in 1832.

A few hundred yards east are two of Dublin's oldest hospitals. **Steevens's Hospital** is in fact the fifth oldest in these islands, yielding to three in London and one in Bath, and the first of its kind in Ireland, endowed by the legacy of a professor of physics who died in 1710. His sister, Grizel, known as Madame Steevens – an eccentric lady who through frequent wearing of a veil gave credence to the rumour that a gypsy's curse had transformed her face into a pig's – took charge of the building and got Thomas Burgh to draw designs. These are like a small version of Kilmainham – a

court enclosed by arcades on four sides. Building began in
1720 and the hospital opened in 1733. Till her death, aged 92,
in 1747, Madame Steevens lived in the rooms to the left of
the gate, spending most of her time showing her face at the
street window to belie her porcine reputation. The hospital
still contains in the Board Room (the work of Edward
Lovett Pearce) the precious library of 4,000 books bequeathed
by Edward Worth, an original trustee. Another benefactor
was Swift's Stella, who endowed a chaplaincy; and Swift
himself was a trustee. Swift also endowed in his will the
neighbouring **St. Patrick's Hospital,** built just after his death
by George Semple and enlarged in 1778 by Cooley. This was
intended 'for lunatics and idiots' – Swift wrote:

> 'He gave the little wealth he had
> To build a house for fools and mad;
> To show by one satiric touch,
> No nation wanted it so much.'

– and is now highly regarded as a psychiatric unit. It is always
known as Swift's Hospital, and contains a collection of relics
of the dean.

There is some interesting wandering to do in this part.
North of Steevens Lane is the handsome Heuston, formerly
Kingsbridge, Station, built in 1844 and terminus of the
Limerick and Cork line. To the south is the murky terminus
and harbour of the Grand Canal. While to the east is the
sixty-acre empire of the House of Guinness, a stone's throw
from the Liffey water that is blessed daily by a majority of
Irishmen, and by those abroad who drink the daily export of
nearly a million pints.

NORTH DUBLIN SUBURBS

Dublin's population has steadily risen this century from
375,000 at the opening to well over 600,000 now. The rise
has meant an ugly creeping of housing estates, shops and
small factories; and the claim that you can walk from the
city centre to open country gets a little less true every day.
Former country houses are now pinnacles in suburbia. The
only relic of the first Earl of Charlemont's seaside house is

surrounded by the bustle of Clontarf, and overlooked by a grandiose red-brick college. This is the famous **Marino Casino**. It was an odd site even in the eighteenth century when Sir William Chambers designed it, being, though ozone-rich, hardly more than a mile from the earl's town house, now the Municipal Gallery. Probably Charlemont was more interested in architectural enterprise than the sensible location of residences, and he had a lifelong association with Chambers – 'the best of men', he called him. The Casino is well worth a visit, a compact, Palladian bid for earthly perfection carried out – with endless plans and counter-plans – between 1758 and 1780 in the grounds of long-vanished Marino House. Utility goes along with aesthetic perfection, for the roof urns are chimneys and the columns hollowed to serve as drains. It is the only building of its kind in Ireland, and cost the builder £60,000.

The outside barely suggests its real size. On the ground floor are a hall, study, bedroom, drawing-room – with magnificent golden sun on the ceiling and fine wood-inlaid floor, remains of sumptuous wall-hangings, gilded pillars, long-mirrors and displays of precious artifacts; there are more bedrooms upstairs, and in the basement a kitchen, cellars, servants' hall and other service rooms in groined brickwork (used by Republicans around 1920 for practice with small arms). The Casino has recently been fully restored after long neglect.

The suburb of **Clontarf** lies to the east, with Clontarf Castle, built in 1835 on the site of an early Pale Castle, and now a hotel in the middle. Several street-names round about incorporate the word Kincora, Brian Boru's half-mythical palace by the shores of Lough Derg. Clontarf was Brian's last victory, in which he – with help from some of Dublin's settled Danes – beat the invading Danes who had some assistance from quisling Irish. It began the end of Danish ambitions, but Brian's death finished the national rule of his own family. Probably the main battle took place nearer city than suburb, but the final chase went out to Howth; and Conquer Hill, a turning off the coast road just beyond Clontarf's Yacht Club, is supposed to have seen the issue decided.

East of Clontarf, the **North Bull Wall** protrudes one and three quarter miles into the bay. It was made in 1819, a hundred years after the building of the harbour which revolutionised Irish trade. Since that year the North Bull itself – a long sandbank that used to trap countless ships driven off course by prevailing winds, and a boon to local peasants who picked the spoils – has grown to three miles and now holds two golf courses, the Royal Dublin and St Anne's, an important bird sanctuary, and splendid beaches. It also has an exceptional variety of wild plants, as well as its own sub-species of house-mouse, *Mus musculus jamesoni*, which has developed a pale coat to blend with the sand.

The coast road continues without excitement past Sutton to **Howth** (pronounced to rhyme with both) a swollen round peninsula with a small harbour on the north side and excellent views from the encircling road, below and above which seabirds nest with cool contempt for gravity. Guarding the eastern entrance to Ireland, Howth is a symbol of home for travelling Irish – 'Delightful to be on the hill of Howth' St Columba sighed in the sixth century, exiled and bidden to convert the Picts of Ireland's eastern colony Argyll,

'Grievous is my errand over the main,
Travelling to Alba of the beetling brows.'

The Dublin road leads straight to village and harbour, passing the demesne of **Howth Castle** on the right. The beautiful gardens, bare rock 150 years ago, are open in spring and summer and are famous for rhododendrons, azaleas, half a mile of thirty-foot high beech hedges dating from 1710, and Ireland's first elm tree, planted in 1585. 2,000 species thrive on this peaty frost-free site, whose original soil was carried up in baskets. The castle is closed to visitors, a break with a tradition that began when the pirate queen, Grace O'Malley, returning to Mayo from a visit to Queen Elizabeth in 1575, was refused admission; and carried off and kept the heir until the owners promised to keep the doors permanently open to needy callers. The resident family is descended in the female line from Sir Almeric Tristram who in 1177 was granted the property by Henry II. Sir Almeric adopted the name St Lawrence after the saint, in answer to his

promise to do so, turned a battle in his favour. The direct
male succession was broken in 1909 – and the earldom and
barony (Ireland's oldest) of Howth died out then; but the
owners are still the Gaisford-St Lawrences. The keep of the
castle, built in 1564, is incorporated in the present castle, a
jumble of styles from different times that includes work by
Francis Bindon, the Morrisons, and Lutyens, whose 1910
restoration made it look, according to H. G. Wells, 'as it
ought to have looked and never had looked in the past.'

Wells also, in *Joan and Peter*, speaks of the view from the
hill – 'one of the most beautiful in the world', with the bay
to the south, the lush midlands to the west, and the Mourne
Mountains sixty miles north, and below them, only a mile
away, Ireland's Eye, a little island-hump of quartzite, popular
with puffins and possessing a restored seventh-century chapel.
Immediately below Howth Hill on the north side is the
village, and beside that the harbour. The Abbey Tavern is
famous for ballad-singing. The ruined abbey church of
St Mary looks over the harbour from steep banks, parts of it
supposedly dating from 1042, but most of the fourteenth to
sixteenth centuries. There is an interesting fifteenth-century
St Lawrence tomb in the south-east chantry. The harbour
itself was built, like Dun Laoghaire, to receive packet-boats
from England in the early nineteenth century, and George IV
landed here in 1821 (drunk, in some reports; though the
death of his wife was the official reason for his cancelling his
scheduled country tour, so disappointing more than one
family that had run up a castle, or at least a ball-room, to
receive him). The harbour soon silted up, and has been used
since only for fishing and sailing-boats; with one famous
exception – the Howth Gun-running of 26th July, 1914,
when Erskine Childers ran in 900 rifles from Germany on his
yacht *Asgard*, in answer to an open arming of Ulster Protestants by Carson and others. A few months later he had joined
British Naval Intelligence, but sided with the Republicans
during the Civil War and was finally shot after a court-martial.

Returning to the mainland we turn right to follow the coast
northwards. There is little dramatic in this flank of County
Dublin's shoreline. The Irish have built mostly south of the

bay and the money and care spent in that direction have
prettified it beyond comparison with the north. What we see
now is a general flatness, with some patches of development,
that a dull day make bleak. But there are good beaches and
dunes and after a little way we are passing the long broad
peninsula that carries Portmarnock's championship golf-
course, and the two-mile Velvet Strand. The next left turn, and a
left and right to follow, bring us to **St Doulough's Church,**
remarkable for its preservation and one of the oldest still in
use – its steep stone roof was built around 1200, though the
tower with its stepped battlements was added in the fifteenth
century. The site was probably that of a seventh-century hermit's
hut, and the inclusion of an anchorite's cell and living quarters
suggest it housed a community. Various walls and other remains
lie about. Opposite is St Doulough's Lodge, where Nathaniel
Hone (1831–1917), the greatest Irish landscape painter of his
time, lived. He had studied in Paris and spent twenty years
at Barbizon, but much of his best work was done on the land
and by the sea between here and Malahide. Most of it lies
unseen in the vaults of the National Gallery.

Malahide is reached by the main road north from St
Doulough's, passing on the left the Hill of Feltrim, once seat
of the Fagans and dubiously claimed as site of the killing of
Ireland's last wolf. Several other places claim the same distinction. **Malahide Castle,** now owned by the Dublin County
Council, and housing an Irish national portrait gallery, (though
excluding modern work), stands before the village on the right.
This was till 1975 the home of the late Baron Talbot de Malahide, by grace of King Edward IV Hereditary Lord Admiral
of Malahide and adjacent seas, and a distinguished ex-diplomat
in his own right. The family had lived here more than 800 years,
with a break in Cromwellian times when a carving of the Virgin
Mary took miraculous flight and returned only with the
restoration of the King to his palace and the Talbots to their
castle. Richard Talbot, Earl of Tyrconnell, lived here, and as
James II's Catholic Lord-deputy tried to turn the Protestant
tide, until after the Battle of the Boyne he fled to die in
France. The family later won a posthumous link with James
Boswell when a Talbot married a descendant of his, and it

was here, in the 1930s and 1940s, that caches of his papers
were found (later bought and published by Yale) showing
that that spunky, tireless, amoral biographer richly deserved
a biography of his own. The castle has traces of the original
moat but little else from before the eighteenth century, the
drum tower to the south-east being late nineteenth century.
The fifteenth-century church of St Sylvester in the grounds –
known as the abbey – was the family vault till 1873. It has
a good altar-tomb of Maud Plunket – 'maid, wife and widow
in one day' since her first husband fell in battle immediately
after the wedding. On the morning of the battle fourteen
Talbots are said to have taken what turned out to be their last
breakfast here.

The nucleus of the present collection is formed by the Talbot
family portraits, including important seventeenth century
works. Many others are on loan from the National Gallery.
There is some rare Irish Georgian furniture, acquired by the
Tourist Board at auction when death duties (since abolished)
after the last baron's death forced his family to sell up; so that
much of the atmosphere of the occupied house survives. There
is also a fine and famous model railway, and in the well maintained garden an interesting collection of shrubs.

Malahide is a small seaside resort, close to the Donabate
golf-links, one of many on this coast rich in sandbanks.
Three miles west is **Swords**, with some interesting antiquities
but little hint of its former importance. St Columba is
supposed to have founded a monastery here and left in charge
St Finan the Leper, who to chasten himself, so the story goes,
had contracted the disease from a child, and suffered from it
thirty years. The monastery rose in importance. Brian Boru's
body lay here a night on the way to Armagh, and later one
of the principal manors of Dublin's Archbishop was built
here. The five-sided ruin of the manorial castle, with towers
at each angle, stands at the north end of the main street,
but having been devastated by Edward Bruce in 1316 it has
little but the gatehouse and west tower of the chapel to show
from before. The stepped battlements of the walls are
characteristically fifteenth century. Down the road are the
Round Tower and steeple of the old abbey church.

The main Swords road takes us directly back to Dublin. Dublin Airport is three miles along on the right, with a very good restaurant to which, for its own sake, people come out from the city. Two miles on is **Santry**, just outside the city boundaries but a suburb in essence. In 1840 Lady Domville built a model village here, a fashionable thing for tidy-minded landlords to do, but it has been swallowed up recently. There is a good church of 1709. A mile and a half farther, in Drumcondra, we pass the broad park of **All Hallows College** on the left. The main part of the building was the work of the neo-Gothic follower of Pugin, J. J. McCarthy, but **Drumcondra House**, built around 1727 by Sir Edward Lovett Pearce, still stands on the south side. It belonged then to Marmaduke Coghill, one of the trustees of Steevens' Hospital. Later that century it passed to the Earl of Charleville, whose widow remarried, after his death, in the Italianate temple built by Alessandro Galilei (architect of Castletown) and still standing in the park. Coghill, having died, according to the inscription, of 'gout in the stomach', was buried in the church of St John the Baptist nearby; his sumptuous monument, by Scheemakers, shows him haughty in the garb of Chancellor of the Irish Exchequer. The most memorable grave is in the churchyard – to James Gandon, who died in 1824 and to whom Dublin owes her greatest buildings. He was interred in the grave of Francis Grose, his close friend and a pioneering antiquarian. Under Grose's epitaph – he died 'whilst in cheerful conversation with his friends' – is Gandon's: 'Also his Friend James Gandon, Architect, Born in 1742 – Died 1824'. That is all; the rest is said by his surviving buildings.

The main road crosses the River Tolka, and straight away we can turn right along Botanic Avenue to the **Botanic Gardens** in Glasnevin. This was once an area of high fashion. Steele lived nearby; Addison – who was twice chief secretary in Ireland – has left his name in the riverside elm-walk; and Swift came frequently to visit his friends, Dr and Mrs Delany, resenting the cost of the coach. Their home, Delville, has left no trace; the Bon Secours Hospital, on the right and over the river, occupies the site of the house, the parterre with its orange trees, bowling-green, grotto, temples, rustic bridges, and paddocks of deer and cattle – the model *ferme ornée*, with a shell-house made by Mrs Delany herself, one of the most charming and informative diarists of her century.

The Botanic Gardens – forty-seven acres of them – were, to start with, the work of that progressive body, the Dublin Society, which, founded in 1731, combined science and philanthropy in its work for farms, farm-workers, and knowledge in general. The gardens were opened in 1794, shortly before a chair in botany was endowed by the society at Trinity. The director's house, a Lebanon cedar and the ancient yew-avenue commemorating Addison are all that survive from that time. In the nineteenth century the gardens were greatly expanded and most of the present buildings, including the fine early cast-iron conservatories, were put up, the 65 feet high Palm House dating from 1884. The Government took direct control in 1877. The gardens can teach and delight. There are beds in which plants are arranged by their scientific families, bringing together unlikely cousins like buttercup, anemone and paeony. There are tropical hothouses with rare ferns, cactuses, lilies, including the seven-foot diameter *Victoria amazonica*, a rich collection of orchids and other exotic plants; pretty herbaceous borders, covered walks and arboreta – containing rich collections of oaks, maples, birches, dwarf conifers – in one of which it is quaint to meet a chubby, affable, marble Socrates on a granite plinth. A small Mexican oak, *Quercus rapanda*, is thought to be the only specimen in these islands. Altogether the gardens, more compact and colourful than Kew, are one of Dublin's finest offerings.

Having seen them, we can go to Glasnevin, strictly **Prospect, Cemetery** by turning right at the main gate and right again. The cemetery has its permanent niche in literature as Paddy Dignam's last resting-place in *Ulysses*, but the list of real-life figures buried here makes a roll-call of Ireland's great – Curran, O'Connell, O'Donovan Rossa, Parnell, Casement, Arthur Griffith, Collins. O'Donovan Rossa died in New York in 1915, but his body was returned here and buried, Patrick Pearse declaiming an emotive funeral oration that helped rally opinion for the rising the following year. Case-

ment's remains were transferred here from London's Penton-
ville Prison, fifty years after his execution for treason. A state
funeral was accorded to the remains, which gruesome prattle
hinted might be blended – owing to the nature of quicklime
burials in prisons – with those of Crippen. The Round Tower
commemorates O'Connell. In 1959 the first record of an
expansive sub-species of the pigeon family, the Collared
Dove, was made in the cemetery. It had appeared in Britain
four years earlier, having swiftly colonised the Continent
from Asia before that. It is now resident all over these islands,
a success comparable to that of the Grey Squirrel.

SOUTH-EAST DUBLIN TO BRAY

The wealth and prestige of the south-east of inner Dublin –
Postal District Two, with Leinster House at its centre –
continues a little dilute to the south-east. From the city to
Dun Laoghaire lies a line of elegant suburbs beside the sea.
Ballsbridge, with Sandymount as its shore flank, is the first,
and from a Dubliner's point of view the most desirable, with
roomy Victorian houses, a leavening of open spaces, broad
streets and, for us, some poles of great interest. In Pembroke
Road, the main through-road, we pass, on the left, the new,
smart Intercontinental Hotel, on the site of Trinity's Botanic
Gardens, and shortly after the rotund American Embassy on
the right. Crossing the Dodder we enter Merrion Road. On
the right is the arena round which all Dublin seems to revolve
in August, the show ground of the **Royal Dublin Society** and
site of the Annual Dublin Horse Show.

Showing off hunters' paces is the least important (except
moneywise) of the society's functions. It is a peculiarly
polymorphic body, whose range of activities evolved in pure
descent from eighteenth-century beginnings. Progressive
landlords and professionals founded it in 1731 'for the
improvement of Husbandry, Manufactures and other useful
Arts'. They offered prizes for schemes and inventions,
circulated books on farming, commerce and industries to
those who could benefit, and gave special encouragement to

linen, which was of mounting importance since the protective English had banned imports of wool. The King took note and helped the society, and soon the Irish Parliament gave large regular grants. At the turn of the century they had created in embryo the National Library, the National History Museum, the National College of Art, the Glasnevin Botanical Gardens, and endowed lectures and professorships. In 1815, having run through a number of headquarters, they bought Leinster House, whose complex of buildings still houses several of their collections. But the Dail, or Irish Parliament, newly-formed and house-hunting in 1922, evicted them, and they have been based here ever since. They keep up scientific work, mainly agricultural but including cancer research, and publish their proceedings. We can see over the buildings, and the hall where they hold winter concerts; and if it is May see their agricultural Spring Show; if August, the Horse Show, one of the world's great equestrian displays.

Sir Alfred Chester Beatty was an American, naturalised British, resident in Dublin, who combined a successful involvement in African and American mining with an interest, as he put it in *Who's Who*, 'in collecting Oriental manuscripts, specialising particularly in manuscripts of artistic merit from the point of view of miniatures and calligraphy'. The product of these combined horizons is the **Chester Beatty Library** in Shrewsbury Road (second right off Merrion Road after the RDS grounds). Open to the public from Tuesday to Saturday, the library comprises two galleries in separate buildings, the older (opened in 1953) and nearer containing a magnificently furnished Chinese Library, Japanese prints and manuscripts, and a unique collection of rare western manuscripts and bindings, ranging from an early ninth-century Italian copy of Bede, to a selection of early printed books, and including some beautiful French and Spanish Books of Hours minutely illustrated. The building at the back (opened 1957) contains the older and most famous manuscripts, notably the Chester Beatty papyri, a group of codices found in Egypt and bought in 1931, many of them from the second and third centuries and a hundred or more years older than the earliest vellum manuscripts. Their significance to scholars is chiefly as evidence for the text of the Greek bible. There is also a unique collection of about 600 Chinese snuff-boxes of various stones including sapphire and garnet, and a collection of Indian, Persian and Middle Eastern manuscripts, paintings, robes, and ornaments.

The road touches the coast at Merrion, and goes on to **Blackrock**. Blackrock College, on the right, is a famous Catholic boys' school founded in 1860, where De Valera was both pupil and master. What is now part of an unbroken line of suburbs was a popular coast and country resort in the eighteenth century, a favourite spot for the new and adventurous sport of bathing. John Scott, Earl of Clonmell and a debauched and venal Lord Chief Justice ('resolve *seriously* to set about learning my profession' he wrote in his revealing diary, six years after his appointment) had a house here, called Neptune, but an enemy bought land nearby, invited the mob of Dublin to chase and catch well-greased pigs in a Grand Olympic Hunt, and thereby succeeded in destroying Neptune's gardens. The villa still stands. Opposite the far end of Blackrock Park is a remnant of the Villa Frescati, occupied by Lord Edward FitzGerald and his wife Pamela in the years before the 1798 Rising and his death. The next right turn but one is Carysfort Avenue, in No. 23 of which Joyce lived for a spell in the 'nineties with his parents; the settings of the *Portrait* and *Ulysses* are numerous along this coast, and probably in all his years of exile no area was ever more familiar to him.

A mile or so farther on we reach **Dun Laoghaire**, pronounced and sometimes written Dunleary, but known as Kingstown for a century after 1821, when George IV took unsteady leave of this part of his kingdom from the new harbour. A stone crown on a ball-based obelisk commemorates the event which fifty thousand turned out to see, though they were disappointed by the King's aborting of various prepared speeches, including O'Connell's, by making some hasty promises to his well-beloved people and hurrying for the boat. The harbour was built to the plans of John Rennie, designer of the London Bridge that was removed to America in 1970, and of old Waterloo Bridge. It has from its inception served the Irish

Mail ferries from and to England. Around it are headquarters of seven yacht clubs, including the Royal Irish and the Royal St George.

Rounding Scotsman's Bay, east of Dun Laoghaire, we come to **Sandycove Point,** with its prominent Martello Tower looking over Dublin Bay to the swollen bastion of Howth. That, too, was Joyce's view. He stayed a short while in 1904 with his elegant medical-student friend, Oliver St John Gogarty, who rented the tower – squat granite relic of British fears of Napoleon – from the War Office for £8 a year. The occasion gave Joyce the opening scene of *Ulysses*, in which Gogarty became 'stately plump Buck Mulligan' and Stephen D. felt left out of things. Joyce's final departure was by night, prompted by Gogarty's firing a pistol at a metal pan to wake a third occupant from a noisy dream. In 1962 Sylvia Beech, who first published *Ulysses*, opened it as a museum, which it remains, with a few notes, photographs and trinkets that try to evoke the giant. Close by is the Forty Foot, a bathing place for men, to which, round the year, come stolid athletes of all ages, some consistently before 8 a.m. when custom allows total nudity. 'Forty Foot Gentlemen Only' reads the sign at the entrance.

Dun Laoghaire leads without break back to **Dalkey,** passing on the right modernised, medieval **Bullock Castle,** one of many which guarded the Dublin approaches, and containing a small museum. Bernard Shaw lived in Torca Cottage, on Dalkey Hill, for several years as a boy, and sometimes returned to the place to stay and write. A pretty, palmy, hilly resort, it provides splendid views of the coastline and mountains behind, and of Dalkey Island, with its Martello tower and the ruined church that dates from Danish times. Dublin at last is falling away and the spirit of the resort is taking over. It continues at **Killiney,** with its excellent Strand and pleasant Victoria Park, and tall Killiney Hill from which granite used to be quarried. From now on the built-up concentration is dissipated, and a few miles on is Bray, one of the strategic gateways to the Wicklow Mountains.

CHAPTER TWO

Boyne Valley and Meath

THE direct road from Dublin to Drogheda is by the T1, but we shall keep mostly to the coast. Beyond Swords and the bridge over Broad Meadow River, we pass a right turn for Donabate, known for its golf links; and another, two miles on, for the little seaside resort of **Portrane**, whose manor house, now near a modern mental hospital, was for a while home of Swift's Stella. The next right turn brings us to **Lusk**, site of a monastery founded in the fifth century, in the first wave of evangelism after St Patrick's mission. The 95-foot Round Tower dates from the last phase of the monastery, which after several Viking assaults was dissolved in the tenth century, though a nunnery of Augustinians continued till the end of the twelfth. The square tower of which the Round Tower seems a part is a belfry of about 1500, built on to an earlier church now replaced by an 1847 construction. There are some good tombs and effigies inside, particularly the florid memorial to the Barnewall family, whose ancestor, Sir Michael de Barneval, landed in Cork in 1172, before Strongbow in Wexford.

Two miles east, outside Rush, is Rogerstown quay from which boats sail to Lambay Island, three miles over the water. (Permission to land must be obtained in advance from the owner, Lord Revelstoke.) The island, rich in breeding sea-birds, has been made a bird sanctuary. There has been a castle here since the fifteenth century, and there was a monastery close on a millennium before that, founded by St Columba. In the aftermath of King William's ousting of James II, some prisoners taken by William's General Ginkel were sent here and died of starvation. (Ignoring their fate a group of hippies in 1969 negotiated to buy a smaller island nearby, planning to live off the land: there were strong local objections and the deal petered out.) Lord Revelstoke's house incorporates the old castle and was designed by Lutyens; it is one of his most subtle works. As elsewhere, Lutyens collaborated with the garden-designer Gertrude Jekyll, founder, with the Irishman William Robinson, of the Surrey School, which shied away from Victorian formalism. Lambay and Howth, a few miles south, are Lutyens's main works in Ireland. The island is valued by naturalists. When Cecil Baring, ancestor of the present owner, bought it in 1902 to celebrate his marriage to an American heiress, his interest in wildlife led him to consult the great botanist Robert Lloyd Praeger who discovered here seventeen species new to British Isles records, and five new to science.

The coast road goes on through Rush, and passes **Kenure Park,** traditional home of the Palmer family, on the left. George Papworth refaced the eighteenth-century house and added the giant Corinthian portico in 1842, and there was fine plasterwork by Robert West inside but the house, empty for years, has been allowed to decay. Four miles on, Skerries has a golf-course and holiday camp. Half a mile beyond the town on the left, Cromwell is said to have camped during the Drogheda massacre, at a place still called the Camps. Balbriggan, the next town along the way, has been known for the making of stockings for two hundred years; Americans sometimes call them balbriggans to this day. The scant Elizabethan ruins north of the town are of a Barnewall castle. Inland from here, around Naul, the hills and their pretty, cave-rich valleys have yielded several finds of objects from the extensive prehistoric Boyne Valley culture. Keeping to the coast, uniformly sandy from here to the Boyne's mouth, we come to **Gormanston,** home of the Prestons, Viscounts Gormanston, from 1363 to 1947 when the castle was taken over by Franciscans for a college. The only gaps in the Preston ownership – in Cromwellian times and for over a century after William's accession – were caused by their tenacious loyalty to Catholicism. Their family vault is under the roofless sixteenth-century chantry chapel, an extension of the now ruined medieval church. From here on the road leads in from the coast and in eight miles reaches the Boyne, County Louth, and the principal town this side of Ulster.

Drogheda, whose population of 20,000 has changed little in the last hundred years, is three miles from the sea. Rising steeply either side of the river, it has a good harbour, well placed for trade with Liverpool, numerous light industries, among them the making of linen and cotton, and a violent history that helped shape its present robust character. A ford across the river made it important enough for the Danes, under their pugnacious king Turgesius, to fortify around AD 911. Like the English later, the Danes have been given little credit for the good things they did in Ireland, among them founding most of the coastal towns. By the end of the eleventh century Drogheda's position attracted the Anglo-Normans who took the place, built a 'bridge over the ford' (the Irish for which gave the town its name), and brought it in two centuries to rank among Ireland's four senior towns, with the right – never exploited – to build a university along the lines of Oxford. In the days of the Pale it was a frontier town, facing the rebellious tribes of Ulster; and Parliaments were often held there as a flourish of authority. The hated Poynings Law, making all Irish laws subject to the king's approval, was passed there in 1495.

Much went awry in the seventeenth century. In the confused warring that went on after the general rebellion of 1641, one attitude was consistent: that of the Parliamentary English, who saw Catholic Ireland as perverse and hostile. Drogheda, held at first for the Parliamentarians, fell later to the Royalists, and it was Cromwell's first target on his arrival at Dublin in 1649. Cromwell came with three sincere convictions – that the 1641 Rising had been the most barbarous massacre the world had seen, that independent Ireland would be a perpetual threat to England, and that God was fully behind him. Taking the town on a third assault he ordered the death of every armed defender. Almost three thousand were massacred – 'a righteous judgment of God upon those barbarous wretches', Cromwell wrote. A hundred who fled to St Peter's steeple for sanctuary were burned inside it, and the few who came off with their lives were transported to Barbados. In 1690 Drogheda again opted for the losing side, sheltering James II before the Battle of the Boyne, but it surrendered to William on the day after the battle and was spared.

Drogheda shared in the eighteenth-century rise and subsequent fall of Irish prosperity. A hundred years ago Thackeray, who devoted forty-five minutes to the place, found it 'smoky, dirty, and lively', with many ruined, shuttered houses pointing up the decay. O'Connell spoke there often, lionised by discontented masses. To-day, suitably, it is a moral stronghold of nationalist feeling and sometimes the scene of municipal wrangles that nobody ignorant of Ireland's recent history can understand.

Streets are narrow and houses jostle each other closely. On the south side of the river, off Barrack Street, which leads up from the bridge, is **Mill Mount**. This is thought to have been a prehistoric mound, perhaps on the scale of Newgrange and Knowth up-river. In the twelfth century a motte was built on it, whose adjoining bailey is now mostly covered by modern barracks. The cross on top was erected during the Holy Year of 1950 and, lit up at night, is visible ten miles out to sea. Nearby is **Butter Gate**, one of two extant thirteenth-century town-gates. There were ten.

From the river bridge the harbour, bounded by the nineteenth-century Boyne Viaduct, can be seen over to the right. Drogheda's other town-gate, **St Laurence's**, commemorates Bishop Laurence O'Toole, who after Strongbow's invasion devoted his life to salvaging native Irish rights. The gate is the best of its kind in Ireland, with two tall drum-towers and a curtain wall intact – the barbican of the original entire gate. The handsome eighteenth-century houses nearby form Drogheda Grammar School. Two hundred yards west, along St Laurence Street is the pretty eighteenth-century **Tholsel**, or market building, now occupied and well preserved, like hundreds of Ireland's best town houses, by a bank. This charming enclave of the town includes the Cornmarket and Market House, both designed by one of Ireland's greatest native architects, Francis Johnston. He also planned the tower and spire of **St Peter's C of I Church** close by. It has interesting monuments and some fine rococo plasterwork in-

side, and a ghoulish cadaver-tombstone on the Golding grave
outside. On the opposite side of West Street is **St Peter's
RC Church,** the memorial church to Saint Oliver Plunket,
seventeenth-century Archbishop of Armagh who was canon-
ised in 1975. Charles II's lenient policy towards Catholics
from time to time met violent reactions, in one of which, in
1681, this gentle Primate was hauled to Westminster, tried
and hanged on a mythical charge. The Irish, whose concern
with mortal remains is greater than Anglo-Saxons' (till quite
recent times it was common practice to lay out bodies for the
payment of last respects and eat baked meats spread on top
of the coffin), preserve his unlovely head embalmed and encased
in full public view, in the North Chapel, far from his body
which is decently buried at Downside Abbey in England.

A short walk along West Street leads to the ruined tower
and other slight remains of St Mary D'Urso's Augustinian
Friary. More graceful remains are those of fifteenth-century
St Mary Magdalene's Dominican Friary to the north. An
unusual feature of Drogheda is the fine modern **Church of
Our Lady of Lourdes** near the Tholsel. The Irish Catholic
clergy, harassed for centuries, have used their comparatively
recent fortune and freedom with an abandon that disfigures
many towns and villages. The main policy seems to have
been the negative one of avoiding any resemblance to traditional Anglican styles. There are in their place a lot of hybrid
and horrid styles, and an exception is well worth a second
look.

Drogheda is just inside Ireland's smallest county, Louth,
less known than it might be owing to its position between
the purlieus of Dublin and the grand countryside of Down.
Its best half is the northern. Apart from Mellifont and
Monasterboice, the southern is eclipsed by the attractions of
the Boyne. It still rewards inspection if there is time.

From the road leading north-east from Drogheda direct to
Termonfeckin, four miles away, a lane turns right to a private
demesne, **Beaulieu.** Its lovely brick-dressed mansion was for
long supposed to have been built by Wren, but it was probably
the work of a Dutchman, working between 1660 and 1666.
The broad eaves show its Dutch inspiration, and it is the only

house of its kind to have survived. Till 1649 this was Plunkett property, a family – Lord Dunsany the author was one – who have innumerable associations in the area. **Termonfeckin** is a quiet village, containing till 1613 the summer residence of the archbishops of Armagh, of which nothing remains. A good High Cross is in the graveyard, and nearby is a fifteenth-century tower with stepped battlements, only survivor of the medieval home of the Dowdalls.

Three miles up the coast, which is mainly flat and dull (but with the odd garish resort) as far as Dundalk, Clogher Head makes a relieving promontory with good views of the Mourne Mountains. The road turns inland to Dunleer, where a right turn on to the main road leads after seven miles to **Castlebellingham**, once famous for its ale. Most of its distinction belongs to the past, since the eighteenth-century Castle Bellingham was turned recently into a hotel and had its grey-painted Gothic façade and gates festooned with neon lights. The park was once well known for yews and beauty, while the Bellingham family included a sixteenth-century Lord Deputy and King William's ADC at the Battle of the Boyne. The Calvary in the village centre, erected in 1904 by Sir Henry Bellingham in memory of his wife, was the first to be put up in Ireland.

Buried in the churchyard is Dr Thomas Guither, a seventeenth-century physician and Fellow of Trinity, Dublin, to whom has been attributed the introduction of frogs into Ireland. It is an issue over which controversy has flared from time to time. After the Ice Age, around 6000 BC, the sea cut off Ireland from Britain, and rather later Britain from the Continent. The frog, now common in Ireland, could have beaten the sea at that time, and there are remains of it in caves in Sligo, side by side with definitely prehistoric bones, that argue it did. However, frogs of a later age could have slipped through cracks in the rock, and so become mixed up with earlier remains. Some say frogs came with the Normans: and Giraldus Cambrensis, who came with them himself, denied their existence before the Normans' arrival. Frogs, he wrote, appeared around Waterford after the Norman landings. His belief tallied with the legend that St Patrick

had expelled all noxious creatures, including frogs, toads
and snakes, in the fifth century. Expert opinion seems to
favour Giraldus on essentials, and Dr Guither, who undoubtedly brought spawn from England and let it develop
in a Trinity pond, seems unlikely to have been the first
introducer.

This central part of Louth has little to pick out except
occasional clusters of antiquities and some pleasing private
houses. General views inland and over Dundalk Bay are
tedious. **Dromiskin**, a couple of miles north of Castlebellingham, breaks the monotony with its stunted Round Tower
(much shortened, recapped, and now used as the parish
church's belfry), a worn and broken High Cross, and a
striking new Catholic church. A backwater now, Dromiskin
can anyway boast that Patrick founded and Vikings occupied
it, and it once contained the relics of St Ronan, whose main
feat was alleged to be restoring to life a mother, stoned to
death, and the child she had allowed to choke with bread.

A mile away to the west is **Milltown Castle**, a fortified
house from Stuart days, private but visible from the road.
This westerly road goes through to **Louth**, another centre
that history abandoned, leaving a few houses and some
impressive ruins. St Patrick founded the first church here,
entrusting it to St Mochta. The church gave place to an abbey
which, being accessible to the coast, was plundered by
Norsemen in the ninth century. The abbey was rebuilt at
Knock, a mile or so south-west, in 1148 and its name spread
so far that the abbot was granted a mitre, usually reserved
for bishops. Louth became a county town, but went down
after the Dissolution. There are remains of a Dominican Friary
of around 1500, and St Mochta's Church, stone-roofed, well
preserved and neatly enclosed by a wall, of about 1100.
Ardpatrick House, a mile east, was once the home of Saint
Oliver Plunket; and Louth Hall, a few miles south, still
belongs to his family, the Barons of Louth.

Louth is on the edge of Cuchulain (pronounced Cer-
hullen) country and the hero's admirers can drive a couple of
miles north-east to see the stone, in a field on the right, to
which he supposedly had himself tied in his last fight in the

long wars between Connaught and Ulster. The scene, though little known, has become a symbol of Ireland's struggle to be free, and is depicted in bronze in Dublin's General Post Office, itself a symbol of resistance.

Cuchulain's greatest exploit took place at **Ardee**, a long, large village (of nearly 3,000 inhabitants) on a broad main street six miles due south of Louth. Here it was, according to legend, that Connaught's Queen Maeve, jealous of her husband Ailill's magic White-Horned Bull, arrived with her army to capture the animal's only equal, the Brown Bull of Cooley. Cooley is now the Carlingford Peninsula and all the men of Ulster would have turned out to resist had they not been laid low by a temporary sickness. Only Cuchulain was fit, a lad of seventeen, who had to smear his chin with blackberry juice to persuade enemies he was of fighting age. The Dee River, wider in the story than it is now (though still an excellent salmon river, free in parts), blocked most of the Connaught men while Cuchulain took them on one at a time, at the ford of Ardee, three hundred yards west of the present bridge. The *Cattle Raid of Cooley*, as the saga is known, tells how, in the intervals of duelling, Cuchulain kills a hundred men a day with his sling, fells a sewing maid incautiously wearing Maeve's head-dress, and destroys an eel, a heifer and a wolf sent against him by the Queen of the Gods, who thereafter befriends him. He was so agile he could turn round in his skin, putting feet and hands behind and buttocks and calves before him. Maeve, much vexed, and failing to seduce the hero, finally orders Ferdia, a childhood friend of Cuchulain's, to fight. A sad duel of three days begins, and at the end of each day both friends embrace and tend the other's wounds, till the prophesied end arrives, Ferdia is killed, and Cuchulain carries him over the river he could not cross alive. A large mound now marks his burial place. At last the Ulster men recover from their epidemic and arrive to take over from Cuchulain, on whose body there is no spot, not even 'the size of a needle-point' without a wound. He lives to fight again. But the Brown Bull has been rustled and carried off to Connaught, where it kills the White-Horned Bull, escapes, returns to Cooley, goes mad, kills all who confront it and finally 'bursts its heart with bellowing and falls dead'.

Ardee keeps an air of the importance it had after the Anglo-Norman invasion, when it was for long periods a crucial outpost of the Pale, though often in native hands. The larger of the two castles was built by Roger Pipard, who held the barony of Ardee in the thirteenth century. Much restored after its violent history, but giving a good idea of a square keep with projecting towers, it now houses the court-house and gaol. Hatch's Castle, a fortified house of the same period just off the main street, could be mistaken for a showy terrace-house. The Hatch family, settled in it by Cromwell, stayed till 1940. Both the Catholic and the pleasing C of I churches are thought to be on the sites of religious foundations of Roger Pipard.

Off a lane a couple of miles south-east of the town, beside a pretty graveyard with yew and holly trees, is the ruin of an oddly athletic building, the 'jumping' **Church of Kildemock**. Little but the wall that jumped still stands, which is strange enough. It stands moreover at a queer angle that baffles most attempts to trace its movement. The picturesque story is that the wall sprang of its own accord to exclude from the church an excommunicated heretic, buried inside. Other verdicts blame a fierce and famous storm of 1715, but it is hard to see how anything short of an earthquake could have caused the move.

A main road goes south from Ardee to Collon, north of which is the demesne of **Oriel Temple,** a house built by John Foster, Speaker of the Irish Parliament in the late eighteenth century, and now the Cistercian Abbey of New Mellifont. Foster, in the prosperous days of Grattan's Parliament, intro-duced a Corn Law which, by protecting Irish grain against cheaper imports, made Ireland for the first time a great tillage country. This changed the face of the country, giving to many a means of earning a living and causing (till the famine of the 1840s broke the system) the building of corn mills whose hollow shells still dot the countryside. Foster gave the house to his sister and her husband, Lord Massereene, in whose family it stayed till the 1930s. Oriel itself was the name of an ancient Irish kingdom. Nowadays adapted for community needs, the house bears little resemblance to the original, and is rather ugly. Foster's main house still stands in the village, where there is also a good C of I church of 1813.

Two remarkable monastic sites remain, before we return to the Boyne. **Monasterboice**, three miles east of Collon, is said to have been founded by St Buithe, a disciple of St Patrick, around AD 500. Like most important early Christian sites its history goes back obscurely into pagan times, as recent digs have shown. St Buithe gave his name to the Boyne (by a complicated conversion from Irish to English). Nothing is known of him, but legend tells that when in old age he wanted to die, angels sent a ladder for him to climb to his quietus. Being near the coast, the abbey suffered from Danish marauders, and in 968 three hundred of them occupied the place, but were overcome and massacred by the Irish High King. A century later the library and Round Tower were burned, but most of the latter still stands, fitted inside with modern staircases leading to a very good all-round view.

In the mid-nineteenth century many scholars came to think that Round Towers, along with anything remotely related in shape, like maypoles, standing stones, and even the Christian cross, were direct descendants of phallic symbols used in an ancient world-wide fertility cult. There may be links, but Dark Ages monks, harried by Vikings, had other things to think of. Their Round Towers were a breakthrough in the art of defence. Entered up a ladder by a door several feet above ground, solidly built and of a shape that deflected missiles, the tower protected its occupants against everything but protracted siege. Which is probably why so many remain. The one in question, topless for a thousand years, is otherwise sound, and its lean from the perpendicular is almost imperceptible.

Monasterboice contains also two church ruins – one thirteenth century – an earlier sundial eight feet high, a graveyard spoiled by hideous modern stones, and three High Crosses, two of which are the best of their kind in Ireland. These richly sculptured pillars are as much Irish landmarks as the Round Towers. The deep relief scenes fitted into panels all over them were used for teaching the scriptures to peasants, but at first their purpose was monumental. The circular stays of the typical Celtic cross suggest that the earliest crosses, made of wood, were carried in procession and needed extra support at the joint. These early crosses had at most some abstract or animal carving at the base, but gradually their use changed, and they became visual aids for open-air sermons. Nowadays they provide one of the best accounts of the development of Celtic art, and the Monasterboice crosses represent their peak. Of the two, Muiredach's Cross is probably the earlier, dating from the early tenth century, but also the better preserved. One side carries scenes from the New Testament, with the Crucifixion in the centre, the other Old Testament scenes and Christ in Judgement. The summit is a model of a contemporary church – a gabled building with shingle roof. The West Cross is one of the tallest in Ireland (21½ feet high) and of rather later date, though in a worse condition. Only about a quarter of the fifty or so panels are intelligible, and they include scenes from the life of David, and episodes in the life, death and resurrection of Christ. It comes as a surprise that, like the grey interiors of our Gothic cathedrals, these panels were at first brightly painted, and that we see them with the polychrome dimension lost.

A rather complicated drive of three miles south-west leads to **Mellifont**, beside the narrow River Mattock, a monastery whose slight but pleasing remains give no idea of its importance in early Irish church history. Giraldus Cambrensis, the bigoted observer who followed his king to Ireland at the Anglo-Norman conquest, found the Irish 'a filthy people, wallowing in vice'. Since its great expansive years of the sixth and seventh centuries the church had certainly declined, but a few years before Giraldus's visit, St Malachy, Archbishop of Armagh and friend of St Bernard of Clairvaux, set in train an effective programme of reform. Using Cistercian monks trained at Clairvaux, and on land provided by the King of Oriel, he founded in 1142 the monastery of Mellifont. He swept away the corruption, immorality and nepotism that had become accepted, and Mellifont's success was closely followed by the founding of daughter establishments all over

Ireland, nine of them within ten years. Other orders soon followed, but Mellifont marks the beginning of religious reform. Moreover, master-masons and workers sent to Mellifont by Bernard brought new architectural ideas to Ireland.

Among its early patrons was Dervorgilla, on whom blame for the English conquest has often been laid. She retired here incognito after the death of Dermot Macmurrough, her second husband. Muirchertach, High King of Ireland, presented 160 cows and sixty ounces of gold to the monastery, at the same time as he gave the glorious site of Cashel to the Munster church. After the Dissolution the place was made over to Edward Moore, ancestor of the Earls of Drogheda, and a fortified house built, but the bases of walls and columns of the original abbey survive. The tall gatehouse, the restored chapter house (miscalled St Bernard's Chapel) with its exquisitely groined roof and foliated capitals, and the octagonal lavabo of about 1200 still give a melancholy idea of former grandeur. This is one of the most moving sites of Leinster.

Hugh O'Neill submitted here to Mountjoy after the Battle of Kinsale had dashed his and Spanish hopes of Irish independence. In the eighteenth century it was bought by the Balfours of nearby Townley Hall, but they never lived in it. A hundred years ago it was used for keeping pigs. Residence to-day is limited to a Youth Hostel and a farmhouse. The Cistercians themselves occupy New Mellifont and leave the ruins to their memories.

The Balfour home, **Townley Hall**, just south of Mellifont, is generally held to be Francis Johnston's best house in the classical style, with a forbidding cut-stone exterior, and some magnificent features inside, including a cantilevered circular central staircase. Trinity College, Dublin, who owned it recently, altered it for the worse, sold off Chinese wall-papers and cut down trees. It is now happily back in private hands. Its demesne is beside the **Boyne River,** and the road round its eastern end leads to all the sites connected with the river's most famous event, the Battle of the Boyne, one of half a dozen main turning-points in Irish history.

Irish Catholics, who before the Commonwealth owned

Trinity College, Dublin: a seat of scholarship at the city's hub.

Muiredach's Cross at Monasterboice, carved in the tenth century.

about three fifths of Irish land, ended that phase with one fifth, 'for fighting' as Swift wrote, 'in defence of their king'. Some of it they got back at the Restoration, but Charles II's reign was a sequence of attempts to please everyone while satisfying none. James II's accession in 1685 gave the Catholics, still barred from government and administration, hopes of recognition and more of what they considered their own land. Some hopes were fulfilled – even the new Viceroy Tyrconnell was a Catholic, and a favourable land reform was on the way when the 'Glorious Revolution' of 1688 tipped James from his throne. Tyrconnell held out for him in Ireland, however, and James planned his come-back from France through Ireland. Early in 1689 he landed with French troops and funds at Kinsale and called a parliament at Dublin which passed various pro-Catholic acts. Protestant opposition massed mainly among the recent Ulster settlers. The English had to act, and what the Irish call 'The War of the Two Kings' began when William landed at Carrickfergus, joined his commander-in-chief Marshal Schomberg and marched south. Much hung in the balance, and not only for these islands.

James fell back from Dundalk, where he had been facing Schomberg's army, to Drogheda, and took up a poor position south of the Boyne, on the north face of the hill of Donore. Of his 25,000 men, 7,000 were French, but the majority were ill-armed Irish irregulars. James himself was a bad general, 'whose weakness, imbecility and bigotry' Sir William Wilde wrote in his florid guide to the Boyne Valley 'had already lost him a crown'. Wilde, however, and many other historians, were themselves bigoted and judged James crudely. He was still no match for William, who pursued him through Ardee and arrived at the Boyne on the thirtieth of June. Taking the high ground that stretches a mile east from Tullyallen, he looked down on the nakedly exposed camp of the Irish, and began to bombard. In spite of a skin-wound received in a rash reconnoitre, he made plans that the short decisive engagement of the first of July fully justified. At dawn that day, he sent 10,000 men three miles west to Rosnaree, burial place of the great Cormac Mac Art, and to Slane, to cross the river and

surprise the Jacobite left flank. This was done by 10.30 am
when he and the remaining forces began crossing the river
below Oldbridge. Only the stump of an obelisk, blown apart
in the Troubles, still marks the stretch. The river, still tidal at
this point, was low, but the crossing was difficult and while
William nearly lost his horse his general Schomberg, a veteran
of the Thirty Years' War, was struck down and killed. There
is a memorial to him by the gates of Oldbridge demesne. As
soon as the main army was across, James's centre and right
wing broke. They fell back first on Donore, then met the
worsted left wing at Duleek, three miles south, where all but
James spent the night. That flouted monarch fled to Dublin,
then south to Waterford, where he made his escape to France
and an old age in exile. His troops dispersed, some to muster
again the following year in the west. The total casualties had
been few, but the real victim was the old English Catholic
aristocracy and what still survived of the Gaelic order and
culture.

Ireland, always a bastion of Catholicism, has often been at
odds with the Pope. It was with a Pope's blessing – Hadrian
IV – that the English occupied Dublin in 1172. After the
Boyne battle, Pope Innocent XI had St Peter's illuminated
and drank a toast to William, for the battle had indirectly
secured Catholic solidarity on the Continent. Irish history is
full of paradox. It could be argued that, ostensibly, the
English were being exploited when a Scotch king fought a
Dutch king on Irish soil for the dominion of England.

Duleek, where the Stuarts finally quitted their throne, is
where the course of the battle has left us. In early days it was
the site of a bishopric founded by St Patrick, often pillaged
by the Norse and once by the Anglo-Normans. After Clontarf,
the body of Brian Boru lay here in state on its way to Armagh.
Late in the twelfth century Hugh de Lacy built a manor and
castle here and probably founded the Augustinian priory
which prospered till the Dissolution, when it was given to the
Moores of Mellifont. There are good effigies and tombs in the
roofless aisle – the best being a decorated fifteenth-century
Bellew family memorial. There are also two worn High Crosses.
The remnant of a cross of different kind stands in the

market place. It was erected by Dame Jennett Dowdall in 1601 in memory of herself and her husband William Bathe of Athcarne, a fortified Elizabethan house still standing three miles south-west of the village. There are several of these crosses in the district, the best of them the White Cross with various New Testament carvings, about half a mile north-west of Athcarne.

The Boyne is a running pageant of Irish history, in no chronological order. Upstream from Oldbridge a lane turns left off the Slane road and leads us zig-zag to the country's grandest prehistoric survivals. On both sides of the valley lie the wooded demesnes of Ireland's richest farming country and here, in a loop of the river, three massive mounds, bare and fence-bound, preserve the memory of ancient power and wealth. The whole area is called the **Brugh Na Bóinne**, a cemetery of Stone Age kings over two miles in length. Its focal points now are the tumuli of Dowth, Newgrange and Knowth. Apart from these, which crown the ridge above the river, there are dozens of mounds and tumps and megaliths in the area. Most have been rifled at some stage, and few if any retain their original shape. Grass grows where stones gleamed white, and over the centuries generations of pasturing cows have flattened the contours.

Not much is known of the creators of this necropolis. They probably sailed from France – Brittany and parts of Spain preserve related remains – in the third millennium BC, bringing the novelty of settled farming and the custom of building passage-graves. From the Boyne they spread west through the midlands to the neighbourhood of Sligo – a line closely packed with their remains. They paid great attention to their dead, enclosing all kinds of trinkets and valuables (but not to be compared with Egyptian funerals) in sometimes colossal tombs. Nothing on the same scale was put up in Ireland till the Normans built their castles. After the neolithic settlements these cities of the dead were used for living in and among, and later, by Norsemen, for plundering. More recently, around 1700, tons of the stones were carted away for road-building, and sometimes trees were planted on top.

Of the big three, we come first to **Dowth**, a mound of

208 feet diameter and 47 feet high. It was twice excavated in the nineteenth century (shortly before, Lord Netterville, who owned nearby Dowth Hall, had put a tea-house on top), when various bones and ornaments came to light. In the main it is a smaller version of **Newgrange,** which now is not only easier to see but has a small, well-arranged museum opposite. Sir William Wilde noted an estimate that 180,000 tons of stones had gone to the building of Newgrange and nobody to my knowledge has revised the figure. Its name, evoking more a cricketing Surrey preparatory school than a heathen mausoleum, means in fact 'the cave of Grainne', a heroine with traces all over Ireland. Her special significance here is unknown, but other mythical figures have clear connections. The river Boyne was always sacred, named after Boann, wife of the chief of the ancient gods known as Tuatha de Danann, or people of Danu. She, from a rash curiosity which it was once permitted to attribute to females in general, approached a sacred well shaded by nine magic hazel trees, whose nuts gave the salmon which ate them the knowledge of everything in the world. The well's waters rose and forced her back. The flood formed the river Boyne in which the salmon, now scattered, wandered forever, seeking their lost hazel trees. The fish in turn imparted knowledge to those who ate them. The gift has probably lapsed now, salmon-eaters seeming no wiser than other people. Boann's son Angus, the god of love, had a magical palace at Brugh na Boinne. Gods killed in battle were buried here, as were kings in later times. Early Christians said that King Cormac mac Art, having switched to Christianity after a long pagan reign, wanted to be buried at the holy Christian site of Rosnaree, a mile upstream. His unregenerate servants placed his coffin here, among his heathen ancestors. Again the river (a convert too) broke its banks and floated the king to the cemetery he wanted.

Newgrange's diameter is 280 feet and it is 44 feet high. Its surface has recently been raised by some six feet, to what is thought to be its original height, and refaced with stones. Bounding the tumulus itself is a series of sculptured kerb-stones. Farther out is an arc of twelve massive standing pillars; traces of others, and the assumption that the arrangement was originally symmetrical, suggests there were originally thirty-six. The best work is inside, for the benefit of the dead. Passing over an enormous greenish stone that partially blocks the entrance we step into a passage, three feet wide and most of its way high enough to walk along, that leads through sixty-two feet to the central chamber. This magnificent room, corbelled up to an apex over nineteen feet high and ten feet across, is constructed of stones on which the megalith builders lavished their art. The abstract markings include spirals and zigzags, lozenges and coils and triangles and other shapes that surpass the contemporary art of other countries. The chamber itself has three recesses containing stone troughs that may have been used for the ashes of cremated kings, or possibly for sacrifice. On only one day of the year, that of the winter solstice, are the sun's rays low enough to penetrate and feebly illuminate the gloom.

Oddly **Knowth** had never been methodically explored till 1962, when Dr George Eogan of University College, Dublin, arrived with his helpers to devote a sequence of ten digging seasons to it. Working inwards from the surround, in which they excavated several smaller tombs, they at last opened up the main passage (114 feet long) and central chamber. The outer tombs were obviously of much later period, perhaps even Early Christian. The massive stones along the 114-foot passage – still bearing the colossal weight of the mound after 4,000 years – were covered with the usual doodle-type motifs. Before the chamber a stone bore a design of rather human aspect, earning it the name 'guardian of the tomb'. Then on 6th August, 1968, the *Irish Times* blazoned the news that, quite by chance and unexpectedly, a *second* passage had been discovered. This rare addition made it one of the most important Neolithic monuments in Europe – a treasury of prehistoric art. It also raised hopes of answers to old questions – the provenance of the first Irish settlers, the source of their fantastic skills, the meaning – if any – of their art. Christianity, when it came, so thoroughly eclipsed the previous culture that everything before is the subject of guesswork. Knowth is helping to reconstruct a former age, not only in Ireland but in Europe too.

At **Slane,** a mile or so up the fertile valley, we are at once back in the eighteenth century, or so it seems standing at the crossroads with a neat three-story Georgian house diagonally placed at each corner. But there is much more to Slane, including a good inn well placed for local fishing as well as sights. The place's name comes from that of Slanius, ruler of Meath, which once comprised slices of the original four Irish kingdoms. High above the village to the north, a line of evocative ruins tops a hill with a sweeping view of the valley, west to Trim and the central plain, south to the Wicklow Mountains, with the Sugar Loaf in clear blue silhouette, east to the puffing chimneys of Drogheda and the sea beyond, north-east to the hills of Louth. These ruins, of a sixteenth-century Franciscan abbey, are where St Patrick supposedly founded a church. A worn tomb in the yard is said to be that of the man he made bishop, St Erc, a semi-legendary divine from the west who daily, summer and winter, is said to have immersed himself in the chill river to recite the psalms. Up to quite modern times coffins brought here for burial were laid for a while by the old shrine. The steep bulge to the west of the ruins, capped with trees and sometimes cows and bounded by a sheer moat, is the remains of a Norman motte.

The road from Slane to Navan runs parallel with the Boyne and passes some beautiful estates. First, on the left, is the wooded demesne of **Slane Castle,** seat of the Marquess of Conyngham. Among the best of the crop of pseudo-castles built at the turn of the eighteenth century, it was mainly designed by James Wyatt, after Capability Brown, Chambers, Gandon and others had been consulted. Wyatt was the most prolific castle-builder of the day, and in his Gothic work he was much the truest to medieval detail, far more so than the Adam brothers, who resented his competition. The stables are Brown's work, and the lodge-gates Francis Johnston's – he added a few features in time for a visit by George IV in 1821. The house contains a restaurant but the rest of it is closed to the public, and the magnificent Gothic library with its tracery ceiling must stay unseen. On the opposite bank **Beauparc House,** built in 1755 probably by

Nathaniel Clements for Lord Belvedere's brother-in-law, stands in its exquisite park. A Miss Lambart of Beauparc once danced a jig in front of Queen Victoria on a visit, and after, Salome-like, begged for Mr Gladstone's head on a salver, typifying the Anglo-Irish loathing of that enlightened statesman.

The sixteenth-century D'Arcy castle ruins of Dunmoe are farther along on the left, and behind them the belfry of **Ardmulchan Church**, scene of a Norse battle; followed on the right by the impressive ruin of Donaghmore with an almost complete Round Tower and more links with the doings of St Patrick. The tower has a striking Romanesque doorway with a crude Crucifixion above it. Finally, before Navan, is the demesne of Blackcastle House, from which sprang Mrs Fitzherbert and many a royal wrangle.

Navan is not very pretty. Like some other Irish towns, it turns its back on the river which alone could make it so. At the confluence of the Blackwater and the Boyne, its position in days of water transport was important, and it figures largely in early Pale history and in the war of the 1640s. Cromwell in punitive mood wrecked its abbey. It recovered from the wars, and built up several industries, among them paper, wool and flax. It had again declined until in the 1970's, a new lead-zinc mining industry restored its bustle and affluence. It is also centrally situated in popular touring country. Until recently its name put people off, for the official Irish spelling – An Uaimh – (hardly easier for Celts than Anglo-Saxons to spell) looked as though it should sound like a stutterer's error; but the inhabitants have voted to return to the anglicised form Navan. A mile south-east, at Athlumney, is the striking ruin of a seventeenth-century manor, with an earlier square keep abutting on the east of the Boyne. It stands much as it stood in the middle of 1690 after Sir Launcelot Dowdall, its owner, deliberately gutted it. He was loyal to the Stuarts and pinned his hopes on James's victory at the Boyne. When news of defeat came to him he declared that William should never rest under his roof. He thereupon set fire to his house, crossed the river and sat all night on the opposite bank watching the flames. Next day he fled to permanent exile in France and

Italy. Four miles south again, grandly overlooking the bank of the Boyne (as many great houses do hereabouts) is one of Richard Castle's last houses, **Bellinter,** now a convent.

There are several more fine houses beside or near the ten-mile road north-west from Navan to Kells. **Ardbraccan House,** by the site where the King of Connaught submitted to King John, was designed in 1776 by James Wyatt, with earlier wings by Richard Castle, who also built the Charter School. The house was used afterwards as the seat of the Church of Ireland Bishops of Meath. A mile north is fifteenth-century Liscartan Castle, with two square towers linked by a hall beside the river bank. Just west of this is the **White Quarry,** source of stone for several of Dublin's finest houses. Turning right off the main road at Finnegan's Crossroads a lane leads up to **Donaghpatrick,** where St Patrick built a church sixty feet long, whose medieval successor is now a ruin. Farther along the main road is **Teltown House,** taking its name from the Palace of Tailte, which used to top the hill beside it. In ancient days and up to the twelfth century, the Olympic Games of Ireland were held here, and parents used this display of the flower of their youth to arrange and negotiate marriages. In 1924 the games were revived in Dublin, changed a bit by the agency of the modern Gaelic movement.

A mile beyond Teltown we can turn right, then left at the crossroads a mile farther on. The grand grounds of Headfort House are on the right; and a lush golf course, sign of the wealth in this area of rich estates within commuting distance of Dublin, is on the left. **Headfort House** belongs to the Marquess of Headfort, whose ancestor came over with Cromwell and bought the land in 1660. The house, of about 1775, closed to the public, may still admit a student of the Adam brothers writing in advance, for they designed some of the interiors, though they never came to Ireland, and Irishmen took over to supervise the work. The outside is plain, and is the work of George Ensor. The dining-room, once painted in many shades of olive and cream and described as Ireland's finest, is blue and cream to-day and much the worse for it. Much of the building is now taken up by a preparatory school. The grounds, sloping down to the Blackwater, contain lovely gardens and a remarkable collection of trees.

Then comes **Kells,** famous for a book probably not made there, and a town of great charm and interest for all that. The Book of Kells (now in Trinity Library) certainly comes into its story, but as a tit-bit in a record of 'plague, pestilence and famine, the sword, fire, battle, murder and sudden death', as Wilde puts it. A local king of pagan times was, it is said, the first to 'dig earth so that water might be in wells', not surprising in view of the wealth of inventors reared in the Irish midlands, from the creator of the hangman's 'drop' to him who patented prefabricated telescopic church steeples. Invention may have been the foundation of Kells's prosperity. In the sixth century it became dominant among the abbeys founded by St Columba in Ireland, and when in 807 the mother abbey in Iona was ransacked with much slaughter by Vikings Kells became the chief of the whole Columban family. It was then that the book, probably made on Iona, was brought here. But the move from Scotland was not justified. No sooner had Abbot Cellach and his surviving brothers arrived than the Vikings attacked Kells too. Someone has reckoned that by the twelfth century the town had been burned twenty-one times and plundered seven, the worst onslaught in 996 by Sigtryg Silk-beard, King of the Dublin Norsemen who later fought and lost at Clontarf.

When the conquering Henry II was recalled from Ireland by the troubles following Becket's murder, he left Hugh de Lacy as viceroy. De Lacy, with half a million acres of Meath to call his own, built castles all over it, one of them at Kells. He also raised walls round the town, bits of which remain. But the stronghold did not last. Baronial and racial struggles over two centuries reduced Kells to a shadow of power, finally snuffed out at the Dissolution in 1551. Its charm now is of the eighteenth century, in Francis Johnston's court-house and Catholic church, and the fashionable (in those days) steeple added to the C of I church's medieval belfry in 1783 by Thomas Cooley.

There are still some remarkable older remains – a good Round Tower over ninety feet high that lacks only its conical cap; it has five instead of the usual four windows at the top,

dubiously explained by the fact that five main approaches to
Kells called for as many look-outs. Beside it but well spaced
are three High Crosses and the base of a fourth, the best and
oldest of which is the south one, or Cross of Patrick and
Columba, with a worn inscription to which it owes its name.
It is beautifully carved with biblical scenes and patterns, not
panelled off as in most later crosses. The animals along the
foot and human figures all over show a sprightly movement
that was seldom improved on. A fifth cross, in the Market
Place, has lost its top in being moved, but though worn is
an excellent collection of relief sculpture. The late history of
the Market Cross is sombre. Swift is said to have salvaged
it and had it put in its present position. Late in the same
century, the English commander of the local garrison had
local rebels in the '98 hanged from it.

Close to the churchyard is a well-preserved building with
stone roof intact, called St Columba's House (or Columcille's
House – there were so many dozens of Colums that a few
important ones are distinguished by altering the name.
Columba is Latin for dove: Columcille means 'Dove of the
Church' and both refer to the Donegal abbot who left Ireland
to found Iona in the sixth century). Built probably in the
ninth century, its cleverly designed walls and the barrel
vaulting that divides two floors have kept it up for 1,100 years
and it is in very good shape still. There are similar buildings
at Killaloe and Glendalough.

From Kells we can drop south to Athboy and begin the
return to Dublin, or bend the arc by continuing along the
Blackwater through the self-consciously pretty town of
Virginia (settled in James I's reign; called after his predecessor
the Virgin Queen); diverting two miles north-east to look at
ruined Cuilcagh House, home of Sheridan and before him of
his feckless and genial grandfather Thomas, author and
impresario, whose friend Swift wrote *Gulliver's Travels*
staying here. We can round Lough Ramor and the lakeside
lands of former Marquesses of Headfort, keep south for the
little market-town of Oldcastle, and continue three miles to
Loughcrew House, now a gutted wreck on the site of the
birthplace of the martyred Archbishop of Armagh, Saint

Oliver Plunket (1629–81).

The point of this extra lap is to see the low ridge of hills (reached from turnings off the Oldcastle–Crossakeel road) that rises north of Loughcrew and runs three miles east. On the three main peaks of these **Loughcrew Hills**, or Slieve Na Calliagh, is a series of over thirty passage-graves and innumerable ring-forts, mounds, megaliths and miscellaneous earthworks. This is a burial ground of some two thousand years back, and a link in the chain of progress, from the Boyne Valley to Sligo, of early Iron Age conquerors. As always, we know them through their death practices – these were cremated – not as living men; and as usual only the bare outlines even of these have come down, since the graves have been pilfered over the centuries and many, up to this century, poorly excavated by amateurs. Consequently, in spite of some impressive abstract patterns engraved on the massive kerbstones (twenty-seven of them in one cairn on the central peak) and of pottery, beads, pins and pendants extracted and now in museums, it is from the eerie splendour of this necropolis, and its command of spiny hills nearby and the whole central plain beyond, that its awesome force comes. In a quiet and subtle way it is one of Ireland's great sights. Most remains are concentrated – you might trip over them in parts – on the west and middle peaks, Carnbane West and Carnbane East, or Hag's Hills.

Back on the road, the L3, we go south-east towards Trim. Athboy is twelve miles on. It was here that Tiernan O'Rourke, who had already lost his wife to Ireland's archetypal traitor, was himself cut down by Hugh de Lacy during a supposed truce and parley. De Lacy's wages came later, in Durrow, Co. Offaly.

A mile to the town's east the **Hill of Ward** rises to 390 feet, topped by an earthwork of four concentric rings. This used to be the scene of an annual gathering and fair on the feast of Samhain (31st October). In 1168 13,000 horsemen blocked the roads on their way there. In pagan times, the festival (replaced by Halloween in the Christian calendar) marked the waning of the sun's powers and the succession of the gods of darkness, winter, and death. To propitiate the latter human sacrifice was offered. Plenty of old sources speak of this happening regularly, and plenty more recent ones deny it. The issue is open, but it remains remotely possible that on this hilltop a third of the healthy children from hereabouts had their throats cut to ward off the worst of winter.

The main Dublin road leads from here to Trim, another great treasure house of Meath. For the view it is best approached from the opposite direction but that requires a detour. Trim is smaller and less active and prosperous than Kells but still more obviously impressive. The streets are neat with brightly painted houses and some good Georgian buildings, and the pillar carrying Wellington's statue of 1817 shows through gaps from most angles. The way in along the Dublin road is the finest, with abbey ruins and two castles rising above sedge and meadowland and the narrow river; even if telephone wires and a building of concrete and corrugated iron obtrude in the middle. Most of the town's history revolves around King John's Castle, the largest Anglo-Norman castle in Ireland, whose eleven-foot thick battlemarked walls and towers enclose over three acres. Of course things happened in Trim before it was built. 'Once upon a time (ten thousand years ago) St Patrick being thirsty as he passed . . .' Thackeray begins a tale about the place which he fails to finish, tired, as all must be, by the continuous popping up of the exemplary patron saint.

Trim came into its own as a stronghold of the Pale. Hugh de Lacy built his main castle here in 1173 but it was knocked down the next year by the Irish resistance. Restored, it soon became the stronghold of a walled town (the 'Sheep Gate' and other remnants still stand between Emmet and Castle Streets). Here came King John in 1210 to scare de Lacy's son, another Hugh, and others back to alliance after the distance from England had lent them the enchanted illusion of being second to none. John took the castle but handed it back five years later in his humbled, post-Magna Carta mood. Roger Pipard rebuilt it in 1220, as he did the castle at Ardee. Thereafter it received many royal visitors. Prince Henry of Lancaster – later Henry IV – was shut up here by Richard II, shortly before the latter's deposition. In 1536 the castle was

seized in Silken Thomas's short campaign against Henry
VIII. In the previous century it housed a mint and several
parliaments, one of which, trying to make English sheep
distinct from Irish goats, enacted that no Englishman was to
wear a moustache or a yellow shirt.

In 1415 Trim's second castle was built by Sir John Talbot,
then Lord Lieutenant of Ireland before going to immortality
in France and the pages of Shakespeare, being finally worsted
by Joan of Arc at Orleans. This 'Scourge of France', 'so
much feared abroad, that with his name the mothers still
their babes', also piously founded Trim's Augustinian Abbey
of St Mary, whose older ruined bell-tower, the 125-foot
Yellow Steeple, commands a splendid view. But his castle,
by Queen Anne's reign, was vacant and decaying. In 1717,
Esther Johnson, Swift's Stella, bought it and sold it to Swift,
who sold it in turn, both at a profit. It then became a diocesan
school (since 1955 Trim is once again seat of a bishop),
attended before Eton by the young Duke of Wellington
(later MP for Trim), and by Sir William Rowan Hamilton,
later inventor of quaternions and Astronomer-Royal. Both
Swift and Wellington have close associations with spots to
the south of Trim. About half a mile east is the beautiful
ruin of Newtown Trim's thirteenth-century cathedral of
SS Peter and Paul, founded in 1206, with some interesting
remains, in spite of the fire that devastated it two centuries
later.

One of the most distinguished old Catholic families of
Ireland, the Barnewalls, Barons Trimleston, had their seat
beside a tributary of the Boyne a couple of miles west of Trim.
Now ruinous, Trimleston Castle housed, in the eighteenth
century, the twelfth baron, who returned from years on the
continent with a collection of rare birds and exotic flowers
which he bred here. He lived in remarkable style, with a
German state coach, and a large eagle chained to the front
door. He knew some medicine, treated his tenants for no
return, and showed a premature perception of psychology
when he had a lady of quality, who complained of the vapours,
shut in a darkened room with four servants who threatened
her with rods.

Laracor is two miles along the Kilcock road (L25) from Trim. Here came Swift in 1700, cheated (as he thought) of the deanery of Derry, to spend twelve years interrupted by long visits to London and Dublin. Even at this time he crops up often and hugely in politics and literature. Here he wrote countless tracts, the *Argument to Prove the Inconvenience of abolishing Christianity*, and vindications of his own suspect position as a churchman, and later, having gone over to the Tories, poured forth squibs and vitriol that helped put the Whigs out of office. In part he wrote the *Journal to Stella* here, a fascinating account of uncensored thought and opinion never intended for publication. Stella – Esther Johnson – came to Laracor as well, and lived primly apart with her chaperon, Mrs Dingley, in vain expectation of an early marriage; just as she lived apart, when Swift did (so it is claimed) finally marry her in Dublin, except when his insane spells called for a resident nurse. The site of her house is pointed out just north of Laracor, beside the gates of Knights-brook House. Nothing remains of the church to which Swift introduced extra services on Wednesdays and Fridays, doing his duty, as Dr Johnson judged 'with great decency and exactness'. And nothing remains of his house, or its well-stocked garden, or the avenues of willows he planted by the banks of the little river, or the surrounding wooden huts of the local Irish whom he championed – though rather like a conservationist with wildfowl, keeping them well clear of the house – or of the grander houses of those 'half-score persons' who formed his congregation. In 1713 Swift became Dean of Dublin's St Patrick's, and though he kept the living here till his death he seldom returned.

Two miles on stand the ruins of **Dangan Castle**, the early home of the Duke of Wellington. Now a long grey shell set beside a copse among pastures and bumpy wastelands (good for boyish battles), the place was inherited from a distant relative by the duke's grandfather, who changed his name from Colley to Wesley out of respect to the donor. (Wellesley was the Duke's change, adding tone and avoiding confusion with perfervid evangelists.) The duke's father, the first Earl of Mornington, was a brilliant musician, liked by everyone,

and became first Professor of Music at Trinity. He ruined
the family fortune, however, by extending his father's landscaping of the grounds here – with canals, trees, enlargement
of the lake, and many ornaments, of which two obelisks on
arches still survive. His two sons, Arthur, the great Duke, and
Richard, Governor-General of India, redeemed the fortunes;
but the house was let, and soon declined.

Somewhere on the southern outskirts of Dangan demesne,
in the **Summerhill** estate, Ambrosio O'Higgins was born in
about 1720. Of a poor Catholic family, he was sent as a boy
to be looked after by his uncle, a Jesuit priest in Cadiz;
then went fortune-hunting in South America. In Peru he
succeeded, rising from pedlar through general to Spanish
Viceroy of Peru and Chile. His natural son, Bernardo O'Higgins, led the Chilean revolt of 1810 and became the new
republic's first president. Summerhill House, home of the
Langford family and built in 1731 by Pearce, was twice
burned down, the last time in the Civil War, and has now
been finally demolished. A bungalow occupies the site, though
one of the splendid rusticated, pedimented arches that flanked
the original façade still survives.

Before going on towards Dublin we return through Laracor
to Tara, if we are to see one of the most famous (if not visually
striking) sites of Ireland. The way leads through **Bective,** a
beautiful abbey-ruin by an old bridge over the Boyne. Founded
in 1147 by Murchard O'Melaghlin, King of Meath, it was
entirely rebuilt a century later. The chapter house and parts
of the church of this second form still stand. Later it was
rebuilt again and adapted as a mansion around 1600. Now the
main surviving buildings surround a central cloister with a
strong battlemented tower at the south-west angle. Bective
was the first daughter house of Mellifont, a distinction that
made its abbot automatically a spiritual peer. Wilde reports
that Bective was said to have been designed by Greek immigrants before the English invasion. Elsewhere he tells that there
was once a Greek church in Trim, more evidence of an influx.
He disclaims firm knowledge, as do present authorities. But
someone at some time had a reason for stating the idea, and
it is attractive to think of Ireland, which then garnered students

and settlers from the nearer parts of Europe, drawing them from Greece as well.

We come now to **Tara**, once the centre of Irish power, source of many of those vivid tales that would have easily matched the Iliad and Odyssey had an Irish Homer been there to give them shape, and now a broad lumpy hilltop, victim of the trampling of millennia of cattle on its rich grass. People have not helped either. Discovery of gold remains in 1810 led to a modified gold rush that hacked the ground about. But Tara remains a symbol of Irish freedom – rebel leaders have always homed to it and it keeps some relics. Its origins are lost altogether, though legends speak of its being founded by Teipe, daughter of the King of Spain, when the Milesians arrived. Tangible remains date from the first few centuries AD, and Roman and oriental goods show how Ireland, though always outside the Roman Empire, dealt and traded with (as well as plundered) those inside. It may have been Roman influence that caused the star pattern of long straight roads that led from Tara to other focal points in the land. At this period Tara rose to its peak of importance. Its kings were priest-kings, and ruled Ireland; the thrice-yearly *Feis* or festival held there involved a ritual marriage between maidens and the king, as nuns later were to marry Christ. King Cormac Mac Art in the third century put up most of the grand wooden buildings where the heroic doings of knights and princes were sung and celebrated and which now have rotted to their earthen stumps. (Stone building seems to have come in about the eighth century.) He built the roads, and schools for history, war and law, and rooted out rivals for a more or less peaceful forty years. *The Wisdom of Cormac the Wise*, written centuries later, may or may not be derived from him, but it contains a splendid ethic of jolly pagan living – high marks for victory, tipple, fornication, poetry and intelligent conversation, and low for bad food, petty quarrels and women aspiring to be anything but bed-mates. Cormac's army, the Fianna or Fenians, sparked off a colourful cycle of tales about Finn McCool the wise leader, Dermot his romantic, at last treacherous colleague, Oisin (or Ossian) the poet, Grania, Cormac's graceful daughter, who seduced Dermot on the eve of her marriage to Finn and led the latter a chase that covered the country, and left a trail of still-surviving place-names. It was very Iliadic and Arthurian, and, in fact, the origin of much of the Round Table romance.

In the fifth century, Tara was taken by Niall of the Nine Hostages, a buccaneering princeling who raided (and took hostages from) the coast of Wales and founded the house of O'Neill, which was to rule Ulster for a thousand years. One of his captives, on a pirate mission to Scotland, was the boy Patrick, who spent some years as a slave before turning evangelist. The O'Neills hung on to the title of High King based on Tara for six centuries until Brian Boru brought an army of such power and prestige from the west that the king gave in without a fight. But Tara's influence declined shortly after Niall. Succession in the old Irish system went to brothers, and so cousins, and quickly dissipated central power. When Patrick lit his paschal fire at Slane, and King Laoghaire saw and marched to snuff out the new religion, Tara's stature had become token, and the last *feis* was held in the mid-sixth century. Laoghaire is said to be buried somewhere here, upright and in full armour, awaiting the armies of the men of Leinster. As an emblem of national unity, Tara lived on, and Tom Moore's 'The harp that once through Tara's halls the soul of music shed . . .' gave it a fresh lease. O'Connell in 1843 chose the hill for one of his monster meetings, urging repeal of the Corn Laws. *The Times* said a million people attended.

There is a map on the site to show where the various remains are – the Fort of the Synods (mutilated, in spite of a Board of Works ban, at the turn of the century by British Israelites in search of the Ark of the Covenant); the Banqueting Hall, 250 yards long, where diners were divided up by feudal laws of precedence; Laoghaire's Fort; and the vast Fort of the Kings, an oval enclosure of about three hundred yards diameter surrounded by a ditch, cut eleven feet into the rock, with a statue of St Patrick and a pillarstone close by. This stone has an ancient, very dubious life history. Most national traditions tended to claim rather forced links with the Bible lands, to attract a greater aura of sanctity. The Irish have some choice wild claims, one of which may have given rise to the Ark quest above. This pillarstone, the story goes, is the same Jacob's pillow on which the patriarch, flying from Esau's hot temper, slept, and dreamed of a ladder rising to heaven. After 586 BC, when Nebuchadnezzar destroyed the old temple, Israelite refugees carried the stone with them to Ireland, where it was used for coronations and uttered a clairvoyant cry if the claimant was the rightful one. Here accounts diverge.

Scottish legend removes it to Scotland, carried by an Ulster king who went to found the colony of Argyll (or Eastern Gael). It passed to Scone, then in 1296 to London, where it now rests under the Confessor's chair in Westminster Abbey on which the British monarch is crowned. Or else it stayed in Ireland on this hill of Tara, with an inscription added to mark the grave of thirty-seven rebels killed in the '98 Rising. Or else, of course, it stayed in Palestine and remains there to this day.

Two neighbouring hills to east and south support, respectively, Skreen Castle, where Columba's relics were brought in 875 and where stands a small medieval church, and the hill-fort of Rath Maeve. From the last we look down on two demesnes, Killeen on the left and **Dunsany** on the right. Both belong to different branches of the Plunkett family, Earls of Fingall and Barons Dunsany. They have done so since Henry VII's reign, when Sir Christopher Plunkett, Deputy Governor of Ireland, married the Cusack heiress of both Castles, later leaving each one to a different son. The boundary was supposed to have been determined by a race between the sons' wives, each running from her own castle towards the other. In Dunsany Castle, till his death in 1957, lived Lord Dunsany, creator in his short stories of Jorkens, the inventive layabout of London clubs. Dunsany discovered and encouraged the young Slane poet Francis Ledwidge, who died in Flanders in 1917. Shortly afterwards, in the 'Troubles', Dunsany Castle was ransacked by a marauding band. 'Who shall I say called?' the butler is reported to have asked as the looters left. It is a story told of many Irish houses, and has to appear once. Dunsany, remodelled in the eighteenth century, has fine plasterwork and a notable staircase. In the grounds is an early fifteenth-century church ruin, with good monuments. During the Penal days, the Protestant Dunsanys kept Killeen in secret trust for their Catholic Fingall cousins who would otherwise have lost their possessions. Killeen, originally a De Lacy castle of about 1190, is one of the many houses remodelled in the early 1800s by Francis Johnston, but it has been sold out of the family, and the Fingall earldom has come to the end of its line. The Dunsanys stay put. Considering their aptitude for backing wrong houses – Simnel, Warbeck, Charles I, James II – and that in the 1921 Troubles one was arrested because he refused to hand in his gun (needing it to shoot snipe) the achievement is remarkable.

The road back to Dublin leads through Dunshaughlin, with a Johnston court-house. To the east lies **Lagore,** a bog that was once a lake, on which was built a crannog, or lake-island, some fifteen hundred years ago. These structures, fairly safe from attack, but for convenience connected with the mainland by a just-submerged causeway, are common in Ireland. They were built up with stones, faggots, peat and timbers dumped inside a ring of upright stakes or piled stones. This particular crannog, a royal residence, yielded good finds when the Howard Archaeological Mission dug in 1934–6 uncovering everything from gang-chains for slaves to animal skulls split lengthwise to obtain the brains. Most of the material is now in the National Museum in Dublin.

Farther on but just off the main road is **Ratoath,** birthplace of Richard Piggott, who forged letters sent to *The Times* incriminating Parnell in the Phoenix Park murders; confessed, and then left for Spain, where he took his own life. A parliamentary commission acquitted Parnell in 1889, and he was cheered when he resumed his seat in the House of Commons. He sued *The Times*, then settled out of court for £5,000. All the same his reputation was harmed; and blackened soon after by the Kitty O'Shea affair. To the east is **Ashbourne,** where Thomas Ashe, a local schoolmaster, led a group of 1916 insurgents. He died a year later in Mountjoy Prison on hunger strike. The second Baron Ashbourne also lived here till his death in 1942. An eccentric patriot, he insisted on wearing a saffron kilt, wrongly thinking it the old national dress, and on speaking Irish in the House of Lords. He died in 1947. From Ashbourne, the straight main road, supposedly built to convey George IV to Slane in 1821, runs twelve miles to Dublin.

CHAPTER THREE

Lakeland

To many people the English Midlands mean coal, smoky cities, and industrial suburbs. The impression is wrong but widely held, and for fear of confusion the tourism authorities for the central plain of Ireland recently changed the official name of the region from Midlands to Lakeland. This they were well justified in doing since large parts of the area north and west of Mullingar are more water than land, and the water provides as much swimming, fishing and boating as could keep happy a hundred times the present number of visitors. Even 'central plain' is a misnomer except for general appearance. Old earth movements crumpled this part less than the coast, but they left it wavy in shape, and here and there gave it small jagged contours. From vantage points like Slane Hill or Slieve Bloom the whole area looks quite flat and monotonous. Below, it is seldom possible to see what the next valley has to offer. The country is pretty rather than grand. Grass, and masses of purple loose-strife, meadow-sweet, orchids, rushes and other damp-loving flowers cover the widespread peat-bog. Lough Ree, a bulge in the River Shannon and reaching a width of seven miles, is the central feature. A boat trip down the Shannon from Carrick, or up from Killaloe is better than roads for getting the taste of the centre, but we shall keep to dry land, since movement is easier, taking Dublin as our starting and finishing point.

The first important town after leaving County Dublin is Maynooth, but a mile or so before it on the right stands **Carton**. (The tall obelisk to the left belongs to Castletown House, described in Chapter Four.) Richard Castle designed Carton, a German who moved to Ireland in 1728 to work with Sir Edward Lovett Pearce on the Parliament House. His other great achievements are Tyrone House and Leinster House in

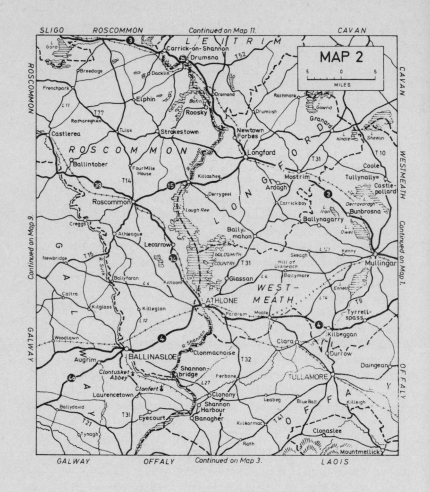

Dublin, and Russborough in County Wicklow, and even though there is a heavy quality about all his work, these are among the country's finest houses. There were two houses at Carton before Castle's time, a standard manor house in the Dutch tradition, and the first Lord Cork's Jacobean Mansion. Commissioned in 1739 by Robert FitzGerald, the nineteenth Earl of Kildare, father of the 1st Duke of Leinster, the architect recast the whole, rebuilding the old curved curtain walks as colonnades terminating in pavilions. He thus fixed it to the predominant Palladian concept. For plaster-work in the superb state apartments the Earl brought in the Francini brothers, whose work abounds still in Dublin. His son later offered Capability Brown £1,000 plus all costs to do the grounds. Brown refused: 'I have not yet finished England.' Nearly a century later Richard Morrison made the front of the house the back and vice versa, adding a splendid Regency dining-room at the same time. It spoiled Castle's work, but pleased Queen Victoria and Prince Albert when they were entertained here in 1849. The Queen slept in the Chinese bedroom, near Morrison's library, but the room has suffered since her time, and the bed she slept in was sold. The Leinster dukes lived in it into the present century, in the early years of which a younger son sold his birthright. He subsequently lost two brothers; and the house was forfeit.

The family connection of the FitzGeralds with **Maynooth** goes back to the Anglo-Norman invasion. Their power and influence left their mark all over Ireland, as family branches drooped and flourished in turn. The stem of the tree was Maurice FitzGerald, who in 1176 built a castle on land stretching from Naas to the Shannon granted him by William the Marshall, who had it from Strongbow. Well into Tudor times the FitzGeralds virtually split power in Southern Ireland with the Butlers of Kilkenny, but they themselves formed two main branches. In Cork, Limerick and Kerry, FitzGeralds rose to supremacy with the titles Earls of Desmond, the White Knights, Knights of Glin and Kerry, Lords of the Decies, and others. The other branch became Earls of Kildare, based on **Maynooth Castle,** whose gatehouse, thirteenth-century keep and great hall, with other fragments, still survive. To Henry VIII the old Anglo-Norman families – FitzGeralds, Butlers, Burkes and others – to whom English interests had become with time too remote to be relevant, were as dangerous as the native Irish. Finding the Earl of Kildare opposed to his break with the Catholic Church, Henry brought him to London in 1534. The earl's son, Silken Thomas (so called from the silk fringes on his troops' helmets) hearing a false rumour that his father had been executed, raised a rebellion but failed to take Dublin Castle and retired to Maynooth. The king's new de-

puty, Sir William Skeffington, besieged the castle for a week
with the first siege-guns ever used in Ireland, then granted the
inmates the 'pardon of Maynooth': a promise of freedom,
followed by exemplary executions. Thomas himself was
dispatched to London to lose his head, and six years later
Henry assumed the title King of Ireland. The castle was later
restored to the Kildare Geraldines but was finally dismantled
in 1647 by Owen Roe O'Neill.

Thackeray spent his short stay in 'the miserable village of
Maynooth' snapping at the priests of the seminary for what
they would do to a young novice who had travelled with
him – 'cramping his mind and biting his tongue, and firing
and cutting at his heart . . . Ah, why didn't he stop home and
dig potatoes.' St Patrick's is Ireland's principal seminary,
and has provided priests and bishops, trained there for at
least eight years, to all parts of the world. It was founded in
1795 with FitzGerald and government money, and through
the efforts of Edmund Burke, who warned the English of the
dangers in a system that since 1538 had forced aspirant
priests to go abroad for training. Its number and scope
increased, and in 1908 it became a recognised College of the
National University. The two quadrangles are respectively
Palladian and Gothic in style, the latter designed in 1845 by
A. W. Pugin; with a chapel – having Ireland's tallest spire –
by J. J. McCarthy. Later buildings, the Great Hall and
Loftus Hall, show only the misfortune of Catholic architecture
in having no native tradition behind it. The museum is
mainly of ecclesiastical interest, though there are some good
paintings, a notable scientific section, and a few of the
inventions – including a machine for shoeing horses – of
Dr Nicholas Callan (1799–1864). Some vestments are ex-
hibited which were made by ladies-in-waiting to Marie
Antoinette and brought across by outlawed French priests
who found employment here. There are also the gifts of
Empress Elizabeth of Austria, sent in return for a kindness
done her by the priests. The first was a large silver statue of
St George, but when it was tactfully remarked that this might
be the wrong saint she sent some superb vestments em-
broidered with golden shamrocks.

As far as Kinnegad the road carries main traffic for Sligo
and Galway. There is little to notice on the way and even
places of former greatness like Clonard have left nothing
more than peculiar contours in the ground. Three miles
beyond Innfield a diversion of five miles can be taken through
Longwood to **Castlerickard,** where next to the church a
decaying pyramid mausoleum engraved with the word
'SWIFTE' marks the grave of the family the dean came from.
The way back to the main road can take in the Boyne Aqueduct, where the infant river passes under the overgrown,
stagnant Royal Canal. A few miles before Kinnegad we pass,
scarcely noticing it, the site of **Clonard,** once the foremost
monastery of Ireland.

It was founded about 530 by St Finnian, an ascetic abbot
known as 'tutor of the saints of Ireland'. It was common then
for monasteries to double as universities, and Clonard drew
students from the Continent as well as Ireland. Brendan the
Navigator, Ciaran of Clonmacnois, Columba and Columbanus, the last two apostles of Christianity in, respectively,
pagan Scotland and barbarian northern Europe, were among
those trained here. The ground-plan was that of a contemporary *rath* or hill-fort, and you can still make out, or make up,
the way the place was ordered.

The road to the left goes to ruined **Ticroghan Castle,**
defended in 1650 by Lady Fitzgarret against the Parliamentary
army. Like many other grass-widows in the Civil Wars, she
defended so efficiently that the besiegers were about to go
away. But her difficulties were acute. Ammunition was
running out, and she had silver forged into bullets. The
Roundheads noticed, deduced, stayed, attacked again, and
won.

Just before Kinnegad we enter Westmeath, and twelve
miles later reach its capital, **Mullingar.** The twin towers of its
modern cathedral (1936–9) by Ralph Byrne provide 140-foot
landmarks, seen for miles across the low country; and there
are dull, decent sculptures inside and out by Albert Power,
who died in 1945. His early work was influenced by Rodin,
but something in Ireland – church patronage or the climate
maybe – stifled the talents of others than him. There is

nothing much to inspire in Mullingar which is kept well-to-do by busy markets where the cattle and other produce of surrounding farms – good hunting country – are sold. But with a pleasant hotel and several farmhouses nearby, it makes a good base.

The district round Mullingar used to be called 'the country of the waters' and it has welcomed for years that stolid and imperturbable race – the anglers. For the coarse fisher the area is ideal. He wants to fish from a bank, not a boat, and with nearly forty centres of coarse angling and innumerable lakes can find congenial lonely positions in all directions. A lake to oneself is no rarity. Visiting anglers could be multiplied by tens and still create no sign of a crowd. Pike, perch, rudd, bream, tench and others exist in plenty for all, and of a size that sometimes defeats the English angler, equipped for the rather smaller fish of his home waters. Game fishing exists, too, and several lakes and rivers have been developed and stocked by the Inland Fisheries Trust. Those most accessible from Mullingar are Loughs Ennell, Owel and Derravaragh, but every local tourist office can supply details of the many more in the region.

Lough Ennell, four miles south of Mullingar, is of more than angling interest. On its eastern shore is **Belvedere**, a mid-eighteenth-century villa built by Richard Castle for the first Earl of Belvedere, Robert Rochfort. The ivy-covered neo-Gothic wall near the house, the Jealous Wall, was built by the earl to block from view Tudenham, his brother George's house next door. 'Jealous' is a posthumous mis-nomer, and most guidebooks explain it wrongly. The earl simply had a row with George, some time in the 1760s. His jealousy was for the middle brother, Arthur, and began in 1743 when both were living at Gaulstown (five miles south-east). Someone told Robert his wife of seven years, whom he adored, was sleeping with Arthur. She confessed. Robert told her father, Viscount Molesworth, who shrugged and said she was a bastard anyway, born before he married her mother. Robert now sued Arthur, and was awarded £20,000 damages. Arthur sailed to England and returned in 1759 to find his brother so far from forgiving that he had Arthur jailed for debt, in which state he stayed till he died. Meanwhile, in 1743, Robert locked his wife inside Gaulstown, and kept her prisoner. She emerged, cracked and haggard, thirty years later when he died. Robert during this time had finished Belvedere, been made an earl, and lived the rest of his days active and very popular with society. The line died out with his son (or more likely Arthur's) the second earl, who built Belvedere House in Dublin.

The last owner of the house was Colonel C. Howard Bury, an Everest climber, who began the quest for the Yeti, or Abominable Snowman, in 1921. He died in 1966, and the fine gardens he cultivated are open to the public once a year or on prior application. South-west of the lake (on which the appearance of the may-fly signals the high fishing season, a good two weeks before it hatches on lakes to the north) is the small ruin of **Lilliput House**, visited by Swift and visitable still down a lane and wooded track. It is said to have given him the name of the island in *Gulliver*. From it can be seen a statue of the White Lady, set on a little island, and to the left Cormorant Island, on which King Malachy II of Meath and Tara died in 1022. Tudenham House was unroofed in 1957.

Back in Mullingar we can continue north-west, along the Ballynacarrigy road, and turn right three miles on for Lough Owel and Lakeland proper, a country of small rounded hills spattered with pretty woods and lakes. Soon Lough Owel comes into view, nearly four miles long, and rich in folklore; and we can walk to its edge by the ruins of **Portloman Castle**, named after St Lomman, a colleague of Patrick, who founded an abbey on whose site, beside the water, ruins still stand. The lake was the scene of the Dane Turgesius's death. It was a time, 845, when the Norse were trying to set up permanent bases in the country. Turgesius arbitrarily 'assumed the sovereignty of all the foreigners in Ireland', kept fleets on Lough Neagh and the Shannon lakes, plundered Clonmacnoise and Armagh and, Minos-like, demanded as tribute from Malachy, King of Meath, his daughter and fifteen virgins. The Dane here met his Theseus, for Malachy dressed up fifteen men as girls, and these took Turgesius, bound him, and waited by Owel for their king's verdict. Malachy had the trussed prisoner drowned. But the victory was partial. Soon the Danes were defending their footholds in Ireland, and in doing so building the country's first cities – Dublin, Waterford and the rest.

After we pass Lough Owel, the first road to the left, then first right, diverts us towards Lough Iron and the romantically ruinous demesne of **Baronstown House**. It used to be the town of Kilbixy, with a de Lacy castle and 'twelve burgesses in their scarlet gowns, a mayor or sovereign, with other officers suitable to so great a port'. There was river traffic along the Inny to Lough Ree, and thence to all Ireland. Now, apart from Francis Johnston's C of I church, there are trees, stones and bog. A mile south, nearer the water, stood **Tristernagh Abbey,** home of the Piers family till Sir William demolished it in 1783. It stood on the site of an Augustinian Priory of 1200, and two tattered arcades still stand. Sir William's son, Sir John Piers, built a cottage here in the early 1800s, surrounded by high walls to keep out law-officers. He had seduced Lady Cloncurry, wife of his close friend, for a bet; and was taken to court and ordered, like Arthur Rochfort, to pay £20,000. The estates were sold out, and he went bankrupt, but redeemed himself by a later marriage. John Betjeman revived the episode in a series of poems ending with the hauntingly evocative *Tristernagh Today:* the house survived till the Troubles; burned accidentally, say most accounts. Even the estate lake has dried up and an artificial island is no more than a pile of stones in dry ground.

Now we can return to the main road – the T3 – past Lough Owel, drive over the crossroads at Bunbrosna, and make for Multyfarnham. Before it, on the right, is **Wilson's Hospital**, a C of I school from whose steps Lough Derravaragh can best be seen to the north. Designed by John Pentland in 1760, the school looks like a model Palladian country house, with the cupola over the central block, and curved wings linking it with pavilions. In 1798 it was occupied for a night by rebels. But Lord Longford came quickly from Pakenham Hall, and caught, hanged, shot or otherwise disposed of every last man.

Beyond Multyfarnham the land slopes down over the

Nugent estate to Donore House and **Lough Derravaragh**
(best seen from the top of Knockeyon, 710 feet high, at the
south-east end of the lake). The Nugents have been linked
with the area since Hugh de Lacy's day, and their old manage-
ment methods made them part-models for the inhabitants of
Castle Rackrent in Maria Edgeworth's novel; though Sir Kit,
who fed his Jewish wife on pork and then, in the Westmeath
way, locked her up for twenty-five years, was based, not on
a Nugent, but a Maguire of Co. Fermanagh. But every
castle hereabouts has a story that borders on fiction. Even
faced with tangible evidence, visitors tend to think Ireland's
recorded past as mythical as the fairies. It is hard to accept
that all these castles could have existed in their pristine
hugeness supporting all those feuding barons; and it is made
harder by the natural exaggeration of the Irish, who call
hillocks mountains, princelings kings, and gang-fights mighty
battles. But there is no doubt many events took place as they
have come down to us.

One that did not was the conversion of the Children of Lir
(an ancient king, possibly the same as Lear) into swans by
their witch stepmother, on the lake here. They spent three
hundred years before moving on to further hardships, and
the story as told in early manuscripts is one of the most
beautiful Celtic romances.

North-east of Derravaragh is **Tullynally**, home of the
Pakenham family, Earls of Longford, and at present of the
seventh earl's son. The last earl was a well-known theatre
manager, playwright, poet and later senator in Dublin. But
it was the second earl who from 1803 onwards gave the house
its present character, employing Francis Johnston to add
another modish Gothic castle to his already considerable list,
giving the old mansion (itself an advanced one, with a central
heating system designed by Maria Edgeworth's father)
towers, a moat and six hundred feet of battlements. That
same earl rejected the future (at that time insolvent) Duke of
Wellington's offer of marriage to his sister Kitty in 1793.
Little but a sense of duty made the duke marry her, unseen for
fourteen years, in 1806, when he returned from India a hero,
and she had meanwhile suffered smallpox and a nervous

breakdown. 'She has grown ugly, by Jove' he whispered to his brother at the wedding. The next earl doubled the battlements (which had not been entirely for show, the second earl being fiercely opposed to Catholic Emancipation) and put in an immense kitchen and servants' hall. Sir Richard Morrison designed the changes. All these and the park and walled gardens are on show at summer weekends.

Continuing east through Castlepollard, the road takes us to **Fore Abbey** in a snug valley under jagged limestone bluffs. The ninth-century church, with its two-and-a-half-ton cross-inscribed lintel stone high above the road, marks the foundation of St Fechin's monastery (about 630) and the only authenticated Benedictine remains in Ireland are across the marshes to the left. There are fragments of the cloister, an old tomb, and a tall tower of the fifteenth century. The gateways of the old town of Fore are beside the road. All the remains repay study, and the whole makes one of Ireland's most beautiful ruins. The place is alive with miracles. St Fechin built his monastery on a quaking bog. To get water, he tapped the rock with his crozier, which disappeared, burrowed half a mile through the rock to Lough Lene, a very pretty lake on the south side, and returned with a gush of water that ran uphill. The saint had the giant lintel (on a doorway as magnificent, according to Petrie, as any in Greece), which workmen failed to shift, wafted to its present position. An ash tree only bore three branches, symbol of the Trinity.

A stone dated 1616 asks for prayers for Patrick Beglan, who, having vowed to live in the tiny anchorite's cell and never leave it, could not resist the sound of a hunting horn, climbed through the window, fell and broke his neck. (One hermit or other occupied the cell till 1764. Hermits were not uncommon in the eighteenth century, and some estate owners had cells built for them, finishing touches to their Arcadian landscapes.) But Fore was burned after the Dissolution and has stayed much as it was since then, happily untouched by restoration.

Returning to Castlepollard we turn right and drive north nine miles, between Lough Sheelin (a good trout, pike and perch lake which takes in parts of three counties, Westmeath,

Cavan and Meath) and Lough Kinale, and turn first left for
Granard, a small village built along the road like many round
here. It has at one end a strangely symmetrical huge mound,
seen from miles around and topped by a statue of St Patrick
since 1932, the supposed fifteen-hundredth anniversary of his
coming for the second time to Ireland. It was fortified by the
Anglo-Normans. From here a diversion can take us through
the Black Pigs Race two miles north-west, remains of a
massive pre-Norman defensive dyke between Loughs Kinale
and Gowna, to Lough Gowna itself, an almost coyly pretty
lake with small fir, chestnut and oak-covered hills around
and hedgerows packed with honeysuckle, hawthorn and
blackberry. Gowna is the source of the River Erne and so starts
the massive Lough Erne complex.

South-west of Granard lies **Mostrim** or Edgeworthstown, a
fading town whose charm is mostly gone. Yet the small
Georgian mansion on the left built by Richard Lovell Edgeworth and now a nursing home run by the Sisters of Mercy,
and the Protestant church with its Edgeworth family vault and
grave of Isola, Oscar Wilde's sister, have a story worth a book.
The Edgeworth family came to Ireland in 1585 and to Mostrim
in James I's reign. Their first representative was a Bishop of
Down. Richard Lovell Edgeworth (1744–1817) was an author,
inventor, MP and father – by one of his four wives – of Maria
and twenty-one other children. He wrote on engineering and
education (his system, based on Rousseau, went beyond
many modern ideas); and invented among countless other
things a telegraph for transmitting horse-racing information
(installed at Lord March's house at Reading), a wheel with
a barrel inside for making walking faster, a horse-carriage
with sails (which frightened the horses), a prototype of
caterpillar wheels, a pebble road surface in advance of
Macadam, an umbrella to cover haystacks, a method of
diverting the Rhône (for which the French gave him land
nearby), a semaphore, velocipede, pedometer, the central
heating system installed at Tullynally, and a prefabricated
spiral of iron for Edgeworthstown's spire. His devoted
daughter Maria – four feet seven inches tall (they tried to
elongate her by hanging when young), with a beaky nose and

ugly eye-disease – won fame in her time for *Castle Rackrent*, *The Absentee*, *Ormond*, and twenty volumes of other writings. Scott wrote that he wanted 'in some distant degree to emulate' her 'admirable Irish portraits' and Turgenev said his own writing was inspired by hers. Her novels and diaries paint a vivid portrait of the area. To get to the Pakenhams', as she liked to do, it was necessary to cross 'a vast Serbonian bog; with a bad road, an awkward ferry, and a country so frightful and so overrun with weeds, that it was aptly called by Mrs Greville "the yellow dwarf's country".'

Ardagh, four miles south-west of Mostrim, is a tidy, dull, model village. Ardagh House, now a convent, is supposedly where Goldsmith, sent to school with a guinea and bent on living it up, was directed when he asked for an inn for the night. It was no inn, but Mr Fetherston's private house, and the ensuing confusion is the basis of *She Stoops to Conquer*.

Longford, the county town, has a nineteenth-century Catholic Cathedral of St Mel in, as they say, the Italian renaissance style, and an efficient hotel, the Longford Arms. A decayed castle of 1627 was pulled down in 1971. It is a good base for Lough Ree and the countryside around, though Longford itself is not as scenic a county as most. Better to turn north for a look at an area that mixes poverty with much beauty – the upper Shannon and south Leitrim. If time is short go west by haunting, deserted Richmond Harbour, alias Clondara, on the Royal Canal, a village that is now being slowly revived, and on across the river to Strokestown.

We pass through Newtown Forbes, with grand, kempt, gothic **Castle Forbes,** first built in 1619, burned and rebuilt in 1830, seat of the Earl of Granard, on the left overlooking the Shannon. The widow of the original Scottish settler, Sir Arthur Forbes (killed in a duel in Hamburg while fighting for Gustavus Adolphus), managed to hold off the Parliamentary forces in the Civil War, for which the family got its earldom. Eight miles to the right we see bare Carn Hill, or Carn Clonhugh, County Longford's highest hill (916 feet), two miles north of which, at **Ballinamuck,** a statue commemorates the French General Humbert's defeat in the last encounter of the 1798 Rising. After it, his troops were gaoled at Longford, then put aboard

The Cross of the Scriptures and O'Rourke's Tower, Clonmacnoise, Offaly.
Below Fore Abbey, Westmeath: Ireland's only Benedictine remains.

Castletown House, Kildare: largest and perhaps the most beautiful
house in Ireland. *Below* the long gallery and its busy decor.

a boat to be sent to Dublin by canal. In the courtly fashion of the time, their band was permitted to play the 'Marseillaise' to the crowds on the bank as they sailed past Mullingar. The road north brings us to the Shannon at Roosky, a small depressed village like many round here; but the economic tide has turned with the injection of capital into the sailing and motor-launch businesses based along the river. We are in Leitrim now, a county with half the population it had at the war's end, where most farms get some of their income from emigrant relations in Britain and America. After Roosky, the pretty Loughs Bofin and Boderg can be seen on the left, divided by the promontory–demesne of **Derrycarne,** once seat of the Gores, Lords Harlech (the Ormsby prefix of the present baron, formerly British Ambassador in Washington, came, by a nineteenth-century marriage, from a wealthy Sligo family – there is nothing Welsh about the Harlechs). A short sharp battle took place here in 1690 between William's and James's troops.

At **Drumsna,** four miles on, Trollope, on a visit as Post Office inspector, got the matter for his first novel, *The Macdermots of Ballycloran*, an excellent and moving story of the decline of a prosperous Catholic family into poverty and tragedy. A mile south of the town on the Roscommon side is a huge, but hard to find, defensive earthwork, in parts a hundred feet thick, known as the Doon of Drumsna, that cut off the same tongue of land as the navigable Jamestown Cut does now. This cut or canal was built in 1848 to avoid a stretch of Shannon rapids, and separated Drumsna from the main river traffic. But the town is prettily set, with views of the Iron Mountains to the north, and an air of nostalgic decay – fine crumbling houses and great gates that lead nowhere but to copses and fields choked with weeds.

Carrick (meaning rock) **-on-Shannon** is Leitrim's capital, with a population well under two thousand. Incorporated by James I it used to have a strongly Protestant reputation, and up to 1826 members of the Corporation had to take the Oath of Supremacy. It saw greater days in the nineteenth century when water transport counted for much. Though the waterways were well advanced in the late eighteenth century, many of the massive locks and waterworks here and elsewhere in Ireland date from the early 1800s, when recurring famines meant cheap labour (the phrase 'famine relief' was devised to make exploitation respectable). But before long railways and roads were the slow death of these schemes. Carrick itself all but died, but was saved by the growing demand for pleasure boating, of which it has become a major centre with a bright future. To get the same density of boats as on the Norfolk Broads, the Shannon would need nearly 200,000 boats. It has a few hundred. People are still rarer than swans and cormorants. Yet for anglers, idlers, and those who like to bask in landscapes like Constable's, no longer possible in England, a motor launch or sailing boat from Carrick, winding down the Shannon, mooring near tiny villages with congenial pubs, hearing tale-telling boatmen and farmers talk and sing local ballads, drifting past castles and deserted hamlets into the rushy paradise of Carnadoc Waters, or on to the sea-like breadth of Lough Ree, is an ideal holiday. (It can be booked in advance through the Bord Failte.)

From Connemara or Sligo, visitors are not likely to come as far inland as Roscommon, so it is a county neglected by tourists. It lacks the beauty of the country and coast to the west, but has much of interest. We can make first for **Elphin**, south-west of Carrick, where Goldsmith's grandfather was curate and the poet himself, as well as Sir William Wilde, Oscar's father, went to school for a while. The seat of a bishop since Patrick consecrated it, it has little but association to keep us, and we go on along the Castlerea road and turn left at the crossroads four miles later for **Rathcroghan**, where a group of earthworks is all that is left of the palace of the kings of Connaught. The view from this windy plateau is imposing for these parts. A hillock with standing stone atop it, due south of Rathcroghan crossroads, marks the royal seat where the goddess-queen Maeve held court with King Aillil. In a bedroom quarrel these two found that, apart from one bull of Aillil's, their possessions were equal. Maeve, piqued, asked an Ulster prince for his bull, and offered to sleep with him in return. He refused. She went to war. The account of this *Cattle Raid of Cooley* constitutes the greatest and most famous of ancient Irish sagas, culminating in the death of

Ulster's hero Cuchulain. Near the hill is the Cave of the Cats, a natural fissure which, maybe two thousand years back, was given a dry-built masonry porch. This was no less than an entrance to the Underworld (Ireland has several others), home of the Morrigu, war goddess of the Celts. Her spirit went abroad in the form of a hooded crow, a bird that peasants used to regard with some awe. (It looks a little like a carrion crow, to which it is closely related, but with a judge's wig on.) From this cave, birds – and sometimes wild pigs – would issue to deal devastation on the land. North of it is a group of mounds, the king's necropolis, where King Conn – from whom Connaught took its name – is among the buried. Most remains probably belong to the first century AD.

Isolated points of interest lie some miles away in all directions. **Frenchpark**, six miles north-west, is a ruined early eighteenth-century mansion, probably by Castle and once the seat of the Lords de Freyne. In 1846, with famine feelings running high, the owner was hanged in effigy opposite the main door. That sort of thing and worse was happening throughout the country. Douglas Hyde was born at the Protestant rectory and is buried in the churchyard. A brilliant, Gaelic poet in his youth, whose songs were sung by peasants from Kerry to Donegal, he lost his poetic genius in Dublin, becoming an academic, the first Professor of Modern History at University College. More memorably, and with Eoin McNeill, he founded in 1893 the Gaelic League, of which he was first president. It aimed at the revival of native Irish language and literature and 'the de-anglicising of Ireland', and was a strong influence on later independance movements. In 1938 Hyde was recalled from retirement to be first President of Ireland.

Strokestown, ten miles east of Rathcroghan, is an imposing village with a long broad avenue taking most of the space. At the east end is the archway entrance to seventeenth-century Strokestown Park, a private house, home of the Mahons, Barons Hartland. Denis Mahon, ancestor of the present owner, inheriting the place from a lunatic uncle just before the famine, offered his tenants free passages to Canada during the worst of it. A false rumour got about that the ship – one of the 'coffin ships' – had foundered with all hands lost. One day soon after, he was shot and killed in his open carriage. Many families suffered from similar episodes. The house, much altered, and refaced, has handsome curved quadrants and wings probably by Castle.

Castlerea, ten miles west of Rathcroghan, was William Wilde's birthplace. Beyond it and beside the River Suck is **Clonalis House,** seat of the O'Conor Don but owned at present – he being a Jesuit who renounced his possessions – by his sister, a regal lady six feet or so tall, who opens the place to the public. It is on the site of a seventeenth century house built on one story, as Catholic houses had to be in penal days. The present house is Victorian – 'We Catholics came into our inheritance late' said Miss Josephine O'Conor, and was built by an ancestor who had married an English Catholic salt heiress. Inside, in a charming atmosphere of cultivated comfort, a fine library of books, manuscripts and other documents depict the history of a family that is traced from Kings of Connaught and High Kings of Ireland.

A few miles north-west is Lough Glinn, in a convent beside which the nuns make what are arguably Ireland's best cheeses. But from Castlerea we keep to the Roscommon Road, and turn left a mile and a half beyond Ballymoe for **Ballintober,** where stand the gatehouses and four polygonal towers of a magnificent castle built in the thirteenth century and, up to the eighteenth, seat of the O'Conors. There is a similar castle at **Roscommon,** about fifteen miles on, situated to the right of the road just before we reach the county town. This castle was built in 1269 by Robert de Ufford, English Justiciar, or administrator, and wrecked in a few years by the then hostile O'Conors, who, having honoured their peaceful alliance with Henry II, had long resented his arbitrary conquest of Connaught. For four hundred years its ownership alternated between English and Irish. In 1652 it was dismantled by the Cromwellian General Reynolds, and later in the century burned and deserted by the Irish after Aughrim. A fine twin-towered gatehouse stands on the east, a subsidiary one on the west, the shell of the state apartments inside, and there is a drum tower at each of the four corners.

There is a Dominican Friary ruin dating from 1453 (bits are two hundred years older) and a courthouse by Richard Morrison, but little else in the town. On the road south to Athlone we get several glimpses of **Lough Ree**, a lake best explored by, boat from Athlone, Lanesborough or Carrick. We can get down to it at several points, including the Rinndown Peninsula, two miles east of Lecarrow (asking permission at the farm where the road turns sharp right) near the colossal overgrown remains of a medieval town and royal castle, built in 1227 as an outpost for the conquest of Connaught; or at Hodson's Bay, by a smart black and white hotel with chalets, boats, a golf course, and Ireland's main water-skiing centre.

The lake is fifteen miles long, seven wide at its widest, and covers ' thirty-nine square miles, the fourth largest in the country. It is popular for game and coarse fishing, with good trout and, besides the usual list of fish, eels that are caught in bulk and sent as far as London. Boats should follow buoys carefully, as squalls rise suddenly and there is little protection on the banks and few landmarks when the lake begins to look more like a sea. Of the twenty-three islands six are of special interest – **Inchcleraun** or Quaker Island with its group of ruined Of the twenty-three islands six are of special interest – **Inchcleraun** or Quaker Island with its group of ruined churches, legendary home of the goddess Ennia, known for eating babies, where the ubiquitous Queen Maeve of Connaught was finally killed while bathing, with a stone from the sling of Forbaid Prince of Ulster in revenge for the death of Cuchulain; and where a Victorian Quaker settled, pulled down a church to make his house, was cursed, and left soon after; **Saints Island**, in fact a peninsula, where there used to be a convent of Poor Clares built by the Dillon family; Inchbofin, with a few good Romanesque remains; the Black Islands, still inhabited; the largest island, Inchmore, with a church ruin on the site of St Liobhan's monastery; and **Hare Island**, where St Ciaran founded a monastery before Clonmacnois and a little church has been adapted as the Dillon mausoleum. (The Dillons, now moved to England, spring from Henry de Leon, who was granted land here at

the Conquest. Catholics, they supported James against Dutch
William, fled to France after the Boyne, kept a family regiment
in the French army, and were finally reconciled to Ireland by
the French Revolution.) Admiralty charts of 1839 (still unsurpassed) show more details of this south-east corner than any
other part; for the surveyor had fallen in love with a local
farmer's daughter and spent most of his time nearby.

Another legend – this one from folklore – has it that the
islands here are for men only, women being ill-advised to
step on them, and even female birds keeping clear – a theme
repeated elsewhere. In fact every inch of the place has a story
to tell. With more space to do so than here, Richard Hay-
ward's *Where the River Shannon Flows* tells many of them,
very well, in a book that any river traveller should obtain.
We pass on to **Athlone**, at the lough's southern tip, and
virtually a border town between west and east Ireland, sitting
as it does astride that geographical and political divider, the
Shannon. The town, almost at Ireland's centre, is of importance as a road, rail, canal and river junction, as a big
market and boat-building centre, a producer of wool and
cotton articles from the riverside factories seen from the
bridge, and the home of a government department. It used to
be a crucial garrison centre in the days when it divided Leinster,
the plain controllable east, from Connaught, the mountainous
undisciplined west; and its military past has left its greatest
legacy, the castle, though the fortifications added when invasion
by Napoleon was feared have been dismantled. For a hundred
years after the Conquest castles came and went on this site till
in 1210 John de Gray, Bishop of Norwich and English Justiciar,
put up the present massive keep and from here the English
tried to control Connaught. In the wars of the 1640s it changed
hands many times – and the town itself never fully recovered.
The castle had another day. After the Battle of the Boyne, it
was attacked by ten thousand Williamites who failed to take
it and a year later by twenty-one thousand. Fifteen hundred
Jacobites defended it then. There followed the heaviest bombardment Ireland ever saw. Fifty tons of powder, six hundred
bombs, twelve thousand cannonballs and tons of stone were
fired. The main body of Jacobites covered others who succeeded

in breaking down the bridge, then plunged in and swam back like Horatius. The Williamites, prevented from substituting a bridge of boats (they were set on fire) sent forces to cross by a deep ford below. This was a brave move but it might have failed had not St Ruth, James's commander, been celebrating what he assumed was victory. The Williamites crossed and won, and the Jacobites moved west to Aughrim for the last scene of the campaign.

The castle has been restored since, though its main towers were lowered to take cannons during the Napoleonic scare (there are remains of other cautious defences nearby). It contains a poor local museum, and washing on lines bespeaks some inhabitants, though the Army has left long since. It seems to stand almost outside Athlone, for this like other towns has its focus away from its river. The town proper has decent shops, good hotels, the house (in the Bawn) where John McCormack, the singer, was born, and another, dated 1628, where the Williamite General Ginkel lived (he became Earl of Athlone after the battle, but the title lapsed, and was later granted to a Prince of Wales), and a domed Renaissance-style church of 1937 which is more imposing from a distance than close to.

The CIE runs boat-cruises on Lough Ree from Athlone. In the opposite direction, about twelve miles by road to the south, and bordering the Shannon, are some of Ireland's finest ruins, those of the monastery of **Clonmacnois**. The Tourist Board has planted an information caravan beside the site, where notes on the individual ruins are available, in more detail than space here allows. To most of us, Clonmacnois appeals more by its setting, history and feel than antiquarian analysis. St Ciaran founded it in 545 – in the burst of monastic foundation that followed Clonard. He was thirty-three when he came and died seven months later. He had earlier founded the church at Hare Island in Lough Ree, which he left to a hermit in more need than himself, and another church whose setting was too luxurious for his ascetic aims. King Dermot (a relief at the foot of the Cross of the Scriptures shows him with Ciaran) gave land and helped build, and the place became the chief monastery in what was then Connaught. Then the Danes came. The fiercest of them, Turgesius, burned it in 844 while his wife recited pagan oracles from the High Altar (no present remain dates from before the ninth century), but it grew till there were around twelve churches in Norman times. One, the Nun's Chapel, some way from the main site, was rebuilt by the pathetic Dervorgilla, Ireland's Helen of Troy, whose infidelity to her husband brought the English in. Clonmacnois suffered all the buffets of Irish medieval history – burned thirteen times, plundered by Vikings eight times, attacked by Irish (while held by others) twenty-seven times. Around 1100 Maelmuirc here wrote *The Book of the Dun Cow*, a collection of old tales and lore, and the oldest extant Gaelic manuscript (it was wrongly said to be written on the skin of St Ciaran's cow, for loss of which Ciaran's servant was barred burial in the cemetery). In 1135 lightning struck off the top half of O'Rourke's tower. A great storm of 1547 damaged many buildings, and agents of the English Dissolution completed the work in 1553 – 'not a bell, large or small, or an image, or an altar, or a book, or a gem, or even glass in a window, was left which was not carried away'. The see was merged with that of Meath, and later attempts at restoration were obliterated by Cromwell.

Of special interest in a brief walk round is the rare collection of monumental grave slabs from the sixth to the eleventh centuries displayed at the entrance; the strange ruins of John de Gray's castle of 1220; and the fine view from it over bog to the Slieve Bloom; the South Cross of about 1000, with a Crucifixion on its west side and other well-preserved carvings; the little church – Eaglais Bheag – under which Ciaran is buried and from a corner of which pilgrims still collect sacred earth; and the late seventeenth-century Temple Dowling, a family chapel; Temple Ri to the north-east, probably the oldest of the churches, with fine east lancet-windows; the cathedral, of about 1100 and later, with a splendid twelfth-century Romanesque doorway, where Ireland's last High King, Rory O'Conor, is buried (the stone-vaulted sacristy was later used as a hedge-school where Catholic children were illicitly and secretly educated

during the Penal years); the Cross of the Scriptures of about
900; the ancient North Cross with a kind of fertility symbol
known as a Sheila-na-gig on it; O'Rourke's Tower with
restored top; the still used C of I church, Temple Conor,
where most of the O'Conors are buried, originally built in
1010 but restored more recently; MacCarthy's Church with
a good small Round Tower as belfry; and, beyond the gate
in the east wall of the new cemetery, the beautiful Nun's
Church that Dervorgilla restored, but was burned again a
few years later – here too, on the chancel arch, is a strangely
revealing Sheila-na-gig (if 'Sheila-of-the-Breasts' can be
allowed to include a figure displaying mainly thighs and
face).

These are the brief facts. They cannot reproduce – and
may even detract from – the beauty of the place, its dreams of
a once famous Catholic university, a glorious and unruly
past, and its now quiet prominence beside a reedy bend of
the Shannon, with hardly a sign of life in sight. A quiet aura
of energy spent and gone is characteristic of this stretch of
the Shannon, between the two large lakes of Ree and Derg.
Covering it by boat becomes monotonous, winding round
bend after sedgy bend. But glimpsed from the land it evokes
something seldom found in Europe nowadays.

Six miles on the road south brings us to **Shannonbridge**,
a sleepy village where the Tullamore-Ballinasloe road crosses
the river by an attractive sixteen-arch bridge. On the west
bank a small nineteenth-century fort recalls again the fear of
Napoleonic invasion, and there are many more scattered
defences. Keeping to the Leinster side of the river we move
to **Clonony** where there is an impressive – though, inside,
badly defaced – tower and bawn from the sixteenth century.
In 1803 workers looking near the tower for stone for the
canal found a limestone slab (still there) covering a double
grave. The slab has an inscription: 'Hereunder Leys Elizabeth
and Mary Bullyn . . .' who were second cousins of Anne
Boleyn, Henry VIII's wife, and cousins of Queen Elizabeth.
Anne herself, who was granddaughter of a Butler and cousin
of the Earl of Ossory, may possibly have been born here.
Her family ties with the Butlers contributed to the king's

favouring that family at the expense of the FitzGeralds.

The road south-west leads to **Shannon Harbour**, a ghost village dominated by the massive ruined Grand Canal Company Hotel. Here the canal begins. It goes to Dublin Harbour. We have already touched at many points the Royal Canal whose stagnating channel lies to the north, from near Longford to Dublin. The Grand is still navigable, part of the complex of waterways on which some of Ireland's best holidays can be had. It seems an absurd extravagance that two canals, giant undertakings, should co-exist in a land never noted for prosperity, but the enthusiasm for building canals in George III's reign was like the acquisition of airlines by semi-bankrupt states in our own day. Canals could have provided cheap transport had the companies building them not lavished money (£30,000 in the case of the Grand) on hotels that could never hope to be full, or had they provided consistent service within them. The Grand Canal (planned partly by John Smeaton, builder of the Forth and Clyde canals and the great third Eddystone lighthouse) was opened bit by bit – having been begun in the 1750s – from 1783 to 1834, and linked the Shannon not only with the sea but with the Barrow and so Waterford as well. The golden age was the first half of the nineteenth century, when hotels and warehouses sprang up and numerous branch lines were built. In 1837 a record 100,695 passengers were carried. Every house in what was then the townlet of Shannon Harbour offered lodging. In all £2 million were spent on the canal, and the investment might have paid had not railways come to supersede boats and the Famine to take the bottom from the Irish economy. In the event the harbour villages were left to rot and slowly turn as picturesque as they are now. The canal was used for commercial transport till 1959 (and in the last war carried a quarter of a million tons of turf). In 1960 it was officially closed. Since then protest and preservation bodies have multiplied, basing their arguments mainly on tourist potential, though other kinds of conveyance could still be cheap. Most people who take a waterways holiday become their instant supporters.

At **Banagher**, three miles south-west, Anthony Trollope,

on his arrival in 1841 as Post Office surveyor, bought a
hunter (and hunted ever after), and started writing novels –
'and since that time who has had a happier life than mine?'
Late Georgian houses with bow-front windows testify to the
wealth the town, now insignificant, once derived from river and
canal traffic and from the strategic importance of its bridge,
fortified at both ends to resist possible invasion from Napoleon's
France. Cuba Court, on the town's east side, brought another
link with the pantheon of English novelists. Built about 1730,
possibly by Edward Lovett Pearce, it was the home in the
nineteenth century of the young Arthur Bell Nicholls; his
uncle was a master at the school it then contained. Later, as
curate to Patrick Brontë, Nicholls proposed – 'trembling,
stirred and overcome' – to Charlotte Brontë, married her in
1854, brought her here for the honeymoon, and made her
happy for the last year of her life. Much of his 50-year widower-
hood was spent at Hill House here. During the last forty years
Cuba Court, described by Maurice Craig as 'perhaps the most
splendidly masculine house in the whole country', has been
allowed to fall into irretrievable ruin. But Cloghan Castle,
three miles southwest, is well maintained round the core of a
twelfth century keep, stronghold of the local O'Madden sept.
   Birr, ten miles away, is one of Ireland's loveliest towns.
But since a line between routes must be drawn we leave it for
another tour to return, deviously, of course, to Athlone and
thence Dublin. We cross the river by the Eyrecourt road
bridge, turn right a mile later, and come to **Clonfert** to see
the diminutive Church of Ireland Cathedral of St Brendan
the Navigator, where that roving saint and precursor of
Columbus is buried. Rebuilt in 1167 by Conor O'Kelly, the
church still displays the tall pedimented west door of that
time – a highlight of Irish Romanesque – with its six orders
of arches, its fantasy of chevron arches, animal and human
heads, and the odd inward slope of the jambs. Inside, the
skeleton of the original building survives, and the fine east
window, but with much addition and nineteenth-century
restoration. Behind the cathedral is a yew walk and the
derelict seventeenth century Bishop's Palace, gutted by fire in
1954 when owned by Sir Oswald Mosley. From the grounds

there is a glimpse of the westernmost stretch of the canal, leading to Ballinasloe. Following it by road we come after five
miles to **Lawrencetown**. There is no trace of Belview House in
the tousled demesne a mile west of the village, but a handsome
triumphal arch, with a sphinx on either side of the pediment,
still stands. It was built in 1783 to comemorate the Volunteers'
convention of the previous year. There are also two decorative
Gothic eyecatchers, built simply to enhance the view.

Five miles north, beside the road to Ballinasloe, are the
well preserved (in spite of a Cromwellian battery) remains
of St Mary's Augustinian Abbey, whose fifteenth-century
west doorway has interesting carvings over the arch. **Ballinasloe** itself, four miles on, has a church partly designed by
Pugin, and a fine mental hospital built in 1838 from Francis
Johnston's designs. The gate-lodge is a disastrous modern
addition. In Thackeray's time the beggars 'were more plen-
teous and more loathsome' here than anywhere else, but they
are gone now. Some good eighteenth-century houses remain,
and every October the town is the setting for Ireland's largest
live-stock fair, which used also to be the largest horse-fair in
Europe. Garbally, to the west, is a pleasant late Georgian
house, now a school, and once the seat of the Trench family,
Earls of Clancarty, who came here in 1632. There is an odd
fluted obelisk in the grounds.

We saw the first aftermath of the Boyne at Athlone.
Aughrim, four miles south-west of Ballinasloe, was the scene
of the last but one act in the war. The still considerable
Jacobite forces under General St Ruth lined almost two
miles of the raised ground running south-east of the village.
On 12th July, 1691, Ginkel and the Williamite forces advanced
against them and were beaten back several times. Irish hopes
were high, when a cannonball struck and killed St Ruth on
the slopes of Aughrim Hill. Meanwhile troops in the castle
(just north of the village) discovered that large supplies of
ammunition did not fit their muskets. Rout followed, and
thousands of Irish lay dead. The remainder, under Patrick
Sarsfield, moved on in tatters to Limerick. St Ruth's body
was probably buried at Kilconnell Friary, four miles north-
west, well worth seeing on its own account. The ruins, north

of the village street, comprise an elegant tower, a nave, choir
and transept with magnificent window tracery, a charming
little arcaded cloister, forty-eight feet square, and some graves
and memorials including the best flamboyant tomb in Ireland,
and the tomb of the seventh Baron Trimleston, a Catholic
aristocrat who 'being transplanted into Conaght with others
by order of the usurper Cromwell, dyed at Moinivae, 1667'.
For the baron and innumerable others, 'To Hell or Connaught' must have rung true.

From here to the west the country grows bleak and
monotonous, better for sheep than tourists. We return
through Ballinasloe to Athlone, and thence by a necessarily
zigzag route to Dublin again, delaying the Far West for a
different and more scenic approach. From Athlone there is
a good direct road for Dublin, but we take the Ballymahon
road north-east and again skirt Lough Ree. This is Leinster
again, and again there are grand houses or their wrecks at
every turn. Moydrum Castle, off our way and two miles
along the first road to the right, is the romantic ruin of a
house designed by Morrison, destroyed like so many others
in the Troubles. To the right, before we enter **Glassan**, is
Waterstown House, the work of Richard Castle, now a ruin
but with an attractive octagonal-spired dovecot and hermitage
in the grounds. Glassan itself begins what is called, with some
exaggeration, Goldsmith country. Turning right in the middle
of the village, and left a mile on we arrive at the Pinnacle,
one of several claimed centres of Ireland. There is a hill of
337 feet and an obelisk on top, put there in 1769, from which
the owner could signal to another estate of his thirty miles
away. How anyone can calculate the centre of such an
anarchic shape as Ireland's is hard to see, and there are at
least three alternative claims – for Birr, the Hill of Uisneach,
and an islet in the south-west corner of Lough Ree.

The lane continues to the hamlet of Kilkenny West,
Goldsmith's father's parish, and the left fork a quarter of a
mile later leads to **Auburn**, or Lissoy, or 'The Deserted
Village' (ostensibly an English village, but with Irish links,
though Macaulay wrote correctly that Goldsmith 'had
assuredly never seen in his native island such a rural paradise,

such a seat of plenty, content and tranquillity, as his Auburn'.)
The Goldsmiths' ruined house is one of the few authenticated
remains in an area subjected to promotional inflation.
Certainly the poet spent his childhood hereabouts. Born near
Pallas (east of Ballymahon) he was at schools at Kilkenny
West, Elphin, Lissoy, Edgeworthstown (where he heard
Carolan the last bard) and Athlone; then at Trinity, Dublin,
for four years, which he ran away from but returned to. His
family had saved to send this maverick to America, and he is
said to have spent the money on the way to Cork harbour.
From then on his career lay in Edinburgh, studying medicine,
and London, where his fame and friendships were always
accompanied by the poverty brought on by generosity. It was
from London he wrote 'I sit and sigh for Lissoy fireside and
"Johnny Armstrong's Last Goodnight" from Peggy Golden...'
The Three Jolly Pigeons just beyond Lissoy on the right has
no material connection with the inn in *She Stoops to Conquer*.

Ballymahon is a pleasant village with a wide street and
modest hotel, a good base for Lough Ree's east side, and the
nearest we come on land to the peninsula of Saints Island.
There are some good houses in the district – Georgian Newcastle two miles east, now a hotel, and Castlecor two miles
west with its extraordinary ground plan – an octagonal central
block with four projecting wings and a rectangular block in
front, copy perhaps of some baroque Italian model. It is a
convent now. We follow the Mullingar road, from which there
are two possible diversions. One, to the left beyond Newcastle,
leads to Abbeyshrule, where are ivy-covered remains of the
1150 Cistercian Abbey, daughter foundation of Mellifont. The
second, five miles later, leads right to the **Hill of Uisneach** (or
Ushnagh), 602 feet high, from the top of which twenty of
Ireland's thirty-two counties are supposedly visible on an
exceptionally fine day. Mentioned by Ptolemy (as the City of
Laberos) and by Giraldus Cambrensis (as Umbilicus Hiberniae,
or navel of Ireland) this hill, spread with antiquities, is the
rival in its place of Tara, Cashel, Rathcroghan and Emain
Macha, and as rich in antique association. The Firbolgs – pre-
Gaelic invaders – divided the country into four provinces
which met here. In the first century the High King, Tuathal,

of the Gaelic race which had conquered the Firbolgs, took an area from each province to create a fifth, Meath (the middle or neck). This centred on an enormous thirty-ton rock, the Cat Stone, on the hill's south-west slope.

The rock, under which the Milesian princess Eriu (who gave her name to Eire) is buried, and many earthworks, pillar stones and souterrains bespeak its importance at that time. It was a royal centre and seat of the fire-cult with its climax at the Beltane, or May-day festival. St Patrick found time to build a church here, and in 984 Brian Boru occupied the hill to challenge and force terms on the High King, who had invaded his own territory.

But nothing is as remarkable as the claim that from here came the Giants' Circle of Stonehenge. Geologists deny it, saying Stonehenge is of rock from Prescelly Mount in Wales. Most other scholars deny it, too, these days, but Geoffrey of Monmouth and after him Giraldus Cambrensis (both of the twelfth century) wrote about it in some detail, and perhaps they had reason to know. According to Geoffrey, African giants originally brought the stones to Ireland and set them up at Killarus, usually thought to be the Hill of Uisneach, which is close to a village called Killare. Nobody would ever have moved them again had not Merlin, when the British King Aurelius wanted some suitable setting for his coronation, obligingly taken them to Wiltshire with a team of fifteen thousand soldiers. There they remained in spite of massive Irish resistance at the time. Nobody in the world would seriously argue for the truth of the tale. But judging by other episodes in Geoffrey's *History*, it is likely some inscrutable truth lies beneath it.

Mullingar is now nine miles off. From there we retrace our route back to Dublin, or switch to the next route at Innfield.

CHAPTER FOUR

Offaly, Laois and North Kildare

FOR most of the year the forty thousand or so acres of flat bog in northern County Kildare are a dull brown colour. In late summer the flowering heather turns the brown into mauve, which prettifies the views from the few hills. There are two kinds of bog, mountain and red, and turf from both kinds is combustible. The **Bog of Allen**, an ill-defined area spanning parts of Kildare, Meath and Offaly, is red, created out of the humid decay of mosses, rushes, grasses and trees in the basin of what was once a lake. Mountain bog (in Wicklow for example) is made in much wetter conditions and supports different flowers and birds. Both owe their existence to large quantities of water being unable to evaporate quickly. Half a century ago everyone dug his own turf (or peat) to burn over the winter, and turbary rights on small acreages were valuable. Now Bord na Mona, the State's turf organisation, has brought monopoly and scientific method to a business that depended much on good weather and available labour, and many farmers buy the Bord's briquettes instead of cutting their own sods. The Bord's turf-run power-stations produce much of Ireland's electricity and will produce more. Bit by bit, too, the Bord is reclaiming bog, for crop-growing, afforestation and cattle pasture.

Walking over bogs barefoot is good for foot-ailments, and rheumatism. It is something in the soil's spring. Enjoying them otherwise calls for sharp eyes. Botanists observant of detail will see bell-heather (dominant on the mountains), duller ling and other heaths, bilberry, cranberry, andromeda, the orange spikes of bog asphodel, bog myrtle, ubiquitous sphagnum moss, pale green reindeer moss, various lichens and a good deal more. Bog is a good wood-preserver, and there have been dramatic finds of prehistoric boats and weapons and of curiously petrified ancient trees. The danger of driving is seeing only a monotony of brown, green and mauve, and the occasional giant power-station like Ferbane or Allenwood. That can be the main impression, for many miles, of the first stage of this journey through the central lowlands, though exceptions abound.

The first exception, after leaving Innfield (fifteen miles west of Dublin) by the Tullamore Road, is **Carbury Hill**, eight miles on and to the right of the road. On the left is Newbury Hall, a good red-brick house of 1760, probably by Nathaniel Clements. The hill, 470 feet high, has various prehistoric mounds and a fortified manor house with graceful clusters of moulded chimneys near the top. This was built in the late sixteenth century by the Cowleys (later Colleys, then Wesleys, finally Wellesleys), ancestors of the Duke of Wellington, on a site previously occupied by a Norman Castle.

Being on the outward edge of the early Pale, this area is thick with castles, and there are many in the vicinity of Edenderry, a pleasant town five miles on. The old castle and demesne of the Blundells lie to the south. Two miles west of the town are the remains, fortified in the sixteenth century, of the Franciscan priory of Monasteroris, founded in 1325, again by a Bermingham. The thick walls are heavily overgrown and there are remains of an early dovecot – a means, in those days, whereby sequestered families could alter the menu.

Half-way to Tullamore we come to **Daingean**, once a county capital that recalls a disappointing phase of Irish history. Native expectations were high when Mary Tudor succeeded Edward VI, restored Catholicism, and absolved some Irish Catholics who had been forced to flee. But her reign showed clearly that religion was no more than a cloak for a persistent English policy of conquest. Married to Philip of Spain, future patron of the Inquisition, Mary took her father's policy even further, confiscated two thirds of Irish land in counties Offaly and Laois (pronounced 'leash') and began the plantations which Elizabeth successfully continued. In honour of which the two counties were renamed King's and Queen's Counties (which they remained till independence)

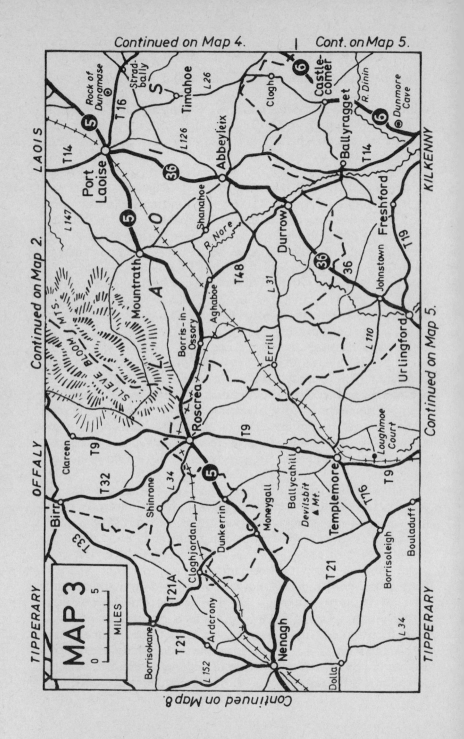

Continued on Map 4.   Cont. on Map 5.

Continued on Map 2.

Continued on Map 5.

Continued on Map 8.

MAP 3

MILES

0   5

LAOIS

OFFALY

KILKENNY

TIPPERARY

TIPPERARY

Rock of Dunamase

Strad-bally

Timahoe

Castle-comer

R. Dinin

Dunmore Cave

Ballyragget

T16

T14

L26

Clogh

L126

Abbeyleix

Port Laoise

Shanahoe

R. Nore

Durrow

Freshford

T14

T19

L147

Mountrath

T48

L31

Johnstown

36

Borris-in-Ossory

Aghaboe

Errill

L110

Urlingford

Clareen

Roscrea

T9

Loughmoe Court

SLIEVE BLOOM MTS.

T32

Shinrone

L34

Dunkerrin

Ballycahill

Devilsbit ▲Mt.

Templemore

T76

T9

Birr

T33

Cloghjordan

Moneygall

Borrisoleigh

Boulad uff

T21A

Ardcrony

T21

Borrisokane

L152

Nenagh

L34

Dolla

with capitals at Philipstown (Daingean) and Maryborough (Port Laoise). Philipstown failed to establish itself. It picked up a castle and a court-house disfigured since but attributed to Gandon, but was superseded as county seat in 1833 by Tullamore.

We can drive on direct to Tullamore, or go by a circular route north of the main road. The latter takes us to **Tyrrells-pass**, an elegant village with a crescent of houses round the green, a spired church with a sumptuous Belvedere monument by John Bacon, and at the west end the tower of Tyrrel Castle. In 1597, in the middle years of the Elizabethan conquest of Ireland, the English met one of a series of reverses when their force of a thousand men, making for a rendezvous with other detachments in the north, was ambushed and cut to pieces by Piers Lacy at this pass through bogland. Five miles west is Kilbeggan, distillery centre and terminus of the last completed branch line of the Grand Canal (1834), now evidently decaying like other places whose importance depended on the waterway. This is one of many encounters with the canal on this route.

Descending, this way, on Tullamore from the north we pass **Durrow Abbey's** ruins on the right, a place abundant with stories but short on tangible remains – a beautifully elaborate tenth-century High Cross, a well, various tomb-stones, and a derelict Protestant church with magnificent west doorway. St Columba of Iona, who should – had not the Scotch a predilection for apostles – have been their country's patron saint, founded Durrow in 551, and Bede mentions it – 'a noble monastery in Ireland known in the Scots (Irish) language as Dearmach, the Field of Oaks, because of the oak forest in which it stands'. (Most of Ireland was covered with trees at that time.) Here, perhaps, the *Book of Durrow*, now in the library of Trinity College, Dublin, was written around AD 700, the subdued masterpiece of the first phase of Celtic illumination, and here Donal, High King of Ireland, was buried in 758. More dramatically, it saw the death of the dynamic Hugh de Lacy whom we met more than once in the Boyne region. In 1186 he came to build a castle, an outpost to the powerful feudal state he had built up in the centre of the country. To obtain the stone, he pulled down the church – even in settled times a tactless move for a Norman among Irishmen – and as he bent to the work an enraged young man, O'Meey, struck off his head at a blow. Much of his binding of the Pale for the Norman cause was undone, in the instant. De Lacy's motte is still to be seen.

Tullamore, Offaly's county town, is a big – for the area – and busy town with proliferating shops and ugly new suburbs. A market town, and centre for distilling and spinning, it nowadays ignores, as it can afford to, the hand that once fed it – the Grand Canal running along its north side (though there are operators for boat-cruise holidays here). Tullamore's nineteenth-century prosperity owes much to the period when it was the canal's terminus and a great distributing centre. Before that it had a short sorry story. It was planned and built at the initiative of the Bury family of Limerick, Earls of Charleville, in the mid-eighteenth century. In 1790 a great balloon was sent up from Charleville (see below) and, instead of floating over, collapsed amid the new town's buildings which were destroyed (the pub, some say by divine intervention, excepted) in the explosion that followed. Rebuilding started soon and the town's more interesting features – some Regency houses and St Catherine's Church by Francis Johnston half a mile to the east, date from the period. **Charleville Castle**, two miles west, is a splendid Gothic structure of 1800–12, with parapets and crenellations by Francis Johnston – the best of several he designed. It was built for Charles Bury, Earl of Charleville, a genial dilettante who caused a scandal by translating Voltaire's scabrous poem on Joan of Arc, *La Pucelle*, into English. Lately owned, like Belvedere to the north, by Colonel Howard Bury, then neglected for a few years, it is now occupied, and restored in essentials. Both outside and inside preserve a rich concentration of Gothic features – the fireplace in the dining-room is modelled on the west door at Oxford's Magdalen College Chapel – and the demesne is well afforested.

Gothic had flourished in Ireland for a long time before Francis Johnston, one of its main Irish practitioners (though he was a master of Palladian classicism as well) designed his remarkable 'pasteboard Gothic' castles in the early 1800s: Slane, Killeen, Glenmore, Pakenham, Charleville and others. In both England and Ireland the strengthened taste for Gothic at this time owed much to the Ossianic revival. Moreover, the need to grow corn for England during the Napoleonic blockade brought Ireland the riches that made the new wave of building possible.

South of Tullamore rise the **Slieve Bloom** mountains, the redeeming feature of the plain County Laois, and one of the loveliest stretches of inner Ireland. They were caused by the folding of sedimentary deposits, especially Old Red Sandstone and calcareous limestone, in the Armorican age – the mountain-building period that followed the Caledonian (in which the Mourne and Wicklow ranges were created). The sandstone, being harder, resisted erosion and remained as a mountainous outcrop – the Galtees and Comeraghs to the south were similarly formed. But limestone, more soluble in water, was eroded and left valleys between the sandstone masses. This pattern recurs throughout the south-west of the country. Slieve Bloom can be crossed by following the main road (T14) south from Tullamore, turning right after four miles towards Clonaslee, and continuing south up the Corragh River valley. Five miles beyond the Cut, a right turn leads to a rougher but more romantic road that climbs north beside the Delour River, then bends north-west to descend on Kinnitty. There are gentle contours, large stretches of wood (where pony-trekking is available) and magnificent views in all directions.

From Kinnitty (which could be reached directly by the T9 from Tullamore) we can go direct to Birr by the main road beside the Camcor River, or south-west to Clareen, where there are ruins of an old monastery on the site of a pagan sanctuary, in which a flame was kept perpetually burning; and there turn right to Birr.

The centre of **Birr** is Emmet – formerly Duke's – Square. In the middle is a tall Doric column with no statue on top. From 1747 it bore the figure of the Duke of Cumberland, who more justly earned the name of 'Butcher' than the £25,000 a year awarded him after Culloden. The statue's erection in what is claimed the very centre of Ireland (a stone – the *Umbilicus Hiberniae* or Ireland's navel, used to be shown till the eighteenth century), matched Hugh de Lacy's bearing at Durrow for want of tact. In the twenties of this century, it was 'found unsafe', and removed. Other reasons would have served. Its removal, however, took away the one sore spot in a small town of unmatched charm, lovely buildings, and an attractive asymmetry.

Birr, founded by St Brendan (of Birr, as opposed to the sailor saint of Clonfert) suffered from customary Danish ravages (we are only ten miles from the Shannon, which was their approach), then rose to importance as an Anglo-Norman outpost. This importance is shown by the claim that, when plague struck the place in 1447, seven hundred clerics died of it. The local Irish royal family was that of O'Carroll, 'a hospitable, fierce, yellow-haired race', one of whom fought with Brian Boru at Clontarf. Their hospitality was sorely tried by the English, who expropriated their lands, first under Henry II and again in the Marian plantations of Laois and Offaly.

Plantation – the policy of setting up enclaves of English by giving land on condition they employed only English servants – got fresh impetus after the Battle of Kinsale (1601) and the Flight of the Earls into exile. In 1620 a thousand acres of Birr were allotted to Laurence Parsons from Norfolk; and his family has remained ever since. Coming from a part of England suspicious of kings and Catholics, they were on Parliament's side in the Civil War, and on William's in the Revolution. This pattern of adherence caused them to lose their castle more than once and brought a charge of high treason under James II, but they ended the century in full possession of their heads and demesne. Laurence did well by the town. Among other things he promoted the manufacture of window and table glass by a Huguenot family at Clonoghill Castle, whose ruins are at Syngefield on the Kinnitty Road. Little survives from the four years' (1623–6) operation of the factory, and what does is highly valued. Parsons was also a martinet; anyone lighting a domestic fire in anything but a stone fireplace was banished by his command, and women serving beer got three days in the stocks.

It was a Sir Laurence Parsons (later second earl of Rosse) who planned the castle's rebuilding after a fire in 1823. But the most famous of the family was the third earl, William Parsons (1800–67). Leaving Oxford with a mathematical first he became MP for King's County (now Offaly) before inheriting his father's title in 1841. Having already improved the techniques of casting reflectors for telescopes he constructed his own – in 1843, at the sixth attempt – of an alloy of copper and tin. Weighing four tons, it remained the world's largest for seventy-five years. With it he revealed that some nebulae of stars have a spiral structure rather like Catherine wheels. It is now in the Science Museum in London (with a fascinating working model to scale). His son, the fourth earl, continued his observations though he moved away from the giant telescope, and another son, Sir Charles Parsons, developed the steam turbine that made ships like *Dreadnought* and *Mauretania* faster than all competitors.

The walls and cylinder – fifty-six feet long – of the telescope stand in the centre of **Birr Castle's** park. (The observer would look into the side of the tube near its upper end.) The grounds themselves (open to the public) are perhaps the best kept in Ireland, with magnificent trees, especially magnolias and maples, shrubs and two century-old box hedges, reputedly the tallest in the world at thirty-four feet. The late earl, a champion of tree-conservation, laid out many of the flower-beds, making excellent use of the waterfalls from the Little Brosna River that flows through the estate. His wife was mother-in-law of Princess Margaret, and her family home is Nymans in Sussex (now a National Trust property) and the couple divided the year between two of the outstanding estates of these islands. Lack of space prevented them from opening the castle (and a good private collection of pictures) to visitors, but it makes an impressive sight outside. Rebuilt in Gothic style with castellated front in the early nineteenth century, it incorporates a small part of the seventeenth-century castle.

Birr's charm lies in its unity, not – apart from the castle – in highlights. Almost the whole of it was laid out in the eighteenth and early nineteenth centuries, a reminder, as with many Irish towns, of the first great age of new-town planning. Opposite the castle gates Oxmantown Mall, with uneven, Georgian houses on the left and a line of chestnuts on the right, leads to the delightful C of I St Brendan's Church. At the end, Emmet Street, with doorway fanlights to match the best of Dublin, leads to Emmet Square, in which, besides the decapitated column already referred to (a statue of St Brendan is planned to replace it), is the Tourist Office, in an upper room of which Melba sang; and Dooley's Hotel, once burned down by tippling guests from the Galway Hunt, who were thereafter known as the 'Blazers'. John's Place and John's Mall lead off to the left, and from the Place a right turn runs up to St Brendan's RC Church, with its fine tower and 124-foot spire designed by Bernard Mullen in 1817. The work was sponsored by the architecturally minded second earl. Next door is a little known work by Pugin, the Convent of Mercy.

South of the castle, the road leads south-west to Borriso-kane, a small town of under a thousand inhabitants, then on again to Nenagh. The route is close to Lough Derg, a beautiful widening of the Shannon, which is described elsewhere. To the south of Nenagh are the Silvermines Mountains, where silver, zinc and lead are mined, and behind them the Slieve Felim. Nenagh is county town of the north of Tipperary, which is divided in two for administration. It is dominated by the cylindrical keep of a Butler Castle built soon after the Anglo-Norman invasion (the Butlers were granted Ormond, an area which corresponds roughly with County Tipperary). Though a Bishop of Killaloe castel-lated it 'after the manner of Windsor' around 1860, it remains the finest of its kind in Ireland. There is also a good nineteenth-century courthouse, and the remains of a friary of 1250. At this time enmity between Irish and English was reflected in the Franciscan order, and Nenagh Friary came to lead the Irish camp. It was destroyed – one almost says 'of course' – by the Cromwellians.

The road to Thurles takes us over the pass between the Devil's Bit Mountain and the Slieve Felim. The former's name is owed to a story that the Devil, furious as he flew south over Ireland that the country was yielding him no souls (a Promised Race complex must be observed in any study of the Irish) took a bite out of a mountain – there is a remarkable cleft – and dropped it on the plain in front of him. The expectoration is the Rock of Cashel. Unfortunately Cashel is limestone, the other old red sandstone.

By turning right three miles after Borrisoleigh and keeping straight on for eight miles we can visit **Holy Cross** before entering Thurles and beginning the return journey to Dublin. Castle keeps and ruined abbeys of various kinds are such a familiar sight in Ireland that those of exceptional interest – Holy Cross, Mellifont, Jerpoint and others – call for a special appeal to the tourist who may be unwilling to go out of his way for another jagged grey silhouette – 'Romanesque against the sky'. Holy Cross, on the banks of the Suir among trees and meadows, is one of the country's best preserved, and certainly among its most beautiful remains. Founded in 1168, it passed soon under the wing of the Cistercians and grew grand and prosperous. Its swift rise was due in part – and its name entirely – to a piece of the True Cross it contained, given by Pope Pascal II to the founder's father. (I know of no other Cross fragment in Ireland, but of enough in Spain, France, Italy and so on to make the original as high as a Round Tower.) These fragments helped the churches that contained them, as lions do Longleat. Holy Cross grew rich as a place of pilgrimage and in the fifteenth century the buildings were remodelled. Even after the Dissolution it was kept intact with Butler protection. It has a typical Cistercian form (cruciform shape, aisled nave, low central tower and an east chapel in each transept). Its treasures include beautiful fifteenth-century sedilia or stone seats, in the presbytery or east end; the east window with its tracery network; some scattered carvings, including a delightful owl, on nave capitals and walls (owls often symbolised evil, as preferring dark to light); a mural painting in the north transept; and a magnificently carved stone shrine, which may have contained the Cross fragment, in the south transept. The Cross fragment itself passed in the nineteenth century to the Ursuline Convent of Cork, where it remains. In 1977 a substantial and harmonious restoration of the abbey was completed, including a re-roofing of the nave for use as a parish church.

Thurles (pronounced Thur-lez), three miles north-east, is a marketing centre on the Suir in the midst of the rich farmlands of north Tipperary. It also manufactures sugar, the beet for which is being developed as another bog enterprise. A Butler town, it has a ruined tower at each end of its broad main street, one of which guards the river bridge. Beyond the east tower is the gleaming RC Cathedral, built by J. J. McCarthy around 1870, with a façade on the model of that at Pisa. Inside, the tabernacle was originally designed in the early 1600s for the Gesu, Rome's gaudiest church.

Two miles north of Thurles and among fine woods is the grand moated folly of **Brittas Castle,** planned by Morrison as a replica of Roscommon but prevented by a fatal fall of stone on the nineteenth-century owner, Mr Langley's, head. Though it is private, permission to view may be given by the owner, and the tower, moat and unfinished walls, and the old house and park rich in trees are well worth seeing. The demesne is on the right of the road to Templemore. Nearly four miles farther a road right leads a mile or so to **Loughmoe Court,** a seventeenth-century fortified mansion, once seat of the Purcells. **Templemore** is a small town described by George Borrow, whose father was stationed here in 1816, in *Lavengro*, with an enormous and lovely park, former demesne of the Carden family, a silted lake, and good walks among the trees. Carden's Folly is a tower just south of the summit of Devil's Bit, which is best approached from here, and gives magnificent views over Offaly and the Suir Valley. Again we take the road north and after a straight drive of eleven miles, with the Devil's Bit to the left and Slieve Bloom straight ahead, arrive at **Roscrea**, a town of ancient and modern importance, and a good alternative base for exploring the Slieve Bloom.

A fortress at Roscrea, guarding the pass between steep mountain ranges, was of first importance to the Normans, who built one in 1212 and replaced it with a better in 1280. From this, and castles at Clonmacnois and Athlone, they could keep a watchful eye on the Shannon approaches, and occasionally cross the river for a show of force. The second castle, built by Edmund Butler, father of the first Earl of Ormonde, in 1280, survives as the town's best ruin, with a solid gate-tower and crumbling drum towers along its massive curtain wall. Inside the bailey is a handsome, three-storey Queen Anne house, home of the Damer family in the eighteenth century, a barracks in the nineteenth, and an unloved dump in the twentieth, until in 1974 the Irish Georgian Society leased and restored it. It is open to the public, and houses good permanent and visiting exhibitions. A computerised genealogical information service is planned. On the east side of the town is the stump of a Round Tower, with a high cross and Romanesque doorway on the other side of the road. These are on the site of one of St Cronan's seventh-century monasteries. The surviving twelfth-century remains were scarred and separated by the laying of the Dublin road. In the valley on the south side of the town is a slender mellowed tower, remnant of a fifteenth-century friary demolished around 1800 and serving now as gate-tower – an appalling contrast – to the RC Gothic Revival Church. The town entices by its ruins, its informality, and the many signs of buildings of great age hidden behind more recent façades and terraces.

St Cronan's first monastery was at the end of a peninsula (Ros-cre) in what was, till drained in the eighteenth century, a shallow lake amid Mona Incha bog. To get to it from Roscrea drive a mile east along the main road, then first right and first left. After a mile the abbey remains, surrounded by trees and a low wall, rise high above the flat meadows. The remains – an exquisite Romanesque church with fine west door, a cross, some gravestones – are mainly twelfth century. As elsewhere in Ireland, bog air used to preserve dead bodies more or less intact, and a smaller island nearby was much hallowed on this account, even regarded as an earthly paradise. Giraldus Cambrensis got the story charmingly wrong. It was impossible to die on the island, he thought; a mixed blessing since some people grew so old that they wanted to die, and 'have to be transported by boat to the larger island. As soon as they touch its ground, they give up the ghost.' He described another of Mona Incha's features: 'No

woman or animal of the female sex could ever enter the island
without dying immediately. This has been proved many
times. A remarkable thing about the birds there is that while
the males settle on the bushes everywhere throughout the
island, the females fly over and leave their mates there and
avoid the island like a plague.'

A couple of miles south, scattered over the Timoney Hills
and Cullaun, is an enigmatic collection of three hundred
standing stones whose arrangement baffles archaeologists,
but they are not easy to see.

We carry on along the main Dublin road to Borris-in-
Ossory, once an important coaching stage, where the ruins of
a Fitzpatrick castle stand. From here we can continue straight
on to Mountrath, a decaying town that shows little sign of
its former monastic, and later linen-manufacturing importance. Its only building of merit (apart from an old-estab-
lished foundry by the bridge), the Courthouse, was recently
demolished, amid council demands for a new public lavatory.

Two miles west, **Roundwood House** is a pretty early eighteenth-century Palladian villa with a rare Chinese fretwork
balcony over the hall. Francis Bindon designed it. Not long
ago it was damp and rotting inside and surrounded by vegetable
anarchy. Then the Irish Georgian Society bought it and
supervised its restoration. It is now a very comfortable guest-
house. Four miles north of Mountrath by the L147 is Ballyfin,
which Mark Bence-Jones calls 'the grandest and most lavishly
appointed early Classical house in Ireland.' It was built for
the Coote family in the 1820s on the site of a house which
had belonged to one of the Duke of Wellington's brothers,
mainly by the Morrisons, father and son. Its heavy, solid,
Roman exterior is matched by a grand use of scagliola columns,
elaborate plasterwork and coffered ceilings inside. It is now a
college run by the Patrician Brothers. From it, a road runs six
miles east to Port Laoise, county town of Laois (or Maryborough, county town of Queen's County, as an older generation still calls it). It has a few points of architectural interest,
but nothing more. Gandon designed the obelisk spire on the
C of I church. Sir Richard Morrison, his pupil, designed the
courthouse, at the back of which is the grotesquely rusticated

old prison. The Pain brothers did the modern prison in 1830, the only one in the Republic exclusively for males. Francis Johnston probably built the lunatic asylum opposite. For all these talents, the town is unexciting.

An alternative route from Borris is to turn right a mile out of the town and come, after four miles, to **Aghaboe**, whose customarily turbulent history before and after the Normans is not at all reflected in the ivy-covered fourteenth-century friary ruins near the parish church. Turning first left after the village, right two miles later and right again at Shanahoe brings us to the Durrow-Abbeyleix road, at which we turn left. On the right is the large demesne of Viscount de Vesci's **Abbey Leix House,** to whose pleasant wooded grounds and gardens pedestrians are admitted. The de Vesci family became lords of Kildare after the break-up of Strongbow's original fief of Leinster in 1243. They lost much of their power soon afterwards by identifying overmuch with the Irish, becoming degenerate as contemporary England saw it, but survived in the area for seven centuries – 'improving' landlords who often promoted the Irish cause. The house, built by James Wyatt in 1773–4, is private but can be seen from the park. The gardens are supposedly modelled on the fantastic estate of Alupka, beside the Black Sea, which once belonged to a Russian ancestor of the de Vesci's. Farther on, **Abbeyleix**, laid out as a model village in the eighteenth century, preserves its charm, with good modest Georgian houses, a market house in the centre of the very broad main street and a crescent of terrace houses behind. The church, with spire by John Semple, was rebuilt by Thomas M. Wyatt, one of myriad architectural kinsmen of the great James, in 1865.

To reach **Timahoe** we follow the Carlow road (L31) and take the second turning left after two miles. On the south side of this tiny village is a very tall Round Tower, almost 100 feet high, the shaft of which is two feet out of true. It has walls four feet thick and a splendid Romanesque doorway, seventeen feet up. The monastery was founded around 650 by St Mochua, a semi-mythical saint whose distinction was to heal others – Colman Elo of loss of memory, Fintan of leprosy – and to keep, among other pets, a fly, which walked along lines of scripture as he read and halted to keep his place when he broke off for thought. In 1970 genealogists were moved to discover that Richard Milhous, great-great-grandfather of Richard Nixon, was born at Timahoe. That was in time for the President's Irish visit.

Stradbally is straight on to the north-east, built along a single mile-long street. It was principal seat of the O'Mores, an Irish sept (a grouping of relations rather broader than a family), who like the O'Connors in Offaly remained unsubdued till the end of the sixteenth century. Long before, the first Tudor confiscations had given their Stradbally lands to Captain Francis Cosby, who turned the friary here into a castle. Little ancient remains in Stradbally, but it does boast the Irish Steam Museum, a collection of engines, cars (including racing), tricycles, fire-engines and other objects in the pageant of steam power; many of which on the first weekend in August participate in an annual Steam Rally that attracts thousands.

Three miles west, north of the Port Laoise road, is the **Rock of Dunamase**, a massive outcrop, 200 feet high, of limestone in a limestone plain; and first, according to the Annals, reported by Ptolemy under the name of Dunum. At no stage of its history was its advantage ignored. Gael fought Gael for it, and lost it to the Anglo-Normans (it went to Strongbow as part of Dermot McMurrough's daughter's dowry). In 1479 the O'Mores retrieved and held it till Mary I's reign and the plantation of Leix. It was in O'More's hands when the Earl of Essex during his ignominious campaign of 1599 marched from Athy to relieve Port Laoise. He decided against occupying it, and instead made his way from Port Laoise towards Kilkenny, but paid dearly for his neglect in the Pass of the Plumes, three miles south-west. Here, ambushed by Owen O'More, he lost hundreds of men before escaping to Wicklow. Cromwellian detachments, more decisive, stormed Dunamase in 1650, took it from Confederate troops and destroyed the buildings. The ruins – of a rectangular thirteenth-century keep and other buildings – are what they left. But the place, from a distance, still looks impregnable.

We can continue north-west to the main Dublin road, turn right on to it, and left a mile after towards Portarlington. The road crosses the Great Heath of Maryborough, and two miles from the main road we pass on the right the church of **Coolbanagher,** designed by Gandon, and one of the most graceful Georgian churches in the country, recently restored. Branching right just farther on we can glimpse **Emo Court,** built also to Gandon's designs just before 1800, for the first Earl of Portarlington, and set in fine grounds with good trees, especially Wellingtonias. The earl was Gandon's first patron. Till recently a Jesuit novitiate college, Emo has now reverted to private hands and a sympathetic restorer. **Portarlington,** a few miles on and beside the Grand Canal, is a pretty Georgian town with the decaying charm and dignity of others in such a position. Under William III, the Marquis de Ruvigny, Earl of Galway, settled many Huguenots here (a little earlier nearby Mountmellick and some other towns were settled as Quaker colonies). Though the 1851 Church of St Paul replaced the French church of 1696, the graveyard still contains many stones inscribed in French, some only a hundred years old. There is a lovely market-house of about 1800 in the centre and many rather earlier houses. Ireland's first turf power-station is north of the town, but we go east, keeping quite close to the canal, seeing Lea Castle on the left after two miles – a towered, thirteenth-century keep of the FitzGeralds, destroyed by Cromwell – and carrying along the straight road. South of Monasterevin, with its handsome houses of merchants enriched by canal trade, is **Moore Abbey,** a magnificent and rare example of mid-eighteenth century gothic architecture. The original house was built by Adam, first Viscount Loftus, lord chancellor of Ireland from 1619 to 1639, who lived here until Wentworth's spiteful legislation forced him to pay a large sum of money to his daughter-in-law, a relation of the lord deputy, in settlement of a very dubious claim. He is said to have held court in the present, much altered, great hall. His own daughter married Charles Moore, later Earl of Drogheda, whose heirs reconstructed the property. Nineteenth century changes imposed a heavier kind of Tudor gothic and made the place notoriously cold. When a particularly heavy portmanteau belonging to a guest, the Earl of Clonmell, fell and burst open on the stairs, it was found to be full of coal. This century the Moores let the house to the singer Count (a papal title) John McCormack, who died in Dublin in 1945. It was sold soon after, and is now a hospital run by the Sisters of Charity of Jesus and Mary.

The good Dublin road now leads straight to Kildare. To the north a group of hills (including Grange Hill, 745 feet, with the **Chair of Kildare,** a limestone outcrop, on top) are the last high ground before the seemingly endless Bog of Allen beyond. From the top, views are good; from bog-level, trees, borders and the occasional Peat Board kiln blot out all displays of countryside. On the southern side there are signs of great wealth in the houses and wealthy demesnes.

Kildare is a town whose history could detain us far longer than its relics. Sedulius Scotus studied here, Vikings plundered, Dermot McMurrough ravaged, Giraldus Cambrensis admired and Confederates bombarded the town. More important, perhaps, St Brigid, founder of the first monastery here, was born nearby about 450, and died here about 520. There is far more to Brigid than a Christian saint with quaint attributes. In the Irish hagiography she ranks second only to St Patrick, which is explained in part by her previous prominence in pagan lore. She was a threefold goddess, daughter of the Dagda, chief of the Celtic gods, and with similarities to Brizo, the moon goddess of Delos. As such she was revered in Gaul (and still is in Brittany) and Britain (as Bride, Brigantia, Brit and other names). Her influence was far too great for fifth-century Christians to deny her existence; and pagan threads were woven into the advancing Christian pattern. Her Christian image constantly harked back to her pagan. At Kildare, unlike other foundations, there were both monks and nuns, and suspicions that, though segregated by a screen in church, they mixed freely in private. One folk-tale even has Brigid proposing to Patrick, and securing from him women's leap-year rights. Also at Kildare a flame burned constantly, from its foundation to the Dissolution, without a break; pagan Brigid was goddess of fire. Moreover, the Irish plainly transferred attributes of the Virgin Mary to

The Cross of Moone,
County Kildare: the
Twelve Apostles.
Below Robertstown,
County Kildare:
a sleepy town once
bustling with canal traffic.

The Round Tower at
Glendalough, County
Wicklow, 110 feet high.
Below A shiela-na-gig at
Cashel, County
Tipperary: probable
tribute to fertility
powers.

Brigid, often known as 'the Virgin of the Gael', and Mary
herself is plainly descended, in some senses, from pre-
Christian deities. Irish devotion to Brigid appears to be due
to the antiquity of her worship, and to the need (in a country
where fathers notoriously influence their children less than
mothers) for a feminine leavening in the stern patriarchy of
the early Christian Trinity.

The **Cathedral of St Brigid** is pleasant enough, with a hotch-
potch of periods in its stones. It was begun in 1229, devastated
in the sixteenth century, and given a new chancel in the
1680s. Then it fell into decay until G. E. Street's restoration
in 1875, which has given its stamp to the whole building.
There are a few good memorials, some of the fourteenth and
fifteenth centuries, inside, and a fine round tower of 106 feet
without (the battlemented top is nineteenth century and
wrong; it should, like others, be a cone). On the far side of
the village square is a fifteenth-century tower, and Lord
Edward FitzGerald lived some years next door in Kildare
Lodge, long since demolished. One mile south-east of the
town is **Tully House**, seat of the National Stud. Its Japanese
Gardens, laid out by Eito and his son in 1906 (Powerscourt's
Japanese Garden was laid out at the same time) are open to
the public; so that one can pass through the Gateway of
Oblivion, past Temptation, over the Hill of Ambition and
through the (uninhabited) Geisha House before proceeding
to the earthier appeal of the Curragh.

The **Curragh**, stretching east from Kildare, is the largest
area (5,000 acres) of unfenced arable-land in the country
(St Brigid's flocks pastured here). The military centre, on the
east side, has been famous since 1646; the racecourse, north
of the Dublin road, for two thousand years. As the headquarters of Irish horse-racing it is surrounded by training
stables and large houses; horse country, with large fields and
impeccable fencing to show the richness, both of land and
owners. The course, in recent times, has had a distinctly
social aura round it; in English days it was necessary to be
an officer or member of a good Dublin social club to attend;
and as lately as 1969 at the Irish Derby held there in early
July, the Duke of Devonshire said approvingly, 'It's the last

racecourse in the world where the waiters wear white gloves –
it's got more *chic* than Ascot.'

The Curragh has seen other sport beside racing. Towards
the east, beyond the camp on the Kilcullen road is Donnelly's
Hollow, a dent in the plain where bare-fist prize fights used
to take place. Dan Donnelly was the champion of the early
nineteenth century – he won his greatest battle, against an
English champion, in 1815 – and his supposed giant footprints
are marked across the area. In 1914 General Gough and the
other officers at the Curragh Barracks threatened to disobey
if ordered to Ulster to fire on Carson's newly formed Ulster
Volunteers, a completely illegal group. Their decision has gone
down as the Curragh Mutiny.

For travellers with a taste for waterways, the next digression
is rewarding. The L180 north from Kildare leads past the
Hill of Allen. The legendary Finn McCool had his stronghold
here. Finn's Fianna (the word means band or company of
soldiers, and appears in the name of, among other groups, one
of the republic's two leading political parties) served the welfare
of Ireland, not individual kings. Their ethic anticipated chivalry.
Each recruit swore never to cheat or harm a woman, never to
turn down a call for help, never to flee before fewer than ten
attackers. He must be able to leap a tree as high as himself and
pass under a branch as low as his knee while running at full
speed. The Fianna punished all wickedness and dishonour and
were themselves above reproach (exceptions included Dermot,
who eloped with Finn's bride Grania on the eve of the wedding).
Their life was war – they even repelled the invasion of Daire
Donn, king of the world, at Ventry – and when there was no
war they hunted, sometimes including all the provinces of
Ireland in a single chase of boar or deer. Their stronghold,
with its halls, couches, golden vats and goblets, armoury and
smithies, is marked, rather unworthily, by an eye-catcher
obelisk erected in 1859.

At Kilmeage, a right turn goes to **Robertstown** on the Grand
Canal, another sleepy canal town – hardly changed except for
the decline of population – with its former huge hotel built to
accommodate 'express' passengers, and steeply humped bridge
over the water. Here and elsewhere there are good walks along

the disused towpaths. Here alone is a splendid Grand Canal festival held in early August, pioneered by the priest and other locals who thought their town should not be allowed to die without resistance. Some of the things offered are the Irish Georgian Society's Annual Cricket Match, played to the rules of 1744, a tour of Kildare period houses, lectures, dances, fishing competitions, and period style, candlelight suppers in the Canal Hotel itself (built at a cost of £7,452; opened in 1803). There is also a permanent exhibition of items connected with the canal.

Having come this way, we could go on to Clane, by the sort of straight road only possible on bogland or desert, through Prosperous, a village named in hopes of wealth to come from its linen mills in the late eighteenth century. These hopes were cut off by the 1798 rebellion. Clane, three miles on, has the remains of a Franciscan Friary to the south-east. If we turn left and continue for a mile we reach on the right the entrance to **Clongoweswood** Jesuit boarding college, founded in 1814. On the north of the demesne, two miles from the college, is the gatehouse of Rathcoffey Castle, seat of the heirs of Sir John de Wogan, Edward I's Justiciar from 1295, who in seventeen years of office settled many wrangles among the, by now, anarchic Anglo-Normans and made the Pale not only self-supporting but also a source of revenue for the Crown, much needed for Scottish wars. The new college chapel is rich in modern Irish art – many stained glass windows by Evie Hone and Michael Healy, and paintings by Sean Keating and others. By contrast to the park, the school inside is dark and sombre, and easy to people with figures from *Portrait of the Artist* – James Joyce was a boy there. He was ragged, perhaps bullied, at the beginning. Asked his age, he replied 'Half past six', and was thereafter known as that. But he enjoyed the school more than *A Portrait* suggests, playing cricket well, winning cups for hurdling, and walking, developing his amazingly methodical mind. 'If that fellow was dropped in the middle of the Sahara', his father wrote at the time, 'he'd sit, be God, and make a map of it.'

Seven miles due south of Clane (a turn right, half-way, leads to the 400-foot-long Leinster Aqueduct, a stately con-

struction for the canal to cross a lovely stretch of the Liffey)
is Kildare's county town, Naas (we could have come straight
here from Kildare). A mile to its west is the evocative ruin of
Jigginstown. Here Lord Deputy Wentworth, later Earl of
Strafford, planned his finest house, fit to lodge the king,
Charles I. He brought over workmen from his Yorkshire
home, and planned a lavish hall with floor of marble (in which
he was an expert), and columns of black Kilkenny marble.
But from building at Jigginstown he was recalled to England to
try to patch (he alone could) the king's splitting kingdom. Instead,
attacked by hostile court factions, many of them Anglo-Irish
offended by his rule, he went as Charles's sacrifice to the
scaffold. Had Wentworth, a loyal servant of Charles, been
allowed to continue in Ireland, he might have settled it – in
his ruthless, tactless way he had already made it richer than
ever before and established some semblance of justice in the
midst of anarchy – and so prevented the apocalyptic alternative
of Cromwell. Half finished Jigginstown fell back into ruin. In
the 1650s all its lead and iron had been stripped for ammunition.
Now the huge vaulted cellars, and gaunt skeleton of brick
walls, 380 feet by 80 feet, with their broad windows, have been
cleared by the Irish Georgian Society and many other volunteers, and subsequently accepted into State care.

There is more zigzagging before the return to Dublin if we
are to see an amazing concentration of grand things in and
around Celbridge. To do this, we take the L25 north from
Naas to Sallins. We turn right in the village on to the minor
road for Celbridge. Six miles on there are impressive views
of **Lyons House** on the right, against a background of hills.
The house was built for £200,000, for Valentine Lawless,
Baron Cloncurry (whose wife Sir John Piers seduced for a
bet, and so kindled a famous court case). It stayed in the
family till recently when, line and title dying out, it was
transformed into an agricultural college. On Lyons Hill
behind, O'Connell fought a duel and killed his man in 1815.
Later that year he was challenged by Robert Peel, young and
in his 'Orange Peel' phase, and accepted. But O'Connell's
wife had him arrested and bound over, to prevent more
blood-spilling.

Closer to the road and beside the Liffey is **Lodge Park**, designed probably by Nathaniel Clements in 1775-7, and, if it was, the last work he did. Its design is unusual – a plain central block with two pavilions, instead of the normal one, on each side. It is privately owned by a Guinness now. Farther on is Killadoon, also possibly built by Clements for his family in the 1770s, and still lived in by his descendants.

After joining the main L2 road to Dublin we come into **Celbridge** past Celbridge Abbey, once owned by Bartholomew Vanhomrigh. He was a Dutchman who came to Ireland with King William as Commissary General to the army. He provisioned the troops before and after the Battle of the Boyne, grew rich on commissions, and bought the abbey; and General Ginkel became godfather to his son. His daughter Esther, on his death in 1709, moved with her mother to London. There she met and fell in love with Swift, and a little later followed him, like her namesake, Esther Johnson, to Ireland. He came to see her often at Celbridge and in the last century the gardener still showed the grotto in a cliff overhanging the river, where they met. 'Swift's Seat' is still to be seen. He called her Vanessa, the other Esther Stella. With the years, his visits tailed off and in 1723 he married Stella, secretly. (The marriage has not been conclusively proved, but there is good evidence for it.) Vanessa heard, and wrote to Stella asking for confirmation. Swift got the letter, rode over, abused, raged, stormed and left. A little later she died here; not before changing her will and leaving her considerable worldly goods to Bishop Berkeley instead of Swift. The present house, rich in gothic detail, was largely built in the late eighteenth century by Henry Grattan's uncle.

Another to make his fortune from the Glorious Revolution was William Conolly, a pub-keeper's son. He acted as agent for beneficiaries of the settlement and took thick slices of their cakes. In 1715 he crowned his ascent in society by being appointed Speaker of the House of Commons, and acted as Lord Justice many times after that. He died in 1729 and his wife had erected a grandiose monument in the Death House, a plain mausoleum in Celbridge's old C of I churchyard. 'He made a modest but splendid use of his great riches . . .'

reads the epitaph. Splendid, but hardly modest, is **Castletown**, the house he built in a large park north of the village – the largest and one of the most beautiful private houses ever built in Ireland.

The main façade, sixty feet tall, is in severe Palladian style, like a Venetian Grand Canal palace bounded by two pavilions. Each of these is joined to the central block by semi-circular colonnades, a popular device that created the longest possible frontage – about 400 feet in this case – and hid utilitarian, farmwork areas beside the house. One pavilion housed the kitchens, the other the horses. A balustrade tops house and colonnades, and the windows of the central course have alternating curved and straight-sided pediments. Broad steps lead to the front door.

The upshot of recent researches is that Alessandro Galilei designed the house (he later did the façade of St John in Lateran in Rome) but that Edward Lovett Pearce, who at first interpreted his plans on the spot, later took a more creative hand. Working for Speaker Conolly was Pearce's first big chance, and probably led him to obtain the commission for the Parliament building in Dublin. His main work is to be seen in the pavilions, and, inside, in the austerely architectural entrance hall and the long gallery. Around 1760 Chambers had an indirect hand in the design of the dining-room and two drawing-rooms downstairs. Numerous crafts-men and masons were employed, among them the Francinis (possibly only one), Simon Vierpyl, and Reynolds's 'little delicate deformed' pupil, Thomas Reily, who painted the designs in the gallery. The festoons of delicate plasterwork by the Francinis by the main staircase – more free and rococo than any they had done before – are as aerial and elegant as any of their kind; but art's prestige was not what it is. Tom Conolly, the owner, who inherited the house from the Speaker's widow, writes grudgingly in 1765 of amounts paid to 'Frankiney stucco man'.

In parts of the house, however, there survives a buoyantly amateurish spirit, the legacy of Tom's wife, Lady Louisa. The Print Room, the only one of its kind in Ireland, is her and her sister Sarah's work, carried out through a winter of the 1770s. There is a natural evolution from this to the gallery, with its painted festoons and garlands and symbols, its Etruscan and Arcadian panels, its niches, bookcases, busts, Venetian chandeliers (the wrong blue, Lady Louisa rightly complained), its deeply compartmented ceiling and, for such large dimensions, a general air of lived-in cosiness. It was, in fact, in Tom's time, the room where most things went on – dancing, eating, card-playing, theatricals and the eternal airing of politics by men and gossip by women. From Lady Louisa's and other letters comes a vivid picture of the primeval distinction between the functions of men and women of society.

Society was a thing old William Conolly could never feel quite part of, though his aspirations and success in getting as near as possible are evident. They stand out in the portraits. The Speaker himself was childless. His nephew William married an earl's daughter and had five daughters and one son. The son, Tom, married the amiable Louisa, daughter of the second Duke of Richmond, himself a grandson of Charles II. Of her sisters one became the Baroness Holland, another the Duchess of Leinster (living over the road at Carton), and another, Sarah, came near to marrying George III, failing which she married first a rustic baronet, then the humbler George Napier, and by him mothered three generals. With Napier she lived in Celbridge, at Oakley Park. Tom's own sisters by their marriages connected him with the Earls of Ross, Buckinghamshire, Bristol, Longford and Clancarty, and Viscounts Howe and Castlereagh – and through them with just about every titled family in Ireland and a good many in England.

The Speaker lived to see none of this, nor, mercifully for him, the second demise of his male line soon after. Tom and Louisa were childless, in their turn. The estate went through their adopted niece to her Pakenham son, who changed his name to Conolly. Family succession lasted to 1965, when the estate was sold to a man bent on redevelopment. For want of other sponsors, Desmond Guinness, President of the Irish Georgian Society, borrowed £93,000, bought the house, and leased it to the society, whose headquarters it is. Nowadays it has concerts, lectures, dances, and seminars, and shares with Carton in June a Festival of Great Irish Houses. It has become a focus of Georgian scholarship. Its main want – of furniture and other chattels – has been slowly remedied by the society's fund-raising and their own cheery brand of importunate begging. When they took it over in 1967 it was empty – even the lead was being stripped from the roof.

There are two curiosities in the demesne, one of which can be seen through the north-west vista from the long gallery. This is the obelisk that the Speaker's widow had Richard Castle design in 1740 (as 'relief work', to use a phrase honoured only by time, after a bitter winter). It was an eye-catcher, to which the family sometimes went out for tea. With its bold pillar surmounting a complex of arches it has been called the only piece of real architecture in Ireland, but that on a narrow and academic definition. The other feature is the Wonderful Barn that ends the north-east vista and comprises four domes, one atop the other, with a spiral staircase outside. It was used probably for storing grain.

The return to Dublin can take us through **Leixlip** (the castle here is the Hon Desmond Guinness's private home) or, more directly, through Lucan, with the beautiful demesne surrounding the Italian embassy on the left. The house was built about 1776 by the local MP, Agmondisham Vesey, with help from Chambers, Wyatt and Michael Stapleton. Four miles on, we are back in the built-up purlieus of Dublin.

CHAPTER FIVE

Wicklow Hills

FOR the Londoner, it is as if the Lake District began at
Golders Green. A dozen miles south of O'Connell Bridge
you can be amid mountains, in furzy, heathery country,
waiting for bent rustic figures to whistle their dogs to clear a
way for your car among sheep or cattle. The population is
confined to a few villages and, except for the highest highlands, where there is no habitation at all, widely scattered
cottages and farmhouses. To reach such dramatic country
again it is necessary to cross Ireland to the west coast or go
north to the Mourne Mountains and Antrim beyond. The
Wicklow Hills form the biggest of the few granite outcrops
in the country, indeed in what one should not call the British
Isles. In times when such things went on, a mass of slaty
(Ordovician) rock evolved through pressure of the sea that
then covered the area. Eruptions and foldings of the Caledonian age followed and threw up masses of molten lava that
solidified as granite – the main body of the Wicklow or
Leinster range. Right down the centre of this range the
granite remained exposed and characteristically rounded, as
the slate and schists were worn away by winds and ice. But
the slate remained on either side, to be weathered into the
irregular shapes of the foothills – deep glens cutting into the
mass, deep lakes hollowed out by ice. Rivers that are small
in comparison with the width of their valley floors are typical
of this glacial action; so are hanging valleys, or glens that cut
laterally across spurs of the hill. These were formed when ice
had cleared from the summits but lay like a blanket several
thousand feet thick all round. New streams from above were
blocked by it and so formed lakes between spurs with ice-
walls as their fronts. In time they both wore away the ground
beneath them, making what later became corries and hanging

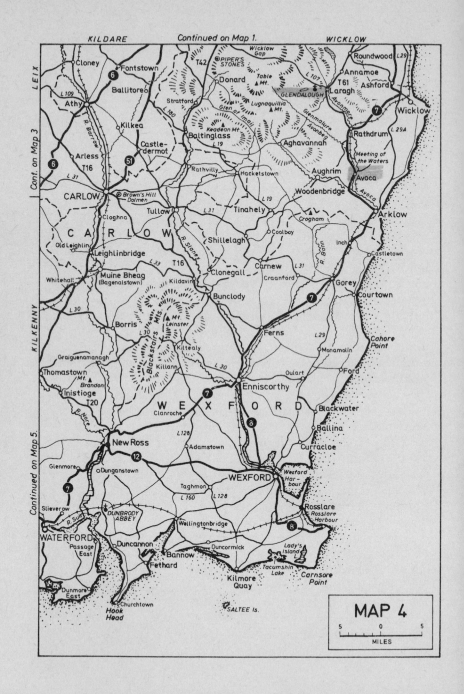

KILDARE Continued on Map 1. WICKLOW

MAP 4

5   0   5
MILES

valleys; and cut new channels to each side along the ice edge, creating the otherwise inexplicable 'dry gaps' of, say, the Glen of the Downs and the Scalp. These formations are best seen on the seaward side of the range. Had it not been for ice, Wicklow would be a dull and lakeless barrier.

There are plenty of decent roads, but the stretch is God's gift to the hiker. The views are rewards of toil (and nowhere is this acute) and best appreciated as such. It was the Wicklow Mountains, said Edward Lear, that decided him to be 'a painter of topographical landscapes'. The hiker has Youth Hostels well placed hereabouts. The folklore is colourful – even though it drove W. M. Thackeray to exclaim, 'The stories are, I am bound to say, abominably stupid and stale.' The history is rich, too, for rugged highlands made an ideal base and retreat for fighters against the English. Some of the best roads date from the '98, when the British built them and barracks to contain the rebels on their own ground.

We can start from Dublin by the road south-west through Tallaght – site of St Maelruan's seventh-century monastery, and of the fourteenth-century country palace of Dublin's archbishops – Brittas, and **Blessington**, a long broad village beside the seven-mile-long Poulaphouca Reservoir, formed by flooding for hydro-electric works. Through the lake the Liffey flows from its source near Sally Gap. A lakeside road has been built all round. In the village a granite drinking fountain with lion's head bears the inscription: 'The water supplied at the cost of a kind and generous LANDLORD for the benefit of his attached and loyal tenants.' It was erected in 1865 as a tribute to the Marquess of Downshire.

About two miles on, to the right, is **Russborough House**, designed by Richard Castle in the 1740s for Joseph Leeson, first Earl of Miltown. Leeson was a great grand-tourer, and filled the house with a rich collection of paintings which went to Ireland's National Gallery at the end of the nineteenth century, when his family and title expired. The house competes with Carton for the distinction of being Castle's best extant work, combining his heavy faults with all his virtues. Its frontage is the longest in Ireland – 700 feet in all – with a central block, long seven-bay wings joined to it by curved

colonnades, and two further wings attached by plain walls
with a baroque gateway in the centre of each. Inside it has fine
stucco work recently ascribed to the Francini brothers, an
unusual spacious landing lit by a large lantern, and a host of
other attractions. The owner, Sir Alfred Beit, not long ago
formed a foundation to manage the house and its collections
and to open them regularly to the public. The paintings, by
Vermeer, Rubens, Goya, Velazquez and others, form one of
the finest collections in these islands, and there is a splendid
collection of Irish silver, much of it from the time – the eighteenth century – when Ireland's silversmiths were the equal of
any in Europe. Four miles further along the main road we pass
Hollywood, and a left turn that leads to the Wicklow Gap.
The road has excellent views; wild and desolate at first,
warmer as it reaches Wicklow's central highlands before
descending, with countless streams and waterfalls, on Glendalough, where we shall rejoin it. Regretting the need to
choose we pass the turn to what was once the Pilgrim's Route
to Glendalough. But views are at no premium in this region.

Half a mile south of Hollywood a left turn takes us into
the Hollywood Glen, a three-mile hanging valley that well
illustrates the effects of the ice-blanket. A mile and a half
down it are remains of St Kevin's Church, on the site perhaps
of the saint's first oratory, set in a 'holy wood'. From here he
moved east to Glendalough. West of the church, and closer
to the T42 road from which we broke away, is one of the
many circles of granite stones known as Piper's Stones –
fourteen boulders (the dancers) and one set away from them.
The legend is that the group were dancing to the piper's tunes
on a Sunday, and were petrified for their sacrilege.

At Donard, we turn left and keep straight on beside the
Leagh River, a tributary of the Slaney, to the end of the
Glen of Imaal, lying at the feet of Table, Lugnaquilla and
Keadeen Mountains. Here stand Leitrim Barracks, erected
in 1798 to cope with the rebellious doings of Michael Dwyer,
whose birthplace, at **Derrynamuck**, two miles south-south-
west, has been reconstructed in traditional style to contain a
small folk museum – in as remote a spot as any fugitive
would choose. The '98 was sustained longest by Wicklow

and Wexford guerrillas, and Dwyer kept the English pre-
occupied with only a small group of men and incredible
daring, marksmanship and resourcefulness. Returning down
the glen we turn left at the main road and reach Baltinglass
after five miles, passing on the right the decayed, elevated
village of Stratford, whose linen factory employed up to a
thousand men in the nineteenth century.

Baltinglass is well situated on the Slaney River, which
here starts a more gradual descent after its mountain origins.
The Cistercian Abbey of Vallis Salutis, founded about 1150
by Dermot MacMurrough, who later brought about the
Norman invasion, stands in ruins to the north, on the east
side of the river. Inside the part of the nave and chancel
walled off to make the C of I church (the square tower is later,
and the cloisters much reconstructed) is the splendid empire-
style mausoleum of the Stratford family, Lords of Baltinglass.
The original Norman Viscounts Baltinglass, FitzEustaces,
forfeited their title in 1586, having joined the Munster rising
that was sparked by the Elizabethan conquest. They were
upheld by a conviction that Mary Queen of Scots was the
rightful monarch. The Stratfords were granted the lapsed
title, and in the eighteenth century John Stratford, Earl of
Aldborough, laid out, enlarged and improved several villages
in the neighbourhood.

At the top of the hill to the north-east is **Rathcoran**, an
Iron Age hill-fort in which is a large passage-grave, from
which various implements, utensils, and fragments of bone
were taken in a 1934 excavation. The countryside hereabouts
is spattered with prehistoric remains.

We cross the bridge and stay with the main road for three
miles, then turn off left and keep going eastwards, with
Lugnaquilla on the left, to Rathdangan and **Aghavannagh
Barracks**, where there is a junction with the old Military
Road to Glenmalure. The Youth Hostel, an ideal base for
climbing the mountain to the north (Lugnaquilla, 3,039 feet,
is the highest mountain in eastern Ireland, third in Ireland),
was originally another of the chain of forts erected by the
British in the 1790s. Later Parnell used it as a shooting lodge –
convenient for his home at Avondale – and afterwards it was

the country home of John Redmond, the moderate leader of the Irish party at Westminster.

Another superb approach to Lugnaquilla is to take the old Military Road to Glenmalure, turning left after four miles at Drumgoff Bridge and going up the valley till the road peters out, at Baravore Ford beside a high waterfall. However, on this quick tour we go back a mile from Aghavannah, then turn left to Aughrim, accompanying the Ow River on its attractive way to the sea. Just before Aughrim the Derry joins the Ow, so making the Aughrim River, and the village of that name is prettily set below the junction. Crossing its bridge we keep to the river's right bank for a mile and a bit, then cross back and pass a trout farm on the way to Woodenbridge. **Croghan** mountain, on the right, has for long been connected with gold. As far back as 2000 BC, soon after workers in the Middle East had learned to melt and mould metal ores prospectors arrived in Ireland to search for metallic ores, and their success is seen in the fact that most local copper works of more recent times had already been worked in prehistoric times. Around Croghan they came on gold and began to create the kind of ornament – crescent-shaped lunulae, sun-discs, cups, torques and so on – well displayed in the National Museum, but the metal was not found without much laborious panning. It seemed for ever impossible to find the motherlode from which the gold came, but there were occasional 'rushes', especially after 1795 when a $21\frac{1}{2}$ oz nugget was discovered. Perhaps a quarter of a million pounds' worth was uncovered in the years that followed, but it was slow work. There have been excitements since, as recently as 1935, but it is unlikely any substantial seam exists. As Praeger says, 'if digging ever produces wealth for this island, it is from peat'. (The destruction of many ancient remains was carried out in the hope of uncovering gold ornaments, but very few have ever been found.

We now arrive at Woodenbridge and the **Vale of Avoca**, which imposes its name on the Aughrim from here to its estuary at Arklow. Though waters meet here, Tom Moore's 'Meeting of the Waters' is supposedly four miles up the Avoca Valley at the confluence of Avonbeg and Avonmore. The delight of this wooded valley, with high, castellated Castle Howard like an Aquitaine crusader castle above it, is spoiled only by the scars of past and present copper pyrites mines and the arid prettifying of the spot that is meant to have inspired Moore. Even in 1836 John Barrow, with experience of the Arctic, China and Africa for comparison, stated coolly, 'I think more has been made of it than either the waters or their meeting deserve', and preferred, as many do, Woodenbridge. There has always been needless controversy about the spot the poet meant: needless, since Moore wrote to an inquirer, 'The fact is, I wrote the song at neither place,' and could not for sure remember which confluence suggested 'There is not in the wide world a valley so sweet . . .'

The main road leads us on towards Rathdrum. Two miles before this, a right turn brings us to Avondale, the lovely square 1799 Georgian home of Charles Stewart Parnell. The Forestry Commission now owns the place and there are still good trees in the park. Parnell was born here in a Protestant, landowning family. Aged 28, he was High Sheriff of the county, then went into politics determined to embarrass the English into granting home rule. He formulated the technique of boycotting. In spite of being once gaoled for seven months by Gladstone his disciplined Irish party of eighty-six became indispensable to the Liberals. He survived several ruthless attacks and an incriminating forgery published by *The Times*, to become uncrowned king of Ireland and Gladstone's close ally, till his adultery with Kitty O'Shea antagonised English non-conformists and Irish Catholics and lost him leadership of the Irish MPs. He campaigned to retrieve it, knowing he was Ireland's only hope, then died, aged 45. During most of the latter years Avondale was deeply mortgaged to cover legal expenses. Gladstone said later 'if these divorce proceedings had not taken place there would be a parliament in Ireland to-day'.

From Rathdrum a main road leads north-north-west to Laragh up the beautiful Clara valley, and so to Glendalough, one of Ireland's most romantic, evocative sights. (We would have reached here from the opposite direction had we crossed the mountains by the Wicklow Gap.) The two lakes, which the word Glendalough means, were scooped out by ice which left a trough much deeper than the water's final outlet. At one stage ice blocked the water in the middle and a lateral stream and bank were formed, the bank remaining as a broad delta to divide the two lakes. The beauty of this steep wooded valley ringed by mountains is most striking, and combined with its remoteness to attract St Kevin to build his solitary cell here in 545, just before St Ciaran founded Clonmacnois, St Brendan Clonfert, and St Comgall Bangor.

Kevin, like most of his contemporary saints, had an empathy with the animal world. The story goes that once, as he sat in his cell (remains by the upper lake, across the bridge near his 'bed' and first church), reading attentively and resting his arm on the window, a blackbird came and, taking his hand to be a nest, laid its eggs there. When the saint at last noticed he was so moved that he kept his open hand in the same position till the young hatched. In memory of this he is often illustrated with a blackbird. After his day the place grew in size and sanctity. There were usual Viking raids but the eastern range of buildings – the cathedral, the barrel-vaulted St Kevin's Kitchen with its belfry, the still almost perfect 110-foot Round Tower (its top is a reconstruction) and several others that survive continued to go up. After the Anglo-Norman invasion the monastery of Glendalough had a chequered history till the Tudor-Stuart conquest of Wicklow finally closed it, and decay began, though some buildings were in use, legally and otherwise, till the nineteenth century. Barrow noted in 1835 that burials of local Catholics took place here regularly. As elsewhere, Penal Laws were no match for peasant persistence. Thackeray as usual found reason to be sceptical. 'There are seven churches' he wrote (as there are, in the lower range) 'whereof the clergy must have been the smallest persons, and have had the smallest benefices and the littlest congregations ever known.'

We return to Laragh and turn left on the T61 towards Dublin. High on the right, two miles on, is Castlekevin, the motte-and-bailey remains of a 1214 Norman castle, in the centre of what used to be O'Toole territory. For centuries a thorn in the flesh of English ambition, it was finally occupied by the Lord Deputy in 1597 and dismantled, to become soon after the ruin it remains. We pass through Annamoe, where the young Laurence Sterne fell into the mill-race; and then through Roundwood, a centre for anglers beside the Vartry reservoir. There are two smaller lakes in the district, Lough Dan and to the north-west Lough Tay in its circular corrie. This is on the steep road up to Sally Gap, with its daunting views. By the top end of the lake is Luggala House, where the house-parties given by Lady Oranmore and Browne for the likes of John Huston, Woodrow Wyatt, Brendan Behan, Claud Cockburn and others have been described in the memoirs of some of them. 'Cyril Connolly was there one year in his red waistcoat,' wrote Behan, 'and I sang rebel ballads for him the whole evening.' Burned down in 1956, the house was rebuilt exactly as before.

Our road lies north from Roundwood. Ten miles on we reach Enniskerry; passing on the way the Great Sugar Loaf, which in spite of stories and appearances is not a volcanic mountain but a stack of quartzite, once covered with slate but now exposed by denudation and weathered into the characteristic quartzite cone. Enniskerry is pretty enough, and it contains the strikingly luxuriant garden of Dargle Cottage, brilliantly conceived by Sir Basil Goulding beside a precipitous stretch of the Dargle. Still, the village is more notable for proximity to Powerscourt, home of the Wingfield family from James I's reign to 1961, when Viscount Powerscourt sold it. The house, rich in plasterwork, marble mantels and inlaid floors, and complete with its original furniture, Waterford chandeliers and Wingfield portraits, was accidentally burned down in 1974. It was to have opened to the public for the first time the following year. Every Irish mansion which survived the Troubles and other depredations is a priceless part of the country's inheritance, but Powerscourt designed by Castle around 1730 and the prominent focus of a fine estate, was specially valuable. Still, the terraces remain, and the magnificent arboretum, lake and prospect of the Sugar Loaf mountain. The terraces were begun in 1745 but the main work dates from the middle of the nineteenth century. Mainly responsible was Daniel Robertson, whose taste was directed both at landscaping and sherry, which he drank as, from a wheelbarrow, he directed the efforts of a hundred men in the 'forties. (There is a peculiar tendency among the Anglo-Irish to exonerate their ancestors by pointing to giant works undertaken during the Famine; they gave work and wages to the needy; but the lasting benefits were all theirs, while labour was cheap – around a halfpenny a day – and easily got since there were no potatoes to dig.)

Powerscourt was almost the last house to be landscaped in the grand manner, before taste and economics dictated a swing from architecture to horticultural gardening. The raw materials could hardly be bettered – the steep slope below the house, a natural lake, and the Wicklow Hills with their rapid colour-changes beyond. The lake was formalised into the present Triton Pool, and work on the terraces began in 1843. From the upper perron, floored with pebbles from Bray beach, and with statues from the Palais Royal which used to breathe fire, five terraces descend to the lake, barred by a grille with winged horses on either side. That is the simple plan, and it is combined with richly varied detail – the bronze Amorini on the perron, the Vine Gate, Bamberg Gate (in *trompe l'oeil* perspective) and other wrought-iron gates, the two Pegasi mentioned, unusually cast in zinc.   Below is a magnificent tree collection – including a 30-foot aromatic *Drimys winteri*, relation of the magnolia, monkey puzzles, a eucalyptus grown to 100 feet in forty years, and a Sitka spruce claimed – like one at Curraghmore – to be Ireland's tallest tree. There is also a Japanese garden of 1908, and some other items of curiosity. Three miles south-south-west of the house is the lovely 400-foot drop of Powerscourt Waterfall – the tallest in these islands – in a deer park. In preparation for a visit by George IV a reservoir was dug at the top to enhance the fall, but the king in the end never came. Unlike other Wicklow cataracts, this costs money to see, but it is the only Wicklow scene Edward Lear painted successfully and is worth the fee.

Instead of making straightway back to Dublin through the picturesque Scalp, we can follow the Glencree River valley west into the hills again, turning right and north at **Glencree Reformatory.** Now a centre for victims of the Northern Ireland troubles, the building began, like others spaced over the hills, as a barracks in 1798, becoming an RC boys' reformatory in 1859. Beside it is a German war cemetery, for Germans whose ships foundered or planes crashed in or near Ireland during the last two wars. Nearby is the source of Dublin's River Dodder, which flows north-west before swinging round through the city's southern suburbs to the sea. Its upper valley is one of the most beautiful and sequestered in the area – it was Synge's favourite walk from Dublin. Four miles along the road from Glencree to Dublin we pass on the left **Montpelier Hill,** on top of which is Speaker Conolly's ruined sporting lodge, built in 1720. (Conolly also owned the Elizabethan Rathfarnham Castle to the north.) On shallow evidence, the lodge is associated with the Hell-Fire Club that was supposed to meet here, and to have at last gutted the place in an effort to ascertain what the members' destination after this life might be like. The club met regularly in the Eagle Tavern by Dublin Castle. In spite of hints of black magic and debauchery, its activities for all we know were confined to heroic intoxication and improper stories.

We enter Dublin through **Rathfarnham,** whose castle to the right was built by Archbishop Loftus in the 1580s. In 1770–1 its new owner, the Earl of Ely, had Chambers as consultant architect for modernisation. Like many of Dublin's suburban grand houses it is kept in a fair state by clerical incumbents, in this case the Jesuits, and preserves beautiful decorations by Angelica Kauffman and others. A mile south of the castle, down Whitechurch Road, is the **Hermitage,** an eighteenth-century house by an unknown architect, with strong national-ist links. Here Robert Emmet courted Sarah Curran, whose father lived in the now ruined priory over the road. In 1910 Patrick Pearse moved his College of St Enda here, building chalets in the grounds when the house overflowed. The enter-prise was bankrupt by the time Pearse was executed for his part in the 1916 Easter Rising. House and grounds were bequeathed to the nation by Pearse's sister. His memory is hallowed by many Irish republicans, and the place has some-thing of the aura of a shrine.

CHAPTER SIX

Dublin–Wexford Coastal: the South-East

THE coast road from Dublin to Wexford runs parallel to an almost unbroken, almost deserted line of sandy seashore. The climate is very respectable, with the lowest year-round rainfall and highest temperatures to be found in Ireland. The Wexford lowlands, with an average 62° F in July, are the warmest part of the country. Inland the country, from the Wicklow Mountains to Wexford's undulating pastures, counts some of Ireland's most quietly beautiful scenery.

The north part of the road does not rival the way through the mountains, but it has attractions of its own. Having emerged from Dublin's coastal trail we come first to **Bray**, a town that evolved from railway needs in the nineteenth century. William Dargan, the 'Railway King', lost his last fortune trying to make it Ireland's Brighton. It has all the trappings of a resort and is a good base for the Wicklow Mountains and some excellent shore and cliff walks round Bray Head. On the right the Little Sugar Loaf rises, conical quartz sister of the Great, making a delightful valley with the long hill of Bray Head. **Kilruddery House**, partly demolished, is on the right, a mock-Tudor mansion built in 1820 by Sir Richard Morrison and his son for the tenth Earl of Meath. Its main boast is the early eighteenth-century formal garden, with lake, canals, cut banks, cliff hedges, a miniature amphitheatre and sumptuous statuary. It is a rare survivor of the French-inspired formal Irish garden. Inside is a magnificent panelled great hall, a fine staircase, and other rooms decorated with elaborate plasterwork. Beyond Delgany (whose C of I church has a magnificent monument to David la Touche, of 1790) the coast road proper is rather dull as far as Wicklow, and the best course is to turn right, come to the T7, the main road, glimpse the beautiful Glen of the Downs to the right, and then head for Newtown Mountkennedy and Ashford. Just before the latter a road leads right for a mile to the Devil's Glen, another scenic Wicklow defile, thickly wooded with oaks and conifers, down which the Vartry River tumbles from its reservoir above. Just beyond Ashford itself, laid out on either side of the Vartry, are **Mount Usher Gardens**, well-known for their rare exotic plants and large collection of trees and shrubs amassed by generations of the Walpole family. The eucalyptus here are said to be the finest in Europe.

Soon the road swings left to **Wicklow** itself, county town but with little to recommend it. It was, like most larger Irish towns, founded by Vikings, though St Patrick is said to have landed here long before and been turned away by the local chief. Its medieval history is much concerned with the O'Byrnes, who with the O'Tooles plagued the English settlement here, exacting 'black rents' from English townsmen till 1542, and later burning the town. There is a good C of I church, and beside the harbour are the grim remains of Black Castle, left to decay since the Cromwellians took it by siege from Confederates in 1649. The fourteen-mile coast road from here to Arklow passes a long succession of good beaches, some of which get crowded by Irish standards in the summer, for this is an easy outing for Dubliners.

Arklow stands at the foot of the Avoca valley, offering a chance to see the part, as far as Woodenbridge, we missed in the last chapter. The drive is a pretty one, again marred only by mining works and the occasional baldness made by tree cutting. **Shelton Abbey**, high on the right, is another mock-Tudor creation of the Morrisons, father and son, with a good rhododendron display in the demesne. From being the family seat of the Earls of Wicklow it has become a State forestry school, beside a large area (spanning the whole Wicklow range) in which most land up to 1,000 feet is given over to forestry. Wicklow is the oldest and most productive forestry area in the country, and trees planted since independence, when a vigorous policy of reafforestation began, have long since been felled to make way for new planting. The national target is to turn a million acres to trees, making the country produce all its own timber and so saving imports from Scandinavia and Canada. Almost all the trees planted, of course, are soft-wood conifers; a pity, since here as elsewhere the old landscape of oak, beech and ash has made way for the foreign look of spruces, pines, firs and larches.

Arklow itself, a centre of boat-building and coaster-owning, has, like Wicklow, a stormy medieval history. In 1315, Edward Bruce, Robert's brother, having accepted the crown of Ulster, marched south to make himself King of all Ireland, and sacked Arklow, then a stronghold of the English. Thereafter the Irish retrieved more and more of their old territory by means of destructive sorties from their mountain fortress, and the town was only preserved by the English at heavy cost to life and money. Like Wicklow, it was occupied by Confederates, and eventually taken and brought into line by Cromwell. It saw another historic drama, when in 1798 Father Michael Murphy, who had raised the Wexford rebellion by killing a British soldier, pitted his brave medley, armed mainly with pitchforks, against Arklow's defences, hoping to link with their Dublin counterparts beyond. Two and a half hours saw the death of Murphy and the end of Wexford hopes. Days later came the hour-long battle of Vinegar Hill, that merely cleared up the fragments. Nothing of note in Arklow survives from those or former times, except a tower and bits of the wall of the original Butler Castle, though there is a good RC church of the nineteenth century. Nor is there any sign of the sea-girt rock reported by Giraldus 'from which the tide ebbs on one side while it flows on the other'. *Pace* the chronicler, who was curious about tides (Wicklow Harbour 'fills up when the tide is ebbing from all other places'), there is very little tidal movement on this coast at all. We go on south by the main road to Gorey passing on the left 833-foot Tara Hill, prominent in its flat surrounds.

Gorey, too, was assaulted by insurgents on their way to Arklow, and gave way, but has little to detain us except St Mark's Church and the Loreto convent, built between 1839 and 1842 by the opinionated, tragi-comic Augustus Welby Pugin, whose devotion to the Gothic revival brought it much of its merit. The road east leads down to the best part of this south-eastern coastline, with several resorts, much sand and few people. (One slight climatic hazard can be the east wind, which can be cool; the prevailing south-west, from which the dunes protect, is warm anyway.) We are now well into County Wexford, whose interior is often called the Garden of Ireland – a name that, while sticking in the throat, gives a correct impression. It is delightfully undramatic, restful country, with enough hills and rivers to give variety. Its coast is unlike any other Irish coast, fairly flat and sandy, with occasional broad inlets. The south-facing section has peculiar fascination. This eastern part is best for bathing. Out to sea, the Glassgorman and other sandbanks and gravel ridges, deposited by the glacial flow on what was land at that time, are a fatal hazard for shipping, and are well lined with lightships. The first seaside village we reach is Courtown (with the finely wooded demesne of Courtown House to the north), a pleasant resort with a harbour that balks fishermen by frequently silting up. Ardamine, two miles south, on the same stretch as Courtown, is unnoticeably notable as the landing place of Ladhra, a companion of Cesair, Noah's granddaughter. The flood did for him, as elsewhere it did for all his companions, barring Fintan.

The coast continues, broken here and there by little villages. Cahore is quiet, in a lovely area of woods and low hills, with the beaches of the Point close by. Blackwater is amazing, not as a competitor for, but a frequent winner of the Tidy Towns competition; tidy it is, of course, but in the luminous colour scheme of its houses, and central religious grotto, something between a village Blackpool and ecclesiastical Clovelly. Curracloe is a pleasant contrast, a village of thatched and whitewashed cottages, with dunes and sandy bay stretching north and south for miles.

We cross the bridge over **Wexford** Harbour and enter the town. The harbour is partly filled with sediment from the Slaney River, whose estuary it forms, and almost blocked from the sea by a long bar of sand and gravel. (Large boats have to use the artificial harbour of Rosslare to the south.) But neither feature could stop the flat-bottomed boats of

Norsemen, who created a trading port (Wexford is a Norse word, 'ford' being the same as 'fjord'); nor the English allies of Dermot MacMurrough, who here began the campaign that created Ireland's main preoccupation for seven hundred years.

The Danes, or Norsemen, appeared in 850 and having conquered stayed for three hundred years. They went down well with the locals, forming treaties, establishing regular merchant shipping lines from Wexford Harbour to Britain, France and beyond, exploiting the sea-fish, building a timber city with lanes leading down to wharves and an earthen wall that later broke the first Norman advance. They erected several churches after their conversion in 1035, and even had the men of Leinster on their side at Clontarf, against Boru.

Robert FitzStephen, heading the Norman influx, arrived at Wexford in May, 1169, and a few days later the Danes surrendered. In 1172 Henry II made the town over to Strongbow, and the king himself spent Lent at Selskar Abbey, continuing his penance for the murder of Becket. Strongbow settled the place with his own countryfolk. By some quirk of history the language of these English speakers was retained by the inhabitants of the barony of Forth till recent times, mixed with a little of the Irish that was spoken all around. It was hardly understood by either Irish or English and eventually died out at the end of last century. After Strongbow the place continued to prosper. The Normans made permanent settlements on Danish foundations, and were followed by the Cistercians, who founded abbeys like Dunbrody and Tintern in the county. New walls and gates went up round Wexford in the fourteenth century and all was well until Cromwell's visit. Early in his progress through southern Ireland, and fresh from his Drogheda bloodbath, the future Protector took Wexford – the Confederates' naval base – by storm, and massacred 1,500 defenders and every available priest in the streets. That left a population of under 400. Cromwell's supposed headquarters are inside the present Woolworth's.

Worse was to follow. In 1798 the United Irishmen made their badly planned bid for independence. In only one quarter

was the rising prolonged, and that where it was least expected
– Wexford and Wicklow. On 26th May Father John Murphy
led his inexperienced soldiery into rebellion. At first they
were successful, and occupied Wexford town, but discipline
was poor. A vandal contingent, under a standard sewn with
the letters MWS – 'Murder without Sin' – without orders
rounded up enemy and suspect. Sir Richard Musgrave wrote
from eye-witness accounts: 'The manner, in general, of
putting them to death was thus: two rebels pushed their
pikes into the breast of the victim, and two into his back,
and in that state (writhing with torture) they held him
suspended, till dead, and then threw him over the bridge into
the water . . .' Meanwhile another, more orderly group of
rebels, under a Protestant landlord, Bagenal Harvey, assaulted
but failed to capture New Ross. Further battles in north
Wexford and Wicklow failed to achieve the rebels' main aim
– to break out of the area and join other fighters in Dublin.
Eventually the English General Lake made for Vinegar Hill,
where a desperate, hour-long engagement was fought.
English – or rather Protestant, for the war had strong religious
undertones – retribution followed. Wexford saw another
scene like the last – more spiking on pikes, and government
troops kicking the severed heads of rebel leaders about the
quays.

In the nineteenth century the harbour was silted further,
and trade and traffic ebbed away. The early 1900s saw the
end of the old oyster trade – three to five shillings a hundred
and rows of eating houses that served them – when a European
virus destroyed the twenty miles of beds along the coast. In
recent years, however, Wexford, with generous Guinness
subsidies, has pulled itself up by its festival. Disdaining high
summer, Wexford waits till the end of October to put on a
programme of lesser known operas with world-class soloists,
Irish TV's orchestra, and the splendid local chorus; as well
as a full complement of films, recitals, exhibitions and so on.
The eighteenth-century theatre is not large, nor indeed is the
town, and a very special intimacy is created between those
who perform and those who watch during this charming week.

For walking round, Wexford has a more historic atmosphere than most Irish cities. Much even of the old Norse arrangement survives in the low alleys leading from the long curving main street to the quay (till 1800 they used to lead straight to wharves). The dull quay, made duller by the barren concrete of Charles Forte's Talbot Hotel, is still magnificently situated on the Slaney estuary. It has a monument to Commodore John Barry, founder of the American Navy, who was born at Ballysampson, some miles south-west. Behind, among the narrow streets and old-fashioned shops, some special monuments stand out. **Selskar** (Holy Sepulchre) **Abbey**, by the West Gate and near remains of the fifteenth-century wall at the town's north-west end beyond Cornmarket and Abbey Street, is where Henry II did penance and Strongbow's daughter (by his first marriage) married Raymond le Gros, his Fitzgerald lieutenant. The Bull Ring, coming south along Main Street, has an excellent 1700 Flemish-gabled house, and the site of the Old Rectory where the Archdeacon father of 'Speranza', Oscar Wilde's poet-mother, lived. The pikeman monument commemorates the '98 and is by Oliver Sheppard (1864–1941), a sculptor who elsewhere pioneered *art nouveau* styles in Ireland. Bull-baiting took place till 1792. Pugin designed the church of St Peter's RC College in Summerhill Road, and his pupil, Robert Pierce, the 'twin churches', both in the upper south-west part of the town. Walks – the Tourist Office lays on very good guided ones – are helped by the system of explanatory plaques arranged at points of interest round the town.

*

We leave Wexford to tour the south coast, a stretch with a peculiar character of its own, where the scenery of lagoons and sandbanks, sea-birds and Norman ghosts make equal claims on our attention. First we drive south-west three miles to **Johnstown Castle**. The castle cluster is nineteenth-century Gothic, designed by Daniel Robertson of Kilkenny, who was responsible for Powerscourt's gardens. The thousand-acre estate has been since 1944 a research institute of the Agricultural Institute, but the grounds are open for the public to drive through. They are worth it for the landscaped garden, herbaceous borders and lakes, and the exceptional collection of trees. Two miles south-south-east stands the mellow ruin of Rathmacknee Castle, one of Wexford's best fifteenth-century remains, with five stories and well-preserved stepped battlements. We can now either make for the coast at **Rosslare** – a developed resort with a good eighteen-hole golf-course and a harbour that receives the ferries from Fishguard, nearly half the total car traffic into Ireland (much different from the days when Shaw could be 'lost in dreams there; one cannot work in a place of such infinite peace'). Or we can bypass Rosslare and head south for **Lady's Island** and **Carnsore Point.** The former, an attractive island on a deep lagoon, reached by a causeway, is the setting of a ruined Augustinian abbey, St Mary's, built like the ruined Lambert Castle close by in the mid-thirteenth century. During a search by troops in Penal times, it is said that a crucifix and statue were discovered and thrown into the lake. Recovered years later, they were restored and make the place a scene of annual pilgrimage (15th August). Three miles south, **Carnsore Point**, an isolated granite outlier from the Leinster chain, makes a secure south-east bastion for the country against the conflicting currents beyond. This mixing of waters, from the south-west Gulf Stream and northerly Labrador current, makes this one of the richest sea areas of these islands, with all kinds of fish represented, including large schools of shark. Currents make it also one of the most dangerous. But sea-fishing trips from several bases within a few miles are under supervision and quite safe. On the landward side is a virtual jungle of fern, gorse and various shrubs. From here to the west the miles of wild fuchsia and escallonia are one of the greatest surprises for the British traveller. Even more startling is that, biologically, these fuchsia flowers by the million are a waste. In our latitudes the plant reproduces only vegetatively – by shoots, chance cuttings and so on – never by seed. St Vogue's well and church remains to the north of the point recall (very little else does) a sixth-century hermit who was reputed to have sailed to Brittany on a stone and died there. The stone is pointed out here. It must have sailed back.

We return past Lady's Island, and then turn left twice to reach **Tacumshane**, which boasts one of Ireland's two windmills. It was built in 1846, of the kind known as tower-mill, with the thatched cap on top revolving to suit the wind-direction. Used till 1936, it was restored in 1952 and is preserved by the State.

Tacumshin Lake, another lagoon cut off from the sea by a long sandbank, is to the west, rich in bird-life. We go north and turn left on the L128 to round the lake, passing at its head Bargy Castle, now a hotel, once the home of Bagenal Harvey who after his part in the '98, and his escape to Saltee Island, was caught, hanged in Wexford and buried at last in Mayglass Church, two miles north-west. The left turn after the castle takes us straight to **Kilmore Quay**, a long and very pretty village in which all the cottages are thatched and whitewashed. From the harbour, with its healthful kelpy smell, there is a pleasing view over the shallow flats that stretch miles to the east. From the harbour, too, fishing-boats go out, for bass and conger-eel and lobsters; and a trip can usually be hired to the **Great Saltee Island**, providing the wind is not strong and northerly. The island is the final rising of a mostly submerged ridge extending from Forlorn Point, by the quay. Apart from being owned by 'Prince Michael the First' (who having achieved his boyhood desire of buying the place, had himself crowned on a limestone throne near the house he inhabits during part of the summer), Great Saltee is one of Ireland's most thriving bird sanctuaries. Here among the wild hyacinths, the sea-campion, sea-pink and scurry-grass dwell, during the nesting period of late spring and early summer, several million birds. Herring, Great and Lesser Black-backed Gulls and Kittiwakes keep mainly towards the rocky scarp on the island's south side. There are besides those relatives of the extinct Great Auk (of which the last Irish specimen was caught at Waterford Harbour in 1846), the Puffin with its Technicolor bill, the Razorbill with a mono-chrome substitute, and the white and dark brown Guillemot with its sinuous neck. Cormorants are there, too, and the superficially gull-like fulmar petrel whose range seems oddly but steadily to expand in this destructive century, unlike that of the peregrine falcon, which used to lord it here but no longer does. In June eggs almost block progress and the noisy birds can be aggressive. By the end of July they have gone to the sea, and the trip is not worth taking. In Saltee most of the handful of Irish records of the nightingale have been made. (In winter there are plenty of geese round Wexford Harbour, not least Greenland white-fronted; the rare and raucous Roseate Tern, with its dark bill and long tail streamers, nests in colonies near Lady's Island and Rosslare.)

We take the minor north road out of Kilmore Quay, turn left after two miles, left again at Duncormick through a land rich in castle ruins to reach Bannow on the extreme west of Ballyteige Bay. At **Bannow**, mounds and sandy humps and the scant ruins of thirteenth-century St Mary's Church mark a lost Norman city, already covered by drifting sands in the seventeenth century. (MPs representing a church and a chimney were still returned to the Irish Parliament till 1798, when £15,000 compensation was.paid.) Beyond is the peninsula of Bannow Island, an island proper in Norman times; and it was here that the Norman Conquest began. Dermot MacMurrough, whose snatching of the willing, mature (she was 44 at the time) Dervorgilla from Tiernan O'Rourke in 1152 had led to the loss of most of his Leinster lands, had meanwhile busied himself finding allies to help him revive. From Henry II of England and France he obtained a letter inviting English knights to help him. The letter had the desired effect of rallying Richard FitzGilbert de Clare, Earl of Pembroke and better known as 'Strongbow' and others to his cause. Strongbow was bribed with an offer of MacMurrough's daughter Eva in marriage and the right of succession to his Leinster territory. In May, 1169, Strongbow's advance guard under Robert FitzStephen arrived at Bannow Island. Days later they held Wexford, and shortly after MacMurrough was secure in his Leinster estates based on Ferns. In the old cemetery beside Bannow Church is said to be Princess Eva's grave.

We follow Bannow Bay round, across Wellingtonbridge, and turn off first left to **Clonmines**, another town that died. In Norse times it had its own mint, for which silver and lead were mined on the opposite river-bank. William the Marshall, Strongbow's son-in-law, fortified it and gave it a Charter of Liberty. It was destroyed at the end of the fourteenth century but, rebuilt soon after, it grew rich again. By 1684 the sands had blocked its access to the sea and silted its harbour. As a thoroughfare it was at an end. But the ruins of three churches and four castles, and its place by the bay, make it an evocative sight. Reverting to the main road we turn off left to round the Hook Peninsula. **Tintern Abbey**, two miles along on the right, was a daughter foundation of its Wye Valley namesake, and was founded by William the Marshall in gratitude for a safe crossing. The ruinous tower and ivied presbytery, showing it aspired to the form of the original, are beautifully set in a copse of trees.

Beyond Fethard the road leads to **Baginbun Head**, where the headland itself is marked off by a large ditch and ramparts – the defences of the second contingent of Norman invaders under Raymond le Gros. They numbered less than a hundred and set themselves to collect a large herd of cows. Soon a force of three thousand Irish and Norse came to send them whence they came (though in old accounts three thousand means simply a large, unspecifiable number). The Normans stampeded the cattle into the attackers and followed up with a charge. Such prisoners as were taken had their limbs broken before being thrown over the cliffs, and the Normans waited confidently for the arrival of Strongbow himself at Passage East, in Waterford. We can continue down the Hook, which was one of two alternative approaches to Waterford for Cromwell when he arrived in 1649. The other was by the west side of Waterford Harbour on which stands a village called Crooke. Either way, Cromwell vowed to take the city, and his words 'By Hook or by Crook' are with us still. Near **Hook Head** is the graceful, crenellated fifteenth-century and later castle of Slade, with its fine tapered tower, assigned by Cromwell to the Loftus family, later Earls of Ely. The drive up the western coast takes us through Duncannon, where the refugee James II, after the rout of the Boyne, took ship for Kinsale before he finally left Ireland to spend his last years at St Germain. The little fortified town was soon after taken by the Williamite officer destined to become first Duke of Marlborough.

Five miles farther north, opposite the point where the River Suir spills into Waterford Harbour, and right beside a creek on its eastern side is the magnificent ruin of **Dunbrody** – a Cistercian abbey built in the early thirteenth century on land granted by one of the first Norman arrivals, Hervey de Montmorency, in 1178. One of its names, St Mary of Refuge, recalls its mother abbey in Dublin and its old sanctuary rights for malefactors, stipulated by the founder. It appears relatively plain, in the Cistercian tradition, with an aisled nave (and its graceful Early English arches), six transept chapels and a low central tower (added, as such towers usually were, in the fifteenth century), and austere cloister buildings. Above all it provides a superb view, especially from the road, and those treasured accompaniments of Irish remains – ivy overgrowth, grass-topped walls, jackdaws above and sheep grazing below – all enhance the effect.

From here, for many miles, our journey is close to the Barrow, one of four major rivers of the south-east. The Barrow is navigable and connects, just above Athy, with the Grand Canal extension, so that it would be possible to get from here to Limerick or Leitrim in the same boat. That requires time and a penchant for uneventful water travel. All the same, to keep to roads that skirt these rivers is almost a guarantee of good scenery, and a lot of the more interesting sights of the country will be met this way – a legacy of the days when forest covered the uplands and valleys were the only means of travel. Most of our travels from now on in the southern hinterland will be based on rivers, from the Slaney in the east to the Lee that recedes almost to the west coast. For the present we follow, more or less, the Barrow and make along the main road for New Ross. Five miles before getting there we can turn right to see the **Kennedy Memorial Park** on the southern slope of Sliabh Coillte. John F. Kennedy's ancestor Patrick is supposed to have come from a farmhouse in Dunganstown, on the left of the main road. The original house has gone, but there is a later one (and distant relatives, postcards and souvenirs) in its place.

The park was sponsored by the Irish in America. It is to be a magnificent arboretum in its time, but it will be several years before most trees reach anything approaching full size. There is still interest in the low grey-stone timber-roofed building in the centre with its fine views and displays, including a bronze map showing the gardens and arboreta of Ireland, and an interesting display of the woods and grains of some 136 different tree species.

The best thing about **New Ross** is its old aura – the tall thin Dutch-type houses of irregular height on the waterfront, the twisting lanes and old steps and cobbled path up the hill, flanked by terraces of charming cottages. It owes its origins to William the Marshall, whose lively abilities in this area matched those of Hugh de Lacy in Meath, with as lasting results. He built the large parish church of St Mary's at the top of the hill, in Early English style, and so paved the way for the import of English Gothic that was the making of Cashel and other cathedrals. Later the town's walls were erected, with everyone compelled to take part in the building.

This was the apogee of the Anglo-Norman occupation. By the end of the thirteenth century they were far flung over the land, but too thinly. In the following century the Irish had learned enough of Norman ways to strike back effectively: and by 1400, after a short-lived settlement by Richard II, last medieval king to land in Ireland, English territory had shrunk to the Pale and had to wait for the Tudors to expand again. One of the chief leaders in this Gaelic resurgence, Art MacMurrough, devastated the town at Richard's coming in 1398, and later regained possession of it, and most of Leinster, earning the title 'most fierce rebel'. He died here in 1418, after token submission to a much weakened English monarchy. In 1649, having supported the Confederacy against Ormonde, the town yielded to Cromwell at his crossing the river by a bridge of boats, preferring not to follow in the wake of Drogheda and Wexford. It did not, however, escape the impact of the '98, and here took place the biggest battle of the whole rebellion. Bagenal Harvey led thousands of rebels in a wild attempt to carry the town. They burned and advanced steadily while the garrisons hailed them with cannon shot.

Jerpoint Abbey, County Kilkenny, with typical Irish battlements.

The Rock of Cashel from the south-east.
Below Cashel Cathedral and Round Tower by night.

Then the government cavalry charged and spread disorder. The initial cohesion of the rebels, once lost, was never restored. Women and children helped them and the tales of bravery and sacrifice are legion. But in the end two thousand rebels were dead, and hardly more than two hundred soldiers, and the net was closing for its final catch at Vinegar Hill. At the end of the battle a nearby barn with dozens of English prisoners in it was set fire to, by some rebel band. Of most interest in the town is the ruin of the original **St Mary's Abbey** with the nineteenth-century C of I church occupying the nave. There are some ghoulish graves and memorials in the crypt and church. The elegant Tholsel, with its domed cupola, in the lower part of the town, was built in 1749. Damaged in 1798 it was rebuilt in 1806 to the old plan.

Keeping to the right or east bank of the river described by Spenser, who knew it well, as 'the goodly Barrow, which doth hoord Great heapes of Salmons in his deep bosome,' we make our way north, through a delightful valley. Woods hang high on either side. There are rare flowers – a cousin of the bluebell, the nettle-leaved bell-flower – among the woods; and the lovely pink trumpeting lily, Meadow Saffron, in damp fields. The first flowers in spring, the second autumn. After eight miles, with conical Mount Brandon looming on the left, we come to **St Mullins,** and the attractive but scanty remains of a monastery founded by St Moling, on a grassy shelf above the river. Moling, who died in 697, is often associated with foxes. The remains include a Round Tower's stump, a High Cross and some rudimentary church ruins, but in spite of the paucity, its position by the river, and the still-used surround of the graveyard, leave a lasting impression.

Farther on the Blackstairs Mountains can be seen on the right, rising to 2,610 feet at Mount Leinster, on whose north slopes (goes a by no means unique claim), the last Irish wolf was killed near Myshall, in 1786. This range is an exposed continuation of the granite of the Wicklow Mountains, as is the heathery Mount Brandon on the other side. Sheltering beneath the latter, on a lovely stretch of the river, is the little town of **Graiguenamanagh** ('Granary of the Monks'), founded by William the Marshall, with picturesque streets (the mountain road west to Inistiogue makes a good diversion). The Cistercian **Abbey of Vallis Sancti Salvatoris,** recently well restored, has much of beauty and interest including the fourteenth-century effigy of a mail-clad knight inside it. The fall of the central tower in 1774, and subsequent spread of rubble, has raised the floor several feet above its original level. The abbey was a copy of, and partly colonised by monks from Strata Florida in Wales, an abbey possessing a wooden bowl claimed by some to be the Holy Grail. Almost the whole of the town is set in the purlieus of the original abbey, the largest Cistercian foundation in Ireland. We can cross here to the west bank and reach Borris, five miles north, by way of **Ullard**, where are the scant remains of seventh-century St Fiachra's monastery and later buildings, which include a good Romanesque doorway and worn tenth-century High Cross. Fiachra went to France from Ireland and died there in 670. His name is for ever associated with haemorrhoids and syphilis, which he allegedly cured, taxis which in French are named after him because the hotel that first hired them out had him as patron, and gardens, because his hermitage at Meaux was admired for its vegetables.

Borris, with its steep wide street and excellent views of the mountains, is beside the demesne of the Kavanaghs, descendants of Art MacMurrough and the Kings of Leinster. In 1778, at heavy, foursquare, battlemented **Borris House,** before its restoration by W. V. Morrison, the Kavanagh family guarded their relation Eleanor Butler after her first scandalous attempt to elope with Sarah Ponsonby. Eleanor escaped after three weeks and tramped the twelve miles southwest to Woodstock where Sarah secreted her in her room before Eleanor's father conceded defeat and sent a carriage to take them to Waterford, whence they sailed to Wales and a lifetime of mutual devotion and fame as the Ladies of Llangollen. A later owner, of the house, Arthur MacMurrough Kavanagh, despite being born with stumps instead of arms and legs, contrived to ride, shoot, marry, sire seven children including the present owner's great-grandfather, serve with effective reforming zeal as an MP, and travel adventurously in remote parts of Asia. Muine Bheag or **Bagenalstown** is seven miles on, with the Bagenal family's former demesne of Dunleckny, which they were granted in the sixteenth century, to the north-east. The present house, Tudor-gothic in style, was built about 1850. Walter Bagenal designed the town in the eighteenth century. He had great ambitions for its architectural splendour and intended it to be called Versailles, but removal of the old coach route left it much as it is, and with a name he would scarcely have approved. There is a good early nineteenth-century Greek-revival court-house. On the west bank, just south of Leighlinbridge is **Dinn Righ,** a rath that marks an ancient seat of the Kings of Leinster; it was the sight of an apocalyptic pre-Gaelic battle. On the opposite bank in the village are the ruins of twelfth-century **Black Castle,** which was destroyed progressively – by Rory Og O'More in 1577, Cromwell in 1649, and some more natural cause in 1892.

Three miles west is the small, sequestered and delightfully casual village of **Old Leighlin.** It comprises a garage, post office, some cottages and the **Cathedral of St Laserian,** relic of the days when it was see of the diocese. Much of the building dates from the thirteenth century. Its overgrown churchyard creates a strong feel of the past, with often-recurring names on the tombstones – Nolan, Bryan, Murphy (and a stone over a '98 victim, that reads simply 'The love is true that I.O.U.'), many of them in the clear and legible lettering of what became a distinct school of tombstone cutters in north Wexford in the early nineteenth century. Inside, the church has some interesting fragments from the original building, and obvious signs of an ill-advised restoration of 1955, including a glass partition between nave and chancel, with retractable doors.

Since St Mullins we have been in the wedge-shaped county of Carlow, and now, half-way up its western border (at this point the river) we come to its namesake county town. In the maze of old Anglo-Irish snobberies, a Carlow address was much superior to a Wexford one. The novelist Molly Keane (M. J. Farrell) was brought up in Wexford, acutely conscious of her address's low rating. It made no difference that her home was almost on the border. **Carlow's** name is odd in that it has no apparent significance – 'four lakes' or 'quadruple

lake' in a part where there is no lake at all. The town is busy
with the smaller industries – shoes and sugar beet (since the
first Irish factory opened here in 1926), though several warehouses stand disused and growing seedier. Its boast is William
the Marshall's castle, Ireland's earliest four-tower keep, of
which survive a curtain wall and two drum towers in the precincts of a factory. Nothing done to it by Art MacMurrough
(in 1405), Rory O'More (in 1577), Cromwell's Ireton or the '98
rebels compared with the achievement of a certain Dr Middleton,
who, deciding it would function well as a lunatic asylum if
only the walls were not quite so thick, used a charge of
dynamite to reduce them and so blew away all but what still
stands. The neo-Gothic RC cathedral, with a statue of the
founder, Bishop Doyle, by John Hogan, and St Mary's C of I
church both date from the early nineteenth century; as does
the fine central classical courthouse by William Vitruvius
Morrison – the finest of all Irish courthouses. The gravel
pits on the west bank are where, after a vain assault on the
town in 1798, over four hundred insurgents were buried in
quicklime.

Two miles east of Carlow (leave by the T16 and turn first
left after the town), in the demesne of eighteenth-century
Browne's Hill House, is the outstanding dolmen of **Browne's
Hill**, the largest in Ireland and perhaps in Europe. (Permission
to view should be asked of the farmer who owns the field in
which it stands.) Its capstone, which measures twenty feet
square by five feet thick, and could weigh as much as a
hundred tons, is supported by smaller stones at each end. It
could be up to five thousand years old. The incredible
achievement of lifting the capstone was obscured by the
builders, who probably covered the whole edifice, with its
royal corpse underneath, with earth or stones, and possibly
a gleaming coat of crystalline quartzite on top. Though
modern archaeologists confess their ignorance of the practices
surrounding dolmens, people in the past were full of theories.
Folklore (and Yeats's 'Faery Song') hold them to be the beds
in which Dermot and Grania, Conchobar's daughter, slept
when pursued by Finn McCool after eloping from Tara.
Just as mythical are the outworn theories that dolmens were

tables on which the Druids laid out human sacrifices in order to apply their knives.

We are about to stray from the south-east, Carlow being half-way between Wexford and Dublin on the inland route west of Wicklow. The river borders have flattened out now for we are coming to the level county of Kildare.

The bustling town of Athy (pronounced Athigh), with its good Georgian market and late sixteenth-century White's Castle defending the bridgehead (private, with lace curtains at its windows), has seen a good deal of warfare due to its position on the border between Kildare and Laois. What is not so usual for an Irish town is the existence of a modern RC church, built in 1963–5, that evokes admiration in many. The Dominicans, whose church it is, are proud of it: 'Revolutionary Style Design' a notice announces outside. Five-sided, and with a hyperbolic roof, it owes something to cinema architecture, but is bright, spacious, and one of the best modern churches in the country. In 1307 Edward Bruce, after defeating a Butler-commanded army three miles north at Ardscull, sacked the town on his journey south. We shall catch him up shortly, but first drive almost due east, seven miles or so, to glimpse the monastery remains of Moone. They stand in private farm ground, but access is public. Chief among them is tall, thin Moone High Cross, of the tenth century, and probably one of the earliest erected. Its well preserved figures are superbly primitive, and the Twelve Apostles, Sacrifice of Isaac, Daniel in the Lions' Den and the Flight into Egypt look like the polished conceptions of a tidy-minded child. Moone House nearby is an elegant eighteenth-century home, raised a story early last century.

Nearly four miles south-west is the grand demesne, with meadows and streams, of Kilkea Castle, an impressive medieval fortress reconstructed, after a fire, in 1849. Until 1960 the property (and after the sale of Carton in 1949 the seat) of the Duke of Leinster, it is now a luxurious hotel. It also has a ghost, that of Gerald, eleventh Earl of Kildare, the pathetic half-brother of Silken Thomas (who lost his head in 1537). Gerald, aged 10 in 1535, when the Geraldines were all but eliminated by Henry VIII, was brought up abroad. For a

time he served under Cosimo de Medici. Later he was restored
to his estates but never regained any of his family's former
power. Every seventh year this 'friendly' (the hotel claims)
ghost rides a white charger into his former study. Kilkea House,
to the south, was the birthplace of Sir Ernest Shackleton, who
accompanied Scott and led later expeditions to the Antarctic
(one of Shackleton's ancestors had founded the Quaker
school at Ballitore, a few miles north, where the boy Edmund
Burke was a pupil). Three miles south-east of Kilkea is
Castledermot, a straggly village with remains, at its south
end, of a monastery founded by St Dermot, in the more
modern churchyard. Dermot is associated with a movement
which, after the great expansive efforts of the early Irish
church had lapsed, tried to revive the vigour, discipline and
scholarship once again. The Culdees, or Friends of God,
began to make themselves felt in the last part of the eighth
century. They banished abuses and took over the running of
the church with military thoroughness. The writings they
concerned themselves with were ascetic rather than aesthetic,
and many that have come down are the rules and records of
the harshest régime in Church history – prescriptions of
beatings, genuflexions by the hundred, long recitations by
heart in awkward postures, spending nights on nettles, or
beside dead bodies. But through their agency a cultural
revival came also. The Book of Kells may owe its existence
to their vigour, though not to their craftsmanship. All that
is known of Dermot is that he was one of them and that,
having founded the monastery about 800, he died in 823.
The Culdees spread from the south, the way we have come,
and moved on to the rest of the country. The monastery
remains include a good Round Tower, two High Crosses,
and the doorway alone of the Romanesque church (from
which the modern church's door is copied). Opposite are the
remains of a Franciscan Friary.

We now drive south-east to **Tullow**, with its narrow main
street and pretty bridge over the Slaney (which replaces, for
us, the Barrow, left to its higher stages in the surrounds of
Slieve Bloom). The town's themes are the familiar ones of
the south-east – Butler dominion, Cromwellian massacre and

'98 troubles (Father John Murphy, its most enterprising leader, was hanged here) – but very little survives. There are good walks, and the river splashes prettily down some rapids beside the bridge. We now go east, diverting for a last look at County Wicklow, but a different quiet, charming corner of it. We reach **Shillelagh** in ten miles. The area is known for its oak forests, but these are much depleted, replaced by conifers, though the local demesne of **Coollattin** keeps the oak growth going. The chief arboreal interest of the place now is a cork oak in the churchyard. In old times this region grew so many òaks that it gave its name to a piece of equipment more essential to the Irishman than an umbrella to an Englishman. 'An Irishman cannot walk or wander, sport or fight, buy or sell comfortably, without an oak stick in his hands.' The shillelagh was used as a walking-stick, for fighting, for hurling, for urging on cattle. But in the eighteenth century English landlords found another use for these oaks. They could sell them, at ten pounds a thousand, as pipe-staves to London dealers. They did, and got their short-lived quick return, and now the blackthorn cudgel, a substitute and nothing to do with the real thing, is sold to credulous tourists as if it were. The house here, built in 1801-4, was till 1977 the Irish seat – his English one is in Yorkshire – of the Earl Fitzwilliam, descendant of a Lord Lieutenant sacked by Pitt for being too liberal, and of a family which once owned and gave its name to some of the most delectable property in Dublin.

Up the valley of the Derry that winds north-east between regular shaped green hills, is Tinahely, and, just across the river, **Fairwood**, the name given by Thomas Wentworth, Earl of Strafford, in 1639 when he was building yet another grand house for himself, amid 'the daintiliest and plenti-fullyest watered country I ever saw'. He planned a park with 1,500 deer, and 'a breed of horses' and an ironworks to give local labour. 'Black Tom's cellars' are the remains of what was only a beginning anyway. We can return to the Slaney through Carnew, where there is a good example of the very reasonable farmhouse accommodation available all over Ireland, this time in a castle; and Clonegall, a lovely village where the Derry joins the Slaney, with a long arched bridge

over the sedgy broadening of the river, and pretty deserted
houses pointing to the movement to towns as farm progress
ousts labour. (Massey-Ferguson enormities are a common
hindrance on these lanes, often far too narrow for them.)
Bunclody (alias Newtownbarry), with its enormous square, is
at the meeting of the Clody and the Slaney and makes a
good base for exploring the bosomy landscape of the Blackstairs Mountains. The last lap of the 2,610-foot Mount
Leinster is closed to cars, but the walk is easy and the view
broader than almost anywhere in Ireland. On Sundays many
locals go up for the walk and view, and pick whortleberries
that abound among the heather.

Ferns, eight miles south-east of Bunclody, was the capital
of Dermot MacMurrough's elastic twelfth-century kingdom.
Worsted for years by his northern rivals, he here, backed by
the first contingents of Normans, received O'Connor's and
O'Rourke's confirmation of his kingship over all Leinster;
and here he died two years later in 1171, rotting alive, it has
been said, according to his deserts, in the priory he had built,
having opened Ireland to the full measure of foreign conquest.
The former capital has become a market village. The thirteenth-
century castle preserves only one and a half drum towers and
a wall, part of which has been converted into a ball-alley.
It was dismantled by Sir Charles Coote in 1641 and part of
its precincts makes a back yard for some seedy houses
backed with corrugated iron. There is a fine chapel, however,
and Round Tower beside it. The Cathedral of St Aodan, or
Maedog, dates from 1817, but contains some interesting
earlier fragments. To the east are the remains of MacMurrough's Augustinian Friary with graceful lancet windows and
a belfry that is curiously square below and becomes a round
tower above. It is on the site of the early monastery founded
by Maedog, who achieved sanctity by, *inter alia*, lying naked
on the cold stone to recite from memory all the psalms each
day of his life. Renunciation also figures at the end of Ferns's
history, for it was here in the nineteenth century that Father
Cullen founded the Pioneer Total Abstinence Association;
so paving the way for the temperance movement that spread
widely in Ireland last century, and is still strong.

Enniscorthy is eight miles south-south-west and lying as it does in the middle of the Wexford farmlands is a thriving market centre with unusual (for Ireland) irregular streets and an old-world look. A statue of Father John Murphy by Oliver Sheppard stands in the market place. It was he who started the rising, striking dead a looting British soldier eight miles away; and beside the town, on Vinegar Hill, the interlude was all but ended, when on 21st June, 1798, General Lake with thirteen thou and men stormed the rebel encampment which had held the town over three weeks, and killed and scattered their force. There is a good view of the town from the hill. Below, the castle and cathedral are worth examining more closely. Raymond le Gros built the castle but it was rebuilt in 1586; shortly afterwards Edmund Spenser leased it for a while. It comes down to us, splendidly solid and little affected by Cromwell or Lake, but restored and modernised in 1900; and now houses the tourist office and a local museum which would benefit from better exhibits (1916 memos, notes, cuttings and artifacts predominate) and arrangement. The RC Cathedral was designed by A. W. Pugin in 1840 and is one of the best examples of Gothic Revival style, with a narrow elevated look inside and out, and a characteristic attention to fine points of detail. Augustus Welby Pugin, son of Augustus Charles, did other work in this area and as far afield as Adare in Limerick, but it brought him little satisfaction. Of the cathedral nave he complains in a letter: 'The new bishop has blocked up the tower and stuck altars under the tower! . . . it could hardly have been worse if it had fallen into the hands of Hottentots.' Two miles south, at Borodale House, Admiral Lord Beatty was born in 1871.

From Enniscorthy we can return to Wexford to complete the circle, through lovely stretches of the Slaney and the low-lying barony of Shelmalier, a wild-fowler's paradise; or drive straight across to New Ross, having already taken the alternative coast-road described at the beginning of the chapter.

CHAPTER SEVEN

Kilkenny and South-East Tipperary, Waterford and Coastline

COUNTY KILKENNY is on the fringe of Leinster, and Tipperary is in Munster. Somewhere here, people stop regarding Dublin as their big city and think of Cork instead. Not so long ago the richer inhabitants ignored both, and saved important shopping, visits to dentist, hairdresser and the like, for trips to London. Leinster, apart from Wicklow, and some smaller rocky outcrops, is a province of large farms and the manor houses and demesnes that go with them. Munster for the most part is mountain and moorland with a rugged rocky coastline that is one of its chief attractions. We are now in a kind of no-man's-land between the two. The farming country of Tipperary's Golden Vale is as rich as any in Ireland, but every fertile stretch is hemmed in by mountains. There is a last majestic scattering of lovely houses and estates before wealth and its signs become the exception. In Kilkenny you would not think of the change. Tipperary shows signs of it, fringed by large mountain ranges; from Waterford west you have moved into another country, and there is more than the landscape to remind you. We can proceed in that order, penetrating far into the interior again, on a circular route that returns us to the coastal road at the city of Waterford.

Again we drive beside a river from New Ross, this time the Nore that spills as prettily down its valley flanked with wooded gorges as the Barrow over to the east. In ten miles we come to Inistioge (pronounced Inisteeg), and just before look left across to the demesne of **Woodstock**, once one of the grandest houses in Kilkenny but burned in the Civil War. 'Never did my imagination paint Paradise itself so full of Nature's sweets' wrote a visiting parson in 1796. In Ireland,

where there has never been a pressure of population to put
scenes of destruction to new uses, the scars remain. Here at
Woodstock, however, the land has been replanted by the
Forestry Department. (The house was built about 1745 by
Francis Bindon, who sometimes collaborated with Richard
Castle, but gave most of his time to portrait painting: at
least eleven of his rather static portraits of Swift survive.) The
house, and Inistioge itself, passed from the Fownes to the Tighe
family in 1778, on the deaths of Sir William and Lady Betty
Fownes, foster parents of Sarah Ponsonby, within weeks of
the furore caused by her elopement from here with Eleanor
Butler to Llangollen in Wales. A graceful monument by
Flaxman to Mary Tighe, a poetess held in repute by the
Victorians, stands in the mausoleum behind the C of I parish
church at the demesne's gates. The delightful ten-arched bridge
we crossed marks the approximate tidal limit of the river.

By turning left two miles on where the main road to
Thomastown crosses the river, we can pass the site of Dysart
Castle, once home of the Berkeley family. The genial
philosopher-bishop George Berkeley was born here in 1685.
Thomastown itself is gone to seed, and a number of empty
warehouses, fragments of town walls and the remains of the
thirteenth-century parish church founded by the Norman
seneschal of Leinster, Thomas FitzAntony, recall its better
times; though some mills are still working. But instead of
crossing its mellowed bridge we turn left and cover the two
miles to the much grander riverside ruin of Jerpoint Abbey,
founded in 1180, a daughter house of Mellifont. The usual
Irish stepped battlements are conspicuous from all angles.
Like other Cistercian foundations, it owes its situation to the
order's rejection of town for country, and a lonely site where
monks could work and pray in peace; and their need for
good sheep pasture nearby, for they traded in wool. Like
others, too, it has an austerity of design in contrast with the
buildings of other orders, but this – as at Boyle, Mellifont,
Holy Cross and Kilcooly (which in turn was colonised by
Jerpoint) – stands out grandly in the rustic setting. Most of
the present buildings date from the fifteenth-century rebuilding, when the central tower was erected, though there

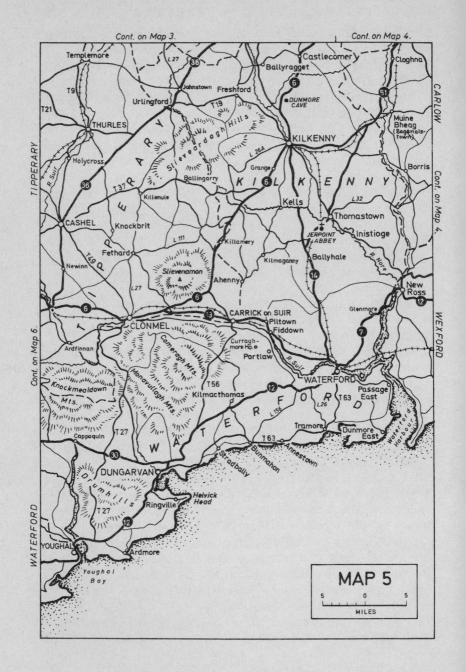

MAP 5

has been partial restoration in the nineteenth century and more recently. Much of Jerpoint's interest lies in its details, the effigy tomb of Felix O'Dullany, twelfth-century Bishop of Ossory, among a collection north of the chancel; and the later effigies of two knights in coats of mail; the Walshe and Butler tombs in the south transept; but especially the carvings of the cloister, each one different (as was normal in medieval work) and of skilled workmanship. The vigour and variety of the characters could make them relief illustrations for Chaucer's tales.

South of Jerpoint the road goes on to join another Kilkenny–Waterford main road, this one over the mountains. There is little to be seen of two curiosities connected with the small valley on this side of the hills, but they deserve mention nevertheless. Some years ago the rock round Kiltorcan was quarried for road-building, and it was possible to walk along the quarry edges picking out fossils of the oldest known plant life of Ireland. They date from the Carboniferous Period, which elsewhere left us our legacy of coal. Here a gradual accumulation of plants and sand under an ancient shallow lake has left a wealth of clear sandstone fossils of primitive plants like club-mosses, horsetails and ferns, some of which in this period grew several feet high. They are still plentiful, but require a careful search. In the same area, around Ballyhale, the people are traditionally supposed to be descended from Welsh settlers of the early centuries AD – 'a clan of Welshes', says Thackeray, who 'maintain themselves in their occupancy of the farms in Tipperary fashion, by simply putting a ball into the body of every man who would come to take a farm over any one of them'.

Seven miles west of Thomastown is **Kells**, nothing to do with the famous Kells in Meath, but the interesting site of a fortified Augustinian priory whose buildings enclosed five acres in the thirteenth century. The need for fortification is seen in the fact that the place was burned by a Bermingham, taken by Edward Bruce and burned by the first Earl of Desmond in the space of a hundred years – the last being occasioned by Kells's owner calling the earl an Irish poet. (Times changed: the earl's grandson was famous for his Irish poetry.) Most of the surviving remains are fifteenth-century towers with connecting walls round the long perimeter, and church – especially cloister – buildings, containing good tombs. Conjuring up the early foundation again points to the great contribution made to the area by the Anglo-Normans and the churchmen who followed them. From here we drive the eight miles due north to **Kilkenny**.

Most of the places we have seen over the last thirty miles came into the possession of the Butler family at the time of the Dissolution. Kilkenny is a Butler headquarters, and since they perpetually crop up hereabouts – throughout Ireland for that matter; from the invasion only the Geraldines have rivalled their status in Ireland – they need some explanation. As FitzWalters, an old Anglo-Norman family, they had gained the honorary title 'Chief Butler of Ireland' (for setting duty on wine imports) from Henry II; in 1328 the seventh Butler married Edward I's daughter and was made Earl of Ormonde. The family soon emerged as one of three great land-owning powers in the south. The other two were both branches of FitzGeralds, one holding the earldom of Kildare, east of Ormonde, the other that of Desmond, to the west. In the fifteenth century the direct male line of Butlers died out (a daughter of the seventh earl married Sir William Boleyn and produced the unfortunate Anne, Queen Elizabeth's mother). A cadet line, with a lot of added Gaelic blood, was after an interval granted the lapsed title, and it was the lining up of the first of these new Ormondes, Piers Roe, with Henry VIII that virtually ended the power of the Kildare FitzGeralds. By now the Ormonde supremacy stretched from the Shannon to Waterford City. Such was the entente between king and Butler that Piers's grandson Thomas was brought up at Windsor with the young Edward VI. Thomas, the 'Black Earl', continued loyal to Elizabeth and, combining wit with strategy, lived to see the destruction of that other rival family, the Desmond FitzGeralds. He was able to do this because, unlike other heads of 'old English' families, he still maintained his English connection and disdained to take on Irish ways. Loyalty survived the Stuarts, and in 1642 was rewarded with a marquisate. Forced to withdraw when the king's fortunes were lost, the future first duke nevertheless brought an army from France in 1650, though he soon had to withdraw. He came back to his dukedom at the Restoration, was twice viceroy, and has remained one of the key figures in Irish history. His son backed the winning side at the Boyne, but later intrigued with Spain over the projected invasion of England in 1714. He was impeached and died in exile in 1745, and his successors, though restored to estates and some titles, never repeated the impact of their ancestors.

Butler history abounds in stone in **St Canice's Cathedral**, in the form of tombs, one of the earliest topped with the effigy of a mail-clad crusader knight, and many of them commemorating Ormonde Butlers. The place is rich in epitaphs from the sixteenth century and later – 'a vertuous mother, and her New-borne Sonne/ (Parted) here meet, and end where they begun . . .' begins a touching tribute of 1631; and the eighteenth century is well represented by rounded heroic couplets. Peter Scheemakers did the memorial to Archbishop Cox's wife in the south transept, which is crowded with good work. The Cox memorial was erected in the archbishop's lifetime with a blank left for an inscription when he came to die. This was taken as an invitation to impiety by young clerics, and a premature epitaph appeared – '. . . This well-known truth, by every tongue confest,/ That by this blank thy life is best express'd.' The statue is in poor shape now, after a fall some years back. The Archbishop is chiefly remembered for the building of Castletown Cox, Ducart's masterpiece in Co. Kilkenny.

St Canice or Kenneth, who founded a monastery here in 577, gave his name to town and cathedral. The latter is primarily thirteenth century, though it incorporates parts of an earlier Romanesque church, whose coneless round tower adjoins the building, and has been vastly altered by later events and restorations. It suffered more than most at the Dissolution through a fanatically iconoclastic bishop, who was nevertheless outdone by the Cromwellians. The bishop of that time recorded that the troops had 'utterly defaced, and ruined' the building. They had 'thrown down all the roof of it, taken away five great goodly bells, broken down all the

windows, and carried away every bit of the glass, and all the
doors of it, that hogs might come and root, and the dogs
gnaw the bones of the dead'. They also stabled their horses
inside. The reconstruction carried out a century later by
Bishop Pococke might have been better had he not used for
his plan the drawings of a man who had never seen the
cathedral. Subsequent restoration has not been faithful to
the original, but the cathedral has the grandeur owed to this
city. It is a pity that the rather stubby central tower should be
lower than the original; but the details of quatrefoil clerestory
windows, the gallery over the west doors, and the rich
collection of memorials and tombs are all of great interest.
North of the cathedral is the plain eighteenth-century Bishop's
Palace and cathedral library of 1679, with a precious collection
of seventeenth- and eighteenth-century books.

Between the cathedral and castle runs the main street,
changing its name from Parliament to High Street half-way,
and then, close to the river, the Parade. Behind Parliament
Street to the left is the Franciscan Friary, a scant ruin close
to Smithwick's Brewery. On the right of Parliament Street,
the Dominican 'Black Abbey' of 1226 was reroofed and
restored to use in 1840. Rothe House, on the right, well
restored and housing the worthy and vigorous Kilkenny
Archaeological Society, is a Tudor merchant's house of 1594
comprising three blocks with courtyards between. It is one
of several surviving Tudor houses of the medieval town;
Kilkenny possesses more than any other Irish town. The
Rothes themselves got the worst of the seventeenth century,
opposing first Cromwell, then William. They left to distinguish themselves in France. Nearly opposite is the courthouse of 1794, much influenced by Gandon's work. Kyteler's
Inn, now a restaurant and an almost complete reconstruction,
was one of many coaching inns in the same street; it was the
home in the early fourteenth century of Dame Alice Kyteler,
a lady of four husbands who, accused of sacrificing cocks
and having communion with the Devil in the cause of witchcraft, fled to England leaving behind a maid, Petronella, to
be burned at the stake. The case is well-documented, and an

intriguing example of medieval judicial practice. The Tholsel,
or Exchange – now the City Hall – is an arcaded building of
1761. In the municipal offices, behind the Great Council
Chamber upstairs, are some interesting old documents
including a thirteenth-century minute book, the Liber Primus.
The city calls for exploratory walks, for it has fine terraces
of Georgian and earlier houses, almshouses, churches and
various medieval monastic remains. It is worth crossing
John's Bridge (just before, on the left of Rose Inn Street, is
Shee's Almshouse, founded 1581) to glimpse Kilkenny
College on the right, which, founded by the Great Duke in
1666, included Swift, Bishop Berkeley, Congreve, Farquhar,
Earl Beatty, and many others among its pupils. The present
building dates from 1782. Excellent guided walks are conducted from the Tourist Office in the Parade, beside the
castle, to which we come in a moment.

In 1844 the town was still officially divided into the distinct
corporations of Irishtown (to the north, around St Canice's),
and Hightown, a pattern repeated in many other cities and
one of the perennial grievances of the native population. It
was, moreover, at Kilkenny that one of the most striking
and effectual examples of English–Irish segregation was
enacted. In 1361 Lionel of Clarence, Edward III's son, was
given the task of restoring to English ways those Anglo-
Norman leaders who were identifying more and more with
the Irish, who surrounded and vastly outnumbered them.
Clarence introduced a code. Its clauses sound absurd to-day
– the English must not marry the Irish or entertain Irish
shanachies (story-tellers), or sell them horses or arms; must
speak English, ride in the English style (i.e. with a saddle),
eschew the game of hurling, and practise the use of English
bows and arrows; and they must keep the Irish from their
churches. But it seemed not at all absurd to the assembled
bishops and archbishops who 'all being present at the said
parliament did fulminate sentence of excommunications
against those contravening the aforesaid statutes'. They were
enacted at Kilkenny, where frequent medieval parliaments
were held.

The place round which history revolved was, of course,

the **Castle**. Strongbow built the first castle in 1172, and this was followed by William the Marshall's sturdier structure of about 1200. To Marshall the town, like many we have seen already, owes its existence. The third Earl of Ormonde bought it in 1391 and from then on it was the chief Butler seat. Marshall's castle remained till the seventeenth century but now only three of his drum towers and the north wall survive. The first duke remodelled it after the Restoration, under the French influence he had been exposed to during exile (the west gateway remains from his work, Ireland's earliest piece of properly classical architecture). When his son was attainted and left the country, it fell into decay, and owes its present state to a major reconstruction by William Robertson in the early 1800s, followed by smaller operations. The city has now bought the castle, and several schemes have been put into effect. In 1967 it was the centre of a massive rally, to which Butlers came from all parts of the world. The grounds have been developed as a National Park, heart of a much bigger park that will take in much of the county. Sadly, the fine paintings collected by successive marquesses have now been scattered, but there is a picture gallery.

Civil servants (the Revenue Commission) also occupy the old Kilkenny Private Theatre opposite the castle, where Gay's opera *Polly* was given its first performance and later Tom Moore acted and met his future wife, sixteen-year-old Bessy Dyke. Nearby are the classical castle stable-buildings, Gibbsian in character, now skilfully converted into the Design Workshops, since 1964 Ireland's centre of industrial design. Only the exhibition hall opens to the public, but in the workshops behind all kinds of prototypes – in silver, linen, wool, copper, pottery, etc – are being prepared by experts for free exploitation by Irish manufacturers.

We now move on from man-made beauties to a locale of natural gloom, the vast and sultry depths of **Dunmore Cave**. This is seven miles north of Kilkenny, at the edge of hilly country abounding in ringforts and giant's graves, off the secondary but most direct road between Kilkenny and Castlecomer. A few years ago one could imagine oneself, were it not for the single iron supporting rail down the steep, long and slippery slope, in unexplored country. Now, lights, paths, viewing-platforms and a car park have removed not only the discomforts but also much of the gothic appeal.

As usual with large caves, this is set in limestone, whose soluble calcium carbonate makes it subject to hollowing. It has, as Mr Thomas Molyneux observed in 1709, a 'dreadful Romantick appearance'. Two English visitors of forty years later wrote: 'when you enter the Mouth, a sudden Chilness seizes all parts of the body, and a Dimness surrounded our lights, as if the Place were filled with a thick fog . . . In several Places were Skulls and human Bones, as it were set in the Crystalline substance.' The cave opens on the left of the descent into an enormous chamber with various evocative rock formations, and then continues through a narrow channel to more subterranean spaces. The place has been famous from prehistoric times. In earliest days, as in other caves, there was supposed to be a monstrous enchanted wild cat living in the entrance, a match for any fighter that challenged it. This probably stemmed from the presence of real wild cats which were still found in Ireland in the nineteenth century. Later it was used for living in, most likely as a refuge in times of war. The Englishman's reference to bones may well link with an entry in the *Annals of the Four Masters* for the year 928: 'Godfrey, grandson of Imhar, with the foreigners of Ath Cliath [Dublin] demolished and plundered Dearc Fearna [Dunmore], where one thousand people were killed in this year.' The 'dreadful Romantick' era followed. Now is the age of lights and amenities.

The land rises to the north to make the dull Kilkenny coalfield, an isolated stretch among the limestone, which has over the ages been mainly stripped of its coal deposits. The town of **Castlecomer**, which we reach having rejoined the main road north, was planned, with its surviving wide streets, by the Wandesford family after they had settled in 1635. It suffered in the '98 and, though pretty, has little left of interest. The Wandesfords exploited the local mines, and smokeless anthracite was till recently produced. We turn left in the town for **Ballyragget**, six miles away. The tower, still roofed, is of a castle built by a Butler of the sixteenth century. Half a mile beyond the village we turn off left to reach Freshford in five miles. Here the eighteenth-century C of I parish church incorporates a fine Romanesque doorway from the monastery first founded by St Lachtan in the seventh century. The appearance of inward lean of the pillars is an obvious characteristic of these Romanesque doorways, but so are the four or five richly carved orders which this lacks. Also unusual is the figured frieze at the top of each outer pilaster. Eight miles west, after turning right in Freshford, we come to Urlingford and, three miles south-south-west (we could, with a map, make a short-cut from the Freshford road) to the remains of the small Cistercian Abbey of **Kilcooly**. It is, characteristically, in a lovely setting of trees at the foot of the Slieve Ardagh Hills and beside a lake. Founded about 1180, with monks from Jerpoint, by Donal O'Brien, King of Thomond (an area that comprised more or less Co. Clare, north of the Shannon estuary), it was destroyed in the mid-fifteenth century and partly rebuilt and enlarged soon after. Inside are several curiosities – the tomb of Piers Butler of Clonamicklon, and his parents and son, with an excellent effigy of a mail-clad knight, and inscrutable apostle figures on the side (the family's ruined, gabled castle is two miles south-west); several other tombs; and some intriguing carvings in the south transept, including a Crucifixion, a St Christopher, and a mermaid pointing invitingly at two fishes. Mermaids are often represented with St Christopher, symbolising the snares in store for the honest traveller. In this carving the dubiously sensual mermaid is trying to entice the fish, which have represented Christians since early churchmen found the initials of the Greek for 'Jesus Christ, son of God' formed the Greek word for fish – ichthus. Outside the abbey is a rounded, corbelled dovecot, doubly useful to farming Cistercians who thereby could have fresh meat in late winter when there was no other available, and could use the lime to improve their soils.

TEMPLEMORE – BORRISOLEIGH – THURLES –
HOLY CROSS

A main road leads direct from Urlingford to Cashel, the romantic, much visited capital of the Kings of Munster, its rock standing prominent for miles in the plain where the Devil spewed it out. But we can turn off the road a few miles before to see **Longfield House**, the home, open to the public, of a man who did as much as anyone in the nineteenth century to open up the country, Charles Bianconi, entrepreneur of the once famous Bianconi cars. Born in Lombardy in 1786 he came to Dublin at the turn of the century as a travelling salesman in cheap prints which he framed himself. By 1815 he had dropped the prints and simply sold travel. His horse-drawn side-cars, starting with the short run between Clonmel and Cahir, soon linked up with the rapidly growing canal services, and before he died covered four thousand miles. By that time, however, the railways were well established, the canals declining, and his virtual monopoly of the Irish road transport system had ceased. The cost to passengers was twopence a mile. The house was built about 1770 by Richard Long, British ambassador to an Indian prince. The last of the Longs was murdered, in the 1820s, supposedly while sitting on the garden lavatory. Bianconi's descendants lived in it till 1968. The last of them in 1962 wrote a book here about her ancestor by the light of an oil-lamp, neither electricity nor central heating being then installed. Following her death, and after a period as a hotel, it reverted to private ownership.

Cashel, in one sense, is a sharp fold of limestone standing a hundred feet above the plain that surrounds it. King Cormac had his Munster capital here in the fourth century, and it became a Christian centre in the fifth, when its king was converted by St Patrick. The saint is said to have spiked his crozier by accident through the king's foot during the baptism, which the monarch took to be a partial re-enactment of the Crucifixion and necessary to the ceremony. Brian Boru was crowned King of Munster here in 977, but maintained his court at Kincora beside Lough Derg, and in 1101 the O'Briens gave the land to the Church. Here in 1127 Cormac MacCarthy, King of Desmond, began to build the little Romanesque church now known as Cormac's Chapel. A cathedral was begun beside this in 1169 and here, two years later, the assembled clergy of Ireland did homage first to Strongbow, then to Henry II himself. Within another hundred years the cathedral was pulled down to make way for that whose shell now dominates the rock – one of the few still standing in Ireland whose dimensions match those of Gothic cathedrals in Britain or the Continent.

In 1495 Garret More, the 'Great' Earl of Kildare and most powerful leader in the country, rebelled against the colonial rule of Sir Edward Poynings, Henry VII's stern viceroy, whose 'Law' once more curtailed native liberties. In the course of his campaign he set fire to Cashel Cathedral, without dire result. Arrested, he explained to the king: 'he thought the archbishop was in it'. 'All Ireland cannot rule this man!' shouted a priest who stood by. 'Then he shall rule all Ireland,' Henry is said to have replied, in one of those reports that make all medieval kings and bishops sound like Oscar Wilde. As it was, Kildare was freed and for the future exercised his influence in the king's favour. More serious damage was done in 1647 by the parliamentarian General Murrough O'Brien, Earl of Inchiquin. When he had done with the place, according to an eye-witness, the altar, steps, chapels, sacristies, seats and numerous passages were piled with the dead.

After Inchiquin's assault, the cathedral fell into disuse. It was restored later in the century, but in the eighteenth, at the instance of Archbishop Agar, ancestor of the Earls of Normanton, who disliked having to climb the hill, the lead roof was removed and the see transferred to St John the Baptist's church in the town. A hundred years later a storm brought down some parts of the buildings which, in 1869, some time after the horse had bolted, were handed over to be preserved by the State.

The entrance to the enclosure is to the left of the fifteenth-century Hall of Vicars Choral, laymen endowed with church lands who helped in chanting the services. A High Cross of the eleventh century, on a carved plinth of the same date (and so *not* the Munster kings' coronation stone, though the mound on which it stands may be the site) has a worn full-length Crucifixion on one side and St Patrick on the other, unlike the complex contents of other crosses. The cathedral is of a simple cruciform pattern, with side chapels on the east of both transepts; the choir is twice as long as the simple aisle-less nave. There are some interesting details – a cross-legged sheila-na-gig (making one incline more to the belief that these curiously obscene little carvings are warnings against lechery than that they carry on some pre-Christian fertility cult), some coats of arms, beasts of the Apocalypse, apostles, several other rather cryptic reliefs, and the tomb of Myler McGrath, Cashel's bishop under Queen Elizabeth, and a notorious pluralist and denominational turncoat. On the north-east corner, adjoining the cathedral, is a round tower, ninety-two feet high and complete after a recent restoration (it was damaged by lightning in 1965). The west end of the nave leads, through a splendid door, into the archbishops' castle, a fourteenth-century addition, with thick walls riddled with passages, whose windows give good views of the country around. On the other, south-east side, cramped between the cathedral and south transept, is the Rock's main treasure and original cathedral, Cormac's chapel.

It is one thing to abstract the features common to Irish Romanesque architecture – the transient style that flourished through the twelfth century before it gave way to Gothic in the next: the high, steeply pitched roofs, the arched windows and doorways with their four, five, or more elaborately carved orders. Or to trace, as is possible, the connection of these features with buildings at Ratisbon, Cologne, and other Rhineland centres where Irish monks had been established since the seventh century or earlier. But it is quite another to pick out the qualities that give the style its individual genius. There seems to be an unsystematic, almost perverse whimsy about essentially Celtic Irish creations, be they book illuminations, jewellery or churches. They are the products more of instinct than of evolved style and as such have died away without greatly influencing the styles that came after. Celtic artists were in a sense rather feminine, going about their creation with a confident intuition. That the western nave arches are off-centre to the chancel, the south tower less massive than the north, the details of design and decoration sited without regard for symmetry – almost with the simple purpose of filling up blank spaces – in every way enhances the building. Even if some of the irregularities resulted from changing needs during the course of building, the way they have been carried out are evidence enough of genius. At the same time this skill in conception goes with a very thorough mastery of technique. For a heavy stone roof to have remained at such an acute angle for nearly nine hundred years shows that; and the barrel vault and corbelling bear it out. It is only sad that other examples of the style only survive in arches and doorways, the body having long ago crumbled. At Cashel, almost alone, one can look on the complete work of art.

The most memorable views of Cashel can be from below, looking from any direction at this outcrop of nature and human inspiration, warmly set in its Tipperary green. Below, too, there are other sights to see in the town. There are ruins of a Dominican priory – other orders followed as Cashel became an ecclesiastical capital; fragments of the fourteenth-century city wall; fifteenth-century Grant's Castle, now a hotel; the eighteenth-century C of I cathedral with a later west front and tower by Richard Morrison; the badly embellished Catholic parish church of St John, on the site of a thirteenth-century Franciscan friary; and the beautiful red brick-fronted Cashel Palace, designed by Sir Edward Lovett Pearce. Oddly, the rear of the building is entirely of stone. It has a fine interior, with the original pine-panelled hall and staircase, and the larger downstairs rooms redecorated in the early nineteenth century, after damage during the 1798 rebellion, with Regency cornices and dadoes. Formerly the Archbishop's Palace, the building was sold by the church in 1962 and restored as a hotel. West of the town are the picturesque ruins of Hore Abbey, originally Benedictine, altered in 1266 for the Cistercians. It is best seen from the Rock.

To our west is Tipperary town, not much of a town, with

the Golden Vale stretching away to the north-west, between
the Galty Mountains and Slieve Felim, and to the south-east
as far as the Comeraghs. But on this route we shall drive due
east, veer south-east and return after Fethard to the Suir,
which we shall follow to Waterford Harbour – the estuary it
shares with its sister rivers the Nore and Barrow. Where the
road bends right, five miles from Cashel, we pass within a
mile of **Knockbrit**, the birthplace (in 1789) of Marguerite
Power, the spirited Countess of Blessington. Her years at
Knockbrit and – from the age of 8 – at Clonmel were tragic.
Her squalid, squandering father was a vicious Catholic
turned Castle agent whose function was to indict his former
friends. He married her to a local wastrel, Captain Farmer,
whose physical cruelty drove her – not yet sixteen – to leave
him after three months. In 1809 she went to England and
later (after her first husband died in a debtor's gaol) married
the Earl of Blessington. From then on her repressed talents
were released. Before the earl's death in 1829 the couple
drained his fortune in Continental travel and as cynosures of
society. After, living in London with the Comte D'Orsay
(estranged husband of her stepdaughter), she wrote essays,
articles, memoirs and novels to pay the heavy costs of enter-
taining all and patronising many of the artistic and social
talents of her day. When the two of them could pay no longer
they left for Paris, hoping Napoleon III, whom they had
helped, would reward the count with office. He did not, and
the count died bankrupt, and she of apoplexy in 1849.

On our left the land is for miles scattered with raths,
mounds and other prehistoric remains. In front rises the
2,368-foot sandstone hill of **Slievenamon** – Mount of the
Women of Finn. Finn McCool, a close parallel and perhaps
predecessor in Celtic myth of King Arthur in English, used
to exercise his little band of warriors, the Fenians (much like
Arthur's Round Table Knights) on the hill. And here, faced
with the necessity of choosing a wife he did it ostensibly by
competitive examination. All the girls who wanted him were
to run up the hill, he sitting on top, and the first to reach
him would win. In secret he knew whom he wanted, and
carried Grania, daughter of Cormac MacArt, to the top the

night before; and so they were betrothed. Later came a disastrous sequel. Finn's close friend Dermot had a beauty spot on his cheek, seeing which any woman fell in love with him. Grania saw and fell. The story of their fatal elopement is told elsewhere.

Fethard is a quiet charming place that turns its back on progress, preserving a few remains of castles and an Augustinian friary. A good diversion can be made two and a half miles east to sixteenth-century Knockelly Castle, the finest of many ruins round here, set on a hill and looking a little like a walled town in southern France.

Risings of the last two centuries before British rule ended can easily confuse the visitor unfamiliar with Irish names and history. (It is extraordinary how little of Irish history is taught in British schools, when it is considered that hardly a single well-known Englishman of the last two centuries did not owe some of his experience, wealth, blood or position to Irish connections or services.) A short-lived one took place in this neighbourhood. In 1848, hundreds of thousands were starving, and still the abundant corn and wheat harvest (only potatoes had failed) was being sent to England to be marketed and fill the pockets of landlords who lived there anyway. The Young Ireland party, ancestor of all subsequent forces for the complete and violent secession of Ireland, directed at the time by a hitherto peaceable landlord called William Smith O'Brien, then raised their standard in tragicomic isolation. Such action as there was took place mainly within a few miles of where we are. On 26th July, with two comrades (most had deserted; a feature of many Irish risings has been that, on the morrow of the call to arms, honest rebels have been loath to inconvenience their employers, and so returned to work), O'Brien advanced to Mullinahone (ten miles east of Fethard) police barracks and called on the occupants to surrender. The constables were cooking breakfast. They asked him kindly to collect more men, to make their surrender less dishonourable to them. He went, and returned to find them fled, with the arms, to a stronger place. The only real action took place on 5th August between thirty-five rebels and a garrison of police, in the garden of the

Widow McCormack, one mile outside Ballingarry (twelve miles north-east of Fethard: the house still stands). The widow cried, O'Brien parleyed with the police, stones were thrown, and shots were fired. A few insurgents fell, the rest hid or fled. O'Brien faced the enemy – 'An O'Brien never turned his back on an enemy' – then fled too. Picked up later, his death sentence at Clonmel was commuted to exile in Tasmania, from which he returned years later to die in Wales.

The Suir has grown to full size, with islands and excellent riverside walks, and a spot where Lady Blessington used to bathe, where we rejoin it at **Clonmel**, capital of the South Riding of Tipperary. (A riding is from the Norse for third; Tipperary has but two, with Nenagh the northern capital). This is one of the largest inland towns in Ireland with a population over eleven thousand, and several flourishing industries. Laurence Sterne was born here, though he spent only a few boyhood years in Ireland, where his father was a soldier. George Borrow lived here for a while, again as a boy, but long enough to learn Irish. Trollope served for a time in the post office; and Bianconi's coaches began from the coach-house at Hearn's Hotel. Founded by a De Burgo in the early thirteenth century, the town passed to the Desmond FitzGeralds, then the Ormondes . The Confederates met here in 1647, and three years later Cromwell arrived on his westerly progress. Under Hugh O'Neill, Owen Roe's nephew, the garrison – 'the stoutest enemy this army had ever met with in Ireland' according to the Ironsides – first repulsed Cromwell, killing 1500 of his men. The inmates escaped that night, and next day the town had to surrender. The operation was carried out with such skill that Cromwell, thinking the town still strong, conceded more generous terms than he allowed others.

O'Connell Street, the main thoroughfare, runs east–west and close to the river. At one end is the **West Gate**, built in 1831 on the site of the medieval one; and at the other the Main Guard, which began as the Court of the Palatinate of Ormonde, later became Tholsel and assize court, and was spoiled last century by a row of shops built into its open ground-floor gallery. The Town Hall, farther on, is modern; beyond that, to the right is the Court House by Sir Richard Morrison, where William Smith O'Brien was sentenced in 1848. The Franciscan friary and St Mary's parish church are both nineteenth century, incorporating interesting parts and details of earlier churches, especially a Butler double effigy in the Franciscan churchyard. Clonmel is headquarters of the Tipperary foxhounds, and well known for its greyhound racing, which being a national institution of growing popularity deserves both a visit (several towns have stadiums) and a moment's attention here.

Dogs have always been important in Ireland. In Roman times the vast, fast Irish wolfhound was exported to the empire and used in the games at Rome; 'all Rome viewed them with wonder and thought they must have been brought hither in iron cages.' In those days they were usually white, and sometimes dyed; blue was a favourite colour, and a white body with purple ears are on record. St Patrick is said to have escaped from boy-slavery in Ireland among a cargo of dogs bound for the Continent. As long as Ireland was beset with wolves, till the eighteenth century, these agile giants (Edmund Campion in 1571 said they were bigger than colts) were bred intensively to catch them, and pedigree specimens were sold all over the world. Then they declined. Export and inactivity did for them in the nineteenth century. But in 1863 an English breeder reconstituted the strain and managed to restore it to fame and the international status it still enjoys. Not among the Irish, however, who respect its memory – it appeared on the sixpenny piece and as the stamp of Belleek China – but enthuse nowadays about that sleek racer, the greyhound. Hundreds of pounds are nightly won and lost on betting, and a large proportion of farmers keep and train the dogs to enter them for the stakes. Here at Clonmel, the Irish Coursing Club has its headquarters by the stadium east of the town in Davis Road. The National Coursing meeting is held nearby early in February.

Davis Road leads out of town and in two miles we come to Two-Mile Bridge, just to the north of which is the unexpected and thoroughly diverting spectacle of the **Falconry of Ireland**,

one of the few of its kind in the world. A German, Ernst
one of the few of its kind in the world. A German, Ernst
Jocher, started it in 1966. On entering, it takes a moment or
two to notice the presence of several massive birds of prey,
tethered to pedestals with perching drums on top, each outside
its own conical hut. There is a Black Vulture, the world's
largest flying bird; a Golden Eagle, a not altogether trust-
worthy bird, which can live to the age of 100, and various owls,
kites, kestrels, buzzards and others. Falcons by definition
include all species which attack and kill with the beak; hawks on
the other hand use their talons. All replacements for the falconry
have to be captured since they are virtually incapable of
breeding in captivity. Falconry itself is one of the world's oldest
sports, and has a lineage in Ireland at least back to Norse days.
Kildare, Wicklow and Meath were considered good hawking
country in late medieval times, since when the activity has
declined, but Clonmel's falconry may herald a revival. There are
daily demonstrations, which can be exciting, and a very decent
bar and restaurant.

   Two miles farther east the road forks and instead of going
straight on to Carrick we can turn left, and three miles later
left again towards the foothills to see the picturesque ruin
of **Kilcash** Castle, once a Butler stronghold, in ruins since
1800, with an old church beside. The church has a Romanesque
south doorway and was for a while in the hands of the
Knights Hospitaller, an order dedicated to the liberation and
guarding of the Holy Land, through funds collected from
estates it owned in Europe. Various metal objects were
stolen from it in 1848 to be forged into bullets for O'Brien's
Young Ireland rising. In the castle James, Earl of Castle-
haven, whom we meet all over the south fighting for the
Catholic Confederates in the 1640s, wrote his memoirs,
which understandably omit his strange boyhood. His father,
Mervyn Touchet, was beheaded in 1631 for what are called
in *Burke's Peerage* 'certain high crimes'. These included a
series of carnal frolics involving Mervyn, his second wife,
his stepdaughter, and at least seven of his servants in most
imaginable combinations in the lordly bed (mainly in Wiltshire but for a while in Co. Down too). In the course of

these young James, scarcely a teenager and kept in ignorance of the family pastimes, was married to his sullied stepsister. When he found out, he wrote his findings to the king, and justice was shortly done. By his soldiering James somewhat redeemed the family name, and the title his father forfeited was restored to him. It died out the following century.

Buried in the Butler mausoleum in the church is Margaret Butler, widow of the Jacobite Viscount Iveagh. She, after the Boyne, protected hunted Catholics from the English and earned the tribute 'The spot where that lady waited, who shamed all women for grace . . .' in a famous Gaelic poem. Returning to the T13 we follow the course of the River Suir eastward, with the wooded slopes of the Comeraghs on the right. Just before Kilsheelan the castellated towers and gables of Gurteen le Poer rise romantically from a beautiful and bosky demesne. This is the ancestral home of the De la Poers (formerly Power; in 1863 they, like many others, reverted to the Norman form of their name, moved by the same passion for medievalism which inspired the courtly, chivalric echoes of this 1868 house). Much of the family's vast territory in County Waterford went, through marriage in 1717, to the Beresfords, later Marquesses of Waterford.

The Suir valley abounds throughout its length in grand Ascendancy houses. Two miles before Carrick we pass on the right the site of Coolnamuck. A story tells that a family which once owned it, having lost their money through extravagance, packed into their coach and drove it over the cliffs at Tramore. **Carrick-on-Suir** is a pleasant town with a well-preserved Butler manor house of 1584 standing beside an older Butler keep overlooking the river. This older castle has been claimed, but so have other sites, as the birthplace of Anne Boleyn, whose grandfather was a Butler. The manor was built by the tenth Earl of Ormonde to entertain her daughter, Queen Elizabeth, but she never came. It is one of the loveliest Tudor remains in the country, and contains Ireland's earliest stucco work, with many armorials and busts of the expected queen. It has been well restored, and now houses a museum. There is little of specific interest in the town, though the memoirs of Dorothea Herbert, a parson's daughter, paint a charming picture of

Protestant provincial life (and her own frustrated love) at the end of the eighteenth century.

A diversion from Carrick takes us due north by the L26. In three miles (one mile beyond Whitechurch, with its C of I church in an ancient enclosure), we pass on the right the entrance to **Castletown House** (often called Castletown Cox, from the name of the first owner, to distinguish it from others). Like its Kildare namesake, it is one of the finest houses in the country, designed in 1767 by Davis Ducart, a Sardinian (whose other work survives in Co. Cork, the city of Limerick, and additions to Florence Court in Fermanagh). Arcaded wings on either side of the main block lead to domed pavilions set forward from the house, and the whole is rich in detail. There is good plasterwork inside, but the house – built for the Archbishop of Cashel of the time – is closed to the public.

Farther along the same road we come to **Ahenny**, on the left, where among the broken gravestones and trees of the churchyard are two very fine high crosses and the base of a third. The worn carvings are still in the main quite recognis- able – animals, monks, some on horseback, a procession of monks carrying a dead body, Daniel in the lions' den, and a typical selection of abstract motifs. These crosses, and several others in the district, belong to the earliest period of cross-building, and may date from the eighth century. The south cross in particular has a wide area of interlacing coils spaced with raised bosses which very much recalls the twisted silver, gold or bronze work with inset gems to be found on Irish metal bowls, ornaments and so on, of the time. There are less distinguished crosses at Killamery, six miles north- north-west, Kilkieran, a mile south, and Tibberaghny, beside the Suir between Carrick and Fiddown. A wide variety of prehistoric objects in the locality and for several miles around point to continual occupation from earliest times.

South of the Suir and on the right of Carrick as we return rise the joined ranges of the Comeragh Mountains and beyond them the Monavullaghs, that together form a beautiful range of cliff-edged Old Red Sandstone. The action of ice and snow in the glacial period is well seen on the eastern side of the mountains, where it has in its descent clawed out precipices from the heads of glens, piling up moraine below and so forming huge deep tarns. **Coomshingaun**, a mile from the main Carrick–Dungarvan road and six hundred feet above it, is the most spectacular of these. A rough path leads up to it from the point where the valley stream reaches the road, through furzy fields in which the little popping sounds in summer are gorse pods bursting to scatter their seeds. The tarn itself, of unknown depth (and associated in local folklore with irresistible currents, evil spirits and the like) is a mile long broadening at the far end as the surrounding cliffs rise spectacularly to a thousand feet over the water. There is a fairly demanding walk along the south side, up a gully that leads off to the left and round the cliffs above the head of the lake. From here the highest point of the Comeraghs is a mile west. One can return down the more gentle slope of the north side, and so back to the road.

Returning to Carrick we cover the four miles east to **Piltown**. This was the site of an important battle in 1462 between the Ormonde Butlers and Desmond FitzGeralds, one of many clashes between these two dominant families of Munster. The pretext was different sympathies in the English Wars of the Roses – Butler supporting Lancastrians and Desmond York. Thomas, Earl of Desmond, won the battle, after which, the Four Masters recorded, 'there were four hundred and ten of the slain of his people interred, besides the number who were devoured by the dogs and birds of prey'. Desmond emerged, for a while, the most powerful man in Ireland.

East of Piltown is the large demesne of **Bessborough House**, which after being burned down in the Civil War in 1923 has been taken over and rebuilt by the Oblate Fathers. Built originally in 1744 by Francis Bindon, it was till this century the seat of the Ponsonbys, Earls of Bessborough – a family that gave the world two remarkable women: Lady Caroline Lamb, daughter of the third earl, who married Lord Melbourne and had a traumatic affaire with Byron in 1813; and Sarah Ponsonby, the first earl's great-niece, who betook herself with Lady Eleanor Butler to Plas Newydd, in

Llangollen, Wales, where the two of them lived long lives in mutual devotion, wore men's clothes, and entertained Scott, Wordsworth, De Quincey and the Duke of Wellington himself. The fourth Earl of Bessborough was Lord Lieutenant during the Great Famine in 1846. The sham castle in the grounds was being erected as a memorial to a Ponsonby presumed killed in the Napoleonic wars. He returned unexpectedly and building was stopped midway.

Two miles farther towards Waterford, **Fiddown Chapel** is set prettily in an overgrown churchyard beside the road. On the other side is a lovely stretch of the river with a long island dividing the stream. The chapel is the mausoleum of the Ponsonby family, adapted from the chancel of a thirteenth-century church. Recently restored by the Irish Georgian Society, it boasts some splendid Bessborough monuments of the early eighteenth century, cleanly classical memorials set against the white background of this sequestered gem. Across the long bridge is the beautifully set village of **Portlaw**. It was founded in the early nineteenth century as a model village for their cotton mill workers by the Quaker family of Malcolmson. The village with its tanneries does not detain us, but the beautiful adjacent demesne of **Curraghmore**, seat of the Beresford family, Marquesses of Waterford, does. The grounds are open on Thursday afternoons. The house itself is mainly eighteenth century but built around a central tower that dates from the twelfth, when Robert Le Poer was granted the surrounding lands by Henry II and made a governor of Ireland jointly with Hugh de Lacy. The Powers, as they became, held most of Co. Waterford till 1717 (in Cromwell's time the fifth Lord Le Poer survived changes of government by going mad). Then the only surviving daughter of the family, Catherine, married Sir Marcus Beresford of a Co. Derry family. It was he who had Curraghmore built as it is, as well as Tyrone House in Dublin. His son (one of thirteen, besides at least two illegitimate sons, one of whom became a general and the other an admiral) was made first Marquess of Waterford, and his descendants – for generations distinguished in the horse-racing world – still live in the house.

Other descendants of Sir Marcus had their effect. His son

John became Commissioner of the Irish Revenue, an architect of the 1800 Act of Union and one of the most hated men in Ireland. Between 1822 and 1885 two successive Beresfords were Archbishops of Armagh and Primates of Ireland.

The house has a long entrance courtyard flanked by low wings. With the tower straight ahead, it has a smack of Blenheim about it, and its architectural ancestry can be traced to Vanbrugh. The actual designer was John Roberts of Waterford. His inspiration is said to have come from Vanbrugh's other palace, Seaton Delaval, in Northumberland. Inside, James Wyatt decorated many of the rooms in the 1780s, and there is earlier plasterwork by the Francinis, and Angelica Kauffman or her husband, Antonio Zucchi, did the ceiling roundels in the dining-room. There is also a magnificent collection of pictures, including Reynolds, Gainsborough and Lawrence, and Astley's portrait of the whole family – eleven of them – painted in about 1760; possibly the largest family portrait in Ireland.

The formal gardens, supposedly laid out to the plans of Versailles, are beautifully set among a vast demesne of woods and with the dramatic background of the Comeraghs. Among the trees is that far from unique specimen, the tallest tree in Ireland – a Sitka Spruce of 156 feet. On the right is a shell-house, the shells put up by Lady Catherine in 261 days of 1754. And inside is a charming statue of her by John van Nost.

Ten miles east of Portlaw lies the city of **Waterford**. We can go north or south of the river, though the northern route allows us to see the broken tower and walls, overlooking the river and Waterford's port, of Granny Castle, two miles west of the town itself. Originally a Le Poer castle, later an Ormonde, it was reduced to its present state by Cromwell, but the thirteenth-century leftovers, with an isolated oriel window, make a romantic ruin.

Waterford is a great meeting-place of historical paths, and it may be the want of any knowledge of this that lets some people pass through the town unmoved and disappointed. It certainly does not give of its best to those who keep to the main through-roads. Behind the wide streets are narrow ones,

hedged with old buildings and historical links that, if they
were not a microcosm of Irish history, might suggest a
Continental town – so used does one get in Ireland to spacious
city layouts. Its first foundation was in 914, by the Vikings,
who came, according to the chronicles, in 'immense floods
and countless sea-vomitings of ships and boats and fleets so
that there was not a harbour nor a land-post nor a dun nor a
fastness in all Munster without floods of Danes and pirates'.
They walled the town, and, after a century, had settled,
turned Christian, and come to depend on the Irish as the
Irish did on them. In 1096, the Norse bishop of Waterford
was consecrated by the Archbishop of Canterbury, but
within seventy-five years the settlement's security was dashed
by the Anglo-Normans' arrival. Their advance guard had
already opened up parts of Wexford when Strongbow, Earl
of Pembroke, landed at Passage East, in Waterford Harbour,
pushed on to the city and after a day of bloody fighting made
the town his own. He promptly claimed the fee due to him,
Eva the daughter of Dermot MacMurrough, who had persuaded him to come, and was married to her in 1170 in the
surviving, though heavily restored, Reginald's Tower. He
then began his effective march north. Three years later
Henry II arrived at Waterford before a triumphal progress
through his new possessions. In 1487 it opposed the Yorkist
pretender, Lambert Simnel, after Henry VII had come to the
English throne. Simnel was crowned Edward VI in Dublin, a
boy of 10, who cannot be supposed to have been the main
force behind his own elevation. In his successful progress
through Ireland Waterford – the only town against him –
managed to survive a six-week siege. In the event Simnel
fought and lost in England, and was deposed to the rank of
kitchen servant. A second siege of twelve days followed in
1495, during Perkin Warbeck's abortive rising. For its double
resistance, the king rewarded Waterford with the motto
Urbs intacta manet.

It remained vainly loyal after Cromwell came in 1649. At
first, its stubborn resistance to his siege broke the spell of
instant conquest that Cromwell had earned. Ireton took
almost all the rest of Munster before he finally broke into

Waterford in August, 1650, giving honourable terms to its citizens. James II, fleeing, passed through the town in 1690, but it yielded to the Williamites soon after. It later shielded a Huguenot influx from France, but in the eighteenth century its significance was small – the elegant cathedral city of a county known for its wealth and the beauty of its Anglo-Irish demesnes.

It also began to manufacture glass, one of many towns to do so. The best period was from the late seventeen-eighties to the early years of the nineteenth century, and examples of its work then, displayed in museums and halls in various parts of Ireland, have an exquisite, minutely opaque quality far removed from the modern products. The factory closed in 1861, and remained closed till 1947. There are now two factories in the town which between them employ 1,200 people but are still a long way from keeping up with orders which swamp them from all parts of the world. A visit is repaid by the splendid, almost medieval sight of busy bare-armed craftsmen deftly shaping, blowing, swinging and appraising all manner of glass forms against a background of glowing furnaces, constant noise, and bustle. All the stages from fashioning the molten glass to the cutting and polishing are seen, and it is possible to glimpse the magnificent specimens of old glass preserved in the building.

A tour of the town could begin at **Reginald's Tower**, built in the twelfth or thirteenth century at the north-east corner of the town walls. The tourist office is downstairs and a museum above. This contains a remarkable collection of town charters from Tudor times on, with the signatures of the sovereigns and illuminated miniatures depicting them above the curvy script. These are in the room where Strong-bow's marriage allegedly took place. There is a tavern beside the tower which incorporates, in an incongruous décor, bits of the city wall.

The **quays,** described in the eighteenth century as the best in Europe, stretch nearly a mile along the Suir. Opposite are precipitous heights with a golf-course and parkland on top, giving good views of the town. The quays, with their railway trucks, ships, wharves and cranes are much more integral to

the city than Dublin's. Behind the buildings, intriguing byways
and sidepaths, with tall crumbling houses of four floors lead off
narrow streets. Among these are the **French Church,** on the site
of a Franciscan Friary whose tower, nave and chancel remain:
and the C of I **Christ Church Cathedral,** built in the 1770s by
John Roberts, whose work is scattered in Waterford as that of
the Pain brothers is in Cork. (It was later twice damaged by
fire and restored in 1891 by Sir Thomas Drew, who also reconstructed St Patrick's Cathedral, Dublin.) The cathedral, with
its strange stepped steeple at the west end, and baroque under-
parts, and the lovely surround provided by the Bishop's Palace
and Deanery, is most impressive. The spacious interior contains
a good selection of plaques, monuments and *memento moris,* of
which the most imposing is that of James Rice, six times
mayor of the town during the difficult York – Lancaster
struggles. His scrawny figure lies atop the decorated sarco-
phagus with worms coiling in and out of his ribs and a frog
at his vitals. (Frogs have an odd connection with Waterford.
Giraldus reports that they were unknown in Ireland till the
Conquest because 'the mud does not contain the seeds from
which green frogs are born'. Then one was found near the
city. 'The English, and more so the Irish, regarded it with
great wonder till the King of Ossory, a man of great wisdom,
with a great shaking of his head and sorrow in his heart,
said "that reptile brings very bad news to Ireland",' which
was taken to foretell the complete conquest.) There is also
a collection of old books and signatures – of Wentworth,
the Great Earl of Cork, Archbishop Ussher and others – on
display. At the entrance is a memorial tablet to an English
lieutenant who in 1799 'volunteered his service in Ireland To
repel an Invading enemy and suppress rebellion.' It makes
an odd but familiar antithesis to the gravestones of Catholic
fighters within a mile of the cathedral, likewise praised but
for fighting on the other side.

The **Catholic Cathedral** is off the quays, in Barronstrand
Street. It, too, most curiously, was built by Roberts, supposedly with funds collected as alms on the steps: but it is in direct
contrast to Christ Church, with heavy pillars, oppressive
expanse of ceiling, and a late dull Corinthian façade. It was

built in its humble setting in Penal times, on land granted by a Protestant corporation. The west front long remained incomplete for want of funds, and its design cannot be blamed on Roberts.

In O'Connell Street, running parallel to the quays, is the fine old **Chamber of Commerce**, once a private house, again by Roberts. It has a beautiful oval, cantilevered staircase and excellent carving within. The **Mall,** leading south-west from Reginald's Tower, has some exceptional Georgian houses, with their essentially Irish fanlights above the doors. Beyond them is Roberts's City Hall, of 1782, containing two pretty theatres, a magnificent old Waterford chandelier and dinner service, other relics and some rather fustian portraits of Waterford and national notables. The theatres house the annual Festival of Light Music, held in late October. Among the relics are some connected with Thomas Francis Meagher, a Young Irelander, and participant in O'Brien's 1848 rising who, condemned to death, escaped to America to win military honours and become Governor of Montana. In the public park opposite is the stolid Court House of 1849, by Terence O'Reilly. It replaces one by James Gandon, who also built the local gaol.

*

Before driving out of town to the east, and so beginning the round of the Waterford coastline, it is worth making the five-mile excursion west to **Mount Congreve,** an early eighteenth-century house (recently extensively refaced and remodelled) off the road to Kilmacthomas. The gardens and woods, over-looking the Suir, are open to the public. The gardens are well known for their spring bulb flowers, rhododendrons and azaleas, the walled gardens for herbaceous and shrub borders.

To the east of Waterford, keeping south of the river, the road leads to Passage East. A diversion to the left leads to Cheekpoint, a hill of 436 feet with excellent views of the town, the various mountain ranges, Dunbrody Abbey to the east and to the south Waterford Harbour – triple estuary of the Suir, Barrow and Nore. **Passage East** is a precipitous little harbour village, most of its gaily painted houses set low and with steep climbs all round. It seems almost too cosy for its

romantic name. It was here that Strongbow landed, content
with the work of his advance parties, to claim, like a fairy
prince in this one respect, the hand of a princess and rights
to a kingdom; and here that Henry II followed him, to
confirm himself at the top of the feudal tree. Crooke, a mile
south, is possibly what gave rise to Cromwell's 'By Hook or by
Crooke'; and was duly occupied by Ireton in 1649. On another
mile, we pass **Geneva Barracks,** where in 1783 the government,
pleased with the influence on the economy of German immigrants in Limerick, and Huguenots and Quakers elsewhere, encouraged Swiss Huguenots to settle, planning a
new city and university. The plan aborted, and the place is
famous for a different episode. The Croppy Boy, a '98 rebel,
came here to confess, but the supposed priest was an army
captain in a cassock, who arrested the boy and had him
hanged. **Woodstown** farther on has a broad shallow sand-
beach, a regency villa once rented by Jacqueline Kennedy,
and like other delectable parts of this coast is free from crowds,
which are only slightly more in evidence at **Dunmore East,**
an anglers' resort delightfully set but beginning to develop,
probably because of its small-port activity. From the hill
behind is an amazing view, neatly combining geology with
aesthetics, of the estuary. The road from here to Tramore is
set back from the sea, the land between being an undulating
duney strip indented with deep bays, stretching out to
Brownstown Head, one of the cusps of Tramore Bay.

   Tramore itself has been a resort since Georgian days, when
George III and his son the Prince Regent made the sea
popular for the first time (a little later Coleridge and the
lake poets took to climbing mountains, so redeeming them
from centuries of dark superstition). People came from as
far as Dublin then, and now from still farther. The length of
the beach, which after half a mile of promenade goes on for
miles along a salt-marsh spit that almost cuts off the inner
part of the bay, prevents it from ever becoming overcrowded,
even during its September festival. It has a caravan park,
amusement arcade, seafood bars, putting green, and other
resort trappings. At the points of Tramore Bay a series of
five tall enigmatic stacks are in fact warnings – or land-based

buoys – erected in Napoleon's time to distinguish the shallow
bay from the navigable Waterford Harbour. The central of
the western ones, from the painted iron statue of a sailor on
it, is known as the Metal Man, and the girl who hops three
times round the base of his pedestal, always keeping one foot
off the ground, will allegedly marry in a year. The walk here
is magnificent, with good views of the coastal cliffs and the
sight, in early summer, of large colonies of sea-birds.

This type of coastal scenery accompanies us for the twenty
miles or so to Dungarvan. There are some rare plants hereabouts and a great wealth of common ones, and villages and
hamlets nestle at the outlets of several rivers. One such is
Annestown, another **Bunmahon**, which has the usual good
beach and small population – both of natives and trippers.
It also has an Irish Language College. There are plenty of
quiet coves for good bathing from rocks. In this neighbourhood there are a number of disused copper mines, which
were worked in the nineteenth century to a depth of 800 feet
below sea level. Most of the labour came from Cornwall,
'the Irish having no great taste for it', according to a contemporary. Irishmen were more easily found to work in the
diving bells, rates of pay being much better. **Kilmacthomas**,
five miles inland from here, was the birthplace in 1797 of
Tyrone Power, actor and comedian. Among his great-
grandsons were his namesake film-star, and the director
Tyrone Guthrie, who lived till his death in 1971 in Co.
Monaghan.

Two changes come over the coast along this stretch. The
high soft grass of Wexford and East Waterford is giving way
gradually to heath and moorland, a wetter climate creating
and maintaining the bog. The climate is the second change.
West of the Monavullagh Mountains, that tail down to the
sea east of Dungarvan, rainfall rises. It is, of course, by a
gradual scale that Dublin's annual twenty inches or so – a
good ten less than Bath's – rise to the forty, sixty, or even
eighty sometimes falling on the top of west coast mountains.
Here, anyway, a jump in that scale is noticeable. The compensation is the warmth of Irish rain; a dowsing to the skin
hardly ever means a chill; and the clarity of light, that with

its bluish tinge in the distance makes outlines starker and
colours bolder. Rain means, besides, cloud. One should make
a mental note to bear clouds in mind when first one steps on
Irish soil, simply for the endless and beautiful variations they
make to the landscape.

Stradbally, four miles on, has another pleasant cove, whose
owner kindly leaves it open to the public. If he did so all the
year he might lose his title to it, on grounds of common usage.
So every year on 14th September he closes it. Stradbally is
one of the last of the larger accessible beaches before we pass
south of the Monavullaghs and cover the last straight stretch
beside Dungarvan Harbour to Dungarvan itself. This is Co.
Waterford's administrative centre (Waterford City only
administers itself). It can hardly be said to hum as a capital
might, though the main square where most activity seems to
begin and end displays illuminated advertisements that might
have their inspiration in Piccadilly Circus. The town is
divided by the River Colligan, which till the nineteenth
century had to be crossed by ferry or on foot. The crossing
was then known as the 'Dungarvan Prospect' because of the
sight of the local women hoisting their skirts to step through
the shallow water. At a cost of £80,000 the Duke of Devonshire had a causeway laid and the two parts – Abbeyside,
with thirteenth-century friary remains, to the east, and the
town proper, with King James's castle ruined by Cromwell,
to the west – were united. Much of the castle's stone was
incorporated in the British barracks, from which, in the
nervy famine times of 1846, Royal Dragoons issued to the
square to fire on a crowd that was complaining of the danger
of harbour work. Two were killed. In 1921 the barracks
itself was destroyed. The vast estuary with its mud-flats
stretching to Helvick Head on the south may seem a pretentious outlet for a river once crossed by barefoot ladies. A
glance at a physical map shows the reason. Two major
west–east valleys run through the long mountain ranges of
Cork, and in glacial times the vast ice-flows which occupied
them must have continued east, and straight to the sea. Later,
when the ice melted, the Rivers Lee and Blackwater found the
effects of glaciation had opened up shorter cuts to the sea. So

that both, instead of staying on the obvious limestone course, turned right, through new clefts in the Old Red Sandstone, and left Dungarvan harbour and Youghal Bay to be spread with silt.

Of interest to dog-fanciers is a memorial, at the junction of main roads three miles north-west of the town, to Master McGrath (McGrath is an old Waterford family; the abbey-side castle was theirs), a greyhound beaten only once in thirty-seven public appearances, who won the Waterloo Cup in 1868, 1869 and 1871. The obelisk, with relief profile of the champion, is said to be the only roadside monument to a dog in Ireland. It is a diversion from which we revert to the coast road south from Dungarvan, round the harbour, then through Ring, noted for its Irish college, and, diverting again, to **Helvick Head**, for the astonishing view of the cliff-edged south Waterford coastline. There is in fact little but views, mainly of beautiful broad sweeps down to the sea, to take our attention as we keep to the coast, rounding the low outcrop of the Drumhills, to reach **Ardmore** twelve miles to the south-west. Here the ruins are among the best, certainly the best placed, of any in Ireland, but the site itself has possibly increased importance as having had a Christian settlement before the evangelising of St Patrick in other parts of the country. Though early manuscript sources point clearly to Patrick's pioneer work being elsewhere, it was probably to the south and east of the country, where contacts with Europe were strongest (and possibly to the west, from Spain), that Christianity first came. Here St Declan was the pioneer. He arrived, after studying in Wales. Old annals say that, finding the place an island and not suitable to his purposes, he pushed the sea back and made it a headland instead. (Nowadays the sea is reclaiming its old ground, due perhaps to the spiritual climate.) The stone on which he sailed still lies on the beach, and at the annual pattern in July (which in 1847 drew fourteen thousand people and still attracts crowds of cure-seekers) pilgrims used to be obliged to crawl under it. This was held to cure rheumatism, though it is arguable that rheumatism would have to have gone before the feat was performed. Declan's activity in converting locals was so successful that later on there was resistance here to St Patrick's more Rome-influenced administration. Of the three main buildings on the site, the **Round Tower**, with subtly tapering walls, a landmark for miles around but seen best from the field above, is perhaps the finest in Ireland, and may also be the latest. Its cap is a recent restoration. **St Declan's House**, a steep-gabled building, is supposed to be his own oratory, though unlikely to be of so early a date. A stone-lined trough dug into the floor is called the Saint's Grave. Most detail of interest is to be found in the **Cathedral**, whose Romanesque nave is probably eleventh-century work, the chancel – with outstanding carved capitals – being two hundred years later. The purpose of the arcading along the north walls of both is not known, but it may have had frescoes on it. There are two ogham stones inside, while on the exterior west wall some figures representing the Judgement of Solomon, the Temptation and other themes may be much earlier than the church itself. Half a mile to the east a few other church remains exist, and here also is the site of a castle occupied by Perkin Warbeck on his second attempt to force his claim to the throne. The castle was in 1649 defended by Catholic Confederates against a besieging force under the Cromwellian Lord Broghill. Forty of the defenders occupied the Round Tower, and two days were enough to force the garrison's surrender. Of the total of 240 prisoners, 117 were hanged on the spot.

Broghill's father was the first 'Great' Earl of Cork whose old haunts and territory we are approaching as we drive nine miles west, crossing the Blackwater to enter Co. Cork and the city of Youghal. Though most parts of Ireland have felt the effect of each architect, or vandal, of national history, each part seems to identify itself particularly with one or other person or phase. Co. Cork, having no monopoly of the period, is stamped deepest with the mark of the Elizabethans. The Great Earl, Spenser, Raleigh are with us now for miles, haunting every valley, lake and castle.

CHAPTER EIGHT

West Waterford: South-West Tipperary: East Cork

YOUGHAL is beside an easily accessible harbour, the gateway to the River Blackwater. This has, in the past, given it greater importance than it enjoys to-day. Founded in the thirteenth century by Anglo-Normans, and included in the barony of Inchiquin, Youghal changed hands a number of times before passing to the Desmond FitzGeralds, whose family catastrophes followed close on those of their Kildare cousins. The policies of Elizabeth were in the main based on peaceful expansion among the 'old English', by now as Irish – and Catholic – as the Irish. Her religion prevented peace, especially after the Pope barred her from Heaven's gates in 1570. Chief among the reactions she sparked was the Munster rebellion begun in 1579, in the course of which the fifteenth and last 'Rebel' Earl of Desmond thoroughly sacked the town of Youghal before moving on to the great reverse at Smerwick. Raleigh was one of the queen's commanders in Munster, and when Elizabeth saw her only hope of lasting success was to plant the area with English colonists he was granted 42,000 acres around Lismore in 1583. In the main the land came from the FitzGeralds. Among his estates was that of Myrtle Grove in Youghal. Having meanwhile tried to form a colony at Virginia in America he returned to Ireland in 1587, exiled from court favour by the rising sun of Essex. But he spent only a few years, and in 1602 sold his estates at a fraction of their market value to a younger man who, arriving earlier in the country with only £27, had found a job conveyancing confiscated lands. This was Richard Boyle, later to become first and 'Great' Earl of Cork. The price he paid for Raleigh's acres was £1,500. Meanwhile Edmund Spenser, who had a

rugged opposite to his poetic side, had accompanied and
found nothing distasteful in the repressive expedition of
1580. He, too, acquired land and in 1588 began to live at
Kilcolman Castle, near Doneraile. He married Boyle's cousin
(and wrote for her his *Epithalamium*) and became friendly
with Raleigh when they both lived in Cork. Each showed
the other his current writing, Spenser his *Faerie Queene* and
Raleigh short poems intended to win back the queen's good
opinion. In the event Raleigh failed to rediscover royal
favour, spent fifteen years in the Tower and ended after a
short and disastrous period of freedom on the scaffold.
Spenser was evicted from Kilcolman in 1598 by insurgents of
the O'Neill rising, and died in poverty in England soon after
(though he was still rightful owner of the demesne and his
grandson later sold it). Only Boyle, the canniest of the three,
kept in with the king, amassed great wealth, on top of
Raleigh's old property, and lived to help Wentworth to his
grave. He divided his land into estates which he leased to
English settlers. He built houses, castles, bridges; put up
factories of various kinds, many of which flourished, and
embellished his own dwellings with works of art both inside
and out. He cut down the great primeval forests of his area
as fuel for the ironworks he inaugurated. He was also an
astute speculator and notorious swindler.

Youghal to-day is a pleasing town by the picturesque
estuary, and with a long gently curving main street over the
middle of which rises the Georgian Clock Gate tower erected
in 1771. Early last century it served as a gaol. North Main
Street, on the side we come in, has some houses of interest –
Tynte's Castle, fifteenth century (one Robert Tynte married
Spenser's widow), altered and used now as a warehouse;
Uniacke or Red House, a rare Irish survival of the Dutch
Renaissance style, built between 1706 and 1715, painted pink;
and a terrace of almshouses built in 1634 by the Great Earl
for six Protestant widows, and still fulfilling the same purpose.
Parallel with the street is another long one to the east which
gives on to quays and warehouses. The finest assembly of
buildings is to the west, landward side of North Main Street –
the Church of St Mary, New College House and **Myrtle**

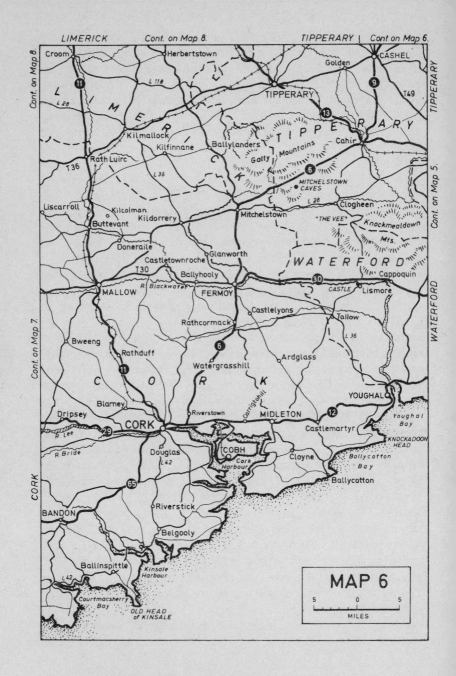

MAP 6

5   0   5
MILES

Grove. The last was owned and inhabited for a while by Raleigh and may be where he entertained Spenser. The house is private. Some say the first potato was planted here by Raleigh, but Killua in Co. Westmeath has a better claim. What is known is that, on the first try, Raleigh ate the plant's berry, which is disgusting. He ordered it to be rooted out, and the gardener discovered the nutritious tuber, ever since an Irish national dish.

New College House is on the site of the medieval college which the Great Earl acquired with the rest and which he put under the care of his brother, the Bishop of Cork. This family connection enabled ninety-five per cent of the college revenues – some £1,000 a year – to reach the earl's pocket. When the reforming Wentworth learned this, in spite of having married his niece to Cork's son, he called him to account. The earl was forced to pay £15,000. Archbishop Laud wrote to Wentworth gleefully: 'No physic is better than a vomit.' But Cork wrote in his diary 'God never forgive the Lord Deputy'; and had the satisfaction a few years later of knowing his own complaints had helped bring Wentworth to the scaffold.

The church is a mixture of styles, from the little that survived Desmond's assault to the giant restoration of the 1850s. Its great appeal is in details. One is the tomb considered to be that of the Countess of Desmond, wife of the twelfth earl who, the story goes, died aged 140 when she fell from a cherry tree at Dromana, up the river. She had danced with Henry VII in London a hundred years before and once visited Elizabeth at her court, walking all the way. The greatest monument is the one erected by himself to the Great Earl. In colourful Italian style it bears carvings of himself, his two wives (the second in ermine, because he was a peer by her time), and mother, and small figures of nine of his sixteen children. These do not include the natural scientist Robert, who appears, however, in the similar chantry in St Patrick's Cathedral, Dublin.

*

We start inland by recrossing the river and keeping close to its east side, either by the main road or the longer lanes that at times run alongside the water. Approaching Cappoquin we pass the demesne of **Dromana** to the left, in which the Methuselah Countess of Desmond was born. This was for centuries a FitzGerald stronghold. In 1676 it came by marriage into the Villiers family, which during that century supplied four kings with favourites – the first and second Dukes of Buckingham, the Duchess of Cleveland, who bore Charles II three Fitzroy dukes, and Elizabeth Villiers, William III's mistress, later Countess of Orkney. In 1802 the Villiers heiress married Henry Stuart, son of the Marquess of Bute; and the Villiers-Stuarts own the place to this day, though a large part of the beautiful waterside demesne has been taken over by the State for forestry.

Henry Stuart's son in 1826 made himself a local hero by ousting the Beresford MP for Waterford, having entertained Daniel O'Connell at the house during the campaign. He was later created Lord Stuart de Decies. He built the exotic gate, in Brighton Regency style, with its onion domes and minarets, across the main entrance to the estate off the Cappoquin road. **Affane,** east of the gate, was in 1564 the scene of one of the last battles in the Butler-Fitzgerald feud. The Geraldines lost and their leader was carried wounded by the Butlers off the field. 'Where is the great Earl of Desmond now?' jeered the Butlers. 'In his proper place, on the necks of the Butlers,' the earl replied.

Raleigh planted cherry trees at Affane, and in Charles II's reign one Valentine Greatraks lived in the castle that preceded the surviving but ruinous Georgian house. He claimed to cure scrofula and other ills by stroking and hypnotism, and the king was one of his patients. Reversing a cliché, an Irishman has called the Rhine Germany's Blackwater. It is full of beauty and history and curiosity, and we shall return to it later. Meanwhile we go on through the village of Cappoquin, where the big house preserves memorials of Lord Keane, who conquered Kabul in 1839, and died before the subsequent rout and massacre of the British in the Khyber Pass; then turn right, and make for the mountains. After five miles we reach **Mount**

Melleray Monastery. Trappists expelled from Brittany in 1832 settled here, cultivated the hard land – and in the 1920s built their Gothic abbey church, using stone from the remains of Mitchelstown Castle. Carlyle came here, venting Protestant bigotry: 'food, glory,' he noted, 'dim notion of getting to heaven, too, I suppose these are motive enough for a man of average Irish insight?' Thackeray was glad to give the place a miss – 'as for seeing shoes made or fields tilled by reverend amateurs, we can find cobblers and ploughboys to do the work better'. He might have thought otherwise had he seen the work, and enjoyed the hospitality of the monks – still dispensed free, though offerings are acceptable. A few miles beyond we join the main road over the **Knockmealdowns**, once known for the eagles and wolves that inhabited them, now more for the magnificent views to north and south to be had from the pass and angular section of main road known as the Vee. Claims have been made that the last wolf in Ireland was killed here in 1770 (though another claim is made for a Carlow catch in 1786). Whenever it was, it long outlived England's last survivor of the species (around 1600) and Scotland's (1743). In Norse and earlier days wolves had been common; and a belief grew up that they had inherited the souls of men who rejected St Patrick's teaching. Giraldus tells of a travelling priest coming on a wolf one evening in the wilderness; after it had 'said some things about God that seemed reasonable' it confirmed the man-wolf theory by peeling its skin to reveal, temporarily, human form – a possible transference from German werewolf lore. (Giraldus also explained the fact that Irish wolves whelp in December as 'a symbol of the evils of treachery and plunder which here blossom before their season'.) In population terms the beasts were decimated by cultivation and wolfhounds, and though Cromwell's depredations gave them a last brief respite, Ireland's eighteenth-century recovery finished them off. Naturally the Great Earl and others like him preferred to hunt deer, for the meat.

On the left, just before the Vee proper, is **Bay Lough**, a tarn of unknown depth, surrounded by rhododendrons and, metaphorically, by rumours of undercurrents and monsters.

It is said to be the influence of Petticoat Loose, a haunting harridan, that caused the road to be built zigzag instead of straight along the old track. The rhododendron (ponticum variety – the only one to grow wild on such a scale) gives a staggering display of colour in late spring, making it hard to believe that the plant was unknown in these islands before George III's day. Missing this view, but presumably appreciating the broad one to the north from the north slope of Sugarloaf Hill (on the other side of the road from the lake), are the earthly remains of Mr Samuel Grubb, a Quaker who owned Castlegrace House on the Tar River below. He was buried upright, as he wished, in a kind of beehive cairn in 1921. In this position he followed the example of King Cormac at Tara, the King of Leinster at Tountinna, and some other examples we shall meet. There is also an orthodox grave on top of the hill, that of Henry Eeles, an early pioneer of electricity.

We descend to the village of Clogheen and turn left towards Ballyporeen, visited in 1984 by Ronald Reagan, in honour of the Irish ancestor no United States president lacks, where a right turn brings us after nearly three miles to **Mitchelstown Caves.** Straight ahead is the splendid line of sandstone gullies and escarpments making the south face of the almost roadless Galty Mountains, which are best climbed from the west side. The caves themselves are the best in Ireland, and divided into two groups, the Old and New. The Old have been known for centuries. James FitzThomas, who claimed to be the Earl of Desmond and was known by Irishmen as the Sugan, or 'straw' earl, sheltered here in the bitter aftermath of the last Munster rising in 1601. Betrayed by the last White Knight, he was taken to the Tower to end both his life and, after a century of decline, the line of Munster Geraldines. Undoubtedly the so-called Old Caves have hidden others than him. The use of caves in prehistoric times is well attested by the bones of animals brought in to eat. (In other Irish caves research on remains has revealed that the Arctic lemming, bear, African wild cat, spotted hyena, and other species rare or undocumented for Europe, once lived in the country.) Though the Old Caves contain the longest chamber of all, 390 feet long and 40 feet high, they are not so remarkable as the New, which were discovered in 1833, and which comprise the normal guided tour. These have spectacular subterranean scenery, a series of chambers that extend nearly a mile and a half, and most evocative formations. All the chambers have been given names which detract from their impact, since the reality never lives up to the fiction.

Burncourt, two miles north of the caves, is the burned out case of a many-gabled, fortified house of 1640. Sir Richard Everard, its builder and a Catholic Confederate, was involved in preparing the defence of Limerick when news came to his wife that Cromwellians were approaching the house. Sooner than let them take it, she set fire to it, almost new as it was. When Limerick was taken the following year Sir Richard was hanged by Ireton. Now, with its four square towers at each corner of the central block, its twenty-six gables, and the holes along the top of the walls to take supports for defensive galleries, it still shows clearly the original concept, better than similar remains in the country. Another shell lies due east of the caves, that of Shanbally Castle, built by John Nash and knocked down after a fire in 1958. North of Burncourt we come to the main Mitchelstown–Cahir road, and turn right, reaching Cahir after about eight miles.

Cahir ('Fort'), a very pretty town, is dominated by a vast central castle, on a rock-island in the Suir. The Castle is the last of a series, as the town's name and literary clues point to the existence of a fortress here at least as early as the third century. The present one, part restored in 1840, was built in the twelfth century but mainly shows the sturdy defences of a fifteenth-century or later reconstruction. It was a Butler base, but of the branch of the family which did not, like the main line, join the king's men and turn Protestant when required; so that Essex besieged it in 1599 and in one of his few successes captured the place after a few days. Cromwell took it in February, 1650, without any trouble, before going to break the stronger back of Clonmel. To the inmates' lack of last-ditch defiance is owed the unusual completeness both of keep and exterior walls. Again restored, it was opened to the public in 1971.

The town is well supplied with Georgian houses; its Gothic Revival C of I church was built in 1817 to designs by Nash, who along with Francis Johnston and Sir Richard Morrison was in high fashion and demand in the Regency period. Nash also planned the *cottage orné* by the River Suir in the Butler demesne that has now become Cahir Park, just south of the town. Known as Swiss Cottage, it can be seen inside and out, and its details – wallpaper showing scenes of the Bosphorus, a wooden spiral staircase, windows engraved with landscapes – display all the cosily rustic aspirations of leisured Georgians.

Leaving Cahir by the Tipperary road (on the right beyond the turn are the ruins of thirteenth-century Augustinian Cahir Abbey), we come after three miles to a signpost pointing left to the Glen of Aherlow, a long fertile valley spread between the Galtees and Slievenamuck to the north. It is not the most dramatic scenery hereabouts, in spite of its reputation, though there is a drive, with views like a geography lesson, over the Slievenamuck range on the north. The glen and the Golden Vale which its eastern end joins are rich farmlands, with fat dark hedges marking the rich green pastures like a chessboard. Together with the plains to the north they make the country's main dairying area, which has meant a change over the last forty years from beef to dairy herds. Pig rearing goes on as a subsidiary, and an increasing acreage is given over to sugar beet. It is all good hunting and shooting country and there are facilities for visitors who want to join in.

Farming activities make **Tipperary** itself, a few miles north, important as a market town, but it might disappoint anyone deserting Leicester Square to see it. A long straggling town, hiding its river, the Ara, behind its back streets, as so many Irish towns do, it harbours a history of spasmodic resistance from the time of King John, who built a castle here, to the Land League agitation of the last century. This movement, begun by Michael Davitt and fostered by Parnell, aimed to thwart landlords at every turn and force the government into granting freeholds to the peasants. Boycotting was one weapon used; murder by the ubiquitous 'Captain Moonlight' was another. In Tipperary the tenants of the major landlord, Smith Barry, simply abandoned their homes and began to build 'New Tipperary' nearby. But they had not the means to survive, and very soon gave up the scheme. If not distinguished, the town has provided the seeds of distinction elsewhere. Hazlitt's grandfather, Eugene O'Neill's father and John O'Leary the Fenian were all born here or nearby.

The road east leads to Golden, passing **Thomastown Castle**, a superb ivy-clad ruin in the Wagnerian mould. Built, with the famous formal garden, in the eighteenth century, it was gothicised and painted blue by Richard Morrison in the 1820s, for the Mathew family, Earls of Llandaff. Father Mathew, who led an effective campaign against liquor in the nineteenth century, was born here. A memorial to him of 1939 stands beside the shell, which itself has recently been bought by Archbishop David Mathew to be preserved as a memorial. Farther on the same road is the ruined Augustinian **St Edmund's Priory** of Athassel, which grew so wealthy after its foundation in 1205 that a town – of which nothing but wall fragments remain – grew round it. The priory's ruins are still most impressive, with interesting details like the doorway to the choir, the chapter house and refectory on a vaulted basement, and the vaulted gate-house.

This is a detour, however, and our way lies west-south-west from Tipperary along the north side of Slievenamuck, turning left after six miles to go over the west end of the hills and see **Moor Abbey** below their southern slopes. Strictly a Franciscan friary, it was built in 1471, burned the next year, and served thereafter more as a fortress than a place of worship, with the friars harbouring outlaws during the Munster conquest and thereby risking, and at least once incurring, death at the hands of the English troops. It saw action in more recent days, too. North Cork was a focus both in the Anglo-Irish War of 1918–21, and again in the Civil War that followed the signing of the Anglo-Irish Treaty. (Soloheadbeg, four miles north of Tipperary, was where the first shots of the guerrilla war were fired.) During the former the abbey was often used as a cover by insurgents, and the

Royal Irish Constabulary made several attempts to blow the place up. We move south from Galbally, the nearby village, close to the higher reaches of the Aherlow, through the eastern pass between the Ballyhoura and Galtees, and come down on Mitchelstown. The Kilworth Mountains, forming the western end of the Knockmealdowns, are straight ahead, and the Nagles in the distance to the right. This is Co. Cork, and we are well within the south-western system of Old Red Sandstone ranges running mainly east–west, with limestone valleys – in this case that of the Blackwater – lying between.

Mitchelstown (some miles west of the caves that were given its name), is a delightful echo of past splendour. Its earlier history is linked with the Clangibbon White Knights, a Limerick branch of the FitzGerald family, sharing a common ancestry with the Desmond FitzGeralds and, ultimately, with the Kildare Fitzgeralds. From the White Knights it passed at the Restoration to the King family, future Earls of Kingston, but by the mid-eighteenth century it was described as wretched and run down. Painstaking Arthur Young, the inventive agriculturalist, whose diaries of his progress round Ireland are one of the best accounts of Irish eighteenth-century life, was the second Earl of Kingston's agent here in 1778, and noted the effects of a system that relied on casual labour. Spalpeens, or freelance farm-workers, would arrive by day or night and 'fix themselves under a dry bank and with a few sticks, furze, fern, etc., make up a hovel much worse than an English pigsty, and support themselves how they can, by work, begging, and stealing'. Soon after, Lord Kingston transformed the town. Schools, a woollen industry, shops – even a salaried physician – were provided; population grew; a model town was built; a Georgian house replaced the old castle as the Kingston residence; and nurserymen were brought from England to landscape the demesne, with generous use of trees. No less than three million mulberries were planted. Since then the town has become one of the big creamery centres in the country. But in the nineteenth century Gothic swept in and the house – 'too large to hang on a watch-chain; too small to live in,' said the third earl – was pulled down to make way for a castle, erected swiftly at a cost of

£100,000 for an expected visit of George IV. The king, detained by good living in Dublin, failed to arrive, and the earl and his heir later lost both reason and fortune. But the castle, by G. R. Pain, remained a pride of Munster till 1922 when it was occupied and burned by Republican troops in the Civil War. The stones were bought for the new church at Mount Melleray, leaving little more than a mound to mark the spot. The town remains, neatly planned round two squares. College Square is flanked on three sides by **Kingston College,** a 1780 foundation for Protestant gentlefolk fallen on hard times: it grants twelve gentlemen and eighteen ladies a house and annuity each.

To the right of the road that accompanies the River Funshion west the countryside is enchanting, and it goes on being so beyond Kildorrery, which is as far as we go with it now. Any direction is good to go in; we are tied by the need to keep more or less to one at a time but will return to the neighbourhood later. It is a good area to stay in, its rich spread of trees concealing lanes and bohreens (the stone-sided tracks built for the moving of cattle), rivers that coil and dip into limestone tunnels, small clearings for farms and grave-yards, a wealth of wild flowers and birds, herons lazily stream-spotting from the air, or standing still and priestlike in the water, waiting to strike. Spenser lived a short way to the west, a little disgruntled, using the lore of the people he despised as the matter for his *Faerie Queene.* In our times Elizabeth Bowen lived just outside **Kildorrery** to which we have come. Bowen's Court was the name of the house and of the sad, scholarly, loving book she wrote about it. It was a high, austere, hip-roofed building of 1776, built by a descendant of the first Bowen settler, an atheist Welshman who came over with Cromwell. That first unsociable Bowen kept hawks, one of which Cromwell is supposed to have strangled in a rage, then compensated him with the land. Like Mitchelstown the Georgian house cost too much, and nineteenth-century Bowens never had enough money to enjoy to the full its size and splendour, the ballroom, the park with its beeches and limes. Elizabeth Bowen, brought up here, came back to live in 1952. Her husband died that same year and it was too much for her. She sold it to a progressive neighbour and the neighbour pulled it down. 'It was a clean end. Bowen's Court never lived to be a ruin,' she wrote, though she had not foreseen the end; and in an access of melodrama, standing by the meadows and trees, in view of the blue Galtees, one can see what she means, a rounded inevitability.

The first Bowens had their land at the expense of Anglo-Norman Roches, whose name lives on in Castletownroche, seven miles south of Kildorrery, beside Spenser's Awbeg River. Two miles before the town, on the right, are the fine, luxuriant gardens of Annes Grove (open to the public at set times) with rare rhododendrons and other shrubs and trees. In 1649 the Lord Roche of the time fled, attainted as a royalist, and his wife – a familiar pattern in Ireland – defended their castle (now **Castle Widenham**) here against Cromwell. They never recovered their fortunes, and the last of the line worked as a stable-boy, refusing wages from pride; though a Limerick branch of the family rose to be the wealthiest merchants in the south in the eighteenth century. The castle now has beautiful gardens. We follow the river on the east side, near its passage through a steep limestone gorge to its attractive meeting with the Blackwater; then turn east with the road to **Ballyhooly,** where stands another Roche castle, restored in the nineteenth century by the Earl of Listowel, impressively seen from the road against the thickness of trees lining the river. The Listowels' other house was Convamore, a mile north-west, built by the Pain brothers in 1833, scene of lavish entertaining, burned down in 1921. Yet another Roche Castle, this one decayed and ivy-covered, stands at **Glanworth** four miles to the north, by a road leading to the left just beyond Ballyhooly; the village is pretty, with an ancient thirteen-arch bridge and ruined Dominican friary. If we continue the detour by taking the direct Fermoy road from Glanworth we pass a magnificent gallery grave on the left at **Labbacallee.** The name means 'Grave of the Old Woman', and at the excavation in 1934 a headless female skeleton was found in the inner chamber at the far end from the road, while the skull was in the larger chamber near the road. This is the most elaborate and largest of several hundred known wedge-shaped gallery tombs in the country, and measures twenty-five feet in length, five feet wide and nine feet at the highest point of its sloping three-slabbed roof. It probably dates to the second half of the third millennium BC and is of a type which, with variations, is found mainly in the south-western counties. The practice appears to have reached the country through Brittany, with those who first brought farming techniques. Two interesting details are the hole clipped out of the corner of the large upright slab that separates the two chambers – thought to have been an escape route for the buried lady's spirit; and the west–east axis (characteristic of these tombs) hinting perhaps at sun-worship. The whole was originally covered with earth. Excavation discovered other skeletons – male – in the outer chamber, which may say something of the society of the day.

When we rejoin the Ballyhooly–Fermoy road, **Castle Hyde** is to the right, on the riverside. A handsome, three-storied eighteenth-century house, with wings, it has a staircase up to its cliff-top garden, where the ruined Condon tower commands astonishing views. But the house is not open to the public, and we continue east to **Fermoy,** a town once noted for the British garrison that occupied the barracks, and which – a rare event in Ireland – faces its river – the Blackwater – on whose southern bank it mostly lies. Till 1791 there was only a village here. It was a time when most Irish towns were owned by great landlords, the inhabitants being no more than tenants. In 1791 one John Anderson, ex-Glasgow labourer made rich by a fishing venture and richer (to the tune of £20,000) by dealing in provisions in Cork, bought most of the now urban land. Restless, kind and canny, he started building: houses, square, theatre, market-house, hotel, livery stable (for Dublin–Cork travellers), bank, brewery, flour and paper mills, and – most important, having induced the government to quarter troops here – a barracks. Trade with the soldiers was the key to prosperity and bustling Fermoy had in 1800 twice its present population, all comparatively well off. He also held to the belief that 'Irish Papists were as well entitled as Protestants to live all the days of their lives,' and encouraged them to build a chapel. The town held its position through the nineteenth century, always a military centre, with the kind of social life bound to thrive round officers and their ladies. Since the British left, the bustle has subsided. The barracks are in ruins, and nice Georgian houses are scant evidence of former glory.

Five miles south of Fermoy is the village of Rathcormack, and a mile south of that, across the River Bride, stands **Kilshannig** House, which must, when finished in 1765, have been one of Ireland's most beautiful houses. Built by Davis Ducart, the Sardinian designer of Castletown in Co. Kilkenny and of the Limerick Customs House it has handsome wings, originally domed, and magnificent plasterwork inside by the Francini brothers.

At **Castle Lyons,** two miles north-east of Rathcormack, are the spindly, ivy-covered ruins of a sixteenth century Barrymore Castle, built on the site of the original stronghold of the Lehane family, chiefs of the surrounding locality of Hy-Lehan (Lyons is the anglicised form of Lehane). Their land, extending over much of east Cork, had been granted to the Barrys after the Conquest. At the end of the sixteenth century, the estate was acquired by the future Earl of Cork, who gave it to his daughter on her marriage to the Earl of Barrymore, to help her 'to buy gloves and pins'. Subsequent Earls of Barrymore restored the building, which became a fashionable mansion of the Ascendancy, till a fire of 1771 left it much as it is now. The village also contains extensive ruins of an early fourteenth-century Carmelite friary, but a more curious ruin is that of the C of I church to the north-west. It stands among the trees and overgrowth of its churchyard, its windows cemented to prevent pilfering that sometimes follows abandonment by a dwindled Protestant congregation. To the east is the mausoleum of the Barrymores, a charming Palladian building of brick and stone, erected around 1750 to house the superb monument, by David Sheehan, to the first earl. Building, sculpture, plaster- and ironwork have recently been well restored.

Returning to Fermoy, we drive east along the north shore of the Blackwater, here broader and faster and best in Ireland for salmon, through the richly wooded valley, to Lismore and catch glimpses of several hoary castles against the long, bosomy backdrop of the Knockmealdowns. Beyond Ballyduff and set in thick woods we pass the elaborate nineteenth-century Gothic gates and castle-bridge of Ballysaggartmore, whose owner, running into debt on their construction, had nothing left for the house he planned to replace the old one. That still stands, ruined and rambling. **Lismore** has little better to show than the first fairy-tale view of its castle from the bridge (mid-eighteenth century; Thomas Ivory's earliest work) we cross before entering the town, for the town gives away little of its former status. In the eighth century it was one of the best known monastic centres of the country, founded by St Carthach or Carthage, who brought both loyal followers and leprosy patients to Lismore, whose prestige soon rose. A century later it was said to have counted young King Alfred among its students, and there are now claims that over twenty calendared saints were buried here. Henry II called soon after his arrival in Ireland, and the future King John picked the riverside site for a castle. This was later handed over to the church authorities, and so came into the possession (as he saw it) of the renegade Myler McGrath, by now in his Protestant phase, who sold a long lease on it in 1589 to Sir Walter Raleigh. Raleigh was more concerned to regain the queen's regard than to exploit the vast areas of tillage, pasture, woods, minerals and fishing that he acquired. He did not stay long in the country, returned to England, offended the queen by making a maid-of-honour – whom he had to marry – pregnant, spent four years in the Tower, explored Trinidad and the Orinoco, and won long-sung victories against the Spanish on their own ground. Unwisely, he did not ingratiate himself with the young heir, James VI of Scotland. Others did, and poisoned the prince's ear against him. He was forced to sell his Irish estates for a song and languished in the Tower from 1603 to his last disastrous expedition to Guiana and subsequent execution in 1618. The beneficiary of his sale, in 1602, was Richard Boyle, future Earl of Cork, who also combined the Elizabethan virtues and vices. To him and Raleigh are owed many existing features – the castles, towns, the division of the land, and the great number of Dorset families who settled at the time and whose descendants, Allen, Coppinger, Mead, Russell, Stout, are still found in the area. The earl lived to become the richest

248 THE COMPANION GUIDE TO IRELAND

man in Ireland and to see the beginning of the Confederate
War, in which his son Roger defended the castle against the
Catholics – a sect despised by the earl himself. He died in
1643. Another son, Robert, born at Lismore, soon went to
England, where he became a founder member of the Royal
Society, author of 'Boyle's law' and the claimed founder of
modern chemistry. The last Lismore Boyle, fourth Earl of
Cork but better known as third Earl of Burlington, was the
Palladian architect whose collaboration with Gibbs produced
the present form of the Royal Academy's headquarters in
London. At his death in 1753, Lismore Castle passed, by the
marriage of his daughter, to the Dukes of Devonshire, with
whom it has remained. From Cork's time, remains include
the gatehouse, the toy-like riding-house (next to the avenue
of pollarded yews planted by the earl's son), the north-west
round tower and the walls of the upper garden; but the basic
work of the period – four gabled ranges round a courtyard –
was 'ruinated' by 1654, according to the *Civil Survey*. As it
stands to-day the castle is owed mainly to the enthusiasm of
the sixth Duke of Devonshire and the skill of his former
gardener, Sir Joseph Paxton, who also designed the Crystal
Palace. Paxton's great river-front dates from the early 1850s,
as does most of the interior, for which Pugin designed much
of the furniture and chimney-pieces, as well as the great
banqueting hall, a sort of miniature House of Lords. Apart
from that the interior is modest and a little disappointing,
but the outside still makes it the most grandiose castle in
Ireland, what the duke himself called 'this quasi-feudal,
ultra regal fortress'.

A younger brother, Lord Charles Cavendish, of the late,
tenth, duke, married in 1932 Adele Astaire (the dancer's
dancing sister), and they owned the castle until his death,
when it reverted to the duke. Lord Charles was buried in the
graveyard of the C of I Cathedral of St Carthage. The medieval
church, reroofed by the Great Earl, had its tall delicate spire
added by G. R. Pain in 1827 – one of the prettiest in the country.
It incorporates a splendid Tudor McGrath monument, Gothic
vaulting, and some eloquent memorials, not least to that
Richard Musgrave who, 'as a Landlord, and a Master, A

Husband, and a Father, A Magistrate, and a Christian, Left behind him few equals, and no Superior . . .' though he *did* leave a treatise on the rebellions Ireland had already seen, with some reflections on how to treat those to come: flogging, burning, and such deterrents. Musgraves are still in evidence in the area. A Sir Richard Musgrave in the 1840s introduced steamers on to the river, and they plied till 1914. Most of the riverside houses have big crumbling jetties.

We return to the river by a scenic route that brings us opposite the most impressive side of Dromana, then over the bridge that crosses the Bride. Six miles west beside the Bride, **Tallow** has Ireland's largest annual horse-fair. The name means Iron Hill, and the Earl of Cork exploited its minerals, making guns and cannons for export and bringing great prosperity to the area. Iron-ore mine shafts abound, and in his day the forges glowed in every village. But all this meant the baring of the land, for thousands of trees were destroyed for charcoal, as well as for shipbuilding, and pipestaves and hogsheads to be sent to France and Spain.

Keeping to the Blackwater, we pass the Pains' hauntingly Gothic Strancally Castle, and the ruined keep beside it where a medieval FitzGerald was given to cutting his guests' throats and dropping there bodies in the river, so as to acquire their lands. Six miles on is the decaying Georgian (1795–7) eleven-bay Ballynatray House, magnificently set in its deer-park by the river, with a ruined abbey on a causewayed island in the demesne. Strongbow's lieutenant Raymond le Gros is said to be buried on the island, and a later owner placed a funeral urn to mark the fact. (Below the abbey is Ireland's only sprat-weir, a wattle contraption for catching sea fish – the river being tidal well above this point.) The Holroyd-Smyths, who owned the house until 1969, were descended from Richard Smyth, who married the Great Earl of Cork's sister Mary from here. Last century they kept the captain's barge from a Napoleonic man-of-war, that had been wrecked off the coast, as a state barge complete with musicians; and a Smyth daughter married the brother of King Ferdinand II of Naples, infuriating the King and condemning herself and her husband, after long diplomatic wrangles, to a life of exile and poverty.

*

The direct road from Youghal to Cork passes through Castle-martyr, ten miles west. The beautiful demesne here had an exacting share of Tudor-Stuart history. It was captured twice for the queen in the Munster invasion, acquired by Raleigh, passed to Boyle, taken by FitzGeralds (the original owners) in the Civil War, enlarged by Boyle's son, the Earl of Orrery, and reduced to ruins in 1688. The gaunt fifteenth-century keep and walls still stand. **Castlemartyr House,** built by the Earl of Shannon, one of Boyle's great-grandsons in the eighteenth century, now belongs to the Carmelites, but may be visited. It has a magnificent double-cube saloon, with plasterwork by Robert West added in the 1760s by the second Earl of Shannon. His father had constructed the impressive watercourse which still snakes through the demesne and round the town.

A road leads south from the village to **Ballycotton Bay,** to which we could have come direct from Youghal by the picturesque coast-road, taking in Knockadoon Head. **Shanagarry,** set a mile back from the sea, has a famous modern pottery. Beside the village is Shanagarry House, with a ruined castle where the Penn family lived after Charles II had given them the land in place of an earlier Cromwellian grant at Macroom. William Penn came in 1666 to sort out estate affairs for his father, the admiral whose bickering with rivals had squashed Cromwell's West Indies ambitions. While staying here William, a Quaker since Oxford days, attended a proscribed Quaker meeting in Cork. He was imprisoned, but soon released, and returned to England to preach, go to gaol again, and finally to leave for the American colony which he named Pennsylvania in his father's honour.

A mile west of Shanagarry is the Ballymaloe House Hotel, a seventeenth-century mansion with one of Ireland's best restaurants in a room with several paintings by Jack Yeats, the poet's brother. East is Ballycotton, a popular resort with good beaches and a pretty harbour, and a base for deep-sea fishing. For a price, anyone can hire a boat for the purpose or accompany an organised fishing trip. Shark, skate, conger, cod, ling and pollock are the species most sought, and a number of Irish records have been established here, though the headquarters of shark fishing is at Kinsale, west of Cork. Quieter interest is to be had at **Cloyne**, a pretty village with a small cathedral, on the way west across this broad peninsula. St Colman, around 600, began the religious tradition here. Colman was such a common name, one story tells, that when once St Carthage, directing a party of monks working beside a river, called 'Into the water, Colman', twelve jumped. This one, a poet some of whose lines survive, was a late vocation, persuaded to take orders by St Brendan the Navigator. Of the medieval church buildings, a ruined oratory and Round Tower remain. In 1734 George Berkeley, the philosopher, was made Bishop of Cloyne. Earlier, with a government grant promised and a legacy from Swift's 'Vanessa', he crossed to Rhode Island bent on 'converting the savage Americans to Christianity'. He founded a college in Bermuda, but the grant never came and he retired to eighteen years of happy home life and philosophy. Though the village had as many people again as it has now, and the diocese stretched to Limerick's hills, he had time for writing, reading, and publishing issues of *The Querist*, in which he advocated economic independence for Ireland. He had earlier, in Sydney Smith's words, 'destroyed this world in one volume octavo' by proposing that things exist only in being perceived. He wrote at Cloyne on the universal benefits to be had from tar water, founded a spinning school and a workhouse, taught improved farming methods, and when the area was swept by a dysentery plague acted the doctor and made large grants to the poor. Cloyne Church (the see is now incorporated with that of Cork) is basically thirteenth century but with the mark of most subsequent styles. It has a fine alabaster statue of Berkeley. He lived in a large house beside it, burned down in 1870.

We rejoin the main Cork road at **Midleton**, where in 1825 the Pain brothers built the C of I church on the site of a Cistercian monastery. Midleton College, rebuilt in 1829, was founded by William III's mistress, Elizabeth Villiers, in 1696 (Swift deplored the king's taste: she 'squinted like a dragon'). The guilt-ridden king, after the Boyne, and the death of his wife, gave her the most valuable grant of land in Ireland –

nearly 100,000 acres, that had been James II's private estates; and she, in an attempt to make herself popular, founded the college.

West of Midleton the road leads straight and wide into Cork, but it is worth diverting left at Carrigtohill. We pass the beautiful and almost insular demesne of **Fota,** formerly belonging to the Smith-Barry family, a cadet branch of the Barrymores. Most of the present house was designed by the Morrisons, father and son, in the early nineteenth century, who disguised the eighteenth century hunting-lodge, which still remains the heart of the building, in stuccoed Regency simplicity. Its interiors are very rich and elaborate: a long scagliola-pillared hall, ornate plasterwork above the staircase (a comparatively small one, being confined within the original house), good furniture and a fine collection of paintings by James Barry, Daniel Maclise, James Arthur O'Connor, Thomas Roberts and others. Owners have always exploited the sheltered, balmy climate, and the gardens, in part reclaimed from the sea, contain many rare subtropical species, among the finest in these islands. A century ago over a hundred thousand plants were bedded in the borders. Such gardening, like the stove house, peach house, melon house and vinery, is of the past. But the magnificent arboretum remains, and a wildlife park has been opened in the grounds. The acres of mud flats around are a great attraction to wildfowl. After six miles we reach **Cobh,** on Great Island in the middle of vast Cork harbour. Cobh, pronounced Cove, was in English days known as Queenstown. 'To give the people the satisfaction of calling the place Queenstown' wrote benign Victoria on her visit in 1849, 'in honour of its being the first spot on which I set foot on Irish ground, I stepped on shore amidst a roar of cannon and enthusiastic shouts of the people.' With a fi ne sense of Irish timing, the mayor had requested the queen to stay on board since preparations were not complete. She refused the delay, and all went well. It has always been Cork's main harbour, and in the eighteenth century lighters and small vessels would take cargoes and passengers hence to the canals of Cork city. It remained in British hands till 1937. From here in 1838 the *Sirius* sailed to make the first Atlantic steamer crossing. Impressive from afar, St Colman's is a depressing Pugin-Ashlin cathedral of 1869 onwards. The town has little to offer; but the island is lovely. Nearly a mile north of Cobh is the churchyard of Clonmel, which harbours the remains of the poet Charles Wolfe, James Verling, sometime surgeon to Napoleon; and many who went down with the *Lusitania* in 1915, in a plainly marked communal grave, maintained by the Cunard Line. Cobh also boasted the world's oldest yacht club, the Royal Cork, founded in 1720 until it recently moved its clubhouse across the water to Crosshaven.

There is no way back but the way we came to rejoin the main Cork road. Six miles further on we pass on the right Dunkathel, or Dunkettle, a handsome house (in a region where rich Cork merchants built many such) of the 1780s, with fine interior plasterwork, friezes and frescoes of the nineteenth century. The next right turn on to the Fermoy road brings us after a couple of miles to **Riverstown,** a house built early in the eighteenth century for Bishop Jemmet Browne of Cork. One room was used for storing potatoes up to a few years ago when the Irish Georgian Society discovered within it some glorious stucco work done by the Francini brothers in 1745. The society restored it with the owner's encouragement. The public are admitted, and several other items of interest have subsequently been unearthed in both house and garden.

CHAPTER NINE

West Cork, Inner Cork and Cork Coast
(Cork to Kenmare)

DUBLINERS are supposed to say that when a Cork man starts smiling at you, it's too late to look for the knife in your back; that Cork is a soft town with a sting in its tail; or that Cork people have a sense of inferiority, which sends them to Dublin or London as soon as they are free, to pass the time singing praises of their native city. A lot of past travellers have found it ugly, gloomy, a 'magazine of nastiness'. Thackeray poured more vitriol on it than he was wont to do on places that disappointed him. He was irked by the populace – 'could they do nothing but stare, swagger and be idle in the streets?'; blown from a concert hall by the blare of a dragoon band; affronted by shabbiness and waste. He published an article in *The Cornhill* that vented his feelings and in answer a Cork potter patented a chamber-pot with an open-mouthed Thackeray decorating the bowl. The line was a grand success and the pots are now prized rarities. (Gladstone was later to receive the same treatment.)

But for every word of abuse there has been more praise. Arthur Young found it pleasant, like a Dutch town with its streets intersected by canals. Wesley thought it 'one of the pleasantest and most ancient cities in the kingdom.' Even Thackeray had selective praise and found the people, even the beggars, cleverer and better-read than most Englishmen. This, according to Padraic Colum, is the city that gives Ireland her journalists, schoolmasters and civil-servants. Away from the overwhelmingly English influence of the Pale (though curiously, architecture shows more English influence than any other part of Ireland), Cork has developed in a highly individual way. From here, and most of the way up the west coast, the fact that people speak English gives little clue to their nature; though the way they speak it, with a lilting sing-song not far removed from a Welsh accent and the unEnglish uses they put English to, indicate the singularity of what lies beneath. For in Cork city and the western part of the country – in spite of the familiar list of English invasions, of plantations, of sporty Anglo-Irish landlords – the highlights of the past are quite different from those of eastern Ireland. Conquerors were more fully absorbed into existing ways. Rebels were welcomed; Perkin Warbeck here acclaimed King of England and provided with men and gold by the mayor, so losing the city its charter and himself his head. The Desmond FitzGeralds, grabbing land from old Irish McCarthys, soon became Irish enough to worry their English lieges. Ignoring the Reformation, they stayed Catholic, and in 1579 the fifteenth FitzGerald earl rebelled against Elizabeth, sacked Youghal, and tried to join with Spanish and Italian forces in Kerry. The subsequent Munster plantation was not a success as that of Connaught was. The Irish kept rallying, and after the Boyne the town, which had backed King James, required a tough assault to bring it to King William's heel. In the eighteenth century it was the Munster Whiteboys, guerrillas campaigning for redress from enclosure, rack-rents, tithes and forced labour, who most terrified their landlord population. A hundred years ago a steady file of emigrants queued for the coffin ships that would, if ship and passengers lasted the journey, take them to America, away from the famine and poverty of Munster and farther afield. Until 1971, a trickle of emigrants catching the transatlantic liners at Cobh recalled the needy flood.

This century's history allots Cork and Munster a copious share of violent political action. One mayor of the city, Thomas MacCurtain, was assassinated in 1920 by Black and Tans, who here most ably fulfilled their Gestapo roles: they were seen, wrote Lord Longford, 'strutting down the streets of Cork, crazy with drink and nerves, lashing passers-by across the face with riding-whips stolen from the shops.' They smashed windows and looted, thugged and raped, and most of what they did was exonerated by leaders who thought brutish reprisal the only way of countering rebellion. The

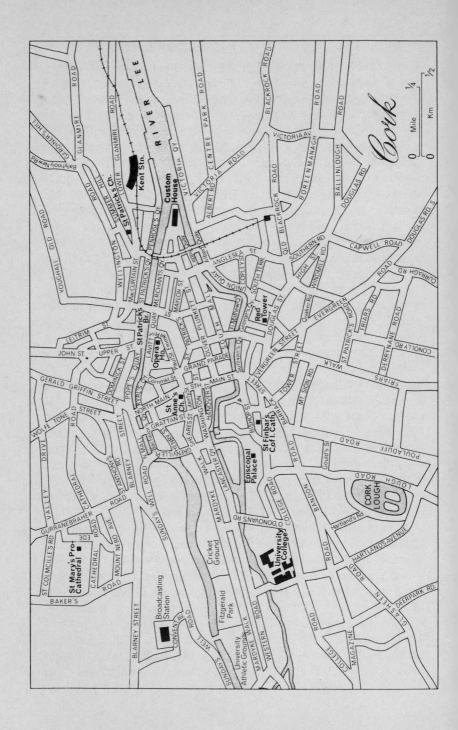

Cork

next mayor, Terence MacSwiney, was imprisoned, went on hunger strike, and died in Brixton after seventy-five days – until recently the longest prison abstinence on record. Both Free Staters and Republicans were based in turn on the city in the Civil War of 1922–3. The uncompromising Volunteers operated from camps in the surrounding hills, and on a narrow lane near Clonakilty the Free State general Michael Collins was killed in an ambush.

Its native writers best express the essence of Cork, whether or not they talk explicitly of it. None were better than Sean O'Faolain (pronounced rather like O'Fwaylan) and Frank O'Connor (pseudonym for Michael O'Donovan), born within three years and a mile of each other, both rising from humble origins by way of humble jobs to dominate the Irish literary scene. O'Faolain was a commercial traveller who fought in the hills for the Republicans before getting an academic training and writing novels, biographies and neat, wry short stories. His life epitomises Cork obstinacy. Having fought for an enlightened republic in 1922 he saw the movement's leaders create a society of 'the most blatant inequalities, the clear absence of equal opportunities for all, a large and flourishing and privileged minority, a bourgeois class utterly devoid of moral courage, an indescribably repressive and obscurantist church, and the most constant and shameless inroads on personal freedom of thought and expression'. Both Church and State attacked his work and banned some of his writing. The words quoted were written in 1966, anniversary of the '16 Rising and execution of those 'whom we are now about to honour fifty years after we have forgotten what they meant to create'.

If O'Faolain is the cussed stubbornness of Cork, O'Connor is the rugged, twinkling-eyed humanity. His autobiography, *An Only Son*, paints the Cork of the 1900s – poverty, wit, songs in grimy Blarney Lane, musty priests, nuns saintly and spiteful, wasting disease, a drunk debased father, incorruptible mother, cramped cabins to live in and wide-eyed glimpses of the tea-cup gentry in large terrace-houses in Sunday's Well; and the silly confused loyalties of the fruitless Civil War. Nothing better paints the nonsense of those times than his

hilarious description of the war's outbreak, issues misunder-
stood, orders miscarried, front lines ignored as fighters on
both sides went to Mass or mother-visiting – a game of overgrown children. Suddenly, for him, the comedy was cut,
when he, imprisoned and not sorry for a rest, saw a fellow
prisoner dying, his arms pierced by an enemy bayonet. Of all
purely Irish writers (O'Connor made excellent English trans-
lations from the Gaelic), his was the highest stature; a story-
teller, rooted to his city and province yet universal like Chekhov
or de Maupassant. Though he, too, was frowned on by official-
dom, his works banned by those he called the 'nervous Nellies';
his funeral in 1966 unattended by top politicians. And he is as
integral to Cork as Dickens to London. He should, through
his writing, be our guide round Cork. But if only out of
respect for copyright, we must keep to our own devices.

Shaw once met an Englishman who thought Cork *was* the
south of Ireland. For him and many others, first arrival at the
city must be disappointing. Like a poor chalice in a plain
church, Cork is fascinating in what it evokes far more than
what it is. It is lively and bustling, Ireland's third largest town
(with the same population as Bath), its seaport facing south
to Spain and France rather than east to the old enemy, and
the nearest major Irish harbour to America. It has factories
for cars (Fords put their first European factory here) and
brewing and distilling and many other processes on the
industrial side – a drab area that swaps its daytime workers
for evening lovers. It has excellent shops, and good wide
streets due to its having, like Dublin, a Wide Streets Commission in the early nineteenth century; and its situation,
where, as Spenser wrote, 'The spreading Lee, that like an
island fayre, Encloseth Corke with his divided flood' is one
of the most charming in Ireland. But war, flood (in 1789 the
houses were nine feet deep in water, which carried many of
them away) and depression have wiped away much that was
best, and few buildings are older than a century and a half.
In Black and Tan times three million pounds' worth of the
city's centre was burned, and the main street, St Patrick's,
can be seen to have one side completely consisting of newer,
taller, nastier buildings than the other.

Though the town has almost none of Dublin's Georgian grandeur it is crammed in unlikely places with domestic architectural curiosities. Nowhere is this more true than north of the river, in the area round **St Anne's, Shandon,** reached from the river by a lovely steep hill with wide steps on either side. The church, like London's St Mary le Bow, is best known for its bells, acclaimed in the lines of Father Prout – 'With thy bells of Shandon, That sound so grand on The pleasant waters of the river Lee.' 'Father Prout' was the invention of a nineteenth-century expelled Jesuit satirist, Francis Sylvester Mahony, and his 'sermons' are a hilarious collection of gossip, banter, Irish bulls, knotted logic, and the fear of God. His doggerel verse trails on in a stream of wit and ready use of most living and some dead languages. He lived and died in Cork and was buried in this graveyard. An oddity of the elegant pepper-pot church tower is that two sides are made of red sandstone and two of white limestone. Around the church are various good buildings including some pleasant antique almshouses – Skiddy's Home – recently saved by a preservation order. West of the church is the unimpressive **St Mary's Pro-Cathedral,** started in 1808, with some interior work by G. R. Pain; and, half a mile north, the much more inspired and modern **Church of the Assumption,** designed and with statues by Seamus Murphy. Whatever its effect on other creative activities, the Catholic Church is nowadays a magnificent patron of the plastic arts, as Murphy's work all about County Cork, as well as that of Evie Hone, Maimie Jellett, Michael Healy, Harry Clarke and many others, testifies. Some stained glass by Hone and Healy is to be seen in the chapel of Collins Barracks, half a mile east of St Anne's.

George Richard and James Pain were sons of an English architect and pupils of John Nash, who brought them to Ireland to help with the construction of Lough Cutra Castle. G. R. Pain's work is specially prominent in Cork. Like Nash, he was adaptable in style, equally at ease in the Gothic Revival that came in the train of the Romantic Movement, and the new emphasis on Greek styles that accompanied the virtual closure of Italy to English travellers during the

Napoleonic war and the subsequent Greek War of Independance. He was not a great architect, nor anything like as prolific as Nash, but his work abounds here. One of the best examples is **St Patrick's Church** on Lower Glanmire Road – with a good pillared portico and roof lantern, let down by the predictable flamboyance of the heavy, marbled interior.

On the central, nearly water-bound area of the city a few scattered points of interest lie behind the main thoroughfares. On the north side, beside Lavitt's Quay, west of St Patrick's Bridge, is the modern **Opera House**, opened in 1965 to replace the one burned down in 1955. Michael Scott built it. Its fare is light – usually a summer season of plays, and music (the jollier operas) kept for the winter. A little to the west is **Coal Quay**, off which leads the old Cornmarket, where in the mornings there is much to see and hear from the old black-shawled women dealers – a treasury of tat in an eighteenth-century arcaded market house. Nearby in Emmet Place is the Crawford Municipal **School of Art** and **Art Gallery**, built on to the eighteenth-century Court House. The exhibition upstairs includes some minor old masters and interesting Irish work – notably by James Barry (1741–1806), a seaman, then artist-protégé of Edmund Burke, who instilled in him an ambition that outstripped his abilities, so that his patchy treatment of great themes, and a temper that got him expelled from the Royal Academy, led to his death in poverty; Sir William Orpen (1878–1931), an anglicised product of County Dublin who, made known and knighted by his official drawings of the First World War, grew bitter as his realistic school faded from the scene; and Sir John Lavery (1856–1951), born in Belfast but trained among the Glasgow school, who suffered the same public fate as Orpen. (Lavery's wife Hazel's portrait, drawn by himself and in the costume of an Irish colleen, decorates the Irish pound notes.) There are also works by Leo Whelan and James Sleator, younger artists in line of descent from Orpen, as well as by Jack Yeats, the poet's brother, including a good pastel self-portrait. A short walk south-west of the Art School is Pugin's RC Church of St Peter and St Paul, a good specimen of Gothic Revival. South-west again, between Grand Parade and South Main

Street, is the C of I **Christ Church,** built in 1720 to replace a church destroyed in John Churchill's (later Duke of Marlborough) siege of 1690 (after the Boyne). Much of the pleasant, plain interior is the work of G. R. Pain. In the church which stood here before, Edmund Spenser is supposed to have married the Earl of Cork's kinswoman, Elizabeth Boyle, 'the soverayne beauty which I do admyre' of his *Amoretti.*

South Mall, leading off the south end of Grand Parade, is the city's financial centre, flanked by smart bank buildings. Near the junction of the two streets is the headquarters of the Cork Film Festival, that unlikely event in the film-world calendar when the sun, tantrums, Martinis and nymphets of the South of France give place to the blarney, threatening damp, Guinness and hospitality of the Irish scene, creating, as the London *Times* said, the best film festival – 'that which draws the film-makers and the people into one.' It takes place in late September, and offers the most perceptively chosen selection of current world cinema. South of South Mall, off Father Mathew Quay, is the Capuchin Church of the Holy Trinity, an ornate G. R. Pain structure with a light and fanciful west front and a pleasantly plain interior. Father Theobald Mathew (1790–1856), the 'apostle of temperance', was first superior of the convent attached to the church.

South of Holy Trinity, across the bridge and east of Mary Street, is one of Cork's few medieval remains, the **Red Tower** of a fourteenth-century Augustinian abbey. From the top of the tower Churchill is said to have watched the progress of his siege in 1690. Half a mile west is the prominent landmark of **St Finbar's C of I Cathedral**, whose spires make impressive skyline silhouettes from many angles around. It is less appealing in close-up. When its Georgian predecessor was pulled down in 1864 the new design was opened to competition, which a heavy-handed lover of French Gothic, William Burges, won. (He also built additions to Cardiff Castle and the Harrow School speech room, as well as designing Hertford College, Connecticut.) His gaining the contract over his nearest rival, William Barre, made the awarding committee, according to a friend of Barre's, 'guilty of the despicable fraud they did unblushingly commit,' though in fact Barre

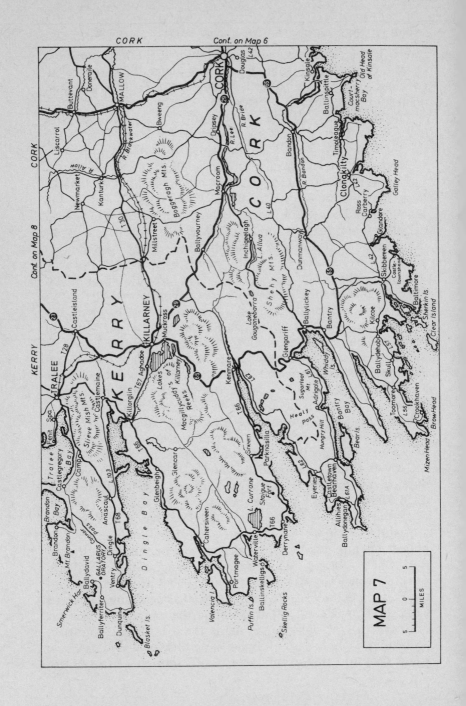

MAP 7

MILES

5   0   5

suffered more from pique than injustice. He might not have
made a better job, but could hardly have made a worse. The
concept is heavy and clumsy, the details poor, evoking little
mental or aesthetic reaction. A detail of interest is the brass
that marks the grave of the first woman Freemason, Elizabeth
Aldworth.

Half a mile west of the cathedral are the grounds of
University College, a constituent college of the National
University. The original 'Queen's colleges' of Dublin, Cork
and Galway were founded in 1845, in response to the demand
for Catholic higher education. Being undenominational, they
did not satisfy the Catholics, who called them the Godless
Colleges and, forming the vast majority, wanted exclusive
seats of learning; and went ahead to found in 1851 their abortive
Catholic University', under Cardinal Newman, in Dublin.
Disraeli, in 1880, tried to satisfy the Catholics with his 'Royal
University', an examining but non-teaching compromise, and
finally in 1908 the National University was founded, with
princely endowments from the British government. The Cork
college was by then well developed, with moderately successful
buildings of the mid-nineteenth century by Sir Thomas Deane's
firm. Macaulay thought them worth a place in Oxford High
Street. Various collections, to be seen on application, are
housed in the faculty buildings, and the college grounds are
delightful. The Pain brothers' Doric-porticoed gaol of 1818
now incorporated in the college (its function changed, it need
hardly be said) is a fine example of the Greek revival. An aspect
of the C of I's attempt, spurred by Gladstone's Disestablishment
in 1869 and the mounting wealth and influence of Catholics,
to show its true and unique descent from the primitive Irish
church, was to patronise the revival of the Irish Romanesque
style which had come to its peak (at Roscrea, Cashel and elsewhere) in the twelfth century. The **Honan Collegiate Chapel** is
a late (1916) example of this revival. Its plan is that of St
Cronan's, Roscrea, and into it is fitted the work of those
considered best in contemporary Irish craftsmanship: stained
glass (by Sarah Purser and Harry Clarke), statues, ironwork,
stonework, carpets, banners and vestments, cross, monstrance
and altar cruets. Together they make a showpiece for the move-

ment. But the general effect lacks the spontaneous vitality of, say, Cormac's Chapel at Cashel: too self-consciously arty. North of the university, along the river, is the **Mardyke,** a once fashionable elm walk with Fitzgerald Park, its fine ornamental gardens and lake, and a small museum of local interest, at the promenade's west end.

Three miles east of the city, just south of the river, stands Blackrock Castle, whose imposing present form – seen magnificently on the road into Cork from the east – is owed to the brothers Pain, but which stands on the site of a fort erected by Lord Mountjoy after the Battle of Kinsale. This was burned in 1872, following an Admiralty dinner. Its dinners have wider renown since 1968, when the place was turned into a restaurant of high quality.

A castle of different, better known appeal is **Blarney,** five miles north-west of the town which, though a crowded tourist haunt, is worth a visit for the beauty of its position and the comparatively good presentation of its complex interior. It stands south-west of the somewhat commercialised village of the same name that houses the Muskerry Hunt kennels and a woollen mill of 1750. 'Blarney', of course, has come to mean a special brand of Irish talk which persuades, deceives even, without actually offending the dupe. The origin of the meaning is supposedly in the procrastination of the then Lord of Blarney, a MacCarthy, when Elizabeth's governors were trying to wean him from dangerous Irish practices. Day to day he made promises 'with fair words and soft speech,' till Elizabeth broke out with the words 'this is all Blarney; what he says he never means,' and Tudor vocabulary was further enriched. The other Blarney tradition of kissing the Blarney Stone at the top of the tower – 'a stone that whoever kisses, O he never misses to grow eloquent' (wrote Prout) is nowadays very commercialised. There is a story that an early MacCarthy, course, has come to mean a special brand of Irish talk which persuades, deceives even, without actually offending the dupe. The origin of the meaning is supposedly in the procrastination of the then Lord of Blarney, a MacCarthy, when Elizabeth's governors were trying to wean him from dangerous Irish practices. Day to day he made promises

'with fair words and soft speech,' till Elizabeth broke out
with the words 'this is all Blarney; what he says he never
means,' and Tudor vocabulary was further enriched. The
other Blarney tradition of kissing the Blarney Stone at the
top of the tower – 'a stone that whoever kisses, O he never
misses to grow eloquent' (wrote Prout) is nowadays very
commercialised. There is a story that an early MacCarthy,
having helped Edward Bruce in his campaign to win the
English crown, was rewarded with a piece of the stone of
Scone, and fixed it on the battlements. A more explicit tale
claims that an old woman, saved from drowning by a king
of Munster, rewarded him with a spell; that if he would kiss
a stone on the castle's topmost wall he would gain a speech
that would win all to him. The best thing about the keep's
summit is the view from it. Eighteenth-century Richard Millikin,
a popular Anglo-Irish poet, made up a song that quaintly caught
its attraction, 'The groves of Blarney, they look so charming,
Down by the purling of sweet silent streams . . .', a faintly
bawdy, beautifully worded poem that James Stephens said
he would sooner have written than anything else in an Irish
anthology. As to the castle itself, it was built in 1446 by
Cormac MacCarthy, whose family, once Kings of South
Munster, repeatedly gained and lost their dominance of
Muskerry (West Cork) from and to the English, till their
departure with the 'Wild Geese' after the Boyne. The tall,
stout tower and keep with good machicolations (open-
bottomed projections from the battlements, through which
stones and possibly boiling oil could be dropped on a besieging
enemy) and some well-preserved rooms on a thick base of
solid granite give a good picture of the fortified house of the
time, and the setting within which family life continued
through spasmodic hostile approaches. The ruin attached to the
keep is of an eighteenth-century addition.

INNER CORK

Cork is the gateway to southern Ireland's most dramatic scenery – the mountainous, deeply indented western coast. Many visitors make straight from the city for the sea. Well they might; but the result is that inner Cork is little patronised, and its great beauty and interest left almost virginal for the benefit of the few who delay, for a day or two, their passage to the sea. Deferring an Atlantic tour, we can drive north from Cork to Mallow, between the Nagles and the Boggeragh Mountains, up the valley of the Martin, to see more of the area begun in the last chapter. The road outside Cork is pretty. We cross a deep glen by a seven-arched viaduct and climb slowly to the 'Red Forge' at Sluggary crossroads, passing through more level country. At Rathduff crossroads, which we cross, two pubs compete for the position of half-way house between Cork and Mallow. Megalithic forts and tombs abound in the area, and that familiar Irish sight, a nipple-like tomb-silhouette on a bosomy hill, comes often into view. Another regular feature is the grandly built estate gate that leads at best to a modest house, more often to nothing. The burning of the houses of the great explains some, but the destruction was not confined to this century's Troubles. The great houses began to decline at the Union, when landlords increasingly grew conspicuous by their absence; but even that does not explain the large number of gates leading almost nowhere. Many are no more than specious symbols of coveted status. Five miles this side of Mallow we pass, on the right, **Mourne Abbey**, a vast area enclosed by defensive walls and towers built in 1216 by the Knights Hospitallers. In its heyday it was a complete little town, with Mayor and Corporation. But this, and Castle Barrett, a short way beyond and on the left, were stage by stage reduced by the Dissolution, the Parliamentarians and King William, and little is left to see.

Mallow itself, a town of just over 5,000, has a long and winding main street which abuts, at its east end, on the castle demesne. It keeps a sneering distance from the Blackwater, which we crossed on entering, in the hydrophobic way of

most inland Irish towns. But water has played a decisive role
in Mallow's history. Founded by Desmond Geraldines in the
thirteenth century, the town was granted in 1584 to Sir
Thomas Norreys, Lord President of Munster, whose tenure
was cut short by the Munster rising of 1598. He had time,
however, to build a fortified house in the new, graceful, frail-
looking style that succeeded the sturdy functional keeps of
Norman and early Tudor times. The style (seen also at
Kanturk and Liscarroll) was not in fact premature, since not
even the former stone masses could withstand assault from
the new cannons of the period; and it was fire, not shot,
which reduced the house to its present skeletal aspect in the
Williamite wars. Meanwhile the demesne had passed by
marriage to the Jephson family, who moved into a stable
block when their house was gutted. The block was thoroughly
adapted for living in after 1837 (with the addition of a new
entrance, true to the 1837 plans and using stones ready cut at
the earlier date, made about 1954), and is now a smart, unpretentious, ten-gabled Tudor-revival residence. It is the Jephson
family's still. The white deer in the park are supposed to descend
from two white harts, the gift of Queen Elizabeth to her god-
child Elizabeth Norreys.

Mallow's look of ordinariness conceals an unusual history.
It is hard to picture, in the days of the six-county border, an
Orange order that throve in this south-western province. Yet
the Moyallow Loyal Protestant Society, founded in the wake
of the 1745 Jacobite scares to maintain loyalty to the Hanover-
ian kings and provide if necessary a militia to fight for them,
grew rich on its unspent funds. An ancestor of Elizabeth
Bowen was one of its presidents, and the minute-book
preserved in her family speaks of festive dinners, Orange
cockades and medals worn, loyal toasts and speeches, and
rewards offered for the arrest of felons. This last was specially
helpful to Mallow's other eighteenth-century distinction, that
of being the prime spa of Ireland, often known as the Irish
Bath. Its warm springs, promoted by Dr Rogers of Cork,
became famous as a cure for consumption, and society of all
ages gathered to take the cure. Arthur Young and Charles
Wesley came, and so did the young blades of the time, those

'Rakes of Mallow' from whom the early-morning Cork coach
was named: 'Beaving, belling, dancing, drinking, Breaking
windows, damning, sinking, Ever raking, never thinking,
Live the Rakes of Mallow.' It lost ground towards the end
of the eighteenth century to the Hot Wells of Bristol, but
Sir Walter Scott came in the early 1800s. Nowadays only the
original Spa House, which is private, and three little spouts
on the Fermoy road, remain from its prosperous days. In
1814 Thomas Davis, founder-member of the Young Irelanders, was born at 72 Thomas Davis Street.

Either side of Mallow, the Blackwater is flecked with the
demesnes and houses, some entire, some ruinous, of old settler
families: Fairy Hill, Woodfort, ruined Dromaneen, Waterloo
and Longueville (now a hotel) to the west; Bearforest, Rook
Forest and Ballymacmoy to the east. Six miles north-west,
beside Cecilstown, is the curious relic of the Perceval family
home, Lohort Castle. Sir Philip Perceval secured over 100,000
acres of north Cork in the early seventeenth century. His
descendant the second Earl of Egmont restored the Lohort's
fifteenth century MacCarthy tower-house. (He thought gunpowder would prove a passing phase, put more faith in bows
and arrows, and equipped the castle with weapons for a hundred
horse; he was also a vigorous advocate of British occupation
of the Falkland Islands: 'the key to the whole Pacific Ocean').
He afforested the demesne in the shape of an octagon, more
apparent now from the map than on the ground. His son
became Prime Minister and was assassinated in 1812. The
Egmont title went astray, to cousins, nephews and so to dor-
mancy, though it was successfully reclaimed by a Canadian
Perceval in 1939. The family abandoned Lohort, which was
badly burned in 1922, but the tower is still occupied.

Eight miles north-north-east of Mallow, **Doneraile Court**,
a handsome house of 1725 in strict Queen Anne style, but
later altered, was the home of Arthur St Leger, first Viscount
Doneraile, whose daughter Mary (later Lady Aldworth), hid
in a large clock to overhear the secret proceedings of his
Freemason lodge meeting. The members, on discovering her,
decided the only solution was to enrol her in the order, and
she thus became the first and one of the only three women

Masons. She is buried in Cork's St Finbar's Cathedral. The son of a later viscount founded in 1776 the famous stakes at Doncaster. In 1969, the St Leger title and line having died out, the Irish Georgian Society tried to preserve the contents and open the house to the public, but they were balked by the trustees. All the contents were sold and the Land Commission took over the estate. Decay and vandalism took their toll. But in 1975 the Commission leased the house, with its stately Ionic Grand Gates, ilex trees and heron-haunted fishponds to the Society, which with its usual brio recruited armies of volunteers to restore the buildings. Provided with large paintings and suitable furniture, it is due to be opened to the public before the end of 1986. The court and small village were part of Edmund Spenser's land, granted him after the Desmond Rebellion. He, Raleigh and Sir Philip Sidney all walked here, 'among the cooly shade of the green alders.' Spenser's home was **Kilcolman Castle,** four miles north of Doneraile, delightfully set in cornfields by a reedy lane and marsh on which seagulls breed in spring. The castle is half a mile from the road. All that remains is a stumpy tower overgrown with ivy, but the view is of a spreading lonely plateau in a mountain-ringed basin. Spenser came to Ireland in 1580 as Lord Deputy Grey's secretary. Grey's mission was to suppress the risings in Ulster and Munster, which he tackled so ruthlessly that he was recalled in 1582. Spenser stayed on, but his feelings for the Irish were much as his master's. In 1588 he came to Kilcolman to live on land forfeited by the Earl of Desmond. He returned the hostile feelings of the natives, and one side of his character is starkly revealed in his *View of the Present State of Ireland*, in which he advocates a policy of elimination akin to Hitler's. (Even the English government refused its publication.) The other facet, the poet's, found fulfilment in a long friendship with Raleigh and a steady output of cantos of *The Faerie Queene*, begun in England, and written mainly at the castle. He also met and married Elizabeth Boyle, and wrote some of his best work for her. In the Munster rising of 1598 unpopular Spenser was besieged at Kilcolman by a ragged mob. He and his family escaped but the castle was burned down. In England at Christmas he addressed the queen:

'Out of the ashes of disolacion and wastnes of this your wretched Realms of Ireland, vouchsafe, most mightie Empresse, our Dred soveraigne, to receive the voices of a few most unhappie Ghostes.' But the queen was deaf to his pleas, and he died destitute in 1599. In Cromwell's time a grandson, Peregrine Spenser, who had reoccupied the land, was threatened with transplantation to Connaught. Cromwell himself intervened to save him, for the sake, not of *The Faerie Queen*, but the *View*.

Two miles west of the castle is **Buttevant**, a town that lies at the northern end of what was the territory of the Barry family, whose earliest title, granted in 1273, was the Viscountcy of Buttevant. It is built along a wide main street. A mile south are the ruins of the Augustinian Abbey of St Thomas, dating from the thirteenth century, with a belfry tower, cloister walls, and a circular dovecot in a field close by. The town itself has a weedy Franciscan friary of 1251, also dedicated to St Thomas, with a rather sinister crypt and sub-crypt below, where bones were recently in evidence. They are said to be the Confederate victims of a Parliamentary army led by the renegade Irishman, Murrough O'Brien. Ruined Buttevant Castle was a good example of the Gothic revival of the early nineteenth century.

Eight miles west-north-west of Buttevant is **Liscarrol**, with one of the three largest Irish medieval castles, built by the Barrys in the thirteenth century. Its massive curtain walls – recently restored – are flanked by two sturdy drum towers and four square ones, reduced to their present ruinous state in 1642, again by Murrough O'Brien. This whole area figured largely in the fighting of the more recent Civil War of 1922. It also appears in Spenser's work, and several of its more musical names were borrowed by him. From here a series of minor roads lead west-south-west ten miles to Newmarket, in the shadow of the desolate Mullaghareirk Mountains to the west. The place is remarkable for little but a link with an often told tale of frustrated love. John Philpot Curran (1750–1817) was born and lived here – at the priory – for several years. In the temporarily halcyon days of the late eighteenth century he studied law, and rose with Grattan to champion Irish Ireland in the Dublin Parliament, often defending the United Irishmen, and fighting the Union – the 'annihilation of Ireland'. Unknown to him his daughter Sarah loved and was loved by Robert Emmet, the callow, hopeless rebel of 1803. Learning of the affair Curran barred Emmet from his house. After the rising he refused to defend him in court. Emmet was beheaded. Sarah later married an Englishman but died abroad in 1808 – of a broken heart, as Moore had it in his poem. Curran's own wife left him for a clergyman. He has an ambiguous position in the story of Irish patriotism.

Kanturk, a few miles south-east, is prettily sited at the meeting of the Allow and Dalua rivers, both in Spenser's *Fairie Queene*. The surrounding country is rich in castles, many dating from the Munster plantations, that can be glimpsed in any drive round local lanes. Far the most magnificent is the shell of early seventeenth-century Mac-Donagh's Court, or **Kanturk Castle**, a mile south of the village. It was no fire or bombardment that reduced it to its present hollow state but the wariness of MacDonagh Mac-Carthy's neighbours, who, suspicious of the purpose of the magnificent rectangular house, heavily fortified with four corner towers, complained to the government. The government, equally disconcerted, ordered an end to the building in 1615. MacCarthy in fury smashed the glass tiles that were ready for the roof, and left the place as it appears now, with empty mullioned windows, brackets for the machicolation, holes for beams, fireplaces, but no floors, no roof, and no history of habitation.

From here we continue south to the main Mallow–Killarney road, turn right along the Blackwater valley, past Dromagh Castle on the right and turn left after four miles. Seven more miles bring us past the demesne of Drishane Castle (now a convent) to Millstreet, a busy but uninteresting village. Its background is the best thing about it, and about the south-ward road we now follow to Macroom. To the right of the rising road the Derrynasaggart Mountains rise from their fringe of bog and stone-fenced fields. To the left are the Boggeraghs, with their highest peak, Musheramore, rising to

2,118 feet in our view. Both mountain chains are full of folklore, supernatural explanations of the standing stones and dolmens that are found across these bleak humps. Leprechauns are not tied to specific places in Ireland but are found all over, though they tend to patronise the prettiest of ruined castles. There is as much chance of meeting one here as elsewhere in the country, and the drill for an encounter needs stating. They are very small people and go around singly. By a confusion of their name, which means 'little people', with the Irish word for shoe, 'brog' or brogue (which by association came to be the name of the Irish accent), they were always taken to be obsessive shoemakers. A leprechaun, if seen at all, is always making shoes for the fairies and taking sips of mountain dew, which is a brand of whisky. It will be a moonlit evening, and he should be approached without a sound, grasped firmly in the hand, fixedly gazed on, and asked where are the crocks of gold. He will try to talk his way out of the question, using immense cunning. If he cannot escape he will give the information. Leprechaun history goes far back into Irish prehistory. Races, once dominant, then superseded by conquering immigrants, were mentally relegated to a low supernatural status. Leprechauns were in better days the conquering Tuatha de Danaan, and ruled all Ireland.

Macroom is a market town, not long ago the capital of Irish-speaking West Cork, made to look bigger than it is by the ribbon development along its main road. Amongst the general ugliness of the place, only the ruined castle, with a longer than usual pedigree of ownership, delays us. In the fifteenth century it was a stronghold of the MacCarthys. In 1649 a force preparing to join the Catholic resurgence of Hugh O'Neill was attacked here and beaten by Lord Broghill. Their leader, Bishop MacEgan, one of several prelates who took military command at the time, was captured, and ordered to tell his garrison at nearby Carrigadrohid to surrender. He refused, and was hanged above the river there. Admiral Penn, the Quaker's father, was granted the land in 1654 at Cromwell's settlement, then deprived of it and compensated with that at Shanagarry by Charles II. The castle subsequently

passed through the hands of several families and was modernised by the Earl of Bantry last century. To little purpose: it
was burned in 1922. Frank O'Connor sat in the grounds, then
an IRA base, in the last stages of the civil war; chatting with
Erskine Childers, who was soon to cross Ireland in an
adventurous bid to escape the Free Staters, be caught in
Wicklow and shot with the callous ceremony that strove to
give dignity to a pointless war. 'You know they will kill you
if they catch you, Mr Childers', said someone on this lawn.
'Oh, why does everyone tell me that?' he snapped irritably.
An Englishman, veteran of the Boer and Great Wars, he
knew, said O'Connor, that 'in a family row it is always the
outsider who gets the blame'. The castle's park is now public,
with parts given over to sports and recreation.

Drives either side of Macroom show the town is the boundary
between the lush, well-farmed east Lee valley and the craggy,
mountain-ringed, boggy west. A round tour that shows off
some of the best of the latter begins from Macroom, along
the Killarney road, turns left at Ballyvourney, zigzags through
hard mountain roads south-west to Gouganebarra Lake,
source of the Lee, and follows the Lee back to Macroom.
This detour begins up the beautiful valley of the Sullane,
and passes, three miles from Macroom, Fairy Land and
fifteenth-century **Carrigaphouca Castle**. This is named from
the existence of a *puca* or goblin; a more recent introduction
to Irish lore than the leprechaun, and probably coming over
with the Danes (from whom the English 'Puck' came too).
The castle's foundation is a clear example of a *roche moutonnée*
or sheep-back, a rock-mound rounded at the end which
faced the glacier's flow. **Ballyvourney**, a few miles farther
along this twisting road with its sheep and rock bluffs, is well
inside the Muskerry Gaeltacht, or Irish-speaking area.
Nearby is the site of a sixth-century nunnery founded by
St Gobnat, a still popular saint whose patterns on 11th
February and Whit Sunday attract enormous crowds. She
was a beekeeper, and is so represented in the statue of 1951
by Seamus Murphy outside the graveyard. The main remains
comprise St Gobnat's House and medieval church, St Gobnat's

Grave and Well. All these fit into a Round, walked by people who still come throughout the year for the cures of the saint, who was adept at healing her nuns and kept the plague from Ballyvourney. Trinkets, offerings, and teacups, put there for the convenience of those drinking the holy water, are much in evidence.

A further climb of nearly four miles leads to a good view across to the MacGillicuddy Reeks above Killarney. But we leave Killarney for a later tour, and drive south-west to reach, after some difficult driving, the sequestered treasure of West Cork, **Lake Gouganebarra**, magnificently set under the sheer heights of the Shehy Mountains. It was on an island of this lake that St Finbar (a well-connected saint who having allegedly crossed the sea to Britain on horseback travelled with St David to Rome), founded an oratory and drowned a monster that St Patrick, in his eviction of reptiles, had over-looked. Finbar went on to work in Cork, but his island remained a sanctuary and the present raised courtyard, save for the 1900 memorial church, inspired – if that is the word – by Cormac's Chapel at Cashel, was built around 1700. The pilgrimage to the site was at its height in the eighteenth century, when Thomas Crofton Croker came and saw, along with the devotion of crowds at prayer in and around the little cells and diseased bathers in the narrow well, a great trade in whiskey and porter, and on the shore the dancing of jigs, an inexorable increase in drunkenness, and brawls breaking out with fists and cudgels. On the mainland lived Teig Buckley and his wife Ansty, whom Eric Cross immortalised in *The Tailor and Ansty*. The holly trees on the island were probably planted for the protective powers of their red berries, which like those of rowan and hawthorn have had a religious significance since prehistoric times. A National Forest Park, opened in 1966, lies to the north of the lake and there are beautiful walks in it, and fine views over Kerry and the western sea from the mountain tops above.

The scenic main road east leads back to Macroom, passing long Lough Allua. A still more attractive minor road leads along the south side of the lake. Beside this southern road, less than a mile before it recrosses the Lee, a plaque stands bearing the inscription 'Altar of Penal Times. Mass was said here 1640–1800'. **Carrignacurra Castle**, a mile east of Inchigeelagh, was an O'Leary property, forfeited by the family, which joined the losing side in the 1641 war. From here the views grow less dramatic, as the road draws near the widening of the Lee above Macroom known as the Gearagh, a swamp of three miles' length, with channels of the river alternating with strips of alder covered by reedy flats. Below Macroom the river widens again, this time from the giant dams erected for hydro-electric purposes. The road passes **Carrigadrohid**, where a castle protrudes into the river beside the bridge. It was here that Bishop MacEgan, staunchly refusing to order his own side to capitulate to Broghill, was hanged after the stronghold was taken, in 1650. The road continues through the pretty valley, edged with forested hills, closely following the river for the remaining eighteen miles to Cork.

CORK TO KENMARE BY COAST

The south-west of Ireland is warm, warmer than anywhere else in Ireland, not only in the climatic sense but also like a seat well sat in. The list of the famous who have been here is inexhaustible. Among those who have recorded their experiences are Tennyson, Macaulay, Thackeray, Scott, Fox, Maria Edgeworth, Alfred Austin, Queen Victoria. More recently Benjamin Britten, Sir Arnold Bax, Françoise Sagan, Charlie Chaplin, Sir Alec Guinness, Sir Bernard Lovell of Jodrell Bank, Gore Vidal and many others have owned land here, and here General de Gaulle came in 1969 at the end of his presidency. What draws people is the complexity of features that make beautiful landscape, a climate where sub-tropical vegetation thrives, an indented coastline that makes almost a thousand miles of what, were it straight, would be a hundred, and in which soft sand alternates with rugged cliff, dune, and rock; a series of sandstone mountain ranges, some with rounded surfaces that look as if you could slide down them, others jagged like a Gothic castle by mad Ludwig of Bavaria, all of them changing their aspect as the light and clouds alter unceasingly; several hundred islands of all shapes, sizes, and states of cultivation; remains from every stage of the least interrupted historical sequence in Europe, a kind people whose instinct for entertainment is unrivalled. And all of it – except for a few square miles round Killarney – is more thinly peopled, either by native or visitor, than any comparable area in Europe.

We approach the far west by the coast road. From Cork we drive due south to **Kinsale**, a historic harbour town, one of the prettiest in Ireland, that grew popular as bathing did in the late eighteenth century and owes much of its charm to that time. Before that, it had had the varied record, common to a west Munster seaport, of exposure both to trade and attack from French and Spanish. The famous Battle of Kinsale took place in 1601. Hugh O'Neill, descendant of the great O'Neill kings, had rebelled in 1595 to defend Ulster and the rest of Ireland against Elizabeth's systematic encroachments. His great victory at the Yellow Ford brought over Mountjoy and a vigorous punishment of the Irish. O'Neill pinned all on the arrival of Spanish allies, who came eventually, not to the north where he needed them, but here to Kinsale in which they secured themselves against Mountjoy's blockade. Forced marches brought O'Neill's army to the scene. Unable to link with the Spanish he had to fight the English alone, and was routed. He escaped, carried on fitful resistance for two years, then submitted. Four years later he and others of the Ulster Irish left Ireland for foreign service in what came to be known as the Flight of the Earls. So that the effects of the battle were to smash the old Irish order for good, to make Ireland temporarily docile and ready for the uprootings of James I's plantation policy, and to make England – an aim from which all her Irish policy inevitably followed – secure from back-door attacks by Catholic Europe. Nearly fifty years later the town saw another frustrated sea-venture. After Charles I's execution in 1649, loyal Ormonde had Charles II proclaimed here, as in all the Munster coast-towns. Prince Rupert entered the harbour to prepare the way for the young king's arrival, with sixteen black-draped ships. But he was blockaded by Parliamentary ships, while young Charles was unable to make the journey for want of funds. Rupert slipped the line and made Lisbon, and within a year elements in Kinsale negotiated with Cromwell and gave up the town quietly. Still later, in 1690, James II sailed out of Ireland and history from Kinsale. In his wake came John Churchill, Marlborough-to-be, and destroyed the walls. Decline set in. From being the only port where the king's ships could be repaired, it lost trade and naval importance to Cork. Its revival came from peacetime activities and is now in full swing, as weekend crowds, some of them yachtsmen and deep-sea anglers, show. It contains some interesting buildings, including the old Dutch-gabled courthouse, of 1706, now a museum; the newly restored Gift Houses of 1682; the sixteenth-century tower house of Desmond Castle, used in Napoleonic times for French prisoners of war; and the curious, much restored thirteenth-century Church of St Multose, with a roofless south transept of 1550; as well as quaint Georgian houses with their bow windows, curved walls and some pretty shaped gables.

All the coastline is delightful on both sides of the harbour, and there is a good drive through Scilly down the east side, through Summer Cove and past Charles's Fort, a monster built in 1677 by Sir William Robinson, often added to and continually occupied by the British till 1922. It was then burned. But we now continue westward from Kinsale, crossing the Bandon River after two miles and making south for the Old Head of Kinsale, a magnificent headland with a ruined castle at its neck and a Napoleonic Wars watchtower on top. The castle belonged to the de Courcy family, Barons Kingsale, premier barons of Ireland who once had the right, exploited under William III, to stand with their hats on in the presence of royalty. Ten miles south of the Head, in 1915, the *Lusitania* was torpedoed by the Germans and more than 1,500 were drowned. For weeks, bodies were washed up on the shore (Edith Somerville recorded six at Castletownshend).

From Ballinspittle (with its prehistoric fort) the coast road goes west, crossing a creek off Courtmacsherry Bay to Timoleague, a village that appears to doze beside the Ardigeen estuary with its spread of mud-flats. Over the wash the thin tower of a large Franciscan friary of 1312 stands out, with other remains from the time when, in 1642, Lord Forbes and an English army burned it out. (Ten miles inland is the larger town of **Bandon**, the Earl of Cork's pride, which he built up till it rivalled Derry in industry. It has a good C of I church of 1610.) **Clonakilty** is six miles west, through lanes thickly hedged with wild flowers and a prospect of hills to north and south. (There is little by way of coast road round the promontory of the Seven Heads, but this, like all headlands and promontories along this coast, offers magnificent views to the walker. The coast is spattered with sandy resorts.) Clonakilty is a market town of little interest, founded by the Earl of Cork (a glance at names on shops shows how lastingly successful the plantations were; English and Scottish names are in parts almost as common as Irish). He established spinning and weaving here, and as late as 1839 there were four hundred looms in the area. Three miles west a signpost points to **Sam's Cross**, and Woodfield, the former a hamlet with a dominant population of Collinses, the latter nearby and the birthplace of Michael Collins (1890–1922). There is a memorial to him by Seamus Murphy at Sam's Cross. Collins had a genius for organising guerrilla warfare, and it was largely this that made the British position untenable in 1921. In that year, he and Arthur Griffith were sent to London for the thorny negotiations with two masters of the art, Lloyd George and Birkenhead. They returned with less than some of their fellows were prepared to accept. Ranks divided, and some, including De Valera, took to the hills. The Civil War followed. In August, 1922, Collins himself was ambushed and killed at Bealnabla (fourteen miles north of Clonakilty, near the Lee). All the same the war made no difference; and within a few years De Valera himself was proscribing those who continued his own fight.

The road continues, and lanes with attractive sea views to the left, often festooned with crimson fuchsia, which is as common here as hawthorn or hazel in England (it has had since the 1780s to grow to such profusion; at that time an English sailor brought it to England from Chile and his wife sold it to a nurseryman in Hammersmith). **Ross Carbery,** a thin village among many trees, and possessing a heavily restored medieval cathedral, is set on a broad inlet. There are pretty coves and beaches nearby but many are spoilt, especially towards Galley Head to the east, where an unplanned litter of caravans and bungalows poisons the front of the demesne of **Castle Freke**, ruined Gothic home of the Barons Carbery. A mile north-west, left of the main road, is the shell of **Derry House** (burned in 1921), home of Charlotte Payne-Townshend, later Mrs Bernard Shaw. Shaw's first visit was in 1905, when he spent the time revising *Captain Brassbound's Conversion*. Charlotte, he wrote, stayed behind, 'doing a round of Bandons and Castletowns and Kingstons and other Irish peers and their castles. I fled to England.'

A minor road from Ross to Glandore takes us past **Coppinger's Court**, a ruined fortified house of the seventeenth century. Set stark and unlikely among gentle hills, with an unusual ground-plan, tall gables and elaborate machicolations, it was attacked and reduced to more or less its present state in the 1640s. **Glandore** is a lovely, quiet fishing village, refurbished by a progressive landlord, James Redmond Barry, in the eighteen-thirties. He and a neighbour, William Thompson, were early socialists, founding cooperatives for industry and fishing, and establishing schools. Thompson earned a footnote in Marx's *Das Kapital*, and some of Barry's planning and building is still evident. Swift stayed a while in 1723 in Rock Cottage, outside Union Hall, a hamlet on the far side of the estuary. Myross, the promontory between here and Castle Haven, was called by Daniel Corkery (whose talk and writings – especially *The Hidden Ireland* – strongly influenced Frank O'Connor) 'one of the most secret places in Ireland, without traffic, almost without pulse of life'. Turning left soon after, we come to **Castletownshend.**

This long village, its main street steeply descending to the water, is where the prolific partnership of Edith Somerville and Martin Ross brought forth the *Irish RM* (or Resident Magistrate) books, the still, in England, reprinted stories of the West Carbery Hunt which, since they failed to show the Irishman always in a serious, patriotic and noble light, have been decried by a respected Irish critic as 'the writings of spiritual nihilists'. With *The Real Charlotte* and *The Big House of Inver* they make a delightful account of the decaying Anglo-

Irish gentry at the turn of this century. Somerville, born in Corfu and educated in Paris, was of an old Castletownshend family. Voilet Martin (Ross's real name) came from Galway. Both had a delighted perception of the ridiculous. They could be a touch ridiculous themselves. An ardent spiritualist, Somerville kept in touch with Martin after the latter's death in 1915, worried her publishers by insisting her work was still the result of transcendental collaboration and must be attributed to them both, and once claimed Martin had teased her by saying she had fallen (in the hereafter) for Tennyson, who sat her on his knee while she called him 'Alf'. She also believed that dogs, unlike horses, had an after life and could be communicated with. Edith's family home was the Georgian mansion Drishane at the entrance to the village, which still belongs to the family. Outside it is a memorial to Admiral Boyle Somerville, her brother, murdered at his door in the 1930s for helping local boys recruit into the Royal Navy. Edith died in 1949 at Tally Ho House, farther on in the village. Both authors were buried at St Barrahane's Church, where in 1923 Edith, to the vicar's consternation, had an alter erected in gratitude for Voilet's ethereal protection during the Troubles. A little before, she recorded a local woman's comment on the end of the Troubles: 'The Black and Tans are gone and the soldiers are gone and now the polis is going and the boys can fight in peace.' Castle Townshend, at the bottom of the village, is a Victorian battlemented mansion with impressive wood panelling in the hall, still the home of the Townshends.

A mile south of the village is **Galleon Point**, off which an engagement between Spanish and English took place in 1601 at the time of Kinsale. The Spanish garrisoned the headland and there is supposed to be a Spanish graveyard here. (Boyle Somerville, also a spiritualist, once had it pointed out to him by a Spanish ghost.) The road continues past a succession of bays and precipitous headlands with pretty beaches. There are signs of hard living among those who inhabit the old cottages, and of high living among those who own the occasional holiday chalets. **Lough Hyne**, south-south-west of Skibbereen, is a charming salt-water lake with a long narrow inlet from the sea which slows the tide so much that it takes three hours

to rise and nine in its imperceptible fall. Recently married
young Julian Huxley stayed here to study the bristle-worm
Sabella, only seen at extra-low water. Beyond is a most attractive, rugged bay. **Baltimore** is an attractive fishing village
built round its harbour, with a ruined sixteenth-century
O'Driscoll castle above. It was here that Algerians, in the
form of privateers, intruded on Irish history in 1631 to
massacre some inhabitants and take others as slaves to
Africa. Spanish Island, opposite the harbour, recalls again
the Spanish expedition of 1601 that ended in the rout of
Kinsale. South-west of it lies Sherkin Island, whose ruined
Franciscan friary of 1460 can be seen from the mainland.
Beyond Sherkin is **Clear Island**, which can be reached by
mailboat from Baltimore. Irish is spoken here, as it is on
many western islands, and there are some interesting antiquities, but in recent years the island has become known for
the work of a small amateur group who in 1959 set up the
Cape Clear Bird Observatory. In season there is never any
difficulty in any island of seeing the best-known sea-species –
the various gulls, kittiwakes, guillemots, puffins, razorbills,
skuas, cormorants and others. But the setting up of new
observatories in Britain and Ireland has shown the local existence of far more sea and land birds than were ever suspected.
Some are strays and casuals, some have always lived on the
sea, out of sight until regular manning of telescopes began.
Cape Clear was a pioneer in sea-bird watching, and has become
known for its sooty, Cary's, and great shearwaters (of which
5,000 were once seen in a single day) – considered rare off these
coasts till the regular watch began. Actual rarities seen here
include the black-browed albatross, little shearwater and,
possibly, Wilson's petrel.

  Clear and Sherkin islands, and farther out lighthouse-
bearing Fastnet Rock, of weather-forecast fame, are the
unsubmerged heights of what was once a long old red sandstone peninsula. From here on our route is a succession of
five such exposed strips, which together make up what rivals
Connemara as Ireland's most dramatic scenery. To reach
the first, we must drive north-east, through the market-village
of Skibbereen, cross the Ilen River and head west again

along the L42. Views improve wherever the road draws near the sea, especially when it overlooks Roaring Water Bay with its hosts of islands and solitary Fastnet in the distance. Inland is wild scrub, sometimes dramatically wild, rising on the right to the shapely peak of Mt Gabriel, from the top of which is seen the best view of the peninsula. Schull (meaning school; monks from Ross Carbery founded one here in the tenth century) has a C of I church with medieval fragments incorporated. J. M. Synge's grandfather was rector here, a man who, in his own words, dedicated his life 'to waging war against Popery in its thousand forms of wickedness'. His church is long since disused.

Mizen Head is the main reason for continuing along the peninsula, with its clearly marked layers of sandstone rock piled into angular cliffs that jut into the Atlantic, and its sequestered signal station, barred to the public, that fires flares at intervals in thick fog to warn off ships. The road back along the north side is of different character, a ruggeder scene of small stone-bordered fields, with harvests carefully tended in patches that anywhere else would be ignored. Poverty has been familiar here for a century and a half, ever since an apparent decline in the fish population deprived many of the means of livelihood. The cause may have been more the Napoleonic Wars, which reduced the foreign markets (including Italy, Portugal and the West Indies) to which Bantry had exported salted, barrelled fish. The land, on which the peasantry was forced back for subsistence, was not fertile enough. Emigration alleviated a problem made more acute by the system of inheritance and primitive farming methods which still included ploughing with the plough attached to a horse's tail, plucking sheep instead of shearing, and burning corn to divide straw from grain, so destroying useful winter fodder and bedding for cattle. In these remote parts the pattern has not changed out of all recognition.

Bantry Bay has been a splendid scene, though the town of Bantry, with its vast desert of a square, has little but the manor-house to recommend it. Unfortunately it is here that giant 326,000-ton tankers bring crude oil for storage on Whiddy Island. Though the terminal tanks were carefully placed half underground, their scarlet roofs still appear to desecrate the surrounds. Colossal sums were spent and gestures made (the new statue of St Brendan: a trip for the Prime Minister to assist launch their first tanker in Japan) by American Gulf Oil Corporation to sweeten the industrial pill. But the jamboree seemed over for the town when employment on building the £10 million terminal came to an end, and now nobody but the Americans is pleased, least of all the visitor. The bay has drawn tourists for as long – maybe two centuries – as tourism of a kind has been known. 'Were such a bay lying upon English shore, it would be the world's wonder', Thackeray wrote and others said as much long before him. Bantry also received visits of a more serious kind. In 1689 a French fleet sailed in to help James II's cause, but turned back after an indecisive battle with William III's navy. In 1796 the French came again, this time with Wolfe Tone on board, who for years in Paris had been planning Ireland's break from England. Out of forty-three ships that left Brest only sixteen got through the channel storms – Tone's diary on board records every variant of wind in hope, gloom and insouciance – '*je m'en fiche*, if ever they hang me, they are welcome to embowel me if they please'. Wind and fog kept them six days in the bay, unable to land. In the end they had to turn back, and it was two years before another attempt could be made. **Bantry House,** above the bay, is a good brick Georgian house of 1765 (enlarged in 1845) at the town's west end, built by Richard White, first Earl of Bantry, ennobled for organising defences against Tone and the French. His son, the second earl, travelled in Europe to amass a collection of paintings, tapestries, furniture, Savonnerie carpets, tiling, fireplaces and trinkets (some from Versailles), which are on view to the public in the musty, dilapidated setting of the house. The garden, laid out in the Italian style with terraces and statuary, gives beautiful views over the bay to the Beara peninsula. The atmosphere is in happy contrast to the modern industrial wonder-working of Whiddy Island opposite. The house is open to the public; was, in fact, the first to be so on a regular basis in the country.

Other good gardens are to be seen on Garinish Island opposite **Glengariff**, after a beautiful drive of some ten miles round the head of the bay (half-way along a right turn leads to Gouganebarra, described elsewhere). The village, with its mellow climate, dense vegetation, fine walks and a plethora of comfortable hotels in and around it, is something of a rest-cure fantasy, marred only by the new crop of bungalows and chalets. It is the climate, frost-free, that makes for the abundance of flowers, some found nowhere else in these islands. But **Ilnacullin Island** is more of a miracle than that. When John Annan Bryce took it over it was almost solid rock. Every spadeful of earth was brought by boat before the gardens could be shaped, in 1910, to the designs of Harold Peto (1854–1933), whose architect's training led him always to use the stone of statuary and masonry in what he thought a just proportion with the plants. State-owned now, it is not at its best, but is one of the most beautiful gardens in the area, with Greek and Roman temples, exotic shrubberies, rock gardens, Japanese gardens, Italian gardens round a lily pond, and some beautiful vistas of the bay and mountain. It was on this island that Shaw wrote much of his *St Joan*.

From here on one soon grows accustomed to luxuriant growth: fuchsia up to twenty-five feet, escallonia with its pink trumpets against thick shiny green foliage, tree-ferns, eucalyptus with its shimmering banana leaves, mountain-ash, oak, holly, yew, Chilean myrtle, *Clethra arborea*, and the famous strawberry tree, *Arbutus unedo*, which grows mainly at Glengarriff and Killarney. The last, otherwise found wild in Europe mainly among the mountains of Spain and on the west coast of France, is made distinct by its flowers (cream, like lily of the valley, and appearing September to October), its leathery glossy leaves, and its prickly scarlet berries, last year's fruit appearing at the same time as this year's flowers. Its specific name, *unedo*, is Latin for 'I eat one'; no more – only its looks are like the strawberry. Less obvious than these plants, but also more or less confined to these parts of Cork and Kerry, are the two rock-loving saxifrages, the delicate pink and ineptly named London Pride, and Kidney-leaved Saxifrage (*Saxifraga hirsuta*); Irish Spurge with little yellow

Ardmore, County Waterford: the best placed ruins in Ireland.
Below Cahir Castle, County Tipperary: a Butler fortress on the Suir.

Cork: the belltower of St Anne's, Shandon.

flowers in early summer and long leaves up to three inches; pale pink Irish Heath, common on moorland in spring; Greater Butterwort with yellow-green leaves and deep purple flowers, enormous compared to their slender stems, on bogs in May – 'the most beautiful member of the Irish flora' wrote Dr Scully, who earlier this century compiled a *Flora of County Kerry*. (The Butterwort is notable also for its feeding on small insects which are trapped on the sticky leaves, digested by a discharge of a kind of gastric juice, and absorbed into the system); July-flowering Blue-eyed Grass with delicate star-shaped flowers at the tips of grassy stems – a botanical problem is that it is found elsewhere mainly in Western America; and the rare fern found at Killarney, *Trichomanes radians*. For most of the flowers, late spring is the best time to arrive; the late-autumn-blooming strawberry tree is an exception.

Beara stands with the Ring of Kerry and Dingle to the north as the most beautiful of the western peninsulas, but it is the least popular. Only a few years ago there were only sixty-five beds available in the forty-mile landstrip. There are more now, but still it is far more rugged and lonely than the other two. The beauty of these craggy peninsulas has to be seen on long drives, and preferably walks. The drive round Beara takes us along the south coast between the island-streaked bay and the Sugarloaf Mountain and other curious, patterned rock formations, results of ancient geological upheaval, beside bog and well-walled oases of grass reserved for some farmstead's few cows. At Adrigole a road branches right to cross the mountains at **Healy Pass**; the road was begun as relief work in Famine Times – fourpence for a twelve-hour day; but a high death-rate and slow progress brought it to a halt. It was begun again in 1928, at the instance of Bantry-born Tim Healy (1855–1931), the most vituperative of those who voted against Parnell, and from 1922–8 first governor-general of the Free State, and opened in 1931. It makes a memorable scenic route passing on the northern descent the dark, islanded, sheer-sided lake of Glanmore. But we continue west from Adrigole, past Hungry Hill (2,251 feet), highest hill of the Caha range and source of the title of Daphne du Maurier's novel, six-mile long Bear Island and the haven that it forms – till 1937 an anchorage of the British Atlantic fleet. Castletown Bearhaven is a long straggling village with a port and sandy beach. Two miles southwest, set back from the road, is the dramatic ruin of **Dunboy Castle,** to which there is admission. It was here in 1602 that Sir George Carew with an English force took and butchered, after a siege, the last Spanish-Irish garrison to hold out after the Battle of Kinsale. Within a year Owen Roe O'Neill had capitulated, and the rising was over. In the 1880s Henry Puxley, owner of the local copper mines, added a huge home in high Victorian style – steep roofs, gangling chimneys, gothic arches and oriel windows – but it was wrecked in the 1920s. The road continues to lovely scenery at the end of the peninsula, and there is an excellent beach at Ballydonegan.

Returning along the north side of the peninsula we pass Allihies and its disused nineteenth-century copper mines (recently worked again for a short time) and drive along a zigzag coast road with splendid sheer drops of rock beside it. The Ring of Kerry makes the north view, with foam-splashed islands and outcrops on the Kenmare River estuary in between, and often (in a climate where in parts and eighty-inch annual rainfall is not uncommon) the addition of a complete rainbow. At **Eyeries** there is a pillar 17½ feet high with ogham inscriptions. Though this is the tallest in the country, over three hundred more exist, many of them, like this, staying *in situ.* They serve in general as gravestones and signs usually record the buried man's name. The script is formed of twenty letters; representing the vowels of the Latin alphabet by notches, and consonants by strokes (slanting or straight). The edge of the stone is used as a line so that strokes and dots go along the edge, up and down. Transliterated, the words are usually found to be Irish. Though they used to be considered proof of a literate society stretching far back into prehistory they are now thought to have been invented in the fourth century in this part of Ireland; from which they spread in a small way to other parts of the country, Wales and Cornwall.

Half-way back we cross, without noticeable difference

between one side and the other, the Cork-Kerry border and five miles later reach the demesne of **Derreen House**, the gardens of which open to the public from April to September. The demesne belongs to descendants, through the Marquesses of Lansdowne, of Sir William Petty, described in the next chapter. It is well worth visiting for the substantial collection of trees, rhododendrons (*Sino grande* and other big-leaved varieties), myrtles, conifers, arbutus, and prolific New Zealand tree ferns, as well as exceptional species like *Embothrium longifolium* and the largest *Cryptomeria elegans* in these islands. The setting, beside Kilmakillogue Harbour and under the symmetrical thousand-foot peak of Knockatee, is unsurpassed anywhere. The house itself was rebuilt after destruction during the Troubles. Its predecessor was rented in 1867 and 1868 by the historian J. A. Froude, and it was here that he wrote most of his *The English in Ireland*, in which he was at pains to show Celts and 'Papists' in sub-Anglo-Saxon colours. Froude's *The Two Chiefs of Dunboy* is a historical novel based on a murder-and-revenge sequence that took place in this region. It has fine descriptions of the scenery, and exciting episodes that bring this area to life.

A few miles farther a lane leads right from the village of Cloonee. The walk up this, past the three Cloonee Loughs – extensions of the river of the same name and in the shadow of Caha Mountain – is one of innumerable superb stretches in these hills. Beyond the lane, our road takes us the remaining eight miles to Kenmare, along one of the most striking stretches of the whole journey.

CHAPTER TEN

Kerry, Limerick Coast Road

'THERE the she-wolf littered, and some half-naked savages, who could not speak a word of English, made themselves burrows in the mud and lived on roots and sour milk . . . scarcely any village, built by an enterprising band of New Englanders far from the dwellings of their countrymen in the midst of the hunting-grounds of the Red Indians, was more completely out of the pale of civilization than Kenmare.' This is Macaulay, showing what had to be overcome by the inventor, anatomist, economist, surveyor and man of several other parts, Sir William Petty (1623–87), to make profitable sense of the region. Petty was granted the land hereabouts by Henry Cromwell as reward for his *Down Survey* of Ireland, the first scientific map of the country, made to facilitate and regulate the rapid changes of ownership of the time. (Sadly, it was destroyed in a Dublin Castle fire in 1711, and only copies and a few county records survive.) In his new estate, he turned his energy to the setting up of iron-works, lead-mines, sea-fisheries and other industries, and in 1670 to the founding of **Kenmare**, then called Nedeen, itself. He also proposed to solve 'the Irish problem': swap 20,000 Irish girls for 20,000 English, and so make sure the next generation of mothers brought up their sons as loyal Englishmen. Though few of his projects survived his death, his great-grandson, the second Earl of Shelburne, short-lived British prime minister (in 1782) and first Marquess of Lansdowne, took what was for the time considerable trouble with his estate, by now approaching 150,000 acres. For him, agriculture was the key to Irish recovery, and he set up an Agricultural Society to spur on his own and others' tenants. The reward of industry was a moral medal, showing on one side barefoot children leaving a smoky, crumbling cabin, and on the other a prospering farm with well-stacked sheaves of corn. He also had his agent build roads and bridges, plant trees, drain bogs, promote fishing, and develop the town of Nedeen, then renamed Kenmare. A quay, a market-house, courthouse, bridewell, spinning factory and inn were built, and the town prospered. Some houses from the time still stand, but none of the major buildings. Nowadays Kenmare expends its wealth on the tourist industry, for only ten miles north is that fantastic complex of lake, mountain, and vegetation that has assumed the name of the small town to its east, Killarney.

Killarney is best approached from Kenmare. The road climbs steeply till the formidable silhouette of MacGillycuddy's Reeks comes into view on the left, with the Gap of Dunloe towards the east. Four miles beyond the sharp right turn the road makes, there is a parking place on the left. This is known as **Ladies View**, and it introduces the two salient points about Killarney. The first is that the region is one of the most beautiful parts of Ireland, as everybody says (though it has rivals). The second is that more tourist amenities are provided than anywhere else in the country; for the simple reason that Killarney draws more tourists than anywhere else. In the season it seethes with people; and with hotels and bars and sweetly smiling guides and souvenir shops. Many visitors, having once seen the sights, swear never to return, and some keep well away in the first place. Some, but not all, of the best sights necessitate walks, which sift tourist sheep from goats. The rest must be seen with the world and his mistress – and with an affable cicerone whose automatic chanting of made-up legend detracts from beauties best seen in silence. These resident experts suffer not at all from the reticence of Arthur Young, writing in 1776 – 'there have been so many descriptions of Killarney written by gentlemen who have resided some time there, that for a passing traveller to attempt the like would be in vain'. He, however, got the better of his fine feelings and went on to write fourteen pages of mauve-to-purple prose.

Killarney really means the series of three lakes lying a mile south-west of the town (very spoilt and of little interest save for the 1842–55 Pugin-McCarthy RC cathedral, recently

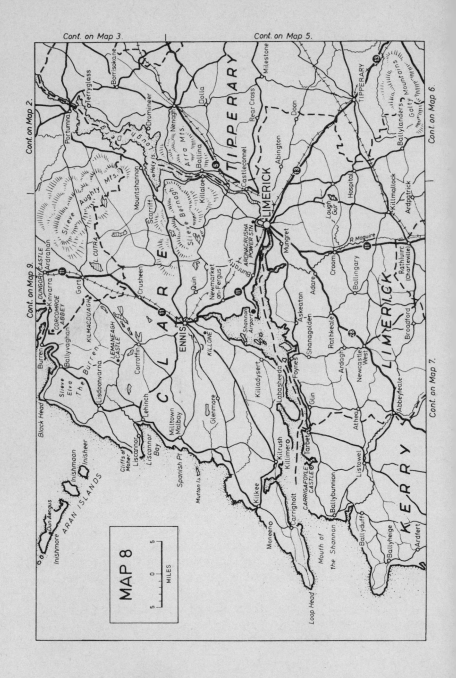

Cont. on Map 3.
Cont. on Map 5.
Cont. on Map 2.
Cont. on Map 6.
Cont. on Map 9.
Cont. on Map 7.

MAP 8

MILES

restored, and some pretty back streets), and the two ranges of
mountains on the west and south-east sides of them. The
arrangement is easily seen from Ladies View. The mountains
to the left, or north, are MacGillycuddy's Reeks with Ireland's
highest peak, Carrauntoohill (3,314 feet), in their midst; their
eastern section, topped by Purple Mt (2,739 feet), is cut off from
the western by a glacial overflow channel, the Gap of Dunloe.
Of the three lakes the Upper Lake, two and a half miles long,
is immediately below Ladies View. A two-and-a-half-mile
river known as the Long Range connects Upper Lake with
Muckross Lake to the north-east, smallest of the three, with
a water level a few feet lower than the Upper Lake's. Muckross
Lake is on the same level as Lough Leane or Lower Lake,
biggest of the three, from which a narrow peninsula, with
part of the Muckross demesne on it, separates it. **Lough Leane**
has over thirty islands on it, including Inisfallen with its old
abbey and the peninsular Ross Island. On the right of the
road rise Torc Mountain and the Mangerton range, with
Lough Guitane beyond. The main historic spots are along
the eastern bank of the Lough – Kenmare demesne, Flesk
Priory, Ross Castle (and offshore the Abbey of Inisfallen),
the ruins of Muckross Abbey and the present house and
demesne of Muckross. The main botanical interest is beside
the Upper Lake, but there are fine tree collections on the
Muckross estate and Governor's Rock, near Ross Castle;
and tree ferns, thorn-apples, bamboos and succulent mesem-
bryanthemums are seen in many gardens. Geological interest
is everywhere, the whole lake complex having been scooped
out by glacial action from the limestone remnants lying in the
valleys of the Old Red Sandstone mountains. The dramatic
scenery of course spreads over the whole area – and to west
and south many miles beyond. Away from the main circuit
of the Gap of Dunloe and the lakes, it becomes proportionally
less crowded and some of the finest walks are to be had around
Mangerton – from Lough Guitane to Horses' Glen and the
deep corrie called Devil's Punchbowl, whose waters, flowing
north by the Owengarriff River, make the splendid tumble of
Torc Waterfall. Black Valley or Cummenduff Glen, south-
west of the southern approach to the Gap of Dunloe, is

another less patronised and beautiful stretch. Short of walking, which takes time in a wide area like this, the best policy for central sightseeing is to fall in with the wishes of official Killarney and travel by jaunting car and boat (which should be arranged beforehand). Cars are not allowed between the main road and lakeside, and though they are technically allowed through the Gap of Dunloe there is militant opposition by the jaunting car drivers to any attempt at passage. Starting from Killarney the best way is through Aghadoe (from which there is a marvellous view of the whole region), north of the lakes to Dunloe Castle. Near the castle is one of the finest collections of ogham stones. The road goes south from here to Kate Kearney's Cottage, that lady having been in late Georgian times one of the 'mountain dew women tribe', or sellers of poteen, who used to pester tourists in the past (the cottage is not the original). From here safely lethargic horses or traps can be hired for the trip through the Gap, with its three lakes and steepening craggy sides to the climactic view at the head. If a boat has not been arranged, return from here can be made back through the Gap. If it has, the way lies on down the southern slope past the entrance to the Black Valley (which leads up to the heart of the Reeks), and round to the head of **Upper Lake**. The water journey goes close to pretty islands with exotic plants, through the Long Range fringed with arbutus and royal fern and a profusion of rare mosses and liverworts, passing the pointed Eagle's Nest on the left. Last century cannons or bugles sounded here to produce a roaring echo. Tennyson heard it in 1848 and the same evening wrote one of his best poems – '. . . The long light shakes across the lakes, And the wild cataract leaps in glory. Blow, bugle, blow, set the wild echoes flying . . .', and Benjamin Britten, who owned a cottage not far away, composed his *Serenade for Tenor, Horn and Strings* to the words. Tennyson's cataract may have been the Torc Cascade, which falls above **Muckross Lake**, entered here beside lush Dinish Island, with its bamboo, eucalyptus, magnolia and other subtropical plants. There are red deer in the woods around the lakes and in the eighteenth century the chief attraction of Killarney to the gentry was hunting them down from the hills and into the water, where the chase continued by boat. The real Colleen Bawn, a girl called Ellen Hanley murdered in 1819 by her husband on the River Shannon, had nothing to do with so-called Colleen Bawn Rock on Muckross Lake, except through a delicate transplantation in Gerald Griffin's novel, *The Collegians.* The boat goes on into Lough Leane and crosses two miles of open water to Ross Castle. The sights on the east shore of the lake are to be seen on foot – by far the best of them the lovely remains of Muckross Franciscan Friary, late fifteenth century, but ruined by Cromwellians, with a magnificent yew in the cloister; Muckross House, a Victorian mansion (1843) in Tudor style, now made into a museum, with lovely grounds which, together with ten thousand acres around, was presented to the nation to be Ireland's first National Park by the previous American owners; fifteenth-century Ross Castle, last place in Munster to be taken by the army Cromwell left behind, in 1652; placed with a good view across the lake; and the various lakeside walks, including that through Kenmare Demesne, site now of luxury hotels, previously the home of the Browne family, Earls of Kenmare. It was Sir Valentine Browne who in Elizabeth's reign bought this and surrounding land stretching into County Cork. The house of his descendant the fourth Earl of Kenmare, a redbrick monster of opulence, built in 1872 on a site supposedly chosen by Queen Victoria (for whose visit a royal barge was sailed from London) and in place of an eighteenth century house a little to the south-east, was gutted in 1913. A replacement to this, known now as Killarney House, was made from the old stable block, and was home of Viscount Castlerosse, later sixth Earl, and doyen of gossip columnists when he worked for Lord Beaverbrook. He designed the picturesque golf-course with the help of Henry Longhurst.

Killarney can be marred by weather. Mangerton in 1903 took 141 inches of rain. Though Killarney town itself and much of the lake area averages between forty to sixty, a point just to the north got an average of eighty-seven inches for each of seventeen years. Charles James Fox, for instance, arrived in heavy rain. Lord Kenmare assured him it was only a shower. It continued raining, Fox staying patient, the earl optimistic.

After five days Fox had to leave, without seeing the views. Three years later Lord Kenmare came to see Fox in London. 'Well, my lord,' said the latter, 'is the *shower* at Killarney over yet?' Queen Victoria, on the other hand, was put out by the heat. In spite of the scenery reminding her 'of *Scotland*, it was *so* fine' she makes constant mention of 'the great heat', 'it was overpoweringly hot' and at Killarney House (where they celebrated Albert's last birthday, she much worried over his health) though 'all the windows were open, there was not a breath of air, and the heat was intense', (she also found 'that peculiar shriek' of the Irish a drawback). But the other old grumble about Killarney, the poor quality and high cost of lodging, is of the past, at least in the first respect. The Germans with three luxury hotels, and the Americans with more, have seen to that.

For the day or days spent in Killarney we will have done well to have stayed nights at or near Kenmare, or on the other side of the Iveragh Peninsula near Killorglin or Glenbeigh. Another tour from Kenmare is the coastal Ring of Kerry, which we can follow clockwise by driving west from the village. The way is past houses of Riviera design, and a few castles, some of both kinds converted into hotels. **Parknasilla,** thirteen miles from Kenmare, has a luxury hotel in its grounds, incorporating the remains of the home of Limerick's C of I bishop, Dr Charles Graves, grandfather of the poet Robert. Shaw stayed and wrote parts of *St Joan* in a private sitting-room in the hotel. **Sneem** is a pretty village with houses in colours that make them look like toys, and an Italianate church of 1865. A boat can be hired to make the trip to Garinish Island, at the mouth of the creek, where many rarities from the southern hemisphere were planted by Lord Dunraven around the turn of the century. Beyond, the road goes inland through a bleak slatey plateau, and returns to the sea and a series of delightful bays and coves. A signposted narrow side road leads three miles to **Staigue Fort,** the most perfectly preserved, though not the biggest, of its kind in the country, set in a commanding amphitheatre among the hills. The skill of the workers who built this vast free-stone fortress with its inward-sloping, eighteen-foot high, thirteen-foot thick walls, points to the

Early Christian period for its construction. Some recent theories put it as much as a thousand years earlier, and till more excavations are done the truth will not be known. However, a fibula found in the walls of Dun Aengus, a similar fortress on the Aran Islands, gave a carbon-14 reading of about 100 B.C. though work at Leacanbuaile supports the first argument. If true, it could have been built under the threat of Norse invasions, which ravaged the coastline from around 800.

Derrynane, farther on, is one of the country's best beaches, close to the island (at low tide linked to the mainland) on which St Finan Cam founded a monastery, a few remains of which still stand. The demesne house was built by Daniel O'Connell (1775–1847), as an extension of his ancestral home, only part of which survives. His additions, which date from 1825 to 1844, include the chapel. Now owned by the Commissioners of Public Works, the house has been restored and opened as a memorial to 'The Liberator'. O'Connell was a p ophet in his own land of Munster, where he was on the court circuit for twenty years, enjoying the dual role of crusader and histrionic performer – 'the great comedian of the Irish race' said Yeats, contrasting him with Parnell, the 'great tragedian'. But the greatest battles of the man who brouoht Ireland from Penal days – when in theory at least a Catholic could not own land, or educate his children at home or abroad, or carry a sword as gentlemen did, or own a horse worth over £10, or take part in his country's lawmaking – to Emancipation, were fought far from here; many at Westminster, of which he said 'I can drive a coach and horses through any act of Parliament.'

Beyond Caherdaniel the road rises over the Pass of Coomakista, revealing for the first time a view of the Skellig Islands, then drops to the little resort of Waterville, standing between the sea and three-mile-long Lough Currane, which makes it popular with anglers. The whole peninsula, like Dingle to the north, is littered with ogham stones, oratories and neolithic graves; and on Church Island in the lake are the sparse ruins of another of St Finan Cam's sixth-century foundations. The saint was credited with introducing wheat into the country, as St Declan of Ardmore was with rye. Ironically, recent research suggests that the building on the

end of the island supposed to have been Finan's cell is a kiln
for drying grain and of much later date. A grand inland road
turns right off the coast road two miles beyond Waterville,
rising along the Inny with the looming prospect of MacGillicuddy's Reeks ahead. But we continue near the sea, and turn
left a mile later, descending on Irish-speaking Ballinskelligs,
a sweet village with a good beach and that familiar occurrence,
the burned out big house. (Animals have to take what they get
in this survival terrain – beating and tight hobbling; and the
use of wooden blinker boards hanging from their horns over
cows' eyes are common sights.) Rounding the north end of
the bay the road climbs to a pass near which one of the finest
views in Ireland can be obtained. In one sweep it takes in the
western half of Dingle Peninsula with each of the Blaskets
looking far less then eighteen miles away; the flat field-
patchwork of Valentia Island, with bosomy swellings at each
end; Portmagee and its new bridge; around to the west the
almost Gothic architecture of the Skelligs – tiny sharp peaks
building up to the great central one in a foamy base; the tip of
Puffin Island near at hand; and far to the south the curved
back of Beara Peninsula.

From the eastern harbour on Valentia Island (reached now
by the Portmagee Bridge) as well as Ballinskelligs and Waterville, boats can be hired to go to the Skelligs. It is a trip that
cannot be counted on till the day since everything depends on
the weather being calm. If this were oftener, the Skelligs would
be almost as much a place of pilgrimage as Cashel or the Giant's
Causeway, but the Atlantic swell, rising and falling up to
twenty feet at the little harbour, makes it otherwise. As it is,
weeks and sometimes months can pass without a decent chance
of access – which is why so many of these south-west coastal
islands have had their populations removed in the present
century. Of all the islands of this outcrop, Little and Great
Skellig Michael, are the two of interest. Little Skellig is often
called, wrongly, the most southerly breeding haunt of gannets in
these islands (there is a small colony on Bull Rock at the tip
of Beara Peninsula), but its population of about 18,000 of the
birds makes it the second biggest in the northern hemisphere,
St Kilda in the Hebrides having more than twice as many.

Besides these goose-sized birds, with their six-foot wing-spans and hundred-foot headlong plunges into the sea for fish, there are predictable quantities of other sea birds – puffins, fulmars, petrels, shearwaters and so on, on this and the other islands. Skellig Michael, patronised by the Archangel as rocky heights generally are, is the site of the best preserved early Irish monastery, founded in the seventh or eighth century by most determined ascetics. The bare rock rises to a peak seven hundred feet above a sheer ninety fathoms of underwater drop, and mist often blots out the mainland altogether. The ruins are about a hundred and twenty feet above sea-level, and comprise six beehive huts or clochans (circular corbelled dry-walled living-quarters, each probably shared by two monks and extraordinarily well preserved), two wells, two circular oratories, some worn primitive High Crosses, and a later medieval Church of St Michael. A wall bounds the monastery and its graveyards from a precipitous drop to the sea. Though earth had to be brought from the mainland and little but sea-pink seems content with the setting, the monks may have had a happier time than the confinement suggests. Birds caught could be eaten, and the sea is rich in fish; herbs were planted and the monastery faced the sun while being well sheltered from winds. A harder time was had by pilgrims of later years, who not only had to risk the wrath of the seventeenth-century Penal Laws which tried to suppress pilgrimages, but also mounted by cruder steps than the present Lighthouse Road; and, having seen the buildings, squeezed through a hole in the rock to ascend the 'Stone of Pain', a smooth sloping rock projecting high over the ocean; finally sitting astride the higher 'spindle', they worked their precarious way along ten feet to recite the Lord's Prayer at the end.

Valentia Island's chief claim to fame is as the eastern terminal of the first transatlantic telegraph cable. Several attempts were made from 1857 onwards, but each time the cable broke, or water penetrated the insulation. In August, 1858, verbal messages could at last be passed from Valentia to Newfoundland, but the line, which was erratic, broke down in October. It was not till 1866 that, with improved

cables, contact became permanent. Thirty years later tele-
graphs were a commonplace across the floors of all the great
oceans. The cable went from near the south-east corner of the
island. On the north coast is Glanleam, seat of Lord Monteagle
and previously of the Knights of Kerry. The nineteenth Knight
(1805–80) succeeded by profuse plantings of windbreak shrubs
(one fuchsia was reported in 1905 to have a ninety-five yard cir-
cumference) in cultivating many South American introductions:
embothriums, drimys, myrtles, escallonias and others; and the
garden remains a fine one. Up to this time the communications
industry was hardly heard of hereabouts. **Caherciveen,** the
town we come to next, was so remote from Irish postal services
that it was reported in 1818 to have better contact with America
than with Dublin, and Dublin newspapers and letters sometimes
arrived via New York. As the century progressed the contact
between the Irish peasantry and America grew rapidly
through forced emigration, and more than one American
politician came to western Ireland to meet the people and
make speeches, knowing their appreciation would be transmitted to his American constituents with far more effect than
his election propaganda. Nowadays, though the biggest town
on the peninsula, it has only two thousand inhabitants, and
contains little of note. O'Connell's ruined birthplace, Carhan
House, is a mile to the east beside a pretty bridge, but the
most interesting remains are to the north-west, across the
bridge over the Valentia River. Near the MacCarthy Castle
of Ballycarbery are two stone ring-forts related to that on the
peninsula's southern side at Staigue. Of the two the better
preserved, **Leacanbuaile,** may like Staigue date back to before 100 B.C. Both forts are placed to cover approach from the
sea, though in this terrain of many humps and hills a stealthy
progress might still have been possible. Yet the forts, in some
ways anticipating the Norman motte-and-bailey, were obviously intended for the protection of a small number – the
chieftain's family – within its walls, and could hardly have
been part of any grand strategy.

The northern road of the Ring of Kerry is less spectacular
than the southern, in spite of good views of Dingle Peninsula.
Kells Bay, between the two ranges of Knockadober (the

initial K is pronounced locally) and Teermoyle Mt, contains a pretty harbour village, in which – as elsewhere hereabouts – some houses are owned by Dubliners and English. Rossbeigh has a magnificent strand along a dune-backed bar that stretches nearly three miles into Dingle Bay (Françoise Sagan has a holiday chalet in the area). **Glenbeigh** is a charming village to which come many anglers, golfers, and refugees from Killarney. Here, too, are the gutted ruins of E. W. Godwin's Gothic Winn's Castle, built in 1867 for Rowland Winn, fourth Lord Headley of Aghadoe. He sued the architect (who had damaged his reputation by eloping with Ellen Terry) on the grounds of leaks and costs. His harsh policy to his tenants resulted in a series of evictions and fights during the Plan of Campaign of 1887. His successor, having married three times, turned Muslim, and made the pilgrimage to Mecca, returning to insist on being known as 'Al Hadji'. In 1925 he claimed to the Press he had been offered the throne of Albania three times – 'but there is no salary attached to it'. Three miles beyond Glenbeigh the road crosses the River Caragh, and a turn to the right leads to the beautiful Glencar, whose lower half is occupied by Lough Caragh under the great natural fortress of MacGillicuddy's Reeks. **Killorglin** is five miles on, on the River Laune, which is the outflow from Killarney's lakes, a town of little distinction save when turned upside down (10th–12th August) by Puck Fair, which centres on its square. During these days a goat, King Puck, which may not appreciate the privilege, is hoisted on to a platform high above the square, and looks down, his horns bedecked with ribbons and rosettes, on the happenings below. These centre round a great cattle, sheep and horse fair, but it is no ordinary fair, for shops and bars stay open day and night and there are possibly more dealings in stout and whiskey than livestock. On the third day the goat is brought down and led round the town and out to be released in the hills from which he came. Though one explanation gives it that goats, like the geese on the Roman Capitol, warned the town's inhabitants of the approach of Cromwell's army by running into its streets, and so saved it, the fair possibly has much older origins. It could date far back to pagan times, and the Festival of

Lughnare, which celebrated the first fruits of the harvest.
There are a few other festivals in Ireland which seem to be
related, and to hark back to the same origins.

DINGLE PENINSULA

To round the spreading flats of Castlemaine Harbour we
drive north-east to the town of Castlemaine, and turn left
towards the southern edge of Dingle Peninsula. Two miles
north of the road the plain begins its slow rise to the rounded
heights of the Slieve Mish range – the Mountains of Phan-
toms. These are the beginning of a continuous chain, the
spine of the Dingle Peninsula, that stretches thirty miles out
to sea and holds, at its tip, the westernmost habitations of
Europe. Richer than the other south-western peninsulas in
some ways – its impressively rugged landscape, an unprettified
natural look, a wealth of ancient remains and links – it is
noticeably short of trees. From the road skirting the giant silted
harbour there are good views of MacGillycuddy's Reeks. Also,
less obvious, there are natterjack toads. These are of interest
here because the northern side of Castlemaine Harbour (and
since 1968 Castlegregory over the other side of the Dingle
Peninsula) are almost their only known habitats in the country.
They, along with all other amphibians and reptiles, are meant
to have been banished by St Patrick (though there are Common
Lizards, Common Newts and Common Frogs). More factually,
they may represent an interesting connection between Ireland
and Spain. A hundred and fifty years ago the discovery of a
natterjack (which has a narrow yellow line down its back,
and shorter legs than the Common Toad) led to long corre-
spondence in nature magazines. Continued patchily for years,
it ended in 1846 with the decision that *Bufo calamita* was
introduced within the last few centuries, thus vindicating the
national saint. They may have been brought by boat and
landed nearby – may even like the frog have been intentionally
introduced. They are nevertheless only one of many species
common to Ireland and the west and south-west coasts of

Europe, known as the Lusitanian flora and fauna. These
included the spotted or Kerry Slug, confined otherwise to
Spain and Portugal; two beetles known only in France; four
Spanish species of woodlouse; and some earthworms, false
scorpions and various molluscs. More apparent are some of
the plants – Arbutus, and some of the saxifrages and heaths
mentioned elsewhere.

Of equal interest is the human link. It is often said that the
people of Dingle and Galway have in general darker, sallower
looks than their compatriots, a result of the flourishing trade
that used to be carried on with Spain, mainly from this west
coast; and also perhaps of survivors from the Armada and
of forces sent by Spain to Smerwick, for instance, to provide
an anti-British foothold in the country. Farther back in time
the links become mythical, but perhaps basically true. Scota
and her son Goidel, descendants of Fenius Farsa, a Scythian
prince – from these three came the whole race of, and three
alternative names for, Gael – were supposed to have reached
Ireland directly from a long stay in Spain. The look of the
place, especially of farms, religious grottoes, statues and
other signs, and the appearance of the people, especially
black-cloaked old women, reinforces the fancy.

We keep going and turn inland with the road for Anascaul,
a lively village, one of whose numerous pubs, the 'South
Pole Inn' used to be the home of Thomas Crean, who trekked
with Scott to the Antarctic. The Dingle road leads away to
the left, and **Dingle** itself is ten miles on. The town spreads
up from the fishing-boat harbour, from which a fleet of about
twenty boats puts out nightly to gather its harvest of mackerel,
bass, plaice and codling. Elizabethan campaigns and Cromwellian ravages wiped out all the town's antiquities, though
there is an interesting Desmond tomb of 1540 in the C of I
church. In a stage-Irish way, the most famous house in the
town no longer exists and its fame accrued from something
that didn't happen. In 1792, James Rice, a papal count in the
Irish Brigade of the French army, planned to rescue Marie
Antoinette from captivity. She was to be brought to Dingle
and there lodged in the count's house, beside the modern RC
presbytery. The queen agreed till she learned her husband

302 THE COMPANION GUIDE TO IRELAND

and children were not to come with her; and in the event
stayed to lose her head.

The great wealth of megalithic tombs and other memorials
in the area records its apparent importance from as far back
as the second millennium BC, a period in which Ireland in
general grew wealthy through, among other things, the
export of gold to parts as distant as the Middle East. But
more abundantly scattered over the area, especially west of
Dingle, are the beehive huts, or clochans, which date from
historic times. Hundreds of these are visible from the road
beyond Ventry. They stand three or four feet high, and people
could only crouch or lie within them. None of them is
mortared. This seems to date them roughly to the sixth, seventh
and eighth centuries, before which most buildings were of wood
and after of mortared stone, though one such hut has been
dated by radio carbon to several centuries earlier. Most of these
may have been used as individual cells by ascetic monks in the
earliest monasteries. The most remarkable group of them is
at Fahan, four miles west of Dingle. To reach this, we pass
through **Ventry** and note a most critical, if half mythical,
event. It was here that Daire Donn, the King of the World
(all but Ireland), swept with his vassals into Ventry Harbour
and advanced up the slope beyond. Finn McCool, that Gaelic
Arthur, and his men fell on the invaders. The clangour,
prowess and gallantry of epic Irish battle went on three days
and nights till Finn, waist deep in blood, fought his way
through to the king and slaughtered him with his remnant
bodyguard. The king's 'grave' is still there, under a ridge that
may conceal a souterrain, or artificially built cave. It is
claimed locally that Ventry was the last Norse foothold in
Ireland and that the story may symbolise their final departure.
But the area is so remarkably rich in remains of various ages
that a dozen explanations could be made to fit.

The road beyond Ventry loops high above sea-level round
Mount Eagle and the western head of the peninsula. The
best view from this dramatic corniche is of the **Blasket
Islands**, the nearest and largest of them lying just over a mile
out to sea. With field-glasses it is possible to make out fat-
tailed sheep grazing round derelict stone cottages and over

decayed gardens. People lived here two thousand years ago.
Fifty years ago Great Blasket was known as the 'next parish
to America'. Life was elemental. There were up to a hundred
and fifty people, a thousand sheep and thirty cows, but no
bulls – cows were taken by delicate curragh to the mainland
for mating. There was no church, no pub, no shop; though
one old woman's house was known and served as the 'Dail'
or talking place. New houses were built from local rock and
furniture from driftwood, but few were needed as the population seldom rose. When a cargo of tea was washed ashore
from a wreck, the leaves being unknown were used as a dye.
In the evenings the people told each other variations of
stories that their ancestors recited a thousand years before.
Three of them wrote down their stories and their life's
account and *Twenty Years A-growing* and *The Islandman*
brought their authors, Maurice O'Sullivan and Tom O'Cro-
han, fame, as did *An Old Woman's Reflections* by Peig
Sayers. After the second world war a visitor noted that the
village was 'a wilderness of nettles and weeds, with hens scratch-
ing in dung and midden heaps, and cows and donkeys browsing
here and there, both in and out of doorways'. By 1953 the
population was shrunken and depressed; no young people
stayed long. The government decided to bring the remaining
villagers to the mainland and resettle them. Boats can be
hired from Dingle and Dunquin to visit the picturesque
ghost-island.

Three miles beyond Slea Head, past country where ravens
and choughs are a common sight, and a mile or so inland,
lies the tiny hamlet of **Dunquin**, comprising a guest house and
a sprinkling of cottages. The guest house was owned till his
death in 1970 by Kruger Kavanagh, a tireless native who
during spells abroad held a commission in the American
Army and counted gangsters, boxers, and politicians among
his friends. Like several others in the region, Mr. Kavanagh
taught Gaelic, to his and the government's mutual benefit.
The remote possibility of making Gaelic the country's first language was still being pursued energetically by the government.
Promotion in the Civil Service, in teaching and the law, was
geared to knowledge of Irish. Even now, a percentage of State

education and of programmes on Radio Eireann are in Irish as are many road-signs, official documents, and bus destinations. Children learn Irish at school and baffle their parents, who learned and forgot. But the demise of Gaelic is now taken for granted by most people. Many who objected to its compulsory use have come to regret its passing. Still in the little enclaves of the Gaeltacht - Gaelic-speaking areas - in Kerry, Mayo, Donegal and elsewhere, there exist Gaelic summer-schools where soil-tillers turn professor to impart their tongue. All the same the number of Irish speakers even in the Gaeltacht continues to decline. Language has always been a political issue, at times bitter: 'Many', said Ralph Brereton Barry, 'have told me how they have gained spiritually by learning Irish. The gain has never been apparent to anyone but themselves.' Certainly Gaelic contains much of charm and beauty, and a rich literature: a language 'if not of a race of poets', Arland Ussher has written, 'at least of a race which has tired the sun with talking a language of quips, hyperboles, cajoleries, endearments, lamentations, blessings, cursings, tirades – and all very often in the same breath'.

North of Dunquin lies the flat open country that leads to Sybil Point and **Smerwick Harbour**. Several tiny villages – Ballyrannig, Ballydavid, Smerwick – lie round the harbour, a huge natural inlet about two miles long and a mile wide. Fishing is the main means of livelihood, and to this end the building of curraghs – especially at Ballydavid – is a thriving craft. These light boats are made of tarred canvas stretched tightly round a wooden frame. Being light and slender they speedily skim the tops of the waves, and their rounded bottoms make them difficult to capsize (though bad weather can hold up fishing for as long as weeks, even in summer). On shore they are carefully tethered, to avoid strong winds hoisting them seaward.

Smerwick was the beautiful setting of an ugly event during the Desmond rebellion. In 1579 a Papal Nuncio and eighty Spaniards built a fort here, with the aim of linking with the rebels. In 1580 they were reinforced by six hundred Italians, and fortified themselves within the ancient Dun an Oir (or Fort of Gold, near which two years earlier a ship of Frobisher's, carrying what he believed to be gold but was in fact pyrites, was wrecked). A vastly superior naval force under Admiral Winter (Raleigh's and Spenser's presence is disputed) sped to the scene, bombarded, took and massacred, using their full repertoire of tortures, though the garrison had surrendered. The treatment, typical of the times, became well known because of the foreigners involved. 'Many years passed,' wrote Kingsley with Aryan satisfaction – he described the affair in *Westward Ho!* – 'before a Spaniard set foot again in Ireland.' On the western side of this neck of land leading to the Three Sisters rocks is **Ferriter's Castle**, whose last owner, Pearce Ferriter, soldier and poet, was the last Kerry commander to submit to the Cromwellians. He was hanged at Killarney in 1653.

Nowadays the course of life is gentle, and rather slow. Leis than a generation ago more people went to church by pony-drawn trap than by car. Pound-notes accumulated under mattresses while old habits persisted. Nowadays every fisherman will possess a cow or two, some sheep on the hills and maybe a goat, but his wife will tend to these. Returned from the sea, he eats his high tea at home, then adjourns for an hour or two to the pub. In winter this will be early, in summer late. Nature requires an elastic respect for the licensing laws. Brendan Behan told the story of a police check-up at a Ballyferriter bar. It was no raid. The sergeant first telephoned to give an hour's notice of arrival. Before he was due the bar's occupants were ushered out politely, for it was after hours, and asked to take their bottles and glasses a little way up the hill. The sergeant came, drank a friendly pint and withdrew, in full knowledge of the facts but appreciating the deference due to his status. Variations on this ritual are common in many parts of Ireland.

Five miles east of Ballyferriter is a remarkable survival from Early Christian times, the **Gallarus Oratory**, or church. A rectangular building about twelve by eighteen feet, and sixteen feet high, it is the most perfect of its kind, better than the two on Skellig Michael. Built by corbelling – making each stone course of smaller measurement than the one beneath so that the courses overlap and eventually meet at

the top – it shows the limitations of a method that was ideal
for circular buildings; for here the roof definitely sags (after
eleven hundred years or so). At Kilmalkedar, a mile away, is
a ruined twelfth-century church with a good Romanesque
doorway, the first building to have been strongly influenced
by Cormac's Chapel at Cashel. It contains an ogham stone,
no rarity in these parts; for the area is packed with such
remains, in their ruinous setting. 'The whole landscape',
wrote Cyril Connolly, 'is expectant and devotional like Iona
or Delphi.'

East of Ballydavid rises Ireland's second highest peak,
Mount Brandon (3,127 feet), and a steep and stony track, the
Saint's Road, follows a zigzag course to the top. The saint
in question, Brandon, or Brendan, was one of the more
daring of those holy Irish stalwarts who left their land in the
sixth and seventh centuries to find God and the Promised
Land, which they took to be located on earth. True or not,
the life story compiled by monks of later centuries is a
colourful one. He was born in 484, in circumstances oddly
akin to those of Christ's birth, with prophecies, cows, a star
and a wise man all playing prominent parts. His boyhood
and youth included a due mixture of study, pilgrimage,
vicious asceticism and miracles. Once ordained, he founded
monasteries throughout Connaught and Munster, then took
himself to lonely meditation atop Mount Brandon, where a
pile of stones is claimed to be the remains of his oratory.
Anyone enjoying the view from this summit is likely to be
moved. St Brendan, his vision enhanced perhaps by a diet of
berries and stream water, resolved to sail the Atlantic and
find the Promised Land. The account of his subsequent seven
years of navigating mentions no identifiable names, of course,
but describes places that uncannily resemble parts of Iceland,
Greenland, the Azores and Bahamas, and the eastern seaboard
of the United States. It became a medieval best-seller, and
was translated from Irish into English, Latin, Welsh, Scots
Gaelic, Breton, French, Saxon and Flemish. The question
whether St Brendan discovered the United States before
Columbus *and* Leif Eriksson will be decided perhaps only if
an Irish equivalent of the Vinland map is unearthed. Some

interpretations of the text confine him to the Irish sea-board,
and make real or mythical islands like Hy-Brasil, and St
Brendan's Island (marked on maps till the nineteenth century,
and the object of Portuguese exploration till the eighteenth)
his western limit. But he stays the patron saint of seamen and
travellers. Brandon Mountain, where he conceived his
project, partakes in his prestige. Till the eighteenth century it
was second only to Croagh Patrick as a place of pilgrimage,
one of the four holy places which serious penitents were
always required to visit. The saint died at Annaghdown in
Galway, and was buried at Clonfert.

The mountain itself and the glens around are ideal country
for walking; the climb to different levels continually peels
away the view of the nearest hill or valley to reveal those
beyond, fields present patterns of brown, green and steel-blue,
little and large basins of land have gathered lakes over the
centuries, and always along the coast black rock is flecked
with white as rollers break and the thunder of waves rumbles
in subterranean channels. But the mountain falls as a steep
cliff to the sea, and to proceed it is necessary to travel south
to Dingle, then north-east, over the Connor Pass, to the edge
of Brandon Bay and Castlegregory. From Connor Pass on a
fine day there is a view not only of the southern Kerry
peninsulas but also of the Clare Coast and Aran Islands to
the north.

Old tales cling to Castlegregory but the village itself is no
more than a pleasant resort with fine bathing and good fishing.
A flat sandy promontory stretching a mile to the north points
to the Magharee Islands, on one of which are the remains
of St Seanach's sixth-century monastery. The road continues
eastward, flanking the south side of Tralee Bay. Near Camp
is the Glen of Galt, with potent spring waters that cure
madness, but there is nothing more to arrest attention before
crossing the trickle which by some geographical hyperbole
was given the name of River Lee (Tralee is named from it).
It was here, at Scota's Glen, that the Scythian Fenius Farsa,
having refused to join the persecution of Jews in Egypt and
fled to Spain, brought his daughter Scota, her husband
Milesius, and their son Goidel, and so established the race

that has been known at different stages as the Fenians, the Scots, the Milesians and the Goidels (or Gaels). A mile beyond lies the chief town of County Kerry, Tralee.

Tralee used to be the chief demesne of the Earls of Desmond, and thirteen of them were buried in the now ruined, almost non-existent, Dominican friary. It was near here that the rebel fifteenth earl, whose waning fortunes are marked at various points across Cork and Kerry, brought the line to an end. At Glenageenty, eight miles east of here, he was wandering with his withered band in the winter of 1583, when an Irish soldier recognised him and cut off his head. His supposed grave is a mound beside the river, but his head, sent to Ormonde (whose family now was undisputedly dominant in southern Ireland) was later spiked on London Bridge, after inspection by the queen. The Desmond estates passed to the Denny family, but the town was twice wrecked in the seventeenth century. Most of the best of Tralee, including the classical courthouse by W. V. Morrison, is Georgian; there is a Victorian RC Church of St John by J. J. McCarthy, a Dominican church by E. W. Pugin and George Ashlin; and little else of interest except inasmuch as it is the biggest town on the south-west coast. A left turn off the Ardfert road north-west of the town leads through the little village of Spa, whose iron-rich spring, guaranteed to 'raise the spirits' and give 'a voracious appetite', attracted visitors in the eighteenth century and later. Fenit, on the corner of land projecting into Tralee Bay, was St Brendan's birthplace, flat and duny, with white sands stretching for miles to the north. It was at an old rath near Banna strand that, on Good Friday of 1916, Sir Roger Casement was arrested, having just landed from a German submarine. His part in the Easter Rising was short and muddled, in spite of months of planning in hospitable Germany. Three months after his arrest he was hanged, but his name, like those of the executed Dublin insurgents, was soon to be a rallying cry, and it was to gratify repeated requests that Harold Wilson allowed the return of his body to Dublin in 1966. The most impressive visible remain of this area is on the site of one of St Brendan's foundations – the hoary, graceful ruins of

medieval **Ardfert Cathedral**, with fine east window and
Romanesque west doorway. The original, founded around
the mid-sixth century, was the saint's first monastery; but
he was soon away to Mt Brandon to make plans for his ocean
journey. In the demesne of Ardfert House, a relic to the east
of the village, are the ruins of a Franciscan friary of 1253,
founded by Thomas FitzMaurice, first Lord Kerry.
The north is the least interesting part of County Kerry,
though the coast road is attractive in parts. At Ballyheige are
the ruins of a house reconstructed in 1809 in grandiose Gothic
by Sir Richard Morrison for the Crosbie family, whose cousins
the Earls of Glandore owned the Ardfert demesne. The original
eighteenth century house is said to have been built with the
silver from a wrecked East Indiaman. The later one was burned
down by Republican forces in 1922. Near Ballyduff is Rattoo
Round Tower, beside the remains of an Augustinian abbey,
and some miles to the north, over the estuary of the River
Feale, is Ballybunion, a resort being developed for the crowds
of tourists, mainly Irish, who descend in summer on its hotels,
amusement places, championship golf-course and beaches. To
the north, as the road rounds with the coast to the east, good
views of Clare's south coast are revealed. Of several castle
remains on this part of the coast, the most impressive is
Carrigafoyle, reached by a narrow causeway from the land.
Till Cromwell's time it belonged to the O'Connor family
and for a while harboured a rebel garrison in the Desmond
rising, till the English took it and hanged the defenders. It
was again taken and finally mutilated by Cromwell's troops.
There are good views from the top. Sir William Pelham, who
led the troops in 1580, and was at the time Lord Justice of
Ireland, had sworn to make this strip of coast, as far as
Limerick 'as bare a country as ever Spaniard set foot in',
and even to-day the success of his mission seems in parts
apparent. But from Tarbert on the scenery grows all the
time prettier, as the river narrows in its last stretch below
Limerick. Six miles on, behind extensive walls to the right
of the road, is **Glin Castle**, a pasteboard Gothic mansion
built between 1790 and 1812, with a long low wing spreading
out, in a rather unbalanced way, to the right. The FitzGerald

Knights of Glin and Kerry, and the White Knight, appear to be the only enduring hereditary knights in British history. They descend from three brothers honoured by Edward III after a battle in 1333, and before that from Maurice, ancestor of all the FitzGerald branches in Ireland. Remote and gaelicised in the far west, the Knights of Glin took part in most of the rebellions against Tudor rule and stayed Catholic and distinctly Irish until the eighteenth century. Then, in common with other families of the west, they were drawn by the lure of English ways to send sons to Winchester, marry English, renounce their religion, bards and stone fortresses, and import architects and decorators to provide suitable accommodation. Glin Castle, with its remarkable plasterwork and a fine double-staircase resembling work by Wyatt, is the result. The present knight, descended from a swashbuckling line that might have been good material for Scott, is a distinguished scholar of Georgian art and architecture. In the village is the stump of an old castle destroyed by Sir George Carew after a siege in 1600, and several Gothic lodges, one of which is an eating-house and shop, surround the demesne.

The village of Foynes is eight miles farther on, under a hill topped by a Celtic cross memorial to Edward Spring-Rice, son of the first, and father of the second Baron Monteagle. Between the town and Foynes Island, is the strip of water once used for the descent of transatlantic seaplanes. Shanagolden is four miles inland, to the south. (The ruined castle of Shanid, two miles south-south-west of it, was built around 1200 by Thomas FitzMaurice, son of the founder of the whole FitzGerald family.) The Angkor-like smothered remains of the thirteenth-century Augustinian nunnery of Old Abbey two miles east of Shanagolden illustrate well those two food sources of self-sufficient orders, the fishpond and the dovecot. Withdrawn from the river and on the edge of the level plain of west County Limerick (well seen from the hills west of Shanagolden) the road goes on from Foynes to Askeaton, whose bridge over the River Deal is its focal point. The castle, another Desmond fortress, was the final refuge of Garrett, the last Earl of Desmond, before his fatal wanderings in the Glenageenty valley. Besieged in 1579, he held out, while the

English under Sir Nicholas Malby sacked the Franciscan friary, with its Desmond tombs, nearby. Next year, with the earl gone, the garrison surrendered, having first in a pacifying gesture set fire to the castle themselves. In the seventeenth-century wars it was taken by Confederates in 1642, and held by them till Cromwellians took it and finally reduced it to its present state – all but a brick building by the keep, added in the eighteenth century for the use of the local Hell Fire Club. From the evidence of the few records, this never attained the excesses of its English counterpart. Most of the big local families were represented, and a Mrs Celinda Blennerhassett, from a local gentry family, was herself not ashamed to belong along with her husband. The friary remains, restored after Malby's time but finally evacuated at the approach of the Cromwellians, include a beautiful cloister.

In the C of I graveyard is buried Aubrey de Vere (1814–1902), the ruin of whose family house, Curragh Chase (burned down in 1941), stands five miles away in a romantic setting of lakes, woods and hills by a lane leading from the Limerick road. It was his poet father, Aubrey (1788–1846), a friend of Wordsworth and married to Mary Spring-Rice, who adopted the surname – he was a Hunt till he succeeded to a baronetcy in 1818. The younger Aubrey, best known for his *The Foray of Queen Maeve*, was in his turn a friend of Tennyson (who came here in 1848), wrote a deal of literary criticism, and under the influences of medievalism, Irish religious history and the Oxford Movement, became a Catholic in 1851. **Dromore Castle,** to the left of the main road three miles beyond the Curragh Chase turning, was built in a hotch-potch style of Gothic with Irish-Romanesque accretions, known quaintly as 'archaeological Gothic', for the Earl of Limerick between 1867 and 1870. Its architect was E. W. Godwin, a friend of Whistler and father, by his mistress Ellen Terry, of Edward Gordon Craig. Inhabited till 1950, then offered for sale, the house – magnificent of its kind – found no takers. With a roof on, according to the destructive Irish law, it was liable for rates; without it, it was free. The roof came off in 1954, and now the building rots in the damp atmosphere. It still makes a most impressive profile. There are several more ancient castles in the area, which from Norse times has guarded the vulnerable back door to Ireland, the Shannon. One of these, Carigogunnel, stands prominent for miles around on a mound of basalt, five miles beyond Dromore. Originally built by the O'Briens of Thomond in the fifteenth century, it was blown up by General Ginkel in 1691, in the closing phase of William III's conquest. North of Dromore is Shannongrove House, close to the river, built around 1709 for the Bury family, later Earls of Charleville and the earliest eighteenth-century house in the county. Flanked by symmetrical wings, it is an elegant example of the Dutch Palladian style. Privately owned, it has superb wood-panelling inside. Just to the east, off Mellon Point, occurs the greatest tidal range in Ireland. The mean spring tide is 18·3 feet.

The last stretch of the Limerick road takes us through the small village of Mungret, where in the sixth century a monastery was founded by St Nessan, about whom nothing is known save the date of his death, 551. The remains of later buildings include a crenellated tower, two churches, a castle, and the nave and choir of the late medieval abbey, sufficient signs of its prestige in early times. From here the road leads four miles north-east to Limerick City.

CHAPTER ELEVEN

Limerick City, Inner Limerick and Lower Shannon

MUNSTER was one of the five provinces or kingdoms of ancient Ireland; but in the semi-feudal administration of pre-Norse times it was divided into two sub-kingdoms, with Desmond in the south and Thomond in the north. Thomond took in parts of Tipperary and Limerick and most of Clare, and was O'Brien territory. When the Danes arrived and built the country's main seaports, **Limerick** was one of them. Strategically placed on the Shannon with easy access to the sea and far into the interior of Ireland, it was a valued prize of the kings who ruled here. These made a name for tyranny and oppression and in the late tenth century Brian Boru, the O'Brien heir, managed to oust them. Based first on Kincora, he made himself king of Munster, and the whole of Ireland his field of action, and in the last ten years of his life revived the power and learning of the monasteries, and reformed the administration of large parts of the country. In 1014 he brought the Viking terror to an end and was himself killed, but the order he created lasted till the Anglo-Norman conquest. In time the O'Brien kingship of Thomond came to settle at Limerick. Brian's descendant, Donal Mor O'Brien, who submitted to Henry II in 1171, was nevertheless first of the Irish chiefs to defeat the Anglo-Normans (at Thurles) when their ambition outran their agreed allotments. In later years, in spite of predictable reverses, the various branches of the O'Brien family held on to power and influence. They became Earls of Inchiquin, Marquesses of Thomond and Barons of Burren; the present Baron Inchiquin is that rare peer, a descendant in unbroken male line from the Gaelic blood of Brian Boru.

It was not long before Limerick came into the hands of the Norman invaders, who proceeded to defend themselves with stout walls on the island known as King's Island, to the north of the main modern town. At this stage they had no intention of mixing with the Irish, whom, following the precepts of Giraldus Cambrensis, they believed to be 'a filthy people, wallowing in vice'. ('They do not avoid incest', he allows himself to go on, 'they do not come to the church with due reverence. Moreover, and this is surely a detestable thing, and contrary not only to the Faith but to any feeling of honour – men in many places in Ireland, I shall not say marry, but rather debauch, the wives of their dead brothers.') Still, the newcomers needed the Irish for menial tasks, and the Irish liked the money they paid, and took to queueing outside the town gates for work, and building their living-quarters nearby. In this way, as in many other Irish cities, two towns grew up – Englishtown and Irishtown – and as such the two areas are still known. At Limerick, as Old English and Irish drew closer together, walls were built round both districts.

It was this combined walled town that Hugh O'Neill defended for six months against the troops of Ireton, who, taking the place in 1652, died of the plague that often gripped a besieged city, in a house in Nicholas Street. A more notable siege came forty years later, after the Boyne, which in William's view had decided the issue finally against James, who, implying agreement, had fled. Patrick Sarsfield (made Earl of Lucan by James) thought otherwise, and picked Limerick as his stronghold. His commander, Tyrconnel, retired to France and so did Sarsfield's French comrade, General Lauzun, saying the city 'could be taken with roasted apples'. William arrived with an army of twenty-six thousand, and waited for his artillery to come up. With inside information Sarsfield broke through the English lines at night and skilfully managed to capture William's convoy of supplies. The cannon were no use to him, so he filled the barrels with powder, buried the mouths in the earth and fired them, destroying the lot; and returned to withstand three weeks of William's assaults, during which the walls were badly breached. In September, the siege was raised and William returned to England. A year passed, and the Irish cause was finally shattered at Athlone, Aughrim and Galway.

When Limerick was attacked again, Sarsfield (who had fought at all the battles, from the Boyne on) held out for a month, then capitulated on what seemed generous terms. Catholics were to enjoy the rights they had held under Charles II, and the Irish army was to be allowed to depart unmolested for France. The treaty was signed on the stone still sited by Thomond Bridge, west of King's Island. The Irish departed – fourteen thousand of them – in what is known as the Flight of the Wild Geese, the second mass emigration, in a century, of capable, ill-led pawns on the board of English and French war policies; to form the Irish Brigade of the French Army and fight with and against the English under the various flags of European powers for a hundred years and more. But the rest of the treaty was soon nullified by an infuriated Protestant parliament. Instead of codified rights, the Catholics got Penal Laws – barring them from parliament, any rank of government office, the law, the army or the navy. And a few years later they were barred from buying land (which the big landlords got over by turning C of I, or trusting their lands to Protestant friends, who in very few cases reneged).

The laws led to hatred, revenge sometimes, and to a lot of fear. Limerick's city gates were locked every night, for sixty years after the siege. Then in the mid-eighteenth century Edmund Sexten Pery, son of a merchant grown rich on the trade brought by 500-ton ships that called at Limerick, began to build outside the town. (He became Speaker of the Irish House of Commons and Viscount Pery, but died without heir. His nephew later became Earl of Limerick.) Limerick's modern centre (really its southern end, locally called the west end) grew up, with the wide streets and large houses and shops growing popular at the time. There were new docks, quays, custom house, theatres (Mrs Siddons appeared here), Exchange, barracks, court-houses. 'You could not in many parts of it help thinking yourself in London, so like are some of the streets and general contour of the houses', wrote Rev. James Hall in 1813. There was a new gaol, too, built by

William Blackburn, a friend of the reformer John Howard, whose other gaols still stand at Dorchester, Gloucester, Liverpool, Oxford, Exeter, Ipswich and elsewhere. The town became one of the smartest in the British Isles. Later, the Grand Canal linked it with Dublin, and crops, cattle, pigs, eggs and so on sailed up the Shannon for export to England. They were sailing still in 1845 when the Famine came and Irishmen died in the streets.

It saw bitter fighting in the Anglo-Irish war and Robert Graves, posted here, wrote that 'it looked like a war-ravaged town. The main streets were pitted with holes like shell-craters and many of the bigger houses seemed on the point of collapse.' He also found out that 'everyone died of drink in Limerick except the Plymouth Brethren, who died of religious melancholia'. Actually the town is noted for its high (over 90 per cent) RC population and Catholic Confraternity.

The reason for the five-line verse being called Limerick is obscure. This use of the word is first recorded in 1898, long after Edward Lear made the form popular and even longer after books of what would now be called limericks had been published. The form, more or less, is found in Shakespeare, Ben Jonson, even Aristophanes. Also in France: and a thin theory suggests that Sarsfield's fellow exiles found it there and that their descendants brought it back to Limerick, whose name it assumed. Others say that in Lear's time people took to inventing these verses, in groups but one at a time. To give the next person time to think, they recited between each attempt – for no known reason – an old river song: '. . . Oh won't you come up, come all the way up, Come all the way up to Limerick?'

All three parts of Limerick have mainly buildings from the eighteenth century on, though each maintains the flavour of a different period. Insular **English Town**, the oldest sector, has the narrow curving streets of the medieval city and contains at its north end, by James Pain's Thomond Bridge, **King John's Castle,** built in 1210, in British times a barracks, re-cently restored from a ruinous state, but none the better for a close crop of council houses. It still makes a good view from across the river. The city and county court-houses, the

Blarney Castle, County Cork: supposed source of Irish fluency.

Castlelyons or Castle Lehane: sixteenth-century seat of the Barrymores. *Below* Bantry House and Bay: the house contents were acquired in post-Revolution France.

city gaol and St Mary's C of I Cathedral are all close together on the south-west of the island. **St Mary's Cathedral**, originally built by Donal Mor O'Brien in 1179, is an amalgam of styles now, with Romanesque restored west doorway and Irish-battlemented tower and a great variety of window styles. The names of seven restorers at least are known. Donal Mor's grave is here in the chancel and a splendid monument to the Great Earl of Thomond, who died in 1624, rebuilt in 1678 after the Cromwellians had sacked it, but with the original effigies. In the choir the seat ends are decorated with twenty-three misericords, probably of around 1500, the only examples of the period in an Irish church. They include some splendid allegorical beasts, among them a lioness, symbol of the Resurrection because she was thought to bring forth lifeless cubs which on the third day she breathed on to waken them. **Irish Town**, across either Mathew or Ball's Bridge (which succeeded one washed away by a high tide of 1775) has less of interest, though it keeps an atmosphere all its own. It does contain the beautiful **Custom House** of 1765–9, designed by the Sardinian Davis Ducart, the town's finest building. but this has to be seen from the waterfront. The RC cathedral is Gothic Revival of the 1850s, by P. C. Hardwick, who worked at Adare. **Newtown Pery**, in the way of the open plan towns of Georgian times, is a little windswept and exposed, and rather heartless-seeming. At the south end, behind O'Connell Street, is Pery Square, with a museum and art gallery beside it. The former has a very mixed bag of trinkets, like most provincial Irish museums. Some old gloves, for which Limerick used to be famous, are displayed, one of them specially packed in a walnut shell to show its thinness; and the usual 'Troubles' collection, with a typed letter from De Valera, some other letters photostated, and bric-à-brac mementoes of the 1916 and later heroes.

INNER LIMERICK COUNTY

Of several trips of interest round Limerick, one is through the rich farming and horse-breeding area that makes up the Plain of Limerick. It used to be known for sheep-rearing and cider, till more profitable uses were found for the land. We take the T11 south-west from Limerick and after eleven miles reach **Adare**, a pretty model village on the River Maigue with many thatched and slated cottages built in the mid-nineteenth century by Edwin, third Earl of Dunraven. An Oxford Movement convert to Catholicism, the earl was a popular and improving landlord. The third earl, for the manor and restoration of the Trinitarian monastery, used as architect P. C. Hardwick, who in London designed the Great Hall of Euston Station, his father having built the recently removed gateway. The monastery with its massive tower was made to incorporate the RC parish church (there is a dovecot behind); while the Augustinian friary, dating from 1315, houses the C of I church, since a renovation of 1807. The demesne, open to the public, includes the beautiful remains of the Franciscan friary founded by the Earl of Kildare in 1464. Nearby, the castle ruins are those of the original Kildare residence which later passed to the Desmonds from whom it takes its name. It owes its parlous state to the Cromwellians. The manor itself is an excellent example of Tudor Gothic revival, added to an eighteenth-century house. Both A. W. Pugin and Hardwick had a hand in it, but the overall plan was due to the second earl and his wife, a Wynd-ham heiress, together with Nash's pupil G. R. Pain. It contains some good works of art and a fine gallery 132 feet long with elaborate wood carving upstairs; and outside, to the south, is a large, handsome and geometrical Box Garden with steps leading down to the river. It was due to the energies of the fourth earl, who died in 1926, and who ran a successful stud here as well as being a war correspondent, competing in the Americas Cup in 1893 and 1895 (and protesting vigorously, like others later, at the way it was run) that the Wyndham Land Act of 1903 was passed which, enabling tenants to buy the land they farmed, began the fragmentation of Ireland's great estates.

Rathkeale, four miles west of Adare, contains the ruins of a FitzGerald castle burned down by a punitive force including Raleigh and Spenser in 1580, and of a thirteenth century Augustinian priory, as well as J. J. McCarthy's Gothic Revival

RC church. The reason why the region hereabouts is still sometimes known as the Palatinate is to be found a mile west, on the T28, at Castle Matrix (formerly Mattress, an enchanting corruption of the original Matres, signifying pagan goddesses). Now refurbished with much flair by its American-Irish owner and open to the public, the castle was for centuries home of the Southwell family, one of whom, the first Baron Southwell, a valiant Williamite, in 1709 gave a home to some twelve hundred German Lutherans evicted from the Rhenish Palatinate. It was a government scheme, aimed in part at spreading foreign skills and crafts; and partly at strengthening Protestantism in die-hard Catholic areas. Its success was qualified. Most of the newcomers kept to themselves, went on speaking German for more than a hundred years, then gradually intermarried with the Irish and became Catholic. But horticulture and agriculture were improved; and two Palatines from Ballingrane, two miles north of Rathkeale, Philip Embury and Barbara Heck (born Ruttle – her family's home still stands) were converted by John Wesley's preaching here and went to introduce Methodism to America. Several common local names – Switzer, Delmege, Teskey, Twiss – have come down from these immigrants. Castle Matrix contains interesting furnishings and a wealth of fascinating documents relating to the Wild Geese, and is open to the public.

Five miles further west on the T28 is **Newcastle West,** with the remains, now partly incorporated in a more recent building, of a large, mainly fifteenth century Desmond castle. Two halls survive. Desmond's Hall is virtually complete, standing on a vaulted basement. The other, eighty feet long, has good trefoil windows. There are also a circualar keep, a tower-house, and part of the curtain wall. The castle was granted at the plantation of Munster, in 1591 to Sir William Courtenay (whose second wife was Francis Drake's widow), ancestor of the present Earl of Devon. In 1641 it was besieged and taken by Confederate Catholics, who burned it. **Croom** is a few miles up the Maigue from Adare, in unpretentious countryside thick with old keeps. The village was the meeting place of a group of local eighteenth century poets, and puts on an annual literary festival. It has a few fragments of a castle built by

Gerald Fitzmaurice, whose brother Thomas was ancestor of the Kildare FitzGeralds. **Monaster,** two miles east, contains the fragmentary ruins of a Cistercian abbey, daughter-foundation of Mellifont, and founded in 1148 by Turlough O'Brien in honour of his victory over the Norse at nearby Rathmore (two miles east again). There are some good Romanesque details in the remains, and the old mill by the bridge is a reminder of the spartan self-sufficiency of this order, which usually chose to settle in most unpromising places. The 863-foot Knockfeerina Hill, seen to the south-west from the Croom-Monaster road, is the other-world seat of the Celtic god Donn Firinne. When the cairn on top was removed by Ordnance Survey researchers in the last century, it was replaced by the local inhabitants. Twelve miles south of Croom, approaching the foothills of the Ballyhoura range, is **Rathluirc,** previously known as Charleville, which name it was given by the Great Earl of Cork's son, Lord Broghill, in honour of Charles II. It was here that Frank O'Connor, unsoldierly recruit to the Republican forces in the Civil War, was captured for the first time. He and his comrades were arrested and lodged in a farmhouse. But captivity was short-lived. A Republican armoured car moved up and battered the house with shells. Captors and captives changed roles, with much waving of white handkerchiefs, and O'Connor was preserved for more confused campaigning.

From Rathluirc we move south along the Buttevant road but turn off left after four miles to go round the northern side of the mountains. At Ardpatrick, where there are a few remains of an early monastery, we can turn right to glimpse, after three miles, the demesne of **Castle Oliver.** The house was rebuilt, but the memory of Marie Gilbert, born here in 1818, lives on under the assumed name of Lola Montez, whose dancing won her a world reputation on the stages of London, St Petersburg, Warsaw, Berlin and Paris; and the title Countess of Landsfeld, given her by Ludwig I of Bavaria, whose mistress she was until the 1848 revolution.

Above the house rises the highest peak of the Ballyhoura range, Mt Seefin, on which Oisin, son of Finn McCool, is supposed to be buried. Oisin was the quiet one of the Finn cycle. A poet (long after, James Macpherson created what he claimed to be Oisin's poetry in his Ossianic forgeries), he fell in love with the Princess Niamh, who carried him over the sea to the Land of Youth, set in the western sea. He stayed there what seemed to him three years but was in reality three hundred, so pleasantly did the time pass. When he returned Finn and the companions of his youth were gone, the country peopled by a race that was mean and diminutive compared with his heroic contemporaries. Christianity had arrived, and he spent long hours arguing the merits of the pagan life with St Patrick. He died unrepentant but, like Virgil, was made by Christians the epitome of pagan virtue, lacking only the grace that Christianity is said to give.

Kilmallock lies seven miles north-north-west. Its few remains – two of the old town gates, a solitary tower of King's Castle, the fifteenth-century church of SS Peter and Paul, and the beautiful ruins of the thirteenth-century Dominican friary beside the river – tell little of its past history or aspect described in the eighteenth century as 'a greater show of magnificence than any other town in the Kingdom'. Originally it was the creation of one branch of the Desmond FitzGeralds, the White Knights. The White Knights died out with the one who betrayed the Sugan Earl of Desmond in his cave sanctuary at Mitchelstown. His memorial is in the Dominican Friary, founded in 1291, mainly of the next two centuries. During his lifetime Kilmallock had risen to its highest importance, with massive walls, four gates and castles, and a crop of gabled fortified houses. Then with the revolt of the fifteenth earl in 1579 it attracted the batteries of the English and was partly burned. But it recovered. Here the rebel earl's son was brought from imprisonment in the Tower, Elizabeth thinking to attract the loyalty of the people away from the rebellious Sugan Earl, his cousin. For a day the plan worked – he was lavishly received by the townsfolk. Next day he went to church, the Protestant Church, and the people turned against him for his heresy. In desperation the English, when they captured the Sugan Earl in 1600, brought him here and at swordpoint in the church forced him to swear allegiance to the queen. He was then lodged in the Tower

till his death in 1608. The town suffered badly in the Confederate War of 1641 and steadily declined, though it could
still, in the eighteenth century, be called 'the Baalbek of
Ireland'. Since then what remained has been broken up for
other buildings. In the demesne, a mile to the south-west, of
Gothic Ash Hill Towers, the Republican army of 1922 had
its temporary front-line headquarters. The house was built,
with its deep stable court before a pedimented main block,
in 1781. There is good plasterwork inside. The rear façade
was reconstructed in the early nineteenth century by the
Pain brothers in fashionable Gothic style.

Hospital, eleven miles north-east, is one of John Betjeman's
favourite towns in Ireland – simply for being called Hospital.
(On the subject of names, that of 'Black and Tans' came
from the nickname of a nearby pack of foxhounds – the
Scarteen, five miles south-east.) The village's name actually
came from the Knights Hospitaller, who owned it from 1215,
and it preserves a thirteenth-century church in which are
some interesting old de Marisco memorials. West of the
town rises the hill of Knockainy (537 feet), otherworld seat of
the goddess Aine or Anu, a Munster goddess of prosperity
and abundance. It was she who gave its scent to the meadow-
sweet. Up to the last century this deity, always friendly to
men (and sometimes more than friendly, as many claims of
descent from her – including that of the fourth Earl of
Desmond – testify) was propitiated here by a magic ritual
on St John's eve. Villagers would carry bunches of burning
hay on poles to the top of the hill, then disperse among the
fields waving the torches over cattle and crops. Her alleged
son, Earl Gerald, was received into the fairy world after
his death, and taken to Lough Gur, which he still circles on
horseback every seventh year. It is not, however, for a sight
of the earl that we move now to the Lough, a few miles
north-west, but to see the centre of an area richer than most
in prehistoric remains.

Lough Gur is Co. Limerick's only lake, set among limestone
hills. Drainage in the nineteenth century greatly reduced its
size, for the two ruined castles beside it used to be on islands.
Drainage also exposed some remains of crannogs, or lake-

dwellings of prehistoric times (these artificial islands were made by piling up peat, faggots, timber and stones inside a ring of stones or stakes. They sometimes continued in use till the Middle Ages.) Here people first tilled the soil of Ireland around 3000 BC – choosing the limestone area thickest with elm trees in the knowledge, perhaps, that this would make the richest soil. Their skills were numerous – they kept cattle, sheep and pigs, spun cloth, hunted birds, adorned themselves, felled trees; and in their place planted cereals. They also made axes, some to be sent as far as southern England. Of their elaborate burial methods numerous remains are in the hills around – stone-circles, cairns, ring-forts, standing-stones, megalithic tombs – though they do not compare with possibly contemporary structures in the Boyne Valley. The largest stone circle in Ireland is at Grange, between the lake's western shore and the Kilmallock–Limerick road. There are altogether twenty-eight monuments under state care, and innumerable more that are not. Various exhibitions, explanations, amenities and a shop have been provided at the north-western corner of the lake. All the same the irregular profusion of humps and tumps and rocky outcrops rising from the bog is fascinating in itself; and it has other treasures, like the spiny-flowered Golden Dock, hardly found elsewhere in Ireland, and the rare Hornwort found growing in the lake. The neighbouring bogs have yielded many remains of the so-called Irish Elk, or Great Deer, a close but giant relation of the Fallow Deer. This it seems lived and died – and attained bigger dimensions in Ireland than anywhere else – before the bogs were formed, for its remains always underlie the bog. It may have died out before men reached the country. Splendid specimens are in the Natural History Museum in Dublin and elsewhere. From Lough Gur, the main road leads twelve miles back to Limerick.

LOWER SHANNON

Ardnacrusha Power Station, three miles north of Limerick, was constructed in 1925 as the first major step in developing the country's natural resources after independence. A German firm was brought in to do the work, which has transformed the Lower Shannon between Limerick and Lough Derg, and indirectly all the rest of the river. In the sixteen-mile stretch between Killaloe and Limerick the river used to fall, by a series of drops and rapids, a total of 100 feet. To harness this potential electric power a canal was built from O'Brien's Bridge to a loop in the river north of Limerick; a weir was made just below the canal intake to block the river and create a reservoir; and the power station was put up at Ardnacrusha to convert the single 100-foot drop of water which had now been contrived beside it. The result is that turbines of over 38,000 horse power are now driven by the water. A side effect (of the removal of 252 million cubic feet of earth and 39 million cubic feet of rock) has been the flooding of a large area of the valley below Killaloe. Navigation there is now an expert business because of church towers and gables lurking under the surface. Ardnacrusha can be seen by the public by previous arrangement, and our drive to Killaloe brings us close to the newly shaped river at several points of its western bank.

Killaloe is a pretty town in a pretty situation, with Slieve Bernagh rising steeply behind it and the neck of Lough Derg bending away to its north. St Molua founded a church here about 600. Nothing of him is known, but a stone oratory he is supposed to have built stood till recently on Friar's Island below the town, till the Shannon Scheme flooding made its removal necessary. It is now beside the RC church. The C of I cathedral occupies the site of Molua's successor, St Flannan's monastery. A pleasant light church, it contains a good Romanesque doorway, blocked off now in the south wall, and said to have been the entrance to King Murtough O'Brien's tomb of 1120, round which the first cathedral was built about 1185. It also has a bilingual stone with ogham and runic inscriptions, a rare combination, probably a memorial to a converted Norseman. In the churchyard is St Flannan's Church, which is the nave of a Romanesque church, containing some early gravestones and sculptures. Nobody knows for sure where the Palace of Kincora, Brian Boru's stronghold, stood, though it was in or around Killaloe. Claims are made for the easily defended site of the RC church, and for the neighbourhood of Beal Boru, an early ring-fort on the lake's west bank a mile and a half north of Killaloe. A rectangular timber house with a central hearth was discovered in a 1961 excavation. It was in this region, living 'in the wild huts of the desert, and on the hard knotty wet roots', that Brian and his brother Mahon and their people, the Dalcassians, who occupied about half modern Clare, began the expulsion of the Norse, killing them progressively 'in twos and threes, and in fives and scores and in hundreds', before moving on to the national scene.

For a few miles north of Killaloe the west-shore road keeps close to the water, then breaks away to return on the north side of Scariff Bay. The scenery along this road, especially on the southern half of the lake, is magnificent, but there are sights which can only be seen from the water (cruises operate from Killaloe and Portumna). One of these, **Holy Island** in Scariff Bay, has on it extensive remains of a monastery originally founded by St Caimin in the seventh century, destroyed by the Norse and rebuilt at the orders of Brian Boru. The pattern (a religious festival, in which pilgrims seek indulgences) associated with it till the 1830s was one of the longest in the country, beginning with seven circuits of the edge of the island (about seven miles) and continuing with visits to the main sites, each of which they circled seven times ending with the well, from which they drank. It was suppressed, like several others, because of the fighting and fornication that came to be connected with it. The remains include a Round Tower and several ancient churches. The largest island of the lake, Illaunmore, also has a few church remains, and it comes into view if we follow any of the lanes leading to the water from the main road after Mountshannon. One of these lanes leads to Williamstown, scene of an ugly episode in the Civil War when the Republicans landed, burned the house, took four Irish Free Staters prisoners to the bridge at Killaloe and there shot them. As we go north the scene gets less dramatic with the levelling out of the mountains into Ireland's vast central plain. Only naturalists are likely to find more pleasure here, for the shores abound in rare plants that include *Inula Salicina* like a small sunflower, found nowhere else in these islands (flowers July–August); Marsh Pea (June–August), with purple flowers and narrow leaves; Water Germander (July–September), with its pale mauve flower – both these last in the soggy parts of the bog; and several others.

Portumna, at the head of the lake, is a pleasant market town in which boat tours of the lake and river can be arranged. The vast demesne of Portumna lies at the west end of the broad main street, and the ruins of the semi-fortified 1609 house (built then for £10,000) preserve some interesting clues to its history. An event that took place here in 1635 was, though its effects could not be foretold, a fatal one for Thomas Wentworth, later Earl of Strafford, who had arrived in 1632 for his eight years as viceroy to Charles I. Pursuing the king's policy of acquiring land from the 'Old English' – by now as big a danger to the Crown as the native Irish – he arranged a hearing at the castle to decide the king's titles to most of the province of Connaught. But Richard de Burgh, Earl of Clanricarde, a patriarchal landlord, who had built the castle, had useful connections at the English court through his marriage to the widow both of Sir Philip Sidney and of the Earl of Essex. He arranged for the jury to contain ten of his kinsmen, and the result was a reverse for Wentworth. Correct but indiscreet, Wentworth brought the sheriff and jurors to Dublin and fined them. Unfortunately for him, the fine was followed straightway, and by chance, by de Burgh's death (he was seventy). Sympathy ebbed from Wentworth, and the new earl was his sworn, and later effective, enemy.

The house, most magnificent of its kind in Ireland, was eventually burned in 1826. A Gothic replacement at the other end of the park was built in 1862. This was burned in 1922. In 1929 Lord Harewood, who had inherited the property, and his wife, the Princess Royal, arrived to restore it, settling for a while in a restored garden house. But they found the stable deliberately burned when they came, and felt perhaps that Ireland at the time was no place for English blood with a royal ingredient. The ruin is a ruin still.

We drive down the east side of the lough, keeping always near the water. The best views come later on, from raised ground, where the Arra Mountains and Slieve Bernagh approach each other, and create the lake by constricting the water-flow. (The mountains are hard red sandstone; limestone has worn away to make the passage and the lough's bed, whose irregularity is caused by this limestone's continued decomposition by water.) The lake's latent powers, now exploited by the Ardnacrusha scheme, were seen over a century ago by a scientist who noted that its level could rise a couple of inches in a day and had been known to rise a foot. A foot would mean 36 million tons of water acquired in a single day – and an average winter would bring 400 million tons.

Terryglass, with its ruined abbey and castle, is the first stopping-point on the return down Lough Derg's eastern shore. Founded soon after Patrick's time by one of the many St Colums, it became a centre of learning and produced, about 1150, the *Book of Leinster*, now in Trinity College, Dublin, an important collection of history tales and poems in Middle Irish including the *Brown Bull of Cooley* saga. A few years later the abbey was the victim of an attack by Galway Irish, and the monks left it for ever, taking their possessions to Lorrha. From the keep of the Norman castle the last of the O'Kennedys, local chiefs, was thrown to his death in the water below. Before, and for many years after this, a banshee wailed and waved her arms on the battlements.

On the right two miles on is Drominagh House, and the castle on the foreshore. The high hill in view miles to the left is Knockshigowna, 689 feet high, the otherworld seat of the Munster fairies. In the ensuing miles we pass castles whose history is lost, and see the dark range of the Slieve Aughty, the lake looking like a pretty fjord where Ree, a few miles above, seems a bleak ocean; Illaunmore, with its fragmentary monastic remains and large new houses of managing directors able to persuade the Land Commission they are not defacing the scenery; the fishing, boating and snipe-shooting resort of Dromineer with its O'Kennedy castle and church, and a new lick of paint and spread of tarmac provided by Bord Failte at a cost of £80,000; and Garrykennedy with its old harbour and ivy-covered ruin and twenty white-washed cottages and bar.

Ahead, the Arra Mountains rise steeply and soon we pass – quite close if we take the mountain road – Tountinna, the highest of them (1,517 feet), with the Graves of the Leinster Men north-east of its summit. The earthworks themselves are Bronze Age chamber tombs – a series of slate slabs – but the place is central to an earlier and a later legend. The first tells how Cesair, great-granddaughter of Noah, came to Ireland – being a place where no sin had been committed since nobody had yet lived here – to avoid the impending flood. She brought with her three men and fifty women. 'In spite of her, for a woman, commendable astuteness', says Giraldus Cambrensis, she failed to escape disaster. One of the men died, and Fintan, of the two survivors, tired doubtless of an unending round of masculine duty, fled to Tountinna. The peak escaped the flood and all the others were drowned, but Fintan was soon joined by other refugees and the race's future assured. Then in Brian Boru's time the King of Leinster, lured hither by Boru's wife's promise of her daughter in marriage, was killed in an ambush prepared by her. Boru, furious, beat his wife, who ran away to the Danes to cause him more mischief. From a distance the mountain, like many in Ireland, looks as if it would be nice to slide down. Good views of Killaloe come into sight and we descend on the small village of Ballina, opposite the town, then continue southwards keeping close to the river bank. Castleconnell has no reason to thank the Shannon Scheme, for it used to be internationally famous for its salmon fishing (salmon do in fact still inhabit the river and a jump has been built for them at the new weir) and for the nearby Doonass falls and rapids, which re-routing the current and flooding have deprived of their force. In the eighteenth century the place was also known as a spa with a medicinal sulphur well. From here to Limerick several derelict demesnes lie between road and river. Ruined

Hermitage is the first, in a wooded demesne that was formerly Lord Massy's. Mount Shannon used to be the home of the Earls of Clare, and its fine Georgian house was enlarged by John Fitzgibbon, who was Attorney-General and Lord Chancellor in the Parliament before Union and later became first earl. A vigorous reactionary, he largely engineered the Parliament of 1799 into voting itself out of existence and back into complete union with Britain. He was known as 'Black Jack'. The house was burned down in 1922. The return to Limerick is five miles along the main road.

CHAPTER TWELVE

Clare and South Galway

COUNTY CLARE is a peninsula on the grand scale, cut off on three of its four sides by Lough Derg, the Shannon estuary, and the Atlantic. It is linked with the rest of Munster by only half a dozen bridges, all of which are in the neighbourhood of Limerick and Killaloe. In many ways it seems more a part of Connaught (in ancient times it was) to which it is joined along forty miles of its north side. It has much of the bleakness and poverty of its northern neighbours, and its population is thinly scattered. But in truth it fits no pattern. It is peculiarly formed. Its eastern half, with the Old Red Sandstone of the Slieve Aughty surrounded by flat limestone, is quite like the counties eastward. But a depression goes through its middle, from the Fergus estuary to Galway, dotted in its northern half by turloughs, lakes that fill and drain away into their limestone beds and never allow plants to creep far down their dry banks without welling up again and submerging them. The western half of the country is in two distinct parts again. The Burren, on the north, comprises a unique desert of limestone with floral peculiarities that have botanists rushing to it in spring. To the south, beyond a broad bed of coal, the county tails off in a glum plain of weathered Millstone Grit. Photographs of Co. Clare tend to be of the coast or specific sights inland. Clare is not a county that photographs well. On the spot, however, and particularly in the north, it can be spectacular.

Cut off as it was, Clare stayed poor. Till well into this century most of the inhabitants had seen neither car nor train. They used the swing-plough, cut meadows with scythes and corn with sickles and spoke Irish universally, as they had done for centuries. There are still many signs of hardship. The ruthless felling of trees, that changed the western landscape in Cromwellian times and after, made bog where there had been pasture. Atlantic gales have never allowed trees to grow in the western part of the county. Things are going in the right direction now, however a visitor used to farms in Leinster or England or America may marvel at the midget stone-bordered fields; but all the same the fight to save the west is not yet won.

But none of this is apparent as we enter the county. Cromwell's agents reserved a five-mile strip round the coast for Protestant settlers. In the event they claimed only about one mile's width and kept to the Shannon estuary. The result is a much richer look on the southern edge of the county; and between Limerick and Ennis – a busy thoroughfare – the estates are richer still. Of recent years the creation of Shannon Airport has shot more wealth into the region, brought by tourists who are offered entertaining package deals for their one, two or three-day stops. Nine miles from Limerick on the main Ennis road we reach the best-known ingredient of these tours, **Bunratty Castle**. Once a centre of the O'Brien Kings of Thomond, it was captured by the Anglo-Norman Thomas de Clare, and the object of constant fighting for two centuries. The building that partly survives was fifteenth-century work, and became once again O'Brien property. It was so grand for its time that the Papal Nuncio Rinuccini, arriving to bolster the Catholics in the Civil War of the 1640s, could write, 'In Italy there is nothing like the palace and grounds of the Lord Thomond'; but the war finished it, the massive keep and little else remaining. Since 1945, when Lord Gort bought it, it has been well restored to its seventeenth-century state and, open to the public by day, it is also used in the evenings for old time banquets, based as nearly on seventeenth-century conventions as to-day's jet travellers would happily countenance. Nearby is the Bunratty Folk Park, a fascinating reconstruction of several traditional kinds of Irish cottage with authentic trimmings. 'Traditional Irish Nights' are held here, in which simple food is followed by folk dances, singing and story-telling. A daytime visit is more informative, giving an intriguing glance at a way of life that is only now finally disappearing. R. A. S. Macalister, one of the greatest Irish archaeologists, wrote that Ireland 'has rendered to Anthropology the unique, inestimable, indispensable service of carrying a primitive European *Precivilisation* down into late historic times and there holding it up for observation and instruction'. The Folk Park makes clear what he meant. On the other side of the main T11 road, beside Sixmilebridge, is Mount Ievers, an enchanting and graceful early eighteenth-century mansion like a doll's house, the height of its three stories accentuated by the fact that each is slightly narrower than the one below. Bricks for one façade (the other is of stone) were shipped from Holland. The house takes paying guests.

Keeping to the L11, on which Sixmilebridge is situated, we continue north and after three miles fork left in the Quin direction. The second right turn after the fork brings us to Craggaunowen, where, around a fortified sixteenth century house, is set an intriguing exhibition of replicas of historic dwellings and other structures, including a bronze age crannog, a ring-fort, furnished farmhouses and a megalithic tomb. There are smaller exhibits in the house. From here the road to Quin takes us on through the lake-spattered plain past Knappogue, a medieval tower extended by a low castellated Victorian gothic range. This is highly commercialised, aims at Shannon coach-trippers, and like Bunratty provides what are called medieval banquets in the evenings. Quin Abbey is one of the best preserved Franciscan friaries in Ireland, built in 1402 (within the four walls of a De Clare castle of 1280) and in use from then till the early nineteenth century, in spite of the suppression of the order in 1541. The last friar died in 1820 and was buried in the north-east corner of the cloister. Good views of surrounding castles are to be had from the slender tower which tapers beautifully in four stages, a characteristic device of Irish building. About fifty of the castles hereabouts were the property of the Macnamaras, including nearby Danganbrack.

About three miles south of Quin and across the Ennis-Limerick railway (during the construction of which in 1854 several hundred prehistoric gold objects were unearthed) is Dromoland Castle, and its lovely sweeping demesne. Till recently this attractive Gothic pile, by James Pain, was the home of Sir Donough Edward Foster O'Brien, Baron Inchiquin, The O'Brien of Thomond, a direct descendant of Brian Boru and one of many O'Briens still owning land in the old Thomond kingdom. It is now a luxury hotel, with old masters in the public rooms. From here the T11 runs north to Ennis, passing on the right, a mile before the town, the lovely 1195 Augustinian friary of Clare Castle.

Ennis itself is Clare's county town, for which it seems small with its population around 6,000. It appears to belong to a different era from the part of Clare we have so far seen. That Irish lives on is seen in the many untranslated inscriptions and street names. It has, in common with the rest of the country, a reputation for rigid politics where politics impinge on the realities of life. It was here that Parnell made the masterly speech that introduced boycotting to the land struggle – 'by isolating him (the evictor) from his kind as if he were a leper of old, you must show him your detestation of the crime he had committed' – a speech that helped Gladstone to put Parnell temporarily away; and here, too, Eamonn de Valera made many speeches, for Clare was the county that kept him in power through all his years as a member of the Dail, 1917 to 1959, and which O'Connell also represented for some years. There is not much to see in the town – some good Georgian houses, a decent court-house of 1854, a statue of O'Connell in unlikely Roman costume, scant ruins of a Franciscan friary with two interesting tombs beside the bridge, and a nineteenth-century RC cathedral. But we are on the brink of some fine country, the best of it to the west and north. We can hurry first round the south-western corner, which is well worth the drive, and for those looking for beaches, resorts and pretty countryside and views an excellent area to stay in.

Three miles out of the town, on the left of the coast-road, is Francis Bindon's Newhall, a good red-brick house of 1745, in whose grounds is the Augustinian nunnery of **Killone**, attractively sited by a lake. Founded by Donal O'Brien around 1190, it was for years ruled by his granddaughter Slaney. It preserves some good details in the church, with its eastern crypt, and a cloister-court. Farther on the estuary of the

Fergus comes into view, spotted with islands, on many of which are monastic remains. Beyond Killadysert the road bends gradually right and passes through Labasheeda, Knock and **Killimer**, where Ellen Hanley, the real 'Colleen Bawn', is buried. Murdered on a boat by her husband in 1819 her body was washed up here and buried by the local schoolmaster. The husband, who had regretted marrying beneath him, was publicly hanged. Her grave-stone, made famous by the novel, play and opera inspired by the story, has been over the years reduced to nothing by tourists. **Kilrush**, five miles farther on, is the largest town of this corner of Clare. It has recently tried to attract attention by a 'Colleen Bawn' Festival, in which a beauty is chosen to stand in for the unhappy heroine and various sporting events take place. Just over the water, and reached by boat from Cappagh Pier a mile south-west of the town, is **Scattery Island**, on which stand remains of the principal monastery founded by St Senan in the early sixth century. Senan was, like many of his holy colleagues, a misogynist (St Brendan thrashed a girl who wanted 'to play her game' with him; St Kevin threw his succubus into the lake at Glendalough), and sternly exiled the virgin Canair who tried to follow him to Scattery, though Tom Moore at least thought he might have yielded to persuasion. Right on the path of the intruding Danes, the monastery suffered in the ninth and tenth centuries, but it grew rich in medieval times. Now the island is dotted with church ruins, some as early as the ninth century. Most impressive is the Angel's Church on the island's summit, incorporating vast undressed boulders in its lower walls.

On a fine day the humped promontory of Dingle to the south-west comes into view on the final western stretch to Loop Head. The main road inland is a dull one, through a flat treeless region of peat bog and rushy swamps. The coastal lane is much better, and brings us to **Carrigaholt,** where there is a college of Irish and an O'Brien (and before them Mac-Mahon) Castle, recently restored in part. Here the last O'Brien Viscount Clare to live in Ireland drilled his Dragoons to save his country for James II; and having lost set sail – one of Sarsfield's Wild Geese – with his troops to win renown in the

Irish brigades of the French army, a tradition continued by successive Viscounts Clare and Counts of Thomond. The last lap to **Loop Head** must be covered by the inland road. The view from the Head itself, a plateau of sea pink enclosed by steep 200-foot cliffs, takes in a vast circuit – MacGillycuddy's Reeks to the south, with Kerry Head near at hand and Dingle's Mount Brandon beyond; and to the north the Aran Islands, and the Twelve Pins of Connemara. From here to Kilkee it is possible to walk, keeping more or less to the cliff-top, for fifteen miles along a varied, indented coastline with strange rock forms to entertain along the way. Ross Bridges, three miles up the coast, are the most spectacular of these, but just before the turn to these the village church of **Moneen** preserves an interesting relic of the campaign of 'Souperism', in which many Protestant groups tried to convert Catholic victims of the Famine with offers of soup. In Penal days the local landlord refused to have a Catholic church on his land. An ark on wheels was constructed and kept on the beach below high-water mark and so legally beyond his clutches. Here an altar was kept and services held. The ark is still preserved in the church.

Twelve miles more brings us to **Kilkee**, a village resort with a good crescent of sandy beach in the arms of a cliff-bordered bay. Here and for several miles northward interest lies along the coast. A short walk to the west leads to the peculiar outcrop of the Duggerna Rocks, neatly patterned strata of shale with what is called the Amphitheatre beyond them. There are other marine curiosities, odd rock formations and puffing-holes, and the only thing to watch out for is the rising tide, which isolates parts of the shoreline. Kilkee has been known as a resort from Victorian times, and Tennyson came here twice. A good way to see the coastline is by hired boat, in calm weather. In bad weather the coast is a great danger to shipping, and there have been several disastrous wrecks in the vicinity.

From here we pass on north-east, keeping as near to the coastline, which becomes more beautiful, as the roads allow. Several side lanes lead down to broad sandy beaches. Spanish Point, about twenty miles beyond Kilkee, recalls the many Armada vessels wrecked along this shore. Most of the Spaniards who survived the wrecks – at Mutton Island to the south-west a thousand men are supposed to have gone down – were caught and executed by Turlough O'Brien on the orders of Sir Richard Bingham, Elizabeth's unscrupulous Governor of Connaught. Indeed the only vessels which can possibly cope with the elements on this part of the coast are curraghs, which require great skill of those who handle them in their pursuit of fish or, in the past, articles to smuggle into the country. In the eighteenth century smuggling was the major source of welfare to the inhabitants. About four-fifths of Irish sheep fleeces, it was thought, were carried to France in exchange for wine, spirits, tobacco, tea and fabrics. The caves that pit the coast provided useful warehouses for this contraband, and many landowners who took the goods in place of rent were happy to turn a blind eye on their provenance. Much the same sort of curraghs were used as those seen beside the sea now, securely tethered against the winds that could easily lift the weight of wood and tarred canvas they comprise. Farther north these tender vessels have been often used for catching the basking shark, a fish – not a maneater – of up to forty feet in length whose liver alone can fill seven or eight barrels.

We round Liscannor Bay and enter a region where in spite of human incursions nature predominates. In the curve of the bay are some small villages – Lahinch, turning itself into a resort with one of Ireland's best golf-courses, and Liscannor, where John Holland (1841–1914), inventor of the submarine, was born. (The inspiration for his work, carried out in New Jersey, was the hope that an American navy might one day be able to sink British warships.) The ruined nineteenth-century Gothic Birchfield House, with rather Moorish features, was the home of Cornelius O'Brien, MP, who laid out the walk above the Moher Cliffs – the only local feature, it was said, that he did not build himself. He also prompted his tenants to erect and pay for the urn-topped column half a mile north-west, complete with its fulsome engraved tribute. As we continue west, then bend north with the coast, the road rises and the inland hills appear more varied. But the great drama is on the seaward side. The **Cliffs of Moher** are one of the grandest natural sights in Ireland: a series of jutting headlands, stretching in all along about five miles, with sheer and clearly stratified faces dropping to the constant slick of creamy spume over the ocean at their feet. At the southern end the view, of the cliffs themselves and over the Aran Islands to Connemara, is magnificent. A tower built as a tea-house by Cornelius O'Brien is restored now, as misplaced as the mock-Tudor café that stood beside Stonehenge years ago. Below, the layers of sandstone topped by a bed of dark shale curve out here and there to spindly stacks, some as high as two hundred feet, living out their last centuries against the Atlantic onslaught. The best views are to be had from O'Brien's Tower, though the cliffs rise to their highest point of 668 feet at the northern end, and a walk, protected from the drop by a fence of tombstone-like slabs put there by the egotistical MP, is well rewarded.

Beside the road north of the Cliffs, thatched and whitewashed cottages set off the views of the Aran Islands. Doolin is a charming fishing village with a pub internationally known for the folk music played in it on most evenings. Augustus John stayed in a cottage here, belonging to his friend Francis Macnamara whose daughter Caitlin, later Dylan Thomas's wife, was brought up in the family home, now a hotel, at Ennistimon. The party called down priestly wrath by bathing naked. Black and Tans later burned the cottage down. From Doolin a road runs inland to Lisdoonvarna, passing poorer farmsteads set in the moorland of the Barony of Burren. This southern part of the Burren is dismal country based on Millstone Grit and coal measures, thought dismal, too, by prehistoric folk, who neglected it but scattered their remains all over the limestone to the north. But Lisdoonvarna's fame rests on the more recent (eighteenth century) discovery of curative, if repellent, sulphurated waters in the area round about. These are alleged to combine with the altitude, the heat caused by sun hitting the bare limestone to the north, and the moisture brought from the Atlantic, to bring relief to rheumatism and related maladies. But the place is not only reserved for aged sufferers. It became a tradition for local bachelor farmers to move into the hotels at the end of the harvest for a period of relaxation. Unmarried girls moved in,

too, and match-making prospered. Match-makers were
professionals till the last century – into this in isolated cases –
and always did good business at fairs and gatherings. Their
main function was diplomatic, reconciling the conflicting
interests of two families, and they needed also the legal
ability to draw up a contract. More recently the town has
become the setting of an annual rock concert.

North and north-east of the town lies the Burren. Lisdoonvarna with its many hotels is a good base. At the homely and
comfortable Keane's the owners are generous with their
knowledge of plants and other local interests. Another is
Gregans Castle Hotel on Corkscrew Hill to the north-east.
The Burren can seem dull on first acquaintance, though at
worst it still appears curious. John likened it to 'an immobilised
rough sea'. Flanked by Galway Bay to the north and the
Atlantic to the west, it is a high (several plateaux of 1,000 feet
and more) expanse of plain grey limestone pavements with
gently sloping sides and a few valleys. Over most of it there
are no trees, no soil, no obvious water – 'savage land', Cromwell's surveyors told him, 'yielding neither water enough to
drown a man, nor a tree to hang him, nor soil enough to bury'.
Yet between the giant clusters of rock are little clefts, chinks
and runnels which continue to support not simply a varied flora
but one that is unique to these islands. How this comes about
is by no means clear, but somehow a combination of thin
peat, a climate kept frostless by very moist sea-winds, and most
effective drainage through the porous limestone favours the
growth of several plants, many of which are rarely found elsewhere in Britain or Ireland. There are the little Spring Gentians
with intense blue five-petalled flowers in spring and early
summer; or Irish Close-flowered Orchid, with its light pink
flowers that are never fully open, another spring bloom often
thought the Burren's main treasure; Hoary Rockrose, a
dwarf with bright yellow flowers found in early summer;
purple-berried Burnet Rose; Vernal Sandwort with narrow
leaves and five white petals, a later summer flower; Dark-red
Helleborine, a midsummer orchid with small elliptic leaves
and a white-ringed red flower; the tall (up to three feet)
Shrubby Cinquefoil with bright yellow flowers, blooming

both in June and August; Bloody Cranesbill; Mountain Avens; Bear-berry and several unusual Saxifrages. Maidenhair Fern with its fan-shaped leaflets is common, too, in the vertical fissures. The range of many of these plants stretches far to the north, in some cases through Galway to Mayo. But the Burren sees them at their most varied and profuse and in particular allows an alpine flora to flourish, probably because shortage of soil prevents other plants growing tall and stifling them. These are mainly to be seen in spring.

Flowers are not the only interest in the Burren. The high clear plateaux have an eerie quality with scattered houses, stony tracks, mazes of grey stone walls, streams and little lakes that come and go with heavy rains, and the rounded hills, some topped by prehistoric cairns. The rock, being limestone, abounds in pots and gorges and complicated caves, many of them long passages not hard for the expert to negotiate, including the Polnagollum complex, Ireland's longest known, on the east side of Slieve Elva, which has been surveyed for nearly seven miles. Many of these caves have been inhabited in the past both by animals and, later, men. Remains found in large quantities have included those of the African Wild Cat which, till the discovery, had not been known to exist in Europe and the Arctic lemming, as well as wolves, bears, reindeer and the giant Irish Elk. To see all the Burren has to offer, a lengthy stay is necessary. A quick tour should include the whole of the coast road from Lisdoonvarna through Doolin, a tiny fishing village, then northwards, round Black Head to Ballyvaghan. Corkscrew Hill, south of Ballyvaghan, leads to the Burren's centre, and any of the lanes to right or left can be taken for the uplands. Prehistoric remains – galley graves, portal dolmens, cairns, ring-forts – are abundant in this hinterland, but their copious survival only means that nobody has since wanted to pull them down for other building or to make way for the plough.

To the south-east is an area of lakes, or turloughs, many of which empty right out in dry weather as the porous limestone absorbs the water. This lowland region, centring on Corrofin, makes a green and pleasant change from the upland karsts. To reach it from Lisdoonvarna we pass through

Kilfenora, whose twelfth century cathedral is partly contained in the later C of I Church. Early remains include altar-tombs and effigies, and in the churchyard is a superb High Cross. The Burren Display Centre here has interesting exhibits and films about the region's geology and wild-life. A mile east the road goes near a vast circular limestone cashel surrounded by a broad *cheval de frise*. After three more miles we pass the haunting ruin of **Leamaneagh Castle.** The castle was the home during the Cromwellian campaign of Conor O'Brien, till he was killed in battle. To save it from confiscation, his wife offered to marry a Cromwellian officer, and an obedient cavalry-man was ordered to comply – a situation that came about more than once. **Corrofin,** in the turlough region, and among innumerable castle ruins of O'Briens and others, is six miles farther on. We approach the area again soon (at Lough Cutra) and meanwhile resume our coastal journey at Ballyvaghan. The eastward road rounds Moneen Mountain and bends left towards the village of Burren. Near the bend, a track leads up to the ruins of the typically sequestered Cistercian abbey of **Corcomroe,** founded about 1180 by that tireless patron of the church, Donal Mor O'Brien, and placed under the rule of Furness Abbey in Lancashire. Dissolved in 1554, the community still continued its discreet existence well into the next century. There are some good effigies and gravestones, many of them of the Burke family, which figures large in the history of Galway, whose border we shall shortly cross. Another fortaste of Co. Galway comes three miles to the north at New Quay beyond Burren village, or 'Burrin Pier' as Shaw called it in *Back to Methuselah*. Under a mile west of the quay is Mount Vernon lodge, holiday house of the Gregory family of Coole, where Shaw and Yeats and many others were entertained by Lady Gregory. Many of the plans of what is known as the Irish Literary renaissance were laid here and in various houses on the plain of Southern Galway. If we continue east and turn left a mile before Kinvarra we come to **Duras House,** on the west of Kinvarra Bay, now a Youth Hostel but in the last years of the nineteenth century the home of the affable Count Florimond de Basterot. This scion of a noble French family that had fled to Ireland at the revolution kept up literary links with his homeland and here entertained de Maupassant, Maurice Barrès and others. Here, too, came his Irish guests, Edward Martyn of Tulira, his cousin, and Yeats and Lady Gregory. It was in the garden that in 1897 the idea of a national theatre – what became the Abbey – was first broached. 'Where, but for that conversation at Florimond de Basterot's,' Yeats mused later, 'had been the genius of Synge?' That idea and others mellowed at Coole, to which we shall come shortly. The Celtic Twilight dominates this region of Galway, but it is far from being its only theme.

Beyond Kinvarra on the left – a narrow-necked promontory in the bay contains the compact, restored castle of **Dunguaire** or Dungory, privately owned but opened in the season for festive dinners arranged by the Shannon Airport Tourist Division. The castle dates to the sixteenth century but is supposedly on the site of seventh-century King Guaire of Connaught's royal palace. A recent owner was the late Christabel Lady Ampthill whose divorce case in the 1920s seemed to indicate she had been blessed with a virgin birth. From Kinvarra a road leads south about seven miles to **Kilmacduagh.** The same King Guaire had a kinsman, Colman MacDuagh, and when Colman was proved by displays of magic to have saintly leanings, the king granted him land to found a monastery, with lovely views across to the Burren hills. The present cathedral ruins are fifteenth century with earlier work incorporated. O'Heyne's Abbey to the north-west contains good thirteenth-century Romanesque work; and there are other remains including a fine 112-foot Round Tower. The saint, however, thought the place too good for him and in old age moved away to Oughtmama near Corcomroe, where he died. From a crossroads south-east of the monastery site a minor road leads south-east towards the southern tip of Lough Cutra. Half a mile up the west shore of this beautifully wooded lake stands **Lough Cutra Castle,** originally built by the Pain brothers to designs of John Nash, who seems to have based them on James Wyatt's Gothic Norris Castle at Cowes, Isle of Wight. The first Viscount Gort was the owner. But his successors fell on hard times during the Famine and sold out to Lord Gough, later made field-marshal and the conqueror both of the Chinese in the Opium War and the Sikhs before the annexation of the Punjab. A hundred years later the present Viscount Gort (who a little later also bought Bunratty and developed it) bought the property back and it has recently been through extensive alterations. It has now been sold again, but the public is still admitted.

Gort, a few miles north along the main road, is a tidy town with a broad main street. Thackeray, in a bad mood, thought it 'looked as if it wondered how the deuce it got itself in the midst of such a desolate country, and seemed to *bore* itself there considerably. It had nothing to do and no society.' Society was on its way. In 1852 Augusta Persse, of an old Northumberland (Percy) family settled in Ireland in Cromwell's time, was born nearby at Roxborough House (on the Loughrea road, but burned down in the Civil War), her family home. When she was twenty-nine she married Sir William Gregory, a diplomat, of **Coole House**, three miles north of Gort, and with him travelled to London, Italy and India. She had a son by him but her husband died seven years after their marriage. As her son grew up she turned her untrained eye to literature, and especially the myth and folklore that were still the currency of the cottages hereabouts. Then she met Yeats at Mount Vernon and found herself precipitated into the literary activity of the 1890s, partly as a patroness – for she was a wealthy widow – and in part as writer – 'Her literary style', wrote Yeats condescendingly, 'became in my ears the best written by a woman.' With Yeats she travelled round the area collecting folklore for her books and plays in Irish. Here at Coole she entertained the leading cultural figures of the day. To-day the house is vanished, but the tree stands where distinguished visitors – Douglas Hyde, Shaw, Yeats, AE, Violet Martin and many others – carved their initials. Yeats himself, who in later years remembered the place 'better than any spot on earth', recalled the art treasures, the Indian artifacts, the signed photographs of Tennyson, Browning, Thackeray, Mark Twain with which it had been crammed. Many of the paintings had been bought in Europe by an eighteenth-century Gregory who, when young, fell in love with a schoolgirl but was debarred from marrying her; he had kept her in a little house on the demesne disguised as a boy till his father died; then they married. The guests were not only literary. Lady Gregory's favourite nephew was Hugh Lane, who often stayed. Here, too, her other nephew, John Shawe-Taylor, decided to organise a conference which led directly to Land Purchase (the rights of tenants to buy the land on which they lived with money lent by the British government). Nowadays the estate, partly given over to forestry, shows no sign of its past activities. Only a few initials on a railed-in copper beech tree recall its greatest years. The house was demolished, for no good reason, in 1941. 'Here, traveller, scholar, poet, take your stand/When all these rooms and passages are gone', wrote Yeats in 1927.

The associations carry further. Four miles east of Coole is a solitary sixteenth-century castle keep, beside a river bridge, amid low woods and slight hills. This is **Thoor Ballylee,** which Yeats bought for £35 in 1917 and restored 'for my wife George' in 1920. A couple of years later he describes life there during the Civil War: '. . . the railway bridges blown up and the roads blocked with stones and trees . . . one never knew what was happening at the other side of the hill or the line of trees. Ford cars passed the house from time to time with coffins standing on end between the seats, and sometimes at night we heard an explosion, and once by day saw the smoke made by the burning of a great neighbouring house.' He gave up the place in 1929 but it has been restored as a Yeats Museum. **Tullira Castle,** to the right of the Galway road eight miles north of Gort, was the ancestral home of Edward Martyn, another notable in the cultural revival. Signs of his lavish patronage of the arts, especially (RC) church decoration, are evident in the region at nearby Laban and at **Loughrea,** eleven miles east, in both of which are stained glass windows by graduates of Sarah Purser's 'Tower of Glass' – A. E. Childe, Michael Healy, Evie Hone and Sarah Purser herself. Loughrea Cathedral was Martyn's patricular interest, and most shows the results of his campaign against the low standard of RC church architecture and ornament. Tullira itself, in a mock-Tudor style that replaced a Georgian house in 1882, was loathed by Yeats – 'Those pillars, that stair, and varnished roof with their mechanical ornament, were among the worst inven-revival', but here he nevertheless, in mystical mood, made his first 'invocation of the moon' and saw in a vision as a reward 'a naked woman of incredible beauty standing upon a pedestal'. Martyn hated the house, too, which his mother had had rebuilt by George Ashlin, but was content to go on living there, among his Impressionists, planning the Catholic artistic renaissance, eating enormously (but only once a day, so thinking himself an ascetic), hating women, worshipping Degas whom he had once known, and arguing often with his irascible and inventive friend George Moore.

A right turn at Ardrahan leads the nine miles to Craugh-well, home of the Galway Blazers. Four miles due north of Craughwell is **Athenry,** once the principal seat of the De Burghs and Berminghams and preserving several medieval ruins – patches of the town walls, a castle keep of 1238, a Dominican Priory and Franciscan Friary in which stands the C of I church. From here the main road west leads straight to Galway city, though a diversion after three miles leads to Clarinbridge, famous for the September Galway Oyster Festival which opens here at Paddy Burke's inn. The miles of Galway Bay oyster beds stretch from Oranmore in the north-east corner of the bay all down the east side to Kinvarra.

Two miles south-west of Clarinbridge, on the south bank of the Kilcolgan's estuary, is the demesne and substantial over-grown ruin of Tyrone House, built in a robust Palladian style in 1779 by Christopher French St. George. The family history shows the hazards of resisting the appeal of absentee land-lordism, for in the nineteenth century they stayed put. Though they hunted and raced fervently, and sired occasional children on local girls, they were by the standards of the age very generous to their many tenants. Gossip gave them a different reputation, of good English stock reverting to peasant bar-barism; and it was this version which Violet Martin heard when in 1912 she visited the house, by then empty. 'If I dared to work up that subject . . .' she wrote to Edith Somerville. The result was one of their best novels, *The Big House of Inver*. In 1972 the Irish Georgian Society bought the ruin.

CHAPTER THIRTEEN

Galway North and West

'As in the body naturall the crisis of the disease is often made by throwing the peccant humor into the extreame parts, soe here the barbarities of Ireland under which it so long laboured, and with which it was soe miserably infected, are all accumulated.' So John Dunton of Galway wrote in a letter to England in 1698. Fifty years earlier Connaught had had been lumped by Cromwell with Hell as a suitable destination for Irishmen. It had had a bad reputation for centuries before this. Though Henry II had acknowledged Irish ownership by the Treaty of Windsor in 1175, his barons had broken his word for him and crossed the Shannon, which till then divided the independent Celts from Anglo-Norman conquerors. The stony flats of Leitrim and Roscommon were left to the Irish. The rest of Connaught became the spoil of Normans, Welsh and Flemings. From them came some of the most common names of the Galway–Mayo bulge – Athy, Bodkin, Blake, Browne, D'Arcy, ffont, ffrench, Joyce, Kirwan, Lynch, Martin, Morris and Skerrett.

These thirteen 'Tribes of Galway' found it hard to maintain their tenure. They had the O'Flaherties and other Irish clans to contend with. Over the west gate of **Galway City** they engraved a prayer: 'From the fury of the O'Flaherties, Good Lord deliver us.' And to preserve the exclusive nature of the city at least they passed a law in 1518: 'no man of this towne shall oste or receive into their housses at Christemas, Easter, nor no feast alles, any of the Burkes, MacWilliams, the Kellies, nor no cepte elles, without license of the mayor and council, on payn to forfeit 5 pounds, that neither o' nor Mac shalle strutte ne swaggere thro the streetes of Galway'. (As lately as the 1940s William Joyce, 'Lord Haw-Haw' thought he might mitigate the penalty for his high treason by remind-

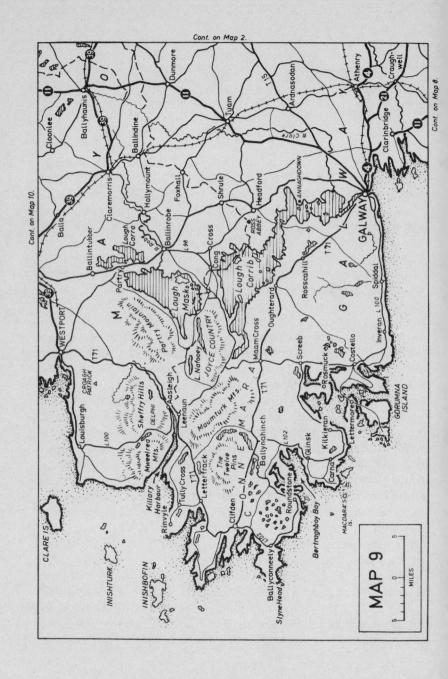

Cont. on Map 2.
Cont. on Map 8.
Cont. on Map 10.

MAP 9

5   0   5
MILES

ing his judges that he had helped suppress the Irish of Galway in Black and Tan times.)

Apartheid, here as elsewhere, worked to some extent as it was intended to. Trade prospered in competition with Limerick, and there was a great deal of mercantile contact with Spain (Columbus, before his Atlantic journey, is supposed to have come here to check on reports of the mythical St Brendan's island). Wine imports and beef, pork, butter and wool exports made Galway one of the greatest commercial towns in the British Isles, till in the 1641 Civil War the citizens made the mistake of backing the king and the Catholic Church. Eleven years later, Cromwell's General Coote took Parliament's revenge, and razed much of the town, recently rebuilt, to the ground. It was after the citizens' second disaster – capture after backing King James – in the same century, that Dunton wrote the biased verdict above. Galway never fully recovered, and the railway, which made Dublin the country's main distribution centre, made sure that the town could never be as important as it had been. In the eighteenth and nineteenth centuries its population was static, even went down a little. Since 1912 it has risen by over a half; and it is now a busy county town with a reviving maritime and tourist trade, and industry. Irish Marble, a company that exports marble all over the world, has become one of Ireland's biggest export firms. And Galway remains what it always has been, the key to the west, between the sea and the longitudinal barrier of Loughs Corrib and Mask.

Lynch is a most distinguished name. In the 170 years before Coote's victory a total of eighty-four mayors had been of that name and it still figures all over the place. One of these mayors, Stephen Lynch, made himself a legend in 1493 when, finding no one willing to hang his son, a condemned murderer, he did the job himself. Or so the story goes. The scene of the hanging is indicated by a memorial beside the churchyard of C of I **St Nicholas's Collegiate Church**, the town's most interesting antiquity. Founded in the early fourteenth century (an Aran man who died in 1580 supposedly aged 220 was said to remember a time when the church did not exist), it has since been much altered and restored, but remains the largest medieval church in Ireland. The curious pyramid-shaped spire was added in 1683 and the parapet restored in 1883. Inside, the simplicity of the cruciform design is pointed up by a number of interesting memorials, not least that of a certain Mr Eyre, who 'was a thorough honest Englishman'. The whole church has recently been restored, perhaps rather too clinically. The other major church, out of the centre on the west bank of the pretty Corrib River, is the **RC Cathedral** built between 1959 and 1965 under the dynamic aegis of the late Bishop of Galway, Dr Browne. The Cathedral seems unhappily to have brought together the worst of several old orders. The building's essentially simple cruciform shape, with an enormous dome, is clumsily rooted to the ground by a cluster of buildings attached at the south side, which disastrously break its line. A mixture of stones in the facing and two vast rosette windows are additional sad features. Inside it is light and vast and refreshing, though again spoiled by inapposite details, as if each member of a committee had had his own favourite idea incorporated in the grand design of this architectural dodo.

Apart from the church of St Nicholas, and some magnificent monuments in the Franciscan Friary, and sixteenth-century Lynch's Castle – now bank offices – only isolated fragments like the Spanish Arch near the quays survive from the old city. The handsome classical courthouse by Sir Richard Morrison dates from about 1800. Up the river is Joseph B. Keane's interesting nineteenth-century University College, in Tudor style, and based on Oxbridge models. There are still good walks through the irregular lanes that each year seem to lose more of their archaic character to the maws of development.

South and west of the town the coast is an ever-lengthening resort area, with promenades, good beaches, and all the relevant trappings. From the harbour there are regular sailings to the **Aran Islands**, and it is possible to make the round trip in a day, though a great deal more time is needed to see even one of the three with any thoroughness. Weather is important. Winds can make a normal two and a half hour journey last six hours, but there are also more expensive regular flights. Jokes about island weather (if you can't see

Brandon Bay, County Kerry, from which St Brendan may have sailed to America.
Below Quin Abbey, County Clare: the abbey survived despite the Dissolution.

The Cliffs of Moher, County Clare: five miles of sheer-sided bays and headlands. *Below* A five-thousand-year-old portal dolmen at Poulnabrone, the Burren, County Clare.

them from the mainland it's raining; if you can, it's going
to rain) are not really justified since they get less rain than the
mainland, where there are mountains to precipitate it. The
islands have got themselves into the paradoxical situation of
being world-renowned for their pure Gaelic culture (though
Liam O'Flaherty, Aran-born novelist, said that many islanders
descend from the ruggedest of Cromwell's troops, put there
to be out of the way, and that 'they still speak English with a
cockney accent'). As a result visitors stream in and out, films
are made and books are written on the islands, and the inhabitants have television and cars. It is hard in such circumstances to maintain Gaelic. When J. M. Synge stayed there (and
wrote a charming account of his stay, during which he sat
often by a crack in the floor of his room and took down the
lyrical conversation of the girls in the kitchen below, using
his notes later for dialogue) he could describe an islander as
shut inside 'a world of individual conceits and theories'.
Nowadays that world embraces Manhattan and Camden
Town, and there is as much worldly wisdom here as anywhere
else. But still Aran retains an outwardly timeless appearance;
and the curraghs that convey goods and people from the
steamer to the two smaller islands, and the rawhide sandals
worn by the islanders *look* unsophisticated even if there is no
sensible alternative to them.

Geologically the islands are the summits of a reef that
stretches out from the limestone surface of Clare and the
Burren (only five miles from the tip of the eastern island,
Inisheer). Inishmore presents a sheer wall of rock, sometimes
400 feet high, to the ocean at the south-west, but on the
north-east all these islands tilt down gradually to the sea.
In the past the land surface was as grey and featureless as
that of the Burren. Gradually, and over centuries, by stopping
up the joints of the limestone with splinters and spreading
sand and seaweed over the bare rock, the islanders have
created a soil that provides them and their stock with grass,
potatoes and cereals. Loose rocks have been used to build
the walls that make a jigsaw of the whole area. In the past
they were used for buildings on the grand scale, especially in
early Christian times.

All three islands abound in monastic remains, including churches, High Crosses and Round Tower remains. Plentiful ruins of another sort survive in the shape of prehistoric forts – of a period unknown but possibly, like Staigue Fort, from the time of Norse invasions, though legends connect them with the original colonisation of Ireland. Of these, **Dun Aengus** on Inishmore was called by Dr Petrie 'the most magnificent barbaric monument in Europe'. It stands above vertical cliffs (a fall of which, it is claimed, reduced the oval form of the fort to its present horseshoe shape) amid three lines of ramparts, the outer of which encloses eleven acres; additional defence was given by the range of outward-pointing sharp stones – the *chevaux de frise* – on the landward side. Both Inishmaan, on which Synge set his *Riders to the Sea*, and Inisheer have forts and monastic remains also, and since it is difficult to visit either without stopping at least for a night, they both preserve an even more sequestered atmosphere. (Neither has a police force on it.) An interesting story attaches to the strip of water between the two bigger islands. Pope Gregory the Great, who sent the officious Augustine on his mission to convert Britain, was known to be a great sympathiser with the Celts even while his official position made it necessary for him to bring their errant church into line with Roman practice. That and his obsessive playing with words ('*Non Angli sed Angeli*' was one of his better puns) endeared him to the Irish, who called him the Goldenmouth, and in time gave him the added distinction of calling him Irish – or the son of an Irishman. The story developed that before his death the Pope ordered his coffined body to be lowered into the Tiber. This was done, and river and sea bore it round Western Europe to these islands, where finally he was buried. The strip of water is known as Gregory's Sound. For a stay of decent length on the islands, which need far more description than space allows here, Thomas H. Mason's *Islands of Ireland* is a pleasant introduction and Synge's *Aran Islands* gives a good picture of the life and way of speech of a past generation.

*

Lough Corrib, due north of Galway, is the second largest lake in Ireland (and in parts as much as 150 feet deep) and contains innumerable islands, many of them of antiquarian interest. This aspect of the local scene was covered with gusto and great scholarship by Oscar Wilde's eccentric father, Sir William, who with his wife 'Speranza' made up a team (as shown in Terence de Vere White's absorbing *Parents of Oscar Wilde*) almost as picturesque as their son. Wilde's book, recently revised and reprinted, is still an excellent detailed guide, though written for an age used to the pace of walking and trap rather than cars, and it serves well on the lake cruises which can be taken from Galway. Here we shall keep to the road and round both lakes – Corrib and Mask – meeting Wilde half-way at his house near Cong. Most noticeable in the trip is the way the lakes divide the flat barren eastern part of the county from the mountainous miles of Connemara and the west, to which we shall shortly come.

The long straight T40 leads north up the east side of the lake and after seven miles a turn to the left leads by a round-about route to **Annaghdown**, where there are evocative crumbling ruins of a Franciscan church, friary and a Norman castle. St Brendan, tired at last by his Atlantic and other travels, died here, in the nunnery he himself had earlier founded, in the arms of his sister Brig, who was its head. The lane leads back to the main road which five miles farther comes to Headford. A mile north-west of the town is **Ross Abbey**, in fact a Franciscan friary refounded in 1498, a time when the neglect of the Church by bishops – often illegitimate sons of great families – put the weight of religious continuity on this and other mendicant orders. They responded with several new foundations and vigorous preaching and many continued long after the official dissolution of the monasteries. Ross, which was wrecked by Cromwell's troops, still shows plainly the characteristic plan of Franciscan houses, being the best preserved friary in Ireland. On the shore a few miles to the south-west are several demesnes and good houses, beside a pretty stretch of the lake. The area is also rich in medieval castle ruins and particularly in prehistoric remains.

From Headford the L98 to the east passes Knockma Hill, one of the many hills in the country that were seats of gods and fairies – this one remains the abode of Finbarra, present king of the fairies. It then goes on to **Tuam**, see of a united Protestant diocese (of Tuam, Killala and Achonry), whose bishop claims the largest area and the smallest community of any in the British Isles. The C of I Cathedral dates back in part to the twelfth century but was totally restored and in parts spoiled during a nineteenth-century restoration by Sir Thomas Deane. It still preserves a superb Romanesque chancel arch, the widest in the country, and sumptuously baroque Italian choir stalls of 1740. The RC Cathedral, outside the town, is duller work of Gothic Revival style. Two miles east is Bermingham House, once seat of the Lords Athenry and from the early nineteenth century home of the Dennis family, one of whom, John Dennis, founded the Galway Blazers. The house is still a hunt headquarters.

Crossing the flat country westwards we return from Tuam through Shrule, with its ruined abbey and castle beside the Black River, to the main lakeside road and make for Cross, where a turn left puts us on the Cong road leading between Loughs Mask and Corrib. The two lakes are connected by sub-terranean channels through the limestone rock and in the Famine a canal was dug, at great cost, in the Famine Relief programme, to link them for boat traffic. The water, which was to debouch into the Corrib at Cong did nothing of the sort, since the porous rock allowed it to sink through; and the dry canal remains as a memorial to improvidence. A mile before Cong an unsignposted lane leads to the (still private) house that Sir William Wilde built and in which he and his family spent long periods. It is a plain gabled house with magnificent views over the lake and its islands, called Moytura, after the prehistoric battlefield Wilde supposed he had identified all round this area. Scholars to-day doubt his findings and some reject them. Some say there were two battles, of which the one here was the first. But his ingenuity in fitting physical remains of mounds, circles and cairns – with which this 'Plain of Moytura' is littered – to literary accounts, was admirable. The battle, if and wherever it took place, was supposed to have been between the Firbolgs, the fourth wave of invaders of Ireland, and the Tuatha de Danaan, or people of the goddess Danu, who arrived after them and here defeated them. The Tuatha were supposed to be the last colonial wave before the Milesians – otherwise known as Gaels – came to displace them and thoroughly settle the country. From the chiefs of the Firbolgs and Tuatha derived many of the shadier gods and spirits, banished in many cases to remote hills and valleys by the introduced Gaelic gods.

Most of the interest of Cong is contained in the demesne of **Ashford Castle**. This large baronial pile in its magnificent grounds was built for Sir Arthur Edward Guinness, son of the brewer-philanthropist Sir Benjamin Lee Guiness and himself created Lord Ardilaun in 1880. The house is now a hotel, one of the best in the country as is its restaurant. Beside the demesne gates are the beautiful and recently restored ruins of Cong Abbey, an early twelfth-century foundation of which part of the chancel and the conventual buildings remain. The cloister is mainly a reconstruction of the 1860s. From Cong can be made the circuit of Lough Mask, with its constant views, on the eastern side, of the Partry Mountains to the west. On the left, four miles along the Ballinrobe road is the lakeside **Lough Mask House,** surrounded by the former estates of Lord Erne, who employed Captain Boycott as his agent in 1873. When the Land League agitation began a few years later the local branch put in a demand for a 25 per cent reduction of their rents. Boycott and his master offered 10 per cent, then 20 per cent, and when this was refused began forceful evictions. A few days before, at Ennis, Parnell had made new proposals for dealing with any evictor; isolate him 'as if he was a leper of old'. Overnight Boycott was a lonely outpost of the Ascendancy. His crops were neglected, as were all his animals, his mail, his laundry. No shop would sell to him or his wife. But he stood his ground, and when his stand was publicised found support in many quarters. Fifty men were dispatched voluntarily by landlords in Monaghan to help him gather his crops, on which the issue turned. Seven thousand police and troops descended to see they were not interfered with. The Irish did nothing. When the crop was gathered the volunteers went away, but the Boycotts went with them. In the event neither side had won, neither lost. A year later the agitation had died down and Boycott returned. The most revealing and least known part of the story is that this time he stayed and soon after found a popularity he had never known before.

Ballinrobe's RC parish church has nine good stained glass windows by Harry Clarke, one of the most notable of the Tower of Glass graduates. A right turn off the main Castlebar road, just out of the town, leads us round Lough Carra and past, after eight miles, the lakeside ruin of **Moore Hall**, decaying among forestry. The Moores were a family of eccentric distinction. In 1798 John Moore was proclaimed first president of the Republic of Connaught on the arrival of French ships to back up the rising of United Irishmen (which had already, over much of the land, been effectively crushed). Humbert's defeat cut short his tenure and he died in prison the following year. George Moore the novelist, friend and enemy of Yeats, Edward Martyn, Leslie Stephen and others, about whom nobody said a good word but everyone told a story more interesting than the last, spent much of his time here in middle age, and described the local scene in the *Ave*, *Salve*, *Vale* trilogy and in *The Lake*. Among many other things, Moore thought himself a gourmet, and was always sending back dishes in restaurants. At Moore Hall, he sacked six cooks in succession. The last protested and returned with a policeman. Moore dragged the baffled constable into the dining-room and put him the judicial question: 'Is there a law in this country to compel me to eat this abominable omelette?' At his death, his ashes were scattered over the lake here.

At the north tip of Lough Carra stands **Ballintubber Abbey**, from 1795 till early this century a possession of the Moores. It was recently thoroughly restored after a turbulent history that included, after its foundation in 1216 by the O'Conor King of Connaught, burning, deroofing by Cromwellians, the subsequent collapse of the tower, and an unbroken tradition of masses held, even during Penal times, for over seven hundred and fifty years. The recent works have left it light, simple and spacious inside, preserving some good

Romanesque details of the early thirteenth century, and a few interesting tombs. Outside, the excavations carried out between 1963 and 1966 show well the transition from Romanesque to Gothic styles that was taking place at the time of its construction. Of the extensive fifteenth-century reconstruction the west doorway (which was removed in the nineteenth century) is one of the most graceful remains.

Driving south down the Galway road and turning right at the village of Partry we come on to the road that leads down the west side of Lough Mask, in country that is in every way different from that to the east. Limestone has given way abruptly to massive beds of Ordovician rock, with small stretches of earlier volcanic rocks. The valleys and tarns, on this western side often surrounded by cliffs 1,000 feet high, are the results of glacial action and can be appreciated by hard walking, especially up the valleys of the Owenbrin; but the drive itself is magnificent, with new vistas opening at each bend of the road. This is **Joyce's Country** (an unofficial title, like Connemara), named from a Welsh family that settled here in the thirteenth century, from whom many of to-day's inhabitants are descended. At the junction by Lough Nafooey we turn right and cross another line of mountains by the pass to descend on the broad and beautiful valley of Joyce's River. Four miles down the valley road we cross the river, and passing Leckavrea Mt on the right come on Maam Cross, a good centre for the lakes and mountain country. Oughterard, ten miles east along the T71 is a bigger pleasant town much given over to the tourist trade. From here the main road continues back to Galway. On the left, four miles out of Oughterard, is Ross Lake with **Ross House** (built 1777) beside it, ancestral home of the Martins of Ross, who were in their time among the greatest landowners of Connaught. Violet Martin, 'Martin Ross' of the *Irish RM* stories, was born in Ross House in 1862. By her time the family had lost its money. She wrote of all the vain attempts to preserve gentility among the big houses roundabout, and how a Miss O'Flaherty nearby used to dress up as a maid to tell people her mistress was out, not wishing them to know she *had* no maid.

GALWAY TO WESTPORT, CONNEMARA

West of Galway the coast road leads straight, fine and rather dull beside a bleak stretch of rugged stony flats and lakes. There are good beaches here and there, and Spiddal, twelve miles along, is a popular seaside resort, with an Irish college, for this is part of the Gaeltacht. When the road eventually bends right and north over twenty miles from Galway, long stony promontories lead down towards a maze of islands stretching for miles to the west. The shore here is dotted with beaches which are all but private, so many there are for so few visitors (the Irish famous tend to come here as a guaranteed escape from crush and bother). From Costelloe a lane to the left crosses to Lettermore Island and hence to the largest of the islands, Gorumna, by shallow causeways. As we continue north there are good views of the Twelve Pins in the heart of Connemara. Four miles west of the junction at Screeb the road passes a turning to **Rosmuck**, on a peninsula, and just past the turning a track leads a quarter of a mile to Patrick Pearse's white thatched cottage, lonely on a small rise. It was here that this Irish patriot son of an English father came for long spells to learn Irish, and then to translate local Irish poetry into English, to write both plays and poems in Irish, and to make 'a little Gaelic kingdom of our own'. The cottage has been much restored to house mementoes of him. A few miles on, the road bends again and follows the coast beside Kilkieran Bay. Behind, the mountains rise up from the plain like a gigantic fortress, rather as MacGillycuddy's Reeks do from the west, or the Wicklow Hills in the east. In common with Wicklow, the whole of south Connemara is granite, the result of volcanic eruptions in the Caledonian period; while the mountains to the north are covered in quartzite, whose hard weathering gives them their jagged, sometimes conical shapes, while gleaming schists, worn down by glaciation, fill the valleys between, or carry on the mountain ranges to the north. The region we are covering now is a strange plain of rock-strewn bog and lake, with a peculiar beauty not usually associated with the name Connemara, but quite as much a part of it. (Connemara is in fact

an unofficial name, anciently one of the divisions of Connaught – Conmacne-mara – and now a term loosely applied
to west Galway.)

Kilkieran, a pretty harbour village where Irish is very much
the first language, is a centre of the seaweed industry. Lobsters,
oysters and scallops make a profitable business on the west
coast of Ireland, but this vegetable harvest from the sea is
also of vital importance. The weed, cut at low tide, by men and
women alike, is used to enrich the stony land, so making
possible crops of potatoes, corn and hay. From Kilkieran
the weed is also exported to Scotland for meal, but this is a
more recent development. All aspects of cultivation are hard
here, for the use of mechanical ploughs is impossible in such
stony soils, and it is difficult – amid the signs of hard hand
industry and frugal living, among people who make English
sound a foreign language and who take more seriously than
most their age-old saint cults and patterns – to remember
that Galway a few miles back is a town of thriving business-
men and international trade. One of the old religious festivals
takes place (on 16th July and 25th September) at St Macdara's
Island, one and a half miles south-west of the peninsula,
where there is an ancient stone church and other remains.
It is still the custom for passing boats to dip their sails three
times when passing the island.

The next main promontory off Connemara, circled by a
continuation of the L102 road, lies between Bertraghboy
Bay and Clifden. The scenery near the road is similar to what
we have seen, but the views of the distant hills are grandly
different. **Roundstone** is one of the nicest resorts in Connemara, with pretty white-washed two-story houses in a line
beside a deep sheltered inlet of sea. It was built in the 1820s
by Alexander Nimmo, a Scotch engineer who settled it with
Scotch fishermen. Lobsters, mackerel and trout, here as
elsewhere, add a dimension to a stay in the district. Above
Roundstone rises the serrated ridge of Errisbeg, and from its
summit (987 feet) can be had perhaps the best panoramic
view of the whole region – the extraordinary complex of rocky
lakes below, the main range of the Twelve Pins, thousands of
islands great and small out to sea, and to the south the coast

of Clare and Kerry, and the Aran Islands standing out against the Cliffs of Moher.

Errisbeg and the country round about is widely known for its rare flora, including several species usually found in America and seldom elsewhere in the British Isles. Three varieties of heath – Irish (miscalled Mediterranean), Mackay's and St Dabeoc's, with its long purple bells – are abundant here. In addition there are plants that have spread from the lime-stone of the Burren. Some more common flowers, here and close to the sea all round the peninsula, are notable for their profusion. Continuing round to the south and west of the promontory we cross the stretch of road described as 'brandy and soda' because of the fresh invigorating wind that blows in from the sea. Dog's Bay, sough of Errisbeg, is one of the most delightful beaches for miles, with its white sand and sheltered position. Beyond Ballyconneely, where an outcrop of land stretches out to Slyne Head, the Derrygimlagh Bog opens out to the east. It was here, in a rocky bog that few pilots would choose for a safe touch-down, that John William Alcock with his co-pilot, Arthur Whitton Brown, crash-landed in June, 1919, after the first transatlantic flight, begun from Newfoundland 16 hours 27 minutes before. (Both were knighted, and Alcock was killed in a plane accident, in the same year.) A simple stone model of an aeroplane wing, a landmark for miles, points towards the spot where they came down. A few miles farther on we enter Clifden, a pleasant resort well protected from Atlantic gales at the head of its own creek. It is a good base for both sea and land sides of Connemara, and in August the Conne-mara Pony Show is held here. The roofless castle, a mile or so to the west, was a Gothic construction for the D'Arcy family, who laid out the town in the early years of the nine-teenth century – a time when the attractions of west Galway began to be realised by the outside world – and several towns, Clifden, Westport, Roundstone, Letterfrack, were built, often for an immigrant population. The D'Arcys were one of the old 'tribes of Galway', but it was another of these, the Martins, whose influence extended furthest, and amounted at times to that of a feudal royal family, a notion they cherished. One Martin boasted to the Prince Regent that the Long Walk at Windsor was badly named. His own drive was thirty miles long, as in a sense it was, for the road from Galway to Ballynahinch, his own residence, was almost entirely flanked by estates he owned.

Ballynahinch Castle, an ugly and restored eighteenth-century house, is beside the lake of the same name, eight miles east of Clifden, and an early stage in one of the most breathtaking circuits of Connemara. (It has one possible drawback: in 1923 Ballynahinch had the highest number of rainy days ever recorded in these islands – 309.) A medieval O'Flaherty demesne, the original castle was confiscated by the ruthless and unloved Sir Richard Bingham, President of Connaught in Elizabeth's reign. Best known of the Martins who ruled here was Colonel Richard Martin (1754–1834), who was mainly responsible for the founding of the RSPCA. Maria Edgeworth came here after his death, but she knew of him, and wrote that as 'King of Connemara' he had ruled over his people 'with absolute power, with laws of his own and setting all other laws at defiance'. His early days were known for innumerable duels. Later he discovered a fondness for animals and introduced a bill to protect them in Parliament. 'Hairtrigger Dick', his early nickname, was dropped for 'Humanity Martin', and the more pious tag has stuck. The Famine broke the family fortunes, and the house went through several owners – including from 1926 Prince Ranjit-sinhji of Nawanagar, an international cricketer who once scored three separate centuries for three separate teams in one day. ('Gentlemen', he was once introduced at a Dublin dinner, 'he might have fished the Ganges; but he prefers the river at Ballynahinch'). In 1945 it became a hotel, which it still remains.

Continuing east on the T71 for six miles beyond Ballynahinch a left turn leads up the valley between the Twelve Pins and the Maumturk Mountains. Ten miles through this valley, with Lough Inagh and the hills from which Connemara marble is quarried on the left, and countless waterfalls on both sides, we reach the T71 again and turn left towards Letterfrack. We are soon passing Kylemore Lake, 'clothed purple and silver under windows lit by the southern sun', as Gogarty wrote in bittersweet mood when his and others' houses were being burned and ransacked by the IRA. Beyond the lake, on the right, is the extraordinary lush demesne of **Kylemore Castle**, since the First World War a convent of Benedictine nuns. (Visitors are welcome.) The castle and the Gothic church to its east were built by a Liverpool millionaire, Mitchell Henry, in the late nineteenth century. He spent thousands of pounds reclaiming adjacent land from the bog, and now the miles of rhododendrons and avenues of fuchsia, best seen in early summer, are one of the outstanding sights of Connemara. Three miles beyond, at Letterfrack, a Quaker settlement of the early nineteenth century, we turn right, and after another three miles branch left at Tully Cross. Beyond the little village of Renvyle, on the right, is **Renvyle House Hotel**, seat of the Blake family till 1883, when it was turned into a hotel. Later it was bought by Oliver St John Gogarty (1878-1957), the doctor turned writer whose racy *As I was Going down Sackville Street* provides the most sensitive and amusing picture that exists of the extraordinary maze of cultural Dublin in the twenties. Here at Renvyle he entertained Yeats (who disliked the house, or rather, was disliked by its dormant spirits, so he considered), Shaw and Augustus John, who called it the most beautiful landscape in in the world and did several paintings here. Then in 1922 the house – 'the long, long house in the ultimate land of the un-discovered West' – was burned by the IRA. 'They say it took a week to burn. Blue china fused like solder.' In the same month the houses of thirty-seven other senators were burned, many of them with priceless treasures inside. Gogarty rebuilt the house in 1930 and opened it as a hotel, which, in different hands, it remains.

A mile and a half west is ruined Renvyle Castle, home successively of the Joyces and O'Flahertys, and once stormed by the autocratic Grace O'Malley. There is a dolmen nearby, and excellent views all round. The large island six miles out to the west is **Inishbofin** (reached by mailboat from Cleggan, on the promontory south-west of here), which possesses several early Christian remains and an interesting early

GALWAY NORTH AND WEST

connection with England. At the Synod of Whitby in 664 St Colman, the Abbot of Lindisfarne, off the Northumberland coast, was worsted by the sly, aggressive arguments of Bishop Wilfrid. It was really a clash between the conformist discipline of Rome and the more quirky, but no less sincere or effective, aspirations of the Irish. Colman retired to Inishbofin with a group of his Irish and English monks, and founded a monastery. Here, according to Bede, the Irish grew perverse in their habits, took little part in the farm work and expected to benefit from the Englishmen's exertions. Rows flared up, and eventually Colman moved with the English to Mayo, where the new foundation gained wide fame and praise. It was still famous in the time of Alcuin, who wrote, in an early example of Ascendancy sentiment, to the monks from the court of Charlemagne, 'Let your light shine among that barbarous nation like a star in the western skies.'

Returning to Tully Cross, we turn left and drive east towards Leenaun, with first the sea at our left, and later Lough Fee lapping the roadside at the right. Turning left at the main road T71 we cover the six miles to Leenaun, with the ten-mile-long dramatic inlet of **Killary Harbour** on the left. The harbour, which is in reality the drowned valley of the Erriff River, was deep (up to eighty feet in its middle passage) enough for the British Channel Fleet that used sometimes to be stationed here, and which was visited by Edward VII and his queen, who landed at Bundorragha opposite. A later visitor was the ascetic mathematician Wittgenstein, who came to live here alone and unravel the problem of numbers. Rather like St Kevin, he would stand so long in deep meditation, according to Bertrand Russell, that the seagulls came to settle on him. (At first he adored Russell, then came to detect a glib facility in his thought; and ingeniously condemned him, along with Wells, as suffering from 'loss of problem'.) At the head of the harbour we cross over the Erriff, a noted salmon river, beside the picturesque Aasle-a-igh waterfall, and enter Mayo.

CHAPTER FOURTEEN

Mayo and West Sligo

NORTH of Killary Harbour the mountains of south-west Mayo are split into three ranges by two valleys. The Mweelrea Mountains on the west are divided from the Sheffry Hills by the deep cut of Delphi Pass and Doo Lough. To the east, the Partry Mountains are divided from the rest by the broad valley of the Erriff River, extended on its western side by a series of glens and lakes that make excellent walking country. The Mweelrea are the highest – with a peak of 2,688 feet – and under their shadow we drive north towards Clew Bay. The road itself – L100 – was the result of so-called Famine Relief, for which perhaps the tourist has more reason to be grateful than the 1840s labourer. Delphi, two miles from the pier at Bundorragha, was so named by a young Marquess of Sligo under the influence of his Grand Tour to classical lands (enthusiasm led to his being imprisoned for a short time for bribing British sailors to convey antiquities in their ships, during war-time). Some of the views in the vicinity are as good as any in Connemara. A few miles north, Croagh Patrick comes into view on the right. The country flattens out but keeps its wild looks – the characteristic of Mayo – and the road descends to Louisburg.

Croagh Patrick, four miles east, is not the highest (it is 2,510 feet) but one of the most famous and quite the holiest of Irish mountains; and Clew Bay, beside which the road now runs is one of the loveliest stretches of coastal scenery, speckled with islands and surrounded by tall mountains. Patrick's connection with the mountain was his withdrawing here to spend the forty days and nights of Lent in fasting and prayer. During that time he supposedly managed to summon together all noxious beasts of the island, 'venomous and monstrous creatures' which stung men and 'not seldom rent and devoured their members' and were often seen 'flying in the air and walking on the earth, loathsome and horrible to behold'. These he persuaded to precipitate themselves to their death down the sheer southern edge of the mountain. The result, if such it is, is that Ireland lacks many of the amphibians and reptiles common in Britain, and certainly has no snakes. (It lacks also that more serious blight, moles.) The story reflects the attempts of early monks to raise their own saints to apostolic rank, for St Paul was credited with similar achievements in Cyprus and Malta (though originally the story goes back to Greek myth for its origins). Nevertheless it was widely believed, and the sagacious Bede held that even when introduced to Ireland snakes would no sooner touch land than die. Moreover, people in England stung by snakes had often been cured by drinking water 'in which scrapings from the leaves of books from Ireland have been steeped'. 'When Patrick drove out the snakes', wrote James Connolly, the 1916 leader, 'they swam the western ocean and turned into Irish Americans.' The sanctity of the mountain has caused it to remain a place of pilgrimage for centuries, and every year on the last Sunday of July, thousands of fasting Catholics throng the roads and the hillside, and climb to the top where services are held. The climb begins at Murrisk Abbey, a ruined Augustinian foundation of the O'Malleys, founded in the fifteenth century.

Westport, six miles east and screened from the bay by the demesne of Westport House – the servants' quarters on an urban scale – is the prettiest town in the county, laid out at a time of growth and hope in the late eighteenth century by Peter Browne, second Earl of Altamont. He was one of the few landlords Arthur Young on his critical tour found he could praise without stint, both for his agricultural activities and for his ambitions with linen manufacture (the rise and fall in the trade of which corresponded with that of the country's self-government). He built enormous warehouses, a first-rate harbour, and houses in the town which were let to weavers, while they were given looms and the money to buy yarn. (James Wyatt may have planned the town, though he never came here.) The Mall, with its central stream, the

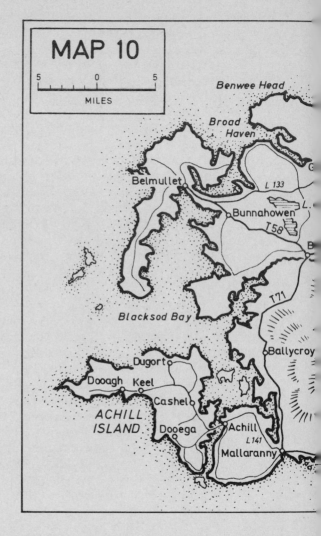

MAP 10

5   0   5
MILES

Benwee Head

Broad Haven

Belmullet

L 133

L.

Bunnahowen

T 58

B

Blacksod Bay

T 71

Ballycroy

Dugort

Dooagh   Keel

Cashel

ACHILL ISLAND

Dooega

Achill

L 141

Mallaranny

Carrowbeg, and avenue of lime-trees, survives in all its
elegance, and there is a pretty C of I church. The warehouses
survive, too, but empty and long disused – the mausoleums of
industry. For, from its peak in the 1830s, when the harbour
was a vital link in Atlantic trade, the town crashed in ten
years, a victim of the Famine, the railway, and the competition

Cont. on Map 11.

Cont. on Map 9.

brought by the industrial revolution. (The dismantled statue in the centre of the Octagon was of George Glendenning, a banker, who helped the town in the 1840s. It was pulled down, and the inscription obliterated, in 1922 by men who liked neither the English nor the thought that some Englishmen were better than others.)

The town's grandest sight is **Westport House**. Underneath are the dungeons of the O'Malley castle that used to stand on the site. The Browne family settled here in 1685, and as Marquesses of Sligo and Earls of Altamont, own it still. It was for them that Richard Castle built the original house in 1731, whose classical east front remains as he designed it. Later, around 1780, Thomas Ivory (designer of Dublin's Blue Coat School) doubled the size of the house and, leaving the east front as it was, added the strangely plain west front and pedimented south front. Inside, the house is rich in the decoration of, among others, Wyatt – the dining-room is one of his masterpieces. There is a lavish, in parts crowded collection of paintings including family portraits by Kneller, Reynolds and Opie and a splendid collection of landscapes by one of the best, and in his time, least appreciated of Irish artists, James Arthur O'Connor (1792–1841); who spent two years pioneering the Irish landscape picture in this part of Ireland before travelling the Continent and dying, in poverty and still obscure, in London. There are also good collections. of silver and Waterford glass. The house is open to the public and with its many shops, camping grounds and other amenities has become an important tourist centre.

The inland road from Westport is not specially rewarding, but **Castlebar**, Mayo's county town twelve miles east-north-east has interesting and curious associations. Founded in James I's reign, it was the scene of an Irish victory in the Civil War of the 1640s (followed by a treacherous butchery of the English), and of a French victory in 1798. Humbert and his 700 French troops, having landed at Killala, and been joined by untrained Irish, put to flight General Lake's garrison and took 1,200 prisoners with such ease that the interlude became known as the Castlebar Races. Later, in 1879, Michael Davitt founded the Land League here in the Imperial Hotel. Hatred of landlords was fierce here because of the ruthless battering-ram evictions ordered by the Earl of Lucan (of Crimea fame), one of the despised Bingham family. The disappearance more recently of the seventh earl, after the violent death of his children's nanny, is said to have given modern tenants the perfect pretext for withholding their

rents. A curious episode culminated here in 1786, the main
part having taken place at **Turlough**, three miles north-east,
where now a Round Tower is the only interesting remain of
the past. In Turlough House was born George Robert
Fitzgerald, descended from the Geraldines on one side and
nephew of the grandiose Earl of Bristol on the other. He
married the sister of Tom Conolly of Castletown, but her
life became hell and she soon left him. His father could not
escape so easily. George kept a pet bear, and after a quarrel
locked his father to the bear (muzzled) in close confinement
and kept him thus for months. He ruled his territory in
feudal state, kept a private army, and fortified the local rath
with guns from a Dutch shipwreck. He also fought over
seventy duels and hunted at night by the light of torches.
Then in the 1780s he was astounded not to be chosen as
Colonel of the Mayo Volunteers. In pique, he captured the
man chosen and murdered him. This time he was arrested
by troops sent for the purpose, tried in Castlebar, and sentenced
to death. His forthcoming execution became one of the
season's events and people flocked to watch. On the day,
he drank a bottle of port, swaggered out of the prison (under
a gate with the solemn inscription 'Without Beware, Within
Amend'), climbed the gallows ladder, sprang off – and
snapped the rope. A new rope was hours in the coming and
his mood changed to gloomy penitence. He was buried at
Turlough.

From Castlebar the L138 leads to **Newport**, a small village
in a valley at the north-east corner of Clew Bay. The 1914
RC parish church, with Romanesque revival details beloved
at that period, contains one of Harry Clarke's best windows
at the east end, with typically glowing colours and a mass of
ghoulish detail in the portrayal of Judgement Day. Taking
the T71 north, then bending west round the coast, we pass
after three miles a lane leading down to Rockfleet Castle,
or **Carrigahooley**, the only ruin that can be positively
associated with Grace O'Malley. This forceful lady illustrates
the special problems facing the Elizabethan English in trying
to get effective control of Connaught. Irish chiefs tended to be
as autocratic and oppressive as English and, even if they

allowed allegiance to Elizabeth herself, would seldom consent to take orders from her envoys and generals. Thus Grace, or Grania, O'Malley was for forty years the stay of all rebellions in the west, and became 'Queen of Clew Bay' by her expert strategy, large private army, and efficient boats. Her headquarters were on Clare Island, but through sons, in-laws and allies she dominated most of the fortresses of the Connaught seaboard. Carrigahooley she came to possess by marrying her second husband, Sir Richard Burke, on a trial basis for a year, at the end of which, having filled the place with her own followers and got herself an heir, she dismissed him. From here she waged war with Sir Richard Bingham and his troops for a while, but later, having lost many of her ships and men, came to an agreement with him and actually travelled to London to meet the queen. She seems to have ended her days loyal, and possessing at most a third of her former empire.

To the north of the road we are on lies the loneliest stretch of all Ireland – the **Nephin Beg** range which, except for the picturesque road from Newport up the east side of Lough Feeagh, comprises over two hundred square miles without road or house at all. In the centre is Nephin Beg itself, 2,065 feet high. At the east end of the range, and cut off from it by a road, is the conical Nephin, 2,646 feet high and commanding magnificent views of the wildest and least peopled county in Ireland, with the great Bog of Erris stretching away to the north. Either way round the range takes us through magnificently desolate country which, though less needs to be said of it because of its want of people and outstanding features, is in some people's eyes the most inspiring part of Ireland.

However, the west coastal road is the more varied, allowing us a sight of Achill Island and the flat indented shores of the Barony of Erris before taking us inland across the bog. We continue west to Mallaranny, a pretty resort festooned with rhododendron and fuchsia, while the Curraun hills to the west are carpeted with juniper, crowberry and Irish heath. There are good beaches here, and plenty more on **Achill**, the largest of Irish islands, twenty yards off the mainland, and

reached by the bridge over Achill Sound. (Before the bridge
was built there were no foxes on the island; after, the islanders
had to construct fences to protect their poultry.) Nowadays
the island shows signs of prosperity, based mainly on tourism
and backed by fishing, but till this century it was one of the
most remote and backward parts of the country. In 1832
corn was still ground by hand between stones. Even in the
early 1900s oats and potatoes were grown in tiny plots barely
able to support the population of 4,000, who relied largely
on a practice that is still important to the Irish economy,
remittances by emigrants to their families at home. The main
target of the fishermen is the basking shark. The season goes
from April to July and the harmless creatures, that can be as
long as forty feet, are caught in nets stretched across the
shoreline at Keem Bay, then speared by fishermen in curraghs.
Later they are cut up for the extraction of oil. (The industry
used to exist on the Aran islands and the director of the film
Man of Aran wanted to show the islanders catching shark.
They had given it up long before and he had to import
experts to teach them how to go about it.) Of the main
centres to-day Dugort is on the north coast, where a colony
of Protestants was settled in 1834 by a C of I clergyman, the
Rev. E. Nangle, of the Church Missionary Society. His battles
with the RC establishment became a national issue, and
occupied no less than fifty pages in the four hundred or so of
John Barrow's *Tour Round Ireland* of 1835. Nangle himself
was obviously a kindly, energetic soul but he was the servant
of an uppish society convinced of its moral superiority.
Untold bigotry and a deal of violence was evinced from either
side. The colony lasted but it never achieved its purpose, and
Achill remains as strongly Catholic as most other regions
hereabouts.

On the slopes of Slievemore above Dugort and among the
hills farther west are to be found the remains of booley-
houses, some of the few to have survived at all (there are
several more in Sligo). Some were still used in living memory.
They were summer milking-houses for the cattle to which
whole families would migrate for the season, living in temporary huts round about. The system probably goes back
to prehistory. It must have been relished by children who

would have found greater freedom than in the villages, and as such Spenser condemned it as leading to 'mischeives and villanyes'. Keel, farther west along the main road, is the principal resort, at the end of a fine two-mile beach. The 'Cathedral rocks' to the east are a splendid work of natural architecture cut into the Menawn Cliffs. To the west the road continues past Corrymore House Hotel (which once belonged to Captain Boycott, and later, from 1924 to 1929, to the American artist Robert Henri) to the delightful, protected Keen Strand, situated under Croaghavn, whose seaward cliffs, over 2,000 feet, are among the highest in Europe. Unfortunately they are best seen from the sea, but there are breathtaking views from the summit, reached by walking past Lough Acorrymore, behind Corrymore House. It was in the waters below them that the Children of Lir, turned into swans, lived out one part of their long exile.

Returning to Mallaranny, we drive north on the long road to Belmullet, with delightful coastal views to the left and mountains to the right till the land levels out in the heart of the Bog of Erris. Just before Bangor, several miles on, we cross the Owenmore River, an anglers' favourite, and in the village turn left to cover the last twelve miles to **Belmullet**. This little town, nothing much in itself, occupies the narrow isthmus between the mainland and the Mullet Peninsula. It has always been a vulnerable area, and when the Famine of the 1840s struck, its inhabitants were reported by a Commissioner to be 'the lowest and most degraded he had ever met with, even among the Ashantees and wild Indians'. Tourism, a golf course and fishing help it along today. To the west of the town lie the sea-beleaguered wilds of the Mullet, forming the two bays of Blacksod and Broad Haven. Apart from the scenery there is little noteworthy, and the scenery is bare enough, there being hardly any trees. Five miles south-west, near the shore are the ruins of a fourteenth-century priory known as Cross Abbey, and offshore from this is Inishglora, an island monastery founded by St Brendan, the preserving air of which was said to save corpses from corruption and even to allow their nails and hair to continue growing. 'Every one there recognises his father and grand-father for a long time after death; and no meat will putrefy on it' wrote the fifteenth-century author of the *Book of Ballymote*.

Returning to Belmullet and along the main road, we break off left after three miles and follow the L133 to a scene that is by contrast most dramatic. **Benwee Head,** off to the left, has magnificent cliffs over 800 feet high and the view from the top gives geographic views over hundreds of miles of coast and out to the Stags of Broadhaven, seven rocks two miles offshore, rising to 300 feet. There are other sheer headlands, difficult to get at, farther east. Beyond Belderg the road approaches the sea and there follow some cliff-bound bays, many with large caves and smooth sandy strands facing the Arctic Circle. Ballycastle, a seaside resort, lies at the head of a long bay which has excellent beaches. Turning left here we carry on round the coast and can, after six miles, turn left again to see Kilcummin Head, at the end of an untarred track. A hilltop memorial on this inhospitable shore marks the landing place of General Humbert's French army that arrived in 1798 to join the Irish insurgents. From here the French made their way to an easy victory at Castlebar, then a decisive defeat at Ballinamuck. A few miles farther on the main road enters **Killala**, where at the time of the invasion the C of I bishop was kept captive by the French in his own house, and afterwards wrote of the extreme courtesy of his warders. The small, gracefully spired C of I cathedral here (the diocese is linked with Tuam and Achonry) was built about 1680 on the site of a medieval church. One original doorway, on the south wall, survives. The pews are really a series of stalls all round. A mile south-east of the town are the unusually complete remains of the 1455 Franciscan friary of Moyne, that survived a turbulent history during Sir Richard Bingham's Elizabethan conquest of Connaught. Another friary, **Rosserk**, is beside the river Moy three miles on. It was founded in 1441 by the Joyces, and it, too, suffered under Bingham. Compactly set in a field beside the water, its church, cloister, refectory and dormitory buildings are among the best preserved in Ireland.

Ballina, though not the county town, is Mayo's biggest, well situated by the salmon-rich Moy with some pleasant demesnes to the north. Apart from the RC cathedral and a broken down fifteenth-century Augustinian friary beside it, there is little of interest in the town, which has declined since it ceased to export from its harbour. There is, however, a good trip to be taken round **Lough Conn**. A new road near the south-eastern corner of the lake leads to a height from which, without walking involved, the lake and its gaunt rocky surrounds, with conical Nephin in the background, can be seen. Three miles south-east is the neat town of Foxford, on the Moy, famous for its woollen factory, begun in the nineteenth century and still run by the Sisters of Charity. It was also the birthplace of Admiral William Brown (1777–1857), like Ambrosio O'Higgins a notable Irish exile to South America; he founded the Argentine navy. Returning to the lough we cross the bridge at Pontoon, where the limestone bed of Lough Conn to the north touches on the granite bed of smaller Lough Cullin, each rock base having a characteristic effect on the plants and scenery. On the hillside just west of the hotel on the far side of Pontoon Bridge is a large granite block, delicately poised. Many stories accrued to this, as to similar phenomena in the district, connecting it with the magic powers of Druids. Unfortunately this one does not rock, as others do, making ideal if hazardous nut-crackers. It was simply shifted by glacial ice and brought to rest by chance at this point. The country and lakes are rich in wildfowl and this is a favourite haunt of shooting and fishing men (there is hardly any hunting in the whole of Connaught apart from two Galway hunts and the Sligo harriers). Lough Conn earlier this century yielded Ireland's record pike – a fifty-three-pounder. From the western road the lake is hidden by intervening demesnes most of the way, but there are tracks leading here and there to the shore. Crossmolina at the north-west corner is a small pretty town, and the circuit is completed by turning right and reaching Ballina again, this time from the west.

We now take the main T40 to the north-east out of the town, and keep to the road round the coast, rather more scenic than the shorter inland route. Four miles on, we leave Mayo and enter County Sligo. Enniscrone is a popular seaside

resort, eight miles from Ballina. Two and a half miles beyond
it, close to the shore, is ruined Castle Firbis, or Lecan Castle,
one of many keeps hereabouts that belonged to the chief
local families – MacFirbis, MacSweeney and O'Dowd. The
building hardly survives at all, but in its day belonged to the
family at the end of whose line came Duald MacFirbis, last
and one of the greatest hereditary Irish genealogists or
shanachies. His book of Genealogies was compiled in St
Nicholas's College, Galway, and he wrote a history of the
Irish – *Chronicon Scotorum*. His family had been prominent
for centuries in this field, and both the Great Book of Lecan
(now in the Royal Irish Academy) and the Yellow Book of
Lecan (now at Trinity College, Dublin,) were compiled here.
The latter contains a version of the old tale of the *Cattle Raid
of Cooley*.

Dromore West, nine miles on, is a pretty village beside the
Dunneill River with the ruins of a medieval church used as a
C of I church in the eighteenth century. Farther on the Ox
Mountains close in on the road from the south. In their
foothills, two miles due south of Skreen and reached by a
lane, is **Lough Achree**, known as Ireland's youngest lake. A
volcano formed it in 1490. The road goes on south of Ballysadare Bay and bends left at Ballysadare to continue to Sligo.

CHAPTER FIFTEEN

Sligo, Leitrim, Fermanagh

THE prehistoric myths of Ireland, as written down by various scribes later, are endlessly complicated in themselves. As with Greek and Roman myths, attempts to tally different versions lead to the marriage of one hero to his great-grandmother and so, maybe, siring his great-aunt. Utter despair must confront the literal mind that goes further and tries to explain the stories of individuals in terms of the movements and histories of peoples. Yet somehow it seems that history does underlie the myth, and there are eminent scholars in Dublin and elsewhere busy showing why. They are a long way behind classical scholars because Celtic scholarship has been afflicted, far more recently than classical, with excess of sentimentality (Tom Moore, etc), forgery (James Macpherson, etc), and anomalous racial bias (a certain brand of nineteenth-century Protestant cleric, etc). When we are confidently told as much about Fir Bolg, Fomorians and Tuatha De Danann as is known, say, about the Minoans, it is certain that the Sligo region will figure large. Every stage of prehistory is represented here, both in myth and archaeological remains. Every local visit from Sligo town takes us back one, two or three thousand years, or even farther, to the dawn of Irish civilisation. Sligo is the western end of an almost unbroken chain of remains stretching from the Royal Cemetery on the Boyne. Four miles west of the town is a landmark that impressively reminds us of this antiquity, and to that pile of 40,000 tons of stone, heaped over the tomb of Queen Maeve and breaking the smooth line of Knocknarea Mountain, we shall go first after a brief glimpse at **Sligo** city itself.

Hardly more than one important building, a hotel, takes notice of the Garavogue River, running to the north of the town's centre between Lough Gill and the harbour. The town is, as a result, less attractive than it might be – its main purpose, from the visitor's point of view, being to serve as a base for sights and beaches in the area. Though the town was fortified in the thirteenth century, nothing remains from the subsequent assaults the walls and castles had to bear, from the early fighting between the Anglo-Norman Maurice FitzGerald and the local septs – notably the O'Donnells – to various changes of hand in the seventeenth-century civil wars. The oldest building is the ruined Dominican friary, known as the Abbey, whose oldest parts go back to 1253 but which was virtually rebuilt in the early fifteenth century. It possesses some fine memorials, including that to the O'Conor Sligo and Lady Eleanor Butler, his wife, who died in 1623, and another of 1616 in the nave, the altar tomb of the O'Creans. The cloisters to the north are in good condition, with some varied carving on the pillars. A quarter of a mile west, in what seems to be the ecclesiastical headquarters of the town, are the RC cathedral and C of I parish church, since 1962 also a cathedral. The one is a copy of a church in Rome, the other an 1812 reworking of a church by Richard Castle – one of the few he did and sadly smothered under Gothic additions.

The road due west out of Sligo leads to Knocknarea past a succession of delightful sandy strands which have attracted Irish and other holiday-makers since the eighteenth century when sea-bathing began as a popular pastime. Strandhill is the best known of these, and beyond it, near the north-west tip of the peninsula, is Killaspugbrone, a ruin on the site of a church founded by St Patrick's disciple, Bishop Bronus. The patron saint allegedly dropped a tooth here one day, which was preserved in the beautiful casket known as the Fiacal Padraig now displayed, albeit toothless, in the National Museum. On the other side of the road the ascent to the summit (1,078 feet) of **Knocknarea** is best made from the eastern side. From its flat top the complexity of inlets and promontories around Sligo Harbour with Inishmurray out to sea twelve miles north, appear like a colourful map below. The great hump of Maeve's Grave is seen to be a vast pile of loose stones, the perimeter of which is about two hundred

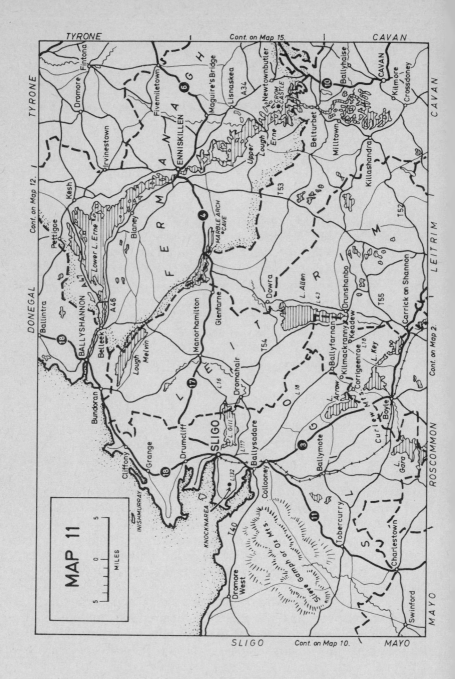

yards. Maeve was the tangled synthesis of a Connaught queen and a Celtic goddess (the same as Mab in British folklore) and the mound is likely to pre-date the Celtic invasions, which makes the name probably misleading. There are, besides, rival claimants for her remains, notably Rathcroghan. Nothing is certain about the matter, but experts are inclined to account it a Bronze Age grave and leave further details to excavation, if ever that takes place. Technical problems and costs would be immense – 40,000 tons of chippings to be removed by hand. It is also said that locals preserve their regard for the queen and might sabotage any attempt to disturb her. Excavation has, however, gone on – too much of it – in the vast megalithic cemetery of Carrowmore, two miles east of the hill, which can be reached after a circuit of Knocknarea and a walk in the extraordinary Glen of Knocknarea (south of the mountain, and through an iron gate just south of the lane that leads off the main road and circles the southern slopes). **Carrowmore** is second only to Carnac in Brittany as a prehistoric graveyard, spreading over a mile and a half. Time, pilferers and amateur archaeologists have reduced the number of identifiable graves from about a hundred to little over half the number. Originally these dolmens, a few of which are visible from the road, were the actual chambers containing the dead, and were covered with earth and stones to make uniform humps over the whole area. Now in most cases only the heavy capstones and their supporting boulders remain. Their place in the scheme of prehistory is obscure, being at the end of a line of related graves that came to Ireland from Brittany, reached their peak in the Boyne Valley and then spread westward. Discoveries in the Boyne Valley threatened to upset fragile preconceptions, but where archaeology is timid, myth feels no restraint. Carrowmore is the burial ground of the dead from the great battle of Northern Moytura, when the Tuatha De Danaan defeated the Fomorians for all time.

The local trip from Sligo on its east side is to **Lough Gill**, which opens out, two and a half miles upstream, from Sligo's Garavogue River. The lake is one of Ireland's prettiest, its surrounding hills rich in woods, till the naked concave shapes

of the limestone mountains take over to the north. What it
shares with Killarney (to which it is often unnecessarily
compared) is a vegetation on some of its islands that includes
arbutus, yew and whitebeam, and on shore among other
rare flowers, the Bird's-nest Orchis and the Yellow Bird's-nest.
On a clockwise circuit of the lake we can turn right two miles
out of the town and see the peninsula which makes up the
demesne of Hazelwood House, a heavy square house with
curving arcades on either side leading to pavilions. Richard
Castle built it, less inspired than he was at Leinster House or
Russborough. It was about to be pulled down when the town
council saved it to become the psychiatric wing of St Columba's
Hospital. They spoiled it with numerous accretions, but then
sold it to an Italian fibre-manufacturing firm which has restored
the house.

Two miles farther along the main road, lanes lead left to
Colgagh Lough, north-east of which is the Deerpark monument, on top of a hill with lovely views over Lough Gill.
The monument is a court cairn, the oldest type of megalithic
tomb, that incorporates an unroofed court, probably used for
ritual purposes. The whole is oval in shape and about 180 feet
long with burial chambers round the sides. The fact that three
pairs of uprights had lintels in place led for a long time to
confusion with Stonehenge, and to the name of the 'Irish
Stonehenge'; more recent research has placed it more
accurately. The whole site has suffered much from farmers,
who used the stones to build stone walls round their fields.
Three miles farther along the main road splendid early
seventeenth-century Parkes Castle comes into view beside
Lough Gill. Beyond it the road bends to the right, and leads
away from the lake to **Dromahair**, chief seat in Anglo-Norman
times of the O'Rourke kings of Breifne. From their castle,
while her husband,Tiernan O'Rourke, was on a pilgrimage to
St Patrick's Purgatory in Lough Derg, Dervorgilla eloped with
Dermot MacMurrough, and so began the fateful sequence of
events that led to the Anglo-Norman Conquest. Most of the
O'Rourke castle was demolished to provide stone for the
fortified house built by Sir William Villiers, half-brother of
Charles I's favourite Duke of Buckingham, in 1626. He was

also given 11,000 acres. The remains of this house stand
behind the Lodge Hotel. Creevelea Friary, founded for
Franciscans by the O'Rourkes in 1508 and containing many
of their tombs, is beside the river half a mile downstream of
the town. A right turn beyond Dromahair brings us after two
miles to a crossroads, where a bohreen (or lane) to the right
leads to the lake's edge and the spot from which a boat is
generally available for a visit to Yeats's little Inisfree island
(in fact the lake's most insignificant isle). The main road
continues for a mile, bends right through the glacial channel
of Slish Gap, and then keeps to the lake for two miles before
breaking away to return to Sligo. To the left, Dooney Rock,
again known for Yeats's use of it, provides excellent views,
from its top, of the whole scene.

SOUTH SLIGO, NORTHERN LEITRIM

Innumerable lakes and rivers feed the Shannon River at its
northern end. The technical source of the river, the Shannon
Pot, is about twenty-five miles east of Sligo. A more interesting
group of lakes with outstandingly beautiful scenery between
them begins about fifteen miles south-west of the town. To
hurry over a cross-section of this area we drive south, past
the eastern end of Ballysadare Bay, and turn right just beyond
the town of Collooney. Collooney Pass, where the limestone
and (hereabouts) quartzite ridge of the Ox Mountains sinks
almost to sea level before rising again to the north-east under
different names, has always been of great importance; for
two rivers, three main roads and the railway share it. A mile
east (off the T3 road to Boyle) is the demesne of **Markree**, an
eighteenth-century house with Gothic enlargements and alterations of 1803 by Francis Johnston. The domed tower of the
old observatory, where stood what was till the 1840s Europe's
largest telescope, still stands. (The telescope is in Hong Kong.)
In 1860 that prolific apostle of 'muscular Christianity', Charles
Kingsley, stayed at the house with his friend Joshua Cooper
(it is still in the same family). There had been a spate of evictions
in South Sligo before his arrival. 'It is a land of ruins and of
the dead', he wrote, and 'it moves me to tears'. But not for

long, there being so many salmon in the river: 'I had magnificent sport this morning. There is nothing like it. The excitement is maddening.' The park is lit with standard gas-lamps, as there used to be a gas-works on the demesne. The house has been consistently inhabited by the Cooper family from Cromwellian times. It is said that Mrs Alexander, writing the lines 'The rich man in his castle. . . . The purple-headed mountain. The river running by . . .' in the hymn All Things Bright and Beautiful, had Markree, where she had stayed, in mind.

We keep to the western road, then branch left on the L11 and come to Ballymote, where once Constance Markievicz, released from a British gaol, received a minutes-long ovation on her return to her home district. (She was born at Lissadell, north-west of Sligo.) The large castle here, built in 1300 by Richard de Burgo, Earl of Ulster, has declined since the Cromwellian campaign into a pleasing ivy-covered ruin. In the ruined Franciscan Friary was written the Book of Ballymote, the largest of all Irish codices, preserved in the Royal Irish Academy and containing numerous current and highly con-trived historical works, including the Book of Invasions.

A few miles beyond Ballymote, beside the same L11, is the 1,168-foot rounded limestone hump of Keshcorran. Half-way up its west face is a row of caves, which were used as habita-tions in prehistoric times – bones of men and various animals have been discovered in methodical excavations, and these include reindeer, Arctic lemming, bears and wolves – all now extinct in the country but common apparently in the Bronze Age – snails, fishes and birds. It was in one of these caves that King Cormac mac Art, the real architect of Tara, was supposed to have been reared by a she-wolf, which had carried him off from his sleeping mother (as, among others, Romulus and Remus, founders of Rome, were also reared – it is not only New Testament stories that are suspiciously echoed in Irish myth). Carrowkeel Mountain is connected to Kesh-corran on the east by a low broad neck. Its broad flat summit has a jagged edge cut by hillside gorges, and on many of the platforms between these gorges are old stone cairns – most of them as prominent over the surrounding country as their builders obviously intended. The total collection – fourteen

The fort of Dun Aengus, on the Aran Island Inishmore.
Below Ashford Castle, beside Lough Corrib, County Galway,
built for a Guinness.

Benbulben, County Sligo, on which the wild boar killed the hero Dermot.
Below Westport House, County Sligo: a different style for each façade.

chambered cairns, two dolmens and many more circles of low stones – has been claimed to have formed a prehistoric village, the only one of its kind in the country. Many of the remains, till excavated earlier this century, had remained untouched down the centuries and so yielded a wealth of Bronze Age objects and several clues as to the old methods of burial. The main road now rises over the Curlew Mountains, and passes the spot where Red Hugh O'Donnell, Hugh O'Neill's spirited lieutenant in the 1599 Rebellion, inflicted his last victory in the war, against Sir Conyers Clifford's advancing army.

Boyle is well situated on a hillside, most of the town being at the foot, but the square at the top containing a good Georgian courthouse. In the courthouse Count G. N. Plunkett was in February, 1917, declared MP for North Roscommon, the first Sinn Feiner to be so; the victory, first of many, marked both the end of Redmond's moderate Home Rule Party and the revival of militant politics. But the town's main treasure is Boyle Abbey. Cistercians founded it here as a daughter of Mellifont in 1161, as usual in a remote and un-peopled place. The town later grew round it and took its name from the abbey. Though badly mutilated in the 1650s by Commonwealth troops, its imposing ruins spread over a wide area and well preserve the basic plan and much of the walls of the abbey cloister and conventual buildings. Of special interest are the eight Norman arches on the south side, probably remnants of an earlier church, and many fine details in capitals, pillars and windows. Among those buried here was Edward King (1612–37), Milton's fellow student, whose early death by drowning off the Welsh coast was the inspira-tion of *Lycidas*.

For people cruising by boat from Carrick-on-Shannon, Boyle is the western upstream limit for their wandering, and makes an ideal base for exploring Lough Key, the most beautiful of local lakes. But the Boyle River, though un-navigable, goes on west to **Lough Gara**, which makes a pretty detour here. Excavations in the lake some years ago yielded evidence of several crannogs – prehistoric lake-dwellings – with many intricately worked artifacts. Coolavin, on the western shore of the lake, was in the eighteenth century all that was left of the estates of the MacDermot family, previously vast landowners but victims of the Penal Laws. Arthur Young in 1780 called at the house of the MacDermot, who making the best of his affairs called himself 'Prince of Coolavin' and 'though he has not even £100 a year will not permit his children to sit down in his presence'. The present gabled house was built in 1898.

From Boyle we drive east and after two miles turn left into the **Rockingham** demesne built originally in the seventeenth century by the Kings, one of whom later became Earl of Kingston, at Mitchelstown in Cork. The most striking view is of Lough Key, almost fragile in its prettiness, studded with wooded islands, with the Curlew Mountains (from which are seen the best views of the lake) rising on the left and further ranges farther north; conjuring up the blades and beauties, the gaiety, boats and lacy parasols of another age. Castle Islands, opposite the site of the old house, was a possession of the MacDermots before their lands dwindled to Coolavin. It still has a castle, but it is crumbling and dangerous. Yeats wanted to make it a Castle of Heroes, a sanctuary to which those who had proved their devotion to Ireland might come and plan Ireland's spiritual rebirth. To the left is Trinity Island, with a ruined abbey in which was composed in the sixteenth century the valuable *Annels of Lough Key*. Rockingham demesne has become a forest park, and the house has disappeared. It had a hectic history. Nash rebuilt it in 1810 for the first Viscount Lorton, brother of the Earl of Kingston. Sacheverell Sitwell called this building one of the two finest Nash houses in Ireland (the other being Caledon). But Lorton, jealous of the size of his brother's house at Mitchelstown, Co. Cork, had the two-storey house spoiled by the addition of a third in 1820. In 1863 the place was accidentally burned down. Rebuilt to its later plan it survived intact till 1957 and was known for its lavish house-parties. Then it was burned again. For a few years its gutted ghost lorded it over the water, and the demesne, the little round battlemented fishing house, the many Gothic follies, Soane's Tiara Lodge, and the ruined church, all added to the unreal quality of the place. Finally the authorities, declaring it beyond repair, demolished it.

From the large and beautiful demesne we drive on east, then fork left off the T3 to follow the lake round its eastern and northern shores. A little further along the main Carrick road is Woodbrook, where in the 1930s young David Thomson went to coach the Kirkwood daughters and stayed, on and off, ten years. His *Woodbrook* published in 1974 beautifully evokes the pleasures, and some of the cares, of rural Anglo-Irish life. At the crossroads of Corrigeenroe we turn right. After two miles and two sharp bends we can divert to the left and visit Moytura, two miles north of the village of Kilmactranny. From the top of the hill there are good views over Lough Arrow, another pretty lake broken up by islands and long promontories. The hillside itself has several megalithic remains and is the claimed site of the second Battle of Moytura, in which the evil sea-spirits, the Fomorians, were finally defeated by the Tuatha De Danaan, precursors of the Milesians, or Celts, themselves.

From Moytura we return through Kilmactranny to the main road, turn left, pass Lough Skean, turn right at the T-junction, continue through Ballyfarnan and part of the demesne of Alderford House on the left; and a mile farther come to the ruined church of **Kilronan** beside Lough Meelagh. Turlough O'Carolan was buried here in 1738 after his death in Alderford House, then a MacDermot property. Born blind, he was, as Goldsmith wrote, 'the last and the greatest' of the old bards, coming at the end of a court tradition that had lasted since the Celtic migrations and before. A bard was a kind of local poet laureate, hired to sing praises, generally of the old Irish aristocracy. Carolan was at once an excellent poet, singer, player and composer – the music of *The Star-spangled Banner* is his. He was also a great drinker, used to whole bottles of whiskey, and it was from this he is supposed to have sickened. On his deathbed he called for a cup, but could not drink; and then he kissed the cup, saying two such old friends could not part without kissing, and died. Later in the eighteenth century his skull was displayed in the church, and then it was lost.

Beyond Keadew the road goes east towards Lough Allen. Up to the left is Arigna, where coal has been mined from the surface in a fitful way for centuries. The product is poor and government backing cannot make it compete with the price of American low-quality coal. We can drive round the southern end of the lake, through the anglers' resort of Drumshanbo and up the east shore under Slieve Anierin, which contains not only coal but bands of iron underlying it. This, too, has been exploited in the past, but the last attempt, in 1765, to smelt iron with pit-coal ended soon after for want of funds. Following the lake, we are also following the Shannon, which can be traced a few miles north-east of Dowra to what is known as its source, the Shannon Pot, though in fact this is supplied from a small lough a mile to the north-east, while the Owenmore River to the south collects the waters from higher up the mountains and more properly deserves the name of source. Nevertheless it is to the Pot that most of the credit and legends attach. At the head of the L43, four miles farther on, we turn left – leaving the Six Counties border to the right till later – and make our way the ten miles or so to **Manorhamilton**. This town, beautifully and strategically set on a high plateau, with main roads running to all four compass points and more, is what strategic centres have often become nowadays, a very good base for the tourist, with fine scenery, a plethora of ancient remains, and easy access to the sea and five other counties. To the north is the ruined seventeenth-century fortified house of Sir Frederick Hamilton, granted large confiscated estates by Charles I. (From here onwards Scotch names like Hamilton figure increasingly in past and present events.) There is a magnificent diversion through the superb Glenade valley and along the southern shore of Lough Melvin, returning by the L16. But we continue west through the delightful valley of Glencar with the almost sculptured forms of its limestone mountains on either side, towards the western end, and the lake itself with several spindly waterfalls dropping into it from the opposite side. Then the road bends round to the south and returns to Sligo.

SLIGO TO BALLYSHANNON

Five miles north of Sligo on the main coast road is **Drumcliff**, whose churchyard is on the site of a monastery supposedly

founded by St Columba, possibly in atonement for the battle
and carnage he caused earlier by refusing to abide by the
High King's verdict in a case of plagiarism involving him.
The battle took place on the slopes of Ben Bulben to the north,
and the High King was worsted. Seeing with horror what he
had caused, Columba took leave for Scotland and settled
there. The stump of a Round Tower and a good High Cross
remain of the medieval monastery. W. B. Yeats is buried in
the C of I churchyard under the epitaph he wrote himself,
and in the midst of countryside every feature of which figures
in his work. He died in France in 1939 and was buried there;
his remains were brought back in 1948, and placed where he
had directed: 'under bare Ben Bulben's head'. The epitaph –
'Cast a cold eye on life, on death. Horseman, pass by!' – was
inspired by annoyance at reading Rilke's ideas on death.
Shapely Ben Bulben has endless links with early myths, and
it was here that the most romantic of early tales found its
resolution. Finn McCool's pursuit of Grania, his old love,
and Dermot, with whom she eloped, is marked up and down
the country by cairns, hills and valleys that bear their names.
At last they were overtly reconciled. Then Finn ordered
Dermot to catch the wild mountain boar that lived on Ben
Bulben, and when he had done so told him to measure its
skin with his bare feet. Dermot, like Achilles, had one
vulnerable point and it, too, was his heel. When he had
measured out the skin one way, Finn told him to check it the
other way, and this was against the boar's bristles. A bristle,
as Finn intended, pierced his heel and killed him.

A left turn just beyond the bridge takes us four miles along
the north of Drumcliff Bay to **Lissadell House**, built in
classical style in the 1830s and with magnificent views across
the water to Knocknarea and the Ox Mountains behind. It is
the home of the Gore-Booths, whose ancestor, Captain Paul
Gore, came to Ireland with Essex. A descendant of his, Sir
Nathaniel Gore, married in the early 1700s Letitia Booth, a
lady of high spirits who forced her coachman at pistol point
to drive her round the Derk of Knocklane, a peninsular
chasm beside the sea at the western tip of the promontory.
She is still said to haunt the place. Sir Robert Gore-Booth
built the present house in 1834, in Grecian style (designed by

Francis Goodwin, who also did the Gothic gates at Markree, and various civic buildings in the north of England). After the Famine, he was accused of having sent hundreds of emigrant tenants to America in an old boat that sank. Many similar reports were made up about Anglo-Irish families, and documentary records speak only of his strenuous efforts and crippling expenditure of £40,000 on his tenants' behalf. His son, Sir Henry, was a distinguished Arctic explorer, and Henry's two daughters rose to high fame in different realms – Eva (1870–1926) as poetess, and Constance (1884–1927), who as Countess Markievicz helped engineer the 1916 Rising and, after imprisonment in England, became the first female British MP, and later Minister of Labour in the Dail's first cabinet of 1919. Sarah Purser painted them here in a portrait (still in the house) that brought her first success. Yeats visited them in 1894 – 'The light of evening, Lissadell,/Great windows open to the south;/Two girls in silk kimonos,/Both beautiful, one a gazelle . . .' The house, among other features remarkable for its hundred-foot-long columnar gallery, is open to the public, and holds many mementoes, and even more ghosts of the family. The tour round it is enhanced by the guide, sometimes a present member of the family and full of reminiscence.

After glimpsing the old Gore castle ruin at Ardtermon Strand, and haunted Knocklane we can drive north-east to rejoin the main road at Grange. A mile before this village a lane leads left to Streedagh Strand, where three ships of the Armada were wrecked – 'I numbered,' wrote Sir Geoffrey Fenton to Lord Burleigh, 'in one strand less than five miles in length eleven hundred dead corpses.' The English descended and caught such survivors as they could and hanged them beside nearby Staad Abbey, whose ruins stand. Some escaped and one, Don Francesco Cuellar, wrote his subsequent adventures, which have more than once been published in English. Turning left at Grange we drive six miles to Cliffoney, where a left turn leads to **Classiebawn**, a neo-Gothic house belonging, till he was murdered by the I.R.A. in a boat off the coast, to Earl Mountbatten, who inherited it from his wife. It belonged in the nineteenth century, with the rest of the 6,000-acre peninsula, to Lord Palmerston, the prime minister, who as a necessarily absentee landlord had a bad reputation for evictions, though he did much for the people and built several Catholic schools. He did not in fact live to see the castle's completion.

Bundoran, seven miles on, is a popular seaside resort with good beaches and views. It is just inside Donegal. Four miles beyond is **Ballyshannon**, which has always been important as the western bridgehead across the River Erne. In 1597 it saw battle between Red Hugh O'Donnell, Lord of Tyrconnell, in league with the rebel Hugh O'Neill, against Essex, and Sir Conyers Clifford, Governor of Connaught, leading an English force. The English, attempting to take the castle (now reduced almost to nothing) were thrown back and made a perilous escape across the rapids, losing many men. In the Mall a plaque marks the birthplace of William Allingham (1824–89), the poet and friend of Rossetti.

LOUGH ERNE AND FERMANAGH

From Ballyshannon the L24 goes south-south-east, keeping to the right of Assaroe Lake and the Power Station, which since 1952 has exploited the force of the reservoir then created by damming. After four miles we cross the border (in normal times an uneventful procedure, sometimes involving a momentary stop, often no formality at all). We now enter Fermanagh, and find ourselves in **Belleek**, a small village with a large china factory. The original nineteenth-century Belleek porcelain, made from feldspar then dug at nearby Castle Caldwell, was often superbly designed and had a rare and elusive glaze. Modern produce, though successfully exported, is unlikely to appeal to any collector, though the tour round the factory seeing every phase of the making is of great interest.

Six miles farther along the north shore road is the demesne of ruined **Castle Caldwell**, one of the many large estates round the lake, now given over to the Forestry Department. This, co-operating with the Royal Society for the Protection of Birds, has created a park that the public, and particularly naturalists, can enjoy, for nature trails are laid out among labelled trees (mainly the too common but profitable Norway and Sitka spruce). There are hides from which to observe the

plentiful wildfowl. (The Common Scoter, which breeds only
in a few places in Scotland and two in northern Ireland, does
so here.) The castle itself was built by a Plantation settler,
Francis Blennerhasset, but passed soon to the Caldwells.
The ageing Sir James Caldwell in 1778, who two years before
had sped Arthur Young on his way in a stately six-oared
barge, colours flying and band playing, wrote to his son, 'you
will have a place universally allowed to be the most beautiful
in England or Ireland'. He kept seventy men employed on his
'improvements'. Early this century the property became
encumbered and passed, via an insurance company, to the
Government. The castle is now in ruins. Four miles beyond
the demesne the road divides and the right fork carries on
over a bridge across long, thin **Boa Island**. A mile from the
bridge a notice on a gate on the right of the road points to
overgrown Caldragh Cemetery, at the bottom of a field near
the lake. It contains two carved squat stone figures, triangular
faces and formalised bodies at back and front, that evoke
glib associations with Polynesian more than Celtic art. Their
double faces suggest a common source with the Roman god
Janus. But they are mysteries, and may be pre-Christian;
nobody feels sure about them, or about superficially similar
figures on White Island.

When the island road rejoins the main road we almost
double back, following the main road to Pettigo and then
turning right, crossing the border, and driving to **Lough Derg**,
a wild stretch of water amid low brown mountains, with no
road or path round most of its shore. (An eighteenth-century
parson of Pettigo called the region 'Siberia.') At the end of
our road is a quay that takes up to 30,000 pilgrims (in June,
July and August) to the island, now encumbered with neo-
Byzantine buildings, from which St Patrick once descended to
Purgatory. The legend is older but was first recorded by an
English monk who described the descent of a Norman knight
Owen, through a cave on the island, across the fields of punish-
ment to the earthly paradise. The legend and site grew in
popularity, being mentioned in the same breath as Santiago de
Compostela; and pilgrims flocked from all over Europe.
Because of the heretic nature of the pilgrimage the Borgia Pope

Alexander VI ordered the cave's destruction. This was carried
out in 1497. It was soon flourishing again; a new cave-mouth
was opened and continued to attract thousands even when
specifically prohibited by English and Irish laws; and even
after the second cave was destroyed. To this day it is the most
revered, and most punishing, pilgrimage in the country,
'such as no man', wrote William Carleton, 'with flesh and
blood capable of suffering . . . could readily forget'.

From here we return to the lake road and continue east, and
then south, to Kesh. The minor road from here close to the
lake passes after two miles the ruins (two stories and a square
turret) of Crevinish Castle, built by Thomas Blennerhasset
before 1618. Two miles on it passes near **White Island** (to
which boat-trips go from Enniskillen or Castle Archdale,
where boats of various kinds may also be hired), which
contains, socketed into the walls of its roofless twelfth-century
Romanesque church, eight grotesque squat figures with rather
more details than the Boa Island figures above. (There are
plans to remove them to a museum, because of damage by
the weather, and replace them with casts.) Some of the things
these figures are carrying point to them being Christian, of
perhaps the ninth or tenth centuries, with the exception of an
obvious Sheila-na-gig, a symbol of some fertility cult. Some
other pagan suggestions and the crudeness of the work appear
to have decided builders of the later church to use them as
masonry, from which role the church's ruin at last released
them. White Island is part of the demesne of Castle Archdale,
to the right of the main road and a bit farther on. The pleasant
Georgian house of 1773, now fallen into ruin, was built near
a Plantation castle of 1615, fragments of which still survive
its 1689 destruction. The park is full of public amenities and a
very modern caravan park, with lounges, television, laundry
and other services laid on. Eleven miles farther on we reach the
busy county town.

Enniskillen, like Ballyshannon, is in a strategic position to
cover Ulster-Connaught traffic, and as such has been a
Protestant stronghold ever since the Tudor and Stuart
plantations ousted the Maguires, then lords of the county.
Weapons found here and at other Erne fords show it saw
innumerable battles before Protestant times. The castle in

Wellington Street beside the river incorporates bits of the original Maguire fortress, and of the construction made by the first Protestant settler, Sir William Cole. He was granted the place in 1612 and with twenty families defended it against the Irish rebels in 1641. Like Derry it became almost a frontier town of loyalist sentiment, and resisted an attack of King James's troops in 1689. Later the townsmen organised themselves into a regiment which was chosen as his personal guard by King William at the Boyne. This led to the formation of two regiments, the Royal Inniskilling Dragoon Guards and the Royal Inniskilling Fusiliers – a distinction shared by no other British city. In the eighteenth century the Cole family became Earls of Enniskillen, with their seat at Florence Court (below). Though prettily situated the town has little of striking interest. The C of I cathedral of 1840 includes a tower of 1637; the Convent of Mercy contains windows by Michael Healy, Sarah Purser, and Beatrice Glenavy. The conspicuous column on top of Fort Hill (from which there are superb views) is to Sir Galbraith Lowry Cole (1772–1842), brother of the second Earl of Enniskillen and Governor of Cape Colony. On the hill west of the town is Portora Royal School, built in 1777 to house a school founded by Charles I in 1626. The hymn writer, M. F. Lyte ('Abide with Me'), and two rather more magical word-spinners, Oscar Wilde and Samuel Beckett, were educated here.

Within a few miles of the city are an ancient and holy island, two of Ireland's finest houses, and a great deal else of beauty and interest. Two miles north-north-west of the town, in lower Lough Erne, is **Devenish Island**, to which cruises run from the town. The remains of the monastery first founded by St Molaisse (who is said to have exiled St Columba to Scotland for causing the Battle of Culdreimne with instructions to convert as many souls as were killed in battle), include a perfect Round Tower (with sculptured heads on a cornice beneath the cap), an ancient house and church, and fifteenth-century St Mary's Abbey. **Castle Coole** is two miles south-east of the town. It dates, like much else of the best of Irish building, to the last years of the eighteenth century when Armar Lowry-Corry, first Earl of Belmore, paid £54,000 altogether to have it erected to the meticulously detailed plans of James Wyatt, whose best work some consider this to be. As with other places associated with his name in Ireland, there is nothing to show that he came here to supervise the work. No expense was spared. Portland stone came by chartered brig from Portland Bill to Ballyshannon, where a special quay had to be built to take it. Thence it was carried by ox-cart. The finest English and continental craftsmen were imported for adornments, including the plasterer Joseph Rose, sculptor Sir Richard Westmacott and marble-worker Dominico Bartoli. When construction was at its height in 1791, no less than twenty-five stonecutters, twenty-six stone-masons, ten stone sawyers, seventeen carpenters and eighty-three labourers were being employed. The earl died in 1802, heavily in debt, but he was not unusual in this; Arthur Young and others often note the grandiose pretensions of the Anglo-Irish gentry who, able to enjoy the service of far more poorly paid servants than the English, wanted the setting to match. The result is superb, from the magnificent 280-foot long façade, with its Doric colonnades and elegant pavilions, to the restrained decoration of the interior, in which every-thing, including the iron stoves in the beautiful circular saloon, share the pevasive spirit of Wyatt in classical, as opposed to neo-Gothic mood. The gardens, which after years of neglect have recently been cleared and replanted, have one rare distinction: on the lake is the only breeding colony of greylag geese, outside Scotland, in the British Isles. House and grounds are owned by the National Trust and open to the public.

There are several other places worth visiting or glimpsing on this side of Upper Lough Erne – Tempo Manor, (home of Bryan, the last of the Maguires and a compulsive duellist who spat a strangers for the joy of a challenge) and possessing a famous garden sometimes open to the public; and Georgian Brookeborough, once the home of Lord Alanbrooke, Chief of the Imperial General Staff during the Second World War, and of Lord Brookeborough, Prime Minister of Northern Ireland from 1943 to 1963; and Crom Castle, the splendid Tudor-revival home and demesne of the Crichtons, Earls of Erne, (see Chapter 20). In the highlands to the east, as to the west of the lake, are large numbers of prehistoric remains of people who had to stay high above what was, before draining, a large expanse of swampy jungle.

After Castle Coole, the other great house of the area is **Florence Court,** six miles south of Enniskillen, by a right turn off the A32. It is the seat of the Coles, original settlers of Enniskillen and since the late eighteenth century Earls of Enniskillen. They still live in the house but it is now the property of the National Trust. Nothing is known of the architect, nor of the exact date of building, probably the middle of the eighteenth century; though the arcaded wings with their terminating pavilions are probably by Davis Ducart, and date from about 1767. The main east front is distinguished by a good deal of detail – deep rustication of the masonry, scrolls, eaved architraves, heavy keystones and pediments over the central doors and windows – that suggest the strong influence of Gibbs, and in the case of the second floor, of Hawksmoor. The two sides and back of the house are plain by comparison, and it is said that the builder, in the manner of the times, ran out of money before he could match them to the front. Inside there is magnificent plasterwork (most of it restored since a bad fire in 1955), best seen from the staircase, and a rich collection of pictures and furniture. The gardens are delightfully wooded and contain an Irish Yew (*Taxus baccata fastigiata*), one of two specimens that in 1780 were discovered on a nearby hill by a farmer who, unused to the erect growth, gave one to Florence Court. From this have been taken – by cutting since, this being a lone female, sexual propagation is impossible – all known Irish yews anywhere. The area hereabouts is, like the Burren, of carbon-iferous limestone, and contains many caves, the result of water's action on the soluble rock. The known caves, like all others in the country, have been listed and described in J. C. Coleman's *The Caves of Ireland.* One of the best and most readily accessible results of water action is Marble Arch, three and a half miles farther along the road on which Florence Court is, and signposted to the left. It is a double natural arch about thirty feet high, at the head of a wooded glen. The ramifications of the caves are endless and not yet fully charted, and a guide is recommended. Another complex of caves is situated north of Boho village, on the north side of Belmore Mountains. Again Coleman's work and a guide are advisable to see the formations, which include Noon's Hole, at 250 feet the deepest pothole in Ireland.

To return to Ballyshannon it is best to go almost all the way into Enniskillen again, then cut across to the A46 that goes along the south shore of Lower Lough Erne. Two and a half miles along we pass the old demesne of **Castle Hume**, the first Irish work of Richard Castle, done for Sir Gustavus Hume, who brought him from London in 1727/8. Only the stable block remains. There are several Plantation castles on or near the road including **Monea Castle**, the most perfect of its kind in Ireland, rectangular in form with two round towers of typical Scottish flavour, three miles inland from Castle Hume. Many of these castles, combining spacious living accommodation with defensive exteriors, show clear influences of the Scottish styles from which they developed. For while Hugh O'Neill, Red Hugh O'Donnell and the other earls had sailed from Ireland in 1607, the native population remained hostile and its grudges later found expression in the 1641 rising. Defensive architecture was still essential. **Tully Castle**, beside the lake six miles beyond Castle Hume, illustrates this well. Built in 1609, it was burned to more or less its present state in 1641. According to survivors they surrendered to Rory Maguire, the rebel chief, on the promise of safe passage, and most were then butchered. It was reports like this, probably inflated over the years, that incited the credulous Cromwell to his vindictive campaign. A mile or so later the road bends westward and the lake broadens to upwards of five miles. To the north the mountains make a superb backdrop to the water. We carry on to Belleek, and thence, crossing the border, return to Ballyshannon.

CHAPTER SIXTEEN

Donegal

DONEGAL is a political oddity. Like Counties Cavan and Monaghan, it belongs to the old nine-county province of Ulster; yet it is not partitioned off from republican Ireland as the other six counties are. The three are, all the same, closely tied to the six counties, and Donegal is only connected to the Republic by a thin neck on either side of Ballyshannon. They are linked to the north by history, trade, family ties, roads, and yet the men they vote into Parliament govern from Dublin. Edward Carson once told Shane Leslie that during the First World War he had planned to include all Ulster in a separate British province. Later he saw his mistake. If his first wish had been granted Northern Ireland would have included a majority of Catholics who, in the course of time, would by democratic means have been able to vote themselves out of union with Britain and into the Republic. This might (or might not) have prevented the tragic conflicts of recent times, but it would not ultimately have suited Carson and his successors. So Donegal and the other two stayed unwanted ugly ducklings. A recently published series of four books on the provinces of Ireland interpreted Ulster as 'the Six'. The three were not covered in any of the books, and that is the sort of humiliation they have to live with.

Donegal is ugly only in the duckling sense. It is one of Ireland's most beautiful counties and some insist it has no rivals. It owes its beauty to a characteristic west-coast land-formation. The rock of its western seaboard half is granite, mixed on the edges with quartzite, and of the eastern half is mainly schists. Before most of the rest of the country's rocks had begun to form, Donegal's western half crumbled in a north-east south-west direction and formed a series of ridges, whose bottoms are still followed by the main inland roads.

Along the Atlantic coast the crumblings have formed into a long series of wild mountainous scarps and craggy inlets with rivers and lakes filling every channel and basin. There is little space for fields (though the Irish are adept at exploiting what space there is) and ocean storms prevent the growing of trees except in unusually protected spots.

But the climate is mild, almost as mild as Kerry's, and such vegetation as there is is luxuriant, and in some cases the rarities of Kerry are found here, too. In addition the quartzite patches, as is their way, have resisted weathering and formed themselves into regularly shaped conical mountains that set off the wilderness of the glacial scene. In the eastern half of the county, and counties farther east, the schists have formed into hilly but less dramatic country. The west coast provides Donegal with her finest scenery, and it is to the coast we shall mainly keep. All this wilderness and rock have tended to keep the county to itself, since until people began to enjoy mountain scenery it was simply too remote or too easily defended to bother with. So its history is peculiar to itself. In the Middle Ages and up to the final conquest and plantation of Ulster, Donegal was the principality of the O'Donnells, who were created, in an early Tudor attempt to win their loyalty to England, Earls of Tyrconnel, the Irish name for their territory. Their eastern neighbours were the O'Neills (created Earls of Tyrone), whose lands included most of central Ulster and were bounded, on the east side, by that of the MacDonnells, Lords of the Isles. Like the O'Neills they descended from Niall of the Nine Hostages and like them, too, they were sporadic patrons of the arts, and sometimes writers themselves. By the shore three and a half miles north-west of Ballyshannon is the ruined castle they gave the O'Clerys, a family of historians and genealogists. Nearer at hand, three-quarters of a mile north-west of the town, are the ruins of Assard Abbey, a foundation whose lands the O'Donnells gave to the Cistercians in the twelfth century. They were, in the main, fighters, and the ruins of the abbey are those that survived an O'Neill sacking in the sporadic feuding that went on between the two families, as well as a later English one.

The O'Clerys are best known for their book *The Annals of*

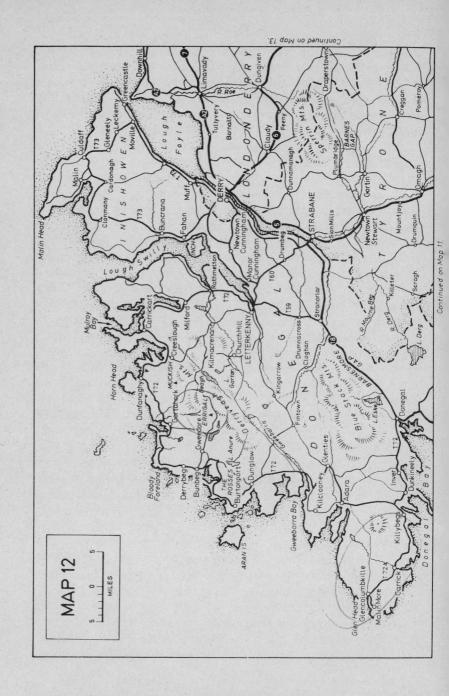

MAP 12

MILES
5   0   5

Malin Head

Downhill

Greencastle
Leckemy
Gleneely
7
Culdaff
Malin   173
Cardonagh
Clonmany   Moville
I N I S H O W E N

Horn Head
Muff
Murroy Bay
Buncrana
173
Fahan
Carrickart
Dunfanaghy
Creeslough
Milford
Rathmelton
INCH
Bunbeg
Derrybeg
172
Gortahork
MUCKISH MTS
Kilmacrenan
Gartan
172
Church Hill
Bloody Foreland
Gweedore
ERRIGAL Beagh
THE ROSSES
Burtonport
AL. Anure
Dunglow
172
Gweebarra Bay

Limavady

R. Roe

Tullyvery
Barnalty

Claudy
Feeny
Dunnamanagh
Dunamangh
Plumbridge

DERRY
Newtown Cunningham
Manor Cunningham
160
Drumbeg
Sion Mills
STRABANE

LONDONDERRY

Sperrin Mts

Dungiven

Draperstown
BARNES GAP

T Y R O N E

Creggan
Pomeroy
Omagh

Gortin
Mountjoy
Newtown Stewart
Drumquin

Lough Foyle
Lough Swilly

L E T T E R K E N N Y

D O N E G A L

Stranorlar
159

Kingarrow
Drummacross
Cloghan
Fintown
Glenties

BARNESMORE GAP
Blue Stack MTS
LESK

Donegal

Kilclooney
Adara
Inver
Dunkineely
Killybegs
Carrick
Malin More
Glencolumbkille
Glen Head

172

R. Mourne Beg
R. Derg
Killeter
Scragh
L. Derg

Dunglow

ARAN IS.

Donegal Bay

Continued on Map 13.

Continued on Map 11.

the Four Masters, written in the 1630s at Donegal, which we
reach after a fourteen-mile drive north from Ballyshannon.
Donegal is a pretty town well set at the north-east corner of
Donegal Bay. The Clerys worked in the friary, founded in
1474, fragments of which survive above a jetty on the estuary;
theirs was the first full account of Gaelic Ireland from what
they took to be its birth through 4,500 years to its apparent
death with the exit of the earls to the Continent, after Kinsale.
The fine fortified house nearby, built in 1610 by Sir Basil
Brooke, grantee of the land, has some good details – bartizan
turrets, gables, mullioned windows and interior carvings –
typical of the period. From Donegal the T18 leads north-east
up to the Gap of Barnesmore, historically one of the principal
links between the county and central Ulster, with excellent
views to the rear over Donegal Bay. But we go north-east
instead and follow the T72 round the coast to one of Ireland's
wildest corners.

Inver, eight miles along, is a fishing village, in the cemetery
of whose roofless, overgrown church is the tomb of Thomas
Nesbit, to whom many Nordic countries owe the invention
of the gun-harpoon for whaling. The road goes on tortuously
through Dunkineely, at the head of a seven-mile long narrow
limestone promontory. Three miles later the road bends to
reveal views of landlocked Killybegs Harbour, with its rocky
coastline. **Killybegs** itself is a charming fishing port also known
for its fish-processing and hand-woven carpet factories, which
since their founding in the nineteenth century have brought
the name Donegal into the first league of carpet trade-names.
The harbour itself, one of the best in western Ireland, has
never been fully exploited, because of its remoteness on the
land side. The area to the west is thickly mountainous and its
cliffs are among the highest in Europe. For sea and cliff
scenery the journey from here has few rivals, but is also
interesting as leading to a valley in the far west of the promontory where a small community has, for a few years, been
pioneering new ways of rural living. On the way there are a
few charmingly sequestered villages, and Carrick with its
colourful houses, is a good centre for the whole promontory.
The Glen River, on which it is situated, opens on the south

side into Teelin Bay, a two-mile long, fjord-like creek down the west side of which runs a road. Following this, we turn right after a mile and a half and come on to a dramatic, narrow, switchback road beside sheer cliffs, pass a lonely castle ruin perched on a narrow headland above the sea, and several oddly shaped lakes among the bog, to reach **Bunglass Head**, with its views of the 1,800-foot high Slieve League cliffs, concave towards the sea, and on a fine day the whole circuit of scenery round to north Mayo. The same and better views – as good as any in Ireland – are to be had from boats that can be hired from Teelin village itself. There is excellent walking country behind the peaks, though guides are advisable for ambitious tours.

From Carrick the road goes on to **Glencolumbkille** through a boggy plateau where turf is cut on a big scale. The village is beautifully set, spread across a valley that widens on its way down to sandy Malin Bay. Unexpectedly, the village adds to its busy turf industry a prolific output of home crafts and now a fascinating Folk Museum, a collection of four cottages that illustrate the peasant way of life at different periods. They help to point up the fact that the cottages in many parts of Ireland are still virtually museums, carrying on characteristics prevalent for centuries. A feature of this kind, found in Donegal and few other places, is the way thatchwork is rounded at the ridge, and the securing ropes over it are often fixed to stone pegs projecting from the walls, both of which devices, protections from the wind, make Donegal cottages more than usually attractive. (A hundred years ago the ropes used to be attached to boulders of sixty pounds' weight that hung below the thatch, keeping the whole roof tautly proof to winds.) Thatchwork is still a useful way of identifying a region, given a knowledge of myriad styles. But the emphasis in the museum is on interior furnishings and fixtures, and throws often startling light on the comforts, potential at least, of the primitive life.

Moving spirit behind Glencolumbkille's renaissance was the Catholic priest, Father McDyer, who, when the issue was even more critical than now, refused to let the west of Ireland die economically without spending his total energies on saving it. His enemies, in his own words, were 'indolence, emigration, cynicism, greed and individualism'. Only the very old and the very young stayed in the west – most of the rest emigrated. In a survey of 1966 it was found that in one part of north Donegal thirty per cent of the farms in a given area were under thirty acres; that sort of size leaves little for one son, let alone two, to inherit. In Mayo, six hundred families a year were closing their farms altogether. Father McDyer's contention was that proper use of the land lying fallow in the west would vastly increase the already considerable contribution of the area to national income. His fight was to get enthusiasm from the people and grants from the government, and it saw steady results. He got basic services going, and helped create a weaving industry, Ireland's first farming co-operative, and a canning plant. The folk museum was part of his plan to lure tourists, and tourism figures large in future hopes. But it is unlikely to overcrowd this busy, scenic backwater.

There is delightful scenery to the north, at Glen Head and Sturrall Head, and to the south, around the quiet sandy resort of Malin Bay. A local legend says Bonnie Prince Charlie came here after Culloden and waited for a ship to take him to sanctuary in France. There is no apparent foundation for it. But Glencolumbkille is scattered with tangible memorials of St Columba, whose favourite retreat this was said to be, and an annual pilgrimage on 9th June brings the devout to follow a three-mile pattern round sites (including his House, Well, Chair and Bed on the Glen Head road) connected with the saint.

A minor road to the east leads us through more of the boggy uplands of the promontory, then down by a series of hairpin bends to the fertile plain around Ardara, centre of the cottage industry of Donegal knitting. It is attractively situated by Loughrosmore Bay with mountain views to east and south. To the north the country becomes flatter inside its curtain of mountains, and often as bleak as north-west Mayo. Five miles north-north-west of Ardara, immediately beyond Kilclooney, we can divert to the left to see the **Bawan**, a huge oval fortress with an eight-foot wide walk at the top of its seventeen-foot walls. The rampart, waterbound in Lough

Doon, can be reached by hire of a boat from a local cottage, or simply seen from the shore. Back on the L81 we keep close to the water past the Gweebarra estuary, cross the bridge, and stay with the T72 close to the coast. The Gweebarra River leads straight to the Derryveagh Mountains and across them to a region of lakes to be visited later. Dungloe, nine miles farther on, is populous for this part, with about eight hundred souls, a fishing port well liked by anglers. To the north is a flattish area, several miles long and broad, known as the Rosses (Irish for promontories) and comprising wind-swept heathery gradients and small but dutifully cultivated fields in a region of innumerable little lakes. The coast road round the west side of this leads to Burtonport, with a fishing fleet and herring-curing station, and a quay from which boats leave for Aran Island (not the better-known Aran Islands), a pleasant island with a wild western seaboard. A prettier way lies north-east of Dungloe past the rock-strewn watery terrain to Lough Anure, a glacial overflow lake both pretty and interesting to geologists for its rock-surrounds – mica slate with coarse granular dolomite – and the wealth of glacial remains including the most common sight hereabouts, moraine debris. Continuing through Creely we come next to Gweedore, on the approach to which are good views, to the right, of Donegal's highest peak, the quartzite cone of Mt Errigal (2,466 feet).

Gweedore is a pleasant and unexpectedly cosy looking village in the heart of this rugged north-western corner of Ireland. It and the land round about were, in the middle of the last century, one of the most backward parts of Ireland, still plagued by the wasteful practice of Rundale, which along with the Booley system had been the basis of all Irish peasant farming up to the early 1900s, and in parts far later. By Rundale, each tenant was allotted small portions of land over the whole expanse of an estate, to make sure he had his fair share of good and bad, and of the different crops grown. But there was no boundary between each man's strips, and since any one tenant might have up to thirty separated plots (and one half acre could sometimes contain the plots of the same number of tenants) terrible confusion and apathy set in. This district was known as one of the poorest, roughest, and in time of famine most desperate in the country – hardly a man of the scores who published descriptions of their Irish tours allowed a word, or any time, to Donegal. Then in 1838 a total of 23,000 acres around Gweedore were bought by Lord George Hill (1801–79), a man who besides possessing a decent level of humanity did the almost unheard-of thing and learned Irish, the better to tackle local problems. Gradually he improved the place out of all recognition, by redividing the land, fencing it, offering premiums for the best crops, and a hundred other things that kept him tied full time to the estate. Crabbed Carlyle, who came in 1849 and found nothing to admire in Donegal landscape nor most of the features of Irish life, still found in Hill a glint of hope. 'In all Ireland', he wrote in his economic prose, 'saw no such beautiful soul.' In the 1880s, after Hill's death, the place regressed, and the Plan of Campaign brought a trail of evictions in neighbouring estates. Maud Gonne was one who came to see the process, rebuilding cabins that the police and troops had battered down; and seeing mothers and babies sleeping under hedges or herded into workhouses, here made a resolve that played a strong part in the later risings – 'It is the English who forced war on us, and the first principle of war is to kill the enemy.'

The country around Errigal Mountain is excellent for walking and climbing, and a favourite but tough climb lies up the Poisoned Glen, a steep-sided corrie running south-east from Dunberry, three miles east of Gweedore. It earns its name from the past presence of Irish spurge, a highly poisonous plant that affects water and can kill fish. In fact it does not seem to grow there any more, but visitors are still advised not to drink water in the glen. To the east the road ascends to the Gap of Dunlewy, from which there are dramatic views on both sides, but again we return to the coast, via Gweedore, to continue our journey through the little ports of Bunbeg, Derrybeg – where the same evictions of 1889 led to a famous murder of a police inspector – and on to Bloody Foreland.

This is best seen at a good sunset, which colours the mountains dramatically golden, if not red, and makes, with the sea strewn with rocks and islands, a magnificent view.

The long island to the north is **Tory**, whose principal trade is lobsters, and which has rich mythical and historic associations. In the days of Ireland's earliest occupation the Fomorians lived here and from this base sallied out to destroy, plunder and exert an evil influence on the colonists. They were exterminated in the second Battle of Moytura, their king, Balor, coming to a horrible end beyond Gortahork, seven miles east of Bloody Foreland. Gortahork itself is a resort well placed for the whole north Donegal mountain complex and for the wealth of beaches along this northern coast. It is also a centre of the Donegal Gaeltacht, or Irish-speaking area, and there is an Irish college nearby. Balor's end came in the demesne of Ballyconnell House, three miles north-east. It had been forecast in a prophecy as the work of a grandson of Balor. Balor, having only one daughter, kept her virginally locked in a tor on the island. An old enemy renamed MacKineely came in disguise to Tory, slept with the girl and got her with child. In revenge Balor caught MacKineely and chopped off his head. The 'Stone of Kineely', a large boulder with red crystalline veins in the demesne, is accounted the blood-stained table he used. Years later the grandson he had been unable to prevent grew up and, in revenge for his father's murder, pierced his malignant eye with a red-hot iron.

Returning to the main road, we go on east by the T72. From Dunfanaghy, seven miles on, a minor road leads west and then north into the promontory of Horn Head, another beauty spot with cliffs at its north end that support many varieties of sea-bird, some rare. On a clear day the Paps of Jura can be seen to the north-east. On the west coast (reached only on foot), which is perforated with caves and tunnels, one called McSweeney's Gun has become well known. Into this the sea in rough weather is supposed to rush with such fury that it creates a bang loud enough to be heard at Derry. Dunfanaghy is a good starting point for climbing Muckish Mountain (2,187 feet) to the south. It has always been a favoured quiet resort, and 'AE' (George Russell, painter, mystic, poet and political writer and a hero and friend of the Gaelic League Members) used to come here for painting holidays. Five miles on, at Cashelmore (beside which is a nineteenth-century bell-tower complete with huge bell but lacking a church) a lane leads left on to the **Ards Peninsula** where, in what used to be described as 'the most beautiful private demesne in the country' the Capuchins have a friary. This can be visited on application. Creeslough is two miles farther along the main road. A left turn here leads along a track two miles to **Doe Castle**, a ruined keep in a well-preserved bawn by the water's edge that was restored and inhabited in the nineteenth century. It was originally a McSweeney stronghold. Red Hugh O'Donnell was fostered here, and though for a while it was granted to English planters it was restored to the Irish family before the Eleven Years War. Owen Roe O'Neill landed here to take his great part in the war, which in the north was, unlike elsewhere, a concerted effort to oust the Planters; but it was taken by the Cromwellian General Coote in 1650. There are good views over the estuary from the top of the precarious steps.

Another left turn from the main road three miles on leads to a lovely drive to Carrigart and the beautiful wild peninsula of **Rosguill**. On the west of the neck leading to this peninsula is Rosapenna, an 1893 hotel built by Lord Leitrim, with good beaches and an eighteen-hole golf-course among the sand dunes. The sand was a disastrous menace in the early part of the last century when Lord Boyne, having built himself a house here, complete with walled gardens, avenues and terraces, found it gradually piled up with sand-drifts. The desperate resistance of relays of workmen was of no avail and eventually the place had to be surrendered to the elements. In 1843 Lord Leitrim bought the property and by planting bent-grass managed to stem the drifts. To the north, yet another superb view is to be had from the 682-foot hill of Ganiamore. Returning to Carrigart we drive on east, along the west side of narrow Mulroy Bay.

Two miles out of the village a lane leads left to Mulroy House, demesne of the Earls of Leitrim, the third of whom, though he gained a notoriety among his tenants and was nicknamed 'Wicked', was no more or less so than countless other landowners. Continuing down the side of Mulroy Bay and past the village of Cranford, we come to Cratlagh Woods.

It was here that this third earl was murdered in 1878, along with his clerk and the driver of his car. He had been known in the army for bravery, fairness and good discipline. Retiring here, he mistook his tenants for private soldiers and while ordering them to do things that were in their own interest, became hated for ordering anything in the first place. Anybody who disobeyed was evicted without question. He prudently travelled armed, and although shot at more than once managed to live to old age. Then in April, 1878, travelling here in the same direction as we are taking, he was ambushed from the woods. Several men were involved and there were struggles. The two employees in his car were shot. The earl was battered to death. Occupants of a following car saw what happened but most evidence at the subsequent trial of three men was confused and contradictory and all were acquitted. 'But one thing is certain,' wrote the novelist Stephen Gwynn twenty years later; every Irish-speaking person within five miles of Milford, and many others, could, and would not, tell you exactly who it was that killed Lord Leitrim'.

Milford is the starting point for the circuit of the **Fanad Peninsula**, with a further succession of mountains, lakes, beaches and views. But for scenery of a different kind we drive south-south-west from Milford, past Lough Fern, to Kilmacrenan. From here it is possible to make one of the most attractive trips into the interior of the county. Taking the road south-west along the Leannan River valley, we turn right after five miles for Church Hill, where turning right we reach Glenveagh Castle, built in 1870, a wonderland baronial pile beside the lough's edge; surrounded by one of the country's great gardens, amid the steeply sloped deer forests of the glen. Terraces, statuary, Italian garden, formal pool, Gothic orangery and an abundance of rare trees and shrubs were all presented to the nation by their owner for the previous forty years, Henry McIlhenny of Philadelphia, and opened to the public in 1984. Two miles on we come down on the neck of land between Loughs Gartan and Akibbon. At St Columb's is the home of the painter Derek Hill, who has given the nation a gallery containing paintings, furnishings, William Morris wall-

papers and many other artifacts. Three-quarters of a mile
north, above the west shore of **Akibbon**, is a roofless church in a
cemetery, traditional burial-place of the Tyrconnel O'Donnells,
on the site of an oratory built by St Columba. The saint's
exact burial place is supposed to be a flagstone some way
south, on the hillside above Lough Gartan, marked by a modern
High Cross.

The saint is one of the best documented of any of his time,
for his life was written – meticulously for the period – by
Adamnan, Abbot of the monastery on Iona which Columba
himself had founded. He comes over as a cold personality,
self-righteous (as most of his saintly contemporaries are
portrayed), and forcing on his monks the hardest of ascetic
lives. His mission to Scotland was prompted by no less than
a fierce battle caused by himself after he had refused to abide
by a High King's judgment. He nevertheless was probably
Scotland's most civilising influence in the Dark Ages. His
exile, though nothing rare in a church that sent hundreds of
proselytising monks to Britain and the Continent in the wake
of the barbarian invasions, caused him to become almost a
patron saint of emigrants. As a result, a night spent on the
flagstone where he was born is said to prevent homesickness,
and has been resorted to by thousands of Irishmen, on the
eves of their departure to make new lives abroad. The area
round about is thick with Columban associations.

We move on from Gartan along the south-west road, up the
valley of the Bullaba to the top of Glenveagh and the Owen-
beagh River valley, a superb position hemmed by mountains
and with long dramatic views down three valleys. From here
we descend to the right on Lough Beagh, between valley
slopes that comprise an enormous deer-park, past the long
thin tree-bordered, islanded lake that is certainly one of the
prettiest in the country. At the foot we turn right and return
to Church Hill and thence to **Kilmacrenan**. Here the O'Donnell
chiefs were inaugurated as Lords of Tyrconnell, and a Holy
Well beside it is still frequented by pilgrims who leave all
manner of tokens behind them. Giraldus Cambrensis, who
never came within a hundred miles of the place, left a vivid
description of the inauguration rites - the gathering of the

406 . THE COMPANION GUIDE TO IRELAND

clan, the chief's embracing of a white mare, the killing of the
mare and cutting its body in pieces, the chief's submersion in
water used to boil the meat and the subsequent feasting on
the meat, the chief remaining all the while in the water.
Where alternatives offered, Giraldus always opted for the
ghoulish.

Just over six miles south of Kilmacrenan is **Letterkenny**,
one of Donegal's larger towns with a population approaching
five thousand. Its late nineteenth-century neo-Gothic-cum-
Irish-Romanesque RC cathedral has several good windows
by Michael Healy. Three miles south-west of the town, by
New Mills, is the ford of Scarriffhollis, where in 1650 Sir
Charles Coote, after several reverses in battle with the fighting
Bishop MacMahon of Clogher, turned the tables on him and
thoroughly routed his depleted forces. This was the end of the
Royalist-Catholic cause in the north. To celebrate it, Coote
had a son of Owen Roe O'Neill clubbed to death outside his
tent and six months later hanged the bishop of Clogher.

We round the head of Lough Swilly and keep on the T59
through Manor Cunningham and Newtown Cunningham,
two miles beyond which we turn left and make for the
Inishowen Peninsula. The conspicuous silhouette on the left
is sixteenth-century Burt Castle, an O'Doherty stronghold
awarded, after it had been taken by the English following the
capture of Derry, to Sir Arthur Chichester, first Baron of
Belfast, and ancestor of the Marquesses of Donegal. Farther
on to the right rises the hill of Greenan, on top of which is
the remarkable **Grianan of Aileach**, a concentric fort built as
the royal seat of the O'Neills, lords of Tyrone (and later most
of Ulster). The fort, with walls $17\frac{1}{2}$ feet thick at the base, is
itself enclosed by three rough earthern ramparts; but its
defence was penetrated in 1101 when Murtagh O'Brien, King
of Munster, came to force the submission of its king, Donal
MacLochlann. The fort was badly restored in the 1870s.

The **Inishowen Peninsula** is known, from the length of the
road round it, as the 'Inishowen 100'. It has also been known
in the past, like much of Donegal, as classic poteen country.
Compared with some of the headlands to the west it offers
less return for more mileage, but it has attractive points and

Malin Head is, if little else, the northernmost point of Ireland. The western coast road passes Inch Island – now an island no more, as a result of drainage – and approaches the waters of Lough Swilly at the pretty resort of Fahan. A holy well and a beautiful and important two-sided cross are all that remain of a seventh-century monastery founded by St Columba. **Lough Swilly** itself has twice in its history been the grave of Irish aspirrations. In 1607 at Rathmullen, opposite Fahan, a ship anchored to take away the 'Earls' – those who had resisted Elizabeth's and James's colonial policies with initial success and ultimate failure at Kinsale. Declared a traitor, Hugh Roe O'Neill, Earl of Tyrone, Red Hugh O'Donnell, his son-in-law and Earl of Tyrconnell, and both their familes, came down to the quay, and with the English at their heels took away into the night the last hopes of Gaelic Ireland. Rejected by France and Spain, which had now made peace with England, they found their way to the papal court where they were made welcome. But with nothing to do and in an unfamiliar climate they languished. Tyrconnell died in 1608, Tyrone in 1616. They were the precursors of many more Irish aristocrats who, backing away from hopeless odds, made their way to Continental courts and often played leading parts in their adopted countries' wars, with special relish against the English. Lough Swilly saw also the end of Wolfe Tone's dreams. With the '98 rebellion already quelled he came with a French squadron to support Humbert's campaign, but the ship he was in was trapped by English frigates and he was arrested the moment he landed, either at Rathmullen or Buncrana. Sentenced to hang, he cut his throat with a penknife in his Dublin gaol.

The castle he was supposedly brought to survives as a solitary tower in Buncrana. Beyond, if we keep to the westward coast road, we cross hilly country and turn inland up the bleak Owenerk valley. In this, a road to the left takes us across the steep Gap of Mamore, with brown barren mountains on each side, and marvellous views from the top. From Raghtin More, a cairn-topped peak to the right, the ubiquitous Finn McCool dispensed his laws. Carndonagh, ten miles on, is the marketing centre of the peninsula, and it has four worn but well decorated early crosses on the roadside. An uninteresting road leads north to Malin Head, with good beaches and rock scenery and a deserted signal tower erected in Napoleonic times. There is a splendidly primitive and remote look about the farms in this northernmost corner of Ireland. We return to Malin village and a mile and a half beyond turn left, through plain boggy country, for Culdaff, where the road bends south and takes us past a circle of standing stones a mile south.

Moville, twelve miles farther, is a seaside resort that used to be a port of call for transatlantic liners, one of the valves through which Irish from this part of the country emigrated. Three miles east-north-east is Greencastle, with a castle, now incorporated in a hotel, that was built in the fourteenth century, passed to the O'Dohertys and in 1610 went, with the rest of the peninsula, to the planter, Sir Arthur Chichester. From this eastern coast-road there are good views across to the north Derry highlands and to the chimneys of Derry to the south. Just beyond Muff we cross the border, both of Donegal and Derry Counties, and move into Northern Ireland.

CHAPTER SEVENTEEN

Derry, West Tyrone and Antrim Coast

GLADSTONE, when he came to power in 1869, seeing that the Protestant Church of Ireland embraced less than one eighth of the Irish population and was unlikely ever to embrace any more, disestablished it. Among those who thought this likely to bring about the world's end was Cecil Frances, the poetic wife of the Bishop of Derry and later Primate of Ireland, Dr William Alexander. Her verse includes *Once in royal David's city* and *There is a green hill far away*. At the Disestablishment she wrote a hymn which her husband caused to be sung in the cathedral – 'Look down, Lord of Heaven, on our desolation!/Fallen, fallen, fallen, is our country's crown;/ Dimly dawns the new year on a churchless nation;/ Amon and Amaleck tread our borders down . . .' It is in the light of that sort of opposition, by no means confined to a fanatic fringe in Derry and other parts of Ulster, that Gladstone's greatness shows up.

Church and commerce have always figured large in **Derry's** history. St Columba founded a monastery in about 546, in an oak-grove (*Daire*) that gave the town its name. In 1164 another famous foundation, Temple More, was built where the RC church of St Columba now stands, probably on the original site. This monastery was destroyed in 1566, in one of the last battles fought by Shane O'Neill, the vain and refractory Lord of Tyrone. A parson led the citizens through what Protestants think of as Derry's finest hour, and a bishop several sizes larger than life adorned the city and Irish history in general in the eighteenth century. The latter, Frederick Augustus Hervey, fourth Earl of Bristol, we shall come to at his home outside Derry. The parson comes at the culmination of the city's seventeenth-century history, which opened with the capture and fortifying of the place by Sir Henry Docwra for the queen. A few years later the dispossessed O'Doherty's rebelled and took it back. But the inexorable project of Plantation followed, Derry was granted to the Irish Society, formed of citizens of London, and her name combined with London's in a form – Londonderry – which official Britain continues and Ireland ignores. The town's walls went up in 1619 and the original cathedral, now much altered, in 1633. Different parts of the country were entrusted to different London guilds and chartered companies, and the Grocers, Fishmongers, Clothworkers and others are still responsible for municipal buildings in many parts. Derry's citizens stayed staunchly Protestant, but the Corporation of London was wanting in efficiency. Wentworth, as impatient with Protestant as with Catholic shortcomings, opened an inquiry and had the Corporation fined £70,000, so adding to the enemies who finally conspired to pull him down. In the Eleven Years War the city inevitably changed hands, at one point welcoming relief from Owen Roe O'Neill, the Catholic commander – such were the partisan confusions of the time. But in 1688, when James II and his Lord Lieutenant Tyrconnell (a Talbot, the O'Donnell earls of the same title having been attainted) were rallying Irish support, Derry stood firm on the Protestant, Williamite side. There were Jacobite sympathisers and these included the governor, who was for handing over to the Jacobite force. But he was expelled, and to prevent further wavering the town's apprentice boys cast the die by seizing the keys of the town and locking the gates. (The gates are closed to this day in an annual ceremony, and the governor, Lundy, burned in effigy.) The siege began in April, 1689, and lasted 105 days, being eventually broken by a Williamite ship sailing in the face of artillery up the Foyle, breaking the besieger's boom, and bringing supplies to the townsmen. The bulwark of the resistance was a forty-three-year-old clergyman from Tyrone, the Rev. George Walker, whose statue, bible in hand, used to stand high on the well-preserved walls. The fullest account of the siege, from which he emerges with heroic stature, is by himself. He also shows that throughout their privations – even forced to eat dogs, cats and tallow – the defenders kept their racial and religious priorities nicely distinct. When the enemy offered them terms, 'they unanimously resolved to eat the Irish and then one another rather than surrender to any but their own King William and Queen Mary'. Walker was killed the following year at the Battle of the Boyne.

Though it throve in the eighteenth century – a Frenchman, remarking on its industry and activity, paid it the intended compliment of having 'no appearance of an Irish city' – it declined in the nineteenth and almost fell asleep with its memories before the recent tragic reaction began. It is tawdry and dull and there is very little obvious life after the day's work is over. Young people go over the border to dance and enjoy themselves in Muff, Co. Donegal. Brendan Behan told of the time he tried to buy a bottle of wine on Sunday from a chemist's shop run by a teetotaller, and had to pose as a Calathumpian, a hastily contrived religious sect that ate the stalks of cabbage but not the leaves and, following biblical practice, drank only wine with their meals. After persuasion the lady decided she wouldn't 'interfere with any man's covenant with God' and gave him the bottle. The town preserves, however, interesting remains as well as memories. The walls, a mile long and neatly enclosing the town centre, are the best preserved in the British Isles. A walk round the top (not allowed until conditions are normal) gives glimpses of the river, the Diamond (a square at the old city's heart), the C of I cathedral, and of a depressing number of decrepit slums. Cannons from the great siege flank the walk.

In the southern sector of the old city is a cluster of the more remarkable buildings. The C of I Cathedral, in a style sometimes called 'Planter's Gothic', contains many relics and some good monuments of the seventeenth century inside and incorporates nineteenth-century restoration work and early twentieth-century additions (the spire, like many in the county, was first erected by the Earl Bishop of Bristol; it fell down and was re-erected in 1823). The Bishop's Gate to the west, commemorating the siege, was built in 1788. In Bishop Street, the Courthouse of 1817 by John Bowden, has a portico modelled on the Erechtheum on the Acropolis, and there are several good Georgian houses nearby. Outside the walls, south-west of Bishop's Gate, is St Columba's RC church, on the supposed site of the saint's original foundation. The **Guildhall** (reached through the walled city along Bishop's Street, the Diamond, and Ship Quay Street, where the playwright George Farquhar was born in 1678) dates from 1911, when it was rebuilt to the plans of its predecessor of 1890, which had burned down in 1908. One of the Victorian Gothic buildings in which Northern Irish cities abound, it contains many stained glass windows showing scenes from the glorious past, and various other musty relics. North of the town is Foyle College, successor of the Free School founded by Planters in 1617. Its alumni include Sir John and Henry Lawrence, the first an enlightened Governor-General of India, the second Governor of Lucknow, killed in the Indian Mutiny in 1857; and the Victorian historian of Greece, Rome and ancient Ireland, John Bagenal Bury. Nearby is Magee University College, founded for the training of Presbyterian ministers in 1857, now part of the new University of Ulster based at Coleraine.

From Derry we cross the river (300 years ago Derry was almost surrounded by water, the Foyle creating watery bog in the lowlands) and follow the valley of the Foyle River along the A5. To the south-east rise the Sperrin Mountains and some of the finest inland countryside of the Six Counties, and a pleasant long diversion is to drive south-east from Derry, along the Faughan valley by the A6, to Claudy and there to cross back south-west to **Strabane**, which, by whatever route, we come to next. It is a busy town with more a Scottish than an Irish look. Granted with 1,000 acres to James Hamilton, later first Earl of Abercorn, at the Plantation, it was besieged in 1641 by Sir Phelim O'Neill, who took the Hamilton castle and abducted the Hamilton Countess of Abercorn. Both were retrieved. A warehouse now covers the site of the castle, and there is little here of interest but associations. In Main Street is Gray's printing-works, with a pretty bow-window, still operating but now the property of the National Trust. Two of its employees helped to make American history. John Dunlop (1747–1812), who served his apprenticeship here, later issued America's first daily paper,

Mussenden Temple, County Derry: the Earl-Bishop's clifftop retreat.
Below Castlecoole, County Fermanagh: seat of the Earls of Belmore.

The Giant's Causeway, County Antrim: Finn's footpath to Scotland.
Below Queen's University, Belfast: stately nineteenth-century Tudor.

the *Pennsylvania Packet*, and was the first printer of the
Declaration of Independence (which was signed by five
emigrant Scotch-Irish delegates and adopted by a Congress
whose secretary was Scotch-Irish). The grandfather of President
Woodrow Wilson also worked here, before emigrating in
1807. His home was at **Dergault**, two miles south-east of
Strabane, where the thatched farmhouse in which he was born
was owned by Wilsons till the National Trust acquired it. The
Ulster contribution to American politics included no less than
a quarter of America's presidents, some of whose birthplaces
we shall come on in due course.

From Strabane the A5 continues south for eight miles to
Newtown Stewart, prettily situated on a coil of the Mourne
River and north of a wooded mountain, Bessy Bell (called,
with nearby Mary Grey, after two Scottish plague victims of
the seventeenth century who became subjects of a nursery
rhyme). Running beside a lake west of the mountain is the
Duke of Abercorn's demesne of **Baronscourt**, with one of
Northern Ireland's best country houses, designed about 1750
by George Steuart, altered and added to by Sir John Soane in
1792, fully restored in the early nineteenth century by W. V.
Morrison and partly pulled down in the twentieth. Individuals
who were granted land in Ulster by James I undertook
to fulfil certain conditions, and were known as *undertakers*.
The first Hamilton undertaker acquired immense estates
in Derry and Tyrone, and the ruin of his castle stands beside the largest of the three lakes. His grandson, fourth
Earl of Abercorn, was aide to James II during his escape
to France, and the anchor of the ship they sailed in is
preserved on the estate. This earl fought for James at Aughrim
in 1691. His successor switched to William's side in time to
save family property and honours, and helped at the relief of
Derry. The present house was built by the eighth earl. His
heir, the first marquess, was a fastidious man. Housemaids
had to wear gloves to make his bed. He tried three times to
find happiness in marriage, but his first wife died young and
his second, a cousin, eloped. He heard of her plans in advance
and wrote one last plea – not that she should stay, but that
she should leave in the family coach. It should never be said a

Lady Abercorn left her husband's roof in a hack chaise. His grandson was created first duke in the 1860s, and was twice Lord Lieutenant. The third duke was Governor of Northern Ireland for twenty-three years after the state's inception in 1922.

The formal gardens are set in a magnificently landscaped and maintained demesne, surrounded by forestry, and are open to the public on all days but Sunday, but the house is not.

On the return to **Newtown Stewart** we pass on the right the scant ruins of Harry Avery's Castle (half a mile west-south-west of the town), an O'Neill stronghold of the fourteenth century. In the town itself are slight remains of a Plantation castle built by Sir Robert Newcomen in 1618. Sir William Stewart, who married Newcomen's daughter, was confirmed in the lands by Charles I and gave the place its name. He was tireless, at the outbreak of the 1641 Rebellion, in organising rescuers of the settlers who were being caught and butchered across all the northern counties (the massacre for which Cromwell regarded his barbarity as recompense). James II was entertained at the castle on his way to and from the siege of Derry, and after the second visit perversely caused it to be burned down, and the town with it. The town was rebuilt in 1722.

Two miles south, off the Omagh road is Camp Hill Cottage, from which in 1808 Thomas Mellon and his parents left for America, he to found a large family, a bank, and the Mellon fortunes. (Paul Getty and Alexander Brown, who founded the oldest American bank still existing, also descended from. Ulster stock.) Close by is the American Folk Park, Mellon-financed, which aims to show the enormous contribution Ulster people made to the expansion of the United States, through an exhibition of real and replica dwellings, a Pennsylvania log-farmstead, a schoolhouse, wagons and so on. **Omagh** itself, seven miles on, is the county town of Tyrone, dominated by a poor nineteenth-century RC Cathedral. In the late middle ages it had an O'Neill castle which was taken in 1602 and garrisoned by Lord Mountjoy, squeezing the Earls of Tyrone out of their titular lands. But it was of no great importance. A survey, for the purpose, of 1666, showed it had twelve hearths, less than half the number in the O'Neill capital Dungannon. The whole county's population then was 12,000 but this northern and western part filled up in the increased confidence of the eighteenth century, and Omagh probably became the county town around 1786. It now contains the museum of the Royal Inniskillen Fusiliers Regiment.

To return to the coast through some of the most attractive scenery in Derry and Tyrone we drive north-north-east along the B48 passing through the great gorge known as Gortin Gap, set in a National Park that provides delightful walks, some of them signposted, in moorland rich in streams and waterfalls. Going on through Gortin we can turn right after one mile and left after another three to cross over Barnes Gap, which has marvellous views over the Gleneely valley to the mountains beyond. Coming down into the valley we turn right on to the B47 and keep going to Draperstown, built and named by its owners, the London Company of Drapers, in 1818. From here a fine stretch of road runs north-north-west to Dungiven, through vast lonely bog-lands. Then, a mile before reaching **Dungiven**, a track leads left to the old ruin of an Augustinian priory founded in 1100 and restored in the late fourteenth century after a fight of some kind of which no details are known. Thereafter it declined, though it was used for C of I services up to 1720. The tomb in the south wall of the chancel is the finest remain, with a beautiful traceried canopy covering the supposed effigy of an O'Cahan, the family which built and patronised the priory. This is one of the most beautiful tombs in the country, well worth the trouble of obtaining the keys from the Post Office. The position of the buildings, 200 feet above the River Roe on a rocky promontory, gives it fine views.

In the town the main landmark, more imposing from a distance than close to, is the nineteenth-century castle, which incorporates part of an earlier structure granted to the London Company of Skinners. An interesting diversion is to **Banagher Old Church**, by a minor south-south-west road beside the castle grounds. The doorway of about 1100 is peculiar, squared off by a lintel outside but rounded inside, implying that the inner part was altered to suit a later rebuilding of the body of the church. The tiny steep-roofed building beside the church is thought to be the tomb of Muiredach O'Heney, a local saint and founder of the church, who may be represented by the little stone figure at the west end. Among his alleged gifts to his O'Heney posterity was making the sand hereabouts a talisman for winning all kinds of contest. It has at times been thrown at racehorses, in pious hopes.

The B192 north from Dungiven takes us nine miles down the Roe valley to Limavady. Half a mile before turning right into the town, on the Derry–Coleraine road, we pass on the right Roe Park. This was the scene of a congress, the Convention of Drumceat, in the year 575, which was important enough to bring St Columba over from Iona to argue various causes. One of these was the preserving of the order of bards, a class firmly founded in the social system, but whose wit and satire made many enemies and brought about a demand for their complete suppression. Columba's pleas and prestige are supposed to have won the day against censorship. But there were also political matters for discussion, among them the status of the Scottish colony of Argyll, which was still forced to pay a tribute to its Ulster overlords. It was absentee landlordism, but not the familiar way round. Again Columba won, and brought back home rule for the Scots. An unlikely account tells that, having sworn when he left Ireland never to step on Irish soil again, he fastened clods of Scottish turf to his shoes to cover himself in this emergency. In the middle ages Roe Park was an O'Cahan stronghold, but their castle was destroyed in 1607. They clung to the ruins, however, and a later English visitor wrote that she found the dowager O'Cahan wrapped in a blanket in the draughts of a gutted hall, brushwood burning on the hearth where lordly logs had blazed.

Limavady is a pleasant Georgian town, officially called Newtown Limavady from the fact that it was bodily moved from the neighbourhood of the castle by an early Planter, Sir Thomas Phillips, to a more savoury distance. Thackeray came here and fell in love with the maid at the inn where he stayed ten minutes, composing later the long and delicate doggerel of 'Peg of Limavaddy'. We leave it by the A2 to follow round the coast. Six miles along, at Tamlaghtard, a narrow lane on the right leads to an old church beside a modern one. In the graveyard is a humble ark-like structure of boulders, put up in the twelfth century but known as St Aodhan's, or Aidan's, Grave. Aidan was one of the most endearing and modest of the early travelling monks, and was appointed from Iona to be first abbot of the new monastery of Lindisfarne in Northumberland, where he died.

Of a very different ecclesiastical cast was Frederick Augustus Hervey (1730–1803), the unorthodox and megalomaniac fourth Earl of Bristol and Bishop of Derry from 1768 to his death. **Downhill**, which we reach as the road bends east between the sea and the hills, was his home, begun in 1776 to be, as he put it, 'about the size of Blenheim'. Mussenden Temple, his classical library atop the precipitous cliffs north of the shell of Downhill Palace, is now the most beautiful reminder of his tastes. In his day he and his buildings adorned the province without rival. Everyone had an opinion of him – Fox thought him mad and dishonest, Voltaire brilliant, Boswell 'learned and ingenious', Lord Charlemont 'a bad father, worse husband', and Wesley, treated by him to roast beef and Yorkshire pudding at Derry, found him admirable. His influence was enormous; it was said 'the world consists of men, women and Herveys', and of his six children two became countesses, one a duchess and one, his heir, a marquess. From the job of chaplain to George III he became, thanks to his brother the Viceroy of Ireland, Bishop of Cloyne, then Bishop of Derry. Revising the lease system he raised the episcopal revenue from £7,000 to near £20,000, and devoted almost all of it, and his other incomes, to buying up antiques and pictures on prolonged visits to Italy. Downhill was built after consultation with Wyatt and Soane though the designs used were by Michael Shanahan, to be the treasure house that held works by Rubens, Tintoretto, Murillo, Correggio, Raphael, Perugino, Van Dyck and others. Outside, sixty acres of bog were transformed by 200 workmen, landscaped to suit the dramatic setting, and planted with 200,000 trees. But Hervey was busy on other schemes, too.

In Derry he repaired the Bishop's Palace, built a bridge over the Foyle, put up parsonage houses and here as elsewhere in the country clapped elegant spires on plain churches. He was concerned about social welfare and started several relief funds, gave numerous individual charities, and worked out a scheme to reform the tithe system (which was more or less adopted in 1838). He entertained his clergy at Downhill and made them race on horseback on the sands below, rewarding the winner with a fatter living. At night he is said to have scattered flour on the floor in the servants' quarters to see from the footprints in the morning who was sleeping with whom. He was a Juanesque lover himself.

He was all for Catholic emancipation, gave grants to RC churches and priests, and fought for their rights in Parliament. Politics brought out his megalomania, and when in true liberal form he put himself at the head of the Volunteers movement in the 1780s, he obviously saw a chance of becoming king in a new independent Ireland. To this end he went to Dublin in 1783, toured streets lined with cheering volunteers in an open landau drawn by six horses, himself dressed in purple with gold tassels and diamond buckles, and surrounded by a squadron of dragoons and his own liveried servants. But he was beaten to the post of chairman of the Convention by Lord Charlemont, and subsequent reforms and government reaction took the life out of the movement. So he built another palace, Ballyscullion, beside Lough Beg just north of Lough Neagh, at a cost of £80,000 and partly modelled on the Pantheon; then another, Ickworth, on the same plan, at his family estate in Suffolk. In his last years he went more dangerously mad, was imprisoned in Italy as a spy by Napoleon's troops, and, released, died outside Rome in 1803.

Downhill, like Ballyscullion, lies in ruins, the first deroofed in 1950, the second deserted since his death. But the National Trust preserves **Mussenden Temple**, with its urn-topped dome, its handsome Corinthian pilasters linked by carved festoons, and interior stucco work; though its walls are no more lined with books for the earl's use when he sat here alone at night, working. The Trust also maintains the attractive Portvantage Glen, to which the roadside Bishop's Gate leads. Close to the

gate, on the left, is the Mausoleum, a memorial to the Earl
Bishop's uncle, based on a Roman original. This, and the
remainder of the demesne are, unlike the Temple and Glen,
in private hands.

We drive on to the east and come after six miles to **Coleraine**,
a handsome harbour town which since 1968 has housed the
University of Ulster on its north side. The Anglo-Normans
had a settlement here and long before the English plantations
there was a county of Coleraine extending from the Bann to
the Glens of Antrim. As English power declined the MacQuillan
family, albeit of Norman origin, rose to lead the Irish as 'Lords
of the Route', and were allied for a while by marriage to the
MacDonnell Lords of the Isles. The old Anglo-Norman
division of the land was forgotten. After the Plantations,
Spenser's 'fishy fruitful Bann' (still famous for salmon) was
again the boundary of a shire that now extended to the east
coast, but Coleraine and the land about it was merged with
Derry. In the eighteenth century Coleraine was a thriving
linen manufacturing town, and the industry continues to-day.
Mount Sandel Fort, beside the river on the south-west of the
town, is the site of one of the two earliest known human settlements in Ireland, dated to about 7000 BC. It has yielded important mesolithic remains of habitations, food, and domestic
bric-a-brac.

The A2 coast road goes north-north-west from here
through the popular, crowded and bungalow-bound resorts
of Portstewart and Portrush, with some good views west to
Inishowen Head. An electric tramway used to run from
Portrush to the Giant's Causeway, beside the sea and next to
the golf-links; and farmers with dying cows used to bring
them here and prop them against the live wires, so that at
least in their going they would bring compensation from the
Tramways Board. Three miles beyond Portrush on the left,
perched precariously and romantically above sheer cliffs, is
Dunluce Castle. The site has yielded traces of both early
Christian and Viking occupation, but the first castle was
built in the thirteenth century, later to become a MacQuillan
stronghold, and finally headquarters of the immigrant
McDonnells, after they had supplanted the MacQuillans at

Ballycastle. It saw much action in Elizabethan times, and was forced to surrender to Shane O'Neill in his loyalist phase by his threat to starve Sorley Boy McDonnell, whom he held prisoner, to death. The castle reverted to the McDonnells after O'Neill's death and Sorley Boy's release in 1567, but was taken and held for a while by the English in 1584, after which the McDonnells came to terms with the queen. Though Randal, Sorley Boy's third son and his successor, sided with Hugh O'Neill for a while at the turn of the century, before throwing in his lot with the English and being eventually created, in 1620, first Earl of Antrim.

In 1639 part of the cliff support at Dunluce gave way, carrying with it into the sea some of the living quarters and eight servants. Restored, it saw sporadic fighting in the Eleven Years War, and was damaged again. When the second Earl of Antrim, Randal's son, came back at the Restoration to his property, he built another (now ruined) house nearby and let the castle crumble. Its large rambling ruins, with barbican, tower and walls of the inner quarters, and even more its perilous position, have changed little since his day. Around it on the chalky ground clusters the pretty blue Meadow Cranesbill in late summer. Hereabouts it is known as the Flower of Dunluce.

Bushmills, a whiskey-distilling (licit) town, is two and a half miles on, and here the road bends north-north-west to come after two miles to Causewayhead, from which the famous **Giant's Causeway** extends two miles towards Benbane Head. Its reputation was born in the eighteenth century after the Dublin Society and the Royal Society had issued illustrated reports. Later the Earl-Bishop of Derry, Frederick Hervey, returned from Italy with a mania for geology – he had seen Vesuvius in eruption, and been hurt in the arm by a steaming stone. He commissioned an artist to paint all aspects of the scene, and began the Causeway's great popularity. Soon various reports, popular and scientific, were being promulgated. One Englishman tried to show the causeway to be the work of Carthaginians. It was the time when the painting of wild landscapes first became popular, and people started to look on mountains and seas as places to climb and bathe in

respectively, not to fear and avoid. A few years before Dr
Johnson decided that, while the causeway might be 'worth
seeing', it was not 'worth going to see'. The discovery of wild
scenery, which was the beginning of the Romantic Movement,
went all against him. Of the causeway a contemporary wrote:
'Here is the temple and altar of Nature, devised by her own
ingenuity, and executed with a symmetry and grace, a grandeur and a boldness which Nature alone could accomplish.
Those cliffs faced with magnificent columns: those broken
precipices of vermilion – coloured rock; yon insulated pillars,
obelisks erected before Greece boasted of her architectural
skill, or Egypt laid the foundations of her Pyramids, proclaim
the power and wisdom of their creator.' And in 1811 the
Rev. William Drummond began a poem on the causeway:
'Ye cliffs and grots where boiling tempests wail,/Ye terraced
capes, ye rocks, ye billows, hail!' and continued for a further
1998 lines. More and more flocked to see the place. Scotland's
Fingal's Cave, being offshore, remained relatively untroubled:
the causeway was often alive with sight-seers, and the trend is
possibly only dying down now as new arrivals realise that the
only way of traversing the scene is on foot, and the walk is a
long one.

The Fingal's Cave connection is more than an aesthetic one.
Both places owe their origins to the same cause, whether myth
or geology is applied. Fingal is the old Irish hero Finn McCool,
and it was Finn who, according to legend, built the causeway
in the first place in order to be able to walk to Scotland.
Geologists see the connection in basalt, a lava rock which,
after it pours out from a volcanic eruption, cools slowly in
the strange columnar forms seen here. The nature of this rock
was the subject of a furious controversy between two scientific
schools in the eighteenth century. Neptunists held, claiming
the Old Testament as their support, that volcanoes are a
modern phenomenon and that basalts, or dolerites, being
ancient, must have been formed by chemical precipitation
within the water. They stated further that all fossils were
formed by water action and could be traced – all of them – to
one universal cataclysm, the Flood. Vulcanites or Plutonians,
on the other hand, insisted that volcanoes had been going

roughly as long as the earth. Much of the argument centred on the nature of basalt, and therefore on the formations of this coast, to which partisans of either side came in large numbers. Among the features that prolonged the argument was an outcrop of basalt at Portrush that had got almost inextricably mixed with a layer of the prevailing lias beds. The lias was, as everyone agreed, thick with fossils. The confusion made it seem that basalt was, too, in which case basalt would be proved to be a sedimentary, not an igneous, rock. This was fine fuel for the Neptunists, reassured in the conviction of their Irish leader, Richard Kirwan, that 'sound geology graduates into religion', and they hammered home their accusations of blasphemy and atheism. In the end the Vulcanists won the day, after a campaign against the fundamentalists that was later to help Darwin considerably.

The extent of the causeway is posted, not only with souvenir stalls and lavatories, but also with maps and explanations of the fanciful names given to individual sights, Giant's Chair, Ladies' Fan, Giant Organ, Coffin and so on. About half-way to Benbane Head is **Spaniards Bay**, a semi-circle of 300-foot vertical cliffs which watched the destruction, in 1588, of the Armada's flagship *Girona*. About twenty Armada vessels were wrecked off Ireland's coasts. The survivors of several had boarded the *Girona* in Donegal and were making their way to Scotland in hopes of Stuart hospitality. At midnight on the 26th October a storm dashed her to pieces here. It was not until July, 1967, that Robert Stenuit traced the wreck and began a unique work of salvage, bringing from a depth of thirty feet a priceless collection of coins, jewellery and weapons. After years of research he had succeeded where others failed by disbelieving contemporary reports of the exact location, which he guessed were put about by local Irish to prevent the English from finding any treasure. This is the most important Armada find to date, and many of the best discoveries are displayed in the Ulster Museum in Belfast.

It is possible to walk several miles round Benbane Head to Dunseverick Castle, all on National Trust property. Somewhere above the track – the exact spot is rightly kept secret – a pair of golden eagles nests. They have, moreover, been seen to do most of their hunting in the Mull of Kintyre, twenty miles away in Scotland.

Whichever way we go, by coast path or road, we come to **Dunseverick Castle** next, a ruined tower on a sheer and narrow headland, site of a castle since Christ's time when its owner, Conal Cearnach, travelled to Rome, as the story goes, joined the Roman army in Palestine, and helped his weakling comrades move the stone from the sepulchre after Christ's crucifixion. The existing ruin may have been built by Anglo-Normans first, and is then known to have changed hands from MacQuillan to O'Cahan to O'Donnell. It was gutted by Cromwellians. A curious discovery made nearby was of the bones of Great Auks and Reindeer amid evidence of a large-scale Bronze Age settlement, showing that both creatures featured in our ancestors' diet. A mile on we turn left on to the main road B15 and shortly after come on the entrance to **White Park Bay**, a strange, quiet, sandy contrast to the Giant's Causeway. The mile long beach of white sand, backed by dunes and a sweeping hill, is impeccably maintained by the National Trust, whose contribution to the attraction of Ulster is incalculable. From the top there are views over Rathlin Island and beyond to the Mull of Kintyre (right) and Islay (left), and of the first part of the magnificent coastline that lies between here and Benbane. Continuing on the road we pass more ruined cliff-top castles, and at **Carrick-a-rede**, less than a mile east of Ballintoy, can walk down to the headland to look at the gigantic rock beyond, separated from the mainland by a sixty-foot wide chasm, and in summer by a rope swing-bridge from which fishermen hang large nets to trap salmon. Five miles more brings us to **Ballycastle**, the limit of the MacQuillans' Route – an old Gaelic territory – and the start of the glens; Glenshesk to the south is the first. The town also marks the border between Ireland's north-east coast of carboniferous limestone and the basalt that adjoins it. Ballycastle is a pretty and popular resort, with a handsome C of I church of 1756, and a good choice for the holiday-maker of fishing, beaches, hills, antiquities and other sights. From here boats go three times a week in fine weather to Rathlin Island. (The race in between is dangerous in rough weather – Niall of the Nine Hostages lost a son and fifty curraghs in a storm here.)

William Petty, in his seventeenth-century survey of Ireland, described **Rathlin Island**'s shape as like 'an Irish stockinge, the toe of which pointeth to the main lande'. It was in a cave on the east coast of the island that Robert Bruce rested in hiding after his defeat at Perth in 1306, and was inspired, by a spider that tried a daring web-swing six times and failed five, to the resolves that led to Bannockburn. Rathlin was the first conquest from the English made by Sorley Boy Mc-Donnell, who in 1573 sent here the women and children of the Glens for safety during the first Desmond Rebellion. For his part, the elder Earl of Essex sent a force of three ships, one captained by Drake, to take the island, which they achieved with little trouble. Everyone, to a total of 600, was butchered, while Sorley looked across helpless from the mainland, and the troops were congratulated for their bravery by the queen herself. In 1642 the McDonnells here were massacred again, this time by the Campbells, come for the purpose from Scotland on the king's orders. It was to this island, from a cottage on the front at Ballycastle, that Marconi transmitted his first wireless signal in 1905. It is rich in bird life, and one of the buzzard's few Irish breeding-places; but the white-tailed sea-eagle, which used to breed on its western cliffs, is found no more.

This north-eastern corner of Ulster – the Route and the Glens – was all McDonnell territory in the late sixteenth century. They were a Scottish family, claiming Lordship of the Isles, and first acquired Irish lands with Henry VIII's backing. Their loyalty was mercurial, the bane both of the English and of more resolute rebels like Hugh O'Neill, who, while keeping both sides guessing, steadily built up to the last great native rising, at the turn of the century. By the time that happened the McDonnells had cast their lot with the English and were subsequently created Earls of Antrim, a title which (by a second creation) they still hold. At **Bonamargy Franciscan Friary**, a mile east of Ballycastle, is a memorial of their duplicity. In 1584 they attacked it, while occupied by the English. But in the mausoleum are tombs of Sorley Boy, his son and grandson, first and second Earls of Antrim, who all died in the glow of English approval.

To the south of the town is the conical basaltic mountain of Knocklayd, 1,695 feet high. In 1788 someone sent a stream of letters to Dublin newspapers, duly printed and taken seriously, about an eruption from the mountain, with detailed circumstantial evidence on the route of the lava, and the people and cattle killed. Though mention was made of the eruption, in print, as late as 1846, the report had no basis at all.

*

From the A2 going east from Ballycastle a lane leads off to the left after nearly three miles to Fair Head, a fantastic sight from the sea and providing excellent scenic walks on land. The headland itself is half slopes of debris running down to the sea and half, above that, sheer basaltic cliffs rising to their height of 636 feet. From here there çan be clear views of western Scotland. The sea below is known as the Waters of Moyle, in which the legendary children of Lir spent three hundred years, working through the curse of their stepmother in the form of swans. A few hundred yards behind the head-land, best found by asking in this unsignposted scrub, is Lough na Cranagh, one of two lakes in the vicinity. In the middle is what appears to be an oddly oval island, which is, in fact, a man-made crannog, a type of Bronze Age habitation common in Ireland and parts of Scotland, but of which few good examples remain. Crannogs were made by stacking peat, stones and anything else available inside a wall of, in this case, stone, but in others of stakes.

Returning to the lane we drive for several miles by a long, steep, winding route, passing Torr Head, only sixteen miles from Scotland, until we descend gradually on the little village of **Cushendun**. From here to the west runs Glendun, which like most of the Glens to the south is worth driving or walking along. The village itself has an excellent beach backed by a green, and the whole is owned by the National Trust. Most of the well-spaced, rather coy village cottages were designed by Clough Williams-Ellis, creator of the exotic enclave of Portmeirion in north Wales. Moira O'Neill, the poetess, lived at Rockport Lodge at the north end of the strand, and John Masefield met his future wife here.

Long ago, in times known only through legend, sorrowful Deirdre and the two sons of Uisneach embarked here for Scotland, fleeing the fury of the king, Conor, balked in his long-laid plans to marry her. Here, too, Shane O'Neill, who had almost rolled up the whole province into his power, was killed by the McDonnells. The occasion was a meeting to which he brought his prisoner and hostage, Sorley Boy, hoping to ally with the McDonnells and so trounce English ambitions. In the old McDonnell castle, whose stumpy ruins lie beside Rockport, a row flared and O'Neill was stabbed to death. His head soon graced the gate of Dublin castle, sent there pickled in a pipkin. As in Norse and Anglo-Norman days, the Irish themselves were the invaders' best ally.

*

Five miles on we come to Cushendall, a rather bigger resort with a number of hotels and an old lock-up tower. A coastal strip of old red sandstone has become apparent already from the road, in exposed flanks of rock. Two miles south it edges the attractive Red Bay whose many caves were inhabited from neolithic to modern times, at the foot of one of the most beautiful of Antrim's glens, **Glenariff**. It runs inland five miles through a heavily wooded valley whose sides flicker with the froth of waterfalls and streams. A fenced-in area near the top (open to the public) contains many waterfalls and trees and is laid out with paths and viewpoints. There is little point in going far into the uplands of Antrim's hinterland, for the coast offers much better scenery.

We return to the coast road, round Garron Point to the east on a splendid corniche, pass Carnlough with its castellated miniature-railway bridge, and three miles later reach **Glenarm**. The glen here comprises the picturesque demesne of the Earls of Antrim, McDonnell descendants of Sorley Boy; and the florid, fanciful, neo-Gothic castle incorporates part of that erected by Randal, the first earl, in 1636, when Dunluce began to show dramatic signs of structural weakness.

The coast road takes us on past the range of mountains

whose western peak, Slemish, is supposed to be where the boy, Saint Patrick, kidnapped from Dunbarton by one of King Niall's pirate parties, worked through his five years of slavery. Eight miles from Glenarm we round Ballygally Head, near the village of Ballygally, whose castle, probably the best example of a Scottish Planter's castle of the early seventeenth century, was converted into a luxury hotel by the Earl of Antrim in the 1930s. Cyril Lord, the ill-starred carpet millionaire, bought the hotel in 1967 for £80,000 and among other things painted each of the twenty-four bedrooms a different colour. He also bought restaurants in and around Belfast.

Four miles beyond is the busy port of **Larne**, Irish terminal of the ferry which nowadays brings ever-increasing shiploads of tourists from Cairnryan. Collectively, it is the tourists who keep Ireland going, being the second biggest money-earner after agriculture, but Larne has seen more momentous arrivals in the past. Edward Bruce, having fought, together with his brother Robert, for Scottish independence, landed here in 1315, to accept the crown offered him by the Ulster chieftains, and begin a campaign which ended with his defeat at Dundalk three years later. In April, 1914, as the likelihood of Home Rule drew nearer, Edward Carson's Ulster Volunteers ran a cargo of 20,000 modern German rifles and much ammunition into the harbour to help ensure that this province, at least, would remain British. In a token show of authority, some British destroyers appeared off the coast, but this was a rebellion the politicians were not, by and large, unhappy to see. Apart from the Round Tower memorial to James Chaine, who introduced the Stranraer steamer service, Larne is notable for the quantity of mesolithic flints and other artifacts found on the Curran, a spit of land to the town's south. These have been so prolific that the word Larnian is used to describe the Irish culture of the period.

From Whitehead, nine miles south-south-east, there is an interesting diversion into the narrow peninsula of **Island Magee**. The cliffs on the east side, especially the Gobbins, make splendid scenery. The woods used to be known for goshawks that bred there, and a Tudor tenant paid a certain number to Queen Elizabeth as his annual rent. At the opening of the Eleven Years War in 1641, the Protestants of this part were said to have been massacred by the rebel Catholics and thrown over these cliffs, but battle has raged ever since over the truth of the accounts. Contemporary depositions filled fourteen volumes, now in Trinity College, Dublin. The peninsula was often noted for witchcraft, the last trial for which in Ireland took place in 1711, after a local girl, Mary Dunbar, plagued by evil spirits, gave descriptions of several women who were causing the trouble. These, accused, pleaded innocent throughout a trial full of ghoulish detail and were eventually imprisoned for a year. One of them, pilloried, had her eye knocked out by missiles thrown by the crowd. In 1808 a certain Mary Butters was charged with the same crime, but was discharged. Then in 1961 some hikers exploring a cave in the Gobbins cliffs came on a cache of cloaks, candles, decanters and the wooden effigy of a snake's head, as well as several documents suggesting the modern existence of a Black Magic cult. But nothing more than speculation about a 'Brotherhood of the Lefthand Path' came to light.

*

Carrickfergus is seven miles south-west of Whitehead. Two miles before it, on the left, is Kilroot, a village in which Dean Swift disconsolately held his first Irish living, worth an annual £100, fresh from Sir William Temple's patronage and London politics. Here he wrote his letters (still preserved) to Miss Waring of Belfast, sister of an old friend of his, and proposed marriage to her, which she refused. The courtship lasted four years. **Carrickfergus** itself once had an importance much greater than that of Belfast. After the Anglo-Normans had completed their conquest of Down in 1177 they picked on the pear-shaped rock promontory here as their base for expansion into Antrim. The magnificent castle, with its vast keep and four defensive D-shaped towers, was built about 1200, the first of its kind in Ireland. 115 years later it was forced, after a year-long siege, to capitulate to Edward Bruce, helped by

reinforcements brought by his brother Robert. With the
recovery of Gaelic power in the fifteenth century, it fell into
disuse, and as that power waned in the sixteenth and seventeenth centuries, recovered in its turn. The older Essex landed
here in 1573 to butcher the natives to submission. In the late
seventeenth century it was the largest town in Ulster. William
III landed here at a spot now marked by a tablet. In 1760 the
town was taken in an unlikely episode of the Seven Years War
by a French raiding party, who were shortly afterwards
ousted. It saw another encounter in the American War of
Independence when the Scottish captain of the American
(and later Russian) navy, Paul Jones, in one of a series of
hazardous exploits, took on and captured an English ship
before the castle. Thereafter, the castle, after use as a prison,
and till 1928 as an English barracks, was allowed the dignity
of an ancient monument and kept in good order. A good
museum of various antiquities is kept inside.

Over the way is the C of I church of St Nicholas. Parts of it
are as old as the castle, but most is the result of a 1640
restoration. Inside, the nave's stained glass on the south and
west sides came in 1800 from Dangan, the Duke of Wellington's ancestral home, the family having fallen on hard times.
In the north transept are the stately monuments in marble
and alabaster of Sir Arthur Chichester and his family.
Chichester, whose impact on seventeenth-century Ireland
matched Wentworth's and Cromwell's – and in terms of lasting
settlement exceeded theirs – is, oddly, far less known. A
Devonian and veteran of Drake's last voyage and various
continental campaigns, he became Lord Deputy in 1604 and
carried out his policies with the fashionable savagery and rare
genius for twelve years. In the wake of the Gunpowder Plot
he reversed his predecessor Mountjoy's liberal policy towards
Catholics. He then turned to Ulster, which before and at his
time had been least amenable to English colonial policies.
His efforts secured three million acres out of a total three and
a half to Protestant immigrants within thirty years, though he
himself retired in 1616, created Baron of Belfast. He died
in 1625 without heir, but from his brother Edward descend
the present Marquess of Donegall and, through the female line,

Lord O'Neill (the name was adopted) of Shane's Castle. If any one man deserves the name, he was the founder of Ulster. His forty-room mansion, Joymount (an inversion of his patron Mountjoy's name), stood in lavish grounds near the church, but fell to ruins in the eighteenth century.

CHAPTER EIGHTEEN

Belfast, Armagh, Lough Neagh and Surrounds

IN 1708 **Belfast** hardly existed. Carrickfergus was the important town of the area. Belfast's history before that had been of continued attempts to grow, frustrated by Edward Bruce (1315), the Lord Deputy Earl of Kildare (1503 and again 1512) and accidental fire (1708). After the demise of the local O'Neills of Clandeboye, Sir Arthur Chichester, granted the land, built the original city and 'a dainty, stately palace' for himself that used 1,200,000 bricks; and took the town's name for his title. But the fire of 1708 sent it all back to the beginning again. In 1790 it was described as 'one of the most trading towns in Ireland'. A Belfast lady wrote to a Dublin doctor: 'You talk of a Dublin merchant paying 1,000 guineas for furnishing a house. I heard a Belfast one's wife say she could not fit up her drawing room for less.' With a population of 20,000, Belfast was in the first league. Its wealth was based on linen, in the production of which in the course of the century it outdistanced Dublin. Bleach fields surrounded the city, and by 1801 it made £2½ million from linen exports. The nineteenth century saw as high a rise in prosperity as in any British city and its population multiplied by over ten. Now, at about half a million, it has doubled again. Murray's *Handbook* eighty years ago listed the town's sights with admiring records of the cost of each building, most of which was covered by the enormous profits of indefatigable, Protestant industrialists. It is still one of the world's main linen producers, and still mercenary, and now includes cigarettes, ships and aeroplanes among its principal industries. Its shipyards are among the world's largest. It is also a political town in which partisan feelings, as recent tragic events have shown,

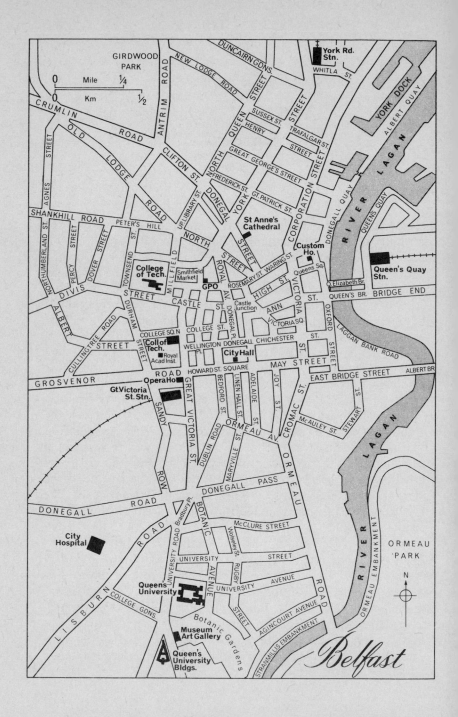

GIRDWOOD PARK

Mile 0 1/4

Km 0 1/2

CRUMLIN ROAD

DUNCAIRN GDNS.

York Rd. Stn.

WHITLA ST.

YORK DOCK

ALBERT QUAY

NEW LODGE ROAD

ANTRIM ROAD

OLD LODGE ROAD

CLIFTON ST.

QUEEN STREET

SUSSEX ST.

HENRY

TRAFALGAR ST.

STREET

RIVER LAGAN

AGNES STREET

SHANKHILL ROAD

PETER'S HILL

NORTH

FREDERICK ST.

GT. PATRICK ST.

UP LIBRARY ST.

DONEGAL STREET

GREAT GEORGE'S STREET

CORPORATION STREET

DONEGALL QUAY

QUEENS QUAY

St Anne's Cathedral

NORTHUMBERLAND ST.

PERCY STREET

DOVER STREET

TOWNSEND STREET

MILLFIELD

College of Tech.

Smithfield Market

GPO

ROYAL AV.

ROSEMARY ST.

WARING ST.

Custom Ho.

Queens Sq.

Q. Elizabeth Br.

Queen's Quay Stn.

DIVIS STREET

ALBERT STREET

DURHAM STREET

CULLINGTREE ROAD

COLLEGE SQ. N.

Coll of Tech.

Royal Acad Inst.

CASTLE ST.

COLLEGE ST.

DONEGAL PL.

Castle Junction

HIGH ST.

ANN ST.

VICTORIA ST.

OXFORD ST.

QUEEN'S BR.

BRIDGE END

LAGGAN BANK ROAD

GROSVENOR ROAD

WELLINGTON PL.

DONEGALL SQUARE

CHICHESTER ST.

City Hall

VICTORIA SQ.

HOWARD ST.

MAY STREET

EAST BRIDGE STREET

ALBERT BR.

Opera Ho.

Gt. Victoria St. Stn.

GREAT VICTORIA ST.

SANDY ROW

LINEN HALL ST.

ADELAIDE ST.

BEDFORD ST.

JOY ST.

CROMAC ST.

McAULEY ST.

STEWART ST.

DUBLIN ROAD

MARYVILLE ST.

ORMEAU AV.

DONEGALL PASS

ORMEAU ROAD

DONEGALL ROAD

City Hospital

BOTANIC

Bradbury Pl.

McCLURE STREET

Wolseley St.

STREET

ORMEAU PARK

UNIVERSITY ROAD

UNIVERSITY AVENUE

UNIVERSITY

RUGBY AVENUE

ORMEAU EMBANKMENT

RIVER LAGAN

Queens University

LISBURN ROAD

COLLEGE GDNS.

Botanic Gardens

STREET

AGINCOURT AVENUE

STRANMILLIS EMBANKMENT

Museum Art Gallery

Queen's University Bldgs.

N

Belfast

run high. It has always been the case that under the smugly respectable Presbyterian façade, the stupendous Victorian buildings, the stern loyalty to king and country (whether the king wanted it or not) lay poverty, resentment and depression – felt most among a class and religion that was seldom given a voice in public affairs. Not surprisingly, it was here that practical Irish republicanism was born, with the formation in 1791 of Wolfe Tone's United Irishmen.

Though much of the town has an ultra-modern look, having been rebuilt after a 1941 blitz which killed 1,000 people and led to the Republic's official contribution to the war – a visit from Dublin's Fire Brigade – it is dominated by two royal ghosts. The first is William III, whose image on a white charger is a familiar painting on the sides of Protestant houses, and whose colour – orange – is a ubiquitous symbol of Protestantism and authority. (In fact the Pope of the day was delighted by William's victory, being at odds, at the time, with James's main allies, the French.) The second ghost is Queen Victoria. She haunts in attitudes, statues, and the styles of buildings. A peak of municipal history was reached in 1849 when she came on a visit. The royal boat was greeted at the quay by thousands cheering. 'A very fine landing place was arranged', wrote the queen in her diary; 'Lord Londonderry came on board and *numerous* deputations with addresses, including the Mayor (whom I knighted), the Protestant Bishop of Down and clergy, the Catholic Bishop (an excellent and modest man), the Sheriff and Members for the County, with Lord Donegal (to whom the greater part of Belfast belongs), Doctor Henry from the new college, and the Presbyterians (of whom there are a *great many* here) . . . the people are a mixture of nations . . . It is really very interesting.'

The plan of the streets and squares in the central part of the city is on a grid system, first put into effect in the late eighteenth century. But in the buildings it is Victorian and modern styles which predominate, and mainly Victorian. John Betjeman, it is said, indulged his enthusiasm for Victoriana once, by placing a chair on the pavement in view of the nineteenth-century gasworks offices (in Ormeau Road, by John Lanyon) and contemplating their magnificence. The dominating building in the middle of Donegall Square, the City Hall, is not quite Victorian – it was built in 1906 – but looks it. A sumptuous pseudo-renaissance building (otherwise impressively known as Edwardian Baroque), it cannot fail to impress outside, but it is dull within.

May Street runs from the south-east corner of the square, and the first turn to the right is Alfred Street, in which is the Catholic church of St Malachy, designed by Thomas Jackson and completed in 1848. An oddity of gables and battlements outside, it has a breathtakingly sumptuous interior, the main feature being the elaborate fan-vaulted ceiling. South-west of Donegall Square runs Bedford Street, thick and stolid with Victorian offices, and containing W. J. Barre's Ulster Hall of 1860. Any of the streets west from Donegall Square leads to College Square East, dominated by the heavy Presbyterian Church House and Assembly Hall, and with the College of Technology built in the early 1900s on the other side. Behind this, and sadly hidden by it, is the **Royal Academical Institution**, always known as 'Inst', and one of the handsomest buildings in Belfast. Completed in 1814, it owed something of its design to Sir John Soane, although the present building is not much like his extant plans. In College Square North are other buildings of the same period or a little later, including the Old Museum, the first museum building in Ireland, and now, as then, headquarters of the Belfast Natural History and Philosophical Society.

Donegall Place runs north from Donegall Square to Castle Junction, the city's focal centre. Royal Avenue leads north from this for six hundred yards. In Rosemary Street, a right turn a third of the way along, is the Old Presbyterian Oval Church, with a most beautiful interior of 1783 (the outside was badly reconstructed in 1833) by Roger Mulholland, who was mainly responsible for the rectangular layout of the city. Farther east, the granite façade of the 1822 Commercial Building faces up Donegall Street, on the right of which, three hundred yards along, is **St Anne's Cathedral**. Begun in 1899, three years before the City Hall, it is still not finished, but collects new stylistic touches as it goes on. Sir Thomas

Drew designed it in Romanesque style, and in spite of some good details it is a prosy pretentious building. In the floor of the nave, which contains a stone from every county of Ireland, is the grave of Edward, Lord Carson (1854–1935), the militant leader of the Unionists and chief architect of partition. Nearby is the College of Art, one of the best post-war buildings in the city.

South-east of the cathedral, through Hill Street and Waring Street (in which the Belfast Bank's head office is the oldest, though much changed, public building in Belfast), we come to the Gothic Albert Memorial 'admitted', the Queen wrote, 'by competent judges to be one of the most graceful monumental erections in the kingdom', and designed by William Barre, whose work abounds in the city. The Custom House beside it dates from 1857, and has a fine E-shaped exterior in palazzo style. In High Street, leading south-west off Queen's Square, is St George's Church, whose interior Barre remodelled. It was built in 1816 by John Bowden, but its best feature is the portico, removed from the Earl Bishop of Derry's redundant palace of Ballyscullion.

On the opposite, western side of Royal Avenue, just behind the Post Office, is Smithfield Market, which unlike its London namesake deals in secondhand books, furniture and general jumble – one of the few of its kind remaining. West of this are the poor residential quarters running between the long dreary radials of Falls Road, Shankill Road and Crumlin Road, whose names have been made familiar to the world by recent tragedies. A quarter of a mile north of Smithfield Market, at the junction of Clifton Street with Donegall Street, is Clifton House, or the Old Charitable Institution. It is arguably the best piece of Georgian work in Belfast. Thomas Cooley was consulted over the design, and it opened in 1774, five years after the Belfast Bank building began life as a market-house. Its Palladian central block and low wings, pedimented at the ends, survive almost as they first appeared.

On the south side of the city, beyond Donegall Square and along Bedford Street and Dublin Road, is the **Queen's University**, independent since 1908, and before that one of the three Queen's Colleges for the education of students not belonging to the Church of Ireland. It numbers about six thousand students now, and is expanding rapidly. The central red-brick Tudor revival building, 600 feet long, was designed by Sir Charles Lanyon, whose work dominated the architectural scene in mid-century; but it is now pressed at the back and sides by later buildings. Within the university precincts, to the south, are the Botanic Gardens, Art Gallery and Ulster Museum – the last two in the same building. Though the art collection is a fine one, including works by Breughel, Turner, Morland, Lawrence, Sickert, Belfast-born Lavery and Jack Yeats, the city has an ambivalent attitude to art, as a walk round the sights so far mentioned will have shown in various ways. Hugh Lane, who found it hard to give Ireland paintings which perceptive collectors would have paid highly for, once offered the Belfast Gallery a distinguished Renaissance *Mother and Child*. It was refused, on the grounds that the mother appeared not to be wearing a wedding ring. The museum houses a fascinating and well-presented collection. Among its best sections are those given over to a history of transport, spinning and weaving machinery, the natural history of these islands, and an exhibition of timepieces down the ages. New buildings, in an impressive style which might be called neomegalithic, have been opened recently.

The Harland and Wolff shipbuilding works, on Queen's Island, a mile north-east of the city, can be reached by crossing either Queen's Bridge or the new Queen Elizabeth Bridge (in very few parts of Belfast is one not reminded of the citizens' loyalty to their female monarchs, or their founding family of Chichester, Marquesses of Donegall). The works were founded in 1859, and now occupy 300 acres and employ (when the economy allows) 11,000 men, making them the largest of their kind in the world. The ill-starred *Titanic* was built here. The yards have headed the world's output of tonnage in no less than twenty-four different years.

Other points of interest on the fringes of and beyond the city are, six miles to the east, **Stormont,** built as seat of the Six Counties' Government, a huge neo-classical building designed by Sir Arnold Thornely and opened in 1932, a present from the British Government. North of Belfast is **Cave Hill**, a landmark of 1,182 feet, and a popular resort of Belfast people at weekends. It contains Bellevue Zoo and Pleasure Gardens, and incorporates the grounds of Belfast Castle, built in 1867 for the Marquess of Donegall: an impressive baronial pile presented to the city in 1934. Of several dolmens and other prehistoric remains in the Belfast area, one fine dolmen with five supports is enclosed in an enormous seven-acre circular earthwork, 600 feet in diameter. It is a mile south of Shaw's Bridge at Ballynahatty, five miles south of the city centre.

TO ARMAGH AND LOUGH NEAGH

A motorway leads from the south-west suburbs of Belfast much of the way to Dungannon, on the west side of Lough Neagh. After six miles there is a turning to **Lisburn,** a neat thriving town built round a triangular market place with a statue of General John Nicholson (1821–57), hero of the siege of Delhi, who was killed at the head of a storming-party there. 'The type of the conquering race', explains his memorial in the cathedral. The town was laid out on its present lines and settled by Sir Fulke Conway, of Conway Castle in Wales. Part of the castle walls he built stands in Castle Gardens, east of the market-place, and between the two is the C of I Christ Church Cathedral, built in 1625 and a good example of so-called 'Planter's Gothic'. The spire was added in 1807. For the last six years of his life, Jeremy Taylor (1613–67) was bishop here. In spite of the pleas for tolerance in his many poetically eloquent works (most written when he, as a royalist, was hunted and sometimes imprisoned), he made himself unpopular by imposing church rituals that were too high for the taste of many, and expelling thirty-six Presbyterian ministers on his arrival here. There is a memorial to him here, though he is buried at Dromore.

Buried in the churchyard is Louis Crommelin, a native of Picardy, who in 1698 brought a colony of French Huguenots to the town, imported a thousand looms from Holland, and founded a thriving linen business. (William III had made concessions to Irish linen production that had been withheld from wool in order to protect the English market.) Twelve

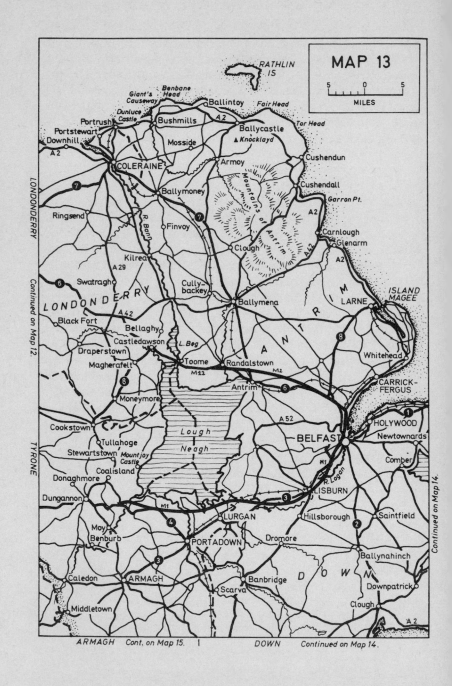

years after his arrival income from production of Irish linen, which had been a small cottage industry before, was valued as a fifth of the whole Irish revenue. Another native of Lisburn, not commemorated by the diocesan authorities, was Laura Bell. She moved to London, grew rich as a courtesan – gossip sheets called her the 'Queen of Whoredom' – and through an affaire with a prince of Nepal did more to end the Indian mutiny than her heroic townsman Nicholson. Then she saw God. Calling herself 'God's Ambassadress', she drew crowds to prayer meetings, and in the end Gladstone himself was a regular attender. The present Technical College used to be the home of Sir Richard Wallace, whose collection of paintings in Hertford House, London (on whose plan this house was built), was given to the nation by his widow as the Wallace Collection.

Hillsborough, four miles south-west of Lisburn, was founded in the 1650s by Sir Arthur Hill, à shrewd Planter who kept friendly both with the Cromwellians and the Restoration government. His descendants grew in wealth and influence till most of the land between Lisburn and Newry was theirs. William III granted them leave, after staying at their castle, to own a private army and the present Marquess of Downshire is still Commander-in-Chief of the only constitutionally recognised private army in the United Kingdom. It numbers one, until 1977 a veteran bugler, who still wore the uniform of the old Dutch Guard. The first Marquess was Wills Hill (1718-93), obstinate and disastrous Secretary of State for the Colonies under George III, and sponsor of Goldsmith's 'Deserted Village'. It was he who caused the building of the cupola-topped market-house, now the courthouse, the present Government House (now the Governor of Northern Ireland's official residence, previously Hillsborough Castle, much restored and added to in the nineteenth century) and St Malachi's Church, rich in monuments. The marquess's ambition was that the church should become the cathedral of Down diocese, but it remains a church. It was much altered by Sir Thomas Drew and others in the nineteenth and present centuries. Among several points of interest inside and out are the grave and memorial to Sir Hamilton Harty, a native of the town, whose father was church organist for forty years; and the Leslie memorial by Nollekens. The original seventeenth-century fort has been much altered, especially by charming eighteenth-century additions – a Strawberry Hill Gothic gazebo above the entrance, and a Gothic gatehouse.

From Hillsborough a minor road leads west to **Moira**. The old estate of the Rawdons, Earls of Moira, to the north-west, saw the first hothouse built in Ireland, the work of Sir Arthur Rawdon in the early seventeenth century, who sent a skilled gardener to Jamaica to collect plants. Five miles north, at Upper Ballinderry, is the simple church Jeremy Taylor built at the end of his life, as Bishop of Dromore, from 1664 on. It contains some original wooden fittings. **Lurgan**, five miles west of Moira, is another Ulster town whose prosperity dates from the introduction of damask weaving in 1691. George Russell (1867–1935), known as 'AE', an oracle to most of the distinguished literary and artistic figures of his day, was born and educated here. The demesne of the original settlers, the Brownlows, is on the east side of the town and is now a public park. The house, built in Tudor style in 1836, is an Orange Lodge. The A26 leads two miles south of Lurgan to Waringstown. William Waring, a linen manufacturer, had Waringstown House built in 1667 and the church in 1681. The three-storied house is charmingly shaped and gabled (the two terminal pavilions were added in the eighteenth century). James Robb, chief mason of the King's Works in Ireland, de-signed the church, though it is chiefly the nave which dates from his day.

Lurgan and Portadown, five miles south-south-west, are gradually being fused in a new city, Craigavon, which will reach north to Lough Neagh. At present **Portadown** is an industrial town, product of the nineteenth century, but famous above all for its roses. The mayor's chain is made of linked gold medals won in rose competitions, mostly by Sam McGredy, best known of Ulster's rose-growers, though he himself has emigrated. At an important junction of road, railway, river and canal, the town is one of Ulster's most prosperous. Its citizens are supposed to be close with their money and have been called 'the Aber-donians of Ireland', a judgement that may have more to do with outside envy than inner character. In a village called The Diamond, four miles west, the Orange Order was founded in 1795.

The main road A3 leads direct from Portadown to **Armagh,** the primatial city of Ireland, and one of the most beautiful. Most of its old building goes back no farther than Georgian times, and that is what is most visually striking about the place. To Victorians, for whom Georgian was simply old-fashioned, Armagh was disappointing. 'No city is so rich in historical associations, and yet has so little to show and tell', wrote the antiquary Bishop William Reeves. Thackeray, who was immensely cheered by the 'wonderful circumstance of the sermon in the cathedral lasting no more than twenty minutes,' summed up the place as having 'the aspect of a good stout old English town'. It is true that little is left to recall the older past, which comes into our knowledge with the first few centuries AD when King Conor and his Red Branch Knights held sway in their capital of **Emain Macha**, a well-preserved rath just over a mile west of the town. The best-known figures of that court, the most powerful in Ireland – petulant Conor, his perfidious wife Maeve, brave Cuchulain, beautiful Deirdre and the sad sons of Uisneach – went to make one of the most evocative story-cycles that have come down from ancient times (James Stephens's *Deirdre* is the most enter-taining version, a very free modern adaptation).

To Armagh came Patrick in the fifth century and, con-verting the king, was given land by him and founded Ireland's first diocese. Later the magnificent *Book of Armagh* (now in Trinity College, Dublin), containing a life of the saint and rivalling in its production the Book of Kells, was written and illuminated here. This was a time of monastic prosperity, and the town soon attracted ravaging Danes, based at Carlingford Lough and Lough Neagh. Burned several times, it became by 989 'the most melancholy spot in the kingdom'. But its prestige remained supreme and Brian Boru, by order of his will, lay in state and was buried here in 1014. After the Conquest it came under the Anglo-Norman mantle and a fourteenth-century decree ruled that Irishmen were not to be raised to the primacy. (A Florentine was appointed in 1478,

and was horrified at his savage surroundings.) But as the
Pale declined its position became less and less secure and
archbishops prudently lived at Termonfeckin, in Co. Louth
and better protected. Wisely, for in the sixteenth century,
after the Reformation had in Catholic eyes annulled the
place's sanctity, the town was destroyed by Shane O'Neill in
his attempt to control all Ulster, and again in the 1641
uprising of Phelim O'Neill. By the middle eighteenth century
it was little more than a village of mud-and-thatch houses
(the material of the majority of Irish houses till far into the
nineteenth century).

Then came Archbishop Richard Robinson (1709–94), a
wealthy prelate whose autocratic ways and generous spending
made him almost the match of his contemporary the Earl-
Bishop of Derry. Already in 1776 he had spent £30,000 on
the beautifying of Armagh. He used Thomas Cooley for
some of the buildings and having put young Francis Johnston
(1761–1829) – a native of the town – to work under him used
him, too, when he emerged from his pupillage. He built as
first priority a splendid episcopal palace, restored the historic
cathedral, built a public library (and gave it a valuable
collection of books), the Royal School (founded on a different
site by Charles II), a public infirmary, gaol and barracks. In
1793 he founded the Observatory. The town's streets were lit
and paved, trees planted, and new three-storey houses built.
The remarkable Robinson, who was created Baron Rokeby
of Armagh in 1777 (his family was from Rokeby in Yorkshire),
intended that Armagh should become capital of Ulster and
seat of a university. It had to be content with the status of a
country town and Ireland's best Georgian treasury outside
Dublin. Robinson died respected by all (including his brother,
Sir William, who out of deference had his shoes made on the
same last, ate the same diet and always took the same
medicines as his brother), though Wesley feared that 'in lieu
of preparing for Heaven he had given too much time to
works of public utility'. The adornment went on, but nothing
that came later was an improvement, except for various
constructions by Francis Johnston – the Courthouse, Market
House and present Bank of Ireland building, originally a

private house. Primate Lord John Beresford (1773–1862), brother of the second Marquess of Waterford, spent £20,000 of his own money, mainly on a complete, clinical and unfortunate overhaul of the C of I cathedral carried out by Lewis Cottingham, who did similar work at Hereford Cathedral. (Much of the work was undone in the 1880s but the decoration that Cottingham cleared was irreplaceable.) Building the Catholic Cathedral occupied the years 1840–1875. But the town remained, above all, Georgian.

Like Rome, the city is built on several hills. On the highest of these is the C of I **Cathedral of St Patrick**, incorporating sections from the thirteenth century on, but virtually the nineteenth-century concept of Cottingham. It is on the site of St Patrick's original church, and of a later monastery, and is the centre of an ancient hill-fort, whose defensive earthworks can be seen in part still. Outside the cathedral's north door is the alleged grave of Brian Boru. There are a few more ancient remains in the north transept including a small female statue which, an old guidebook explains, 'is naked, except for a girdle, and is therefore probably not of Christian origin'. The chancel is very slightly out of line with the nave, which may be for technical reasons but has been explained as symbolising the inclination of Christ's head on the cross. The memorials are a treasury of the work of great sculptors, including a statue, by the west door, of Sir Thomas Molyneux, physician and zoologist, by Roubiliac; a magnificent seventeenth-century likeness of Dean Drelincourt, by Rysbrack; Sir Francis Chantrey's statue of Primate Stuart; and a bust, by the amiable Nollekens, of the greatest benefactor, Primate Robinson, Baron Rokeby; besides effigies of Primate Lord John George Beresford, and his cousin Marcus, who succeeded him in 1862; and, in the north transept, seventeenth-century memorials to the Caulfields, Earls of Charlemont. North-west of the cathedral, beside the eighteenth-century houses of Vicar's Hill, is the **Public Library**, designed for Robinson by Cooley in 1771 and extended in 1820, containing 20,000 valuable books and manuscripts. George Ensor's Infirmary of 1774 stands behind it to the right.

The handsome, unpretentious **Archbishops' Palace** is on the

444 THE COMPANION GUIDE TO IRELAND

south side of the hill, off Dobbin Street. The work of Ducart, Cooley and, later, of Johnston, who added the unadorned second floor almost identical to the first, it contains a collection of paintings of kings and primates. A little removed from the palace is its chapel of 1783, also by Cooley, and with a remarkable interior added by Johnston, who did some of his best work for his native town. In the demesne, part of which is now a golf-course, are remains of a thirteenth-century Franciscan friary, the only medieval ruin in the city.

A few yards from Dobbin Street's east end is the Bank of Ireland office, built by Johnston as a family house for the Dobbins. To the right the **Mall** opens up, once a racecourse, now an elegant square with its green, walks, lime-trees and differently designed Georgian terraces, and Johnston's Courthouse at the far end, hideously defaced by some concrete accretion. On the Mall's east side is the well-arranged **County Museum** of 1833, with good archaeological displays and an exhibition of Orange Order appurtenances. The Royal School (founded in 1608, though the main building is of 1774) and Observatory (to see which written application should be made), both by Cooley, are on College Hill, off to the right at the Mall's north end. The imposing Gothic **RC Cathedral** is on the city's north-west side, standing on its own hill and the work, mainly, of J. J. McCarthy. Its handsome exterior belies the garish nature of its more modern – Italian – interior decoration.

From Armagh we can visit, seven miles south-east by the A28, Gosford Castle, the grim and massive former home of the Earls of Gosford, one of whose extravagance led earlier this century to the sale of the valuable library and much furniture. Apart from its singularly forbidding aspect, it is the first Norman revival house in either Ireland or Britain, having been built in 1820. Another interesting diversion from Armagh takes us fourteen miles south-west by the A3 main road, crossing the border into Co. Monaghan (in Ulster, but like Cavan and Donegal not in the six counties). Half a mile beyond the border we turn right for the charming village of **Glaslough,** whose manorial demesne, Castle Leslie, is the home of the Leslie family. The first of the line in Ireland was a Protestant

Castleward, County Down: classical this side, gothic the other.
Below Ardress House, County Armagh: an elegant country mansion
of the 1770s.

The Mountains of Mourne, County Down, from Dundrum Bay.
Below Killyleagh Castle: a ground-rent of gold spurs.

rector who, unable to reconcile fighting his king (James) with his principles, went on later to visit the old Pretender in exile and to try and convert him. The previous house on the demesne was Georgian but the ruling Leslie of the 1870s, granted a baronetcy by Disraeli, built the present extravagant baronial mansion in honour of his elevation, and filled it with a magnificent collection of Italian paintings and objets d'art, styling part of the house and garden in the Italian manner. The last baronet – he died in 1970 – was Sir Shane Leslie, a cousin and boyhood friend of Winston Churchill, some relics of whom are preserved in the house. His younger brother Norman was the last serving officer in the British army to fight a duel. He spent the summer of 1910 practising his sword-play on the lawn here, then went to Paris and honourably allowed himself to be wounded by Ysoury Pasha, a relative of the Egyptian khedive, whose wife he had seduced. Sir Shane himself was in his time an old-school eccentric, an IRA sympathiser, a Catholic convert and a prolific and witty writer with a special interest in ghosts. The public who come to this remote part to take advantage of the house's opening hours are likely to be shown round by a member of the family.

Recrossing the state border (we must return by the way we came, as that is the nearest 'approved road') we reach **Caledon,** in Co. Tyrone, a model village beside the grand demesne of the same name. Originally known as Kenard, it was an O'Neill headquarters till the war of the 1640s. At the Ulster rising of 1641 which he led, Phelim O'Neill brought Lord Caulfeild here a prisoner and killed him. In 1747 the castle and demesne came to John Boyle, fifth Earl of Orrery (1707–62), descendant of the Earl of Cork and friend and biographer of Swift, through his second wife, a Hamilton. 'Caledon has changed me into a Hibernian,' he wrote, and created a magnificent garden with all the new features William Kent (protégé of his kinsman the fourth earl, also Earl of Burlington) was advocating to create romantic effect. These included a hermit's cell made from tree roots, a popular device of the time, complete with matting couch, stools, table with manuscript on it, pair of spectacles, leathern bottle, bowls, hourglass, books and mathematical instruments – everything but a hermit, though some landowners went so far as to hire one. He also put up Latin tags on the rustic buildings which, in combination with naked classical statues, roused suspicion of paganism in the Presbyterian peasants; but told them all the tags were different phrases of welcome, and all was well. The present house (not open to the public) was the work of Thomas Cooley, but was considerably revised in 1812 by John Nash, who added wings, Ionic portico and colonnades outside and created one of his masterpieces, the oval drawing-room, within. The grounds, too, are magnificent, and include a large herd of deer, introduced by James Alexander, fourth Earl of Caledon, along with wapiti and small black bears. The park is also noted for its avenue of araucaria, or monkey-puzzle trees, a curiosity that became wildly popular after 1844 when William Lobb sent back seeds from Chile. Field-Marshal Earl Alexander of Tunis, younger brother of the fifth Earl of Caledon, was born here in 1891.

Eight miles north-east of Caledon (by the B45 then the B128) is **Benburb**, with a ruined Plantation castle and C of I church built by Sir Richard Wingfield, ancestor of the Powerscourt family, in 1613. This was the scene of the crushing victory of Owen Roe O'Neill, nephew of Hugh, rebel Earl of Tyrone, over General Munro's Parliamentary Army in 1646, a victory whose effect was nullified by the bickering of the Confederate Council, which should have consolidated Irish interests. From this time on the Irish forces, under whatever guise, began to decline, and the death of O'Neill himself three years later, combined with Cromwell's arrival, put paid to all their hopes. Three miles north-east is **The Moy**, a model village laid out by James Caulfeild, first Earl of Charlemont (1728–99) in 1754, on a plan close to that of Marengo in Lombardy. It used to be famous for a horse fair. Between this and Charlemont, just to the south-east, run the county boundary and the Blackwater River, overlooked by the remains of a fort of 1602 which, though demolished in the 1920s, still shows excellently, through the surviving earthworks, the defensive arrangements of a Plantation stronghold. The British housed a garrison here till 1858. In the Roxborough demesne to the north of the village there stood the grandiose mansion – massive, mansard-roofed, rather Ritz-like – that had been the home of the successors of Lord Charlemont. It was burned down in 1922; as was the pretty fort-governor's house built for the Earl's ancestor, Sir Toby Caulfeild, early in the seventeenth century. This was situated across the river at Charlemont, in County Armagh. A left turn off the B28, followed by another on to the Derrycaw road, leads to The Argory, a handsome 1820 house, well set among parkland and woods, administered by the National Trust. It contains an outstanding collection of modern art, and maintains splendid fin-de-siècle effects including gas lighting provided by a private acetylene gas plant in the stable yard.

Four miles east of Charlemont on the B28 is **Ardress House**, originally a farmhouse of Restoration times, and remodelled and transformed into a modestly elegant country house in the 1770s by its architect-owner, George Ensor. He worked at Armagh for Archbishop Robinson, and his brother was Richard Castle's assistant. Some gables and other features belong to the original building and give it a seventeenth-century look. But its greatest feature, the drawing-room, is very much of the eighteenth century. Michael Stapleton, whose work still abounds in Dublin, did the superb plasterwork of the ceiling which shows the influence of Italian stuccodores as well as of Adam. There is a good collection of pictures in the only other room shown, on loan from Lord Castlestewart. The house is owned by the National Trust which took it over in 1960 and restored it from an advanced state of decay.

Returning to The Moy, we drive due north-west to **Dungannon**, a town which was till the end of the sixteenth century a principal seat of the O'Neills. Though it has a number of buildings of various periods, none of them (except perhaps a decaying coaching inn attached to the Technical College) is of great distinction. Hugh Roe O'Neill, Earl of Tyrone, preparing his long and vigorous campaign against Queen Elizabeth's army, professed to be improving his ancestral home here by reroofing it with lead. The English later learned the lead was in fact for making bullets. Nothing of the old castle survives.

Donaghmore, three miles north-west of Dungannon, was the parish of the Rev. George Walker before Derry called him to immortality. From 1818 to 1821 Charles Wolfe, poet of 'The Burial of Sir John Moore after Corunna', was rector. (The poem was acclaimed, and credited to Byron and others before its real author was known.) The church was at **Castle Caulfeild**, two miles south, and preserves good seventeenth-century details, though it was much altered in 1838. South of the village are the remains of a castle erected by Sir Toby Caulfeild, later Lord Charlemont, in 1619 and burned down in the 1641 rebellion. A few good mullioned windows and chimneys remain.

The A29 out of Dungannon leads north to Coalisland, centre of the Tyrone coalfield which, in spite of holding an estimated thirty million tons of coal, has never, because of technical difficulties and distribution costs, been profitably mined. An eighteenth-century canal links the town with Lough Neagh on the south-east, but the railways that came later brought English coal at less cost to the region. We take the B161 east-north-east and nearing the lake pass **Mountjoy Castle** on the left. Built by Sir Francis Roe, a Tyrone undertaker, or colonist, in 1602, it changed hands several times in the wars of the 1640s and was eventually dismantled by Parliamentarians in 1648. Poorly kept, beside a chicken run and farm buildings, it still shows well the ground plan and brick construction of a Tudor Castle.

Lough Neagh, which we skirt for a while now and see from different angles, has been the biggest single natural influence on the way Ulster has developed, a vast sheet of water – 153 square miles and the biggest in the British Isles – abutting on five of the present six counties. Ten rivers flow into it but only one out – the Bann, that reaches the sea below Coleraine, due north. The edge on all sides slopes gently to a depth of a few feet, then drops abruptly to a uniform depth of forty or fifty feet except for a narrow basin in the north-west which goes down 120 feet. In the past, before drainage, its periodic floods would cover up to 30,000 acres all round its shores.

In legend, it began as a simple stream – the Bann – and people could jump from one side to the other. The stream's flow was controlled by a lid over the source which always had to be watched. One day, the watcher left her task. The spring overflowed, and filled the valley. All the houses and villages around were flooded, and ever since Round Towers and other buildings have been seen by fishermen, Abu-Simbel-like beneath the water. Giraldus Cambrensis, who took old tales seriously, supplied the crucial reason; bestiality among the peasants. 'It looked,' he wrote, 'as if the author of nature had judged that a land which had known such filthy crimes against nature was not worthy, not only of its first inhabitants, but of any others for the future.' Yet another account ascribed it to the hero Finn McCool, who, chasing a Scottish giant away from Ireland, picked up a lump of earth and threw it after him. The lump left a hole in the earth which is the lake's basin. The mud itself missed its target, landed in the sea, and formed the Isle of Man.

In more recent years scientists and locals, including the eminent botanist R. Lloyd Praeger, have heard loud bangs that continue, sometimes for hours, coming from the lake with no normal explanation. Biologists in search of diatoms and more visible rarities like the American *Spiranthes stricta*, a species of Lady's Tresses known elsewhere in only one part of Scotland, find plenty on the shore. The lake supports a large number of wildfowl, four thousand geese winter on it, and there is a period of days in late autumn when hundreds of Whooper Swans, after a direct 800-mile flight from their Icelandic breeding lakes, fly in and remain till they split into smaller groups and disperse to smaller lakes. It abounds in salmon, trout and eels – one of the few delicacies of this province. Yet for all its curiosities, Lough Neagh is the least picturesque of Irish lakes, has almost no islands, and need not hold us.

We turn left at the first opportunity, pass Stuart Hall, the Irish seat of Lord Castlestewart, turn left again for Stewartstown, then right for Cookstown. Two miles south of the town, on the right of the road beyond **Tullaghoge**, is a hilltop ring-fort mostly covered with trees. This prehistoric sanctuary used to have a stone on it which was used as the inauguration throne of the O'Neills, all of whom up to Hugh Roe were sworn in as chieftains. (As a ruling royal family the O'Neills lasted seven centuries, longer than any other family in Europe except the Wittelsbachs of Bavaria.) In 1602 Lord Mountjoy destroyed the chair while his successors destroyed and exiled the family. A right turn into a lane just after we enter Cookstown leads to **Killymoon** castle, a castellated Gothic building designed for Colonel William Stewart in 1807 by the versatile John Nash who, like most successful practitioners of his period, moved from classical styles (Rockingham and Caledon) to Gothic (here and Lough Cutra) and back with great facility. This designer of one of the five longest lists of English houses and public buildings in the record of distinguished English architects, also planned the Italianate rectory of Lissan, two miles north-east of the town. Killymoon once belonged to the Prince Regent, who won it in a game of cards. The present owner paid £100 for it, at a time when it was thrown in with some land he was buying. **Cookstown** itself is built along a forty-yard wide, mile-long main street, laid out by William Stewart, ancestor of the original Killymoon Stewart in 1724. It is an early model village on a very large scale, but the width of the road was not designed for traffic – more as an elegant promenade.

Four miles north-east of Cookstown by the A29 is Moneymore, a town founded in James I's reign by the London Draper's Company, and elegantly redeveloped by them about 1840. A mile south-east of it is the delightfully simple late seventeenth-century (probably) house, **Springhill**, now owned by the National Trust. It used to belong to the Conynghams, an Ayrshire family, which, like the Caulfeilds and other seventeenth-century Ulster settlers, was later to spread its interests over all Ireland. From the beech avenue at the front it looks like a doll's house with a façade of large plain windows and one central gable window in the roof. The two wings were added in the eighteenth century by the builder's great-nephew, William, who made other additions, too, and renovated the original house. This contains a good collection of furniture, in an arrangement and on a scale that put comfort before spectacle. There are some interesting portraits, including two of William III and Queen Mary presented by the king for loyal Protestant service. The outbuildings include a barn that now houses a collection of carriages, a model traditional Irish cottage and several rooms given over to a collection of old costumes. The gardens are unpretentious and contain a circular dovecot rather like a stunted Round Tower.

Midway between Slieve Gallion and Lough Neagh the A31 takes us to Magherafelt, a small village where anglers like to stay, then continues past Castledawson to Bellaghy. To the east of this small village is the diminished ruin of Bally-scullion, Bishop Hervey's greatest Irish building, conceived on a heroic scale, and left to crumble as soon as he died. There is little to see, and the detour is no more than a pilgrimage to one of this remarkable man's relics. Two miles south, on peninsular Church Island, are remains of a fourteenth-century church, with spire and tower added, as frequently in the region, by the Earl-Bishop himself. Coming down to the north-west corner of Lough Neagh we turn left and cross the river Bann, the Lough's only considerable outlet, at Toome Bridge, mentioned in one of those maudlin 1798 rebel songs – 'There's never a tear in the blue, blue eyes; both glad and bright are they,/As Roddy McCorley goes to die on the Bridge of Toome today' – that still appear to take the fancy of the Irish young as much as British and American pop creations. Randalstown, six miles east, stands inland from the old lakeside demesne of the O'Neills. On the southern side of the romantically decaying demesne is **Shane's Castle** on its rocky foundations, accidentally destroyed in an 1816 fire. It took its name from Shane MacBrian O'Neill, one-time comrade of the rebel Earl of Tyrone, but later pledged and loyal to the English crown. He died in 1619. From him descend the present Barons O'Neill, though the male succession was broken when an only surviving daughter in the eighteenth century married a Chichester, a plantation family to whom O'Neills had once been implacably hostile. The present O'Neills live in a modern (1964) classical house on the site of a Georgian mansion burned in the twenties.

Antrim is six miles east-south-east. Like many towns in the interior of the county its economy is based mainly on linen, but it is one of the oldest religious sites in the province, and possesses one of Ulster's two near-perfect Round Towers (the other is on Devenish Island). From the name given to this one by original English settlers comes the name of the local townland, 'The Steeple'. A Tudor gateway at the west end of the main street leads into the demesne of Antrim Castle, built in the early 1600s, enlarged in 1662 by Sir John Clotworthy, created Viscount Massereene by Charles II, and since 1922 a hollow shell surrounded by its once magnificent park, now public and shabbily kept up by the local authority. The wars of the seventeenth century brought action here, and there was even a naval battle on the lake in 1642. The 1798 Rebellion saw a nearly successful move here by the insurgents, when they assaulted the town from three angles and almost had the dragoons and yeomen worsted before lack of communication between the various parties led to panic and flight. Henry Joy McCracken led the first attack. He was one of many Presbyterians who, downtrodden as much as the Catholics by laws that gave all preference to the Church of Ireland, conceived and carried through the Rising, often in liaison with Catholic allies in the south. McCracken was later caught and hanged in Belfast.

From Antrim the A6 to Belfast takes us after five miles past **Castle Upton**, seat of the Upton family, Viscounts Templetown since 1776. The house, which incorporates a refectory dating from the twelfth century, was built in 1611. In 1793 Robert Adam came to do one of his few Irish works, refurnishing the house inside and out and adding extensions. Little of this was appreciated in the nineteenth century when Victorian fireplaces replaced Adam ones. Early this century the place fell into decay, was sold to a farmer who replaced the crenellated top floor with a plain one, used the rubble to fill the lake and filled Adam's courtyard with styes for 1,000 pigs. New owners have saved what could be saved over the last few years and carried out extensive rebuilding on the eighteenth-century pattern. Adam's beautiful Upton Mausoleum adjoining the demesne is in the hands of the National Trust, and is the only building on the estate regularly open to the public. The house's gardens sometimes are. The return to Belfast from here is about eleven miles.

CHAPTER NINETEEN

Down

THE south side of Belfast Lough is, naturally enough, the scene of Belfast citizens' relaxation and entertainment, especially at weekends. It is, as a result, a long stretch of resorts, with all the amenities resorts should have, but with many of the more interesting constructions of the past obscured by modern development. **Holywood**, five miles from the capital, preserves (apart from what is claimed to be Ireland's only Maypole) some remains of a sixteenth-century Franciscan friary. It was also the home of General Stonewall Jackson's ancestors, who emigrated in 1748. The nineteenth-century Bishop's Palace here has become the Culloden Hotel, with a reputation as high as any in Ireland. **Cultra**, to the north-east, has become the site of the magnificent **Ulster Folk Museum**, with outdoor exhibitions of past ways of life – buildings, machinery, furniture and implements. This is worth a trip on its own. On the right of the main road four miles on **Clandeboye**, seat of the Marquess of Dufferin and Ava, who traces his descent from Sir James Hamilton, an unscrupulous Scotch settler who, having ingratiated himself with his compatriot king, James I, persuaded him that the large and rich Clandeboye estates, improperly granted to another Scotch family at the expense of the native O'Neills, could rightly be given to himself. The eighteenth-century house was enlarged in 1820 by Sir Richard Morrison; but the first Marquess (1826–1902), later Viceroy of India (Ava is the name of the ancient capital of Burma) altered the interior and the grounds in the 1850s, until his money ran out. He was thus prevented from executing plans for a grandiose conversion to Gothic towers, battlements and pinnacles; but was able to build, in 1861, the so-called Helen's Tower, in memory of his mother, on whom he doted. (She, an early widow, was

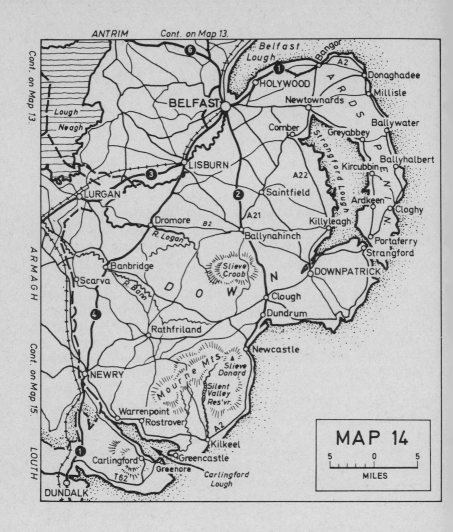

ANTRIM   Cont. on Map 13.

Cont. on Map 13.

ARMAGH   Cont. on Map 15.   LOUTH

Belfast Lough

Bangor

A2

Donaghadee

Millisle

HOLYWOOD

BELFAST

Newtownards

Comber

Greyabbey

Ballywater

Ballyhalbert

A22

Kircubbin

Ardkeen

Cloghy

LISBURN

Saintfield

Killyleagh

Portaferry

Strangford

LURGAN

A21

Dromore   B2

Ballynahinch

DOWNPATRICK

R. Logan

Slieve Croob

DOWN

Banbridge

R. Bann

Scarva

Clough

Dundrum

Rathfriland

Newcastle

Slieve Donard

NEWRY

Silent Valley Res'vr.

Warrenpoint

Rostrover

A2

Kilkeel

Carlingford

Greencastle

Greenore

T62

Carlingford Lough

DUNDALK

Strangford Lough

ARDS PEN.

Mourne Mts.

MAP 14

5   0   5

MILES

eighteen years his senior; 'My mother and I,' he said, 'shared our youth.') There is one room on each of three floors and a roof-bastion on top. The middle room is hung with golden tablets on which poems written (to order) by Tennyson, Browning and others are engraved. From the top there are superb views of the loughs, sea and Scotland beyond. North of the main road is the Marquess's baronial railway station, of 1865, with a private waiting-room for the family.

The next town, **Bangor,** is the site of one of the most famous early Irish monasteries, founded in 559 by St Comgall, a saint said to have been graced with miraculous saliva. His spit could shatter a rock, and more than once a gobbet turned to gold. His greatest pupil was St Columbanus, who like others left to preach on the Continent. His oak-like obstinacy earned him much praise and many memories, and he left behind him at least three monastic foundations in France and one, Bobbio, which still exists, near Milan. St Gall, his companion, also Bangor-trained, was too weak to cross the Alps with him and remained on the north side to found the Swiss monastery of St Gall. Nothing remains of Comgall's or the medieval house which was left to decay at the Dissolution. Beyond Bangor a long stretch of attractive coastline as far as Ballymacormack Bay is owned by the National Trust.

Rounding the headland we come after four miles to **Donaghadee,** another resort town with an attractive harbour from and to which the Scottish packet-boat crossed in the eighteenth and nineteenth centuries. Scotland is visible from here in good weather, and it was from Scotland that John Keats arrived with his friend Charles Brown in 1818, intending to visit the Giant's Causeway, which he had been advised was forty-eight miles of walking. But, as he wrote, living in Ireland was 'thrice the expense of Scotland . . . Moreover we found those 48 miles to be Irish ones which reach to 70 English. So having walked to Belfast on one day and back to Donoghadee the next we left Ireland with a fair breeze.' To the south from here stretches the **Ards Peninsula.** The forty-mile circuit of this is a picturesque tour but of less interest than others around Belfast. The two points of great interest are towards the north of the western road, running along the shores of Strangford Lough. In a pleasant garden beside the village of **Grey Abbey** are the remains of the abbey itself – an aisleless church, with interesting medieval and seventeenth-century Montgomery monuments, and a refectory building, in Early English style. It was founded in 1193 by Affreca, daughter of the King of Man, under John de Courcy's patronage. Dissolved in 1537 it was burned by the O'Neills later in the century, to prevent its becoming a shelter to English settlers. It was re-roofed in the seventeenth century and used as a parish church till 1778. One of the effigies is thought to represent the foundress.

Two miles north is the demesne of **Mount Stewart**, home of the Marquess of Londonderry. The land was bought in 1744 by the grandfather of Lord Castlereagh, who was born here in 1769 – and became in 1797 Pitt's Chief Secretary for Ireland and a reviled architect of Union. He succeeded his father as second Marquess in 1821, a year before his suicide. The gardens are owned by the National Trust and open to the public. Because of the sheltered position and high humidity, they almost match Kerry in the profusion of fuchsia, tree-sized heathers, eucalyptus, mimosa palms, bottle-brushes and many others. On the same side of the road a short way south is the Temple of the Winds, a lovely octagonal garden house overlooking the lough which was designed by James 'Athenian' Stuart and built in 1780. It came to the National Trust in 1962 and was subsequently restored.

Newtownards stands inland from the head of Strangford Lough, and dates from the thirteenth century when a Dominican priory, whose ruins remain, was founded here. All traces of the old town implied by its name seem to have vanished. The priory, parts of which were refurbished in the early seventeenth century, incorporates the Londonderry family vault. There is a pleasant town hall of 1765, with cupola and pedimented entrance. A mile north-east of the town are the few remains of **Moville Abbey**, which in the sixth century flourishing of Irish monasticism towered above most others in scholarship. Finnian, its founder, had studied at the early Scottish monastery of Candida Casa, in Galloway. He ruled his monks with an iron hand. At his first foundation seven monks died of hunger and cold. But Moville brought novices from all over Ireland and often abroad, and included some of the greatest saints in its numbers.

The straight A22, down the west side of Strangford Lough, leads from Comber direct to County Down's capital, Downpatrick, passing through **Killyleagh** where, as at Clandeboye, a house was built by Sir James Hamilton in the early seventeenth century. It was, he wrote, 'ane vera strong castle; the lyk is not in the northe'. His grandson, something of an imbecile, married the first Earl of Drogheda's daughter, a lady who, determined to annexe the property for her own family, poisoned her husband and destroyed his will. After a long lawsuit the estate was divided between two branches of Hamiltons, and remained so until the Marquess of Dufferin, inheriting both Clandeboye and half Killyleagh in 1841, gave the latter to the owner of the other half in return for an annual tribute – he was a great lover of Walter Scott – of gold spurs and roses. The solid castle, with pointed pinnacle-roofs on each tower, still bulks impressively over the village and lough beyond. It was thoroughly restored and enlarged around 1850 by Sir Charles Lanyon. Sir Hans Sloane (1660–1753), who after a lifetime of collecting gave his collection of 50,000 volumes, 3,560 manuscripts and scientific items to be the nucleus of the British Museum, was a native of the village.

Downpatrick is rich in ancient associations, and the country around is full of prehistoric remains. In 1177, in what amounted to a Norman Conquest of his own, the freebooter John de Courcy, without licence from the king, took the then kingdom of Down in a rapid, skilful campaign. His first target was Downpatrick, which he surprised, took, and made the site of his principal castle. A few years later he decided to excavate three famous tombs, those of St Patrick, St Brigid and St Columba. They were found, according to Giraldus Cambrensis, 'through divine revelation'. It may or may not have been true. St Patrick's tomb is claimed by Glastonbury, St Brigid's by Kildare, and St Columba's has been by Iona, and other parts of Ireland. Holy bones were a good bait for pilgrims, who brought money to the shrines; and claims were often made lightly. Nevertheless the town is forever linked with the name of St Patrick, who may well have founded a church and diocese here. An early monastery certainly existed, and de Courcy's action enabled him to invoke the church's blessing on his transfer of the see of the diocese from Bangor. He also built an abbey for Benedictines. This and most of the subsequent buildings were destroyed by an earthquake in 1245, again by Edward Bruce in 1316, and once more by the English in 1538. They lay in ruins for centuries but with the town's considerable expansion in the eighteenth century the need for a restoration became urgent. Between 1790 and 1826 most of the old ruins were swept away irrevocably, the Round Tower being used to provide masonry for the new church tower. Part of the body of the Benedictine cathedral survives in Charles Lilly's restoration, with a few fragments set into the wall. But the stone outside, inscribed with the letters PATRIC to mark his alleged grave, was made to order in 1900. The town, pleasantly set in hilly surrounds (with the huge Dun sixty feet high to the north – from which comes Down's name), has some good Georgian houses and Southwell School, an almshouse and school of 1733, possibly designed by Edward Lovett Pearce.

Saul, where St Patrick arrived on his mission to Ireland, is two miles north-east. It preserves a few remains of a twelfth-century abbey, supposedly on the site of his first foundation, and it was here that he died. To the south are the holy and curative wells of Struel, with ruins of a chapel and various medieval buildings covering a Drinking Well, an Eye Well, and tanks for the total immersion of men and women. Pilgrims still come here on the night of 23rd June. The wells owe their powers, naturally, to St Patrick. Five miles east of Saul, outside Strangford, is Castleward House, one of the best preserved Georgian Houses in Ulster, and in the keeping of the National Trust. Built between 1760 and 1780, it is the result of a compromise between Bernard Ward, Lord Bangor, an admirer of the Palladian style of architecture, and his wife Anne, daughter of the first Lord Darnley, whose taste was for Strawberry Hill Gothic. The house combines both styles, the south-west front following Lord Bangor's preference – classical, and with a pillared, pedimented portico – and the north-east his wife's – Gothic, with seven bays of ogee windows, under a row of battlements. Both are exceptional of their kinds and the interior, which contains some fine and curious plasterwork, also reflects the two styles. (This combination of styles was made elsewhere at that period – in Ireland at Westport House.) In the grounds, which stretch down to the shore of Strangford Lough, are an early canal, a Palladian garden temple and near the water a neat little tower-house of about 1610. After all this the Bangors were unable to get on together, and parted.

We go south-west, either returning to Downpatrick and continuing along the A25, or by the coast road through some pretty fishing villages. Clough, six miles from Downpatrick, has scanty ruins of a thirteenth-century castle. **Dundrum**, three miles farther, possesses the greatest of County Down's castles. Strategically situated by road and navigable water, it was built about 1230 by John de Courcy on the site of an older fortification, and was intended by him to play the same part in Down as Carrickfergus in Antrim. It had a not unusual turbulent history, changing hands and burning many times. 'I assure your lordship,' Lord Deputy Grey wrote in 1553 to the Lord Privy Seal, 'as yt standeth, ys one of the strongyst holtes that ever I sawe in Irelande, and moost commodios for defence in the hole countre, both by see and lande.' In view of which, Cromwellians dismantled it in 1652. It had probably, before that, served as quarry for the construction of an Elizabethan mansion nearer the shore. Now it stands as a majestic ruin, surrounded by its moat cut in the rock.

Newcastle, four miles south-south-west, is the gateway to the **Mourne Country**, whose mountains well deserve the reputation they have all over the world. The coast road, the northern road that borders them, and the steep road that splices them in two between Newcastle and Kilkeel, are all equally good ways to see them, but the best views are obtained by walking. From Newcastle the ascent of Slieve Donard on foot up the Glen river takes an able-bodied climber two hours or less. From this the broadest views can be had. The northern fringe of Slieve Bearnagh is contained in the **Tollymore Forest Park**, a forestry area which, as elsewhere in Northern Ireland, provides various amenities for tourists as well as getting on with the business of growing and cutting wood. From a fine old arboretum, centre of the former demesne of the Earls of Roden, marked paths go in various directions, past streams and waterfalls and through woods. There are also camping and caravan sites, discreetly placed so as not to spoil the natural scene. From here we can continue west and after three miles turn left to cross the mountains, by the pass between Pigeon Rock Mountain and Slieve Muck, close to which is the source of the River Bann. The highest of the range, Slieve Donard, 2,796 feet, overlooking the sea, is some miles to the left. On the far side the road leads down to Kilkeel, a pleasant seaside resort with a good beach and pretty fishing-fleet harbour. An alternative on the descent is to turn left, pass close to the Silent Valley reservoir which supplies Belfast's water, and follow down the reservoir's outflow, the River Kilkeel. Seven miles south-west of Kilkeel is Greencastle, with an impressively sited ruin of a fourteenth-century English fortress. The road west from Kilkeel goes close to the steep south-western slopes of the mountains on the edge of Carlingford Lough. After five miles it crosses Causeway Water, on whose right bank, 500 yards from the road, is the Kilfeaghan Dolmen, its 35-ton capstone supported by two stones. Rostrevor, with its statue of General Ross, who died of wounds after commanding the British capture of Washington in 1812, and Warrenpoint two miles farther, are very attractively situated resorts. Beyond Warrenpoint the lough narrows into the creek of the Newry River, which we follow five miles to Newry itself.

Newry, almost on the border between the Republic and the six counties, came into Hugh de Lacy's territories in the early thirteenth century. It was an ancient foundation and had at the time a large Cistercian Abbey. But it was subject to a full list of medieval setbacks, being destroyed by Edward Bruce in 1315 and again by Shane O'Neill in 1566. It changed hands twice in the Eleven Years War and was burned down by the Jacobites, retreating after the arrival at Donaghadee of William's General Schomberg. When Swift saw it a few years later the steeple of St Patrick's church (the first C of I church built as such in Ireland), was all that was left, and it was of Newry he wrote the lines 'High church, low steeple,/Dirty town, proud people'. Later buildings have not much enhanced the town and St Colman's Cathedral is an uninspired pseudo-Gothic work. John Mitchell (1815–75), a recruit to the Young Irelanders, whose advocacy of force to effect complete

separation revived a tradition forgotten since Emmet's day,
is buried in the Unitarian churchyard, off High Street to the
east of the town's centre. Two and a half miles west-north-
west of the town is **Derrymore**, a charming thatched mansion
preserved by the National Trust. A one-story house formed
around a courtyard, it is of a type often constructed by minor
eighteenth-century gentry, but of which no others survive.
It was built by Isaac Corry, Chancellor of the Irish Exchequer,
in the 1770s. Here the Earl of Charlemont, Henry Grattan,
Lord Castlereagh and others are supposed to have gathered to
sign the Act of Union, though this is little more than an
arguable tradition.

Newry is surrounded by delightful hilly countryside, the
Mourne Mountains to the east and Slieve Gullion to the west,
all of them worth a good deal of time and scrutiny. But to
complete the round tour from Belfast we keep to the Valley
of the Canal (begun in 1729, the first ever built in the British
Isles) which connects Carlingford Lough with Lough Neagh.
At Scarva we turn right and cross the river. Scarva House is
the scene of an annual charade on 13th July, when a mock
battle is staged to commemorate the Boyne. It was here that
King William's forces rallied on their way to the battle in
1689. Also in the demesne is the best surviving stretch of the
Dane's Cast, a prehistoric dyke that marked off the ancient
Ulster kingdom, more or less confined to Down. Eleven miles
north-east is the cathedral town of **Dromore**, seat of a small
C of I bishopric, and heart of the Magennis country, an old
Irish clan of which the famous Guinness family may be a
modern branch. Jeremy Taylor was bishop here from 1661 and
it was he who built the core of the present cathedral, for the
old one had been in ruins since the town was burned in the
1641 rising. Thomas Percy, editor of the '*Reliques of Ancient
English Poetry*', whose ballads were a seminal influence on
Scott, became bishop in 1781 and in 1808 carried out a major
restoration of the cathedral. Both Percy and Taylor are
buried here.

East from Dromore, the straight B2 goes direct to Ballynahinch, passing on the right the attractive range of Slieve
Croob, whose sides contain many prehistoric remains. From

Ballynahinch the A21 goes north-north-east to Saintfield, a mile before which is **Rowallane House**, a National Trust property with one of the finest gardens in the country. Fifty years ago it was rocky scrubland. Then Hugh Armytage Moore set to work on a vast reclamation plan and the result is a series of self-contained gardens spread over a fifty-acre estate. There are exotic Chilean and Chinese shrubs, a large and varied collection of rhododendrons, magnolias, cherries, wall plants, as well as expanses of lawn and woodland. From Saintfield, the A7 and A24 return us to Belfast.

CHAPTER TWENTY

Carlingford Peninsula, Dundalk, Co. Monaghan

THE strategic route between the richest part of Ulster and the rest of Ireland has always been through Newry. But a line of mountains lies to the south and west of the town and only a few valleys, or the long way round the Carlingford Peninsula, allow reasonable access. When Hugh Roe O'Neill, Earl of Tyrone, came out in full rebellion against the English at the end of the sixteenth century, he was wise enough to block the Moyry Pass, where the railway now goes, so holding up his enemies for five years. Three hundred years before Edward Bruce, recently crowned in Dundalk, and a real threat to Norman Ireland, was killed by Sir John Bermingham just to the south of the pass. A thousand years before that, the long half-mythical struggles between Ulster and Connaught reached their peak in the Cattle-raid of Cooley, in the epic account of which (recently newly translated from the Gaelic by Thomas Kinsella) Irish literature also reached a peak. The Ulster hero of the campaign was Cuchulain. Cooley was the Carlingford Peninsula. Throughout it, names and relics recall that seminal struggle.

We drive south from Newry along the west side, first of the Newry Canal, then of Carlingford Lough, and cross the Six Counties border after seven miles. The water is said to be a good medium for the smuggling that goes on (changing its nature as prices and taxes fluctuate on either side). **Carlingford** itself is a much diminished town, but it keeps several remains from its medieval importance. It claims the arrival of St Patrick in 432. Its main feature is so-called King John's Castle, built in the shape of a D by John de Courcy about 1210, and impressively overhanging the sheer rock drop beside the harbour. There are superb views from here of the

Mourne Mountains over the water. Because of the town's position, the burghers who built their houses here later made them tough to resist attack, and several have survived. Taaffe's Castle is one, best seen from the shore. Beyond is the old Tholsel, once a town gate. The Mint, of the fifteenth century, has interesting interlacing patterns round the windows. The parish church has a medieval tower, once part of the walls; while the ruinous Dominican abbey, built in 1305, preserves a scant tower and turrets.

Above the town rises the steep slope of Carlingford Mountain, almost two thousand feet high, with superb views from its summit. It is better seen from Greenore, two miles south-east, a sleepy seaside resort with a golf-links and poor shingle beach in a generally depressed area of coastline. Three miles south, off one of a complex of lanes in the extremity of the peninsula, is the old Bagenal stronghold of Ballug, but only the walls remain from the fifteenth century, when that minor colonist family encroached on the ancestral lands of the O'Neills, later to be horrified and implacable when Hugh O'Neill won and married a Bagenal daughter, and took her to what they considered the barbarities of his fortress at Dungannon.

The mountain shows up well from the main road on the west which takes us back to wealthier land and eventually to **Dundalk**, built on the flat marshy ground at the head of Dundalk Bay. The town is big and busy for this part of the Republic and it has been an important port. Its history is, for the foreigners and most Irish, a drearily confusing catalogue of attacks and sieges, mounted in every century to get command of its dominating position on the road to Ulster. In the graveyard of the C of I church of St Nicholas is a memorial to Robert Burns's sister, who is buried here. The church itself has a fourteenth-century tower and some windows of a century later, but the Georgian character of Francis Johnston's renovations dominate. Minor changes of the last few years and the splashing of green and maroon paint at points inside have not added much. The Catholic church of St Patrick owes its inspiration to the design of King's College, Cambridge, but nobody would fancy himself in the university

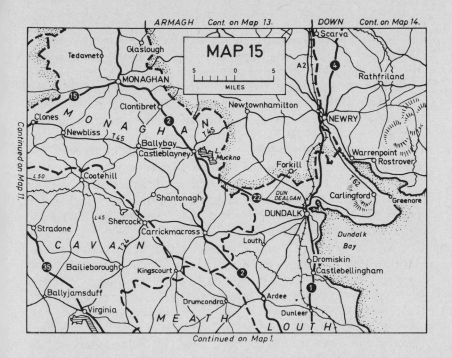

MAP 15

5   0   5
MILES

Continued on Map 11.

Continued on Map 1.

at the sight of it. There is a dignified, austere courthouse in granite, and scant remains of a medieval Augustinian friary.

To the north lies the southern bulge of County Armagh and those hills which made Dundalk in medieval times the extreme of the Pale. Over the border is the battle site mentioned above – the **Moyry**, where in 1601 the soon to be victorious Mountjoy erected a still extant castle to guard the pass. Three miles west is Forkill, outside which an actual domestic problem illustrates a common anomaly about the artificial border. The house of one John Morgan is in part inside each country. He gets his post from both – that from the Republic through the back door, from Ulster through the front. Officially he is in neither country. There are many like him. One in Ballyconnell gets electricity from the Republic and water from the north. More seriously, many of these people are cut off from their natural markets and have to travel miles to another.

Between Forkill and Dundalk, a mile south of the border,

is the village of **Faughart**. St Brigid, one of the three primary saints of Ireland, was supposedly born here in 450, and a hideously garish shrine marks the spot by the stream where the Virgin Mary appeared to her. It might be said to be in the Lourdes-Butlins style. On the hill of Faughart above is the grave of Edward Bruce, brother of Robert and an almost equal menace to the Plantagenets, whose attempt to raise the Irish in support of the Scotch reached its climax in his crowning at Dundalk, then collapsed in 1318 with his defeat and death here. It was a heroic failure, and Edward deserves better than to be eclipsed by his brother's reputation. But this ruined shrine does him some justice. The whole of Leinster lies visible below, like a chart of his campaigns.

A mile west of Dundalk, south of the T22 which we now follow into the county of Monaghan, is Castletown, otherwise known as Bellew's Castle, home of a fifteenth-century colonist and with some elegant parapets remaining. Nearby **Dun Dealgan** – Delga's Fort – from which name Dundalk derives, is supposedly the birthplace of Cuchulain. Somewhere hereabouts this mythical hero died in battle, once again defending Ulster and its king, Conchobar, and the Red Branch Knights from invasion by the malevolent queen of Connaught, Maeve. Wounded, he bound himself to a pillar-stone in order to die standing. His horse, the Gray of Macha, in a final fury killed fifty men who came to finish him off. But the hero's face turned pale as 'a one-night's snow' and he died, and the importance of Ulster with him; for the time being, it has to be said.

We drive on west for a hurried inland tour. A right turn at the crossroads three miles on brings us to Roche Castle, an imposing, almost triangular ruin of the thirteenth century. Two miles farther the T22 crosses the border into Northern Ireland, but this way being closed for the present we have to turn left at Rassanmore and then keep right until we resume the T22 in County Monaghan. The name Monaghan means 'little shrubbery' which, though originally applied to the town alone, is apt for the generally unexciting county. The north, edged by the desolate boglands of Slieve Beagh, is hardly worth a visit, and we keep to the centre and south, which has

some pretty lakes and undulations. Castleblayney, sixteen
miles from Dundalk, is named after a settler of James I's time.
Lake Muckno beside it is the county's longest and prettiest
and offers good fishing for brown trout, pike, perch and rudd.
Hope Castle, the guest-house of the Franciscan Convent, is
in the Hope demesne to the town's south.

Monaghan itself is twelve miles on by the T2. Half-way
there we pass through the little village of Clontibret, where in
1595, early in his rebellion, Hugh Roe O'Neill ambushed an
English force under his reluctant brother-in-law, Sir Henry
Bagenal, and roundly defeated them. **Monaghan** is a busy
and attractive county town built round a central diamond.
James I incorporated the town in 1614 but it has few historic
remains. The market house of 1792 is an elegant building
and the RC cathedral of St Macartan is a good Gothic-
revival building of the last half of the nineteenth century, by
the indefatigable disciple of Pugin, J. J. McCarthy. Much of
the town's building, including the market-house, is due to the
patronage of the Westenra family, Barons Rossmore since
the eighteenth century, who originally settled in Ireland from
Holland in the time of Charles II. Their demesne, Rossmore, is
a mile or so south of the town, but the house is no more than
an imposing Gothic ruin surrounded by an estate now given
over to forestry.

West of Monaghan, nearly a mile along the T15, the minor
L44 breaks off to the left and gives us a pretty drive to Newbliss, where we can turn right for Clones.Annaghmakerrig
House, two miles south of Newbliss, was the home, till his
death in 1971, of Sir Tyrone Guthrie, the theatrical director.
Descended, like the film-star Tyrone Power, from a famous
Waterford actor of the eighteenth century, he put most of his
money and enthusiasm in his last years into a jam factory
established by him in the village. It went out of business a
month before his death. The house is now a residential centre
for artists, writers and musicians.

Clones is a busy little agricultural centre with a history
going back at least to sixth-century St Tigernach, first bishop
and founder of a monastery here, who died of the plague in
549. The place grew in importance and an Augustinian abbey

was built in the twelfth century. A topless round tower and some church ruins containing a church-shaped tomb survive from this. In the Diamond is a weathered high cross, probably comprising bits of two tenth-century crosses.

We can cross the national border at Clontivrin, a mile west of the town, and make for **Newtown Butler**, in a part of County Fermanagh that Upper Lough Erne and its liquid outposts makes more water than land. On the outskirts of the town in 1690 an Irish army on King James's side was defeated by a force from Enniskillen supporting King William. A hundred years before, the land to the north, which had for centuries belonged to the Maguires and which guarded one of the main approaches to Ulster from Connaught, was the scene of repeated attempts by that callous hothead Sir Richard Bingham to break into the last enclave of native Irish power. The Maguires held on till the 1590s. When they broke, the crafty Earl of Tyrone showed his hand fully on the side of the Irish, and raised the last and most critical of Gaelic rebellions. Maguire's Bridge, twelve miles north, recalls the old lords of Fermanagh. Lisnaskea, two miles this side of it, was another Maguire centre, and on a nearby rath, Cornashee Mount, half a mile north, they were inaugurated as princes by the O'Neill, their overlord. Aghalurcher church, a mile and a half south of Lisnaskea is where, in 1484, one Maguire killed another, at the altar, in a clannish feud. The ruin, the yews, and the macabre, untidy graves give it a haunting air.

The best sight near Newtown Butler is **Crom Castle**, four miles south-west of the town and magnificently sited in the Earl of Erne's wooded demesne by the lake. The earl's seat is a grandly battlemented Tudor-revival castle of 1829, built by Scott's friend Edward Blore. In the grounds, which flank one of the hundreds of inlets of the lough, is old Crom Castle, the quintessence of a romantic ivy-covered ruin, built in 1611, scene of Jacobite assaults in 1689, and destroyed by fire in 1764.

The relevant cross-border roads are closed at present and to reach Belturbet, due south of Newtown Butler in County Cavan, we have to return to Clones, turn right on to the L45, and keep turning right, on to the L44 and L50 successively, hugging the border on the Republic's side. Belturbet is a pretty little village on the River Erne. Keeping to the T52 we come next to Milltown. Off a lane half a mile south of the village are the attractive remains of a medieval church and round tower, built on the site of a monastery founded in the sixth century by St Mogue, a disciple of Wales's St David. From Milltown we round Lough Oughter, turning left on to the L3 at Killashandra, and left again on to the L15 at Crossdoney. Here and there are glimpses of the lake itself, a mazy complex of channels, islands, and peninsulas extending from the channel of the River Erne. Like all the lakeland complex of County Cavan, this inland archipelago draws many anglers, often coming regularly to their favourite spots.

Three miles before the county town we pass on the left **Kilmore** C of I cathedral, a neo-Gothic building that incorporates a Romanesque doorway. William Bedell, a seventeenth-century bishop buried in the churchyard, was the first translator of the Bible into Irish. In **Cavan** itself is the imposing and elaborate RC cathedral, built in 1942. Beside it is the heavily classical courthouse built in the early nineteenth century by John Bowden. The ground rises just north of the town, and we get delightful views over the watery patchwork, interspersed with woods and fields and the odd spire piercing the horizon. Almost due west, and reached by a road off the L15 which skirts the lakeside demesne of the Maxwells, Lords Farnham, is the circular fourteenth-century tower of **Clough Oughter**, one of the best preserved of its kind in the country. Well set on a small island, it was scene of the short imprisonment of the translator Bishop Bedell in 1641, and eight years later of the death of Owen Roe O'Neill, last and greatest hope of the Confederate Catholics. One year later Cromwell arrived in Ireland, and there was no leader to match him.

Cavan's new cathedral replaces a neo-Gothic one. This old building was transported to **Ballyhaise** and most of it re-erected as the parish church. We reach Ballyhaise by driving five miles north of Cavan along the L44. North of the village is a fine house built by Richard Castle in about 1732 – an attractive combination of red brick and stone. It is now an agricultural college, and around the building are some inept additions.

We now swing to the east, first driving two miles south-east to rejoin the L15, and coming in another ten miles to **Cootehill**, a town founded in 1662 by Colonel Thomas Coote, son of a notorious military adventurer, in the heart of O'Reilly territory. Thomas's successor married in 1697 Ann Lovett, aunt of the architect Edward Lovett Pearce, which is how the almost perfect Palladian villa, **Bellamont Forest**, came to be built a mile north of the town, in about 1730. Nearly square, and in red brick, with a massive Doric pedimented portico, it contains rooms of beautiful proportions and superb compartmented plasterwork ceilings. The Coote family produced several generals, among them Sir Eyre, Clive's comrade and successor in India, and another whose dealings with the boys of Christ's Hospital led to a public scandal in 1815 and his retirement as colonel of his regiment. Another soldiering Coote, who lived at Bellamont, became Earl of Bellamont in 1767, by which time he was father of innumerable illegitimate children. But he wanted a legal heir, the likelihood of which was not enhanced, it was thought, by a wound in the groin received in a duel with the ex-Viceroy of Ireland, Lord Townshend, in 1772. Two years later, however, he married Emily, daughter of the first Duke and Duchess of Leinster; but since the Duchess, by this time a widow, was rumoured to be secretly married to Mr Ogilvie, her children's tutor, and an unredeemed commoner, the earl refused to speak to her at the wedding. The marriage was a failure except in so far as it produced an heir; but he died young. The father had his body brought back to Bellamont, where it lay in state for three full days, and was then buried in the church, an enormous procession being arranged to follow the hearse. The earl maintained his eccentric ways – calling the Irish 'Hottentots', making his maiden speech in the Irish House of Commons in his favourite language, French, and siring natural children – until his death in 1800. The house remained in the hands of his illegitimate family till 1874, when poverty forced them to sell up. It is owned now by an architect, probably the only house built by Pearce still in private hands.

A mile north is the **Dartrey** demesne – now a state forest – whose Tudor revival house has been completely demolished.

However, a mausoleum by James Wyatt still stands among the young fir trees, and it contains a beautiful monument to Lady Anne Dawson in a niche inside, erected after 1770 by her husband, the first Lord Dartrey. The statues – of Lord Dartrey and his young son looking up at an angel guarding a funeral urn – are the work of Joseph Wilton, a protégé of Lord Charlemont.

From Cootehill we drive south-east on the L46 to Shercock, passing on the left after three miles the ancient burial cairn known as the Cohaw Giants Grave. Shercock itself, and Bailieborough to the south, and Ballybay seven miles north-east, are famous centres of fishing; as is **Carrickmacross**, ten miles east of Shercock on the T24. The Earl of Essex, granted lands by Queen Elizabeth, built a castle here, but the materials were used for a market-house in 1780. There is a steepled C of I church of the same period, and the RC church has ten good lights by Harry Clarke, pupil of Sarah Purser at her Tower of Glass studio. The road continues direct to Dundalk, a few miles south of which, at Castlebellingham, we rejoin the route described in Chapter 2.

History

Ancient Ireland was rich, from gold and other minerals, and as remote as anywhere in Europe. Its richness brought it trade and other contacts with Europe, while isolation spared it Roman invasion. The most enduring import from the Continent was Christianity, of a mainly monastic kind which well suited the structure of Irish society. From the fifth century on, the Church grew in influence and for a time, after the barbarian invasions, carried the lamp of civilisation back to Europe. Nevertheless it remained, like the society around it, fragmented. Chief fought chief, abbot fought abbot, and all movement towards feudal unity was halted by rivalries and quarrels. High Kings were sovereign in name only, and even the Norse settlers of the ninth and tenth centuries, while building the country's first cities and promoting trade around the coasts, gave up trying to run the inland Irish. These, God-fearing as they were, still proved an administrative and doctrinal bane to their spiritual head, the Pope.

An Irish prince invited the Anglo-Normans to Ireland in 1169. A pope, the Anglo-Saxon Hadrian IV, gave the invaders his blessing. Seven hundred years of Irish history follow directly from that partially successful campaign. Beyond the Pale, an area around Dublin which stayed in English hands, a consistent pattern lasted for three centuries. Almost as fast as they were given lands and built their castles, English settlers adopted the ways and loyalties of their new surroundings and turned on their old masters; and native chiefs who were persuaded to pledge loyalty to the king redeemed the pledge whenever it suited them. Until the Tudors came, there was spasmodic anarchy.

The Tudors saw Ireland's potential value to an enemy, especially Spain. That being so, the Irish stood no chance of being free. Colonisation was more ruthless and resolute, and it was not just English grandees who were given land, but retiring soldiers, artisans, merchants and adventurers. Natives were eliminated, absorbed, or forced to the far west, and Elizabeth's reign ended with the last mass Irish rising. The result was a vast exodus of Gaelic aristocrats, and the virtual end of the old Gaelic order.

Rebellion had been stiffest in the north, and to remedy this James I allocated all the best land of Ulster to Scottish settlers whose tenacious hold on their grants has lasted among their descendants. These new Presbyterian Scotch-Irish were soon protesting against laws which boosted British farming and industry at the expense of their own. Many of them went to America. At home, a republican tradition grew strong, and much subsequent rebellion has been conceived in the north. Elsewhere in the seventeenth century, Cromwell's campaign of 1649, the most vicious the country saw, left enduring scars and resentment. But it was no more than a continuation of Tudor policy, and in its own terms it succeeded. After a final Catholic rallying to James II's tattered flag in 1690, the country settled into what Yeats called 'the one Irish century that escaped from darkness and confusion'. The Catholics and poor, shackled by the Penal Laws, would not have agreed.

The eighteenth was the century of the Ascendancy, when the Anglo-Irish could not only dominate but – rebellion being dormant – build beautiful houses all over the country. Industry, agriculture and foreign trade boomed, roads and canals opened up the country. Money was made – fortunes by many – and society glittered. Dublin, Kilkenny, Armagh, Birr and other towns were virtually built anew. Then once again the English in Ireland began to feel independent of England, and called for Home Rule. In 1782 they were given a measure of it, but that little succeeded only in raising the hopes of radicals. The French Revolution fomented the hopes, and with the rising of 1798 England, fearing as always that independent Ireland could make friends of England's enemies, brought all power back to London.

After rising to a peak in the early nineteenth century, the country's prosperity ebbed away, and many English left for good. The labouring classes, which had gained least from previous riches, now worked, when there *was* work, for generally niggardly landlords they seldom even saw. Work or no work, they paid rents. A blight in successive years on their staple food, the potato, worsened their plight. In the middle of the century five years of death and mass emigration reduced the population from 8½ to 6½ million. By 1901 it was under 4½ million.

Concessions arrived during the century; Catholic emancipation, extended suffrage, repeal of the Corn Laws, the spread of education, and at last the right of tenants to buy the land they worked with money borrowed from the government. But now the call for Home Rule was loud at all levels. It might in the end have been given, but too many English promises had been false. Between 1916 and 1921 the Irish snatched power by force.

The six counties of the new Northern Ireland, still one third Presbyterian, were the exception. With no cause to love the English, whose laws had acted against non-conformists as much as Catholics, the majority liked popery still less. Discarding the three mainly Catholic counties of the province, a diminished Ulster stayed united with Britain, though it, too, had to use force to do so. It was a precarious basis for lasting union.

APPENDIX II

Language

All the conquests, plantations and settlements – Norse, Norman, English, Scotch – and many smaller immigrations of Spanish, Huguenots, Swiss and Germans have so deeply diluted Celtic blood that there is probably none of the real thing left. This has not prevented – has possibly caused – a nostalgic move, since independence, towards a Celtic culture, and in particular the revival of the Irish language, still spoken early in the nineteenth century by over half the population, but dead by the end, except in outlying parts of the country and among the academic Gaelic League. The 1937 Irish Constitution declared Irish to be the first official language of a people most of whom knew hardly a word of it. Now it is taught in all schools and used widely on the radio and television, on bus and street signs, in government and other official papers, and so on.

There is, however, no denying that English remains the language of the people, and very little doubt that it always will. Even patriots like O'Connell saw it as the language of progress and urged people to speak it. In the Gaeltacht, the poor areas scattered round the south and west coasts where Irish has always been first language, it is now artificially bolstered by a system of grants, so that students from other parts may come and learn it. It has to be subsidised. The language, like primitive farming methods, has been isolated in areas of traditional poverty.

The tourist needs no Irish at all. Those who speak it normally – scarcely 30,000 of them – switch politely to English when one of the company does not understand it. Even if he took the trouble to learn it, the visitor would find that Waterford Irish is substantially different from Kerry Irish, Kerry from Galway, and the official language a modern hybrid. He would find, too, that large numbers of people have no time for it, and agree with the member of the Dail who once said its revival would make most people illiterate in two languages. And it may surprise him to find that, before leaving school to forget it, many Irish children not only learn Irish, but also in the upper school grades do some of their lessons through the medium of the language. Nevertheless, its revival is deeply bound up with the earnest search of a new state for its own identity, and it has, moreover, an old and vivid literature of its own which nobody wants to see buried with Latin in musty libraries.

The language was probably introduced into the country by the Goidels, Gaelic settlers of the last few centuries BC, though no writing survives from before the sixth century AD, and the earliest which does uses the Roman alphabet. The only exception is the curious ogham script, whose letters, in the form of notches on memorial stones, itself derives from the Roman alphabet. In time this Gaelic language evolved and modern scholars classify it into periods: Old Irish (which stands to Modern much as Latin to French) gave way in the tenth century to Middle Irish; Middle to Early Modern in the thirteenth century, and that to Late Modern in the seventeenth.

Until recently it had a written alphabet, of only eighteen letters, formed by symbols different from ours. Though still found all over the country, Irish script is disappearing after an official decision to adopt normal Roman letters. It is, in fact, an old decorative script known as uncial, and was used a lot in medieval monasteries.

It is an extremely difficult language. Like Latin and German it is inflected, its nouns and adjectives changing their endings, and sometimes other parts, depending on the case or number being used. *Fir*, for instance, means 'men' (it is often seen in public places), but its singular, 'man', is *fear*. English has similar irregularities – 'man' and 'men' is an example – but not nearly so many. Verbs are also complicated; and while there are two meaning 'to be' there is none meaning 'to have', so that possession is often indicated by what seems to others to be circumlocution. 'I have a dog' is expressed in Irish 'a dog is at me'.

Nor are there words with the range of meanings of our 'yes' and 'no'. This lack leads Irishmen to express a positive or negative in English as they are used to in Irish. A question opening 'Will you . . . ?' gets the English answer 'I will not' or 'I will', seldom 'no' or 'yes'. Other idioms spring from the same cause. 'After' doing something always means a temporal 'after', never a statement of intent. The existence in the Irish verb 'to be' of a 'habitual' tense leads to such phrases (they are very common) as Synge's 'the like of the holy prophets, do be straining the bars of paradise to lay eyes on the Lady Helen'. Which is to say they they are not simply straining now, but make a habit of it.

There are other problems. Aspiration, as long as Irish script was used, was shown by a dot over the letter in question (instead of the English habit of inserting an *h*). Then the official decision to replace Irish letters with Roman led to the adoption of the English practice, which in turn caused clumsy letter-sequences like *seachtmhain*, meaning 'week'. In 1948 a reformed spelling was introduced, which simplified the same word to *seachtain* (pronounced 'shochdin').

Eclipsis, in which the sound of the first letter of a word is eclipsed in certain contexts by one placed before it, this alone being pronounced, has no parallel in English and would take too long to explain. Among the many causes of eclipsis is when the word in question follows any of the numerals seven to ten, but does not follow the numerals three to six, unless in the genitive case. From things like this, opposition to revival gets much of its armour.

Pronunciation varies in the different Irish-speaking areas. Difficult cases are explained where they occur in this book, or in the Glossary, which contains some Irish words in everyday use.

Over the centuries English and Irish have left marks on each other. Plenty of what appear to be cryptic and complicated Irish spellings conceal ordinary English words, and several Gaelic words, like 'poteen', have been absorbed into English. Sometimes transference has led to confusion, as when people sought for some mythical explanation of the phoenix of

Phoenix Park, when in fact the word is an English approximation to the original Irish *fionn uisge*, meaning clear water.
Sometimes, too, a word may seem to have three alternative
spellings: Irish, an English approximation to the Irish pronunciation, and an English version pronounced differently.
The word *ruadh* (red) might be spelt Roo-a to show how
roughly it is pronounced. At the same time it has been
absorbed into English as 'Roe.' So *ruadh*, roo-a, roe and red
all mean the same.

There are also words which, while not Gaelic, are not
strictly the English of England either. Expressions like
jackeen, shoneen, and gossoon (a boy-servant, from the
French *garçon*) are really Anglo-Irish. Other words – strand,
demesne, undertaker, tinker, turf – while being thoroughly
English, have either changed their meaning minutely in Irish
use, or are used more commonly there than anywhere else.

All these fluid processes at times make the spelling of
place-names confusing. Old Irish, Norse, Norman, and
various English versions of these have resulted sometimes in
alternative modern spellings of the same name (Navan and
An Uaimh are examples) which do not seem to represent the
same sound at all. In looking for a standard, people usually go
to the Ordnance Survey half-inch maps, but there are cases
where common or local usage is different. The rule in this book
has been to follow the Ordnance Survey except in cases which
would sound wrong to most Irish ears. There are necessarily
examples which leave room for argument.

More confusion stems from the gradual change, over the
centuries, of family names and titles from each other, and from
the names of places from which they derive. Kinsale becomes
Kingsale, Palmerstown Palmerston, Clonmel Clonmell, and
so on. Different branches of families use different spellings:
Plunket or Plunkett, McDonnell or MacDonnell, Power or
Le Poer. Even standard reference books, not to mention other
sources, occasionally contradict each other. This insouciance
towards spelling is tied to the importance, in Ireland, of the
spoken word in relation to the written. It should dismay only
the literally literal mind.

Climate

No one season is clearly better than all others for going to Ireland. On average its climate is warmer than Britain's, and it hardly ever sees settled snow. The south-east gets most warmth and sunshine; the mountainous west is rainiest. July and August are good for warmth and beaches, but there are more tourists about. There can be serious crowds in and around Dublin, but the worst effect in most other parts (except at festival times) is that long stretches of beach have to be shared with a few others. September and October choke the hedges and moors with berries and greenery. But late spring is prettiest, and on average May and June have more sunshine than other months (several hotels and services offer discounts in May).

The main blight at any time can be rain or drizzle, especially in the far west and to a lesser extent along the north and south coasts. But rain is not what it is elsewhere. It is soft, and often dries quickly in sun and winds. It adds a blueness to distant hills and a richness to all natural colours. The clouds that bring it, endlessly changing the greater part of any landscape, are one of the finest sights of the country. On arrival it is worth making a mental note to watch clouds.

Food and Drink

Dublin's best restaurants and hotels provide as good wine and food as is to be found in England. The same goes for the handful of top-class hotels spread around the country. But they offer little that is especially Irish because Ireland had no tradition of gastronomy; though native beef, lamb, pork, salmon, trout, eels and Dublin Bay prawns are superb raw materials.

The 1840s famines had the curious effect of making people associate free or cheap country food with poverty. They tried to get away from them, and now things like vegetables and salads that can be grown for almost nothing, and others that are free – blackberries, whortleberries, wild raspberries and strawberries – are astonishingly rare in middle- and lower-range restaurants. For the same reason, some Irish seem to find it incredible that visitors should want traditional cottage fare. You are more likely to be offered fried fish and chips, or the universal and so-called Limerick ham (which *can* be very good) with a pittance of salad, than Irish stew which, with its base of mutton neck, potatoes and onions, can when properly cooked be delicious.

The Irish eat rather fewer potatoes per head than the English, but in country districts they eat them differently, boiled and served – often as a separate course – in their skins, sometimes with butter. Bacon and cabbage, boiled together, make another traditional dish. You can still get soda bread, made with sour milk and raised with bread soda, but most of the best is made in homes, and fast giving way to sliced loaves. Oysters, a poor man's food until disease killed the oyster beds of Wexford and Carlingford early this century, are returning. The largest beds are in Galway, and new ones

are being laid in Carlingford Lough. Oysters make a gastron-
omic combination with Guinness.

Most of the traditional milk products are made no more.
There used to be a vast range of curds, butter and cream –
'whitemeats' they were sometimes called – but the home dairy
has gone the way the bread oven is going now. Cheese was
hardly eaten. It was looked on askance as a kind of tallow,
and even now the variety of cheeses sold in most shops is
disappointing.

Irish drinks are well enough known. People say that
Guinness, the most popular dark stout, tastes better in Ireland
than anywhere else, and offer Liffey water as explanation,
but its qualities vary widely from pub to pub (and the Liffey
was never the source of the water anyway). At its creamy
best it can be as great as a great wine. Irish whiskey (usually
spelt with the 'e') is made mainly from malted barley, like
Scotch, but in a pot-still to which heat is applied directly by
anthracite, as opposed to the Scotch patent-still (invented by
an Irishman, Aeneas Coffey), in which the direct heat is
provided by steam. Few people dispute the superiority of
Scotch single-malt whiskies, but these apart the differences
are matters for taste. Irish whiskies vary more than Scotch,
and Paddy may suit many whom Jameson does not.

Scotch's world-wide reputation is something new. In
Trollope's novels and much later, gentlemen take a drop of
Irish. Irish whiskey is always used in Irish coffee, a beverage
drunk more by tourists than natives. It is made by pouring into
a pre-heated glass first a measure of whiskey, then one or two
teaspoons of sugar, then hot black coffee. The mixture is
stirred before whipped cream, poured on over the back of a
spoon, tops the whole with a layer of white.

Information and Accommodation

Ireland's Tourist Board, or *Bord Fáilte*, is one of the best organised and most helpful in the world. It has permanent offices in the big cities, and seasonal offices (from May to October, often in centrally placed caravans) in smaller ones. It publishes numerous booklets and brochures, and goes out of its way to give information on sights, cultural events, festivals, sports, fishing, tours, transport and so on. It sells cheap, comprehensive lists of approved hotels, guest houses, hostels and farmhouse accommodation. What can be more important, each office reserves Board-approved accommodation of whatever kind and cost is desired; locally or far afield, in advance or on the day. From its offices in foreign cities it also arranges and makes bookings for various kinds of holiday – touring, fishing, cruising, hunting and others – as well as for the main festivals. It remains astonishingly true that the Board, like most of the people, see their interests served best by serving yours. The Northern Ireland Tourist Board is not so extensive. It publishes and distributes a lot of information, and has bureaux all over the province but it does not have an accommodation service to match that of its neighbours.

Addresses of main offices:

Irish Tourist Board,
Baggot Street Bridge, Dublin 2.
(Offices also in London, Manchester, Birmingham, Glasgow, New York, Chicago, San Francisco, Toronto, Montreal, Paris, Frankfurt.)

Northern Ireland Tourist Information Centre,
6 Royal Avenue, Belfast BD1 1DQ.
(Other offices in London, Dublin and Glasgow, and at all British Travel Association offices throughout the world.)

Glossary

Adventurer	One who subscribed money to Parliament for the reduction of Ireland from 1642 onward, and stood to gain lands confiscated from rebels.
Antae	Short projections of walls beyond the corner of a building. Singular, anta, is rare.
Árd Rí	(pron. 'Aurd ree') High King, a title claimed and disputed by ruling Irish families from the fifth to the twelfth centuries.
Ascendancy	The period of Anglo-Irish domination of Ireland from the seventeenth to nineteenth centuries.
Bailey	Enclosed courtyard of a Norman or later castle, beside the keep or mote.
Bally	(from Irish *baile*). Settlement, town.
Bartizan	Small turret projecting from the angle of a parapet or tower, or half-way up it.
Bawn	Fortified enclosure of a castle.
Beg	(Irish *beag*). Small.
Beehive hut	Small circular structure, made from rough stones and by corbelling, q.v.
Bivallate	Enclosed by two concentric banks.
Bohreen	Path, usually flanked by stone walls, originally for driving cows through.
Bord Failte	Irish for 'Board of the Welcomes'. Irish Tourist Board.
Bull, Irish	Proposition whose comic inconsistency is not seen by the speaker, e.g. 'I must stop making resolutions'.
Bullaun	Stone, often found in early monasteries, with smooth depression in the side, probably used as a mortar.
Caher	Stone fort of dry masonry.
Carrig, or Carrick	Rock.
Cashel	Stone-walled enclosure, round a ring-fort, church or monastery.

Celsius	The name officially used in Ireland for the Centigrade scale, after its inventor.
Cheval-de-Frise	Irregular, defensive arrangement of sharp stones or stakes in front of a fortress. (First used in Frisia.)
Clochan	See Beehive hut.
Coade Stone	A very hard patent composition made in London from 1769 to 1836, and used for architectural mouldings and sculptures.
Corbel	A stone projecting from a wall as a support. Beehive huts and other buildings were built by corbelling, each course of masonry projecting over that below until the walls met at the top.
Crannog	A usually artificial island in a lake or marsh, belted by a ring of stakes or stones, and sometimes having a causeway to the land, just out of sight below water level.
Currach	Keelless small boat made by stretching tarred canvas – in ancient times hide – over a framework of laths.
Dáil Éireann	(pron. 'Dau-il airan') The lower house, or House of Representatives, in the Irish Parliament (*Oireachtas*).
Derg	(Irish *dearg*) Red.
Demesne	The word usually used for the enclosed park round a big house; from the Latin *Dominicus*, 'belonging to a lord'.
Derry	(Irish *doire*) Tree or wood of oak.
Diamond	The word used in Ulster for a town's central square.
Dolmen	Stone chamber of a neolithic tomb, usually consisting of a capstone supported on vertical stones, originally covered by a mound of earth.
Drum	(Irish *druim*) Ridge.
Dub, or Doo	(Irish *dubh*) Black.
Dun	Fort.
Ennis	(Irish *inis*) Island.
Esker	Long ridge of gravel, sand and other alluvial deposits, which was once the bed of a river in the ice-sheet.
Eye-catcher	Tower, obelisk or folly designed simply to catch the eye in a landscaped garden.
Feis	(pron. 'fesh') Festival.

Fianna Fáil   (pron. 'fee-anna fau-il') 'Sons of destiny'; name of one of the two main political parties.

Fine Gael   (pron. 'finna gale') 'Race of the Irish'; name of one of the two main political parties.

Finial   Stone ornament at the top of a spire, pinnacle, gable or other similar feature.

Gaeltacht   Area in which Irish is the vernacular language.

Gallaun   Standing stone, usually isolated.

Gallery grave   Megalithic chamber tomb, either rectangular or wedge-shaped, sometimes divided into compartments by stones.

Gallowglass   Mercenary soldier from Scotland, used in Ireland from the thirteenth to the fifteenth centuries.

Garda   (pron. 'gorda') Guard; policeman.

Grianan   (pron. 'greenan') Palace.

High Cross   Tall, stone (usually Celtic) cross, dating from the early tenth to the thirteenth century, generally with carvings.

Inch, or Innis   (Irish *inis*) Island.

Jackeen   Useless braggart.

Kill   (Irish *cill*) Small church or cell.

Knock   (Irish *cnoc*) Hill.

Liberty   Urban district which was not under the jurisdiction of the mayor.

Lis   (Irish *lios*) Earthen fort, or enclosure.

Mor, More   Big, great.

Og   Young.

Ogee   Double-curve, as in the letter *s*.

Ogham   A script formed of lines representing twenty letters of the Latin alphabet, used around the fifth century AD to notch memorial inscriptions on standing stones; the earliest known Irish script.

Oireachtas   Irish national parliament, comprising the President, Dáil and Seanad.

Pale   The area, of varying borders but focused round Dublin, to which effective English control was confined from the twelfth to sixteenth centuries.

Passage-grave   Megalithic grave in which a passage leads to the tomb-chamber.

Pattern   Festival commemorating a local saint, in which indulgences can be won by various acts of worship and endurance.

Pillarstone	Megalithic standing stone.
Plantation	Used to describe effects of the planting of Ulster in James I's reign, especially architectural styles which introduced many features from Scotland.
Poteen	Illicitly distilled Irish whiskey.
Quadrant	Curved connection, in the shape of a quarter-circle, between the main block of a Palladian house and its wings or pavilions.
Rath	Earthen fort or enclosure.
Scoil	Irish word for School.
Seanad Éireann	Senate, or Upper House, of the Irish Parliament, or Oireachtas.
Sedilia	Seats, generally three and built into the wall, for clergy, situated on the south side of the chancel.
Sept	A large family grouping, comprising people who lived in one area, had the same surname, and traced their descent to common ancestors.
Shanachie	Genealogist, or story-teller.
Sheila-na-gig	Carving of a – usually naked – woman in religious or secular buildings, generally thought to be connected with a fertility rite.
Shoneen	Fraterniser with the British.
Sinn Fein	(pron. 'Shin fane') 'We Ourselves'; political party founded in 1905 for the furtherance of Home Rule, periodically illegal since independence.
Skerry	Rock.
Slieve (Irish *sliabh*)	Mountain.
Souterrain	Underground series of chambers, found often in ring-forts, whose purpose is unknown, but was probably for storage and perhaps sometimes refuge.
Strand	Word most commonly used in Ireland for beach.
Tanist	Heir of a chieftain, elected by his sept. The *Tánaiste* to-day is the Deputy Taoiseach, or Prime Minister.
Taoiseach	(pron. 'Tee-shook') Prime Minister.
Teachta Dala	Member of the Dáil, usually abbreviated TD.
Tholsel	Town hall.
Tra, or Tráigh	(pron. 'traw') Irish for Beach.
Turf	Word normally used where peat or peat-fuel would be used in Britain.

Uachtarán   President of the Republic of Ireland.
Undertaker   Mainly Scottish colonists of Ulster in James I's
               time, who agreed to observe certain conditions
               in accepting land-grants.

Maps

The best for general touring are Bartholomew's quarter-inch maps which cover the whole country in five sheets. For route-planning, Bartholomew's Touring Map, twelfth-inch to the mile, covers the whole country in one sheet and also shows contours by colour. More detail on specific areas is on the Irish Ordnance Survey half-inch maps, of which twenty-five cover the country. They are very useful but not always quite as full or even accurate as they might be; though the Northern Ireland series, published by the British Ordnance Survey, are more recently revised and improved. A recent series of Irish Ordnance Survey maps – their 'Holiday Maps' – shows the whole country on four sheets at a scale of a quarter-inch to the mile. Well presented and showing many interesting features, they are maddeningly short on place-names. Bartholomew remains the best.

Further Reading

Becket, J. C.: The Making of Modern Ireland. Faber,1966.

Behan, Brendan: Brendan Behan's Island. Hutchinson, 1962.

Bence-Jones, Mark: Burke's Guide to Country Houses, Volume 1: Ireland. Burke's Peerage, 1978.

Boylan, Henry: A Dictionary of Irish Biography. Gill and Macmillan, 1978.

Carty, James: Ireland, A Documentary Record (in three volumes), Fallon, Dublin, 1951 and 1952.

Caulfield, Max: The Easter Rebellion. Muller, 1964.

Charlesworth, J. K.: The Geology of Ireland. Oliver and Boyd, 1963.

Chart, D. A.: The Story of Dublin. Dent, 1932.

Clarke, Desmond: Dublin. Batsford, 1977.

Coleman, J. C.: The Caves of Ireland. Anvil Books, Tralee, 1965.

Corkery, Daniel: The Hidden Ireland. 3rd ed, Gill, Dublin, 1941.

Craig, Maurice: Dublin 1660-1860. Hodges, Figgis, Dublin; Cresset Press, London, 1952.

Craig, Maurice, and the Knight of Glyn: Ireland Observed; Mercier Press, Cork, 1970.

Craig, Maurice: The Architecture of Ireland. Batsford, 1982.

Crookshaok, Anne, and the Knight of Glin: The Painters of Ireland. Barrie and Jenkins, 1978.

Curran, C. P.: Dublin Decorative Plasterwork. Tiranti, 1967.

Curtis, Edmund: A History of Ireland. 6th ed, Methuen, 1950.

Danaher, Kevin: In Ireland Long Ago. Mercier Press, Cork, 1962.

De Paor, M. and L.: Early Christian Ireland. Thames and Hudson, 1958.

Dillon, Myles: The Cycle of the Kings. OUP, 1946.

Dillon, Myles, and Nora Chadwick: The Celtic Realms. Weidenfeld and Nicolson, 1967.

Dudley Edwards, Ruth: An Atlas of Irish History. Methuen, 1973.

Evans, Estyn: Irish Folk Ways. Routledge and Kegan Paul, 1957.

Evans, Estyn: The Irish Heritage. Dundalgan Press, 1942.

FitzGerald, Brian: The Anglo-Irish, 1602-1745. Staples Press, 1952.

Flower, Robin: The Irish Tradition. OUP, 1947.

Gibbings, Robert: Lovely is the Lee. Dent, 1949.

Gibbings, Robert: Sweet Cork of Thee. Dent, 1951.

Giraldus Cambrensis: The Topography of Ireland. Dundalgan Press, Dundalk, 1951.

Gogarty, Oliver St John: As I Was Going Down Sackville Street. Sphere, 1968.

Guinness, Hon. Desmond and William Ryan: Irish Houses and Castles. Weidenfeld and Nicolson, 1971.

Guinness, Desmond: Georgian Dublin. Batsford, 1982.

Harvey, John: Dublin. Batsford, 1949.

Henry, Françoise: Irish Art in the Early Christian Period. Methuen, 1965.

Hone, Joseph: W. B. Yeats. 2nd ed, Macm illan, 1962.

Inglis, Brian: The Story of Ireland. Faber, 1956.

Kennelly, Brendan (ed): The Penguin Book of Irish Verse. Penguin, 1970.

Killanin, Lord, and Michael V. Duignan: Shell Guide to Ireland. 2nd ed, Ebury Press, 1967.

Leask, H. G.: Irish Castles. 3rd ed, Dundalgan Press, Dundalk, 1951.

Leask, H. G.: Irish Churches and Monastic Buildings. (3 vols). Dundalgan Press, Dundalk, 1955-60.

Lecky, W. E. H.: A History of Ireland in the Eighteenth Century. (5 vols). Longmans, 1895.

Lehane. Brendan: The Quest of Three Abbots. John Murray, 1968.

Lehane, Brendan: Dublin. Time-Life, 1979.

Lydon, James, and MacCurtain, Margaret (editors): The Gill History of Ireland. (11 vols). Gill and Macmillan, 1972-1975.

Lyons, F. S. L.: Ireland since the Famine. Collins, 1973.

Macardle, Dorothy: The Irish Republic. 4th ed., Irish Press, Dublin, 1951.

MacLysaght, Edward: Irish Life in the Seventeenth Century. 2nd ed, Talbot Press, Dublin, 1950.

Malins, Edward, and Bower, Patrick: Irish Gardens and Demesnes from 1830. Barrie and Jenkins, 1980.

Malins, Edward, and the Knight of Glin: Lost Demesnes. Barrie and Jenkins, 197?.

Mason, T. H.: Islands of Ireland. Paperbacked, Mercier Press, Cork, 1967.

Maxwell, Constantia: Dublin under the Georges, 3rd ed, Harrap, 1946.

Maxwell, Constantia: Country and Town in Ireland under the

Georges. New ed, Dundalk, 1950.

Mitchell, Frank: The Irish Landscape. Collins, 1976.

Moody, T. W. and F. X. Martin: The Course of Irish History. Mercier Press, Cork, 1967.

Moriarty Christopher: A Guide to Irish Birds. Mercier Press, Cork, 1967.

Murphy, Dervla: A Place Apart. Murray, 1978.

O'Connor, Frank: A Book of Ireland. Collins, 1959.

O'Connor, Ulick: Oliver St John Gogarty. Cape, 1964.

O'Faolain, Sean: The Great O'Neill. Longmans, 1942.

O'Faolain, Sean: The Irish, Penguin, 1947.

O'Rourke, Fergus J.: The Fauna of Ireland. Mercier Press, Cork, 1970.

O'Sullivan, Maurice: Twenty Years A-growing. OUP (World's Classics edition) 1953.

Pakenham, Frank: Peace By Ordeal. Cape, 1935.

Pakenham, Thomas: The Year of Liberty. Hodder, 1969.

Pochin Mould, Daphne D. C.: The Irish Saints. Burns and Oates, 1964.

Praeger, Robert Lloyd: The Way that I Went. Paperback edition. Allen Figgis, Dublin, 1959.

Praeger, Robert Lloyd: The Natural History of Ireland. Collins, 1950.

Rolt, L. T. C.: Green and Silver. Allen and Unwin, 1949.

Somerville-Large, Peter: The Coast of West Cork. Gollancz, 1974.

Somerville-Large, Peter: Irish Eccentrics. Hamish Hamilton, 1975.

Taylor, Geoffrey: The Emerald Isle. Evans Bros, 1952.

Thackeray, W. M.: Irish Sketch Book. London, 1842.

Webb, D. A.: An Irish Flora. Dundalgan Press, Dundalk, 1943.

White, Terence de Vere: The Parents of Oscar Wilde. Hodder and Stoughton, 1967.

White, Terence de Vere: A Fretful Midge. Routledge and Kegan Paul, 1957.

Wilde, William R.: Beauties of the Boyne and Blackwater. New edition, Sign of the Three Candles, Dublin, 1949.

Wilde, William R.: Loch Coirib. New edition, Three Candles, Dublin, 1955.

Woodham-Smith, Cecil: The Great Hunger. Hamish Hamilton, 1962.

Houses, Castles and Gardens Regularly Open to the Public

Note: Times and dates of opening may be checked at any tourist office. Information on some other houses and gardens open from time to time may be obtained from the Royal Horticultural Society of Ireland, 16 St Stephen's Green, Dublin 2.

Antrim

Carrickfergus Castle, Carrickfergus	Daily, all year.
Templetown, Templepatrick	

Armagh

Ardress House, Annaghmore	Sat to Thurs, April to September.
The Argory, Moy	Sat to Thurs, April to September.

Clare

Bunratty Castle, Bunratty	Daily, February to November.
Knappogue Castle, Quin	Daily, April to October.

Cork

Bantry House, Bantry	Daily, all year.
Blarney Castle, Blarney	Daily, all year.
Dunkathe, Glanmire	Wed, Thurs, Sat, Sun, May to September.
Fota, Carrigtwohill	Daily, Monday to September; Sat and Sun, October to February.
Riverstown, Glanmire	Thurs to Sun, May to Sept.

(Gardens only):

Annesgrove, Castletownroche	Sun to Fri, Easter to September.
Ilnacullin, Glengarriff	Daily, March to October.
Creagh, Skibbereen	Daily, Easter to September.
Castle Gardens, Timoleague	Daily, June to August.

Derry

Hezlett House, Coleraine	Sat to Thurs, April to September.
Mussenden Temple, Downhill	Sat to Thurs, April to September.
Springhill, Moneymore	Sat to Thurs, April to September.

Donegal

Glenveagh Castle, Church Hill	Daily, July to September.
St Columb's, Church Hill	Daily, July to September.

Down

Castleward, Strangford	Sat to Thurs, April to September.
Mount Stewart, Newtownards	Sat to Thurs, April to September.

Gardens only:
Castlewellan, Castlewellan
Rowallane, Saintfield   Sat to Thurs, April to September.

Dublin

Casino Marino	Daily, mid-June to September.
Dublin Castle	Daily, all year.
James Joyce Tower, Sandycove	Daily, May to September.
Malahide Castle, Malahide	Daily, all year.

Gardens only:

Fernhill, Sandyford	Tues to Sun, March to October.
Howth Castle, Howth	Daily, all year.
Marlay Grange, Rathfarnham	
National Botanic Gardens, Glasnevin	Daily, all year.
St Anne's, Clontarf	

Fermanagh

Castlecoole, Enniskillen	Sat to Thurs, April to September.
Florence Court, Enniskillen	Sat to Thurs, April to September.

Galway

Dun Guaire Castle, Kinvara	Daily, April to September.
Kylemore Abbey, Letterfrack	Daily, April to October.
Thoor Ballylee, Gort	Daily, May to September.

Kerry
  Derrynane, Caherdaniel
  Muckross House, Killarney   Daily, 17 March to Oct;
                                     Tues to Sun, Nov to 16 March.

  Gardens only:
  Derreen, Lauragh   Tues, Thurs, Sun, April to
                                     September.
Kildare
  Castletown, Celbridge   Wed, Sat, Sun, April to
                                     September.
                                     Sun, January to March.

  Gardens only:
  Japanese Gardens, Tully   Daily, Easter to October.

Kilkenny
  Edward Rice's birthplace,
    Westcourt, Callan
  Kilkenny Castle, Kilkenny   Daily, mid-June to 30
                                     September; Tues to Sun,
                                        October to mid-June.
  Rothe House, Kilkenny   Daily, April to October;
                                     Sun, November to March.

  Gardens only:
  Water Garden Ladywell,
    Thomastown   Daily, May to September.

Laois
  Gardens only:
  Abbey Leix, Abbeyleix   Daily, Easter to September.
                                     Daily, Easter to October.
  Emo Court, Emo   Daily, Easter to October.

Limerick
  Castle Matrix, Rathkeale   Sat to Tues, 15 May to
                                     15 September.

Offaly
  Gardens only:
  Birr Castle, Birr   Daily, all year

Roscommon
  Clonalis, Castlerea   Sat and Sun, May and June;
                                     Tues to Sun, July to
                                     9 September

Sligo
Lissadell, Carney — Daily, May to September.

Tipperary
Cahir Castle, Cahir — Daily, mid-June to
30 September; Tues to Sun,
October to mid-June.
Damer House, Roscrea — Daily, April to October.
Manor House,
Carrick-on-Suir — Daily, all year.

Tyrone
Mellon House, Mountjoy
Wilson House, Strabane

Waterford
Gardens only:
Curraghmore, Portlaw — Thurs, April to September.
Lismore Castle, Lismore — Sun to Fri, 7 May to
14 September.

Westmeath
Gardens only:
Tullynally Castle,
Castlepollard — Sun to Fri, June to September.

Wexford
Gardens only:
Johnstown Castle — Daily, all year.

Wicklow
Avondale, Rathdrum — Daily, May to August;
Fri to Mon, September.
Russborough, Blessington — Sun, Wed, Sat, July and August;
Sun, Wed, June; Sun,
Easter to May.

Gardens only:
Dargle Glen — Sun, May to September.
Mount Usher Gardens,
Ashford — Daily, 17 March to September.
Powerscourt, Enniskerry — Daily, Easter to October.

Some Regular Events

March:	St Patrick's Day (17th)
April:	Irish Grand National, Fairyhouse Circuit of Ireland Motor Rally
May:	Cork International Choral and Folk Dance Festival 2,000 and 1,000 Guineas, Curragh Kilkenny Beer Festival Galway Arts Festival Killarney Pan Celtic Week
June:	An Fleadh Nua. Traditional music and dancing, Dublin Cork Film Festival Festival in Great Irish Houses, Castletown, Co. Kildare and others Listowel Writers Week Festival of Tipperary Dublin International Organ Festival Malahide Festival National Rowing Regatta, Carlow International Motor Rally, Co. Donegal
July:	Irish Sweeps Derby, Curragh Guinness Oaks, Curragh Wexford Strawberry Fair Fleadh Cheoil na hEireann. Traditional music competition, Listowel, Co. Kerry Croagh Patrick Pilgrimage, Co. Mayo Open Tennis Championships of Ireland, Dublin
August:	Robertstown Grand Canal Fiesta, Robertstown, Co. Kildare Wicklow Regatta Festival

Steam Rally, Stradbally, Co. Laois
Claddagh Festival, Galway
Carrolls Irish Open Golf Championship
Dublin Horse Show
Puck Fair, Killorglin, Co. Kerry
Yeats Summer School, Sligo
Connemarra Pony Show, Clifden, Co. Galway
Birr Vintage Week, Birr, Co. Offaly
Letterkenny International Folk Dance Festival, Co.
  Donegal

September: Festival of Kerry, Tralee, Co. Kerry
Irish St Leger, Curragh
Killarney Arts Festival
Oyster Festival, Galway
Phoenix Park International Motor Race
International Festival of Light Opera, Waterford
All-Ireland Hurling Final, Croke Park, Dublin
All-Ireland Football Final, Croke Park, Dublin
Liffey Descent Canoe Race

October: Horse Fair, Ballinasloe, Co. Galway
Wexford Opera Festival
Cork Jazz Festival

Index